CompTIA®
Linux+™

Study Guide
Second Edition

Roderick W. Smith

WILEY

John Wiley & Sons, Inc.

Senior Acquisitions Editor: Jeff Kellum
Development Editor: Alexa Murphy
Technical Editors: Ross Brunson and Kevin Glendenning, FOSSter.com
Production Editor: Eric Charbonneau
Copy Editor: Kim Wimpsett
Editorial Manager: Pete Gaughan
Production Manager: Tim Tate
Vice President and Executive Group Publisher: Richard Swadley
Vice President and Publisher: Neil Edde
Media Project Manager 1: Laura Moss-Hollister
Media Associate Producer: Marilyn Hummel
Media Quality Assurance: Josh Frank
Book Designer: Judy Fung
Proofreader: Candace Cunningham
Indexer: Ted Laux
Project Coordinator, Cover: Katherine Crocker
Cover Designer: Ryan Sneed

Copyright © 2013 by John Wiley & Sons, Inc., Indianapolis, Indiana

Published simultaneously in Canada

ISBN: 978-1-118-53174-7
ISBN: 978-1-118-61130-2 (ebk.)
ISBN: 978-1-118-57034-0 (ebk.)
ISBN: 978-1-118-57048-7 (ebk.)

Dear Reader,

Thank you for choosing *CompTIA Linux+ Study Guide, Second Edition*. This book is part of a family of premium-quality Sybex books, all of which are written by outstanding authors who combine practical experience with a gift for teaching.

Sybex was founded in 1976. More than 30 years later, we're still committed to producing consistently exceptional books. With each of our titles, we're working hard to set a new standard for the industry. From the paper we print on to the authors we work with, our goal is to bring you the best books available.

I hope you see all that reflected in these pages. I'd be very interested to hear your comments and get your feedback on how we're doing. Feel free to let me know what you think about this or any other Sybex book by sending me an email at nedde@wiley.com. If you think you've found a technical error in this book, please visit http://sybex.custhelp.com. Customer feedback is critical to our efforts at Sybex.

Best regards,

Neil Edde
Vice President and Publisher
Sybex, an Imprint of Wiley

Acknowledgments

Although this book bears my name as author, many other people contributed to its creation. Without their help, this book wouldn't exist, or at best would exist in a lesser form. Jeff Kellum was the acquisitions editor and so helped get the book started. Alexa Murphy, the developmental editor, and Eric Charbonneau, the production editor, oversaw the book as it progressed through all its stages. Ross Brunson and Kevin Glendenning were the technical editors who checked the text for technical errors and omissions—but any mistakes that remain are my own. Kim Wimpsett, the copy editor, helped keep the text grammatical and understandable. The proofreader, Candace Cunningham, checked the text for typos. I'd also like to thank Neil Salkind and others at Studio B, who helped connect me with Wiley to write this book.

About the Author

Roderick W. Smith is a Linux consultant and author. He has written more than 20 books on Linux, FreeBSD, and computer networking, including *Linux Essentials, the LPIC-2 Study Guide, and Linux Administrator Street Smarts* (all from Sybex). He can be reached at rodsmith@rodsbooks.com.

Contents at a Glance

Contents

Table of Exercises

CompTIA Certification

It Pays to Get Certified

CompTIA.

In a digital world, digital literacy is an essential survival skill. Certification proves you have the knowledge and skill to solve business problems in virtually any business environment. Certifications are highly valued credentials that qualify you for jobs, increased compensation, and promotion.

IT is Everywhere	IT Knowledge and Skills Get Jobs	Job Retention	New Opportunities	High Pay-High Growth Jobs
IT is mission critical to almost all organizations and its importance is increasing.	Certifications verify your knowledge and skills that qualifies you for:	Competence is noticed and valued in organizations.	Certifications qualify you for new opportunities in your current job or when you want to change careers.	Hiring managers demand the strongest skill set.
• 79% of U.S. businesses report IT is either important or very important to the success of their company	• Jobs in the high growth IT career field • Increased compensation • Challenging assignments and promotions • 60% report that being certified is an employer or job requirement	• Increased knowledge of new or complex technologies • Enhanced productivity • More insightful problem solving • Better project management and communication skills • 47% report being certified helped improve their problem solving skills	• 31% report certification improved their career advancement opportunities	• There is a widening IT skills gap with over 300,000 jobs open • 88% report being certified enhanced their resume

Certification Helps Your Career

CompTIA Linux+ Powered by LPI certification is held by many IT staff members in organizations—25 percent of IT staff within a random sampling of U.S. organizations within a cross section of industry verticals have earned CompTIA Linux+ certification.

CompTIA Linux+ Powered by LPI Validates the fundamental knowledge and skills required of junior Linux administrators. The exams cover system architecture, GNU and UNIX commands, user interfaces and desktops, and Linux installation and package management.

Candidate Job Roles   Includes junior Linux administrator, junior network administrator, systems administrator, Linux database administrator, and web administrator.

Dual Certification   If you choose, certification in CompTIA Linux+ Powered by LPI, attained by passing CompTIA exams LX0-101 and LX0-102, enables you to become certified in LPIC-1 as well.

Starting Salary   The average salary for CompTIA Linux+ Powered by LPI certification holders is $76,000 (USD).

Mandated/Recommended by Organizations Worldwide   Companies such as Dell, HP, IBM, Lenovo, and Xerox recommend or require CompTIA Linux+ Certification.

CompTIA Career Pathway

CompTIA offers a number of credentials that form a foundation for your career in technology and allow you to pursue specific areas of concentration. Depending on the path you choose to take, CompTIA certifications help you build upon your skills and knowledge, supporting learning throughout your entire career.

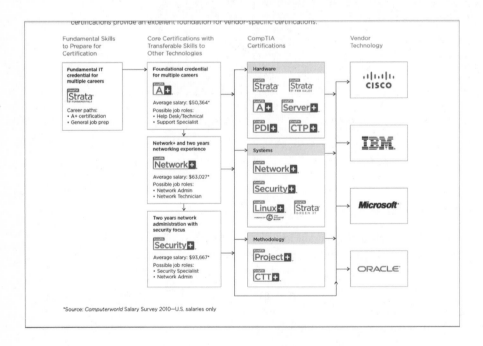

Steps to Certification

Four Steps to Getting Certified and Staying Certified

1. Review the exam objectives.	Review the certification objectives to make sure you know what is covered on the exam: `http://www.comptia.org/certifications/testprep/examobjectives.aspx`.
2. Practice for the exam.	After you have studied for the certification, take a free assessment and sample test to get an idea what type of questions might be on the exam: `http://www.comptia.org/certifications/testprep/practicetests.aspx`.
3. Purchase an exam voucher.	Purchase exam vouchers on the CompTIA Marketplace, which is located at `http://www.comptiastore.com`.
4. Take the test!	Select a certification exam provider and schedule a time to take your exam. You can find exam providers here: `http://www.comptia.org/certifications/testprep/testingcenters.aspx`.

Join the Professional Community

The free IT Pro online community (`http://itpro.comptia.org`) provides valuable content to students and professionals.

- Career IT job resources
    - Where to start in IT
    - Career assessments
    - Salary trends
    - U.S. job board
- Forums on networking, security, computing, and cutting-edge technologies
- Access to blogs written by industry experts
- Current information on cutting-edge technologies
- Access to various industry resource links and articles related to IT and IT careers

Content Seal of Quality

This courseware bears the seal of CompTIA Approved Quality Content. This seal signifies this content covers 100 percent of the exam objectives and implements important instructional design principles. CompTIA recommends multiple learning tools to help increase coverage of the learning objectives.

Why CompTIA?

Global Recognition   CompTIA is recognized globally as the leading IT nonprofit trade association and has enormous credibility. Plus, CompTIA's certifications are vendor-neutral and offer proof of foundational knowledge that translates across technologies.

Valued by Hiring Managers   Hiring managers value CompTIA certification because it is a vendor- and technology-independent validation of your technical skills.

Recommended or Required by Government and Businesses   Many government organizations and corporations either recommend or require technical staff to be CompTIA certified (for example, Dell, Sharp, Ricoh, the U.S. Department of Defense, and many more).

Three CompTIA Certifications Ranked in the Top 10   In a study by DICE of 17,000 technology professionals, certifications helped command higher salaries at all experience levels.

How to Obtain More Information

Visit CompTIA online   Visit http://www.comptia.org to learn more about getting CompTIA certified.

Contact CompTIA   Call 866-835-8020 ext. 5 or email questions@comptia.org.

Join the IT Pro Community   Visit http://itpro.comptia.org to join the IT Pro community to get relevant career information.

Connect with Us   Learn more about us via LinkedIn, Facebook, Twitter, Flickr, and YouTube.

Introduction

Why should you learn about Linux? It's a fast-growing operating system, and it is inexpensive and flexible. Linux is also a major player in the small and mid-sized server field, and it's an increasingly viable platform for workstation and desktop use as well. By understanding Linux, you'll increase your standing in the job market. Even if you already know Windows or Mac OS and your employer uses these systems exclusively, understanding Linux will give you an edge when you're looking for a new job or you're looking for a promotion. For instance, this knowledge will help you to make an informed decision about if and when you should deploy Linux. The Computing Technology Industry Association (CompTIA) promotes the Linux+ exam as an introductory certification for people who want to enter careers involving Linux. The exam is meant to certify that an individual has the skills necessary to install, operate, and troubleshoot a Linux system and is familiar with Linux-specific concepts and basic hardware.

The purpose of this book is to help you pass the Linux+ exams (LX0-101 and LX0-102) updated in 2012. Because these exams cover basic Linux installation, configuration, maintenance, applications, networking, and security, those are the topics that are emphasized in this book. You'll learn enough to get a Linux system up and running and to configure it for many common tasks. Even after you've taken and passed the Linux+ exams, this book should remain a useful reference.

In 2010, CompTIA announced a partnership with Linux Professional Institute, the organization behind the popular LPI Certification (LPIC) program. With this partnership, CompTIA offers the LPIC Level 1 exams under the Linux+ umbrella. The exams and the exam objectives are identical for the two programs; however, Linux+ candidates have the option of receiving their LPIC-1 as well as the Novell Certified Linux Administrator certification by passing the CompTIA Linux+ exams.

What Is Linux?

Linux is a clone of the Unix operating system (OS) that has been popular in academia and many business environments for years. Formerly used exclusively on large mainframes, Unix and Linux can now run on small computers—which are actually far more powerful than the mainframes of just a few years ago. Because of its mainframe heritage, Unix (and hence also Linux) scales well to perform today's demanding scientific, engineering, and network server tasks.

Linux consists of a kernel, which is the core control software, and many libraries and utilities that rely on the kernel to provide features with which users interact. The OS is available in many different distributions, which are collections of a specific kernel with specific support programs.

Why Become Linux Certified?

Several good reasons to get your Linux certification exist. There are four major benefits:

Relevance   The exams were designed with the needs of Linux professionals in mind. This was done by performing surveys of Linux administrators to learn what they actually need to know to do their jobs.

Quality   The exams have been extensively tested and validated using psychometric standards. The result is an ability to discriminate between competent administrators and those who must still learn more material.

Neutrality   CompTIA is an organization that doesn't itself market any Linux distribution. This fact removes the motivation to create an exam that's designed as a way to market a particular distribution.

Support   The exams are supported by major players in the Linux world.

How to Become Certified

The certification is available to anyone who passes the two required exams: LX0-101 and LX0-102. You don't have to work for a particular company. It's not a secret society.

The exam is administered by Pearson VUE. The exam can be taken at any Pearson VUE testing center. If you pass, you will get a certificate in the mail saying that you have passed. Contact (877) 551-PLUS (551-7587) for Pearson VUE contact information.

To register for the exam with Pearson VUE, call (877) 551-PLUS (551-7587), or register online at www.vue.com/comptia. However you do it, you'll be asked for your name, mailing address, phone number, employer, when and where you want to take the test (i.e., which testing center), and your credit card number (arrangement for payment must be made at the time of registration).

As noted above, if you take and pass the CompTIA Linux+ exams, you do have the option of also obtaining your LPIC-1 certification from LPI, as well as your Novell Certified Linux Administrator (CLA) certification at the same time. All that is required is authorization to submit your information to LPI. You are given this option at the testing site.

Who Should Buy This Book

Anybody who wants to pass the certification exams may benefit from this book. This book covers the material that someone new to Linux will need to learn the OS from the beginning, and it continues to provide the knowledge you need up to a proficiency level sufficient to pass the two exams. You can pick up this book and learn from it even if you've never used Linux before, although you'll find it an easier read if you've at least casually used Linux for a few days. If you're already familiar with Linux, this book can serve as a review and as a refresher course for information with which you might not be completely familiar. In either case, reading this book will help you to pass the exams.

This book is written with the assumption that you know at least a little bit about Linux (what it is, and possibly a few Linux commands). I also assume you know some basics about computers in general, such as how to use a keyboard, how to insert a disc into an optical drive, and so on. Chances are, you have used computers in a substantial way in the past—perhaps even Linux, as an ordinary user, or maybe you have used Windows or Mac OS. I do not assume that you have extensive knowledge of Linux system administration, but if you've done some system administration, you can still use this book to fill in gaps in your knowledge.

As a practical matter, you'll need a Linux system with which to practice and learn in a hands-on way. Neither the exams nor this book covers actually installing Linux on a computer from scratch, although some of the prerequisites (such as disk partitioning) are covered. You may need to refer to your distribution's documentation to learn how to accomplish this task. Alternatively, several vendors sell computers with Linux pre-installed.

How This Book Is Organized

This book consists of 10 chapters plus supplementary information: an online glossary, this introduction, and the assessment test after the introduction. The chapters are organized as follows:

- Chapter 1, "Exploring Linux Command-Line Tools," covers the basic tools you need to interact with Linux. These include shells, redirection, pipes, text filters, and regular expressions.

- Chapter 2, "Managing Software," describes the programs you'll use to manage software. Much of this task is centered around the RPM and Debian package management systems. The chapter also covers handling shared libraries and managing processes (that is, running programs).

- Chapter 3, "Configuring Hardware," focuses on Linux's interactions with the hardware on which it runs. Specific hardware and procedures for using it include the BIOS, expansion cards, USB devices, hard disks, and the partitions and filesystems used on hard disks.

- Chapter 4, "Managing Files," covers the tools used to manage files. This includes commands to manage files, ownership, and permissions, as well as Linux's standard directory tree and tools for archiving files.

- Chapter 5, "Booting Linux and Editing Files," explains how Linux boots up and how you can edit files in Linux. Specific topics include the GRUB Legacy and GRUB 2 boot loaders, boot diagnostics, runlevels, and the Vi editor.

- Chapter 6, "Configuring the X Window System, Localization, and Printing," describes the Linux GUI and printing subsystems. Topics include X configuration, managing GUI logins, configuring location-specific features, enabling accessibility features, and setting up Linux to use a printer.

- Chapter 7, "Administering the System," describes miscellaneous administrative tasks. These include user and group management, tuning user environments, managing log files, setting the clock, and running jobs in the future.

- Chapter 8, "Configuring Basic Networking," focuses on basic network configuration. Topics include TCP/IP basics, setting up Linux on a TCP/IP network, and network diagnostics.

- Chapter 9, "Writing Scripts, Configuring Email, and Using Databases," covers these miscellaneous topics. Scripts are small programs that administrators often use to help automate common tasks. Email, of course, is an important topic for any computer user, particularly on Linux, which often runs an email server for local or remote use. Linux can run databases that help you store and retrieve information, and these tools can be very important ones on many Linux systems.

- Chapter 10, "Securing Your System," covers security. Specific subjects include network security, local security, and the use of encryption to improve security.

Chapters 1 through 5 cover the LX0-101 exam, while Chapters 6 through 10 cover the LX0-102 exam. These make up Part I and Part II of the book, respectively.

Each chapter begins with a list of the exam objectives that are covered in that chapter. The book doesn't cover the objectives in order. Thus, you shouldn't be alarmed at some of the odd ordering of the objectives within the book. At the end of each chapter, you'll find a couple of elements you can use to prepare for the exam:

Exam Essentials   This section summarizes important information that was covered in the chapter. You should be able to perform each of the tasks or convey the information requested.

Review Questions   Each chapter concludes with 20 review questions. You should answer these questions and check your answers against the ones provided after the questions. If you can't answer at least 80 percent of these questions correctly, go back and review the chapter, or at least those sections that seem to be giving you difficulty.

 The review questions, assessment test, and other testing elements included in this book are *not* derived from the actual exam questions, so don't memorize the answers to these questions and assume that doing so will enable you to pass the exam. You should learn the underlying topic, as described in the text of the book. This will let you answer the questions provided with this book *and* pass the exam. Learning the underlying topic is also the approach that will serve you best in the workplace—the ultimate goal of a certification.

To get the most out of this book, you should read each chapter from start to finish and then check your memory and understanding with the chapter-end elements. Even if you're already familiar with a topic, you should skim the chapter; Linux is complex enough that there are often multiple ways to accomplish a task, so you may learn something even if you're already competent in an area.

Additional Study Tools

Readers of this book can access a Web site that contains several additional study tools, including the following:

 Readers can access these tools by visiting http://www.sybex.com/go/linuxplus2e.

Sample Tests All of the questions in this book will be included, including the Assessment Test at the end of this introduction and the 200 from the review sections at the end of each chapter. In addition, there are two 50-question bonus exams. The test engine runs on Windows, Linux, and Mac OS.

Electronic Flashcards The additional study tools includes 150 questions in flashcard format (a question followed by a single correct answer). You can use these to review your knowledge of the exam objectives. The flashcards run on both Windows and Linux.

Glossary of Terms as a PDF File In addition, there is a searchable glossary in PDF format, which can be read on all platforms that support PDF.

Conventions Used in This Book

This book uses certain typographic styles in order to help you quickly identify important information and to avoid confusion over the meaning of words such as on-screen prompts. In particular, look for the following styles

- *Italicized text* indicates key terms that are described at length for the first time in a chapter. (Italics are also used for emphasis.)

- A `monospaced font` indicates the contents of configuration files, messages displayed at a text-mode Linux shell prompt, filenames, text-mode command names, and Internet URLs.

- *`Italicized monospaced text`* indicates a variable—information that differs from one system or command run to another, such as the name of a client computer or a process ID number.

- **`Bold monospaced text`** is information that you're to type into the computer, usually at a Linux shell prompt. This text can also be italicized to indicate that you should substitute an appropriate value for your system. (When isolated on their own lines, commands are preceded by non-bold monospaced $ or # command prompts, denoting regular user or system administrator use, respectively.)

In addition to these text conventions, which can apply to individual words or entire paragraphs, a few conventions highlight segments of text:

A note indicates information that's useful or interesting but that's somewhat peripheral to the main text. A note might be relevant to a small number of networks, for instance, or it may refer to an outdated feature.

 A tip provides information that can save you time or frustration and that may not be entirely obvious. A tip might describe how to get around a limitation or how to use a feature to perform an unusual task.

 Warnings describe potential pitfalls or dangers. If you fail to heed a warning, you may end up spending a lot of time recovering from a bug, or you may even end up restoring your entire system from scratch.

Sidebar

A sidebar is like a note but longer. The information in a sidebar is useful, but it doesn't fit into the main flow of the text.

 Real World Scenario

Real World Scenario

A real world scenario is a type of sidebar that describes a task or example that's particularly grounded in the real world. This may be a situation I or somebody I know has encountered, or it may be advice on how to work around problems that are common in real, working Linux environments.

EXERCISE: EXERCISE

An exercise is a procedure you should try on your own computer to help you learn about the material in the chapter. Don't limit yourself to the procedures described in the exercises, though! Try other commands and procedures to really learn about Linux.

The Exam Objectives

Behind every computer industry exam you can be sure to find exam objectives—the broad topics in which exam developers want to ensure your competency. The official exam objectives are listed here. (They're also printed at the start of the chapters in which they're covered.)

 Exam objectives are subject to change at any time without prior notice and at CompTIA's sole discretion. Please visit CompTIA's Web site (http://certification.comptia.org/home.aspx) for the most current listing of exam objectives.

Exam LX0-101 Objectives

The following are the areas in which you must be proficient in order to pass the LX0-101 exam. This exam is broken into four topics (101–104), each of which has three to eight objectives. Each objective has an associated weight, which reflects its importance to the exam as a whole. The four main domains are

Domain	% of Exam
101 System Architecture	14%
102 Linux Installation and Package Management	18%
103 GNU and Unix Commands	43%
104 Devices, Linux Filesystems, Filesystem Hierarchy Standard	25%
Total	100%

101 System Architecture

101.1 Determine and Configure hardware settings (Chapter 3)

- Enable and disable integrated peripherals
- Configure systems with or without external peripherals such as keyboards
- Differentiate between the various types of mass storage devices
- Set the correct hardware ID for different devices, especially the boot device
- Know the differences between coldplug and hotplug devices
- Determine hardware resources for devices

- Tools and utilities to list various hardware information (e.g., lsusb, lspci, etc.)
- Tools and utilities to manipulate USB devices
- Conceptual understanding of sysfs, udev, hald, dbus
- The following is a partial list of the used files, terms, and utilities: /sys, /proc, /dev, modprobe, lsmod, lspci, lsusb

101.2 Boot the System (Chapter 5)

- Provide common commands to the boot loader and options to the kernel at boot time
- Demonstrate knowledge of the boot sequence from BIOS to boot completion
- Check boot events in the log file
- The following is a partial list of the used files, terms and utilities: /var/log/messages, dmesg, BIOS, bootloader, kernel, init

101.3 Change runlevels and shutdown or reboot system (Chapter 5)

- Set the default run level
- Change between run levels including single user mode
- Shutdown and reboot from the command line
- Alert users before switching run levels or other major system events
- Properly terminate processes
- Knowledge of basic features of systemd and Upstart
- The following is a partial list of the used files, terms and utilities: /etc/inittab, shutdown, init, /etc/init.d, telinit

102 Linux Installation and Package Management

102.1 Design hard disk layout (Chapter 3)

- Allocate filesystems and swap space to separate partitions or disks
- Tailor the design to the intended use of the system
- Ensure the /boot partition conforms to the hardware architecture requirements for booting
- Knowledge of basic features of LVM
- The following is a partial list of the used files, terms and utilities: / (root) filesystem, /var filesystem, /home filesystem, swap space, mount points, partitions

102.2 Install a boot manager (Chapter 5)

- Providing alternative boot locations and backup boot options
- Install and configure a boot loader such as GRUB Legacy
- Perform basic configuration changes for GRUB 2
- Interact with the boot loader
- The following is a partial list of the used files, terms, and utilities, `/boot/grub/menu
.1st`, `grub.cfg` and other variations, `grub-install`, MBR, superblock

102.3 Manage shared libraries (Chapter 2)

- Identify shared libraries
- Identify the typical locations of system libraries
- Load shared libraries
- The following is a partial list of the used files, terms and utilities, `ldd`, `ldconfig`, `/etc/
ld.so.conf`, `LD_LIBRARY_PATH`

102.4 Use Debian package management (Chapter 2)

- Install, upgrade and uninstall Debian binary packages
- Find packages containing specific files or libraries which may or may not be installed
- Obtain package information like version, content, dependencies, package integrity and installation status (whether or not the package is installed)
- The following is a partial list of the used files, terms and utilities: `/etc/apt/sources
.list`, `dpkg`, `dpkg-reconfigure`, `apt-get`, `apt-cache`, `aptitude`

102.5 Use RPM and YUM package management (Chapter 2)

- Install, re-install, upgrade and remove packages using RPM and YUM
- Obtain information on RPM packages such as version, status, dependencies, integrity and signatures
- Determine what files a package provides, as well as find which package a specific file comes from
- The following is a partial list of the used files, terms and utilities: `rpm`, `rpm2cpio`, `/etc/
yum.conf`, `/etc/yum.repos.d/`, `yum`, `yumdownloader`

103 GNU and Unix Commands

103.1 Work on the command line (Chapter 1)

- Use single shell commands and one line command sequences to perform basic tasks on the command line

- Use and modify the shell environment including defining, referencing and exporting environment variables
- Use and edit command history
- Invoke commands inside and outside the defined path
- The following is a partial list of the used files, terms and utilities: ., bash, echo, env, exec, export, pwd, set, unset, man, uname, history

103.2 Process text streams using filters (Chapter 1)

- Send text files and output streams through text utility filters to modify the output using standard UNIX commands found in the GNU textutils package
- The following is a partial list of the used files, terms and utilities: cat, cut, expand, fmt, head, od, join, nl, paste, pr, sed, sort, split, tail, tr, unexpand, uniq, wc

103.3 Perform basic file management (Chapter 4)

- Copy, move and remove files and directories individually
- Copy multiple files and directories recursively
- Remove files and directories recursively
- Use simple and advanced wildcard specifications in commands
- Using find to locate and act on files based on type, size, or time
- Usage of tar, cpio, and dd
- The following is a partial list of the used files, terms and utilities: cp, find, mkdir, mv, ls, rm, rmdir, touch, tar, cpio, dd, file, gzip, gunzip, bzip2, file globbing

103.4 Use streams, pipes and redirects (Chapter 1)

- Redirecting standard input, standard output and standard error
- Pipe the output of one command to the input of another command
- Use the output of one command as arguments to another command
- Send output to both stdout and a file
- The following is a partial list of the used files, terms and utilities: tee, xargs

103.5 Create, monitor and kill processes (Chapter 2)

- Run jobs in the foreground and background
- Signal a program to continue running after logout
- Monitor active processes
- Select and sort processes for display
- Send signals to processes

- The following is a partial list of the used files, terms and utilities: &, bg, fg, jobs, kill, nohup, ps, top, free, uptime, killall

103.6 Modify process execution priorities (Chapter 2)

- Know the default priority of a job that is created
- Run a program with higher or lower priority than the default
- Change the priority of a running process
- The following is a partial list of the used files, terms and utilities: nice, ps, renice, top

103.7 Search text files using regular expressions (Chapter 1)

- Create simple regular expressions containing several notational elements
- Use regular expression tools to perform searches through a filesystem or file content
- The following is a partial list of the used files, terms and utilities: grep, egrep, fgrep, sed, regex(7)

103.8 Perform basic file editing operations using *vi* (Chapter 5)

- Navigate a document using vi
- Use basic vi modes
- Insert, edit, delete, copy and find text
- The following is a partial list of the used files, terms and utilities: vi, /, ?, h, j, k, l, i, o, a, c, d, p, y, dd, yy, ZZ, :w!, :q!, :e!

104 Devices, Linux Filesystems, Filesystem Hierarchy Standard

104.1 Create partitions and filesystems (Chapter 3)

- Use various mkfs commands to set up partitions and create various filesystems such as: ext2, ext3, xfs, reiserfs v3, vfat
- The following is a partial list of the used files, terms and utilities: fdisk, mkfs, mkswap

104.2 Maintain the integrity of filesystems (Chapter 3)

- Verify the integrity of filesystems
- Monitor free space and inodes
- Repair simple filesystem problems
- The following is a partial list of the used files, terms and utilities: du, df, fsck, e2fsck, mke2fs, debugfs, dumpe2fs, tune2fs, xfs tools (such as xfs_metadump and xfs_info)

104.3 Control mounting and unmounting of filesystems (Chapter 3)

- Manually mount and unmount filesystems
- Configure filesystem mounting on bootup
- Configure user mountable removeable filesystems
- The following is a partial list of the used files, terms and utilities: /etc/fstab, /media, mount, umount

104.4 Manage disk quotas (Chapter 4)

- Set up a disk quota for a filesystem
- Edit, check and generate user quota reports
- The following is a partial list of the used files, terms and utilities: quota, edquota, repquota, quotaon

104.5 Manage file permissions and ownership (Chapter 4)

- Manage access permissions on regular and special files as well as directories
- Use access modes such as suid, sgid and the sticky bit to maintain security
- Know how to change the file creation mask
- Use the group field to grant file access to group members
- The following is a partial list of the used files, terms and utilities: chmod, umask, chown, chgrp

104.6 Create and change hard and symbolic links (Chapter 4)

- Create links
- Identify hard and/or soft links
- Copying versus linking files
- Use links to support system administration tasks
- The following is a partial list of the used files, terms and utilities: ln

104.7 Find system files and place files in the correct location (Chapter 4)

- Understand the correct locations of files under the FHS
- Find files and commands on a Linux system
- Know the location and propose of important file and directories as defined in the FHS
- The following is a partial list of the used files, terms and utilities: find, locate, updatedb, whereis, which, type, /etc/updatedb.conf

Exam LX0-102 Objectives

The 102 exam comprises six topics (105–110), each of which contains three or four objectives. The six major topics are weighted as follows:

Domain	% of Exam
105 Shells, Scripting and Data Management	17%
106 User Interfaces and Desktops	8%
107 Administrative Tasks	20%
108 Essential System Services	17%
109 Networking Fundamentals	23%
110 Security	15%
Total	100%

105 Shells, Scripting and Data Management

105.1 Customize and use the shell environment (Chapter 9)

- Set environment variables (e.g., PATH) at login or when spawning a new shell
- Write BASH functions for frequently used sequences of commands
- Maintain skeleton directories for new user accounts
- Set command search path with the proper directory
- The following is a partial list of the used files, terms, and utilities: /etc/profile, env, export, set, unset, ~/.bash_profile, ~/.bash_login, ~/.profile, ~/.bashrc, ~/.bash_logout, function, alias, lists

105.2 Customize or write simple scripts (Chapter 9)

- Use standard sh syntax (loops, tests)
- Use command substitution
- Test return values for success or failure or other information provided by a command
- Perform conditional mailing to the superuser
- Correctly select the script interpreter through the shebang (#!) line
- Manage the location, ownership, execution and suid-rights of scripts
- The following is a partial list of the used files, terms, and utilities: for, while, test, if, read, seq

105.3 SQL data management (Chapter 9)

- Use of basic SQL commands
- Perform basic data manipulation
- The following is a partial list of the used files, terms, and utilities: `insert`, `update`, `select`, `delete`, `from`, `where`, `group by`, `order by`, `join`

106 User Interfaces and Desktops

106.1 Install and configure X11 (Chapter 6)

- Verify that the video card and monitor are supported by an X server
- Awareness of the X font server
- Basic understanding and knowledge of the X Window configuration file
- The following is a partial list of the used files, terms, and utilities: `/etc/X11/xorg.conf`, `xhost`, `DISPLAY`, `xwininfo`, `xdpyinfo`, `X`

106.2 Setup a display manager (Chapter 6)

- Turn the display manager on or off
- Change the display manager greeting
- Change default color depth for the display manager
- Configure display managers for use by X-stations
- The following is a partial list of the used files, terms, and utilities: `/etc/inittab`; plus xdm, kdm, and gdm configuration files

106.3 Accessibility (Chapter 6)

- Keyboard Accessibility Settings (AccessX)
- Visual Settings and Themes
- Assistive Technology (ATs)
- The following is a partial list of the used files, terms, and utilities: Sticky/Repeat Keys, Slow/Bounce/Toggle Keys, Mouse Keys, High Contrast/Large Print Desktop Themes, Screen Reader, Braille Display, Screen Magnifier, On-Screen Keyboard, Gestures (used at login, for example gdm), Orca, GOK, `emacspeak`

107 Administrative Tasks

107.1 Manage user and group accounts and related system files (Chapter 7)

- Add, modify and remove users and groups
- Manage user/group info in password/group databases

- Create and manage special purpose and limited accounts
- The following is a partial list of the used files, terms, and utilities: /etc/passwd, /etc/shadow, /etc/group, /etc/skel, chage, groupadd, groupdel, groupmod, passwd, useradd, userdel, usermod

107.2 Automate system administration tasks by scheduling jobs (Chapter 9)

- Manage cron and at jobs
- Configure user access to cron and at services
- The following is a partial list of the used files, terms, and utilities: /etc/cron.{d,daily,hourly,monthly,weekly}, /etc/at.deny, /etc/at.allow, /etc/crontab, /etc/cron.allow, /etc/cron.deny, /var/spool/cron/*, crontab, at, atq, atrm

107.3 Localization and internationalization (Chapter 6)

- Locale settings
- Timezone settings
- The following is a partial list of the used files, terms, and utilities: /etc/timezone, /etc/localtime, /usr/share/zoneinfo, environment variables (LC_*, LC_ALL, LANG, TZ), /usr/bin/locale, tzselect, tzconfig, date, iconv, UTF-8, ISO-8859, ASCII, Unicode

108 Essential System Services

108.1 Maintain system time (Chapter 7)

- Set the system date and time
- Set the hardware clock to the correct time in UTC
- Configure the correct timezone
- Basic NTP configuration
- Knowledge of using the pool.ntp.org service
- The following is a partial list of the used files, terms, and utilities: /usr/share/zoneinfo, /etc/timezone, /etc/localtime, /etc/ntp.conf, date, hwclock, ntpd, ntpdate, pool.ntp.org

108.2 System logging (Chapter 7)

- Syslog configuration files
- syslog
- standard facilities, priorities and actions

- The following is a partial list of the used files, terms, and utilities: `syslog.conf`, `syslogd`, `klogd`, `logger`

108.3 Mail Transfer Agent (MTA) basics (Chapter 9)

- Create e-mail aliases
- Configure e-mail forwarding
- Knowledge of commonly available MTA programs (postfix, sendmail, qmail, exim) (no configuration)
- The following is a partial list of the used files, terms, and utilities: `~/.forward`, sendmail emulation layer commands, `newaliases`, `mail`, `mailq`, postfix, sendmail, exim, qmail

108.4 Manage printers and printing (Chapter 6)

- Basic CUPS configuration (for local and remote printers)
- Manage user print queues
- Troubleshoot general printing problems
- Add and remove jobs from configured printer queues
- The following is a partial list of the used files, terms, and utilities: CUPS configuration files, tools and utilities; `/etc/cups`; `lpd` legacy interface (`lpr`, `lprm`, `lpq`)

109 Networking Fundamentals

109.1 Fundamentals of internet protocols (Chapter 8)

- Demonstrate an understanding network masks
- Knowledge of the differences between private and public "dotted quad" IP-Addresses
- Setting a default route
- Knowledge about common TCP and UDP ports (20, 21, 22, 23, 25, 53, 80, 110, 119, 139, 143, 161, 443, 465, 993, 995)
- Knowledge about the differences and major features of UDP, TCP and ICMP
- Knowledge of the major differences between IPv4 and IPV6
- Knowledge of the basic features of IPv6
- The following is a partial list of the used files, terms, and utilities: `/etc/services`, `ftp`, `telnet`, `host`, `ping`, `dig`, `traceroute`, `tracepath`

109.2 Basic network configuration (Chapter 8)

- Manually and automatically configure network interfaces
- Basic TCP/IP host configuration

- The following is a partial list of the used files, terms, and utilities: /etc/hostname, /etc/hosts, /etc/resolv.conf, /etc/nsswitch.conf, ifconfig, ifup, ifdown, route, ping

109.3 Basic network troubleshooting (Chapter 8)

- Manually and automatically configure network interfaces and routing tables to include adding, starting, stopping, restarting, deleting or reconfiguring network interfaces
- Change, view or configure the routing table and correct an improperly set default route manually
- Debug problems associated with the network configuration
- The following is a partial list of the used files, terms, and utilities: ifconfig, ifup, ifdown, route, host, hostname, dig, netstat, ping, traceroute

109.4 Configure client side DNS (Chapter 8)

- Demonstrate the use of DNS on the local system
- Modify the order in which name resolution is done
- The following is a partial list of the used files, terms, and utilities: /etc/hosts, /etc/resolv.conf, /etc/nsswitch.conf

110 Security

110.1 Perform security administration tasks (Chapter 10)

- Audit a system to find files with the suid/sgid bit set
- Set or change user passwords and password aging information
- Being able to use nmap and netstat to discover open ports on a system
- Set up limits on user logins, processes and memory usage
- Basic sudo configuration and usage
- The following is a partial list of the used files, terms, and utilities: find, passwd, lsof, nmap, chage, netstat, sudo, /etc/sudoers, su, usermod, ulimit

110.2 Setup host security (Chapter 10)

- Awareness of shadow passwords and how they work
- Turn off network services not in use
- Understand the role of TCP wrappers
- The following is a partial list of the used files, terms, and utilities: /etc/nologin, /etc/passwd, /etc/shadow, /etc/xinetd.d/*, /etc/xinetd.conf, /etc/inetd.d/*, /etc/inetd.conf, /etc/inittab, /etc/init.d/*, /etc/hosts.allow, /etc/hosts.deny

110.3 Securing data with encryption (Chapter 10)

- Perform basic OpenSSH 2 client configuration and usage
- Understand the role of OpenSSH 2 server host keys
- Perform basic GnuPG configuration and usage
- Understand SSH port tunnels (including X11 tunnels)
- The following is a partial list of the used files, terms, and utilities: ssh, ssh-keygen, ssh-agent, ssh-add, ~/.ssh/id_rsa and id_rsa.pub, ~/.ssh/id_dsa and id_dsa.pub, /etc/ssh/ssh_host_rsa_key and ssh_host_rsa_key.pub, /etc/ssh/ssh_host_dsa_key and ssh_host_dsa_key.pub, ~/.ssh/authorized_keys, /etc/ssh_known_hosts, gpg, ~/.gnupg/*

Assessment Test

1. The following line appears in your X server's mouse configuration area. What can you conclude?

    ```
    Option      "Protocol" "PS/2"
    ```

    A. The mouse is connected to the PS/2 hardware mouse port.

    B. The mouse uses the PS/2 software communication standard.

    C. The computer is an ancient IBM PS/2 system.

    D. The mouse was designed for use with IBM's OS/2.

    E. A slash (/) is invalid in a protocol name, so the mouse won't work.

2. How can you tell whether your system is using `inetd` or `xinetd` as a super server? (Select two.)

    A. Type `ps ax | grep inetd`, and examine the output for signs of `inetd` or `xinetd`.

    B. Type `superserver` to see a report on which super server is running.

    C. Look for the `/etc/inetd.conf` file or `/etc/xinetd.d` subdirectory, which are signs of `inetd` or `xinetd`, respectively.

    D. Examine the `/etc/inittab` file to see which super server is launched by `init`, which is responsible for this task.

    E. Type `netstat -a | grep inet` and examine the output for signs of `inetd` or `xinetd`.

3. How does the `lpc` utility for CUPS differ from its counterpart in BSD LPD and LPRng?

    A. The `lpc` utility is unique to CUPS; it doesn't ship with BSD LPD or LPRng.

    B. CUPS doesn't ship with an `lpc` command, but BSD LPD and LPRng do.

    C. CUPS's `lpc` is much more complex than its counterpart in BSD LPD and LPRng.

    D. CUPS's `lpc` is much simpler than its counterpart in BSD LPD and LPRng.

    E. The `lpc` utility is identical in all three of these printing systems.

4. What file would you edit to restrict the number of simultaneous logins a user can employ?

    A. `/etc/pam.d/login-limits`

    B. `/etc/bashrc`

    C. `/etc/security/limits.conf`

    D. `/etc/inittab`

    E. `/etc/passwd`

5. Which of the following are required when configuring a computer to use a static IP address? (Select two.)

    A. The IP address of the DHCP server

    B. The hostname of the NBNS server

    C. The computer's IP address

    D. The network mask

    E. The IP address of the NTP server

6. What does the following command accomplish?

    `$ wc report.txt | tee wc`

    A. It launches the wc editor on both the `report.txt` and `wc.txt` files; each file opens in its own window.

    B. It displays a count of the windows in which the `report.txt` file is displayed and shows that information in a new window called wc.

    C. It creates a count of newlines, words, and bytes in the `report.txt` file and then displays a count of these statistics about the report it just generated.

    D. It cleans up any memory leaks associated with the `tee` program's use of the `report.txt` file.

    E. It displays a count of newlines, words, and bytes in the `report.txt` file and copies that output to the wc file.

7. Which of the following characters defines the end of an OS or kernel definition in /boot/grub/grub.cfg?

    A. ;

    B.)

    C. }

    D. */

    E. None of the above; the definition ends with the `title` line beginning the next entry

8. What does the number 703 represent in the following /etc/passwd entry?

    george:x:703:100:George Brown:/home/george:/bin/tcsh

    A. The account's human ID (HID) number

    B. The account's process ID (PID) number

    C. The account's group ID (GID) number

    D. The account's globally unique ID (GUID) number

    E. The account's user ID (UID) number

9. What does the `grep` command accomplish?

    A. It creates a pipeline between two programs.

    B. It searches files' contents for a pattern.

    C. It concatenates two or more files.

    D. It displays the last several lines of a file.

    E. It locates files on the hard disk.

10. Which of the following are journaling filesystems for Linux? (Select three.)

    A. HPFS

    B. ReiserFS

    C. Ext2fs

    D. Ext3fs

    E. XFS

11. You've configured your computer to use SMTP and IMAP via a tunneled SSH connection to your ISP's email server for improved security. Why might you still want to use GPG encryption for your emails on top of the encryption provided by SSH?

    A. The SSH tunnel reaches only as far as the first email server; GPG encrypts data on all the computers all the way to or from your email correspondents.

    B. SSH encryption is notoriously poor for email, although it's perfectly adequate for login sessions; thus, adding GPG encryption improves security.

    C. SSH doesn't encrypt the headers of the email messages; GPG encrypts the headers to keep snoopers from learning your correspondents' identities.

    D. Using GPG guarantees that your email messages won't contain unwanted viruses or worms that might infect your correspondents' computers.

    E. Configured in this way, SSH will encrypt the email headers and bodies, but not any attachments to your email.

12. Which of the following ports are commonly used to retrieve email from an email server computer? (Select two.)

    A. 110

    B. 119

    C. 139

    D. 143

    E. 443

13. You're experiencing sporadic problems with a Secure Shell (SSH) login server—sometimes users can log in, and sometimes they can't. What might you try immediately after a failure to help diagnose this problem?

   A. On the server computer, type **http://localhost:631** into a Web browser to access the SSH configuration page and check its error subpage for error messages.

   B. Type **diagnose sshd** to run a diagnostic on the SSH server daemon (**sshd**).

   C. Type **tail /var/log/messages** to look for error messages from the server.

   D. Examine the **/dev/ssh** device file to look for error messages from the server.

   E. On the server computer, type **sshd** to view SSH's diagnostic messages.

14. What is the function of the ~/.profile file?

   A. It's the user configuration file for the ProFTP server.

   B. It's one of a user's **bash** startup scripts.

   C. It's the user configuration file for the ProFile file manager.

   D. Its presence tells **tcsh** to ignore file modes.

   E. It holds the user's encrypted password.

15. You want your computer to remind you to get your car inspected in two years. What is the best way to do this, of the specified options?

   A. Create a program that repeatedly checks the time and, when two years have passed, displays a message to get your car inspected.

   B. Type **cal** *day month year*, where *day*, *month*, and *year* specify the date of the future inspection, to have Linux run a program that you then specify on that date.

   C. Create a **cron** job that runs hourly. This job should check the date and, when the correct date comes up, use **mail** to notify you of the need for a car inspection.

   D. Use the NTP GUI calendar program to create an alarm for the specified date. The program will then display the message you enter at the specified date and time.

   E. Type **at** *date*, where *date* is a date specification. You can then specify a command, such as **mail** with appropriate options, to notify you of the need to get your car inspected.

16. How would you configure a computer to use the computer whose IP address is 172.24.21.1 as a gateway for all network traffic that's not otherwise configured?

   A. **gateway default 172.24.21.1**

   B. **gateway 172.24.21.1**

   C. **route gateway 172.24.21.1**

   D. **route add default gw 172.24.21.1**

   E. **gw 172.24.21.1**

17. What software can you use to drive a Braille display device? (Select two.)

    A. Emacspeak

    B. BRLTTY

    C. A 2.6.26 or later kernel

    D. GOK

    E. A framebuffer driver

18. Which is true of source RPM packages?

    A. They consist of three files: an original source tarball, a patch file of changes, and a PGP signature indicating the authenticity of the package.

    B. They require programming knowledge to rebuild.

    C. They can sometimes be used to work around dependency problems with a binary package.

    D. They are necessary to compile software for RPM-based distributions.

    E. They always contain software that's licensed under terms of the GPL.

19. Which utility should you use by itself to rename the file `pumpkin.txt` to `lantern.txt`?

    A. dd

    B. rm

    C. cp

    D. mv

    E. ln

20. You want to run a lengthy scientific simulation program, called `simbigbang`, which doesn't require any user interaction; the program operates solely on disk files. If you don't want to tie up the shell from which you run the program, what should you type to run `simbigbang` in the background?

    A. `start simbigbang`

    B. `simbigbang &`

    C. `bg simbigbang`

    D. `background simbigbang`

    E. `nice simbigbang`

21. Which of the following commands will install an RPM package file called `theprogram-1.2.3-4.i386.rpm` on a computer? (Select two.)

    A. `rpm -Uvh theprogram-1.2.3-4.i386.rpm`

    B. `rpm -i theprogram-1.2.3-4.i386.rpm`

    C. `rpm -U theprogram`

    D. `rpm -e theprogram-1.2.3-4.i386.rpm`

    E. `rpm -Vp theprogram-1.2.3-4.i386.rpm`

22. What tool can diagnose and fix many common Linux filesystem problems?

    A. mkfs

    B. fsck

    C. chkdsk

    D. scandisk

    E. fdisk

23. You've just installed MySQL, and you intend to use it to store information about the animals in a zoo, from the anteaters to the zebras. What command are you likely to use first, once you start MySQL?

    A. CREATE DATABASE animals;

    B. USE animals;

    C. CREATE TABLE animals;

    D. INSERT INTO animals;

    E. UPDATE animals;

24. Which of the following commands displays help on *topic*, when typed in a Linux shell? (Select two.)

    A. manual *topic*

    B. man *topic*

    C. ? *topic*

    D. info *topic*

    E. hint *topic*

25. A computer's hardware clock keeps track of the time while the computer is powered off. In what formats may this time be stored on an x86 Linux system? (Select two.)

    A. Coordinated Universal Time (UTC)

    B. Internet Time

    C. Local time

    D. 12-hour time

    E. Mars time

26. You want to know what kernel modules are currently loaded. What command would you type to learn this information?

    A. insmod

    B. depmod

    C. modprobe

    D. lsmod

    E. modinfo

27. You want to enable all members of the `music` group to read the `instruments.txt` file, which currently has 0640 (`-rw-r-----`) permissions, ownership by `root`, and group ownership by `root`. How might you accomplish this goal? (Select two.)

    A. Type `chown music instruments.txt` in the file's directory.

    B. Type `chgrp music instruments.txt` in the file's directory.

    C. Type `chgroup music instruments.txt` in the file's directory.

    D. Type `chmod 0600 instruments.txt` in the file's directory.

    E. Type `chown :music instruments.txt` in the file's directory.

28. You want to create a link to the `/usr/local/bin` directory in another location. Which of the following statements is true?

    A. You can do this only if `/usr/local/bin` is on a journaling filesystem.

    B. You must own `/usr/local/bin` to create the link.

    C. You can create the link only if the link's location is on the same filesystem as the original directory.

    D. Only the system administrator can do this.

    E. The link will probably have to be a symbolic link.

29. Which of the following, when typed in Vi's command mode, saves a file and quits the program? (Select two.)

    A. `:rq`

    B. `:wq`

    C. `:re`

    D. `:we`

    E. `ZZ`

30. A user's home directory includes a file called `~/.forward` that consists of one line: `|~/junkme`. What is the effect of this configuration?

    A. The user's incoming mail is forwarded to the `junkme` user on the same system.

    B. The user's incoming mail is stored in the `~/junkme` file.

    C. The user's incoming mail is sent through the `~/junkme` program file.

    D. The user's incoming mail is flagged as spam and deleted.

    E. The user's incoming mail is forwarded to the same user on the `junkme` computer.

Answers to the Assessment Test

1. B. "PS/2" can refer to both a hardware interface and a software protocol, but used in the context of the `Protocol` option, it unambiguously refers to the software protocol. Thus, option B is correct. Option A *might* be correct, but the specified line is insufficient evidence of that; USB mice generally use the PS/2 protocol or a variant of it, such as the Intellimouse PS/2 protocol. Although the PS/2 hardware port and protocol originated with the IBM PS/2 computer mentioned in option C, many other computers now use them. Mice that use the PS/2 protocol may be used with just about any OS, not just IBM's OS/2, so option D is incorrect. A slash (/) is valid as part of the PS/2 protocol name, so option E is incorrect. For more information, please see Chapter 6, "Configuring the X Window System, Localization, and Printing."

2. A, C. Examining a process listing (obtained from `ps`) for signs of the super server is the most reliable way to determine which one is actually running, so option A is correct. The presence of the super server's configuration file or files (as in option C) is also a good diagnostic, although some older systems that have been upgraded may have both sets of configuration files. There is no standard `superserver` utility to report on which one is used, so option B is incorrect. Most distributions launch the super server through a SysV startup script; the `/etc/inittab` file isn't directly involved in this process, so examining it would be pointless, and option D is incorrect. Although the output of `netstat -ap`, when typed as `root`, will include an indication of any instance of `inetd` or `xinetd` that's listening for connections, option E omits the critical –p option, which causes the program to display process names. Thus, option E is incorrect. For more information, please see Chapter 10, "Securing Your System."

3. D. The `lpc` utility is used to start, stop, change the priority of, and otherwise control jobs in a print queue. CUPS ships with an `lpc` utility, but it's quite rudimentary compared to the `lpc` utilities of BSD LPD and LPRng. Instead, CUPS relies on its Web-based interface to provide the ability to control print jobs. Thus, option D is correct, and the remaining options must logically all be incorrect. For more information, please see Chapter 6, "Configuring the X Window System, Localization, and Printing."

4. C. The `/etc/security/limits.conf` file defines various limits on user resources, including the number of simultaneous logins individual users are permitted. Thus, option C is correct. The `/etc/pam.d/login-limits` file (option A) is fictitious, although login limits do rely on the `pam_limits` module to the Pluggable Authentication System (PAM). The `/etc/bashrc` file (option B) is a global `bash` startup script file, but it's not normally used to impose login limits. The `/etc/inittab` file (option D) is a key Linux startup file, but it doesn't have any direct bearing on imposing login limits. The `/etc/passwd` file (option E) defines many key account features, but login limits are not among these. For more information, please see Chapter 10, "Securing Your System."

5. C, D. The computer's IP address (option C) and network mask (aka subnet mask or netmask; option D) are the most critical components in TCIP/IP network configuration. (Additional information you may need to provide on many networks includes the IP addresses of one to three DNS servers, the hostname or IP address of a router, and the computer's

(DHCP) server (option A)—and if a DHCP server is present, chances are you should be using DHCP rather than static IP address assignment. A NetBIOS Name Service (NBNS) server (option B) converts between names and IP addresses on NetBIOS networks. The hostname of such a computer isn't likely to be a critical configuration element, although you may need to provide this information to Samba for some operations to function correctly when sharing files. A Network Time Protocol (NTP) server (option E) helps you maintain system time on all your computers, but this isn't required for basic network configuration. For more information, please see Chapter 8, "Configuring Basic Networking."

6. E. The `wc` command displays a count of newlines, words, and bytes in the specified file (`report.txt`). Piping this data through `tee` causes a copy of the output to be stored in the new file (`wc` in this example—you shouldn't run this command in the same directory as the `wc` executable file!). Thus, option E is correct. Contrary to option A, `wc` is not an editor, and the remaining syntax wouldn't cause two files to open in separate windows even if `wc` were an editor. Contrary to option B, `wc` doesn't count windows or open a new window. Option C describes the effect of `wc report | wc`—that is, it overlooks the `tee` command. Contrary to option D, `wc` has nothing to do with cleaning up memory leaks, and `tee` doesn't directly use the `report.txt` file. For more information, please see Chapter 1, "Exploring Linux Command-Line Tools."

7. C. The `grub.cfg` filename indicates a GRUB 2 configuration file. In such files, each OS or kernel stanza begins with a `menuentry` line and an open curly brace (`{`) and ends with a close curly brace (`}`). Thus, option C is correct. Some configuration files and programming languages use semicolons (`;`) at the end of most lines, but this isn't true of GRUB 2, so option A is incorrect. Although close parentheses (`)`) are used to terminate some types of options in some configuration files, including disk identifiers in GRUB 2's configuration file, they aren't used to terminate whole OS or kernel definitions in this file, so option B is incorrect. The string `*/` terminates comments in C program files, but isn't commonly used in GRUB 2 configuration files, so option D is incorrect. Option E would be correct if the question had asked about a GRUB Legacy configuration file (`menu.lst` or `grub.conf`), but the question specifies a GRUB 2 configuration file (`grub.cfg`); the two boot loaders terminate their OS/kernel stanzas differently, so option E is incorrect. For more information, please see Chapter 5, "Booting Linux and Editing Files."

8. E. The third field of `/etc/passwd` entries holds the UID number for the account, so option E is correct. Linux doesn't use any standard identifier called a human ID (HID; option A), although the acronym HID stands for human interface device, a class of USB devices. Accounts don't have PID numbers (option B); those belong to running processes. The account's GID number (option C) is stored in the fourth field of `/etc/passwd`—100 in this example. Linux accounts don't use globally unique ID (GUID) numbers, so option D is incorrect. For more information, please see Chapter 7, "Administering the System."

9. B. The `grep` command scans files to find those that contain a specified string or pattern, as described by option B. In the case of text files, `grep` displays the matching line or lines; for binary files, it reports that the file matches the pattern. The method of creating a pipeline (option A) involves separating two commands with a vertical bar (`|`). The `grep` command can be used in a pipeline, but it doesn't create one. The command that concatenates files (option C) is `cat`, and the command that displays the last several lines of a file (option D) is `tail`. Several commands, such as `find`, `locate`, and `whereis`, locate files (option E), but

`grep` is not among these commands. For more information, please see Chapter 1, "Exploring Linux Command-Line Tools."

10. B, D, E. ReiserFS (option B) was written from scratch for Linux. The Third Extended Filesystem (ext3fs; option D) is a journaling filesystem based on the older non-journaling Second Extended Filesystem (ext2fs; option C). The Extents Filesystem (XFS; option E) is a journaling filesystem written by SGI for Irix and later ported to Linux. The High-Performance Filesystem (HPFS; option A) is a non-journaling filesystem designed by Microsoft for OS/2. For more information, please see Chapter 3, "Configuring Hardware."

11. A. Option A correctly describes the features of SSH and GPG in this context. Option B is incorrect because SSH should do a fine job of encrypting your email so that it can't be decoded between your system and your ISP's email server. Option C has it backward; email transferred via SSH will be completely encrypted, including both headers and body. GPG doesn't encrypt headers, just message bodies. Option D is incorrect because GPG isn't a virus scanner, just an encryption tool. Option E is incorrect because the SSH tunnel will encrypt everything in the SMTP transfer, including email attachments. For more information, please see Chapter 10, "Securing Your System."

12. A, D. Port 110 (option A) is assigned to the Post Office Protocol (POP), and port 143 (option D) is assigned to the Internet Message Access Protocol (IMAP), both of which may be used to retrieve email messages from an email server system. Port 119 (option B) is assigned to the Network News Transfer Protocol (NNTP), port 139 (option C) is assigned to the Server Message Block/Common Internet File System (SMB/CIFS) protocol, and port 443 (option E) is assigned to the Hypertext Transfer Protocol with SSL encryption (HTTPS), none of which is commonly used for email retrieval. For more information, please see Chapter 8, "Configuring Basic Networking."

13. C. Log files, such as `/var/log/messages` and sometimes others in `/var/log`, often contain useful information concerning server errors. The `tail` program displays the last few lines of a file, so using it to examine log files immediately after a problem occurs can be a useful diagnostic procedure. Option C correctly combines these features. The `http://localhost:631` URL of option A accesses the Common Unix Printing System (CUPS) configuration utility, which has nothing to do with SSH. There is no standard `diagnose` utility (option B) to help diagnose server problems, and there is no standard `/dev/ssh` file (option D). The **sshd** program is the SSH server itself, so option B will simply launch the server. For more information, please see Chapter 5, "Booting Linux and Editing Files."

14. B. The `~./profile` file is one of several `bash` startup scripts, as stated in option B. It has nothing to do with the ProFTP server (option A) or the `tcsh` shell (option D). The ProFile file manager mentioned in option C is fictitious. Users' encrypted passwords (option E) are usually stored in `/etc/shadow`. For more information, please see Chapter 9, "Writing Scripts, Configuring Email, and Using Databases."

15. E. The `at` utility was created to run programs at one specified point in the future. Thus, option E will accomplish the stated goal. Options A and C might also work; but neither is the *best* way to accomplish this goal. Option A will tie up CPU time, and if the program crashes or the system is shut down during the intervening two years, the message will never display. Option C would be more reliable, but it adds unnecessary complexity to your

hourly `cron` job schedule. The `cal` program displays a text-mode calendar, enabling you to identify the days of a week for a given month; it doesn't schedule future jobs, as option B suggests. A GUI calendar program, as specified in option D, might work; but NTP is the Network Time Protocol, a protocol and like-named program for synchronizing clocks across a network. Thus, NTP isn't the tool for the job, and option D is incorrect. For more information, please see Chapter 7, "Administering the System."

16. D. Option D provides the correct command to add 172.24.21.1 as the default gateway. Options A and B both use the fictitious `gateway` command, which doesn't exist and therefore won't work unless you create a script of this name. Option C uses the correct `route` command, but there is no `gateway` option to `route`; you must use `add default gw`, as in option D. There is no standard `gw` command, so option E is incorrect. For more information, please see Chapter 8, "Configuring Basic Networking."

17. B, C. The BRLTTY package is an add-on daemon for handling a Braille display device, and some features for using these devices have been added to the 2.6.26 kernel, so options B and C are correct. Emacspeak (option A) is speech-synthesis software; it can be used to "speak" a text display to a user, but it doesn't interface with Braille displays. GOK (option D) is an on-screen keyboard, not a Braille display tool. Framebuffer drivers (option E) are kernel drivers for managing conventional video cards; they aren't used to drive Braille displays. For more information, please see Chapter 6, "Configuring the X Window System, Localization, and Printing."

18. C. Some dependencies result from dynamically linking binaries to libraries at compile time and so can be overcome by recompiling the software from a source RPM, so option C is correct. Option A describes Debian source packages, not RPM packages. Recompiling a source RPM requires only issuing an appropriate command, although you must also have appropriate compilers and libraries installed. Thus, option B is overly pessimistic. Source tarballs can also be used to compile software for RPM systems, although this results in none of RPM's advantages. Thus, option D is overly restrictive. The RPM format doesn't impose any licensing requirements, contrary to option E. For more information, please see Chapter 2, "Managing Software."

19. D. The `mv` utility can be used to rename files as well as move them from one location to another, so option D is correct. The `dd` utility (option A) is used to copy files to backups, `rm` (option B) is used to remove (delete) files, `cp` (option C) copies files, and `ln` (option E) creates links. For more information, please see Chapter 4, "Managing Files."

20. B. Appending an ampersand (&) to a command causes that command to execute in the background. The program so launched still consumes CPU time, but it won't monopolize the shell you used to launch it. Thus, option B is correct. The `start` (option A) and `background` (option D) commands are fictitious. Although `bg` (option C) does place a job into the background, it doesn't launch a program that way; it places a process that's been suspended (by pressing Ctrl+Z) into the background. The `nice` utility (option E) launches a program with modified priority, but a program so launched still monopolizes its shell unless you take additional steps. For more information, please see Chapter 2, "Managing Software."

21. A, B. The -Uvh parameter (option A) issues an upgrade command (which installs the program whether or not an earlier version is installed) and creates a series of hash marks to display the command's progress. The –i parameter (option B) installs the program if it's not already installed but causes no progress display. Option C uses a package name, not a complete filename, and so it will fail to install the package file. The -e option (option D) removes a package. Option E's -Vp option verifies the package file but doesn't install it. For more information, please see Chapter 2, "Managing Software."

22. B. Option B, fsck, is Linux's filesystem check utility. It's similar in purpose to the DOS and Windows CHKDSK and ScanDisk utilities (similar to options C and D), but these DOS and Windows utilities don't work on Linux filesystems like ext2fs or ReiserFS. Option A, mkfs, creates new filesystems; it doesn't diagnose or fix filesystem problems. Option E, fdisk, is a tool for creating or modifying disk partitions; it doesn't manage the filesystems they contain. For more information, please see Chapter 3, "Configuring Hardware."

23. A. A freshly installed MySQL database is unlikely to have a ready-made database of animals, so your first task is to create that database with the CREATE DATABASE command, as shown in option A. (You could call the database something other than animals, of course.) The USE command in option B will be useful only once the database has been created. Once the database is created, you can use CREATE TABLE, as in option C, to create a table; however, you'll need an existing database first, and this command also requires information about the type of data to be stored, which option C doesn't provide. Option D's INSERT INTO command stores data into a table once it's been created, so it's far from the first command you'll use. It also requires additional specification of the data to be stored, so it's incomplete. Option E's UPDATE command modifies existing entries, so you'll use this command only after you've created the database and added at least one animal to it. (Option E is also an incomplete command even then.) For more information, please see Chapter 9, "Writing Scripts, Configuring Email, and Using Databases."

24. B, D. The correct answers, man and info (options B and D), are two common Linux help packages. Although ? (option C) is a common help command within certain interactive programs, it isn't a help command in bash or other common Linux shells. There is no common command called manual (option A) nor is hint (option E) a valid bash command or common program name. For more information, please see Chapter 1, "Exploring Linux Command-Line Tools."

25. A, C. Unix systems traditionally store time in UTC (aka Greenwich Mean Time), and Linux may do so as well. Thus, option A is correct. Most other *x*86 PC OSs traditionally store time as the local time, however, so Linux also supports this option, and option C is also correct. Internet Time (option B) is an alternative to the 24-hour clock in which the day is broken into 1,000 "beats." Standard PC BIOSs don't support this time format. Likewise, a 12-hour clock isn't terribly useful to computers because it doesn't differentiate a.m. from p.m., making option D incorrect. Although the length of the Martian day is similar to that of Earth (24 hours and 37 minutes), those wanting to colonize Mars will have to wait for PC clocks to support setting time for the Red Planet; option E is incorrect. For more information, please see Chapter 7, "Administering the System."

26. D. Typing lsmod (option D) produces a list of the modules that are currently loaded. The insmod (option A) and modprobe (option C) programs both load modules—either a single module or a single modules and all those on which it depends, respectively. The `depmod` command (option B) generates the `modules.dep` file that contains module dependency information. The `modinfo` command (option E) displays information, such as its version number and author, on a single module. For more information, please see Chapter 3, "Configuring Hardware."

27. B, E. The `chgrp` and `chown` commands can both change the group ownership of a file. The `chgrp` command takes a group name and a filename as parameters, as in option B. The `chown` command normally changes a file's owner; but if you provide a group name preceded by a dot (.) or a colon (:), as in option E, it changes the group of a file. The `chown` command shown in option A will change the primary ownership of the file to the `music` user, if such a user exists on the system; it won't change the group ownership. There is no standard `chgroup` command, as in option C. Option D will change the permissions to 0600 (`-rw-------`), which will be a step backward with respect to the goal state. For more information, please see Chapter 4, "Managing Files."

28. E. Hard links to directories are not permitted by most filesystems, so you'll probably have to create a symbolic link, as noted in option E. Links don't rely on a filesystem journal, so option A is incorrect. Contrary to option B, anybody may create a link, not just the original's owner. Option C describes a restriction of hard links; but because this link will probably have to be a symbolic link, this restriction is unimportant and option C is incorrect. Option D describes a more severe restriction than option B, but it's incorrect for the same reasons. For more information, please see Chapter 4, "Managing Files."

29. B, E. The colon (:) starts ex mode, from which you can enter commands. In ex mode, `r` includes a file in an existing one, `w` writes a file, `e` loads an entirely new file, and `q` quits the program. Thus, the desired combination is `:wq` (option B). As a special case, ZZ does the same thing, so option E is also correct. For more information, please see Chapter 5, "Booting Linux and Editing Files."

30. C. The `~/.forward` file is a user email forwarding file. The vertical bar character (|) at the start of such a file is a code to send the email through the specified program file, so option C is correct. To do as option A describes, the file would need to read `junkme` or `junkme@`*hostname*, where *hostname* is the computer's hostname. To do as option B describes, the leading vertical bar would have to be omitted. It's conceivable that the `~/junkme` script does as option D describes, but there's no way of knowing this for certain. To do as option E describes, the file would have to read *user*`@junkme`, where *user* is the username. For more information, please see Chapter 9, "Writing Scripts, Configuring Email, and Using Databases."

Exam 1

PART

I

Chapter

1

Exploring Linux Command-Line Tools

THE FOLLOWING EXAM OBJECTIVES ARE COVERED IN THIS CHAPTER:

- ✓ 1.103.1 Work on the command line
- ✓ 1.103.2 Process text streams using filters
- ✓ 1.103.4 Use streams, pipes, and redirects
- ✓ 1.103.7 Search text files using regular expressions

Linux borrows heavily from Unix, and Unix began as a text-based operating system (OS). Unix and Linux retain much of this heritage, which means that to understand how to use and, especially, administer Linux, you must understand at least the basics of its command-line tools. Thus, this book begins with an introduction to Linux *shells* (the programs that accept and interpret text-mode commands) and many of the basic commands and procedures you can use from a shell.

This chapter begins with basic shell information, including shell options and procedures for using them. From there, this chapter covers streams, pipes, and redirection, which you can use to shunt input and output between programs or between files and programs. These techniques are frequently combined with text processing using *filters*—commands you can use to manipulate text without the help of a conventional text editor. Sometimes you must manipulate text in an abstract way, using codes to represent several different types of text. This chapter therefore covers this topic.

Understanding Command-Line Basics

Before you do anything else with Linux, you should understand how to use a Linux shell. Several shells are available, but most provide similar capabilities. Understanding a few basics will take you a long way in your use of Linux, so I describe some of these techniques and commands. You should also understand shell *environment variables*, which are placeholders for data that may be useful to many programs. Finally, on the topic of command-line basics, you should know how to get help with commands you're trying to use.

Exploring Your Linux Shell Options

As with many key software components, Linux provides a range of options for shells. A complete list would be quite long, but the more common choices include the following:

bash   The GNU Bourne Again Shell (bash) is based on the earlier Bourne shell for Unix but extends it in several ways. In Linux, bash is the most common default shell for user accounts, and it's the one emphasized in this book and on the exam.

bsh   The Bourne shell upon which bash is based also goes by the name bsh. It's not often used in Linux, although the bsh command is sometimes a symbolic link to bash.

tcsh   This shell is based on the earlier C shell (csh). It's a fairly popular shell in some circles, but no major Linux distributions make it the default shell. Although it's similar to bash in many respects, some operational details differ. For instance, you don't assign environment variables in the same way in tcsh as in bash.

csh   The original C shell isn't much used on Linux, but if a user is familiar with csh, tcsh makes a good substitute.

ksh   The Korn Shell (ksh) was designed to take the best features of the Bourne shell and the C shell and extend them. It has a small but dedicated following among Linux users.

zsh   The Z shell (zsh) takes shell evolution further than the Korn Shell, incorporating features from earlier shells and adding still more.

In addition to these shells, dozens more obscure ones are available. In Linux, most users run bash because it's the default. Some other OSs use csh or tcsh as the default, so if your users have backgrounds on non-Linux Unix-like OSs, they may be more familiar with these other shells. You can change a user's default shell by editing the account, as described in Chapter 7, "Administering the System."

The file /bin/sh is a symbolic link to the system's default shell—normally /bin/bash for Linux. This practice enables you to point to a shell (say, at the start of a simple shell script, as described in Chapter 9, "Writing Scripts, Configuring E-mail, and Using Databases") and be assured that a shell will be called, even if the system's available shells change. This feature is particularly important when developing shell scripts that might be run on other computers, as described in Chapter 9.

Using a Shell

Linux shell use is fairly straightforward for anybody who's used a text-mode OS before: You type a command, possibly including options to it, and the computer executes the command. For the most part, Linux commands are external—that is, they're separate programs from the shell. A few commands are internal to the shell, though, and knowing the distinction can be important. You should also know some of the tricks that can make using the command shell easier—how to have the computer complete a long command or filename, retrieve a command you've recently run, or edit a command you've recently used (or haven't yet fully entered).

One class of commands—those for handling basic file management—is very important but isn't described here in great detail. For more information on these commands, consult Chapter 4, "Managing Files."

Starting a Shell

If you log into Linux using a text-mode login screen, chances are you'll be dropped directly into your default shell—the shell is what presents the prompt and accepts subsequent commands.

If you log into Linux using a graphical user interface (GUI) login screen, though, you'll have to start a shell manually. Some GUIs provide a menu option to start a program called a terminal, xterm, Konsole, or something similar. These programs enable you to run text-mode programs within Linux, and by default they come up running your shell. If you can't find such a menu option, look for one that enables you to run an arbitrary command. Select it, and type xterm or konsole as the command name; this will launch an xterm-type program that will run a shell.

Using Internal and External Commands

Internal commands are, as you might expect, built into the shell. Most shells offer a similar set of internal commands, but shell-to-shell differences do exist; consult your shell's man page (as described later, in "Getting Help") for details, particularly if you're using an exotic shell. Internal commands you're likely to use enable you to perform some common tasks:

Change the Working Directory   Whenever you're running a shell, you're working in a specific directory. When you refer to a file without providing a complete path to the file, the shell works on the file in the current working directory. (Similar rules apply to many programs.) The cd command changes the current working directory. For instance, typing cd /home/sally changes to the /home/sally directory. The tilde (~) character is a useful shortcut; it stands for your home directory, so typing cd ~ will have the same effect as cd /home/sally if your home directory is /home/sally.

Display the Working Directory   The pwd command displays ("prints" to the screen) the current working directory.

Display a Line of Text   The echo command displays the text you enter; for instance, typing echo Hello causes the system to display the string Hello. This may seem pointless, but it's useful in scripts (described in Chapter 9), and it can also be a good way to review the contents of environment variables (described later in this chapter, in "Using Environment Variables").

Execute a Program   The exec command runs an external program that you specify, as in exec myprog to run myprog. In most cases, this is better accomplished by typing the name of the program you want to run. The exec command has one special feature, though: Rather than create a new process that runs alongside the shell, the new process *replaces* the shell. When the new process terminates, it's as if you terminated the shell.

Time an Operation   The time command times how long subsequent commands take to execute. For instance, typing time pwd tells you how long the system took to execute the pwd command. The time is displayed after the full command terminates. Three times are displayed: total execution time (aka real time), user CPU time, and system CPU time. The final two values tell you about CPU time consumed, which is likely to be much less than the total execution time.

Set Options   In its most basic form, set displays a wide variety of options relating to bash operation. These options are formatted much like environment variables, but they aren't the same things. You can pass various options to set to have it affect a wide range of shell operations.

Terminate the Shell The `exit` and `logout` commands both terminate the shell. The `exit` command terminates any shell, but the `logout` command terminates only login shells—that is, those that are launched automatically when you initiate a text-mode login as opposed to those that run in `xterm` windows or the like.

This list isn't complete. Later sections of this chapter and later chapters describe some additional internal commands. Consult your shell's documentation for a complete list of its internal commands.

Some of these internal commands are duplicated by external commands that do the same thing, but those external commands aren't always installed on all systems. Even when those external commands are installed, the internal command takes precedence unless you provide the complete path to the external command on the command line, as in typing **/bin/pwd** rather than **pwd**.

 Real World Scenario

Confusion over Internal and External Commands

When duplicate internal and external commands exist, they sometimes produce subtly different results or accept different options. These differences can occasionally cause problems. For instance, consider the pwd command and symbolic links to directories. (Symbolic links are described in more detail in Chapter 4. For now, know that they're files that point to other files or directories and for most intents and purposes can be accessed just like the files or directories to which they point.) Suppose you create a symbolic link to /bin within your home directory and then cd into that directory. You then want to know where you are. The pwd command that's internal to bash will produce a different result from the external pwd command:

```
$ pwd
/home/sally/binlink
$ /bin/pwd
/usr/bin
```

As you can see, bash's internal pwd shows the path via the symbolic link, whereas the external command shows the path to which the link points. Sometimes these differences can cause confusion, such as if you read the man page or other documentation that describes one version but you use the other and a difference is important. You may wonder why the command isn't operating as you expect. If in doubt, look up the documentation for, and type the complete path to, the external command to be sure you use it.

When you type a command that's not recognized by the shell as one of its internal commands, the shell checks its *path* to find a program by that name to execute it. The path is a list of directories in which commands can be found. It's defined by the PATH environment variable, as described shortly in "Using Environment Variables." A typical user account has about half a dozen or a dozen directories in its path. You can adjust the path by changing the PATH environment variable in a shell configuration file, as described in "Exploring Shell Configuration."

You can run programs that aren't on the path by providing a complete path on the command line. For instance, typing **./myprog** runs the myprog program in the current directory, and typing **/home/arthur/thisprog** runs the thisprog program in the /home/arthur directory.

 WARNING   The root account should normally have a shorter path than ordinary user accounts. Typically, you'll omit directories that store GUI and other user-oriented programs from root's path in order to discourage use of the root account for routine operations, thus minimizing the risk of security breaches related to buggy or compromised binaries being run by root. Most important, root's path should never include the current directory (./). Placing this directory in root's path makes it possible for a local miscreant to trick root into running replacements for common programs, such as ls, by having root change into a directory with such a program. Indeed, omitting the current directory from ordinary user paths is also generally a good idea. If this directory must be part of the ordinary user path, it should appear at the end of the path so that the standard programs take precedence over any replacement programs in the current directory.

In the case of both programs on the path and those whose complete paths you type as part of the command, the program file must be marked as executable. This is done via the execute bit that's stored with the file. Standard programs are marked as executable when they're installed, but if you need to adjust a program's executable status, you can do so with the chmod command, as described in Chapter 4.

Performing Some Shell Command Tricks

Many users find typing commands to be tedious and error-prone. This is particularly true of slow or sloppy typists. For this reason, Linux shells include various tools that can help speed up operations. The first of these is *command completion*: Type part of a command or (as an option to a command) a filename, and then press the Tab key. The shell tries to fill in the rest of the command or the filename. If just one command or filename matches the characters you've typed so far, the shell fills it in and adds a space after it. If the characters you've typed don't uniquely identify a command or filename, the shell fills in what it can and then stops. Depending on the shell and its configuration, it may beep. If you press the

Tab key again, the system responds by displaying the possible completions. You can then type another character or two and, if you haven't completed the command or filename, press the Tab key again to have the process repeat.

The most fundamental Linux commands have fairly short names—mv, ls, set, and so on. Some other commands are much longer, though, such as traceroute or sane-find-scanner. Filenames can also be quite lengthy—up to 255 characters on many filesystems. Thus, command completion can save a lot of time when you're typing. It can also help you avoid typos.

The most popular Linux shells, including bash and tcsh, support command and filename completion. Some older shells, though, don't support this helpful feature.

Another useful shell shortcut is the *history*. The history keeps a record of every command you type. If you've typed a long command recently and want to use it again or use a minor variant of it, you can pull the command out of the history. The simplest way to do this is to press the Up arrow key on your keyboard; this brings up the previous command. Pressing the Up arrow key repeatedly moves through multiple commands so you can find the one you want. If you overshoot, press the Down arrow key to move down the history. The Ctrl+P and Ctrl+N keystrokes double for the Up and Down arrow keys, respectively.

Another way to use the command history is to search through it. Press Ctrl+R to begin a backward (reverse) search, which is what you probably want, and begin typing characters that should be unique to the command you want to find. The characters you type need not be the ones that begin the command; they can exist anywhere in the command. You can either keep typing until you find the correct command or, after you've typed a few characters, press Ctrl+R repeatedly until you find the one you want. The Ctrl+S keystroke works similarly but searches forward in the command history, which might be handy if you've used a backward search or the Up arrow key to look back and have overshot. In either event, if you can't find the command you want or if you change your mind and want to terminate the search, press Ctrl+G to do so.

Frequently, after finding a command in the history, you want to edit it. The bash shell, like many shells, provides editing features modeled after those of the Emacs editor:

Move Within the Line Press Ctrl+A or Ctrl+E to move the cursor to the start or end of the line, respectively. The Left and Right arrow keys move within the line a character at a time. Ctrl+B and Ctrl+F do the same, moving backward and forward within a line. Pressing Ctrl plus the Left or Right arrow key moves backward or forward a word at a time, as does pressing Esc and then B or F.

Delete Text Pressing Ctrl+D or the Delete key deletes the character under the cursor, whereas pressing the Backspace key deletes the character to the left of the cursor. Pressing Ctrl+K deletes all text from the cursor to the end of the line. Pressing Ctrl+X and then Backspace deletes all the text from the cursor to the beginning of the line.

Transpose Text   Pressing Ctrl+T transposes the character before the cursor with the character under the cursor. Pressing Esc and then T transposes the two words immediately before (or under) the cursor.

Change Case   Pressing Esc and then U converts text from the cursor to the end of the word to uppercase. Pressing Esc and then L converts text from the cursor to the end of the word to lowercase. Pressing Esc and then C converts the letter under the cursor (or the first letter of the next word) to uppercase, leaving the rest of the word unaffected.

Invoke an Editor   You can launch a full-fledged editor to edit a command by pressing Ctrl+X followed by Ctrl+E. The bash shell attempts to launch the editor defined by the $FCEDIT or $EDITOR environment variable or Emacs as a last resort.

These editing commands are just the most useful ones supported by bash; consult its man page to learn about many more obscure editing features. In practice, you're likely to make heavy use of command and filename completion, the command history, and perhaps a few editing features.

If you prefer the Vi editor to Emacs, you can use a Vi-like mode in bash by typing **set -o vi**. (Vi is described in Chapter 5, "Booting Linux and Editing Files.")

The history command provides an interface to view and manage the history. Typing **history** alone displays all the commands in the history (typically the latest 500 commands); adding a number causes only that number of the latest commands to appear. You can execute a command by number by typing an exclamation mark followed by its number, as in !210 to execute command 210. Typing **history -c** clears the history, which can be handy if you've recently typed commands you'd rather not have discovered by others, such as commands that include passwords.

The bash history is stored in the .bash_history file in your home directory. This is an ordinary plain-text file, so you can view it with a text editor or a command such as less (described later, in "Paging Through Files with less").

Because your bash history is stored in a file, it can be examined by anybody who can read that file. Some commands enable you to type passwords or other sensitive data on the same line as the commands themselves, which can therefore be risky. The ~/.bash_history file does *not* record what you type in response to other programs' prompts, just what you type at the bash prompt itself. Thus, if you have a choice, you should let commands that require passwords or other sensitive data prompt you themselves to enter this data, rather than enter such information as options to the command at the bash prompt.

In Exercise 1.1, you'll experiment with your shell's completion and command-editing tools.

EXERCISE 1.1

Editing Commands

To experiment with your shell's completion and command-editing tools, follow these steps:

1. Log in as an ordinary user.

2. Create a temporary directory by typing `mkdir test`. (Directory and file manipulation commands are described in more detail in Chapter 4.)

3. Change into the test directory by typing `cd test`.

4. Create a few temporary files by typing `touch one two three`. This command creates three empty files named one, two, and three.

5. Type `ls -l t`, and without pressing the Enter key, press the Tab key. The system may beep at you or display two three. If it doesn't display two three, press the Tab key again, and it should do so. This reveals that either two or three is a valid completion to your command, because these are the two files in the test directory whose filenames begin with the letter t.

6. Type `h`, and again without pressing the Enter key, press the Tab key. The system should complete the command (`ls -l three`), at which point you can press the Enter key to execute it. (You'll see information on the file.)

7. Press the Up arrow key. You should see the `ls -l three` command appear on the command line.

8. Press Ctrl+A to move the cursor to the beginning of the line.

9. Press the Right arrow key once, and type `es` (without pressing the Enter key). The command line should now read `less -l three`.

10. Press the Right arrow key once, and press the Delete key three times. The command should now read `less three`. Press the Enter key to execute the command. (Note that you can do so even though the cursor isn't at the end of the line.) This invokes the `less` pager on the three file. (The `less` pager is described more fully later, in "Paging Through Files with `less`.") Because this file is empty, you'll see a mostly empty screen.

11. Press the Q key to exit from the `less` pager.

Exploring Shell Configuration

Shells, like many Linux programs, are configured through files that hold configuration options in a plain-text format. The bash configuration files are actually bash shell scripts, which are described more fully in Chapter 9. For now, you should know that the ~/.bashrc and ~/.profile files are the main user configuration files for bash, and /etc/bash.bashrc and /etc/profile are the main global configuration files.

Even without knowing much about shell scripting, you can make simple changes to these files. Edit them in your favorite text editor, and change whatever needs changing. For instance, you can add directories to the $PATH environment variable, which takes a colon-delimited list of directories.

Be careful when changing your bash configuration, particularly the global bash configuration files. Save a backup of the original file before making changes, and test your changes immediately by logging in using another virtual terminal. If you spot a problem, revert to your saved copy until you can learn the cause and create a working file.

Using Environment Variables

Environment variables are like variables in programming languages—they hold data to be referred to by the variable name. Environment variables differ from programs' internal variables in that they're part of the environment of a program, and other programs, such as the shell, can modify this environment. Programs can rely on environment variables to set information that can apply to many different programs. For instance, many text-based programs need to know the capabilities of the terminal program you use. This information is conveyed in the $TERM environment variable, which is likely to hold a value such as xterm or linux. Programs that need to position the cursor, display color text, or perform other tasks that depend on terminal-specific capabilities can customize their output based on this information.

Chapter 9 describes environment variables and their manipulation in more detail. For the moment, you should know that you can set them in bash by using an assignment (=) operator followed by the export command:

```
$ NNTPSERVER=news.abigisp.com
$ export NNTPSERVER
```

You can combine these two commands into a single form:

```
$ export NNTPSERVER=news.abigisp.com
```

Either method sets the $NNTPSERVER environment variable to news.abigisp.com. (When setting an environment variable, you omit the dollar sign, but subsequent references include a dollar sign to identify the environment variable as such.) Thereafter, programs that need this information can refer to the environment variable. In fact, you can do so from the shell yourself, using the echo command:

```
$ echo $NNTPSERVER
news.abigisp.com
```

Some environment variables, including the $TERM environment variable, are set automatically when you log in. If a program uses environment variables, its documentation should say so. The $NNTPSERVER variable is used by some Usenet news clients, which enable participation in a type of online discussion group that predates Web forums.

You can also view the entire environment by typing **env**. The result is likely to be several dozen lines of environment variables and their values. Chapter 9 describes what many of these variables are in more detail.

To delete an environment variable, use the unset command, which takes the name of an environment variable (without the leading $ symbol) as an option. For instance, **unset NNTPSERVER** removes the $NNTPSERVER environment variable.

Getting Help

Linux provides a text-based help system known as man. This command's name is short for *manual*, and its entries (its man pages) provide succinct summaries of what a command, file, or other feature does. For instance, to learn about man itself, you can type **man man**. The result is a description of the man command.

The man utility uses the less pager to display information. This program displays text a page at a time. Press the spacebar to move forward a page, Esc followed by V to move back a page, the arrow keys to move up or down a line at a time, the slash (/) key to search for text, and so on. (Type **man less** to learn all the details, or consult the upcoming section "Paging Through Files with less.") When you're done, press Q to exit less and the man page it's displaying.

Linux man pages are organized into several sections, which are summarized in Table 1.1. Sometimes a single keyword has entries in multiple sections; for instance, passwd has entries under both section 1 and section 5. In most cases, man returns the entry in the lowest-numbered section, but you can force the issue by preceding the keyword by the section number. For instance, typing **man 5 passwd** returns information on the passwd file format rather than the passwd command.

TABLE 1.1 Manual sections

Section number	Description
1	Executable programs and shell commands
2	System calls provided by the kernel
3	Library calls provided by program libraries
4	Device files (usually stored in /dev)
5	File formats
6	Games
7	Miscellaneous (macro packages, conventions, and so on)
8	System administration commands (programs run mostly or exclusively by root)
9	Kernel routines

Some programs have moved away from man pages to info pages. The basic purpose of info pages is the same as that for man pages, but info pages use a hypertext format so that you can move from section to section of the documentation for a program. Type **info info** to learn more about this system.

Both man pages and info pages are usually written in a terse style. They're intended as reference tools, not tutorials; they frequently assume basic familiarity with the command, or at least with Linux generally. For more tutorial information, you must look elsewhere, such as this book or the Web. The Linux Documentation Project (http://tldp.org) is a particularly relevant Web-based resource for learning about various Linux topics.

Using Streams, Redirection, and Pipes

Streams, *redirection*, and *pipes* are some of the more powerful command-line tools in Linux. Linux treats the input to and output from programs as a stream, which is a data entity that can be manipulated. Ordinarily, input comes from the keyboard and output goes to the screen (which in this context can mean a full-screen text-mode login session, an xterm or a similar window, or the screen of a remote computer via a remote login session). You can redirect these input and output streams to come from or go to other sources, though, such as files. Similarly, you can pipe the output of one program into another program. These facilities can be great tools to tie together multiple programs.

Part of the Unix philosophy to which Linux adheres is, whenever possible, to do complex things by combining multiple simple tools. Redirection and pipes help in this task by enabling simple programs to be combined together in chains, each link feeding off the output of the preceding link.

Exploring Types of Streams

To begin understanding redirection and pipes, you must first understand the different types of input and output streams. Three are most important for this topic:

Standard Input   Programs accept keyboard input via *standard input*, or stdin. In most cases, this is the data that comes into the computer from a keyboard.

Standard Output   Text-mode programs send most data to their users via *standard output* (aka stdout), which is normally displayed on the screen, either in a full-screen text-mode session or in a GUI window such as an xterm. (Fully GUI programs such as GUI word processors don't use standard output for their regular interactions, although they might use standard output to display messages in the xterm from which they were launched. GUI output isn't handled via an output stream in the sense I'm describing here.)

Standard Error   Linux provides a second type of output stream, known as *standard error*, or stderr. This output stream is intended to carry high-priority information such as error messages. Ordinarily, standard error is sent to the same output device as standard output, so you can't easily tell them apart. You can redirect one independently of the other, though, which can be handy. For instance, you can redirect standard error to a file while leaving standard output going to the screen so that you can interact with the program and then study the error messages later.

Internally, programs treat these streams just like data files—they open them, read from or write to the files, and close them when they're done. Put another way, ordinary files are streams from a program's point of view. The standard input, output, and error streams just happen to be the ones used to interact with users.

Redirecting Input and Output

To redirect input or output, you use symbols following the command, including any options it takes. For instance, to redirect the output of the echo command, you would type something like this:

```
$ echo $NNTPSERVER > nntpserver.txt
```

The result is that the file nntpserver.txt contains the output of the command (in this case, the value of the $NNTPSERVER environment variable). Redirection operators exist to achieve several effects, as summarized in Table 1.2.

TABLE 1.2   Common redirection operators

Redirection operator	Effect
>	Creates a new file containing standard output. If the specified file exists, it's overwritten.
>>	Appends standard output to the existing file. If the specified file doesn't exist, it's created.
2>	Creates a new file containing standard error. If the specified file exists, it's overwritten.
2>>	Appends standard error to the existing file. If the specified file doesn't exist, it's created.
&>	Creates a new file containing both standard output and standard error. If the specified file exists, it's overwritten.
<	Sends the contents of the specified file to be used as standard input.
<<	Accepts text on the following lines as standard input.
<>	Causes the specified file to be used for both standard input and standard output.

Most of these redirectors deal with output, both because there are two types of output (standard output and standard error) and because you must be concerned with what to do in case you specify a file that already exists. The most important input redirector is <, which takes the specified file's contents as standard input.

A common trick is to redirect standard output or standard error to /dev/null. This file is a device that's connected to nothing; it's used when you want to get rid of data. For instance, if the whine program is generating too many error messages, you can type `whine 2> /dev/null` to run it and discard its error messages.

One redirection operator that requires elaboration is <<. This operator implements a *here document*, which takes text from the following lines as standard input. Chances are you won't use this redirector on the command line, though; the following lines *are* standard input, so there's no need to redirect them. Rather, you might use this command as part of a script in order to pass data to an interactive program. Unlike most redirection operators, the text immediately following the << code isn't a filename; instead, it's a word that's used to mark the end of input. For instance, typing **someprog << EOF** causes someprog to accept input until it sees a line that contains *only* the string EOF (without even a space following it).

> Some programs that take input from the command line expect you to terminate input by pressing Ctrl+D. This keystroke corresponds to an end-of-file marker using the American Standard Code for Information Interchange (ASCII).

A final redirection tool is the tee command. This command splits standard input so that it's displayed on standard output and on as many files as you specify. Typically, tee is used in conjunction with data pipes so that a program's output can be both stored and viewed immediately. For instance, to view and store the output of someprog, you might type this:

```
$ someprog | tee output.txt
```

> The vertical bar (|) is the pipe character. It implements a pipe, as described in the next section.

Ordinarily, tee overwrites any files whose names you specify. If you want to append data to these files, pass the -a option to tee.

Piping Data Between Programs

Programs can frequently operate on other programs' outputs. For instance, you might use a text-filtering command (such as the ones described shortly, in "Processing Text Using Filters") to manipulate text output by another program. You can do this with the help of redirection operators; send the first program's standard output to a file, and then redirect the second program's standard input to read from that file. This solution is awkward, though, and it involves the creation of a file that you might easily overlook, leading to unnecessary clutter on your system.

The solution is to use data pipes (aka pipelines). A pipe redirects the first program's standard output to the second program's standard input and is denoted by a vertical bar (|):

```
$ first | second
```

For instance, suppose that *first* generates some system statistics, such as system uptime, CPU use, number of users logged in, and so on. This output might be lengthy, so you want to trim it a bit. You might therefore use *second*, which could be a script or command that echoes from its standard input only the information in which you're interested. (The grep command, described in "Using grep," is often used in this role.)

Pipes can be used in sequences of arbitrary length:

```
$ first | second | third | fourth | fifth | sixth [...]
```

Generating Command Lines

Sometimes you'll find yourself constructing a series of commands that are similar to each other but not similar enough to enable you to use their normal options to substitute a single command. For instance, suppose you want to remove every file in a directory tree with a name that ends in a tilde (~). (This filename convention denotes backup files created by certain text editors.) With a large directory tree, this task can be daunting; the usual file-deletion command (rm, described in more detail in Chapter 4) doesn't provide an option to search for and delete every file in a directory tree that matches such a specific criterion. One command that can do the search part of the job, though, is find, which is also described in more detail in Chapter 4. This command displays all the files that match criteria you provide. If you could combine the output of find to create a series of command lines using rm, the task would be solved. This is precisely the purpose of the xargs command.

The xargs command builds a command from its standard input. The basic syntax for this command is as follows:

```
xargs [options] [command [initial-arguments]]
```

The *command* is the command you want to execute, and *initial-arguments* is a list of arguments you want to pass to the command. The *options* are xargs options; they aren't passed to *command*. When you run xargs, it runs *command* once for every word passed to it on standard input, adding that word to the argument list for *command*. If you want to pass multiple options to the command, you can protect them by enclosing the group in quotation marks.

For instance, consider the task of deleting all those backup files, denoted by tilde characters. You can do this by piping the output of find to xargs, which then calls rm:

```
$ find ./ -name "*~" | xargs -d "\n" rm
```

The first part of this command (**find ./ -name "*~"**) finds all the files in the current directory (./) or its subdirectories with a name that ends in a tilde (*~). This list is then piped to xargs, which adds each input value to its own rm command. Problems can arise if filenames contain spaces, since by default xargs uses both spaces and newlines as item delimiters. The -d "\n" option tells xargs to use only newlines as delimiters, thus avoiding this problem in this context. (The find command separates each found filename with a newline.)

A tool that's similar to xargs in many ways is the backtick (`), which is a character to the left of the 1 key on most keyboards. The backtick is *not* the same as the single quote character ('), which is located to the right of the semicolon (;) on most keyboards.

Text within backticks is treated as a separate command whose results are substituted on the command line. For instance, to delete those backup files, you can type the following command:

```
$ rm `find ./ -name "*~"`
```

The backtick solution works fine in some cases, but it breaks down in more complex situations. The reason is that the output of the backtick-contained command is passed to the command it precedes as if it had been typed at the shell. By contrast, when you use xargs, it runs the command you specify (rm in these examples) once for each of the input items. What's more, you can't pass options such as -d "\n" to a backtick. Thus, these two examples will work the same in many cases, but not in all of them.

Processing Text Using Filters

In keeping with Linux's philosophy of providing small tools that can be tied together via pipes and redirection to accomplish more complex tasks, many simple commands to manipulate text are available. These commands accomplish tasks of various types, such as combining files, transforming the data in files, formatting text, displaying text, and summarizing data.

Many of the following descriptions include input-file specifications. In most cases, you can omit these input-file specifications, in which case the utility reads from standard input instead.

File-Combining Commands

The first group of text-filtering commands are those used to combine two or more files into one file. Three important commands in this category are cat, join, and paste, which join files end to end, based on fields in the file, or by merging on a line-by-line basis, respectively.

Combining Files with cat

The cat command's name is short for *concatenate*, and this tool does just that: It links together an arbitrary number of files end to end and sends the result to standard output. By combining cat with output redirection, you can quickly combine two files into one:

```
$ cat first.txt second.txt > combined.txt
```

Although cat is officially a tool for combining files, it's also commonly used to display the contents of a short file. If you type only one filename as an option, cat displays that file. This is a great way to review short files; but for long files, you're better off using a full-fledged pager command, such as more or less.

You can add options to have cat perform minor modifications to the files as it combines them:

Display Line Ends   If you want to see where lines end, add the -E or --show-ends option. The result is a dollar sign ($) at the end of each line.

Number Lines   The -n or --number option adds line numbers to the beginning of every line. The -b or --number-nonblank option is similar, but it numbers only lines that contain text.

Minimize Blank Lines   The -s or --squeeze-blank option compresses groups of blank lines down to a single blank line.

Display Special Characters   The -T or --show-tabs option displays tab characters as ^I. The -v or --show-nonprinting option displays most control and other special characters using carat (^) and M- notations.

The tac command is similar to cat, but it reverses the order of lines in the output.

Joining Files by Field with *join*

The join command combines two files by matching the contents of specified fields within the files. Fields are typically space-separated entries on a line, although you can specify another character as the field separator with the -t *char* option, where *char* is the character you want to use. You can cause join to ignore case when performing comparisons by using the -i option.

The effect of join may best be understood through a demonstration. Consider Listings 1.1 and 1.2, which contain data on telephone numbers; Listing 1.1 shows the names associated with those numbers, and Listing 1.2 shows whether the numbers are listed or unlisted.

Listing 1.1: Demonstration File Containing Telephone Numbers and Names

```
555-2397 Beckett, Barry
555-5116 Carter, Gertrude
555-7929 Jones, Theresa
555-9871 Orwell, Samuel
```

Listing 1.2: Demonstration File Containing Telephone Number Listing Status

```
555-2397 unlisted
555-5116 listed
555-7929 listed
555-9871 unlisted
```

You can display the contents of both files using join:

```
$ join listing1.1.txt listing1.2.txt
555-2397 Beckett, Barry unlisted
555-5116 Carter, Gertrude listed
555-7929 Jones, Theresa listed
555-9871 Orwell, Samuel unlisted
```

By default, join uses the first field as the one to match across files. Because Listings 1.1 and 1.2 both place the phone number in this field, it's the key field in the output. You can specify another field by using the -1 or -2 option to specify the join field for the first or second file, respectively, as in `join -1 3 -2 2 cameras.txt lenses.txt` to join using the third field in cameras.txt and the second field in lenses.txt. The -o *FORMAT* option enables more complex specifications for the output file's format; consult the man page for join for more details.

The join command can be used at the core of a set of simple customized database-manipulation tools using Linux text-manipulation commands. It's very limited by itself, though; for instance, it requires its two files to have the same ordering of lines. (You can use the sort command to ensure this is so.)

Merging Lines with *paste*

The paste command merges files line by line, separating the lines from each file with tabs, as shown in the following example, using Listings 1.1 and 1.2 again:

```
$ paste listing1.1.txt listing1.2.txt
555-2397 Beckett, Barry 555-2397 unlisted
555-5116 Carter, Gertrude        555-5116 listed
555-7929 Jones, Theresa 555-7929 listed
555-9871 Orwell, Samuel 555-9871 unlisted
```

You can use paste to combine data from files that aren't keyed with fields suitable for use by join. Of course, to be meaningful, the files' line numbers must be exactly equivalent. Alternatively, you can use paste as a quick way to create a two-column output of textual data; however, the alignment of the second column may not be exact if the first column's line lengths aren't exactly even, as shown in the preceding example.

File-Transforming Commands

Many of Linux's text-manipulation commands are aimed at transforming the contents of files. These commands don't actually change files' contents, though; rather, they send the changed file to standard output. You can then pipe this output to another command or redirect it into a new file.

 An important file-transforming command is sed. This command is very complex and is covered later in this chapter, in "Using sed."

Converting Tabs to Spaces with *expand*

Sometimes text files contain tabs but programs that need to process the files don't cope well with tabs; or perhaps you want to edit a text file in an editor that uses a different amount of horizontal space for the tab than did the editor that created the file. In such cases, you may want to convert tabs to spaces. The expand command does this.

By default, expand assumes a tab stop every eight characters. You can change this spacing with the -t *num* or --tabs=*num* option, where *num* is the tab spacing value.

Displaying Files in Octal with *od*

Some files aren't easily displayed in ASCII; most graphics files, audio files, and so on use non-ASCII characters that look like gibberish. Worse, these characters can do strange things to your display if you try to view such a file with cat or a similar tool. For instance, your font may change, or your console may begin beeping uncontrollably. Nonetheless, you may sometimes want to display such files, particularly if you want to investigate the structure of a data file. You may also want to look at an ASCII file in a way that eliminates certain ambiguities, such as whether a gap between words is a tab or several spaces. In such cases, od (whose name stands for *octal dump*) can help. It displays a file in an unambiguous format—octal (base 8) numbers by default. For instance, consider Listing 1.2 as parsed by od:

```
$ od listing1.2.txt
0000000 032465 026465 031462 033471 072440 066156 071551 062564
0000020 005144 032465 026465 030465 033061 066040 071551 062564
0000040 005144 032465 026465 034467 034462 066040 071551 062564
0000060 005144 032465 026465 034071 030467 072440 066156 071551
0000100 062564 005144
0000104
```

The first field on each line is an index into the file in octal. For instance, the second line begins at octal 20 (16 in base 10) bytes into the file. The remaining numbers on each line represent the bytes in the file. This type of output can be difficult to interpret unless you're well versed in octal notation and perhaps in the ASCII code.

Although od is nominally a tool for generating octal output, it can generate many other output formats, such as hexadecimal (base 16), decimal (base 10), and even ASCII with escaped control characters. Consult the man page for od for details on creating these variants.

Sorting Files with *sort*

Sometimes you'll create an output file that you want sorted. To do so, you can use a command that's called, appropriately enough, sort. This command can sort in several ways, including the following:

Ignore Case   Ordinarily, sort sorts by ASCII value, which differentiates between uppercase and lowercase letters. The -f or --ignore-case option causes sort to ignore case.

Month Sort   The -M or --month-sort option causes the program to sort by three-letter month abbreviation (JAN through DEC).

Numeric Sort   You can sort by number by using the -n or --numeric-sort option.

Reverse Sort Order   The -r or --reverse option sorts in reverse order.

Sort Field   By default, sort uses the first field as its sort field. You can specify another field with the -k *field* or --key=*field* option. (The *field* can be two numbered fields separated by commas, to sort on multiple fields.)

As an example, suppose you wanted to sort Listing 1.1 by first name. You could do so like this:

```
$ sort -k 3 listing1.1.txt
555-2397 Beckett, Barry
555-5116 Carter, Gertrude
555-9871 Orwell, Samuel
555-7929 Jones, Theresa
```

The sort command supports a large number of additional options, many of them quite exotic. Consult sort's man page for details.

Breaking a File into Pieces with *split*

The split command can split a file into two or more files. Unlike most of the text-manipulation commands described in this chapter, this command requires you to enter an output filename—or more precisely, an output filename prefix, to which is added an alphabetic code. You must also normally specify how large you want the individual files to be:

Split by Bytes   The -b *size* or --bytes=*size* option breaks the input file into pieces of *size* bytes. This option can have the usually undesirable consequence of splitting the file mid-line.

Split by Bytes in Line-Sized Chunks   You can break a file into files of no more than a specified size without breaking lines across files by using the -C=*size* or --line-bytes=*size* option. (Lines will still be broken across files if the line length is greater than *size*.)

Split by Number of Lines   The -l *lines* or --lines=*lines* option splits the file into chunks with no more than the specified number of lines.

As an example, consider breaking Listing 1.1 into two parts by number of lines:

```
$ split -l 2 listing1.1.txt numbers
```

The result is two files, numbersaa and numbersab, that together hold the original contents of listing1.1.txt.

If you don't specify any defaults (as in split listing1.1.txt), the result is output files split into 1,000-line chunks, with names beginning with x (xaa, xab, and so on). If you don't specify an input filename, split uses standard input.

Translating Characters with *tr*

The tr command changes individual characters from standard input. Its syntax is as follows:

```
tr [options] SET1 [SET2]
```

You specify the characters you want replaced in a group (*SET1*) and the characters with which you want them to be replaced as a second group (*SET2*). Each character in *SET1* is replaced with the one at the equivalent position in *SET2*. Here's an example using Listing 1.1:

```
$ tr BCJ bc < listing1.1.txt
555-2397 beckett, barry
555-5116 carter, Gertrude
555-7929 cones, Theresa
555-9871 Orwell, Samuel
```

 The tr command relies on standard input, which is the reason for the input redirection (<) in this example. This is the only way to pass the command a file.

This example translates some, but not all, of the uppercase characters to lowercase. Note that *SET2* in this example was shorter than *SET1*. The result is that tr substitutes the last available letter from *SET2* for the missing letters. In this example, the J in Jones became a c. The -t or --truncate-set1 option causes tr to truncate *SET1* to the size of *SET2* instead.

Another tr option is -d, which causes the program to delete the characters from *SET1*. When using -d, you can omit *SET2* entirely.

The tr command also accepts a number of shortcuts, such as [:alnum:] (all numbers and letters), [:upper:] (all uppercase letters), [:lower:] (all lowercase letters), and [:digit:] (all digits). You can specify a range of characters by separating them with dashes (-), as in A-M for characters between A and M, inclusive. Consult tr's man page for a complete list of these shortcuts.

Converting Spaces to Tabs with *unexpand*

The unexpand command is the logical opposite of expand; it converts multiple spaces to tabs. This can help compress the size of files that contain many spaces and can be helpful if a file is to be processed by a utility that expects tabs in certain locations.

Like expand, unexpand accepts the -t *num* or --tabs=*num* option, which sets the tab spacing to once every *num* characters. If you omit this option, unexpand assumes a tab stop every eight characters.

Deleting Duplicate Lines with *uniq*

The uniq command removes duplicate lines. It's most likely to be useful if you've sorted a file and don't want duplicate items. For instance, suppose you want to summarize Shakespeare's vocabulary. You might create a file with all of the Bard's works, one word per line. You can then sort this file using sort and pass it through uniq. Using a shorter example file containing the text to be or not to be, that is the question (one word per line), the result looks like this:

```
$ sort shakespeare.txt | uniq
be
is
not
or
question
that
the
to
```

Note that the words to and be, which appeared in the original file twice, appear only once in the uniq-processed version.

File-Formatting Commands

The next three commands—fmt, nl, and pr—reformat the text in a file. The first of these is designed to reformat text files, such as if a program's README documentation file uses lines that are too long for your display. The nl command numbers the lines of a file, which can be helpful in referring to lines in documentation or correspondence. Finally, pr is a print-processing tool; it formats a document in pages suitable for printing.

Reformatting Paragraphs with *fmt*

Sometimes text files arrive with outrageously long line lengths, irregular line lengths, or other problems. Depending on the difficulty, you may be able to cope simply by using an appropriate text editor or viewer to read the file. If you want to clean up the file a bit, though, you can do so with fmt. If called with no options (other than the input filename, if you're not having it work on standard input), the program attempts to clean up paragraphs, which it assumes are delimited by two or more blank lines or by changes in indentation. The new paragraph formatting defaults to no more than 75 characters wide. You can change this with the *-width*, -w *width*, or --width=*width* options, which set the line length to *width* characters.

Numbering Lines with *nl*

As described earlier, in "Combining Files with cat," you can number the lines of a file with that command. The cat line-numbering options are limited, though, so if you need to do complex line numbering, nl is the tool to use. In its simplest case, you can use nl alone to accomplish much the same goal as cat -b achieves: numbering all the non-blank lines in a file. You can add many options to nl to achieve various special effects:

Body Numbering Style   You can set the numbering style for the bulk of the lines with the -b *style* or --body-numbering=*style* option, where *style* is a style format code, described shortly.

Header and Footer Numbering Style   If the text is formatted for printing and has headers or footers, you can set the style for these elements with the -h *style* or --header-numbering=*style* option for the header and -f *style* or --footer-numbering=*style* option for the footer.

Page Separator   Some numbering schemes reset the line numbers for each page. You can tell nl how to identify a new page with the -d=*code* or --section-delimiter=*code* option, where *code* is a code for the character that identifies the new page.

Line-Number Options for New Pages   Ordinarily, nl begins numbering each new page with line 1. If you pass the -p or --no-renumber option, though, it doesn't reset the line number with a new page.

Number Format   You can specify the numbering format with the -n *format* or --number-format=*format* option, where *format* is ln (left justified, no leading zeros), rn (right justified, no leading zeros), or rz (right justified with leading zeros).

The body, header, and footer options enable you to specify a numbering style for each of these page elements, as described in Table 1.3.

TABLE 1.3   Styles used by nl

style code	Description
t	The default behavior is to number lines that aren't empty. You can make this default explicit by using a *style* of t.
a	This *style* causes all lines to be numbered, including empty lines.
n	This *style* causes all line numbers to be omitted, which may be desirable for headers or footers.
p*REGEXP*	This option causes only lines that match the specified regular expression (*REGEXP*) to be numbered. Regular expressions are described later, in "Using Regular Expressions."

As an example, suppose you've created a script, buggy, but you find that it's not working as you expect. When you run it, you get error messages that refer to line numbers, so you want to create a version of the script with lines that are numbered for easy reference. You can do so by calling nl with the option to number all lines, including blank lines (-b a):

```
$ nl -b a buggy > numbered-buggy.txt
```

Because the input file doesn't have any explicit page delimiters, the output will be numbered in a single sequence; nl doesn't try to impose its own page-length limits.

The `numbered-buggy.txt` file created by this command isn't useful as a script because of the line numbers that begin each line. You can, however, load it into a text editor or display it with a pager such as `less` to view the text and see the line numbers along with the commands they contain.

Preparing a File for Printing with *pr*

If you want to print a plain-text file, you may want to prepare it with headers, footers, page breaks, and so on. The pr command was designed to do this. In its most basic form, you pass the command a file:

```
$ pr myfile.txt
```

The result is text formatted for printing on a line printer—that is, pr assumes an 80-character line length in a monospaced font. Of course, you can also use pr in a pipe, either to accept input piped from another program or to pipe its output to another program. (The recipient program might be lpr, which is used to print files, as described in Chapter 6, "Configuring the X Window System, Localization, and Printing.")

By default, pr creates output that includes the original text with headers that include the current date and time, the original filename, and the page number. You can tweak the output format in a variety of ways, including the following:

Generate Multi-column Output   Passing the *-numcols* or `--columns=`*numcols* option creates output with *numcols* columns. Note that pr doesn't reformat text; if lines are too long, they're truncated or run over into multiple columns.

Generate Double-Spaced Output   The `-d` or `--double-space` option causes double-spaced output from a single-spaced file.

Use Form Feeds   Ordinarily, pr separates pages by using a fixed number of blank lines. This works fine if your printer uses the same number of lines that pr expects. If you have problems with this issue, you can pass the `-F`, `-f`, or `--form-feed` option, which causes pr to output a form-feed character between pages. This works better with some printers.

Set Page Length   The `-l` *lines* or `--length=`*lines* option sets the length of the page in lines.

Set the Header Text   The `-h` *text* or `--header=`*text* option sets the text to be displayed in the header, replacing the filename. To specify a multi-word string, enclose it in quotes, as in `--header="My File"`. The `-t` or `--omit-header` option omits the header entirely.

Set Left Margin and Page Width   The `-o` *chars* or `--indent=`*chars* option sets the left margin to *chars* characters. This margin size is added to the page width, which defaults to 72 characters and can be explicitly set with the `-w` *chars* or `--width` *chars* option.

These options are just the beginning; pr supports many more, which are described in its man page. As an example of pr in action, consider printing a double-spaced and numbered version of a configuration file (say, `/etc/profile`) for your reference. You can do this by piping together cat and its -n option to generate a numbered output, pr and its -d option to double-space the result, and lpr to print the file:

```
$ cat -n /etc/profile | pr -d | lpr
```

The result should be a printout that might be handy for taking notes on the configuration file. One caveat, though: If the file contains lines that approach or exceed 80 characters in length, the result can be single lines that spill across two lines. The result will be disrupted page boundaries. As a workaround, you can set a somewhat short page length with -l and use -f to ensure that the printer receives form feeds after each page:

```
$ cat -n /etc/profile | pr -dfl 50 | lpr
```

The pr command is built around assumptions about printer capabilities that were reasonable in the early 1980s. It's still useful today, but you might prefer to look into GNU Enscript (http://www.codento.com/people/mtr/genscript/). This program has many of the same features as pr, but it generates PostScript output that can take better advantage of modern printer features.

File-Viewing Commands

Sometimes you just want to view a file or part of a file. A few commands can help you accomplish this goal without loading the file into a full-fledged editor.

As described earlier, the cat command is also handy for viewing short files.

Viewing the Starts of Files with *head*

Sometimes all you need to do is see the first few lines of a file. This may be enough to identify what a mystery file is, for instance; or you may want to see the first few entries of a log file to determine when that file was started. You can accomplish this goal with the head command, which echoes the first 10 lines of one or more files to standard output. (If you specify multiple filenames, each one's output is preceded by a header to identify it.) You can modify the amount of information displayed by head in two ways:

Specify the Number of Bytes   The -c *num* or --bytes=*num* option tells head to display *num* bytes from the file rather than the default 10 lines.

Specify the Number of Lines   You can change the number of lines displayed with the -n *num* or --lines=*num* option.

Viewing the Ends of Files with *tail*

The tail command works just like head, except that tail displays the *last* 10 lines of a file. (You can use the -c/--bytes and -n/--lines options to change the amount of data displayed, just as with head.) This command is useful for examining recent activity in log files or other files to which data may be appended.

The tail command supports several options that aren't present in head and that enable the program to handle additional duties, including the following:

Track a File   The -f or --follow option tells tail to keep the file open and to display new lines as they're added. This feature is helpful for tracking log files because it enables you to see changes as they're made to the file.

Stop Tracking on Program Termination   The --pid=*pid* option tells tail to terminate tracking (as initiated by -f or --follow) once the process with a process ID (PID) of *pid* terminates. (PIDs are described in more detail in Chapter 2, "Managing Software.")

Some additional options provide more obscure capabilities. Consult tail's man page for details.

You can combine head with tail to display or extract portions of a file. For instance, suppose you want to display lines 11–15 of a file, sample.txt. You can extract the first 15 lines of the file with head, and then display the last five lines of that extraction with tail. The final command would be head -n 15 sample.txt | tail -n 5.

Paging Through Files with *less*

The less command's name is a joke; it's a reference to the more command, which was an early file pager. The idea was to create a better version of more, so the developers called it less.

The idea behind less (and more, for that matter) is to enable you to read a file a screen at a time. When you type **less *filename***, the program displays the first few lines of *filename*. You can then page back and forth through the file:

- Pressing the spacebar moves forward through the file a screen at a time.

- Pressing Esc followed by V moves backward through the file a screen at a time.

- The Up and Down arrow keys move up or down through the file a line at a time.

- You can search the file's contents by pressing the slash (/) key followed by the search term. For instance, typing **/portable** finds the first occurrence of the string portable after the current position. Typing a slash followed by the Enter key moves to the next occurrence of the search term. Typing **n** alone repeats the search forward, while typing **N** alone repeats the search backward.

- You can search backward in the file by using the question mark (?) key rather than the slash key.

- You can move to a specific line by typing **g** followed by the line number, as in **g50** to go to line 50.

- When you're done, type **q** to exit from the program.

Unlike most of the programs described here, less can't be readily used in a pipe, except as the final command in the pipe. In that role, though, less is very useful because it enables you to conveniently examine lengthy output.

 Although less is quite common on Linux systems and is typically configured as the default text pager, some Unix-like systems use more in this role. Many of less's features, such as the ability to page backward in a file, don't work in more.

One additional less feature can be handy: Typing **h** displays less's internal help system. This display summarizes the commands you may use, but it's long enough that you must use the usual less paging features to view it all! When you're done with the help screens, type **q,** just as if you were exiting from viewing a help document with less. This action will return you to your original document.

File-Summarizing Commands

The final text-filtering commands I describe are used to summarize text in one way or another. The cut command takes segments of an input file and sends them to standard output, while the wc command displays some basic statistics on the file.

Extracting Text with *cut*

The cut command extracts portions of input lines and displays them on standard output. You can specify what to cut from input lines in several ways:

By Byte   The -b *list* or --bytes=*list* option cuts the specified list of bytes from the input file. (The format of a *list* is described shortly.)

By Character   The -c *list* or --characters=*list* option cuts the specified list of characters from the input file. In practice, this method and the by-byte method usually produce identical results. (If the input file uses a multi-byte encoding system, though, the results won't be identical.)

By Field   The -f *list* or --fields=*list* option cuts the specified list of fields from the input file. By default, a field is a tab-delimited section of a line, but you can change the delimiting character with the -d *char*, --delim=*char*, or --delimiter=*char* option, where *char* is the character you want to use to delimit fields. Ordinarily, cut echoes lines that don't contain delimiters. Including the -s or --only-delimited option changes this behavior so that the program doesn't echo lines that don't contain the delimiter character.

Many of these options take a *list*, which is a way to specify multiple bytes, characters, or fields. You make this specification by number; it can be a single number (such as 4), a closed range of numbers (such as 2-4), or an open range of numbers (such as -4 or 4-). In this final case, all bytes, characters, or fields from the beginning of the line to the specified number or from the specified number to the end of the line are included in the list.

The cut command is frequently used in scripts to extract data from some other command's output. For instance, suppose you're writing a script and the script needs to know the hardware address of your Ethernet adapter. This information can be obtained from the ifconfig command (described in more detail in Chapter 8, "Configuring Basic Networking"):

```
$ ifconfig eth0
eth0      Link encap:Ethernet   HWaddr 00:0C:76:96:A3:73
          inet addr:192.168.1.3  Bcast:192.168.1.255  Mask:255.255.255.0
          inet6 addr: fe80::20c:76ff:fe96:a373/64 Scope:Link
          UP BROADCAST NOTRAILERS RUNNING MULTICAST  MTU:1500  Metric:1
          RX packets:7127424 errors:0 dropped:0 overruns:0 frame:0
          TX packets:5273519 errors:0 dropped:0 overruns:0 carrier:0
          collisions:0 txqueuelen:1000
          RX bytes:6272843708 (5982.2 Mb)  TX bytes:1082453585 (1032.3 Mb)
          Interrupt:10 Base address:0xde00
```

Unfortunately, most of this information is extraneous for the desired purpose. The hardware address is the 6-byte hexadecimal number following HWaddr. To extract that data, you can combine grep (described shortly, in "Using grep") with cut in a pipe:

```
$ ifconfig eth0 | grep HWaddr | cut -d " " -f 11
00:0C:76:96:A3:73
```

Of course, in a script you would probably assign this value to a variable or otherwise process it through additional pipes. Chapter 9 describes scripts in more detail.

Obtaining a Word Count with *wc*

The wc command produces a word count (that's where it gets its name), as well as line and byte counts, for a file:

```
$ wc file.txt
 308  2343  15534 file.txt
```

This file contains 308 lines (or, more precisely, 308 newline characters); 2,343 words; and 15,534 bytes. You can limit the output to the newline count, the word count, the byte count, or a character count with the --lines (-l), --words (-w), --bytes (-c), or --chars (-m) option, respectively. You can also learn the maximum line length with the --max-line-length (-L) option.

For an ordinary ASCII file, the character and byte counts will be identical. These values may diverge for files that use multi-byte character encodings.

Using Regular Expressions

Many Linux programs employ *regular expressions*, which are tools for describing or matching patterns in text. Regular expressions are similar in principle to the wildcards that can be used to specify multiple filenames. At their simplest, regular expressions can be plain text without adornment. Certain characters are used to denote patterns, though. Because of their importance, I describe regular expressions here. I also cover two programs that make heavy use of regular expressions: grep and sed. These programs search for text within files and permit editing of files from the command line, respectively.

Understanding Regular Expressions

Two forms of regular expression are common: basic and extended. Which form you must use depends on the program; some accept one form or the other, but others can use either type, depending on the options passed to the program. (Some programs use their own minor or major variants on either of these classes of regular expression.) The differences between basic and extended regular expressions are complex and subtle, but the fundamental principles of both are similar.

The simplest type of regular expression is an alphabetic string, such as Linux or HWaddr. These regular expressions match any string of the same size or longer that contains the regular expression. For instance, the HWaddr regular expression matches HWaddr, This is the HWaddr, and The HWaddr is unknown. The real strength of regular expressions comes in the use of non-alphabetic characters, which activate advanced matching rules:

Bracket Expressions   Characters enclosed in square brackets ([]) constitute bracket expressions, which match any one character within the brackets. For instance, the regular expression b[aeiou]g matches the words bag, beg, big, bog, and bug.

Range Expressions   A range expression is a variant on a bracket expression. Instead of listing every character that matches, range expressions list the start and end points separated by a dash (-), as in a[2-4]z. This regular expression matches a2z, a3z, and a4z.

Any Single Character   The dot (.) represents any single character except a newline. For instance, a.z matches a2z, abz, aQz, or any other three-character string that begins with a and ends with z.

Start and End of Line   The carat (^) represents the start of a line, and the dollar sign ($) denotes the end of a line.

Repetition Operators   A full or partial regular expression may be followed by a special symbol to denote how many times a matching item must exist. Specifically, an asterisk (*)

denotes zero or more occurrences, a plus sign (+) matches one or more occurrences, and a question mark (?) specifies zero or one match. The asterisk is often combined with the dot (as in .*) to specify a match with any substring. For instance, A.*Lincoln matches any string that contains A and Lincoln, in that order—Abe Lincoln and Abraham Lincoln are just two possible matches.

Multiple Possible Strings   The vertical bar (|) separates two possible matches; for instance, car|truck matches either car or truck.

Parentheses   Ordinary parentheses (()) surround subexpressions. Parentheses are often used to specify how operators are to be applied; for example, you can put parentheses around a group of words that are concatenated with the vertical bar, to ensure that the words are treated as a group, any one of which may match, without involving surrounding parts of the regular expression.

Escaping   If you want to match one of the special characters, such as a dot, you must *escape* it—that is, precede it with a backslash (\). For instance, to match a computer hostname (say, twain.example.com), you must escape the dots, as in twain\.example\.com.

The preceding descriptions apply to extended regular expressions. Some details are different for basic regular expressions. In particular, the ?, +, |, (, and) symbols lose their special meanings. To perform the tasks handled by these characters, some programs, such as grep, enable you to recover the functions of these characters by escaping them (say, using \| instead of |). Whether you use basic or extended regular expressions depends on which form the program supports. For programs, such as grep, that support both, you can use either; which you choose is mostly a matter of personal preference.

Regular expression rules can be confusing, particularly when you're first introduced to them. Some examples of their use, in the context of the programs that use them, will help. The next couple of sections provide such examples.

Using *grep*

The grep command is extremely useful. It searches for files that contain a specified string and returns the name of the file and (if it's a text file) a line of context for that string. The basic grep syntax is as follows:

```
grep [options] regexp [files]
```

The *regexp* is a regular expression, as just described. The grep command supports a large number of options. Some of the common options enable you to modify the way the program searches files:

Count Matching Lines   Instead of displaying context lines, grep displays the number of lines that match the specified pattern if you use the -c or --count option.

Specify a Pattern Input File   The -f *file* or --file=*file* option takes pattern input from the specified file rather than from the command line.

Ignore Case   You can perform a case-insensitive search, rather than the default case-sensitive search, by using the -i or --ignore-case option.

Search Recursively   The -r or --recursive option searches in the specified directory and all subdirectories rather than simply the specified directory. You can use rgrep rather than specify this option.

Use an Extended Regular Expression   The grep command interprets *regexp* as a basic regular expression by default. To use an extended regular expression, you can pass the -E or --extended-regexp option. Alternatively, you can call egrep rather than grep; this variant command uses extended regular expressions by default.

A simple example of grep uses a regular expression with no special components:

```
$ grep -r eth0 /etc/*
```

This example finds all the files in /etc that contain the string eth0 (the identifier for the first Ethernet device on most Linux distributions). Because the example includes the -r option, it searches recursively, so files in subdirectories of /etc are examined in addition to those in /etc itself. For each matching text file, the line that contains the string is printed.

> Some files in /etc can't be read by ordinary users. Thus, if you type this command as a non-root user, you'll see some error messages relating to grep's inability to open files.

Ramping up a bit, suppose you want to locate all the files in /etc that contain the string eth0 or eth1. You can enter the following command, which uses a bracket expression to specify both variant devices:

```
$ grep eth[01] /etc/*
```

A still more complex example searches all files in /etc that contain the hostname twain.example.com or bronto.pangaea.edu and, later on the same line, the number 127. This task requires using several of the regular expression features. Expressed using extended regular expression notation, the command looks like this:

```
$ grep -E "(twain\.example\.com|bronto\.pangaea\.edu).*127" /etc/*
```

This command illustrates another feature you may need to use: shell quoting. Because the shell uses certain characters, such as the vertical bar and the asterisk, for its own purposes, you must enclose certain regular expressions in quotes lest the shell attempt to parse the regular expression and pass a modified version of what you type to grep.

You can use grep in conjunction with commands that produce a lot of output in order to sift through that output for the material that's important to you. (Several examples throughout this book use this technique.) For example, suppose you want to find the process ID (PID) of a running xterm. You can use a pipe to send the result of a ps command (described in Chapter 2) through grep:

```
# ps ax | grep xterm
```

The result is a list of all running processes called xterm, along with their PIDs. You can even do this in series, using grep to further restrict the output on some other criterion, which can be useful if the initial pass still produces too much output.

Using *sed*

The sed command directly modifies the contents of files, sending the changed file to standard output. Its syntax can take one of two forms:

```
sed [options] -f script-file [input-file]
sed [options] script-text [input-file]
```

In either case, *input-file* is the name of the file you want to modify. (Modifications are temporary unless you save them in some way, as illustrated shortly.) The script (*script-text* or the contents of *script-file*) is the set of commands you want sed to perform. When you pass a script directly on the command line, the *script-text* is typically enclosed in single quote marks. Table 1.4 summarizes a few sed commands that you can use in its scripts.

TABLE 1.4 Common sed commands

Command	Addresses	Meaning
=	0 or 1	Display the current line number.
a*text*	0 or 1	Append *text* to the file.
i*text*	0 or 1	Insert *text* into the file.
r *filename*	0 or 1	Append text from *filename* into the file.
c*text*	Range	Replace the selected range of lines with the provided *text*.
s/*regexp*/*replacement*	Range	Replace text that matches the regular expression (*regexp*) with *replacement*.
w *filename*	Range	Write the current pattern space to the specified file.
q	0 or 1	Immediately quit the script, but print the current pattern space.
Q	0 or 1	Immediately quit the script.

Table 1.4 is incomplete; sed is quite complex, and this section merely introduces this tool.

The Addresses column of Table 1.4 requires elaboration: sed commands operate on addresses, which are line numbers. Commands may take no addresses, in which case they operate on the entire file; one address, in which case they operate on the specified line; or two addresses (a range), in which case they operate on that range of lines, inclusive.

In operation, sed looks something like this:

```
$ sed 's/2012/2013/' cal-2012.txt > cal-2013.txt
```

This command processes the input file, cal-2012.txt, using sed's s command to replace the first occurrence of 2012 on each line with 2013. (If a single line may have more than one instance of the search string, you must perform a global search by appending g to the command string, as in s/2012/2013/g.) By default, sed sends the modified file to standard output, so this example uses redirection to send the output to cal-2013.txt. The idea in this example is to quickly convert a file created for the year 2012 so that it can be used in 2013. If you don't specify an input filename, sed works from standard input, so it can accept the output of another command as its input.

Although it's conceptually simple, sed is a very complex tool; even a modest summary of its capabilities would fill a chapter. You can consult its man page for basic information, but to fully understand sed, you may want to consult a book on the subject, such as Dale Dougherty and Arnold Robbins's *sed & awk, 2nd Edition* (O'Reilly, 1997).

Certain sed commands, including the substitution command, are also used in Vi, which is described more fully in Chapter 5.

 **Real World Scenario**

Doing One Thing in Many Ways

As you become experienced with Linux and compare notes with other Linux administrators, you may find that the way you work is different from the way others work. This is because Linux often provides multiple methods to solve certain problems. For instance, ASCII text files use certain characters to encode the end of a line. Unix (and Linux) use a single line feed character (ASCII 0x0a, sometimes represented as \n), whereas DOS and Windows use the combination of a carriage return (ASCII 0x0d or \r) and a line feed. When moving ASCII files between computers, you may need to convert from one form to the other. How can you do this?

One solution is to use a special-purpose program, such as dos2unix or unix2dos. You could type **dos2unix file.txt** to convert file.txt from DOS-style to Unix-style ASCII, for instance. This is usually the simplest solution, but not all computers have these utilities installed.

Another approach is to use tr. For instance, to convert from DOS style to Unix style, you might type this:

```
$ tr -d \\r < dosfile.txt > unixfile.txt
```

This approach won't work when converting from Unix style to DOS style, though. For that, you can use sed:

```
sed s/$/"\r"/ unixfile.txt > dosfile.txt
```

Variants on both the tr and sed commands exist. For instance, sometimes the quotes around \r may be omitted from the sed command; whether they're required depends on your shell and its configuration.

Yet another approach is to load the file into a text editor and then save it using different file-type settings. (Not all editors support such changes, but some do.)

Many other examples exist of multiple solutions to a problem. Sometimes one solution stands out above others as being superior, but other times the differences may be subtle, or each approach may have merit in particular situations. Thus, it's best to be at least somewhat familiar with all the alternatives. I describe many such options throughout this book.

Summary

The command line is the key to Linux. Even if you prefer GUI tools to text-mode tools, understanding text-mode commands is necessary to fully manage Linux. This task begins with the shell, which accepts commands you type and displays the results of those commands. In addition, shells support linking programs together via pipes and redirecting programs' input and output. These features enable you to perform complex tasks using simple tools by having each program perform its own small part of the task. This technique is frequently used with Linux text filters, which manipulate text files in various ways—sorting text by fields, merging multiple files, and so on.

Exam Essentials

Summarize features that Linux shells offer to speed up command entry.   The command history often enables you to retrieve an earlier command that's similar or identical to the one you want to enter. Tab completion reduces typing effort by letting the shell finish long command names or filenames. Command-line editing lets you edit a retrieved command or change a typo before committing the command.

Describe the purpose of the man command.   The man command displays the manual page for the keyword (command, filename, system call, or other feature) that you type. This documentation provides succinct summary information that's useful as a reference to learn about exact command options or features.

Explain the purpose of environment variables.   Environment variables store small pieces of data—program options, information about the computer, and so on. This information can be read by programs and used to modify program behavior in a way that's appropriate for the current environment.

Describe the difference between standard output and standard error.   Standard output carries normal program output, whereas standard error carries high-priority output, such as error messages. The two can be redirected independently of one another.

Explain the purpose of pipes.   Pipes tie programs together by feeding the standard output from the first program into the second program's standard input. They can be used to link together a series of simple programs to perform more complex tasks than any one of the programs could manage.

Summarize the structure of regular expressions.   Regular expressions are strings that describe other strings. They can contain normal alphanumeric characters, which match the exact same characters, as well as several special symbols and symbol sets that match multiple different characters. The combination is a powerful pattern-matching tool used by many Linux programs.

Review Questions

1. You type a command into bash and pass a long filename to it, but after you enter the command, you receive a `File not found` error message because of a typo in the filename. How might you proceed?

    A. Retype the command, and be sure you type the filename correctly, letter by letter.

    B. Retype the command, but press the Tab key after typing a few letters of the long filename to ensure that the filename is entered correctly.

    C. Press the Up arrow key, and use bash's editing features to correct the typo.

    D. Any of the above.

    E. None of the above.

2. Which of the following commands is implemented as an internal command in bash?

    A. `cat`

    B. `less`

    C. `tee`

    D. `sed`

    E. `echo`

3. You type `echo $PROC`, and the computer replies `Go away`. What does this mean?

    A. No currently running processes are associated with your shell, so you may log out without terminating them.

    B. The remote computer PROC isn't accepting connections; you should contact its administrator to correct the problem.

    C. Your computer is handling too many processes; you must kill some of them to regain control of the computer.

    D. Your central processing unit (CPU) is defective and must be replaced as soon as possible.

    E. You, one of your configuration files, or a program you've run has set the $PROC environment variable to `Go away`.

4. What does the pwd command accomplish?

    A. It prints the name of the working directory.

    B. It changes the current working directory.

    C. It prints wide displays on narrow paper.

    D. It parses Web page URLs for display.

    E. It prints the terminal's width in characters.

5. In an xterm window launched from your window manager, you type **exec gedit**. What will happen when you exit from the gedit program?

   A. Your shell will be a root shell.

   B. The gedit program will terminate, but nothing else unusual will happen.

   C. Your X session will terminate.

   D. The xterm window will close.

   E. A new instance of gedit will be launched.

6. What is the surest way to run a program (say, myprog) that's located in the current working directory?

   A. Type ./ followed by the program name: **./myprog**.

   B. Type the program name alone: **myprog**.

   C. Type **run** followed by the program name: **run myprog**.

   D. Type /. followed by the program name: **/.myprog**.

   E. Type the program name followed by an ampersand (&): **myprog &**.

7. How does man display information by default on most Linux systems?

   A. Using a custom X-based application

   B. Using the Firefox Web browser

   C. Using the info browser

   D. Using the Vi editor

   E. Using the less pager

8. You want to store the standard output of the ifconfig command in a text file (file.txt) for future reference, and you want to wipe out any existing data in the file. You do *not* want to store standard error in this file. How can you accomplish these goals?

   A. ifconfig < file.txt

   B. ifconfig >> file.txt

   C. ifconfig > file.txt

   D. ifconfig | file.txt

   E. ifconfig 2> file.txt

9. What is the effect of the following command?

   ```
   $ myprog &> input.txt
   ```

   A. Standard error to myprog is taken from input.txt.

   B. Standard input to myprog is taken from input.txt.

   C. Standard output and standard error from myprog are written to input.txt.

   D. All of the above.

   E. None of the above.

10. How many commands can you pipe together at once?

    A. 2

    B. 3

    C. 4

    D. 16

    E. An arbitrary number

11. You want to run an interactive script, `gabby`, which produces a lot of output in response to the user's inputs. To facilitate future study of this script, you want to copy its output to a file. How might you do this?

    A. `gabby > gabby-out.txt`

    B. `gabby | tee gabby-out.txt`

    C. `gabby < gabby-out.txt`

    D. `gabby &> gabby-out.txt`

    E. `gabby `gabby-out.txt``

12. A text-mode program, `verbose`, prints a lot of spurious "error" messages to standard error. How might you get rid of those messages while still interacting with the program?

    A. `verbose | quiet`

    B. `verbose &> /dev/null`

    C. `verbose 2> /dev/null`

    D. `verbose > junk.txt`

    E. `quiet-mode verbose`

13. How do the > and >> redirection operators differ?

    A. The > operator creates a new file or overwrites an existing one; the >> operator creates a new file or appends to an existing one.

    B. The > operator creates a new file or overwrites an existing one; the >> operator appends to an existing file or issues an error message if the specified file doesn't exist.

    C. The > operator redirects standard output; the >> operator redirects standard error.

    D. The > operator redirects standard output; the >> operator redirects standard input.

    E. The > operator writes to an existing file but fails if the file doesn't exist; the >> operator writes to an existing file or creates a new one if it doesn't already exist.

14. What program would you use to display the end of a configuration file?

    A. `uniq`

    B. `cut`

    C. `tail`

    D. `wc`

    E. `fmt`

15. What is the effect of the following command?

```
$ pr report.txt | lpr
```

   A. The file `report.txt` is formatted for printing and sent to the `lpr` program.

   B. The files `report.txt` and `lpr` are combined together into one file and sent to standard output.

   C. Tabs are converted to spaces in `report.txt`, and the result is saved in `lpr`.

   D. The file `report.txt` is printed, and any error messages are stored in the file `lpr`.

   E. None of the above.

16. Which of the following commands will number the lines in `aleph.txt`? (Select three.)

   A. `fmt aleph.txt`

   B. `nl aleph.txt`

   C. `cat -b aleph.txt`

   D. `cat -n aleph.txt`

   E. `od -nl aleph.txt`

17. Which of the following commands will change all occurrences of dog in the file `animals.txt` to mutt in the screen display?

   A. `sed -s "dog" "mutt" animals.txt`

   B. `grep -s "dog||mutt" animals.txt`

   C. `sed 's/dog/mutt/g' animals.txt`

   D. `cat animals.txt | grep -c "dog" "mutt"`

   E. `fmt animals.txt | cut 'dog' > 'mutt'`

18. You've received an ASCII text file (`longlines.txt`) that uses no carriage returns within paragraphs but two carriage returns between paragraphs. The result is that your preferred text editor displays each paragraph as a very long line. How can you reformat this file so that you can more easily edit it (or a copy)?

   A. `sed 's/Ctrl-M/NL/' longlines.txt`

   B. `fmt longlines.txt > longlines2.txt`

   C. `cat longlines.txt > longlines2.txt`

   D. `pr longlines.txt > longlines2.txt`

   E. `grep longlines.txt > longlines2.txt`

19. Which of the following commands will print lines from the file `world.txt` that contain matches to changes and changed?

A. `grep change[ds] world.txt`

B. `sed change[d-s] world.txt`

C. `od "change'd|s'" world.txt`

D. `cat world.txt changes changed`

E. `find world.txt "change(d|s)"`

20. Which of the following regular expressions will match the strings dog, dug, and various other strings but not dig?

A. `d.g`

B. `d[ou]g`

C. `d[o-u]g`

D. `di*g`

E. `d.ig`

Chapter

2

Managing Software

THE FOLLOWING EXAM OBJECTIVES ARE COVERED IN THIS CHAPTER:

- ✓ 1.102.3 Manage shared libraries
- ✓ 1.102.4 Use Debian package management
- ✓ 1.102.5 Use RPM and Yum package management
- ✓ 1.103.5 Create, monitor, and kill processes
- ✓ 1.103.6 Modify process execution priorities

A Linux system is defined largely by the collection of software it contains. The Linux kernel, the libraries used by many packages, the shells used to interpret commands, the X Window System GUI, the servers, and more all make up the system's software environment. Many of the chapters of this book are devoted to configuring specific software components, but they all have something in common: tools used to install, uninstall, upgrade, and otherwise manipulate the software. Ironically, this commonality is a major source of differences between Linux systems. Two major Linux package management tools exist: RPM Package Manager (RPM) and Debian packages. (Several less-common package management systems also exist.) With few exceptions, each individual Linux computer uses precisely one package management system, so you'll need to know only one to administer a single system. To be truly fluent in all things Linux, though, you should be at least somewhat familiar with both of them. Thus, this chapter describes both.

This chapter also covers *libraries*—software components that can be used by many different programs. Libraries help reduce the disk space and memory requirements of complex programs, but they also require some attention; if that attention isn't given to them, they can cause problems by their absence or because of incompatibilities between their and their dependent software's versions.

Package management, and in some sense library management, relates to programs as files on your hard disk. Once run, though, programs are dynamic entities. Linux provides tools to help you manage running programs (known as *processes*)—you can learn what processes are running, change their priorities, and terminate processes you don't want running.

Package Concepts

Before proceeding, you should understand some of the principles that underlie Linux package management tools. Any computer's software is like a house of cards: One program may rely on multiple other programs or libraries, each of which relies on several more, and so on. The foundation on which all these programs rely is the Linux kernel. Any of these packages can theoretically be replaced by an equivalent one; however, doing so sometimes causes problems. Worse, removing one card from the stack could cause the whole house of cards to come tumbling down.

Linux package management tools are intended to help build and modify this house of cards by tracking what software is installed. The information that the system maintains helps avoid problems in several ways:

Packages   The most basic information that package systems maintain is information about software *packages*—that is, collections of files that are installed on the computer. Packages are usually distributed as single files that are similar to *tarballs* (archives created with the tar utility and usually compressed with gzip or bzip2) or zip files. Once installed, most packages consist of dozens or hundreds of files, and the package system tracks them all. Packages include additional information that aids in the subsequent duties of package management systems.

Installed File Database   Package systems maintain a database of installed files. The database includes information about every file installed via the package system, the name of the package to which each of those files belongs, and associated additional information.

Dependencies   One of the most important types of information maintained by the package system is *dependency* information—that is, the requirements of packages for one another. For instance, if SuperProg relies on UltraLib to do its work, the package database records this information. If you attempt to install SuperProg when UltraLib isn't installed, the package system won't let you do so. Similarly, if you try to uninstall UltraLib when SuperProg is installed, the package system won't let you. (You can override these prohibitions, as described later in "Forcing the Installation." Doing so is usually inadvisable, though.)

Checksums   The package system maintains checksums and assorted ancillary information about files. This information can be used to verify the validity of the installed software. This feature has its limits, though; it's intended to help you spot disk errors, accidental overwriting of files, or other non-sinister problems. It's of limited use in detecting intrusions, because an intruder could use the package system to install altered system software.

Upgrades and Uninstallation   By tracking files and dependencies, package systems permit easy upgrades and uninstallation: Tell the package system to upgrade or remove a package, and it will replace or remove every file in the package. Of course, this assumes that the upgrade or uninstallation doesn't cause dependency problems; if it does, the package system will block the operation unless you override it.

Binary Package Creation   Both the RPM and Debian package systems provide tools to help create binary packages (those that are installed directly) from source code. This feature is particularly helpful if you're running Linux on a peculiar CPU; you can download source code and create a binary package even if the developers didn't provide explicit support for your CPU. Creating a binary package from source has advantages over compiling software from source in more conventional ways, because you can then use the package management system to track dependencies, attend to individual files, and so on.

Both the RPM and Debian package systems provide all of these basic features, although the details of their operation differ. These two package systems are incompatible with one another in the sense that their package files and their installed file databases are different; you can't directly install an RPM package on a Debian-based system or vice versa. (Tools to convert between formats do exist, and developers are working on ways to better integrate the two package formats.)

Most distributions install just one package system. It's possible to install more than one, though, and some programs (such as alien) require both for full functionality. Actually *using* both systems to install software is inadvisable because their databases are separate. If you install a library using a Debian package and then try to install an RPM package that relies on that library, RPM won't realize that the library is already installed and will return an error.

Using RPM

The most popular package manager in the Linux world is the RPM Package Manager (RPM). RPM is also available on non-Linux platforms, although it sees less use outside the Linux world. The RPM system provides all the basic tools described in the preceding section, "Package Concepts," such as a package database that allows for identifying conflicts and ownership of particular files.

RPM Distributions and Conventions

Red Hat developed RPM for its own distribution. Red Hat released the software under the General Public License (GPL), however, so others have been free to use it in their own distributions—and this is precisely what has happened. Some distributions, such as Mandriva (formerly Mandrake) and Yellow Dog, are based on Red Hat, so they use RPMs as well as many other parts of the Red Hat distribution. Others, such as SUSE, borrow less from the Red Hat template, but they do use RPMs. Of course, all Linux distributions share many common components, so even those that weren't originally based on Red Hat are very similar to it in many ways other than their use of RPM packages. On the other hand, distributions that were originally based on Red Hat have diverged from it over time. As a result, the group of RPM-using distributions shows substantial variability, but all of them are still Linux distributions that provide the same basic tools, such as the Linux kernel, common shells, an X server, and so on.

Red Hat has splintered into three distributions: Fedora is the downloadable version favored by home users, students, and businesses on a tight budget. The *Red Hat* name is now reserved for the for-pay version of the distribution, known more formally as Red Hat Enterprise Linux (RHEL). CentOS is a freely redistributable version intended for enterprise users.

RPM is a cross-platform tool. As noted earlier, some non-Linux Unix systems can use RPM, although most don't use it as their primary package-distribution system. RPM supports any CPU architecture. Red Hat Linux is or has been available for at least five CPUs: *x*86, *x*86-64 (aka AMD64, EM64T, and x64), IA-64, Alpha, and SPARC. Among the distributions mentioned earlier, Yellow Dog is a PowerPC distribution (it runs on Apple PowerPC-based Macs and some non-Apple systems), and SUSE is available on *x*86, *x*86-64, and PowerPC systems. For the most part, source RPMs are transportable across architectures—you can use the same source RPM to build packages for *x*86, AMD64, PowerPC, Alpha, SPARC, or any other platform you like. Some programs are composed of architecture-independent scripts and so need no recompilation. There are also documentation and configuration packages that work on any CPU.

The convention for naming RPM packages is as follows:

packagename-a.b.c-x.arch.rpm

Each of the filename components has a specific meaning:

Package Name   The first component (*packagename*) is the name of the package, such as `samba` or `samba-server` for the Samba file and print server. Note that the same program may be given different package names by different distribution maintainers.

Version Number   The second component (*a.b.c*) is the package version number, such as 3.6.5. The version number doesn't have to be three period-separated numbers, but that's the most common form. The program author assigns the version number.

Build Number   The number following the version number (*x*) is the *build number* (also known as the *release number*). This number represents minor changes made by the package maintainer, not by the program author. These changes may represent altered startup scripts or configuration files, changed file locations, added documentation, or patches appended to the original program to fix bugs or to make the program more compatible with the target Linux distribution. Many distribution maintainers add a letter code to the build number to distinguish their packages from those of others. Note that these numbers are *not* comparable across package maintainers—George's build number 5 of a package is *not* necessarily an improvement on Susan's build number 4 of the same package.

Architecture   The final component preceding the `.rpm` extension (*arch*) is a code for the package's architecture. The `i386` architecture code is common; it represents a file compiled for any *x*86 CPU from the 80386 onward. Some packages include optimizations for Pentiums or newer (`i586` or `i686`), and non-*x*86 binary packages use codes for their CPUs, such as `ppc` for PowerPC CPUs or `x86_64` for the *x*86-64 platform. Scripts, documentation, and other CPU-independent packages generally use the `noarch` architecture code. The main exception to this rule is source RPMs, which use the `src` architecture code.

As an example of RPM version numbering, the Fedora 17 distribution for *x*86-64 ships with a Samba package called `samba-3.6.5-86.fc17.1.x86_64.rpm`, indicating that this is build 86.fc17.1 of Samba 3.6.5, compiled with *x*86-64 optimizations. These naming conventions are just that, though—conventions. It's possible to rename a package how-ever you like, and it will still install and work. The information in the filename is retained within the package. This fact can be useful if you're ever forced to transfer RPMs using a medium that doesn't allow for long filenames. In fact, early versions of SUSE eschewed long filenames, preferring short filenames such as `samba.rpm`.

In an ideal world, any RPM package will install and run on any RPM-based distribution that uses an appropriate CPU type. Unfortunately, compatibility issues can crop up from time to time, including the following:

- Distributions may use different versions of the RPM utilities. This problem can completely prevent an RPM from one distribution from being used on another.

- An RPM package designed for one distribution may have dependencies that are unmet in another distribution. A package may require a newer version of a library than is present on the distribution you're using, for instance. This problem can usually be overcome by installing or upgrading the depended-on package, but sometimes doing so causes problems because the upgrade may break other packages. By rebuilding the package you want to install from a source RPM, you can often work around these problems, but sometimes the underlying source code also needs the upgraded libraries.

- An RPM package may be built to depend on a package of a particular name, such as `samba-client` depending on `samba-common`; but if the distribution you're using has named the package differently, the `rpm` utility will object. You can override this objection by using the `--nodeps` switch, but sometimes the package won't work once installed. Rebuilding from a source RPM may or may not fix this problem.

- Even when a dependency appears to be met, different distributions may include slightly different files in their packages. For this reason, a package meant for one distribution may not run correctly when installed on another distribution. Sometimes installing an additional package will fix this problem.

- Some programs include distribution-specific scripts or configuration files. This problem is particularly acute for servers, which may include startup scripts that go in `/etc/rc.d/init.d` or elsewhere. Overcoming this problem usually requires that you remove the offending script after installing the RPM and either start the server in some other way or write a new startup script, perhaps modeled after one that came with some other server for your distribution.

In most cases, it's best to use the RPMs intended for your distribution. RPM meta-packagers, such as the Yellow Dog Updater, Modified (Yum), can simplify locating and installing packages designed for your distribution. If you're forced to go outside of your distribution's officially supported list of packages, mixing and matching RPMs from different distributions usually works reasonably well for most programs. This is particularly true if the distributions are closely related or you rebuild from a source RPM. If you have trouble with an RPM, though, you may do well to try to find an equivalent package that was built with your distribution in mind.

The *rpm* Command Set

The main RPM utility program is known as rpm. Use this program to install or upgrade a package at the shell prompt. The rpm command has the following syntax:

```
rpm [operation][options] [package-files|package-names]
```

Table 2.1 summarizes the most common rpm operations, and Table 2.2 summarizes the most important options. Be aware, however, that rpm is a complex tool, so this listing is necessarily incomplete. For information about operations and options more obscure than those listed in Tables 2.1 and 2.2, see the man pages for rpm. Many of rpm's less-used features are devoted to the creation of RPM packages by software developers.

TABLE 2.1　Common rpm operations

Operation	Description
-i	Installs a package; system must *not* contain a package of the same name
-U	Installs a new package or upgrades an existing one
-F or --freshen	Upgrades a package only if an earlier version already exists
-q	Queries a package—finds whether a package is installed, what files it contains, and so on
-V or --verify	Verifies a package—checks that its files are present and unchanged since installation
-e	Uninstalls a package
-b	Builds a binary package, given source code and configuration files; moved to the rpmbuild program with RPM version 4.2
--rebuild	Builds a binary package, given a source RPM file; moved to the rpmbuild program with RPM version 4.2
--rebuilddb	Rebuilds the RPM database to fix errors

TABLE 2.2 Most-important rpm options

Option	Used with operations	Description
--root *dir*	Any	Modifies the Linux system having a root directory located at *dir*. This option can be used to maintain one Linux installation discrete from another one (say, during OS installation or emergency maintenance).
--force	-i, -U, -F	Forces installation of a package even when it means overwriting existing files or packages.
-h or --hash	-i, -U, -F	Displays a series of hash marks (#) to indicate the progress of the operation.
-v	-i, -U, -F	Used in conjunction with the -h option to produce a uniform number of hash marks for each package.
--nodeps	-i, -U, -F, -e	Specifies that no dependency checks be performed. Installs or removes the package even if it relies on a package or file that's not present or is required by a package that's not being uninstalled.
--test	-i, -U, -F	Checks for dependencies, conflicts, and other problems without actually installing the package.
--prefix *path*	-i, -U, -F	Sets the installation directory to *path* (works only for some packages).
-a or --all	-q, -V	Queries or verifies all packages.
-f *file* or --file *file*	-q, -V	Queries or verifies the package that owns *file*.
-p *package-file*	-q	Queries the uninstalled RPM *package-file*.
-i	-q	Displays package information, including the package maintainer, a short description, and so on.
-R or --requires	-q	Displays the packages and files on which this one depends.
-l or --list	-q	Displays the files contained in the package.

To use `rpm`, you combine one operation with one or more options. In most cases, you include one or more package names or package filenames as well. (A package filename is a complete filename, but a package name is a shortened version. For instance, a package filename might be `samba-3.6.5-86.fc17.1.x86_64.rpm`, whereas the matching package name is `samba`.) You can issue the `rpm` command once for each package, or you can list multiple packages, separated by spaces, on the command line. The latter is often preferable when you're installing or removing several packages, some of which depend on others in the group. Issuing separate commands in this situation requires that you install the depended-on package first or remove it last, whereas issuing a single command allows you to list the packages on the command line in any order.

Some operations require that you give a package filename, and others require a package name. In particular, `-i`, `-U`, `-F`, and the rebuild operations require package filenames; `-q`, `-V`, and `-e` normally take a package name, although the `-p` option can modify a query (`-q`) operation to work on a package filename.

When you're installing or upgrading a package, the `-U` operation is generally the most useful because it enables you to install the package without manually uninstalling the old one. This one-step operation is particularly helpful when packages contain many dependencies; `rpm` detects these and can perform the operation should the new package fulfill the dependencies provided by the old one.

To use `rpm` to install or upgrade a package, issue a command similar to the following:

```
# rpm -Uvh samba-3.6.5-86.fc17.1.x86_64.rpm
```

You can also use `rpm -ivh` in place of `rpm -Uvh` if you don't already have a `samba` package installed.

WARNING   It's possible to distribute the same program under different names. In this situation, upgrading may fail or it may produce a duplicate installation, which can yield bizarre program-specific malfunctions. Red Hat has described a formal system for package naming to avoid such problems, but they still occur occasionally. Therefore, it's best to upgrade a package using a subsequent release provided by the same individual or organization that provided the original.

Verify that the package is installed with the `rpm -qi` command, which displays information such as when and on what computer the binary package was built. Listing 2.1 demonstrates this command. (`rpm -qi` also displays an extended plain-English summary of what the package is, which has been omitted from Listing 2.1.)

Listing 2.1: RPM query output

```
$ rpm -qi samba
Name        : samba
Epoch       : 2
```

```
Version     : 3.6.5
Release     : 86.fc17.1
Architecture: x86_64
Install Date: Mon 16 Jul 2012 12:28:51 PM EDT
Group       : System Environment/Daemons
Size        : 18503445
License     : GPLv3+ and LGPLv3+
Signature   : RSA/SHA256, Fri 04 May 2012 11:03:50 AM EDT, Key ID↵
              50e94c991aca3465
Source RPM  : samba-3.6.5-86.fc17.1.src.rpm
Build Date  : Fri 04 May 2012 08:42:51 AM EDT
Build Host  : x86-06.phx2.fedoraproject.org
Relocations : (not relocatable)
Packager    : Fedora Project
Vendor      : Fedora Project
URL         : http://www.samba.org/
Summary     : Server and Client software to interoperate with Windows machines
```

Extracting Data from RPMs

Occasionally you may want to extract data from RPMs without installing the package. For instance, this can be a good way to retrieve the original source code from a source RPM for compiling the software without the help of the RPM tools or to retrieve fonts or other non-program data for use on a non-RPM system.

RPM files are actually modified `cpio` archives. Thus, converting the files into `cpio` files is relatively straightforward, whereupon you can use `cpio` to retrieve the individual files. To do this job, you need to use the `rpm2cpio` program, which ships with most Linux distributions. (You can use this tool even on distributions that don't use RPM.) This program takes a single argument—the name of the RPM file—and outputs the `cpio` archive on standard output. So, if you want to create a `cpio` archive file, you must redirect the output:

```
$ rpm2cpio samba-3.6.5-86.fc17.1.src.rpm > samba-3.6.5-86.fc17.1.src.cpio
```

> The redirection operator (>) is described in more detail in Chapter 1, "Exploring Linux Command-Line Tools," as is the pipe operator (|), which is mentioned shortly. Chapter 4, "Managing Files," describes `cpio` in more detail.

You can then extract the data using `cpio`, which takes the `-i` option to extract an archive and `--make-directories` to create directories:

```
$ cpio -i --make-directories < samba-3.6.5-86.fc17.1.src.cpio
```

Alternatively, you can use a pipe to link these two commands together without creating an intermediary file:

```
$ rpm2cpio samba-3.6.5-86.fc17.1.src.rpm |  cpio -i --make-directories
```

In either case, the result is an extraction of the files in the archive in the current directory. In the case of binary packages, this is likely to be a series of subdirectories that mimic the layout of the Linux root directory—that is, `usr`, `lib`, `etc`, and so on, although precisely which directories are included depends on the package. For a source package, the result of the extraction process is likely to be a source code tarball, a `.spec` file (which holds information RPM uses to build the package), and perhaps some patch files.

> When you're extracting data from an RPM file using `rpm2cpio` and `cpio`, create a holding subdirectory and then extract the data into this subdirectory. This practice will ensure that you can find all the files. If you extract files in your home directory, some of them may get lost amidst your other files. If you extract files as `root` in the root (`/`) directory, they could conceivably overwrite files that you want to keep.

Another option for extracting data from RPMs is to use `alien`, which is described later in "Converting Between Package Formats." This program can convert an RPM into a Debian package or a tarball.

Using Yum

Yum (`http://yum.baseurl.org`), mentioned earlier, is one of several meta-packagers—it enables you to easily install a package and all its dependencies using a single command line. When using Yum, you don't even need to locate and download the package files, because Yum does this for you by searching in one or more repositories—Internet sites that host RPM files for a particular distribution.

Yum originated with the fairly obscure Yellow Dog Linux distribution, but it's since been adopted by Red Hat, CentOS, Fedora, and some other RPM-based distributions. Yum isn't used by all RPM-based distributions, though; SUSE and Mandriva, to name just two, each use their own meta-packagers. Debian-based distributions generally employ the Advanced Package Tools (APT), as described later in "Using `apt-get`." Nonetheless, because of the popularity of Red Hat, CentOS, and Fedora, knowing Yum can be valuable.

The most basic way to use Yum is with the `yum` command, which has the following syntax:

```
yum [options] [command] [package...]
```

Which options are available depend on the command you use. Table 2.3 describes common `yum` commands.

TABLE 2.3 Common yum commands

Command	Description
install	Installs one or more packages by package name. Also installs dependencies of the specified package or packages.
update	Updates the specified package or packages to the latest available version. If no packages are specified, yum updates every installed package.
check-update	Checks to see whether updates are available. If they are, yum displays their names, versions, and repository area (updates or extras, for instance).
upgrade	Works like update with the --obsoletes flag set, which handles obsolete packages in a way that's superior when performing a distribution version upgrade.
remove or erase	Deletes a package from the system; similar to rpm -e, but yum also removes depended-on packages.
list	Displays information about a package, such as the installed version and whether an update is available.
provides or whatprovides	Displays information about packages that provide a specified program or feature. For instance, typing **yum provides samba** lists all the Samba-related packages, including every available update. Note that the output can be copious.
search	Searches package names, summaries, packagers, and descriptions for a specified keyword. This is useful if you don't know a package's name but can think of a word that's likely to appear in one of these fields but not in these fields for other packages.
info	Displays information about a package, similar to the rpm -qi command.
clean	Cleans up the Yum cache directory. Running this command from time to time is advisable, lest downloaded packages chew up too much disk space.
shell	Enters the Yum shell mode, in which you can enter multiple Yum commands one after another.
resolvedep	Displays packages matching the specified dependency.
localinstall	Installs the specified local RPM files, using your Yum repositories to resolve dependencies.
localupdate	Updates the system using the specified local RPM files, using your Yum repositories to resolve dependencies. Packages other than those updated by local files and their dependencies are not updated.
deplist	Displays dependencies of the specified package.

In most cases, using Yum is easier than using RPM directly to manage packages, because Yum finds the latest available package, downloads it, and installs any required dependencies. Yum has its limits, though; it's only as good as its repositories, so it can't install software that's not stored in those repositories.

WARNING   If you use Yum to automatically upgrade all packages on your system, you're effectively giving control of your system to the distribution maintainer. Although Red Hat or other distribution maintainers are unlikely to try to break into your computer in this way, an automatic update with minimal supervision on your part could easily break something on your system, particularly if you've obtained packages from unusual sources in the past.

If you don't want to install the package but merely want to obtain it, you can use yumdownloader. Type this command followed by the name of a package, and the latest version of the package will be downloaded to the current directory. This can be handy if you need to update a system that's not connected to the Internet; you can use another computer that runs the same distribution to obtain the packages and then transfer them to the target system.

If you prefer to use GUI tools rather than command-line tools, you should be aware that GUI front-ends to yum exist. Examples include yumex and kyum. You can use the text-mode yum to install these front-ends, as in **yum install kyum**.

Exercise 2.1 runs you through the process of managing packages using the rpm utility.

EXERCISE 2.1

Managing Packages Using RPM

To manage packages using the rpm utility, follow these steps:

1. Log into the Linux system as a normal user.

2. Acquire a package to use for testing purposes. You can try using a package from your distribution that you know you haven't installed; but if you try a random package, you may find it's already installed or has unmet dependencies. This lab uses as an example the installation of zsh-4.3.17-1.fc17.x86_64.rpm, a shell that's not installed by default on most systems, from the Fedora 17 DVD onto a Fedora 17 system. You must adjust the commands as necessary if you use another RPM file in your tests.

3. Launch an xterm from the desktop environment's menu system if you used a GUI login.

4. Acquire root privileges. You can do this by typing **su** in an xterm, by selecting Session ➢ New Root Console from a Konsole window, or by using sudo (if it's configured) to run the commands in the following steps.

EXERCISE 2.1 *(continued)*

5. Type **rpm -q zsh** to verify that the package isn't currently installed. The system should respond with the message package zsh is not installed.

6. Type **rpm -qpi zsh-4.3.17-1.fc17.x86_64.rpm**. (You'll need to provide a complete path to the package file if it's not in your current directory.) The system should respond by displaying information about the package, such as the version number, the vendor, the hostname of the machine on which it was built, and a package description.

7. Type **rpm -ivh zsh-4.3.17-1.fc17.x86_64.rpm**. The system should install the package and display a series of hash marks (#) as it does so.

8. Type **rpm -q zsh**. The system should respond with the complete package name, including the version and build numbers. This response verifies that the package is installed.

9. Type **zsh**. This launches a Z shell, which functions much like the more common bash and tcsh shells. You're likely to see your command prompt change, but you can issue most of the same commands you can use with bash or tcsh.

10. Type **rpm -V zsh**. The system shouldn't produce any output—just a new command prompt. The verify (-V or --verify) command checks the package files against data stored in the database. Immediately after installation, most packages should show no deviations. (A handful of packages will be modified during installation, but zsh isn't one of them.)

11. Type **rpm -e zsh**. The system shouldn't produce any output—just a new command prompt. This command removes the package from the system. Note that you're removing the zsh package while running the zsh program. Linux continues to run the zsh program you're using, but you'll be unable to launch new instances of the program. Some programs may misbehave if you do this because files will be missing after you remove the package.

12. Type **exit** to exit zsh and return to your normal shell.

13. Type **rpm -q zsh**. The system should respond with a package zsh is not installed error because you've just uninstalled the package.

14. Type **yum install zsh**. The system should check your repositories, download zsh, and install it. It will ask for confirmation before beginning the download.

15. Type **rpm -q zsh**. The results should be similar to those in step 8, although the version number may differ.

16. Type **rpm -e zsh**. This step removes **zsh** from the system but produces no output, just as in step 11.

The final three steps will work only if your distribution uses Yum. If you're using a distribution that uses another tool, you may be able to locate and use its equivalent, such as zypper for SUSE.

RPM and Yum Configuration Files

Ordinarily, you needn't explicitly configure RPM or Yum; distributions that use RPM configure it in reasonable ways by default. Sometimes, though, you may want to tweak a few details, particularly if you routinely build source RPM packages and want to optimize the output for your computer. You may also want to add a Yum repository for some unusual software you run. To do so, you typically edit an RPM or Yum configuration file.

The main RPM configuration file is /usr/lib/rpm/rpmrc. This file sets a variety of options, mostly related to the CPU optimizations used when compiling source packages. You shouldn't edit this file, though; instead, you should create and edit /etc/rpmrc (to make global changes) or ~/.rpmrc (to make changes on a per-user basis). The main reason to create such a file is to implement architecture optimizations—for instance, to optimize your code for your CPU model by passing appropriate compiler options when you build a source RPM into a binary RPM. This is done with the optflags line:

```
optflags: athlon -O2 -g -march=i686
```

This line tells RPM to pass the -O2 -g -march-i686 options to the compiler whenever building for the athlon platform. Although RPM can determine your system's architecture, the optflags line by itself isn't likely to be enough to set the correct flags. Most default rpmrc files include a series of buildarchtranslate lines that cause rpmbuild (or rpm for older versions of RPM) to use one set of optimizations for a whole family of CPUs. For x86 systems, these lines typically look like this:

```
buildarchtranslate: athlon: i386
buildarchtranslate: i686: i386
buildarchtranslate: i586: i386
buildarchtranslate: i486: i386
buildarchtranslate: i386: i386
```

These lines tell RPM to translate the athlon, i686, i586, i486, and i386 CPU codes to use the i386 optimizations. This effectively defeats the purpose of any CPU-specific optimizations you create on the optflags line for your architecture, but it guarantees that the RPMs you build will be maximally portable. To change matters, you must alter the line for your CPU type, as returned when you type **uname -p**. For instance, on an Athlon-based system, you might enter the following line:

```
buildarchtranslate: athlon: athlon
```

Thereafter, when you rebuild a source RPM, the system will use the appropriate Athlon optimizations. The result can be a slight performance boost on your own system, but reduced portability—depending on the precise optimizations you choose, such packages may not run on non-Athlon CPUs. (Indeed, you may not even be able to install them on non-Athlon CPUs!)

Yum is configured via the /etc/yum.conf file, with additional configuration files in the /etc/yum.repos.d/ directory. The yum.conf file holds basic options, such as the directory to which Yum downloads RPMs and where Yum logs its activities. Chances are you won't need to modify this file. The /etc/yum.repos.d/ directory, on the other hand, potentially holds several files, each of which describes a Yum repository—that is, a site that holds RPMs that may be installed via Yum. You probably shouldn't directly edit these files; instead, if you want to add a repository, you should manually download the RPM that includes the repository configuration and install it using rpm. The next time you use Yum, it will access your new repository along with the old ones. Several Yum repositories exist, mostly for Red Hat, CentOS, and Fedora, such as the following:

Livna   This repository (http://rpm.livna.org/) hosts multimedia tools, such as additional codecs and video drivers.

KDE Red Hat   Red Hat, CentOS, and Fedora favor the GNU Network Object Model Environment (GNOME) desktop environment, although they ship with the K Desktop Environment (KDE), too. The repository at http://kde-redhat.sourceforge.net provides improved KDE RPMs for those who favor KDE.

Fresh RPMs   This repository (http://freshrpms.net) provides additional RPMs, mostly focusing on multimedia applications and drivers.

Many additional repositories exist. Try a Web search on terms such as *yum repository*, or check the Web page of any site that hosts unusual software you want to run to see whether it provides a Yum repository. If so, it should provide an RPM or other instructions on adding its site to your Yum repository list.

RPM Compared to Other Package Formats

RPM is a very flexible package management system. In most respects, it's comparable to Debian's package manager, and it offers many more features than tarballs do. When compared to Debian packages, the greatest strength of RPMs is probably their ubiquity. Many software packages are available in RPM form from their developers and/or from distribution maintainers.

Distribution packagers frequently modify the original programs in order to make them integrate more smoothly into the distribution as a whole. For instance, distribution-specific startup scripts may be added, program binaries may be relocated from default /usr/local subdirectories, and program source code may be patched to fix bugs or add features. Although these changes can be useful, you may not want them, particularly if you're using a program on a distribution other than the one for which the package was intended.

The fact that there are so many RPM-based distributions can be a boon. You may be able to use an RPM intended for one distribution on another, although as noted earlier, this isn't certain. In fact, this advantage can turn into a drawback if you try to mix and match too much—you can wind up with a mishmash of conflicting packages that can be difficult to disentangle.

The RPMFind Web site, `http://rpmfind.net`, is an extremely useful resource when you want to find an RPM of a specific program. Another site with similar characteristics is Fresh RPMs, `http://freshrpms.net`. These sites include links to RPMs built by programs' authors, specific distributions' RPMs, and those built by third parties. Adding such sites as Yum repositories can make them even easier to use.

Compared to tarballs, RPMs offer much more sophisticated package management tools. This can be important when you're upgrading or removing packages and also for verifying the integrity of installed packages. On the other hand, although RPMs are common in the Linux world, they're less common on other platforms. Therefore, you're more likely to find tarballs of generic Unix source code, and tarballs are preferred if you've written a program that you intend to distribute for other platforms.

Using Debian Packages

In their overall features, Debian packages are similar to RPMs; but the details of operation for each differ, and Debian packages are used on different distributions than are RPMs. Because each system uses its own database format, RPMs and Debian packages aren't interchangeable without converting formats. Using Debian packages requires knowing how to use the dpkg, dselect, and apt-get commands. A few other commands can also be helpful.

Debian Distributions and Conventions

As the name implies, Debian packages originated with the Debian distribution. Since that time, the format has been adopted by several other distributions, including Ubuntu, Linux Mint, and Xandros. Such distributions are derived from the original Debian, which means that packages from the original Debian are likely to work well on other Debian-based systems. Although Debian doesn't emphasize flashy GUI configuration tools, its derivatives tend to be more GUI-centric, which makes these distributions more appealing to Linux novices. The original Debian favors a system that's as bug-free as possible, and it tries to adhere strictly to open source software principles rather than invest effort in GUI configuration tools. The original Debian is unusual in that it's maintained not by a company that is motivated by profit, but rather by volunteers who are motivated by the desire to build a produce they want to use.

Like RPM, the Debian package format is neutral with respect to both OS and CPU type. Debian packages are extremely rare outside Linux, although various systems that used the Debian package system and software library atop non-Linux kernels have been attempted, and largely abandoned, with the exception of kFreeBSD (http://www.debian.org/ports/kfreebsd-gnu/)

The original Debian distribution has been ported to many different CPUs, including *x*86, *x*86-64, IA-64, ARM, PowerPC, Alpha, 680*x*0, MIPS, and SPARC. The original architecture was *x*86, and subsequent ports exist at varying levels of maturity. Derivative distributions generally work only on *x*86 or *x*86-64 systems, but this could change in the future.

Debian packages follow a naming convention similar to that for RPMs; but Debian packages sometimes omit codes in the filename to specify a package's architecture, particularly on *x*86 packages. When these codes are present, they may differ from RPM conventions. For instance, a filename ending in i386.deb indicates an *x*86 binary, powerpc.deb is a PowerPC binary, and all.deb indicates a CPU-independent package, such as documentation or scripts. As with RPM files, this file-naming convention is only that— a convention. You can rename a file as you see fit, to either include or omit the processor code. There is no code for Debian source packages because, as described in the upcoming section "Debian Packages Compared to Other Package Formats," Debian source packages consist of several separate files.

The *dpkg* Command Set

Debian packages are incompatible with RPM packages, but the basic principles of operation are the same across both package types. Like RPMs, Debian packages include dependency information, and the Debian package utilities maintain a database of installed packages, files, and so on. You use the dpkg command to install a Debian package. This command's syntax is similar to that of rpm:

dpkg [*options*][*action*] [*package-files*|*package-name*]

The *action* is the action to be taken; common actions are summarized in Table 2.4. The options (Table 2.5) modify the behavior of the action, much like the options to rpm.

TABLE 2.4   dpkg primary actions

Action	Description
-i or --install	Installs a package
--configure	Reconfigures an installed package: runs the post-installation script to set site-specific options
-r or --remove	Removes a package but leaves configuration files intact

`-P` or `--purge`	Removes a package, including configuration files
`--get-selections`	Displays currently installed packages
`-p` or `--print-avail`	Displays information about an installed package
`-I` or `--info`	Displays information about an uninstalled package file
`-l` *pattern* or `--list` *pattern*	Lists all installed packages whose names match *pattern*
`-L` or `--listfiles`	Lists the installed files associated with a package
`-S` *pattern* or `--search` *pattern*	Locates the package(s) that own the file(s) specified by *pattern*
`-C` or `--audit`	Searches for partially installed packages and suggests what to do with them

TABLE 2.5   Options for fine-tuning dpkg actions

Option	Used with actions	Description
`--root=`*dir*	All	Modifies the Linux system using a root directory located at *dir*. Can be used to maintain one Linux installation discrete from another one, say during OS installation or emergency maintenance.
`-B` or `--auto-deconfigure`	`-r`	Disables packages that rely on one that is being removed.
`--force-`*things*	Assorted	Overrides defaults that would ordinarily cause dpkg to abort. Consult the dpkg man page for details of *things* this option does.
`--ignore-depends=`*package*	`-i`, `-r`	Ignores dependency information for the specified package.
`--no-act`	`-i`, `-r`	Checks for dependencies, conflicts, and other problems without actually installing or removing the package.
`--recursive`	`-i`	Installs all packages that match the package-name wildcard in the specified directory and all subdirectories.
`-G`	`-i`	Doesn't install the package if a newer version of the same package is already installed.
`-E` or `--skip-same-version`	`-i`	Doesn't install the package if the same version of the package is already installed.

As with rpm, dpkg expects a package name in some cases and a package filename in others. Specifically, --install (-i) and --info (-I) both require the package filename, but the other commands take the shorter package name.

As an example, consider the following command, which installs the samba_2:3.6. 3-2ubuntu2.3_amd64.deb package:

```
# dpkg -i samba_2:3.6.3-2ubuntu2.3_amd64.deb
```

If you're upgrading a package, you may need to remove an old package before installing the new one. To do this, use the -r option to dpkg, as in the following:

```
# dpkg -r samba
```

To find information about an installed package, use the -p parameter to dpkg, as shown in Listing 2.2. This listing omits an extended English description of what the package does.

Listing 2.2:   dpkg package information query output

```
$ dpkg -p samba
Package: samba
Priority: optional
Section: net
Installed-Size: 22862
Maintainer: Ubuntu Developers <ubuntu-devel-discuss@lists.ubuntu.com>
Architecture: amd64
Version: 2:3.6.3-2ubuntu2.3
Replaces: samba-common (<= 2.0.5a-2)
Depends: samba-common (= 2:3.6.3-2ubuntu2.3), libwbclient0↵
  (= 2:3.6.3-2ubuntu2.3), libacl1 (>= 2.2.51-5), libattr1 (>= 1:2.4.46-5),↵
  libc6 (>= 2.15), libcap2 (>= 2.10), libcomerr2 (>= 1.01), libcups2↵
  (>= 1.4.0), libgssapi-krb5-2 (>= 1.10+dfsg~), libk5crypto3 (>= 1.6.dfsg.2),↵
  libkrb5-3 (>= 1.10+dfsg~), libldap-2.4-2 (>= 2.4.7), libpam0g↵
  (>= 0.99.7.1), libpopt0 (>= 1.14), libtalloc2 (>= 2.0.4~git20101213),↵
  libtdb1 (>= 1.2.7+git20101214), zlib1g (>= 1:1.1.4), debconf (>= 0.5)↵
  | debconf-2.0, upstart-job, libpam-runtime (>= 1.0.1-11),↵
  libpam-modules, lsb-base (>= 3.2-13), procps, update-inetd,↵
  adduser, samba-common-bin
Recommends: logrotate, tdb-tools
Suggests: openbsd-inetd | inet-superserver, smbldap-tools, ldb-tools,↵
  ctdb, ufw
Conflicts: samba4 (<< 4.0.0~alpha6-2)
Size: 8042012
```

Debian-based systems often use a pair of somewhat higher-level utilities, apt-get and dselect, to handle package installation and removal. These utilities are described later in "Using apt-get" and "Using dselect, aptitude, and Synaptic." Their interfaces can be very useful when you want to install several packages, but dpkg is often more convenient when you're manipulating just one or two packages. Because dpkg can take package file-names as input, it's also the preferred method of installing a package that you download from an unusual source or create yourself.

Using *apt-cache*

The APT suite of tools includes a program, apt-cache, that's intended solely to provide information about the Debian package database (known in Debian terminology as the *package cache*). You may be interested in using several features of this tool:

Display Package Information   Using the showpkg subcommand, as in **apt-cache showpkg samba**, displays information about the package. The information displayed is different from that returned by dpkg's informational actions.

Display Package Statistics   You can learn how many packages you've installed, how many dependencies are recorded, and various other statistics about the package database by passing the stats subcommand, as in **apt-cache stats**.

Find Unmet Dependencies   If a program is reporting missing libraries or files, typing **apt-cache unmet** may help; this function of apt-cache returns information about unmet dependencies, which may help you track down the source of missing-file problems.

Display Dependencies   Using the depends subcommand, as in **apt-cache depends samba**, shows all of the specified package's dependencies. This information can be helpful in tracking down dependency-related problems. The rdepends subcommand finds reverse dependencies—packages that depend on the one you specify.

Locate All Packages   The pkgnames subcommand displays the names of all the packages installed on the system. If you include a second parameter, as in **apt-cache pkgnames sa**, the program returns only those packages that begin with the specified string.

Several more subcommands and options exist, but these are the ones you're most likely to use. Several apt-cache subcommands are intended for package maintainers and debugging serious package database problems rather than day-to-day system administration. Consult the man page for apt-cache for more information.

Using *apt-get*

APT, with its apt-get utility, is Debian's equivalent to Yum on certain RPM-based distributions. This meta-packaging tool enables you to perform easy upgrades of pack-ages, especially if you have a fast Internet connection. Debian-based systems include a file, /etc/apt/sources.list, that specifies locations from which important packages can be obtained. If you installed the OS from a CD-ROM drive, this file will initially list directories on the installation CD-ROM in which packages can be found. There are also likely to be a few lines near the top, commented out with hash marks (#), indicating directories on an FTP site or a Web site from which you can obtain updated packages. (These lines may be uncommented if you did a network install initially.)

> Don't add a site to /etc/apt/sources.list unless you're sure it can be trusted. The apt-get utility does automatic and semiautomatic upgrades, so if you add a network source to sources.list and that source contains unreliable programs or programs with security holes, your system will become vulnerable after upgrading via apt-get.

Although APT is most strongly associated with Debian systems, a port to RPM-based systems is also available. Check http://apt4rpm.sourceforge.net for information about this port.

The apt-get utility works by obtaining information about available packages from the sources listed in /etc/apt/sources.list and then using that information to upgrade or install packages. The syntax is similar to that of dpkg:

apt-get [*options*][*command*] [*package-names*]

Table 2.6 lists the apt-get commands, and Table 2.7 lists the most commonly used options. In most cases, you won't use *any* options with apt-get—just a single command and possibly one or more package names. One particularly common use of this utility is to keep your system up to date with any new packages. The following two commands will accomplish this goal if /etc/apt/sources.list includes pointers to up-to-date file archive sites:

```
# apt-get update
# apt-get dist-upgrade
```

TABLE 2.6   apt-get commands

Command	Description
update	Obtains updated information about packages available from the installation sources listed in /etc/apt/sources.list.
upgrade	Upgrades all installed packages to the newest versions available, based on locally stored information about available packages.
dselect-upgrade	Performs any changes in package status (installation, removal, and so on) left undone after running dselect.

dist-upgrade	Similar to upgrade, but performs "smart" conflict resolution to avoid upgrading a package if doing so would break a dependency.
install	Installs a package by package name (not by package filename), obtaining the package from the source that contains the most up-to-date version.
remove	Removes a specified package by package name.
source	Retrieves the newest available source package file by package filename using information about available packages and installation archives listed in /etc/apt/sources.list.
check	Checks the package database for consistency and broken package installations.
clean	Performs housekeeping to help clear out information about retrieved files from the Debian package database. If you don't use dselect for package management, run this from time to time in order to save disk space.
autoclean	Similar to clean but removes information only about packages that can no longer be downloaded.

TABLE 2.7 Most-useful apt-get options

Option	Used with commands	Description
-d or --download-only	upgrade, dselect-upgrade, install, source	Downloads package files but doesn't install them.
-f or --fix-broken	install, remove	Attempts to fix a system on which dependencies are unsatisfied.
-m, --ignore-missing, or --fix-missing	upgrade, dselect-upgrade, install, remove, source	Ignores all package files that can't be retrieved (because of network errors, missing files, or the like).
-q or --quiet	All	Omits some progress indicator information. May be doubled (for instance, -qq) to produce still less progress information.
-s, --simulate, --just-print, --dry-run, --recon, or --no-act	All	Performs a simulation of the action without actually modifying, installing, or removing files.

TABLE 2.7 Most-useful apt-get options *(continued)*

Option	Used with commands	Description
-y, --yes, or --assume-yes	All	Produces a "yes" response to any yes/no prompt in installation scripts.
-b, --compile, or --build	source	Compiles a source package after retrieving it.
--no-upgrade	install	Causes apt-get to *not* upgrade a package if an older version is already installed.

WARNING   If you use APT to automatically upgrade all packages on your system, you're effectively giving control of your computer to the distribution maintainer. Although Debian or other distribution maintainers are unlikely to try to break into your computer in this way, an automatic update with minimal supervision on your part could easily break something on your system, particularly if you've obtained packages from unusual sources in the past.

In Exercise 2.2, you'll familiarize yourself with the Debian package system.

EXERCISE 2.2

Managing Debian Packages

To manage Debian packages, follow these steps:

1. Log into the Linux system as a normal user.

2. Acquire a package to use for testing purposes. You can try using a package from your distribution that you know you haven't installed; but if you try a random package, you may find it's already installed or has unmet dependencies. This lab uses as an example the installation of zsh_4.3.17-1ubuntu1_amd64.deb, a shell that's not installed by default on most systems, obtained using the –d option to apt-get on an Ubuntu 12.04 system. You must adjust the commands as necessary if you use another package, distribution, or architecture in your tests.

3. Launch an xterm from the desktop environment's menu system if you used a GUI login.

4. Acquire root privileges. You can do this by typing **su** in an xterm, by selecting Session ➢ New Root Console from a Konsole window, or by using sudo (if it's configured) to run the commands in the following steps.

5. Type **dpkg -L zsh** to verify that the package isn't currently installed. This command responds with a list of files associated with the package if it's installed or with an error that reads Package `zsh' is not installed if it's not.

6. Type **dpkg -I zsh_4.3.17-1ubuntu1_amd64.deb**. (You'll need to add a complete path to the package file if it's not in your current directory.) The system should respond by displaying information about the package, such as the version number, dependencies, the name of the package maintainer, and a package description.

7. Type **dpkg -i zsh_4.3.17-1ubuntu1_amd64.deb**. The system should install the package and display a series of lines summarizing its actions as it does so.

8. Type **dpkg -p zsh**. The system should respond with information about the package similar to that displayed in step 6.

9. Type **zsh**. This launches a Z shell, which functions much like the more common bash and tcsh shells. You're likely to see your command prompt change slightly, but you can issue most of the same commands you can use with bash or tcsh.

10. Type **dpkg -P zsh**. This command removes the package from the system, including configuration files. It may produce a series of warnings about non-empty directories that it couldn't remove. Note that you're removing the zsh package while running the zsh program. Linux continues to run the zsh program you're using, but you'll be unable to launch new instances of the program. Some programs may misbehave because files will be missing after you remove the package.

11. Type **exit** to exit from zsh and return to your normal shell.

12. Type **dpkg -L zsh**. The system should respond with a Package `zsh' is not installed error because you've just uninstalled it.

13. Type **apt-get install zsh** to install zsh using the APT system. Depending on your configuration, the system may download the package from an Internet site or ask you to insert a CD-ROM. If it asks for a CD-ROM, insert it and press the Enter key. The system should install the package.

14. Type **dpkg -p zsh**. The system should respond with information about the package similar to that displayed in step 6 or 8.

15. Type **dpkg -P zsh**. This command removes the package from the system, as described in step 10.

Using *dselect, aptitude,* and Synaptic

The dselect program is a high-level package browser. Using it, you can select packages to install on your system from the APT archives defined in /etc/apt/sources.list, review the packages that are already installed on your system, uninstall packages, and upgrade packages. Overall, dselect is a powerful tool, but it can be intimidating to the uninitiated because it presents a lot of options that aren't obvious, using a text-mode interactive user interface.

Although dselect supports a few command-line options, they're mostly obscure or minor (such as options to set the color scheme). Consult dselect's man page for details. To use the program, type **dselect**. The result is the dselect main menu, as shown running in a KDE Konsole window in Figure 2.1.

FIGURE 2.1   The dselect utility provides access to APT features using a menu system.

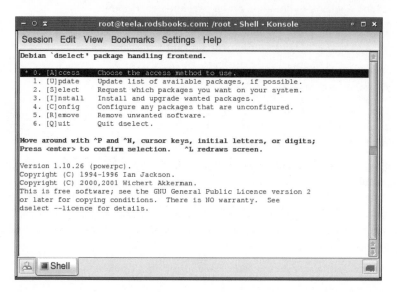

Another text-based Debian package manager is aptitude. In interactive mode, aptitude is similar to dselect in a rough way, but aptitude adds menus accessed by pressing Ctrl+T and rearranges some features. You can also pass various commands to aptitude on the command line, as in **aptitude search samba**, which searches for packages related to Samba. Features accessible from the command line (or the interactive interface) include the following:

Update Package Lists   You can update package lists from the APT repositories by typing **aptitude update**.

Install Software   The install command-line option installs a named package. This command has several variant names and syntaxes that modify its action. For instance, typing **aptitude install zsh** installs the zsh package, but typing **aptitude install zsh-** (with a trailing dash) and **aptitude remove zsh** both uninstall zsh.

Upgrade Software   The full-upgrade and safe-upgrade options both upgrade all installed packages. The safe-upgrade option is conservative about removing packages or installing new ones and so may fail; full-upgrade is less conservative about these actions and so is more likely to complete its tasks, but it may break software in the process.

Search for Packages   The `search` option, noted earlier, searches the database for packages matching the specified name. The result is a list of packages, one per line, with summary codes for each package's install status, its name, and a brief description.

Clean Up the Database   The `autoclean` option removes already-downloaded packages that are no longer available, and `clean` removes all downloaded packages.

Obtain Help   Typing **`aptitude help`** results in a complete list of options.

Broadly speaking, `aptitude` combines the interactive features of `dselect` with the command-line options of `apt-get`. All three programs provide similar functionality, so you can use whichever one you prefer.

A tool that's similar to `dselect` and `aptitude` in some ways is Synaptic, but Synaptic is a GUI X-based program and as such is easier to use. Overall, `dselect`, `aptitude`, and Synaptic are useful tools, particularly if you need to locate software but don't know its exact name—the ability to browse and search the available packages can be a great boon. Unfortunately, the huge package list can be intimidating.

Reconfiguring Packages

Debian packages often provide more-extensive initial setup options than do their RPM counterparts. Frequently, the install script included in the package asks a handful of questions, such as querying for the name of an outgoing mail relay system for a mail server program. These questions help the package system set up a standardized configuration that has nonetheless been customized for your computer.

In the course of your system administration, you may alter the configuration files for a package. If you do this and find you've made a mess of things, you may want to revert to the initial standard configuration. To do so, you can use the `dpkg-reconfigure` program, which runs the initial configuration script for the package you specify:

```
# dpkg-reconfigure samba
```

This command reconfigures the `samba` package, asking the package's initial installation questions and restarting the Samba daemons. Once this is done, the package should be in something closer to its initial state.

Debian Packages Compared to Other Package Formats

The overall functionality of Debian packages is similar to that of RPMs, although there are differences. Debian source packages aren't single files; they're groups of files—the original source tarball, a patch file that's used to modify the source code (including a file that controls the building of a Debian package), and a `.dsc` file that contains a digital "signature" to help verify the authenticity of the collection. The Debian package tools can combine these and compile the package to create a Debian binary package. This structure makes Debian source packages slightly less convenient to transport because you must move at least two files (the tarball and patch file; the .dsc file is optional) rather than just one. Debian source packages also support just one patch file, whereas RPM source packages may contain multiple patch files. Although you can certainly combine multiple patch files into one, doing so makes it less clear where a patch comes from, thus making it harder to back out of any given change.

These source package differences are mostly of interest to software developers. As a system administrator or end user, you need not normally be concerned with them unless you must recompile a package from a source form—and even then, the differences between the formats need not be overwhelming. The exact commands and features used by each system differ, but they accomplish similar overall goals.

Because all distributions that use Debian packages are derived from Debian, they tend to be more compatible with one another (in terms of their packages) than RPM-based distributions are. In particular, Debian has defined details of its system startup scripts and many other features to help Debian packages install and run on any Debian-based system. This helps Debian-based systems avoid the sorts of incompatibilities in startup scripts that can cause problems using one distribution's RPMs on another distribution. Of course, some future distribution could violate Debian's guidelines for these matters, so this advantage isn't guaranteed to hold over time.

As a practical matter, it can be harder to locate Debian packages than RPM packages for some exotic programs. Debian maintains a good collection at `http://www.debian.org/distrib/packages`, and some program authors make Debian packages available as well. If you can find an RPM but not a Debian package, you may be able to convert the RPM to Debian format using a program called `alien`, as described shortly in "Converting Between Package Formats." If all else fails, you can use a tarball, but you'll lose the advantages of the Debian package database.

Configuring Debian Package Tools

With the exception of the APT sources list mentioned earlier, Debian package tools don't usually require configuration. Debian installs reasonable defaults (as do its derivative distributions). On rare occasions, though, you may want to adjust some of these defaults. Doing so requires that you know where to look for them.

The main configuration file for dpkg is /etc/dpkg/dpkg.cfg or ↩/.dpkg.cfg. This file contains dpkg options, as summarized in Table 2.5, but without the leading dashes. For instance, to have dpkg always perform a test run rather than actually install a package, you'd create a dpkg.cfg file that contains one line:

```
no-act
```

For APT, the main configuration file you're likely to modify is /etc/apt/sources.list, which was described earlier in "Using apt-get." Beyond this file is /etc/apt/apt.conf, which controls APT and dselect options. As with dpkg.cfg, chances are you won't need to modify apt.conf. If you do need to make changes, the format is more complex and is modeled after those of the Internet Software Consortium's (ISC's) Dynamic Host Configuration

Protocol (DHCP) and Berkeley Internet Name Domain (BIND) servers' configuration files. Options are grouped together by open and close curly braces ({ }):

```
APT
{
  Get
  {
    Download-Only "true";
  };
};
```

These lines are equivalent to permanently setting the `--download-only` option described in Table 2.7. You can, of course, set many more options. For details, consult `apt.conf`'s man page. You may also want to review the sample configuration file, `/usr/share/doc/apt/examples/apt.conf`. (The working `/etc/apt/apt.conf` file is typically extremely simple, or may be missing entirely and therefore not be very helpful as an example.)

You should be aware that Debian's package tools rely on various files in the `/var/lib/dpkg` directory tree. These files maintain lists of available packages, lists of installed packages, and so on. In other words, this directory tree is effectively the Debian installed file database. As such, you should be sure to back up this directory when you perform system backups and be careful about modifying its contents.

Converting Between Package Formats

Sometimes you're presented with a package file in one format, but you want to use another format. This is particularly common when you use a Debian-based distribution and can find only tarballs or RPM files of a package. When this happens, you can keep looking for a package file in the appropriate format, install the tools for the foreign format, create a package from a source tarball using the standard RPM or Debian tools, or convert between package formats with a utility like `alien`.

This section focuses on this last option. The `alien` program comes with Debian and a few other distributions but may not be installed by default. If it's not installed on your system, install it by typing **apt-get install alien** on a system that uses APT, or use the Rpmfind or Debian package Web site to locate it. This program can convert between RPM packages, Debian packages, Stampede packages (used by Stampede Linux), and tarballs.

You need to be aware of some caveats. For one thing, `alien` requires that you have appropriate package manager software installed—for instance, both RPM and Debian to convert between these formats. The `alien` utility doesn't always convert all dependency information completely correctly. When converting from a tarball, `alien` copies the files directly as they had been in the tarball, so `alien` works only if the original tarball has files that should be installed off the root (/) directory of the system.

Although `alien` requires both RPM and Debian package systems to be installed to convert between these formats, `alien` doesn't use the database features of these packages unless you use the `--install` option. The presence of a foreign package manager isn't a problem as long as you don't use it to install software that might duplicate or conflict with software installed with your primary package manager.

The basic syntax of `alien` is as follows:

```
alien [options] file[...]
```

The most important options are `--to-deb`, `--to-rpm`, `--to-slp`, and `--to-tgz`, which convert to Debian, RPM, Stampede, and tarball format, respectively. (If you omit the destination format, `alien` assumes you want a Debian package.) The `--install` option installs the converted package and removes the converted file. Consult the `alien` man page for additional options.

For instance, suppose you have a Debian package called `someprogram-1.2.3-4_i386 .deb`, and you want to create an RPM from it. You can issue the following command to create an RPM called `someprogram-1.2.3-5.i386.rpm`:

```
# alien --to-rpm someprogram-1.2.3-4_i386.deb
```

If you use a Debian-based system and want to install a tarball but keep a record of the files it contains in your Debian package database, you can do so with the following command:

```
# alien --install binary-tarball.tar.gz
```

It's important to remember that converting a tarball converts the files in the directory structure of the original tarball using the system's root directory as the base. Therefore, you may need to unpack the tarball, juggle files around, and repack it to get the desired results *prior to* installing the tarball with `alien`. For instance, suppose you have a binary tarball that creates a directory called `program-files`, with `bin`, `man`, and `lib` directories under this. The intent may have been to unpack the tarball in `/usr` or `/usr/local` and create links for critical files. To convert this tarball to an RPM, you can issue the following commands:

```
# tar xvfz program.tar.gz
# mv program-files usr
# tar cvfz program.tgz usr
# rm -r usr
# alien --to-rpm program.tgz
```

By renaming the `program-files` directory to `usr` and creating a new tarball, you've created a tarball that, when converted to RPM format, will have files in the locations you want—`/usr/bin`, `/usr/man`, and `/usr/lib`. You might need to perform more extensive modifications, depending on the contents of the original tarball.

Package Dependencies and Conflicts

Although package installation often proceeds smoothly, sometimes it doesn't. The usual sources of problems relate to unsatisfied dependencies or conflicts between packages. The RPM and Debian package management systems are intended to help you locate and resolve such problems, but on occasion (particularly when mixing packages from different vendors), they can actually cause problems. In either event, it pays to recognize these errors and know how to resolve them.

 If you use a meta-packager, such as Yum or APT, for all your package management, you're much less likely to run into problems with package dependencies and conflicts. These problems are most likely to arise when you install lone packages, especially those from unusual sources.

Real and Imagined Package Dependency Problems

Package dependencies and conflicts can arise for a variety of reasons, including the following:

Missing Libraries or Support Programs   One of the most common dependency problems is caused by a missing support package. For instance, all KDE programs rely on Qt, a widget set that provides assorted GUI tools. If Qt isn't installed, you won't be able to install any KDE packages using RPMs or Debian packages. Libraries—support code that can be used by many different programs as if it were part of the program itself—are particularly common sources of problems in this respect.

Incompatible Libraries or Support Programs   Even if a library or support program is installed on your system, it may be the wrong version. For instance, if a program requires Qt 4.8, the presence of Qt 3.3 won't do much good. Fortunately, Linux library-naming conventions enable you to install multiple versions of a library in case you have programs with competing requirements.

Duplicate Files or Features   Conflicts arise when one package includes files that are already installed and that belong to another package. Occasionally, broad features can conflict as well, as in two Web server packages. Feature conflicts are usually accompanied by name conflicts. Conflicts are most common when mixing packages intended for different distributions, because distributions may split files across packages in different ways.

Mismatched Names   RPM and Debian package management systems give names to their packages. These names don't always match across distributions. For this reason, if one package checks for another package by name, the first package may not install on another distribution, even if the appropriate package is installed, because that target package has a different name.

Some of these problems are very real and serious. Missing libraries, for instance, must be installed. (Sometimes, though, a missing library isn't quite as missing as it seems, as described in the upcoming section "Forcing the Installation.") Others, like mismatched package names, are artifacts of the packaging system. Unfortunately, it's not always easy to tell into which category a conflict fits. When using a package management system, you may be able to use the error message returned by the package system, along with your own experience with and knowledge of specific packages, to make a judgment. For instance, if RPM reports that you're missing a slew of libraries with which you're unfamiliar, you'll probably have to track down at least one package—unless you know you've installed the libraries in some other way, in which case you may want to force the installation.

Workarounds for Package Dependency Problems

When you encounter an unmet package dependency or conflict, what can you do about it? There are several approaches to these problems. Some of these approaches work well in some situations but not others, so you should review the possibilities carefully. The options include forcing the installation, modifying your system to meet the dependency, rebuilding the problem package from source code, and finding another version of the problem package.

Forcing the Installation

One approach is to ignore the issue. Although this sounds risky, it's appropriate in some cases involving failed RPM or Debian dependencies. For instance, if the dependency is on a package that you installed by compiling the source code yourself, you can safely ignore the dependency. When using rpm, you can tell the program to ignore failed dependencies by using the --nodeps parameter:

```
# rpm -i apackage.rpm --nodeps
```

You can force installation over some other errors, such as conflicts with existing packages, by using the --force parameter:

```
# rpm -i apackage.rpm --force
```

Do *not* use --nodeps or --force as a matter of course. Ignoring the dependency checks can lead you into trouble, so you should use these options only when you need to do so. In the case of conflicts, the error messages you get when you first try to install without --force will tell you which packages' files you'll be replacing, so be sure you back them up or are prepared to reinstall the packages in case of trouble.

If you're using dpkg, you can use the `--ignore-depends=`*package*, `--force-depends`, and `--force-conflicts` parameters to overcome dependency and conflict problems in Debian-based systems. Because there's less deviation in package names and requirements among Debian-based systems, these options are less often needed on such systems.

Upgrading or Replacing the Depended-on Package

Officially, the proper way to overcome a package dependency problem is to install, upgrade, or replace the depended-upon package. If a program requires, say, Qt 4.8 or greater, you should upgrade an older version (such as 4.4) to 4.8. To perform such an upgrade, you'll need to track down and install the appropriate package. This usually isn't too difficult if the new package you want comes from a Linux distribution, especially if you use a meta-packager such as Yum or APT; the appropriate depended-on package should come with the same distribution.

One problem with this approach is that packages intended for different distributions sometimes have differing requirements. If you run Distribution A and install a package that was built for Distribution B, the package will express dependencies in terms of Distribution B's files and versions. The appropriate versions may not be available in a form intended for Distribution A; and by installing Distribution B's versions, you can sometimes cause conflicts with other Distribution A packages. Even if you install the upgraded package and it works, you may run into problems in the future when it comes time to install some other program or upgrade the distribution as a whole—the upgrade installer may not recognize Distribution B's package or may not be able to upgrade to its own newer version.

Rebuilding the Problem Package

Some dependencies result from the libraries and other support utilities installed on the computer that compiled the package, not from requirements in the underlying source code. If the software is recompiled on a system that has different packages, the dependencies will change. Therefore, rebuilding a package from source code can overcome at least some dependencies.

If you use an RPM-based system, the command to rebuild a package is straightforward: You call `rpmbuild` (or `rpm` with old versions of RPM) with the name of the source package and use `--rebuild`, as follows:

```
# rpmbuild --rebuild packagename-version.src.rpm
```

Of course, to do this you must have the source RPM for the package. This can usually be obtained from the same location as the binary RPM. When you execute this command, `rpmbuild` extracts the source code and executes whatever commands are required to build a new package—or sometimes several new packages. (One source RPM can build multiple binary RPMs.) The compilation process can take anywhere from a few seconds to several hours, depending on the size of the package and the speed of your computer. The result should be one or more new binary RPMs in `/usr/src/`*distname*`/RPMS/`*arch*, where *distname* is a distribution-specific name (such as `redhat` on Red Hat or `packages` on SUSE) and *arch* is your CPU architecture (such as `i386` or `i586` for x86 or `ppc` for PowerPC). You can move these RPMs to any convenient location and install them just as you would any others.

Source packages are also available for Debian systems, but aside from sites devoted to Debian and related distributions, Debian source packages are rare. The sites that do have these packages provide them in forms that typically install easily on appropriate Debian or related systems. For this reason, it's less likely that you'll rebuild a Debian package from source.

Be aware that compiling a source package typically requires you to have appropriate development tools installed on your system, such as the GNU Compiler Collection (GCC) and assorted *development libraries*. Development libraries are the parts of a library that enable programs to be written for the library. Many Linux installations lack development libraries even when the matching binary libraries are installed. Thus, you may need to install quite a few packages to recompile a source package. The error messages you receive when you attempt but fail to build a source package can help you track down the necessary software, but you may need to read several lines of error messages and use your package system to search for appropriate tools and development libraries. (Development libraries often include the string dev or devel in their names.)

Locating Another Version of the Problem Package

Frequently, the simplest way to fix a dependency problem or package conflict is to use a different version of the package you want to install. This could be a newer or older official version (4.2.3 rather than 4.4.7, say), or it might be the same official version but built for your distribution rather than for another distribution. Sites like Rpmfind (http://www.rpmfind .net) and Debian's package listing (http://www.debian.org/distrib/packages) can be very useful in tracking down alternative versions of a package. Your own distribution's Web site or FTP site can also be a good place to locate packages.

If the package you're trying to install requires newer libraries than you have and you don't want to upgrade those libraries, an older version of the package may work with your existing libraries. Before installing such a program, though, you should check to be sure that the newer version of the program doesn't fix security bugs. If it does, you should find another way to install the package.

The main problem with locating another version of the package is that sometimes you really need the version that's not installing correctly. It may have features you need, or it may fix important bugs. On occasion, other versions may not be available, or you may be unable to locate another version of the package in your preferred package format.

Startup Script Problems

One particularly common problem when trying to install servers from one distribution in another is getting startup scripts working. In the past, most major Linux distributions used

SysV startup scripts, but these scripts weren't always transportable across distributions. Today, alternatives to SysV are common, which further complicates this problem. The result is that the server you installed may not start up. Possible workarounds include modifying the startup script that came with the server, building a new script based on another one from your distribution, and starting the server through a local startup script like `/etc/rc.d/rc.local` or `/etc/rc.d/boot.local`. Chapter 5, "Booting Linux and Editing Files," describes startup scripts in more detail.

Startup script problems affect only servers and other programs that are started automatically when the computer boots; they don't affect typical user applications or libraries.

Managing Shared Libraries

Most Linux software relies heavily on *shared libraries*. The preceding sections have described some of the problems that can arise in managing shared library packages—for example, if a library isn't installed or is the wrong version, you may have problems installing a package. Library management goes beyond merely configuring them, though. To understand this, you must first understand a few library principles. You can then move on to setting the library path and using commands that manage libraries.

Library Principles

The idea behind a library is to simplify programmers' lives by providing commonly used program fragments. For instance, one of the most important libraries is the C *library* (libc), which provides many of the higher-level features associated with the C programming language. Another common type of library is associated with GUIs. These libraries are often called *widget sets* because they provide the on-screen *widgets* used by programs—buttons, scroll bars, menu bars, and so on. The GIMP Tool Kit (GTK+) and Qt are the most popular Linux widget sets, and both ship largely as libraries. Libraries are chosen by programmers, not by users; you usually can't substitute one library for another. (The main exceptions are minor version upgrades.)

Linux uses the *GNU C library (glibc)* version of the C library. Package-manager dependencies and other library references are to glibc specifically. As of glibc 2.15, for historical reasons the main glibc file is usually called `/lib/libc.so.6` or `/lib64/libc.so.6`, but this file is sometimes a symbolic link to a file of another name, such as `/lib/libc-2.15.so`.

In principle, the routines in a library can be linked into a program's main file, just like all the object code files created by the compiler. This approach, however, has certain problems:

- The resulting program file is huge. This means it takes up a lot of disk space, and it consumes a lot of RAM when loaded.

- If multiple programs use the library, as is common, the program-size issue is multiplied several times; the library is effectively stored multiple times on disk and in RAM.

- The program can't take advantage of improvements in the library without recompiling (or at least relinking) the program.

For these reasons, most programs use their libraries as shared libraries (aka *dynamic libraries*). In this form, the main program executable omits most of the library routines. Instead, the executable includes references to shared library files, which can then be loaded along with the main program file. This approach helps keep program file size down, enables sharing of the memory consumed by libraries across programs, and enables programs to take advantage of improvements in libraries by upgrading the library.

 Linux shared libraries are similar to the dynamic link libraries (DLLs) of Windows. Windows DLLs are usually identified by .DLL filename extensions; but in Linux, shared libraries usually have a .so or .so.*version* extension, where *version* is a version number. (.so stands for *shared object*.) Linux *static libraries* (used by linkers for inclusion in programs when dynamic libraries aren't to be used) have .a filename extensions.

On the downside, shared libraries can degrade program load time slightly if the library isn't already in use by another program, and they can create software management complications:

- Shared library changes can be incompatible with some or all programs that use the library. Linux uses library numbering schemes to enable you to keep multiple versions of a library installed at once. Upgrades that shouldn't cause problems can overwrite older versions, whereas major upgrades get installed side by side with their older counterparts. This approach minimizes the chance of problems, but sometimes changes that *shouldn't* cause problems *do* cause them.

- Programs must be able to locate shared libraries. This task requires adjusting configuration files and environment variables. If it's done wrong or if a program overrides the defaults and looks in the wrong place, the result is usually that the program won't run at all.

- The number of libraries for Linux has risen dramatically over time. When they're used in shared form, the result can be a tangled mess of package dependencies, particularly if you use programs that rely on many or obscure libraries. In most cases, this issue boils down to a package problem that can be handled by your package management tools.

- If an important shared library becomes inaccessible because it was accidentally over-written, due to a disk error or for any other reason, the result can be severe system problems. In a worst-case scenario, the system might not even boot.

In most cases, these drawbacks are manageable and are much less important than the problems associated with using static libraries. Thus, dynamic libraries are very popular.

Static libraries are sometimes used by developers who create programs using particularly odd, outdated, or otherwise exotic libraries. This enables them to distribute their binary packages without requiring users to obtain and install their oddball libraries. Likewise, static libraries are sometimes used on small emergency systems, which don't have enough programs installed to make the advantages of shared libraries worth pursuing.

Locating Library Files

The major administrative challenge of handling shared libraries involves enabling programs to locate those shared libraries. Binary program files can point to libraries either by name alone (as in `libc.so.6`) or by providing a complete path (as in `/lib/libc.so.6`). In the first case, you must configure a *library path*—a set of directories in which programs should search for libraries. This can be done both through a global configuration file and through an environment variable. If a static path to a library is wrong, you must find a way to correct the problem. In all of these cases, after making a change, you may need to use a special command to get the system to recognize the change, as described later in "Library Management Commands."

Setting the Path Systemwide

The first way to set the library path is to edit the `/etc/ld.so.conf` file. This file consists of a series of lines, each of which lists one directory in which shared library files may be found. Typically, this file lists between half a dozen and a couple dozen directories. Some distributions have an additional type of line in this file. These lines begin with the `include` directive; they list files that are to be included as if they were part of the main file. For instance, Ubuntu 12.04's `ld.so.conf` begins with this line:

```
include /etc/ld.so.conf.d/*.conf
```

This line tells the system to load all the files in `/etc/ld.so.conf.d` whose names end in `.conf` as if they were part of the main `/etc/ld.so.conf` file. This mechanism enables package maintainers to add their unique library directories to the search list by placing a `.conf` file in the appropriate directory.

Some distributions, such as Gentoo, use a mechanism with a similar goal but different details. With these distributions, the `env-update` utility reads files in `/etc/env.d` to create the final form of several `/etc` configuration files, including `/etc/ld.so.conf`. In particular, the `LDPATH` variables in these files are read, and their values make up the lines in `ld.so.conf`.

Thus, to change ld.so.conf in Gentoo or other distributions that use this mechanism, you should add or edit files in /etc/env.d and then type **env-update** to do the job.

Generally speaking, there's seldom a need to change the library path systemwide. Library package files usually install themselves in directories that are already on the path or add their paths automatically. The main reason to make such changes would be if you installed a library package, or a program that creates its own libraries, in an unusual location via a mechanism other than your distribution's main package utility. For instance, you might compile a library from source code and then need to update your library path in this way.

After you change your library path, you must use ldconfig to have your programs use the new path, as described later in "Library Management Commands."

In addition to the directories specified in /etc/ld.so.conf, Linux refers to the trusted library directories, /lib and /usr/lib. These directories are always on the library path, even if they aren't listed in ld.so.conf.

Temporarily Changing the Path

Sometimes, changing the path permanently and globally is unnecessary and even inappropriate. For instance, you might want to test the effect of a new library before using it for all your programs. To do so, you could install the shared libraries in an unusual location and then set the LD_LIBRARY_PATH environment variable. This environment variable specifies additional directories the system is to search for libraries.

Chapter 9, "Writing Scripts, Configuring Email, and Using Databases," describes environment variables in more detail.

To set the LD_LIBRARY_PATH environment variable using the bash shell, you can type a command like this:

```
$ export LD_LIBRARY_PATH=/usr/local/testlib:/opt/newlib
```

This line adds two directories, /usr/local/testlib and /opt/newlib, to the search path. You can specify as few or as many directories as you like, separated by colons. These directories are added to the *start* of the search path, which means they take precedence over other directories. This fact is handy when you're testing replacement libraries, but it can cause problems if users manage to set this environment variable inappropriately.

You can set this environment variable permanently in a user's shell startup script files, as described in Chapter 9. Doing so means the user will *always* use the specified library paths in addition to the normal system paths. In principle, you could set the LD_LIBRARY_PATH globally; however, using /etc/ld.so.conf is the preferred method of effecting global changes to the library path.

Unlike other library path changes, this one doesn't require that you run ldconfig for it to take effect.

Correcting Problems

Library path problems usually manifest as a program's inability to locate a library. If you launch the program from a shell, you'll see an error message like this:

```
$ gimp
gimp: error while loading shared libraries: libXinerama.so.1: cannot↵
 open shared object file: No such file or directory
```

This message indicates that the system couldn't find the libXinerama.so.1 library file. The usual cause of such problems is that the library isn't installed, so you should look for it using commands such as find (described in Chapter 4, "Managing Files"). If the file isn't installed, try to track down the package to which it should belong (a Web search can work wonders in this task) and install it.

If, on the other hand, the library file is available, you may need to add its directory globally or to LD_LIBRARY_PATH. Sometimes the library's path is hard-coded in the program's binary file. (You can discover this using ldd, as described shortly in "Library Management Commands.") When this happens, you may need to create a symbolic link from the location of the library on your system to the location the program expects. A similar problem can occur when the program expects a library to have one name but the library has another name on your system. For instance, the program may link to biglib.so.5, but your system has biglib.so.5.2 installed. Minor version-number changes like this are usually inconsequential, so creating a symbolic link will correct the problem:

```
# ln -s biglib.so.5.2 biglib.so.5
```

You must type this command as root in the directory in which the library resides. You must then run ldconfig, as described in the next section.

Library Management Commands

Linux provides a pair of commands that you're likely to use for library management. The ldd program displays a program's shared library dependencies—that is, the shared libraries that a program uses. The ldconfig program updates caches and links used by the system for locating libraries—that is, it reads /etc/ld.so.conf and implements any changes in that file or in the directories to which it refers. Both of these tools are invaluable in managing libraries.

Displaying Shared Library Dependencies

If you run into programs that won't launch because of missing libraries, the first step is to check which libraries the program file uses. You can do this with the ldd command:

```
$ ldd /bin/ls
        librt.so.1 => /lib/librt.so.1 (0x0000002a9566c000)
        libncurses.so.5 => /lib/libncurses.so.5 (0x0000002a95784000)
        libacl.so.1 => /lib/libacl.so.1 (0x0000002a958ea000)
        libc.so.6 => /lib/libc.so.6 (0x0000002a959f1000)
        libpthread.so.0 => /lib/libpthread.so.0 (0x0000002a95c17000)
        /lib64/ld-linux-x86-64.so.2 (0x0000002a95556000)
        libattr.so.1 => /lib/libattr.so.1 (0x0000002a95dad000)
```

Each line of output begins with a library name, such as librt.so.1 or libncurses.so.5. If the library name doesn't contain a complete path, ldd attempts to find the true library and displays the complete path following the => symbol, as in /lib/librt.so.1 or /lib/libncurses.so.5. You needn't be concerned about the long hexadecimal number following the complete path to the library file. The preceding example shows one library (/lib64/ld-linux-x86-64.so.2) that's referred to with a complete path in the executable file. It lacks the initial directory-less library name and => symbol.

The ldd command accepts a few options. The most notable of these is probably -v, which displays a long list of version information following the main entry. This information may be helpful in tracking down which version of a library a program is using, in case you have multiple versions installed.

Keep in mind that libraries can themselves depend on other libraries. Thus, you can use ldd to discover what libraries are used by a library. Because of this potential for a dependency chain, it's possible that a program will fail to run even though all its libraries are present. When using ldd to track down problems, be sure to check the needs of all the libraries of the program, and all the libraries used by the first tier of libraries, and so on, until you've exhausted the chain.

The ldd utility can be run by ordinary users, as well as by root. You must run it as root if you can't read the program file as an ordinary user.

Rebuilding the Library Cache

Linux (or, more precisely, the ld.so and ld-linux.so programs, which manage the loading of libraries) doesn't read /etc/ld.so.conf every time a program runs. Instead, the system relies on a cached list of directories and the files they contain, stored in binary format in /etc/ld.so.cache. This list is maintained in a format that's much more efficient than a plain-text list of files and directories. The drawback is that you must rebuild that cache every time you add or remove libraries. These additions and removals include both changing the contents of the library directories and adding or removing library directories.

The tool to do this job is called ldconfig. Ordinarily, it's called without any options:

```
# ldconfig
```

This program does, though, take options to modify its behavior:

Display Verbose Information   Ordinarily, ldconfig doesn't display any information as it works. The -v option causes the program to summarize the directories and files it's registering as it goes about its business.

Don't Rebuild the Cache   The -N option causes ldconfig to *not* perform its primary duty of updating the library cache. It will, though, update symbolic links to libraries, which is a secondary duty of this program.

Process Only Specified Directories   The -n option causes ldconfig to update the links contained in the directories specified on the command line. The system won't examine the directories specified in /etc/ld.so.conf or the trusted directories (/lib and /usr/lib).

Don't Update Links   The -X option is the opposite of -N; it causes ldconfig to update the cache but not manage links.

Use a New Configuration File   You can change the configuration file from /etc/ld.so .conf by using the -f *conffile* option, where *conffile* is the file you want to use.

Use a New Cache File   You can change the cache file that ldconfig creates by passing the -C *cachefile* option, where *cachefile* is the file you want to use.

Use a New Root   The -r *dir* option tells ldconfig to treat *dir* as if it were the root (/) directory. This option is helpful when you're recovering a badly corrupted system or installing a new OS.

Display Current Information   The -p option causes ldconfig to display the current cache—all the library directories and the libraries they contain.

Both RPM and Debian library packages typically run ldconfig automatically after installing or removing the package. The same thing happens as part of the installation process for many packages compiled from source. Thus, you may well be running ldconfig more than you realize in the process of software management. You may need to run the program yourself if you manually modify your library configuration in any way.

Managing Processes

When you type a command name, that program is run, and a *process* is created for it. Knowing how to manage these processes is critical to using Linux. Key details in this task include identifying processes, manipulating foreground and background processes, killing processes, and adjusting process priorities.

Understanding the Kernel: The First Process

The Linux kernel is at the heart of every Linux system. Although you can't manage the kernel process in quite the way you can manage other processes, short of rebooting the computer, you can learn about it. To do so, you can use the uname command, which takes several options to display information:

Node Name   The -n or --nodename option displays the system's node name—that is, its network hostname.

Kernel Name   The -s or --kernel-name option displays the kernel name, which is Linux on a Linux system.

Kernel Version   You can find the kernel version with the -v or --kernel-version option. Ordinarily, this holds the kernel build date and time, not an actual version number.

Kernel Release   The actual kernel version number can be found via the -r or --kernel-release option.

Machine   The -m or --machine option returns information about your machine. This is likely to be a CPU code, such as i686 or x86_64.

Processor   Using the -p or --processor option may return information about your CPU, such as the manufacturer, model, and clock speed; in practice, it returns unknown on many systems.

Hardware Platform   Hardware platform information is theoretically returned by the -i or --hardware-platform option, but this option often returns unknown.

OS Name   The -o or --operating-system option returns the OS name—normally GNU/Linux for a Linux system.

Print All Information   The -a or --all option returns all available information.

In practice, you're most likely to use uname -a at the command line to learn some of the basics about your kernel and system. The other options are most useful in multi-platform scripts, which can use these options to quickly obtain critical information to help them adjust their actions for the system on which they're running.

Examining Process Lists

One of the most important tools in process management is ps. This program displays processes' status (hence the name, ps). It sports many helpful options, and it's useful in monitoring what's happening on a system. This can be particularly critical when the computer isn't working as it should be—for instance, if it's unusually slow. The ps program supports an unusual number of options, but just a few of them will take you a long way. Likewise, interpreting ps output can be tricky because so many options modify the program's output. Some ps-like programs, most notably top, also deserve attention.

Using Useful *ps* Options

The official syntax for ps is fairly simple:

```
ps [options]
```

This simplicity of form hides considerable complexity because ps supports three different *types* of options, as well as many options within each type. The three types of options are as follows:

Unix98 Options   These single-character options may be grouped together and are preceded by a single dash (-).

BSD Options   These single-character options may be grouped together and must *not* be preceded by a dash.

GNU Long Options   These multi-character options are never grouped together. They're preceded by two dashes (--).

Options that may be grouped together may be clustered without spaces between them. For instance, rather than typing **ps -a -f**, you can type **ps -af**. The reason for so much complexity is that the ps utility has historically varied a lot from one Unix OS to another. The version of ps that ships with major Linux distributions attempts to implement most features from all these different ps versions, so it supports many different personalities. In fact, you can change some of its default behaviors by setting the PS_PERSONALITY environment variable to posix, old, linux, bsd, sun, digital, or various others. The rest of this section describes the default ps behavior on most Linux systems.

Some of the more useful ps features include the following:

Display Help   The --help option summarizes some of the more common ps options.

Display All Processes   By default, ps displays only processes that were run from its own terminal (xterm, text-mode login, or remote login). The -A and -e options cause it to display all the processes on the system, and x displays all processes owned by the user who gives the command. The x option also increases the amount of information that's displayed about each process.

Display One User's Processes   You can display processes owned by a given user with the -u *user*, U *user*, and --User *user* options. The *user* variable may be a username or a user ID.

Display Extra Information   The -f, -l, j, l, u, and v options all expand the information provided in the ps output. Most ps output formats include one line per process, but ps can display enough information that it's impossible to fit it all on one 80-character line. Therefore, these options provide various mixes of information.

Display Process Hierarchy   The -H, -f, and --forest options group processes and use indentation to show the hierarchy of relationships between processes. These options are useful if you're trying to trace the parentage of a process.

Display Wide Output   The ps command output can be more than 80 columns wide. Normally, ps truncates its output so that it will fit on your screen or xterm. The -w and w options tell ps not to do this, which can be useful if you direct the output to a file, as in **ps w > ps.txt**. You can then examine the output file in a text editor that supports wide lines.

You can combine these ps options in many ways to produce the output you want. You'll probably need to experiment to learn which options produce the desired results because each option modifies the output in some way. Even those that would seem to influence just the selection of processes to list sometimes modify the information that's provided about each process.

Interpreting ps Output

Listings 2.3 and 2.4 show a couple of examples of ps in action. Listing 2.3 shows **ps -u rodsmith --forest**, and Listing 2.4 shows **ps u U rodsmith**.

Listing 2.3:   Output of **ps -u rodsmith --forest**

```
$ ps -u rodsmith --forest
  PID TTY          TIME CMD
 2451 pts/3    00:00:00 bash
 2551 pts/3    00:00:00 ps
 2496 ?        00:00:00 kvt
 2498 pts/1    00:00:00 bash
 2505 pts/1    00:00:00  \_ nedit
 2506 ?        00:00:00      \_ csh
 2544 ?        00:00:00          \_ xeyes
19221 ?        00:00:01 dfm
```

Listing 2.4:   Output of **ps u U rodsmith**

```
$ ps u U rodsmith
USER        PID %CPU %MEM   VSZ  RSS TTY      STAT START   TIME COMMAND
rodsmith  19221  0.0  1.5  4484 1984 ?        S    May07   0:01 dfm
rodsmith   2451  0.0  0.8  1856 1048 pts/3    S    16:13   0:00 -bash
rodsmith   2496  0.2  3.2  6232 4124 ?        S    16:17   0:00 /opt/kd
rodsmith   2498  0.0  0.8  1860 1044 pts/1    S    16:17   0:00 bash
rodsmith   2505  0.1  2.6  4784 3332 pts/1    S    16:17   0:00 nedit
rodsmith   2506  0.0  0.7  2124 1012 ?        S    16:17   0:00 /bin/cs
rodsmith   2544  0.0  1.0  2576 1360 ?        S    16:17   0:00 xeyes
rodsmith   2556  0.0  0.7  2588  916 pts/3    R    16:18   0:00 ps u U
```

The output produced by ps normally begins with a heading line, which displays the meaning of each column. Important information that may be displayed (and labeled) includes the following:

Username   This is the name of the user who runs the programs. Listings 2.3 and 2.4 restricted this output to one user to limit the length of the listings.

Process ID   The process ID (PID) is a number that's associated with the process. This item is particularly important because you need it to modify or kill the process, as described later in this chapter.

Parent Process ID   The parent process ID (PPID) identifies the process's parent. (Neither Listing 2.3 nor Listing 2.4 shows the PPID.)

TTY   The teletype (TTY) is a code used to identify a terminal. As illustrated by Listings 2.3 and 2.4, not all processes have TTY numbers—X programs and daemons, for instance, don't. Text-mode programs do have these numbers, which point to a console, xterm, or remote login session.

CPU Time   The TIME and %CPU headings are two measures of CPU time used. The first indicates the total amount of CPU time consumed, and the second represents the percentage of CPU time the process is using when ps executes. Both can help you spot runaway processes—those that are consuming too much CPU time. Unfortunately, what constitutes "too much" varies from one program to another, so it's impossible to give a simple rule to help you spot a runaway process.

CPU Priority   As described shortly, in "Managing Process Priorities," it's possible to give different processes different priorities for CPU time. The NI column, if present (it's not in the preceding examples) lists these priority codes. The default value is 0. Positive values represent *reduced* priority, whereas negative values represent *increased* priority.

Memory Use   Various headings indicate memory use—for instance, RSS is resident set size (the memory used by the program and its data), and %MEM is the percentage of memory the program is using. Some output formats also include a SHARE column, which is memory that's shared with other processes (such as shared libraries). As with CPU-use measures, these columns can help point you to the sources of difficulties; but because legitimate memory needs of programs vary so much, it's impossible to give a simple criterion for when a problem exists.

Command   The final column in most listings is the command used to launch the process. This is truncated in Listing 2.4 because this format lists the complete command, but so much other information appears that the complete command won't usually fit on one line. (This is where the wide-column options can come in handy.)

As you can see, a lot of information can be gleaned from a ps listing—or perhaps that should be the plural *listings*, because no single format includes all of the available information. For the most part, the PID, username, and command are the most important pieces of information. In some cases, though, you may need specific other components. If your system's memory or CPU use has skyrocketed, for instance, you'll want to pay attention to the memory or CPU use column.

It's often necessary to find specific processes. You might want to find the PID associated with a particular command in order to kill it, for instance. This information can be gleaned by piping the ps output through grep, as in **ps ax | grep bash** to find all the instances of bash.

Although you may need a wide screen or xterm to view the output, you may find **ps -A --forest** to be a helpful command in learning about your system. Processes that aren't linked to others were either started directly by init or have had their parents killed, and so they have been "adopted" by init. (Chapter 5 describes init and the boot procedure in more detail.) Most of these processes are fairly important—they're servers, login tools, and so on. Processes that hang off several others in this tree view, such as xeyes and nedit in Listing 2.3, are mostly user programs launched from shells.

top: A Dynamic *ps* Variant

If you want to know how much CPU time various processes are consuming relative to one another or if you want to quickly discover which processes are consuming the most CPU time, a tool called top is the one for the job. The top tool is a text-mode program, but of course it can be run in an xterm or similar window, as shown in Figure 2.2; there are also GUI variants, like kpm and gnome-system-monitor. By default, top sorts its entries by CPU use, and it updates its display every few seconds. This makes it a very good tool for spotting runaway processes on an otherwise lightly loaded system—those processes almost always appear in the first position or two, and they consume an inordinate amount of CPU time. Looking at Figure 2.2, you might think that FahCore_65.exe is such a process, but in fact, it's legitimately consuming a lot of CPU time. You'll need to be familiar with the purposes and normal habits of programs running on *your* system in order to make such determinations; the legitimate needs of different programs vary so much that it's impossible to give a simple rule for judging when a process is consuming too much CPU time.

FIGURE 2.2   The top command shows system summary information and information about the most CPU-intensive processes on a computer.

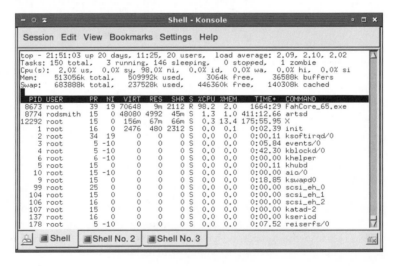

Like many Linux commands, top accepts several options. The most useful are listed here:

-d *delay*   This option specifies the delay between updates, which is normally five seconds.

-p *pid*   If you want to monitor specific processes, you can list them using this option. You'll need the PIDs, which you can obtain with ps, as described earlier. You can specify up to 20 PIDs by using this option multiple times, once for each PID.

-n *iter*   You can tell top to display a certain number of updates (*iter*) and then quit. (Normally, top continues updating until you terminate the program.)

-b   This option specifies batch mode, in which top doesn't use the normal screen-update commands. You might use this to log CPU use of targeted programs to a file, for instance.

You can do more with top than watch it update its display. When it's running, you can enter any of several single-letter commands, some of which prompt you for additional information. These commands include the following:

h and **?**   These keystrokes display help information.

k   You can kill a process with this command. The top program will ask for a PID number, and if it's able to kill the process, it will do so. (The upcoming section "Killing Processes" describes other ways to kill processes.)

q   This option quits from top.

r   You can change a process's priority with this command. You'll have to enter the PID number and a new priority value—a positive value will decrease its priority, and a negative value will increase its priority, assuming it has the default 0 priority to begin with. Only root may increase a process's priority. The renice command (described shortly, in "Managing Process Priorities") is another way to accomplish this task.

s   This command changes the display's update rate, which you'll be asked to enter (in seconds).

P   This command sets the display to sort by CPU usage, which is the default.

M   You can change the display to sort by memory usage with this command.

More commands are available in top (both command-line options and interactive commands) than can be summarized here; consult top's man page for more information.

One of the pieces of information provided by top is the *load average*, which is a measure of the demand for CPU time by applications. In Figure 2.2, you can see three load-average estimates on the top line; these correspond to the current load average and two previous measures. A system on which no programs are demanding CPU time has a load average of 0.0. A system with one program running CPU-intensive tasks has a load average of 1.0. Higher load averages reflect programs competing for available CPU time. You can also find the current load average via the uptime command, which displays the load average along with information on how long the computer has been running. The load average can be useful in detecting runaway processes. For instance, if a system normally has a load average of 0.5 but suddenly gets stuck at a load average of 2.5, a couple of CPU-hogging processes may have hung—that is, become unresponsive. Hung processes sometimes needlessly consume a lot of CPU time. You can use top to locate these processes and, if necessary, kill them.

Most computers today include multiple CPUs or CPU cores. On such systems, the load average can equal the number of CPUs or cores before competition for CPU time begins. For instance, on a quad-core CPU, the load average can be as high as 4.0 without causing contention. Typically, one program can create a load of just 1.0; however, *multi-threaded* programs can create higher load averages, particularly on multi-core systems.

jobs: Processes Associated with Your Session

The jobs command displays minimal information about the processes associated with the current session. In practice, jobs is usually of limited value, but it does have a few uses. One of these is to provide job ID numbers. These numbers are conceptually similar to PID numbers, but they're not the same. Jobs are numbered starting from 1 for each session, and in most cases, a single shell has only a few associated jobs. The job ID numbers are used by a handful of utilities in place of PIDs, so you may need this information.

A second use of jobs is to ensure that all your programs have terminated prior to logging out. Under some circumstances, logging out of a remote login session can cause the client program to freeze up if you've left programs running. A quick check with jobs will inform you of any forgotten processes and enable you to shut them down.

Understanding Foreground and Background Processes

One of the most basic process-management tasks is to control whether a process is running in the foreground or the background—that is, whether it's monopolizing the use of the terminal from which it was launched. Normally, when you launch a program, it takes over the terminal, preventing you from doing other work in that terminal. (Some programs, though, release the terminal. This is most common for servers and some GUI programs.)

If a program is running but you decide you want to use that terminal for something else, pressing Ctrl+Z normally pauses the program and gives you control of the terminal. (An important point is that this procedure suspends the program, so if it's performing real work, that work stops!) This can be handy if, say, you're running a text editor in a text-mode login and you want to check a filename so you can mention it in the file you're editing. You press Ctrl+Z and type **ls** to get the file listing. To get back to the text editor, you then type **fg**, which restores the text editor to the foreground of your terminal. If you've suspended several processes, you add a job number, as in **fg 2** to restore job 2. You can obtain a list of jobs associated with a terminal by typing **jobs**, which displays the jobs and their job numbers.

A variant on fg is bg. Whereas fg restores a job to the foreground, bg restores a job to running status, but in the background. You can use this command if the process you're running is performing a CPU-intensive task that requires no human interaction but you want to use the terminal in the meantime. Another use of bg is in a GUI environment—after launching a GUI program from an xterm or similar window, that shell is tied up servicing the GUI program, which probably doesn't really need the shell. Pressing Ctrl+Z in the xterm window will enable you to type shell commands again, but the GUI program will be frozen. To unfreeze the GUI program, type **bg** in the shell, which enables the GUI program to run in the background while the shell continues to process your commands.

As an alternative to launching a program, using Ctrl+Z, and typing **bg** to run a program in the background, you can append an ampersand (&) to the command when launching the program. For instance, rather than edit a file with the NEdit GUI editor by typing **nedit myfile.txt**, you can type **nedit myfile.txt &**. This command launches the nedit program in the background from the start, leaving you able to control your xterm window for other tasks.

Managing Process Priorities

Sometimes, you may want to prioritize your programs' CPU use. For instance, you may be running a program that's very CPU-intensive but that will take a long time to finish its work, and you don't want that program to interfere with others that are of a more interactive nature. Alternatively, on a heavily loaded computer, you may have a job that's more important than others that are running, so you may want to give it a priority boost. In either case, the usual method of accomplishing this goal is through the nice and renice commands. You can use nice to launch a program with a specified priority or use renice to alter the priority of a running program.

You can assign a priority to nice in any of three ways: by specifying the priority preceded by a dash (this works well for positive priorities but makes them look like negative priorities), by specifying the priority after a -n parameter, or by specifying the priority after an --adjustment= parameter. In all cases, these parameters are followed by the name of the program you want to run:

nice [*argument*] [*command* [*command-arguments*]]

For instance, the following three commands are all equivalent:

```
$ nice -12 number-crunch data.txt
$ nice -n 12 number-crunch data.txt
$ nice --adjustment=12 number-crunch data.txt
```

All three of these commands run the number-crunch program at priority 12 and pass it the data.txt file. If you omit the adjustment value, nice uses 10 as a default. The range of possible values is –20 to 19, with negative values having the highest priority. Only root may launch a program with increased priority (that is, give a negative priority value), but any user may use nice to launch a program with low priority. The default priority for a program run without nice is 0.

If you've found that a running process is consuming too much CPU time or is being swamped by other programs and so should be given more CPU time, you can use the renice program to alter its priority without disrupting the program's operation. The syntax for renice is as follows:

```
renice priority [[-p] pids] [[-g] pgrps] [[-u] users]
```

You must specify the *priority*, which takes the same values this variable takes with nice. In addition, you must specify one or more PIDs (*pids*), one or more group IDs (*pgrps*), or one or more usernames (*users*). In the latter two cases, renice changes the priority of all programs that match the specified criterion—but only root may use renice in this way. Also, only root may increase a process's priority. If you give a numeric value without a -p, -g, or -u option, renice assumes the value is a PID. You may mix and match these methods of specification. For instance, you might enter the following command:

```
# renice 7 16580 -u pdavison tbaker
```

This command sets the priority to 7 for PID 16580 and for all processes owned by pdavison and tbaker.

Killing Processes

Sometimes, reducing a process's priority isn't a strong enough action. A program may have become totally unresponsive, or you may want to terminate a process that shouldn't be running. In these cases, the kill command is the tool to use. This program sends a signal (a method that Linux uses to communicate with processes) to a process. The signal is usually sent by the kernel, the user, or the program itself to terminate the process. Linux supports many numbered signals, each of which is associated with a specific name. You can see them all by typing **kill -1**. If you don't use -1, the syntax for kill is as follows:

```
kill -s signal pid
```

Although Linux includes a kill program, many shells, including bash and csh, include built-in kill equivalents that work in much the same way as the external program. If you want to be sure you're using the external program, type its complete path, as in /bin/kill.

The -s *signal* parameter sends the specified signal to the process. You can specify the signal using either a number (such as 9) or a name (such as SIGKILL). The signals you're most likely to use are 1 (SIGHUP, which terminates interactive programs and causes many daemons to reread their configuration files), 9 (SIGKILL, which causes the process to exit without performing routine shutdown tasks), and 15 (SIGTERM, which causes the process to exit but allows it to close open files and so on). If you don't specify a signal, the default is

15 (SIGTERM). You can also use the shortened form *-signal*. If you do this and use a signal name, you should omit the SIG portion of the name—for instance, use KILL rather than SIGKILL. The *pid* option is, of course, the PID for the process you want to kill. You can obtain this number from ps or top.

> The kill program will kill only those processes owned by the user who runs kill. The exception is if that user is root; the superuser may kill any user's processes.

Real World Scenario

Running Programs Persistently

Signals can be passed to programs by the kernel even if you don't use the kill command. For instance, when you log out of a session, the programs you started from that session are sent the SIGHUP signal, which causes them to terminate. If you want to run a program that will continue running even when you log out, you can launch it with the **nohup** program:

$ **nohup** *program options*

This command causes the program to ignore the SIGHUP signal. It can be handy if you want to launch certain small servers that may legitimately be run as ordinary users.

A variant on kill is killall, which has the following form:

killall [*options*] [--] *name* [...]

This command kills a process based on its name rather than its PID number. For instance, **killall vi** kills all the running processes called vi. You may specify a signal in the shortened form (*-signal*) or by preceding the signal number with -s or --signal. As with kill, the default is 15 (SIGTERM). One potentially important option to killall is -i, which causes it to ask for confirmation before sending the signal to each process. You might use it like this:

$ **killall -i vi**
Kill vi(13211) ? (y/n) y
Kill vi(13217) ? (y/n) n

In this example, two instances of the Vi editor were running, but only one should have been killed. As a general rule, if you run killall as root, you should use the -i parameter; if you don't, it's all too likely that you'll kill processes that you shouldn't, particularly if the computer is being used by many people at once.

Some versions of Unix provide a killall command that works very differently from Linux's killall. This alternate killall kills all the processes started by the user who runs the command. This is a potentially much more destructive command, so if you ever find yourself on a non-Linux system, *do not* use killall until you've discovered what that system's killall does (say, by reading the killall man page).

Summary

Linux provides numerous tools to help you manage software. Most distributions are built around the RPM or Debian package systems, both of which enable installation, upgrade, and removal of software using a centralized package database to avoid conflicts and other problems that are common when no central package database exists. You can perform basic operations on individual files or, with the help of extra tools such as Yum and APT, keep your system synchronized with the outside world, automatically or semi-automatically updating all your software to the latest versions.

No matter how you install your software, you may need to manage shared libraries. These software components are necessary building blocks of large modern programs, and in the best of all possible worlds they operate entirely transparently. Sometimes, though, shared libraries need to be upgraded or the system configuration changed so that programs can find the libraries. When this happens, knowing about critical configuration files and commands can help you work around any difficulties.

Beyond managing packages and libraries, Linux software management involves manipulating processes. Knowing how to manipulate foreground and background processes, adjust process priorities, and kill stray processes can help you keep your Linux system working well.

Exam Essentials

Identify critical features of RPM and Debian package formats.   RPM and Debian packages store all files for a given package in a single file that also includes information about what other packages the software depends on. These systems maintain a database of installed packages and their associated files and dependencies.

Describe the tools used for managing RPMs.   The rpm program is the main tool for installing, upgrading, and uninstalling RPMs. This program accepts operations and options that tell it precisely what to do. The Yum utility, and particularly its yum command, enables installation of a package and all its dependencies via the Internet, rather than from local package files.

Describe the tools used for managing Debian packages.   The dpkg program installs or uninstalls a single package or a group of packages you specify. The apt-get utility retrieves programs from installation media or from the Internet for installation and can automatically upgrade your entire system. The dselect program serves as a menu-driven interface to apt-get, enabling you to select programs you want to install from a text-mode menu.

Summarize tools for extracting files and converting between package formats.   The rpm2cpio program can convert an RPM file to a cpio archive, enabling users of non-RPM systems to access files in an RPM. The alien utility can convert in any direction between Debian packages, RPMs, Stampede packages, and tarballs. This enables the use of packages intended for one system on another.

Summarize the reasons for using shared libraries.   Shared libraries keep disk space and memory requirements manageable by placing code that's needed by many programs in separate files from the programs that use it, enabling one copy to be used multiple times. More generally, libraries enable programmers to use basic "building blocks" that others have written without having to constantly reinvent code.

Describe methods available to change the library path.   The library path can be changed systemwide by editing the /etc/ld.so.conf file and then typing **ldconfig**. For temporary or per-user changes, directories may be added to the path by placing them in the LD_LIBRARY_PATH environment variable.

Explain the difference between foreground and background processes.   Foreground processes have control of the current terminal or text-mode window (such as an xterm). Background processes don't have exclusive control of a terminal or text-mode window but are still running.

Describe how to limit the CPU time used by a process.   You can launch a program with nice or use renice to alter its priority in obtaining CPU time. If a process is truly out of control, you can terminate it with the kill command.

Review Questions

1. Which of the following is *not* an advantage of a source package over a binary package?

    A.   A single source package can be used on multiple CPU architectures.

    B.   By recompiling a source package, you can sometimes work around library incompatibilities.

    C.   You can modify the code in a source package, thus altering the behavior of a program.

    D.   Source packages can be installed more quickly than binary packages can.

    E.   You may be able to recompile source code for a non-Linux Unix program on Linux.

2. Which is true of using both RPM and Debian package management systems on one computer?

    A.   It's generally inadvisable because the two systems don't share installed-file database information.

    B.   It's impossible because their installed-file databases conflict with one another.

    C.   It causes no problems if you install important libraries once in each format.

    D.   It's a common practice on Red Hat and Debian systems.

    E.   Using both systems simultaneously requires installing the `alien` program.

3. Which of the following statements is true about binary RPM packages that are built for a particular distribution?

    A.   License requirements forbid using the package on any other distribution.

    B.   They may be used in another RPM-based distribution only when you set the `--convert-distrib` parameter to `rpm`.

    C.   They may be used in another RPM-based distribution only after you recompile the package's source RPM.

    D.   They can be recompiled for an RPM-based distribution running on another type of CPU.

    E.   They can often be used on another RPM-based distribution for the same CPU architecture, but this isn't guaranteed.

4. An administrator types the following command on an RPM-based Linux distribution:

   `# rpm -ivh megaprog.rpm`

   What is the effect of this command?

   A. If the `megaprog` package is installed on the computer, it is uninstalled.

   B. If the `megaprog.rpm` package exists, is valid, and isn't already installed on the computer, it is installed.

   C. The `megaprog.rpm` source RPM package is compiled into a binary RPM for the computer.

   D. Nothing; `megaprog.rpm` isn't a valid RPM filename, so `rpm` will refuse to operate on this file.

   E. The `megaprog.rpm` package replaces any earlier version of the package that's already installed on the computer.

5. Which of the following commands will extract the contents of the `myfonts.rpm` file into the current directory?

   A. `rpm2cpio myfonts.rpm | cpio -i --make-directories`

   B. `rpm2cpio myfonts.rpm > make-directories`

   C. `rpm -e myfonts.rpm`

   D. `alien --to-extract myfonts.rpm`

   E. `rpmbuild --rebuild myfonts.rpm`

6. To use dpkg to remove a package called `theprogram`, including its configuration files, which of the following commands would you issue?

   A. `dpkg -e theprogram`

   B. `dpkg -p theprogram`

   C. `dpkg -r theprogram`

   D. `dpkg -r theprogram-1.2.3-4.deb`

   E. `dpkg -P theprogram`

7. Which of the following describes a difference between `apt-get` and dpkg?

   A. `apt-get` provides a GUI interface to Debian package management; dpkg doesn't.

   B. `apt-get` can install tarballs in addition to Debian packages; dpkg can't.

   C. `apt-get` can automatically retrieve and update programs from Internet sites; dpkg can't.

   D. `apt-get` is provided only with the original Debian distribution, but dpkg comes with Debian and its derivatives.

   E. `apt-get` works only with Debian-based distributions, but dpkg can work with both RPMs and Debian packages.

8. What command would you type to obtain a list of all installed packages on a Debian system?

   A. `apt-get showall`

   B. `apt-cache showpkg`

   C. `dpkg -r allpkgs`

   D. `dpkg -i`

   E. `dpkg--get-selections`

9. As root, you type **apt-get update** on a Debian system. What should be the effect of this command?

   A. None; update is an invalid option to `apt-get`.

   B. The APT utilities deliver information about the latest updates you've made to the APT Internet repositories, enabling you to share your changes with others.

   C. The APT utilities download all available upgrades for your installed programs and install them on your system.

   D. The APT utilities retrieve information about the latest packages available so that you may install them with subsequent `apt-get` commands.

   E. The APT utilities update themselves, ensuring you're using the latest version of APT.

10. Which of the following commands would you type to update the `unzip` program on a Fedora system to the latest version? (Select all that apply.)

    A. `yum update unzip`

    B. `yum upgrade unzip`

    C. `yum -u unzip`

    D. `yum -U unzip`

    E. `yum check-update unzip`

11. How should you configure a system that uses Yum to access an additional Yum software repository?

    A. Edit the `/etc/apt/sources.list` file to include the repository site's URL, as detailed on the repository's Web site.

    B. Download a package from the repository site and install it with RPM, or place a configuration file from the repository site in the `/etc/yum.repos.d` directory.

    C. Use the `add-repository` subcommand to `yum` or the Add Repository option in the File menu in `yumex`, passing it the URL of the repository.

    D. Edit the `/etc/yum.conf` file, locate the `[repos]` section, and add the URL to the repository after the existing repository URLs.

    E. Edit the `/etc/yum.conf` file, locate the `REPOSITORIES=` line, and add the new repository to the colon-delimited list on that line.

12. What is the preferred method of adding a directory to the library path for all users?

   A. Modify the LD_LIBRARY_PATH environment variable in a global shell script.

   B. Add the directory to the /etc/ld.so.conf file, and then type **ldconfig**.

   C. Type **ldconfig /new/dir**, where /new/dir is the directory you want to add.

   D. Create a symbolic link from that directory to one that's already on the library path.

   E. Type **ldd /new/dir**, where /new/dir is the directory you want to add.

13. You prefer the look of GTK+ widgets to Qt widgets, so you want to substitute the GTK+ libraries for the Qt libraries on your system. How would you do this?

   A. You must type **ldconfig --makesubs=qt,gtk**. This command substitutes the GTK+ libraries for the Qt libraries at load time.

   B. You must uninstall the Qt library packages and re-install the GTK+ packages with the **--substitute=qt** option to **rpm** or the **--replace=qt** option to **dpkg**.

   C. You must note the filenames of the Qt libraries, uninstall the packages, and create symbolic links from the Qt libraries to the GTK+ libraries.

   D. You can't easily do this; libraries can't be arbitrarily exchanged for one another. You would need to rewrite all the Qt-using programs to use GTK+.

   E. You must reboot the computer and pass the **subst=qt,gtk** option to the kernel. This causes the kernel to make the appropriate substitutions.

14. A user types **kill -9 11287** at a **bash** prompt. What is the probable intent, assuming the user typed the correct command?

   A. To cut off a network connection using TCP port 11287

   B. To display the number of processes that have been killed with signal 11287 in the last nine days

   C. To cause a server with process ID 11287 to reload its configuration file

   D. To terminate a misbehaving or hung program with process ID 11287

   E. To increase the priority of the program running with process ID 11287

15. What programs might you use to learn what your system's load average is? (Select two.)

   A. ld

   B. load

   C. top

   D. uptime

   E. la

16. Which of the following commands creates a display of processes, showing the parent-child relationships through links between their names?

    A. `ps --forest`

    B. `ps aux`

    C. `ps -e`

    D. `ps --tree`

    E. All of the above

17. You use `top` to examine the CPU time being consumed by various processes on your system. You discover that one process, `dfcomp`, is consuming more than 90 percent of your system's CPU time. What can you conclude?

    A. Very little; `dfcomp` could be legitimately consuming that much CPU time, or it could be an unauthorized or malfunctioning program.

    B. No program should consume 90 percent of available CPU time; `dfcomp` is clearly malfunctioning and should be terminated.

    C. This is normal; `dfcomp` is the kernel's main scheduling process, and it consumes any unused CPU time.

    D. This behavior is normal *if* your CPU is less powerful than a 2.5GHz EM64T Pentium, but on newer systems, no program should consume 90 percent of CPU time.

    E. This behavior is normal *if* your CPU has at least four cores, but on systems with fewer cores than this, no program should consume 90 percent of CPU time.

18. You type `jobs` at a `bash` command prompt and receive a new command prompt with no intervening output. What can you conclude?

    A. The total CPU time used by your processes is negligible (below 0.1).

    B. No processes are running under your username except the shell you're using.

    C. The `jobs` shell is installed and working correctly on the system.

    D. The system has crashed; `jobs` normally returns a large number of running processes.

    E. No background processes are running that were launched from the shell you're using.

19. Which two of the following commands are equivalent to one another? (Select two.)

    A. `nice --value 10 crunch`

    B. `nice -n -10 crunch`

    C. `nice -10 crunch`

    D. `nice 10 crunch`

    E. `nice crunch`

20. Which of the following are restrictions on ordinary users' abilities to run `renice`? (Select two.)

A. Users may not modify the priorities of processes that are already running.

B. Users may not modify the priority of their programs launched from anything but their current shells.

C. Users may not decrease the priority (that is, increase the priority value) of their own processes.

D. Users may not modify the priorities of other users' processes.

E. Users may not increase the priority (that is, decrease the priority value) of their own processes.

Chapter

3

Configuring Hardware

THE FOLLOWING EXAM OBJECTIVES ARE COVERED IN THIS CHAPTER:

- ✓ 1.101.1 Determine and configure hardware settings
- ✓ 1.102.1 Design hard disk layout
- ✓ 1.104.1 Create partitions and filesystems
- ✓ 1.104.2 Maintain the integrity of filesystems
- ✓ 1.104.3 Control mounting and unmounting of filesystems

All OSs run atop hardware, and this hardware influences how the OSs run. Most obviously, hardware can be fast or slow, reliable or unreliable. Somewhat more subtly, OSs provide various means of configuring and accessing the hardware—partitioning hard disks and reading data from *Universal Serial Bus* (USB) devices, for instance. You must understand at least the basics of how Linux interacts with its hardware environment in order to effectively administer a Linux system, so this chapter presents that information.

This chapter begins with a look at firmware, which is the lowest-level software that runs on a computer. A computer's firmware begins the boot process and configures certain hardware devices. This chapter then moves on to expansion cards and USB devices.

This chapter concludes with an examination of disk hardware and the filesystems it contains—disk interface standards, disk partitioning, how to track disk usage, how to tune filesystems for optimal performance, how to check filesystems' internal consistency, and how to repair simple filesystem defects. Assuming a filesystem is in good shape, you must be able to mount it to be able to use it, so that topic is also covered here. (One disk topic, boot managers, is covered in Chapter 5, "Booting Linux and Editing Files.")

Configuring the Firmware and Core Hardware

All computers ship with a set of core hardware—most obviously, a *central processing unit* (CPU), which does the bulk of the computational work, and *random access memory* (RAM), which holds data. Many additional basic features help glue everything together, and some of these can be configured both inside and outside of Linux. At the heart of much of this hardware is the firmware, which provides configuration tools and initiates the OS booting process. You can use the firmware's own user interface to enable and disable key hardware components, but once Linux is booted, you may need to manage this hardware using Linux utilities. Key components managed by the firmware (and, once it's booted, Linux) include interrupts, I/O addresses, DMA addresses, the real-time clock, and *Advanced Technology Attachment* (ATA) hard disk interfaces.

Understanding the Role of the Firmware

Many hardware devices include firmware, so any given computer can have many types of firmware installed—for the motherboard, for a plug-in disk controller, for modems, and so on. The most important firmware, though, is installed on the computer's motherboard. This firmware initializes the motherboard's hardware and controls the boot process. In the past, the vast majority of *x86-* and *x86-64*-based computers have used a type of firmware known as the *Basic Input/Output System* (BIOS). Beginning in 2011, though, a new type of firmware, known as the *Extensible Firmware Interface* (EFI) or the *Unified EFI* (UEFI), has become all but standard on new computers. Some older computers also use EFI. Despite the fact that EFI isn't technically a BIOS, most manufacturers refer to it by that name in their documentation. The exam objectives refer to the BIOS, but not to EFI. Nonetheless, in the real world you're likely to encounter EFI on newer computers. The differences between BIOS and EFI are particularly important in booting the computer, as described in Chapter 5. For many of the setup tasks described in this chapter, the two types of firmware behave very similarly, although EFI implementations sometimes provide flashier graphical user interfaces; most BIOSs, and some EFIs, provide only text-mode user interfaces.

In this book, I use the term *EFI* to refer both to the original EFI and to the newer UEFI, which is effectively EFI 2.*x*.

The motherboard's firmware resides in *electronically erasable programmable read-only memory* (EEPROM), aka flash memory. When you turn on a computer, the firmware performs a *power-on self-test* (POST), initializes hardware to a known operational state, loads the boot loader from the boot device (typically the first hard disk), and passes control to the boot loader, which in turn loads the OS.

Historically, a further purpose of a BIOS was to provide fundamental input/output (I/O) services to the operating system and application programs, insulating them from hardware changes. Although the Linux kernel uses the BIOS to collect information about the hardware, once Linux is running, it doesn't use BIOS services for I/O. In theory, some EFI services can be used by the OS, but as of the 3.5.0 kernel, Linux takes advantage of few of these EFI features. Linux system administrators require a basic understanding of the BIOS or EFI because of the key role it plays in configuring hardware and in booting.

Most *x86* and *x86-64* computers use a BIOS or an EFI; however, some computers use radically different software in place of these types of firmware. Older PowerPC-based Apple computers, for instance, use OpenFirmware. (Intel-based Macs use EFI.) Although OpenFirmware, EFI, and other firmware programs differ from the traditional (some now say "legacy") *x86* BIOS, these systems all perform similar tasks. If you must administer a computer with an unusual firmware, you should take some time to research the details of how its firmware operates; however, this won't greatly affect how Linux treats the hardware at the level of day-to-day system administration.

Although firmware implementations vary from manufacturer to manufacturer, most BIOSs and EFIs provide an interactive facility to configure them. Typically, you enter this setup tool by pressing the Delete key or a function key early in the boot sequence. (Consult your motherboard manual or look for onscreen prompts for details.) Figure 3.1 shows a typical BIOS setup main screen. You can use the arrow keys, the Enter key, and so on to move around the BIOS options and adjust them. Computers usually come delivered with reasonable BIOS defaults, but you may need to adjust them if you add new hardware or if a standard piece of hardware is causing problems.

FIGURE 3.1   A BIOS setup screen provides features related to low-level hardware configuration.

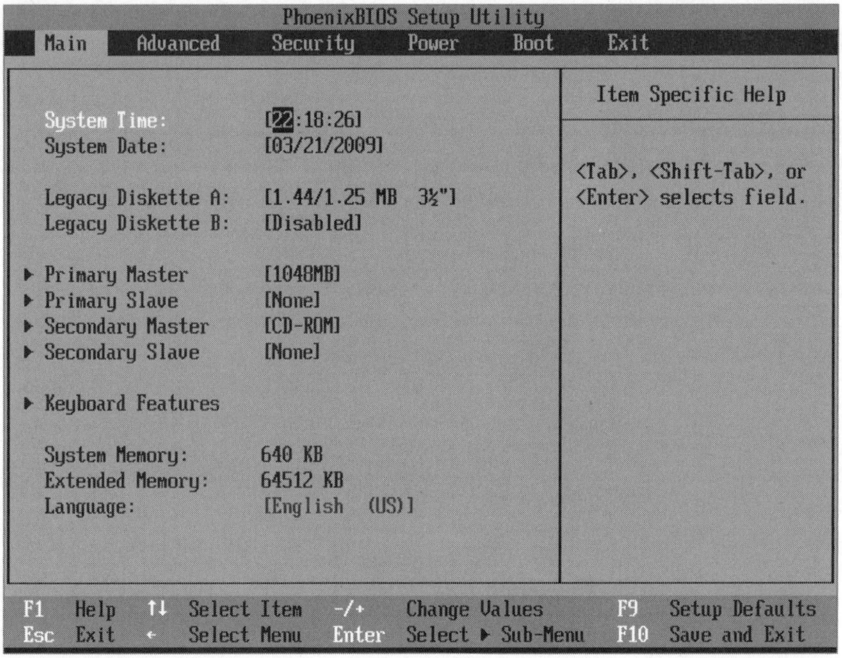

```
                        PhoenixBIOS Setup Utility
    Main     Advanced    Security    Power    Boot    Exit

                                             ┌──────────────────────────┐
                                             │    Item Specific Help     │
      System Time:        [22:18:26]         │                          │
      System Date:        [03/21/2009]       │                          │
                                             │  <Tab>, <Shift-Tab>, or   │
      Legacy Diskette A:  [1.44/1.25 MB  3½"]│  <Enter> selects field.   │
      Legacy Diskette B:  [Disabled]         │                          │
                                             │                          │
    ▶ Primary Master      [1048MB]           │                          │
    ▶ Primary Slave       [None]             │                          │
    ▶ Secondary Master    [CD-ROM]           │                          │
    ▶ Secondary Slave     [None]             │                          │
                                             │                          │
    ▶ Keyboard Features                      │                          │
                                             │                          │
      System Memory:      640 KB             │                          │
      Extended Memory:    64512 KB           │                          │
      Language:           [English  (US)]    │                          │

    F1   Help   ↑↓  Select Item   -/+   Change Values    F9   Setup Defaults
    Esc  Exit   ←   Select Menu   Enter  Select ▶ Sub-Menu  F10  Save and Exit
```

PCs with EFIs may provide setup utilities similar to the one shown in Figure 3.1. As noted earlier, though, some EFIs feature flashier GUIs rather than a text-based user interface. Others are organized in a very different way, as shown in Figure 3.2. The variability makes it impossible to provide simple instructions on how to locate specific features; you may need to read your manual or explore the options your firmware provides.

FIGURE 3.2 Firmware user interfaces vary greatly from one to another; you may need to spend some time exploring yours.

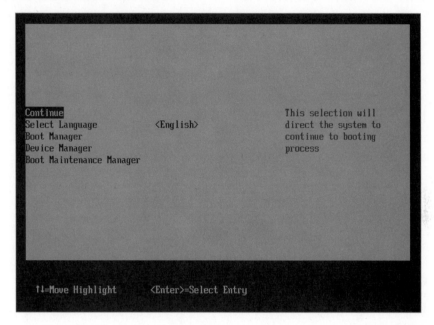

One key ability of the firmware is to enable or disable on-board hardware. Modern motherboards provide a wide range of hardware devices, including floppy disk controllers, hard disk controllers, RS-232 serial ports, parallel ports, USB ports, Ethernet ports, audio hardware, and even video hardware. Usually, having this hardware available is beneficial, but sometimes it's not. The hardware may be inadequate, so you'll want to replace it with a more capable plug-in card; or you may not need it. In such cases, you can disable the device in the firmware. Doing so keeps the device from consuming the hardware resources that are described shortly, reducing the odds of an unused device interfering with the hardware you do use.

Precisely how to disable hardware in the firmware varies from one computer to another. You should peruse the available menus to find mention of the hardware you want to disable. Menus entitled Integrated Peripherals or Advanced are particularly likely to hold these features. Once you've spotted the options, follow the onscreen prompts for hints about how to proceed; for instance, Figure 3.1 shows an Item Specific Help area on the right side of the screen. Information about keys to press to perform various actions appears here. (Although not identified as a help area, the right side of the screen in Figure 3.2 provides similar hints.) Once you're finished, follow the onscreen menus and prompts to save your changes and exit. When you do so, the computer will reboot.

Once Linux boots, it uses its own drivers to access the computer's hardware. Understanding the hardware resources that Linux uses will help you determine when you may want to shut down, boot into the firmware, and disable particular hardware devices at such a low level.

 Real World Scenario

Booting Without a Keyboard

Most PCs have keyboards attached to them; however, many Linux computers function as servers, which don't require keyboards for day-to-day operation. In such cases, you may want to detach the keyboard to reduce clutter and eliminate the risk of accidental key-presses causing problems.

Unfortunately, many computers complain and refuse to boot if you unplug the keyboard and attempt to boot the computer. To disable this warning, look for a firmware option called Halt On or something similar. This option tells the firmware under what circumstances it should refuse to boot. You should find an option to disable the keyboard check. Once you select this option, you should be able to shut down, detach the keyboard, and boot normally. Of course, you'll need to be able to access the computer via a network connection or in some other way to administer it, so be sure this is configured before you remove the keyboard!

IRQs

An *interrupt request* (IRQ), or interrupt, is a signal sent to the CPU instructing it to suspend its current activity and to handle some external event such as keyboard input. On the $x86$ platform, IRQs are numbered from 0 to 15. More modern computers, including $x86$-64 systems, provide more than these 16 interrupts. Some interrupts are reserved for specific purposes, such as the keyboard and the real-time clock; others have common uses (and are sometimes overused) but may be reassigned; and some are left available for extra devices that may be added to the system. Table 3.1 lists the IRQs and their common purposes in the $x86$ system. (On $x86$-64 systems, IRQs are typically assigned as in Table 3.1, but additional hardware may be assigned to higher IRQs.)

TABLE 3.1   IRQs and their common uses

IRQ	Typical use	Notes
0	System timer	Reserved for internal use.
1	Keyboard	Reserved for keyboard use only.

2	Cascade for IRQs 8–15	The original *x*86 IRQ-handling circuit can manage just 8 IRQs; 2 are tied together to handle 16 IRQs, but IRQ 2 must be used to handle IRQs 8–15.
3	Second RS-232 serial port (COM2: in Windows)	May also be shared by a fourth RS-232 serial port.
4	First RS-232 serial port (COM1: in Windows)	May also be shared by a third RS-232 serial port.
5	Sound card or second parallel port (LPT2: in Windows)	
6	Floppy disk controller	Reserved for the first floppy disk controller.
7	First parallel port (LPT1: in Windows)	
8	Real-time clock	Reserved for system clock use only.
9	Open interrupt	
10	Open interrupt	
11	Open interrupt	
12	PS/2 mouse	
13	Math coprocessor	Reserved for internal use.
14	Primary ATA controller	The controller for ATA devices such as hard drives; traditionally /dev/hda and /dev/hdb under Linux.[1]
15	Secondary ATA controller	The controller for more ATA devices; traditionally /dev/hdc and /dev/hdd under Linux.[1]

[1]Most modern distributions treat ATA disks as SCSI disks, which changes their device identifiers from /dev/hdx to /dev/sdx.

IRQ 5 is a common source of interrupt conflicts on older computers because it's the default value for sound cards as well as for second parallel ports. Modern computers often use a higher IRQ for sound cards and also often lack parallel ports.

The original *Industry Standard Architecture* (ISA) bus design makes sharing an interrupt between two devices tricky. Ideally, every ISA device should have its own IRQ. The more recent *Peripheral Component Interconnect* (PCI) bus makes sharing interrupts a bit easier, so PCI devices frequently end up sharing an IRQ. The ISA bus has become rare on computers made since 2001 or so.

Once a Linux system is running, you can explore what IRQs are being used for various purposes by examining the contents of the /proc/interrupts file. A common way to do this is with the use of the cat command:

```
$ cat /proc/interrupts
            CPU0
   0:          42    IO-APIC-edge      timer
   1:      444882    IO-APIC-edge      i8042
   4:          12    IO-APIC-edge
   6:          69    IO-APIC-edge      floppy
   8:           0    IO-APIC-edge      rtc
   9:           0    IO-APIC-fasteoi   acpi
  14:     3010291    IO-APIC-edge      ide0
  15:    11156960    IO-APIC-edge      ide1
  16:   125264892    IO-APIC-fasteoi   eth0
  17:           0    IO-APIC-fasteoi   cx88[0], cx88[0]
  20:     3598946    IO-APIC-fasteoi   sata_via
  21:     4566307    IO-APIC-fasteoi   uhci_hcd:usb1, uhci_hcd:usb2, ehci_hcd:usb3
  22:      430444    IO-APIC-fasteoi   VIA8237
 NMI:           0    Non-maskable interrupts
 LOC:   168759611    Local timer interrupts
 TRM:           0    Thermal event interrupts
 THR:           0    Threshold APIC interrupts
 SPU:           0    Spurious interrupts
 ERR:           0
```

The /proc filesystem is a *virtual filesystem*—it doesn't refer to actual files on a hard disk but to kernel data that's convenient to represent using a filesystem. The files in /proc provide information about the hardware, running processes, and so on. Many Linux utilities use /proc behind the scenes; or you can directly access these files using utilities like cat, which copies the data to the screen when given just one argument.

This output shows the names of the drivers that are using each IRQ. Some of these driver names are easy to interpret, such as floppy. Others are more puzzling, such as cx88 (it's a driver for a video capture card). If the purpose of a driver isn't obvious, try doing a Web search on it; chances are you'll find a relevant hit fairly easily. Note that the preceding output shows interrupts numbered up to 22; this system supports more than the 16 base *x*86 interrupts.

The /proc/interrupts file lists IRQs that are in use by Linux, but Linux doesn't begin using an IRQ until the relevant driver is loaded. This may not happen until you try to use the hardware. Thus, the /proc/interrupts list may not show all the interrupts that are configured on your system. For instance, the preceding example shows nothing for IRQ 7, which is reserved for the parallel port, because the port hadn't been used prior to viewing the file. If the parallel port were used and /proc/interrupts viewed again, an entry for IRQ 7 and the parport0 driver would appear.

Although IRQ conflicts are rare on modern hardware, they do occasionally still crop up. When this happens, you must reconfigure one or more devices to use different IRQs. This topic is described shortly, in "Configuring Expansion Cards."

I/O Addresses

I/O addresses (also referred to as *I/O ports*) are unique locations in memory that are reserved for communications between the CPU and specific physical hardware devices. Like IRQs, I/O addresses are commonly associated with specific devices and should not ordinarily be shared. Table 3.2 lists some Linux device filenames along with the equivalent names in Windows, as well as the common IRQ and I/O address settings.

TABLE 3.2 Common Linux devices

Linux device	Windows name	Typical IRQ	I/O address
/dev/ttyS0	COM1	4	0x03f8
/dev/ttyS1	COM2	3	0x02f8
/dev/ttyS2	COM3	4	0x03e8
/dev/ttyS3	COM4	3	0x02e8
/dev/lp0	LPT1	7	0x0378-0x037f
/dev/lp1	LPT2	5	0x0278-0x027f
/dev/fd0	A:	6	0x03f0-0x03f7
/dev/fd1	B:	6	0x0370-0x0377

Although the use is deprecated, older systems sometimes use /dev/cuax (where *x* is a number 0 or greater) to indicate an RS-232 serial device. Thus, /dev/ttyS0 and /dev/cua0 refer to the same physical device.

Once a Linux system is running, you can explore what I/O addresses the computer is using by examining the contents of the /proc/ioports file. A common way to do this is with the cat command:

```
$ cat /proc/ioports
0000-001f : dma1
0020-0021 : pic1
0040-0043 : timer0
0050-0053 : timer1
0060-006f : keyboard
0070-0077 : rtc
0080-008f : dma page reg
00a0-00a1 : pic2
00c0-00df : dma2
00f0-00ff : fpu
```

This example truncates the output, which goes on for quite a way on the test system. As with IRQs, if your system suffers from I/O port conflicts, you must reconfigure one or more devices, as described in "Configuring Expansion Cards." In practice, such conflicts are rarer than IRQ conflicts.

DMA Addresses

Direct memory addressing (DMA) is an alternative method of communication to I/O ports. Rather than have the CPU mediate the transfer of data between a device and memory, DMA permits the device to transfer data directly, without the CPU's attention. The result can be lower CPU requirements for I/O activity, which can improve overall system performance.

To support DMA, the *x*86 architecture implements several DMA channels, each of which can be used by a particular device. To learn what DMA channels your system uses, examine the /proc/dma file:

```
$ cat /proc/dma
 2: floppy
 4: cascade
```

This output indicates that DMA channels 2 and 4 are in use. As with IRQs and I/O ports, DMA addresses should not normally be shared. In practice, DMA address conflicts are rarer than IRQ conflicts, so chances are you won't run into problems. If you do, consult the upcoming section "Configuring Expansion Cards."

Boot Disks and Geometry Settings

Most firmware implementations enable you to choose the order in which devices are booted. This is an area in which BIOS and EFI differ, and there are substantial implementation-to-implementation differences, too. Generally speaking, though, the rules are as follows:

BIOS   The BIOS boot process begins by reading a *boot sector* (typically the first sector) from a disk and then executing that code. Thus, boot options for BIOS-based computers are limited; you can only select the order in which various boot devices (hard disks, floppy disks, optical disks, USB devices, and so on) are examined to find a boot sector.

EFI   Under EFI, the boot process involves reading a boot loader file from a filesystem on a special partition, known as the *EFI System Partition* (ESP). This file either can take a special default name or can be registered in the computer's NVRAM. Thus, EFI computers often present an extended range of boot options, involving both default boot loader files from various devices (to enable granting precedence to a bootable USB flash drive, for example) and multiple boot loaders on the computer's hard disks. Some primitive EFI implementations, though, present simple BIOS-like boot options.

Many EFI implementations support a BIOS compatibility mode and so can boot media intended for BIOS-based computers. This feature, intended to help in the transition from BIOS to EFI, can complicate firmware setup and OS installation because it creates extra boot options that users often don't understand.

Although boot sequences involving removable disks are common, they have their problems. For instance, if somebody accidentally leaves a floppy disk in the drive, this can prevent the system from booting. Worse, some viruses are transmitted by BIOS boot sectors, so this method can result in viral infection. Using removable disks as the default boot media also opens the door to intruders who have physical access to the computer; they need only reboot with a bootable removable disk or CD-ROM to gain complete control of your system. For these reasons, it's better to make the first hard disk (or a boot loader on a hard disk's ESP, in the case of EFI) the only boot device. (You must change this configuration when installing Linux or using an emergency boot disk for maintenance.) Most modern computers make temporary changes easier by providing a special key to allow a one-time change to the boot sequence. On older computers, to change the boot sequence, you must locate the appropriate firmware option, change it, and reboot the computer. It's usually located in an Advanced menu, so look there.

Another disk option is the one for detecting disk devices. Figure 3.1 shows three disk devices: the A: floppy disk (/dev/fd0 under Linux), a 1048MB primary master hard disk, and a CD-ROM drive as the secondary master. In most cases, the firmware detects and configures hard disks and CD-ROM drives correctly. In rare circumstances, you must tell a BIOS-based computer about the hard disk's *cylinder/head/sector (CHS) geometry.*

The CHS geometry is a holdover from the early days of the *x*86 architecture. Figure 3.3 shows the traditional hard disk layout, which consists of a fixed number of read/write heads that can move across the disk surfaces (or platters). As the disk spins, each head marks out a circular track on its platter; these tracks collectively make up a cylinder. Each track is broken down into a series of sectors. Thus, any sector on a hard disk can be uniquely identified by three numbers: a cylinder number, a head number, and a sector number. The *x*86 BIOS was designed to use this three-number CHS identification code. One consequence of this configuration is that the BIOS must know how many cylinders, heads, and sectors the disk has. Modern hard disks relay this information to the BIOS automatically; but for compatibility with the earliest hard disks, BIOSs still enable you to set these values manually.

FIGURE 3.3   Hard disks are built from platters, each of which is broken into tracks, which are broken into sectors.

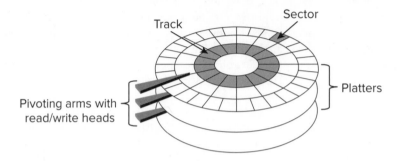

The BIOS will detect only certain types of disks. Of particular importance, SCSI disks and (on some older computers) serial ATA (SATA) disks won't appear in the main BIOS disk-detection screen. These disks are handled by supplementary firmware associated with the controllers for these devices. Some BIOSs do provide explicit options to add SCSI devices into the boot sequence, so you can give priority to either ATA or SCSI devices. For those without these options, SCSI disks generally take second seat to ATA disks.

CHS geometry, unfortunately, has its problems. For one thing, all but the earliest hard disks use variable numbers of sectors per cylinder—modern disks squeeze more sectors onto outer tracks than inner ones, fitting more data on each disk. Thus, the CHS geometry presented to the BIOS by the hard disk is a convenient lie. Worse, because of limits on the numbers in the BIOS and in the ATA hard disk interface, plain CHS geometry tops out at 504MiB, which is puny by today's standards. Various patches, such as CHS geometry translation, can be used to expand the limit to about 8GiB. Today, though, the preference is to use *logical block addressing* (LBA) mode. (Some sources use the expansion *linear block addressing* for this acronym.) In this mode, a single unique number is assigned to each sector on the disk, and the disk's firmware is smart enough to read from the correct head and cylinder when given this sector number. Modern BIOSs typically provide an option to use LBA mode, CHS translation mode, or possibly some other modes with large disks. EFI doesn't use CHS addressing at all, except in its BIOS compatibility mode; instead, EFI uses LBA mode exclusively. In most cases, LBA mode is the best choice. If you must retrieve data from very old disks, though, you may need to change this option.

Because of variability in how different BIOSs handle CHS translation, moving disks between computers can result in problems because of mismatched CHS geometries claimed in disk structures and by the BIOS. Linux is usually smart enough to work around such problems, but you may see some odd error messages in disk utilities like fdisk. If you see messages about inconsistent CHS geometries, proceed with caution when using low-level disk utilities lest you create an inconsistent partition table that could cause problems, particularly in OSs that are less robust than Linux on this score.

Coldplug and Hotplug Devices

Whenever you deal with hardware, you should keep in mind a distinction between two device types: *coldplug* and *hotplug*. These device types differ depending on whether they can be physically attached and detached when the computer is turned on (that is, "hot"), versus only when it's turned off ("cold").

Coldplug devices are designed to be physically connected and disconnected only when the computer is turned off. Attempting to attach or detach such devices when the computer is running can damage the device or the computer, so do not attempt to do so.

Traditionally, components that are internal to the computer, such as the CPU, memory, PCI cards, and hard disks, have been coldplug devices. A hotplug variant of PCI, however, has been developed and is used on some computers—mainly on servers and other systems that can't afford the downtime required to install or remove a device. Hot-plug SATA devices are also available.

Modern external devices, such as Ethernet, USB, and IEEE-1394 devices, are hotplug; you can attach and detach such devices as you see fit. These devices rely on specialized Linux software to detect the changes to the system as they're attached and detached. Several utilities help in managing hotplug devices:

Sysfs The *sysfs* virtual filesystem, mounted at /sys, exports information about devices so that user-space utilities can access the information.

A *user space* program is one that runs as an ordinary program, whether it runs as an ordinary user or as root. This contrasts with *kernel space* code, which runs as part of the kernel. Typically, only the kernel (and hence kernel-space code) can communicate directly with hardware. User-space programs are the ultimate users of hardware, though. Traditionally, the /dev filesystem has provided the main means of interface between user-space programs and hardware; however, the tools described here help expand on this access, particularly in ways that are useful for hotplug devices.

HAL Daemon   The *Hardware Abstraction Layer (HAL) Daemon*, or `hald`, is a user-space program that runs at all times (that is, as a daemon) that provides other user-space programs with information about available hardware.

D-Bus   The *Desktop Bus* (D-Bus) provides a further abstraction of hardware information access. Like `hald`, D-Bus runs as a daemon. D-Bus enables processes to communicate with each other as well as to register to be notified of events, both by other processes and by hardware (such as the availability of a new USB device).

udev   Traditionally, Linux has created device nodes as conventional files in the /dev directory tree. The existence of hotplug devices and various other issues, however, have motivated the creation of udev: a virtual filesystem, mounted at /dev, which creates dynamic device files as drivers are loaded and unloaded. You can configure udev through files in /etc/udev, but the standard configuration is usually sufficient for common hardware.

These tools all help programs work seamlessly in a world of hotplug devices by enabling the programs to learn about hardware, including receiving notification when the hardware configuration changes.

Older external devices, such as parallel and RS-232 ports, are officially coldplug in nature. In practice, many people treat these devices as if they were hotplug, and they can usually get away with it; but there is a risk of damage, so it's safest to power down a computer before connecting or disconnecting such a device. When RS-232 or parallel port devices are hotplugged, they typically aren't registered by tools such as udev and `hald`. Only the ports to which these devices connect are handled by the OS; it's up to user-space programs, such as terminal programs or the printing system, to know how to communicate with the external devices.

Configuring Expansion Cards

Many hardware devices require configuration—you must set the IRQ, I/O port, and DMA addresses used by the device. (Not all devices use all three resources.) Through the mid-1990s, this process involved tedious changes to jumpers on the hardware. Today, though, you can configure most options through software.

NOTE   Even devices that are built into the motherboard are configured through the same means used to configure PCI cards.

Configuring PCI Cards

The PCI bus, which is the standard expansion bus for most internal devices, was designed with Plug-and-Play (PnP)–style configuration in mind; thus, automatic configuration of PCI devices is the rule rather than the exception. For the most part, PCI devices configure themselves automatically, and there's no need to make any changes. You can, though, tweak how PCI devices are detected in several ways:

- The Linux kernel has several options that affect how it detects PCI devices. You can find these in the kernel configuration screens under Bus Options. Most users can rely on the options in their distributions' default kernels to work properly; but if you recompile your kernel yourself and if you're having problems with device detection, you may want to study these options.

- Most firmware implementations have PCI options that change the way PCI resources are allocated. Adjusting these options may help if you run into strange hardware problems with PCI devices.

- Some Linux drivers support options that cause them to configure the relevant hardware to use particular resources. You should consult the drivers' documentation files for details of the options they support. You must then pass these options to the kernel using a boot loader (as described in Chapter 5) or as kernel module options.

- You can use the setpci utility to directly query and adjust PCI devices' configurations. This tool is most likely to be useful if you know enough about the hardware to fine-tune its low-level configuration; it's not often used to tweak the hardware's basic IRQ, I/O port, or DMA options.

In addition to the configuration options, you may want to check how PCI devices are currently configured. You can use the lspci command for this purpose; it displays all information about the PCI busses on your system and all devices connected to those busses. This command takes several options that fine-tune its behavior. Table 3.3 lists the most common of these.

TABLE 3.3 Options for lspci

Option	Effect
-v	Increases verbosity of output. This option may be doubled (-vv) or tripled (-vvv) to produce yet more output.
-n	Displays information in numeric codes rather than translating the codes to manufacturer and device names.
-nn	Displays both the manufacturer and device names and their associated numeric codes.
-x	Displays the PCI configuration space for each device as a hexadecimal dump. This is an extremely advanced option. Tripling (-xxx) or quadrupling (-xxxx) this option displays information about more devices.
-b	Shows IRQ numbers and other data as seen by devices rather than as seen by the kernel.
-t	Displays a tree view depicting the relationship between devices.

TABLE 3.3 Options for lspci *(continued)*

Option	Effect
-s [[[[*domain*]:]*bus*]:] [*slot*][.[*func*]]	Displays only devices that match the listed specification. This can be used to trim the results of the output.
-d [*vendor*]:[*device*]	Shows data on the specified device.
-i *file*	Uses the specified file to map vendor and device IDs to names. (The default is /usr/share/misc/pci.ids.)
-m	Dumps data in a machine-readable form, intended for use by scripts. A single -m uses a backward-compatible format, whereas doubling (-mm) uses a newer format.
-D	Displays PCI domain numbers. These numbers normally aren't displayed.
-M	Performs a scan in bus-mapping mode, which can reveal devices hidden behind a misconfigured PCI bridge. This is an advanced option that can be used only by root.
--version	Displays version information.

Learning about Kernel Modules

Hardware in Linux is handled by kernel drivers, many of which come in the form of *kernel modules*. These are stand-alone driver files, typically stored in the /lib/modules directory tree, that can be loaded to provide access to hardware and unloaded to disable such access. Typically, Linux loads the modules it needs when it boots, but you may need to load additional modules yourself.

You can learn about the modules that are currently loaded on your system by using lsmod, which takes no options and produces output like this:

```
$ lsmod
Module              Size  Used by
isofs              35820  0
zlib_inflate       21888  1 isofs
floppy             65200  0
nls_iso8859_1       5568  1
nls_cp437           7296  1
vfat               15680  1
fat                49536  1 vfat
sr_mod             19236  0
ide_cd             42848  0
cdrom              39080  2 sr_mod,ide_cd
```

This output has been edited for brevity. Although outputs this short are possible with certain configurations, they're rare.

The most important column in this output is the first one, labeled `Module`; this column specifies the names of all the modules that are currently loaded. You can learn more about these modules with `modinfo`, as described shortly, but sometimes their purpose is fairly obvious. For instance, the `cdrom` module provides access to the optical drive.

The `Used by` column of the `lsmod` output describes what's using the module. All the entries have a number, which indicates the number of other modules or processes that are using the module. For instance, in the preceding example, the `isofs` module (used to access CD-ROM filesystems) isn't currently in use, as revealed by its 0 value; but the `vfat` module (used to read VFAT hard disk partitions and floppies) is being used, as shown by its value of 1. If one of the modules is being used by another module, the using module's name appears in the `Used by` column. For instance, the `isofs` module relies on the `zlib_inflate` module, so the latter module's `Used by` column includes the `isofs` module name. This information can be useful when you're managing modules. For instance, if your system produced the preceding output, you couldn't directly remove the `zlib_inflate` module because it's being used by the `isofs` module; but you could remove the `isofs` module, and after doing so, you could remove the `zlib_inflate` module. (Both modules would need to be added back to read most CD-ROMs, though.)

The `lsmod` command displays information only about kernel modules, not about drivers that are compiled directly into the Linux kernel. For this reason, a module may need to be loaded on one system but not on another to use the same hardware because the second system may compile the relevant driver directly into the kernel.

Loading Kernel Modules

Linux enables you to load kernel modules with two programs: `insmod` and `modprobe`. The `insmod` program inserts a single module into the kernel. This process requires you to have already loaded any modules on which the module you're loading relies. The `modprobe` program, by contrast, automatically loads any depended-on modules and so is generally the preferred way to do the job.

In practice, you may not need to use `insmod` or modprobe to load modules because Linux can load them automatically. This ability relies on the kernel's module auto-loader feature, which must be compiled into the kernel, and on various configuration files, which are also required for modprobe and some other tools. Using `insmod` and modprobe can be useful for testing new modules or for working around problems with the auto-loader, though.

In practice, insmod is a fairly straightforward program to use; you type its name followed by the module filename:

```
# insmod /lib/modules/2.6.26/kernel/drivers/block/floppy.ko
```

This command loads the floppy.ko module, which you must specify by filename. Modules have module names, too, which are usually the same as the filename but without the extension, as in floppy for the floppy.ko file. Unfortunately, insmod requires the full module name.

You can pass additional module options to the module by adding them to the command line. Module options are highly module-specific, so you must consult the documentation for the module to learn what to pass. Examples include options to tell an RS-232 serial port driver what interrupt to use to access the hardware or to tell a video card framebuffer driver what screen resolution to use.

Some modules depend on other modules. In these cases, if you attempt to load a module that depends on others and those other modules aren't loaded, insmod will fail. When this happens, you must either track down and manually load the depended-on modules or use modprobe. In the simplest case, you can use modprobe much as you use insmod, by passing it a module name:

```
# modprobe floppy
```

As with insmod, you can add kernel options to the end of the command line. Unlike insmod, you specify a module by its module name rather than its module filename when you use modprobe. Generally speaking, this helps make modprobe easier to use, as does the fact that modprobe automatically loads dependencies. This greater convenience means that modprobe relies on configuration files. It also means that you can use options (placed between the command name and the module name) to modify modprobe's behavior:

Be Verbose   The -v or --verbose option tells modprobe to display extra information about its operations. Typically, this includes a summary of every insmod operation it performs.

Change Configuration Files   The modprobe program uses a configuration file called /etc/modprobe.conf (or multiple files in /etc/modprobe.d). You can change the configuration file or directory by passing a new file with the -C *filename* option, as in **modprobe -C /etc/mymodprobe.conf floppy**.

Perform a Dry Run   The -n or --dry-run option causes modprobe to perform checks and all other operations *except* the actual module insertions. You might use this option in conjunction with -v to see what modprobe would do without loading the module. This may be helpful in debugging, particularly if inserting the module is having some detrimental effect, such as disabling disk access.

Remove Modules   The -r or --remove option reverses modprobe's usual effect; it causes the program to remove the specified module and any on which it depends. (Depended-on modules are *not* removed if they're in use.)

Force Loading   The -f or --force option tells modprobe to force the module loading even if the kernel version doesn't match what the module expects. This action is potentially dangerous, but it's occasionally required when using third-party binary-only modules.

Show Dependencies   The --show-depends option shows all the modules on which the specified module depends. This option doesn't install any of the modules; it's purely informative in nature.

Show Available Modules   The -l or --list option displays a list of available options whose names match the wildcard you specify. For instance, typing **modprobe -l v*** displays all modules whose names begin with v. If you provide no wildcard, modprobe displays all available modules. Like --show-depends, this option doesn't cause any modules to be loaded.

This list of options is incomplete. The others are relatively obscure, so you're not likely to need them often. Consult the modprobe man page for more information.

Removing Kernel Modules

In most cases, you can leave modules loaded indefinitely; the only harm that a module does when it's loaded but not used is to consume a small amount of memory. (The lsmod program shows how much memory each module consumes.) Sometimes, though, you may want to remove a loaded module. Reasons include reclaiming that tiny amount of memory, unloading an old module so you can load an updated replacement module, and removing a module that you suspect is unreliable.

The work of unloading a kernel module is done by the rmmod command, which is basically the opposite of insmod. The rmmod command takes a module name as an option, though, rather than a module filename:

```
# rmmod floppy
```

This example command unloads the floppy module. You can modify the behavior of rmmod in various ways:

Be Verbose   Passing the -v or --verbose option causes rmmod to display some extra information about what it's doing. This may be helpful if you're troubleshooting a problem.

Force Removal   The -f or --force option forces module removal even if the module is marked as being in use. Naturally, this is a very dangerous option, but it's sometimes helpful if a module is misbehaving in some way that's even more dangerous. This option has no effect unless the CONFIG_MODULE_FORCE_UNLOAD kernel option is enabled.

Wait Until Unused   The -w or --wait option causes rmmod to wait for the module to become unused, rather than return an error message, if the module is in use. Once the module is no longer being used (say, after a floppy disk is unmounted if you try to remove the floppy module), rmmod unloads the module and returns. Until then, rmmod doesn't return, making it look like it's not doing anything.

A few more rmmod options exist; consult the rmmod man page for details.

Like insmod, rmmod operates on a single module. If you try to unload a module that's depended on by other modules or is in use, rmmod will return an error message. (The -w option modifies this behavior, as just described.) If the module is depended on by other modules, rmmod lists those modules, so you can decide whether to unload them. If you want to unload an entire *module stack*—that is, a module and all those upon which it depends—you can use the modprobe command and its -r option, as described earlier in "Loading Kernel Modules."

Configuring USB Devices

USB is an extremely popular (perhaps the most popular) external interface form. This fact means you must understand something about USB, including USB itself, Linux's USB drivers, and Linux's USB management tools.

USB Basics

USB is a protocol and hardware port for transferring data to and from devices. It allows for many more (and varied) devices per interface port than either ATA or SCSI and gives better speed than RS-232 serial and parallel ports. The USB 1.0 and 1.1 specifications allow for up to 127 devices and 12Mbps of data transfer. USB 2.0 allows for much higher transfer rates—480Mbps, to be precise. USB 3.0, introduced in 2010, supports a theoretical maximum speed of 4.8Gbps, although 3.2Gbps is a more likely top speed in practice. USB 3.0 devices require a new physical connector.

Data transfer speeds may be expressed in bits per second (bps) or multiples thereof, such as megabits per second (Mbps) or gigabits per second (Gbps); or in bytes per second (B/s) or multiples thereof, such as megabytes per second (MB/s). In most cases, there are 8 bits per byte, so multiplying or dividing by 8 may be necessary if you're trying to compare speeds of devices that use different measures.

USB is the preferred interface method for many external devices, including printers, scanners, mice, digital cameras, flash drives, and music players. USB keyboards, Ethernet adapters, modems, speakers, hard drives, and other devices are also available, although USB has yet to dominate these areas as it has some others.

Most computers ship with four to eight USB ports. (A few years ago, two USB ports were more common.) Each port can handle one device by itself, but you can use a *USB hub* to connect several devices to each port. Thus, you can theoretically connect huge numbers of USB devices to a computer. In practice, you may run into speed problems, particularly if you're using USB 1.*x* for devices that tend to transfer a lot of data, such as scanners, printers, or hard drives.

If you have an older computer that lacks USB 3.0 support and you want to connect a high-speed USB 3.0 device, you can buy a separate USB 3.0 board. You can continue to use the computer's built-in USB ports for slower devices.

Linux USB Drivers

Several different USB controllers are available, with names such as UHCI, OHCI, EHCI, and R8A66597. Modern Linux distributions ship with the drivers for the common USB controllers enabled, so your USB port should be activated automatically when you boot the computer. The UHCI and OHCI controllers handle USB 1.*x* devices, but most other controllers can handle USB 2.0 devices. You need a 2.6.31 or newer kernel to use USB 3.0 hardware. Note that these basics merely provide a means to access the actual USB hardware and address the devices in a low-level manner. You'll need additional software—either drivers or specialized software packages—to make practical use of the devices.

You can learn a great deal about your devices by using the lsusb utility. A simple use of this program with no options reveals basic information about your USB devices:

```
$ lsusb
Bus 003 Device 008: ID 0686:400e Minolta Co., Ltd
Bus 003 Device 001: ID 0000:0000
Bus 002 Device 002: ID 046d:c401 Logitech, Inc. TrackMan Marble Wheel
Bus 002 Device 001: ID 0000:0000
Bus 001 Device 001: ID 0000:0000
```

In this example, three USB busses are detected (001, 002, and 003). The first bus has no devices attached, but the second and third each have one device—a Logitech TrackMan Marble Wheel trackball and a Minolta DiMAGE Scan Elite 5400 scanner, respectively. (The scanner's name isn't fully identified by this output, except insofar as the ID number encodes this information.) You can gather additional information by using various options to lsusb:

Be Verbose The -v option produces extended information about each product.

Restrict Bus and Device Number Using the -s [[*bus*]:][*devnum*] option restricts output to the specified bus and device number.

Restrict Vendor and Product You can limit output to a particular vendor and product by using the -d [*vendor*]:[*product*] option. The *vendor* and *product* are the codes just after ID on each line of the basic lsusb output.

Display Device by Filename Using -D *filename* displays information about the device that's accessible via *filename*, which should be a file in the /proc/bus/usb directory tree. This directory provides a low-level interface to USB devices, as described shortly.

Tree View The -t option displays the device list as a tree so that you can more easily see what devices are connected to specific controllers.

Version The -V or --version option displays the version of the lsusb utility and exits.

Early Linux USB implementations required a separate driver for every USB device. Many of these drivers remain in the kernel, and some software relies on them. For instance, USB disk storage devices use USB storage drivers that interface with Linux's SCSI support, making USB hard disks, removable disks, and so on look like SCSI devices.

Linux provides a USB filesystem that in turn provides access to USB devices in a generic manner. This filesystem appears as part of the /proc virtual filesystem. In particular, USB device information is accessible from /proc/bus/usb. Subdirectories of /proc/bus/usb are given numbered names based on the USB controllers installed on the computer, as in /proc/bus/usb/001 for the first USB controller. Software can access files in these directories to control USB devices rather than use device files in /dev as with most hardware devices. Tools such as scanner software and the Linux printing system can automatically locate compatible USB devices and use these files.

USB Manager Applications

USB can be challenging for OSs because it was designed as a hot-pluggable technology. The Linux kernel wasn't originally designed with this sort of activity in mind, so the kernel relies on external utilities to help manage matters. Two tools in particular are used for managing USB devices: usbmgr and hotplug.

The usbmgr package (located at http://freecode.com/projects/usbmgr) is a program that runs in the background to detect changes on the USB bus. When it detects changes, it loads or unloads the kernel modules that are required to handle the devices. For instance, if you plug in a USB Zip drive, usbmgr will load the necessary USB and SCSI disk modules. This package uses configuration files in /etc/usbmgr to handle specific devices and uses /etc/usbmgr/usbmgr.conf to control the overall configuration.

With the shift from in-kernel device-specific USB drivers to the USB device filesystem (/proc/bus/usb), usbmgr has been declining in importance. In fact, it may not be installed on your system. Instead, most distributions rely on the Hotplug package (http://linux-hotplug.sourceforge.net), which relies on kernel support added with the 2.4.x kernel series. This system uses files stored in /etc/hotplug to control the configuration of specific USB devices. In particular, /etc/hotplug/usb.usermap contains a database of USB device IDs and pointers to scripts in /etc/hotplug/usb that are run when devices are plugged in or unplugged. These scripts might change permissions on USB device files so that ordinary users can access USB hardware, run commands to detect new USB disk devices, or otherwise prepare the system for a new (or newly removed) USB device.

Configuring Hard Disks

Hard disks are among the most important components in your system. Three different hard disk interfaces are common on modern computers: *Parallel Advanced Technology Attachment* (PATA), aka ATA; *Serial Advanced Technology Attachment* (SATA); and *Small*

Computer System Interface (SCSI). In addition, external USB and IEEE-1394 drives are available, as are external variants of SATA and SCSI drives. Each has its own method of low-level configuration.

Configuring PATA Disks

PATA disks once ruled the roost in the *x*86 PC world, but today SATA disks have largely supplanted them. Thus, you're most likely to encounter PATA disks on older computers— say, from 2005 or earlier. PATA disks are still readily available, though.

As the full name implies, PATA disks use a parallel interface, meaning that several bits of data are transferred over the cable at once. Thus, PATA cables are wide, supporting a total of either 40 or 80 lines, depending on the variety of PATA. You can connect up to two devices to each PATA connector on a motherboard or plug-in PATA controller, meaning that PATA cables typically have three connectors—one for the motherboard and two for disks.

PATA disks must be configured as masters or as slaves. This can be done via jumpers on the disks themselves. Typically, the master device sits at the end of the cable, and the slave device resides on the middle connector. All modern PATA disks also support an option called *cable select*. When set to this option, the drive attempts to configure itself automatically based on its position on the PATA cable. Thus, your easiest configuration is usually to set all PATA devices to use the cable-select option; you can then attach them to whatever position is convenient, and the drives should configure themselves.

For best performance, disks should be placed on separate controllers rather than configured as master and slave on a single controller, because each PATA controller has a limited throughput that may be exceeded by two drives. Until recently, most motherboards have included at least two controllers, so putting each drive on its own controller isn't a problem until you install more than two drives in a single computer.

All but the most ancient BIOSs auto-detect PATA devices and provide information about their capacities and model numbers in the BIOS setup utilities. In the past, most motherboards would boot PATA drives in preference to other drives, but modern firmware usually provides more options to control your boot preferences.

In Linux, PATA disks have traditionally been identified as /dev/hda, /dev/hdb, and so on, with /dev/hda being the master drive on the first controller, /dev/hdb being the slave drive on the first controller, and so on. Thus, gaps can occur in the numbering scheme—if you have master disks on the first and second controllers but no slave disks, your system will contain /dev/hda and /dev/hdc but no /dev/hdb. Partitions are identified by numbers after the main device name, as in /dev/hda1, /dev/hda2, and so on.

The naming rules for disks also apply to optical media, except that these media typically aren't partitioned. Most Linux distributions also create a link to your optical drive under the name /dev/cdrom or /dev/dvd. Removable PATA disks, such as Zip disks, are given identifiers as if they were fixed PATA disks, optionally including partition identifiers.

Most modern Linux distributions favor newer PATA drivers that treat PATA disks as if they were SCSI disks. Thus, you may find that your device filenames follow the SCSI rules rather than the PATA rules even if you have PATA disks.

Configuring SATA Disks

SATA is a newer interface than PATA, and SATA has largely displaced PATA as the interface of choice. New motherboards typically host four or more SATA interfaces and frequently lack PATA interfaces.

SATA disks connect to their motherboards or controllers on a one-to-one basis—unlike with PATA, you can't connect more than one disk to a single cable. This fact simplifies configuration; there typically aren't jumpers to set, and you needn't be concerned with the position of the disk on the cable.

As the word *serial* in the expansion of *SATA* implies, SATA is a serial bus—only one bit of data can be transferred at a time. SATA transfers more bits per unit of time on its data line, though, so SATA is faster than PATA (1.5–6.0Gbps for SATA vs. 128–1064Mbps for PATA, but these are theoretical maximums that are unlikely to be achieved in real-world situations). Because of SATA's serial nature, SATA cables are much thinner than PATA cables.

Modern firmware detects SATA disks and provides information about them just as for PATA disks. The firmware may provide boot order options, too. Older BIOSs are likely to be more limited. This is particularly true if your motherboard doesn't provide SATA support but you use a separate SATA controller card. You may be able to boot from an SATA disk in such cases if your controller card supports this option, or you may need to use a PATA boot disk.

Most Linux SATA drivers treat SATA disks as if they were SCSI disks, so you should read the next section, "Configuring SCSI Disks," for information about device naming. Some older drivers treat SATA disks like PATA disks, so you may need to use PATA names in some rare circumstances.

Configuring SCSI Disks

There are many types of SCSI definitions, which use a variety of different cables and operate at various speeds. SCSI is traditionally a parallel bus, like PATA, although the latest variant, Serial Attached SCSI (SAS), is a serial bus like SATA. SCSI has traditionally been considered a superior bus to PATA; however, the cost difference has risen dramatically over the past decade or two, so few people today use SCSI. You may find it on older systems or on very high-end systems.

SCSI supports up to 8 or 16 devices per bus, depending on the variety. One of these devices is the SCSI host adapter, which either is built into the motherboard or comes as a plug-in card. In practice, the number of devices you can attach to a SCSI bus is more restricted because of cable-length limits, which vary from one SCSI variety to another. Each device has its own ID number, typically assigned via a jumper on the device. You must ensure that each device's ID is unique. Consult its documentation to learn how to set the ID.

If your motherboard lacks built-in SCSI ports, chances are it won't detect SCSI devices. You can still boot from a SCSI hard disk *if* your SCSI host adapter has its own firmware that supports booting. Most high-end SCSI host adapters have this support, but low-end SCSI host adapters don't have built-in firmware. If you use such a host adapter, you can still attach SCSI hard disks to the adapter, and Linux can use them, but you'll need to boot from a PATA or SATA hard disk.

SCSI IDs aren't used to identify the corresponding device file on a Linux system. Hard drives follow the naming system /dev/sd*x* (where *x* is a letter from a up), SCSI tapes are named /dev/st*x* and /dev/nst*x* (where *x* is a number from 0 up), and SCSI CD-ROMs and DVD-ROMs are named /dev/scd*x* or /dev/sr*x* (where *x* is a number from 0 up).

SCSI device numbering (or lettering) is usually assigned in increasing order based on the SCSI ID. If you have one hard disk with a SCSI ID of 2 and another hard disk with a SCSI ID of 4, they will be assigned to /dev/sda and /dev/sdb, respectively. The real danger is if you add a third SCSI drive and give it an ID of 0, 1, or 3. This new disk will become /dev/sda (for an ID of 0 or 1) or /dev/sdb (for ID 3), bumping up one or both of the existing disks' Linux device identifiers. For this reason, it's usually best to give hard disks the lowest possible SCSI IDs so that you can add future disks using higher IDs.

The mapping of Linux device identifiers to SCSI devices depends in part on the design of the SCSI host adapter. Some host adapters result in assignment starting from SCSI ID 7 and working down to 0 rather than the reverse, with Wide SCSI device numbering continuing on from there to IDs 14 through 8.

Another complication is when you have multiple SCSI host adapters. In this case, Linux assigns device filenames to all of the disks on the first adapter, followed by all those on the second adapter. Depending on where the drivers for the SCSI host adapters are found (compiled directly into the kernel or loaded as modules) and how they're loaded (for modular drivers), you may not be able to control which adapter takes precedence.

Remember that some non-SCSI devices, such as USB disk devices and SATA disks, are mapped onto the Linux SCSI subsystem. This can cause a true SCSI hard disk to be assigned a higher device ID than you'd expect if you use such "pseudo-SCSI" devices.

The SCSI bus is logically one-dimensional—that is, every device on the bus falls along a single line. This bus must not fork or branch in any way. Each end of the SCSI bus must be *terminated*. This refers to the presence of a special resistor pack that prevents signals from bouncing back and forth along the SCSI chain. Consult your SCSI host adapter and SCSI devices' manuals to learn how to terminate them. Remember that both ends of the SCSI chain must be terminated, but devices mid-chain must *not* be terminated. The SCSI host adapter qualifies as a device, so if it's at the end of the chain, it must be terminated. Termination is a true hardware requirement; it doesn't apply to SATA or USB disk devices, even though they use Linux SCSI drivers.

Incorrect termination often results in bizarre SCSI problems, such as an inability to detect SCSI devices, poor performance, or unreliable operation. Similar symptoms can result from the use of poor-quality SCSI cables or cables that are too long.

Configuring External Disks

External disks come in several varieties, the most common of which are USB, IEEE-1394, and SCSI. SCSI has long supported external disks directly, and many SCSI host adapters have both internal and external connectors. You configure external SCSI disks just like internal disks, although the physical details of setting the SCSI ID number and termination may differ; consult your devices' manuals for details.

Linux treats external USB and IEEE-1394 disks just like SCSI devices, from a software point of view. Typically, you can plug in the device, see a /dev/sdx device node appear, and use it as you would a SCSI disk. This is the case for both true external hard disks and media such as solid-state USB flash drives.

External drives are easily removed, and this can be a great convenience; however, you should never unplug an external drive until you've unmounted the disk in Linux using the umount command, as described in Chapter 5. Failure to unmount a disk is likely to result in damage to the filesystem, including lost files. In addition, although USB and IEEE-1394 busses are hot-pluggable, most SCSI busses aren't, so connecting or disconnecting a SCSI device while the computer is running is dangerous. (Inserting or ejecting a removable SCSI disk, such as a Zip disk, is safe, however.)

Designing a Hard Disk Layout

Whether your system uses PATA, SATA, or SCSI disks, you must design a disk layout for Linux. If you're using a system with Linux preinstalled, you may not need to deal with this task immediately; however, sooner or later you'll have to install Linux on a new computer or one with an existing OS or upgrade your hard disk. The next few pages describe the $x86$ partitioning schemes, Linux mount points, and common choices for a Linux partitioning scheme. The upcoming section "Creating Partitions and Filesystems" covers the mechanics of creating partitions.

Why Partition?

The first issue with partitioning is the question of why you should do it. The answer is that partitioning provides a variety of advantages, including the following:

Multi-OS Support   Partitioning enables you to keep the data for different OSs separate. In fact, many OSs can't easily co-exist on the same partition because they don't support each other's primary filesystems. This feature is obviously important mainly if you want the computer to boot multiple OSs. It can also be handy to help maintain an emergency system—you can install a single OS twice, using the second installation as an emergency maintenance tool for the first in case problems develop.

Filesystem Choice   By partitioning your disk, you can use different *filesystems*—data structures designed to hold all the files on a partition—on each partition. Perhaps one filesystem is faster than another and so is important for time-critical or frequently accessed files, but another may provide accounting or backup features you want to use for users' data files.

Disk Space Management   By partitioning your disk, you can lock certain sets of files into a fixed space. For instance, if you restrict users to storing files on one or two partitions, they can fill those partitions without causing problems on other partitions, such as system partitions. This feature can help keep your system from crashing if space runs out. On the other hand, if you get the partition sizes wrong, you can run out of disk space on just one partition much sooner than would be the case if you'd used fewer partitions.

Disk Error Protection   Disks sometimes develop problems. These problems can be the result of bad hardware or of errors that creep into the filesystems. In either case, splitting a disk into partitions provides some protection against such problems. If data structures on one partition become corrupted, these errors affect only the files on that partition. This separation can therefore protect data on other partitions and simplify data recovery.

Security   You can use different security-related mount options on different partitions. For instance, you might mount a partition that holds critical system files read-only, preventing users from writing to that partition. Linux's file security options should provide similar protection, but taking advantage of Linux filesystem mount options provides redundancy that can be helpful in case of an error in setting up file or directory permissions.

Backup   Some backup tools work best on whole partitions. By keeping partitions small, you may be able to back up more easily than you could if your partitions were large.

In practice, most Linux computers use several partitions, although precisely how the system is partitioned varies from one computer to another. (The upcoming section "Common Partitions and Filesystem Layouts" describes some possibilities.)

Understanding Partitioning Systems

Partitions are defined by data structures that are written to specified parts of the hard disk. Several competing systems for defining these partitions exist. On *x*86 and *x*86-64 hardware, the most common method up until 2010 had been the *Master Boot Record* (MBR) partitioning system, so called because it stores its data in the first sector of the disk, which is also known as the MBR. The MBR system, however, is limited to partitions and partition placement of 2 tebibytes (TiB; 1TiB is 2^{40} bytes), at least when using the nearly universal sector size of 512 bytes. The successor to MBR is the *GUID Partition Table* (GPT) partitioning system, which has much higher limits and certain other advantages. The tools and methods for manipulating MBR and GPT disks differ from each other, although there's substantial overlap.

Still more partitioning systems exist, and you may run into them from time to time. For instance, Macintoshes that use PowerPC CPUs generally employ the Apple Partition Map (APM), and many Unix variants employ Berkeley Standard Distribution (BSD) disk labels. You're most likely to encounter MBR and GPT disks, so those are the partitioning systems covered in this book. Details for other systems differ, but the basic principles are the same.

MBR Partitions

The original *x*86 partitioning scheme allowed for only four partitions. As hard disks increased in size and the need for more partitions became apparent, the original scheme was extended in a way that retained backward compatibility. The new scheme uses three partition types:

- *Primary partitions*, which are the same as the original partition types
- *Extended partitions*, which are a special type of primary partition that serves as a placeholder for the next type
- *Logical partitions*, which reside within an extended partition

Figure 3.4 illustrates how these partition types relate. Because logical partitions reside within a single extended partition, all logical partitions must be contiguous.

FIGURE 3.4   The MBR partitioning system uses up to four primary partitions, one of which can be a placeholder extended partition that contains logical partitions.

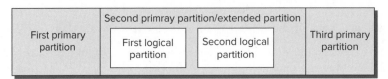

For any one disk, you're limited to four primary partitions, or three primary partitions and one extended partition. Many OSs, such as DOS, Windows, and FreeBSD, *must* boot from primary partitions, and because of this, most hard disks include at least one primary partition. Linux, however, is not so limited, so you could boot Linux from a disk that contains no primary partitions, although in practice few people do this.

The primary partitions have numbers in the range of 1–4, whereas logical partitions are numbered 5 and up. Gaps can appear in the numbering of MBR primary partitions; however, such gaps cannot exist in the numbering of logical partitions. That is, you can have a disk with partitions numbered 1, 3, 5, 6, and 7 but not 1, 3, 5, and 7—if partition 7 exists, there must be a 5 and a 6.

In addition to holding the partition table, the MBR data structure holds the primary BIOS boot loader—the first disk-loaded code that the CPU executes when a BIOS-based computer boots. Thus, the MBR is extremely important and sensitive. Because the MBR exists only in the first sector of the disk, it's vulnerable to damage; accidental erasure will make your disk unusable unless you have a backup.

You can back up your MBR partitions by typing **sfdisk -d /dev/sda >** **sda-backup.txt** (or similar commands to specify another disk device or backup file). You can then copy the backup file (sda-backup.txt in this example) to a removable disk or another computer for safekeeping. You can restore the backup by typing **sfdisk -f /dev/sda < sda-backup** **.txt**. Be sure you're using the correct backup file, though; a mistake can generate incorrect or even impossible partition definitions!

MBR partitions have type codes, which are 1-byte (2-digit hexadecimal) numbers, to help identify their purpose. Common type codes you may run into include 0x0c (FAT), 0x05 (an old type of extended partition), 0x07 (NTFS), 0x0f (a newer type of extended partition), 0x82 (Linux swap), and 0x83 (Linux filesystem).

Although the MBR data structure has survived for three decades, its days are numbered because it's not easily extensible beyond 2TiB disks. Thus, a new system is needed.

GPT Partitions

GPT is part of Intel's EFI specification, but GPT can be used on computers that don't use EFI, and GPT is the preferred partitioning system for disks bigger than 2TiB. Most EFI-based computers use GPT even on disks smaller than 2TiB.

GPT employs a *protective MBR*, which is a legal MBR definition that makes GPT-unaware utilities think that the disk holds a single MBR partition that spans the entire disk. Additional data structures define the true GPT partitions. These data structures are duplicated, with one copy at the start of the disk and another at its end. This provides redundancy that can help in data recovery should an accident damage one of the two sets of data structures.

GPT does away with the primary/extended/logical distinction of MBR. You can define up to 128 partitions by default (and that limit may be raised, if necessary). Gaps can occur in partition numbering, so you can have a disk with three partitions numbered 3, 7, and 104, to name just one possibility. In practice, though, GPT partitions are usually numbered consecutively starting with 1.

GPT's main drawback is that support for it is relatively immature. The fdisk utility (described shortly in "Partitioning a Disk") doesn't work with GPT disks, although alternatives to fdisk are available. Some versions of the GRUB boot loader also don't support it. The situation is worse in some OSs—particularly older ones. Nonetheless, you should be at least somewhat familiar with GPT because of MBR's inability to handle disks larger than 2TiB.

Like MBR, GPT supports partition type codes; however, GPT type codes are 16-byte GUID values. Disk partitioning tools typically translate these codes into short descriptions, such as "Linux swap." Confusingly, most Linux installations use the same type code for their filesystems that Windows uses for its filesystems, although a Linux-only code is available and is likely to begin seeing heavier use beginning in 2013.

An Alternative to Partitions: LVM

An alternative to partitions for some functions is logical volume management (LVM). To use LVM, you set aside one or more partitions and assign them MBR partition type codes of 0x8e (or an equivalent on GPT disks). You then use a series of utilities, such as pvcreate, vgcreate, lvcreate, and lvscan, to manage the partitions (known as *physical volumes* in this scheme), to merge them into volume groups, and to create and manage logical volumes within the volume groups. Ultimately, you then access the logical volumes using names you assigned to them in the /dev/mapper directory, such as /dev/mapper/myvol-home.

LVM sounds complicated, and it is. Why would you want to use it? The biggest advantage to LVM is that it enables you to easily resize your logical volumes without worrying about the positions or sizes of surrounding partitions. In a sense, the logical volumes are like files in a regular filesystem; the filesystem (or volume group, in the case of LVM) manages the allocation of space when you resize files (or logical volumes). This can be a great boon if you're not sure of the optimum starting sizes of your partitions. You can also easily add disk space, in the form of a new physical disk, to expand the size of an existing volume group.

On the downside, LVM adds complexity, and not all Linux distributions support it out of the box. LVM can complicate disaster recovery, and if your LVM configuration spans multiple disks, a failure of one disk will put all files in your volume group at risk. It's easiest to configure a system with at least one filesystem (dedicated to /boot, or perhaps the root filesystem containing /boot) in its own conventional partition, reserving LVM for /home, /usr, and other filesystems.

Despite these drawbacks, you might consider investigating LVM further in some situations. It's most likely to be useful if you want to create an installation with many specialized filesystems and you want to retain the option of resizing those filesystems in the future. A second situation where LVM is handy is if you need to create very large filesystems that are too large for a single physical disk to handle.

Mount Points

Once a disk is partitioned, an OS must have some way to access the data on the partitions. In DOS and Windows, this is done by assigning a drive letter, such as C: or D:, to each partition. (DOS and Windows use partition type codes to decide which partitions get drive letters and which to ignore.) Linux, though, doesn't use drive letters; instead, Linux uses a unified directory tree. Each partition is *mounted* at a *mount point* in that tree. A mount point is a directory that's used as a way to access the filesystem on the partition, and mounting the filesystem is the process of linking the filesystem to the mount point.

For instance, suppose that a Linux system has three partitions: the root (/) partition, /home, and /usr. The root partition holds the basic system files, and all other partitions are accessed via directories on that filesystem. If /home contains users' home directories, such as sally and sam, those directories will be accessible as /home/sally and /home/sam once this partition is mounted at /home. If this partition were unmounted and remounted at /users, the same directories would become accessible as /users/sally and /users/sam.

Partitions can be mounted just about anywhere in the Linux directory tree, including on directories on the root partition as well as directories on mounted partitions. For instance, if /home is a separate partition, you can have a /home/morehomes directory that serves as a mount point for another partition.

The upcoming section "Mounting and Unmounting Filesystems" describes the commands and configuration files that are used for mounting partitions. For now, you should be concerned only with what constitutes a good filesystem layout (that is, what directories you should split off into their own partitions) and how to create these partitions.

Common Partitions and Filesystem Layouts

So, what directories are commonly split off into separate partitions? Table 3.4 summarizes some popular choices. Note that typical sizes for many of these partitions vary greatly depending on how the system is used. Therefore, it's impossible to make recommendations on partition size that will be universally acceptable.

TABLE 3.4   Common partitions and their uses

Partition (mount point)	Typical size	Use
Swap (not mounted)	One to two times the system RAM size	Serves as an adjunct to system RAM; is slow but enables the computer to run more or larger programs.
/home	200MiB–3TiB (or more)	Holds users' data files. Isolating it on a separate partition preserves user data during a system upgrade. Size depends on the number of users and their data storage needs.
/boot	100–500MiB	Holds critical boot files. Creating it as a separate partition lets you circumvent limitations of older BIOSs and boot loaders, which often can't boot a kernel from a point above a value between 504MiB and 2TiB.
/usr	500MiB–25GiB	Holds most Linux program and data files; this is sometimes the largest partition, although /home is larger on systems with many users or if users store large data files. Changes implemented in 2012 are making it harder to create a separate /usr partition in many distributions.
/usr/local	100MiB–3GiB	Holds Linux program and data files that are unique to this installation, particularly those that you compile yourself.
/opt	100MiB–5GiB	Holds Linux program and data files that are associated with third-party packages, especially commercial ones.

TABLE 3.4   Common partitions and their uses *(continued)*

Partition (mount point)	Typical size	Use
/var	100MiB–3TiB (or more)	Holds miscellaneous files associated with the day-to-day functioning of a computer. These files are often transient in nature. Most often split off as a separate partition when the system functions as a server that uses the /var directory for server-related files like mail queues.
/tmp	100MiB–20GiB	Holds temporary files created by ordinary users.
/mnt	N/A	Not a separate partition; rather, it or its subdirectories are used as mount points for removable media like floppies or CD-ROMs.
/media	N/A	Holds subdirectories that may be used as mount points for removable media, much like /mnt or its subdirectories.

Some directories—/etc, /bin, /sbin, /lib, and /dev—should *never* be placed on separate partitions. These directories host critical system configuration files or files without which a Linux system can't function. For instance, /etc contains /etc/fstab, the file that specifies what partitions correspond to what directories, and /bin contains the mount utility that's used to mount partitions on directories. Changes to system utilities in 2012 are making it harder, but not impossible, to split off /usr as a separate partition.

The 2.4.*x* and newer kernels include support for a dedicated /dev filesystem, which obviates the need for files in a disk-based /dev directory; so, in some sense, /dev can reside on a separate filesystem, although not a separate partition. The udev utility controls the /dev filesystem in recent versions of Linux.

Creating Partitions and Filesystems

If you're installing Linux on a computer, chances are it will present you with a tool to help guide you through the partitioning process. These installation tools will create the partitions you tell them to create or create partitions sized as the distribution's maintainers believe appropriate. If you need to partition a new disk you're adding, though, or if you want to create partitions using standard Linux tools rather than rely on your distribution's installation tools, you must know something about the Linux programs that accomplish this task. Partitioning involves two tasks: creating the partitions and preparing the partitions to be used.

In Linux, these two tasks are usually accomplished using separate tools, although some tools can handle both tasks simultaneously.

 Real World Scenario

When to Create Multiple Partitions

One problem with splitting off lots of separate partitions, particularly for new administrators, is that it can be difficult to settle on appropriate partition sizes. As noted in Table 3.4, the appropriate size of various partitions can vary substantially from one system to another. For instance, a workstation is likely to need a fairly small /var partition (say, 100MiB), but a mail or news server may need a /var partition that's gigabytes in size. Guessing wrong isn't fatal, but it is annoying. You'll need to resize your partitions (which is tedious and dangerous) or set up symbolic links between partitions so that subdirectories on one partition can be stored on other partitions. LVM can simplify such after-the-fact changes, but as noted earlier, LVM adds its own complexity.

For this reason, I generally recommend that new Linux administrators try simple partition layouts first. The root (/) partition is required, and swap is a very good idea. Beyond this, /boot can be helpful on hard disks of more than 8GiB with older distributions or BIOSs but is seldom needed with computers or distributions sold since 2000. Aside from user data (in /home or elsewhere), most Linux installations in 2012 require 5–25GiB, so setting root (/) to a value in this range makes sense. An appropriate size for /home is often relatively easy for new administrators to guess, or you can devote all your disk space after creating root (/) and swap to /home. Beyond these partitions, I recommend that new administrators proceed with caution.

As you gain more experience with Linux, you may want to break off other directories into their own partitions on subsequent installations or when upgrading disk hardware. You can use the du command to learn how much space is used by files within any given directory.

Partitioning a Disk

The traditional Linux tool for disk partitioning is called fdisk. This tool's name is short for *fixed disk*, and the name is the same as a DOS and Windows tool that accomplishes the same task. (When I mean to refer to the DOS/Windows tool, I capitalize its name, as in FDISK. The Linux tool's name is always entirely lowercase.) Both DOS's FDISK and Linux's fdisk are text-mode tools to accomplish similar goals, but the two are very different in operational details.

Although fdisk is the traditional tool, several others exist. One of these is GNU Parted, which can handle several different partition table types, not just the MBR that fdisk can handle. If you prefer fdisk to GNU Parted but must use GPT, you can use GPT fdisk (http://www.rodsbooks.com/gdisk/); this package's gdisk program works much like fdisk but on GPT disks. Although fdisk is the tool covered by the exam, some administrators prefer the related cfdisk (or the similar cgdisk for GPT), which has a friendlier user interface. The sfdisk (or sgdisk for GPT) tool is useful for writing scripts that can handle disk partitioning tasks.

Using *fdisk*

To use Linux's fdisk, type the command name followed by the name of the disk device you want to partition, as in **fdisk /dev/hda** to partition the primary master PATA disk. The result is an fdisk prompt:

```
# fdisk /dev/hda

Command (m for help):
```

At the Command (m for help): prompt, you can type commands to accomplish various goals:

Display the Current Partition Table   You may want to begin by displaying the current partition table. To do so, type **p**. If you *only* want to display the current partition table, you can type **fdisk -l /dev/hda** (or whatever the device identifier is) at a command prompt rather than enter fdisk's interactive mode. This command displays the partition table and then exits.

Create a Partition   To create a partition, type **n**. The result is a series of prompts asking for information about the partition—whether it should be a primary, extended, or logical partition; the partition's starting cylinder; the partition's ending cylinder or size; and so on. The details of what you're asked depend in part on what's already defined. For instance, fdisk won't ask you if you want to create an extended partition if one already exists. Older versions of fdisk measure partition start and end points in cylinders, not megabytes. This is a holdover from the CHS measurements used by the *x*86 partition table. Recent versions of fdisk use sectors as the default unit of measure, although you can specify a partition's size by using a plus sign, number, and suffix, as in **+20G** to create a 20GiB partition.

WARNING   In the past, partitions were aligned on CHS cylinders. This was beneficial given the hardware of the 1980s, but today it's detrimental. Many modern disks require partition alignment on 8-sector or larger boundaries for optimum performance. Recent partitioning programs begin partitions on 1MiB (2048-sector) boundaries for this reason. Failure to align partitions properly can result in severe performance degradation. See http://www .ibm.com/developerworks/linux/library/l-4kb-sector-disks/ for more on this topic.

Delete a Partition   To delete a partition, type **d**. If more than one partition exists, the program will ask for the partition number, which you must enter.

Change a Partition's Type   When you create a partition, `fdisk` assigns it a type code of 0x83, which corresponds to a Linux filesystem. If you want to create a Linux swap partition or a partition for another OS, you can type **t** to change a partition type code. The program then prompts you for a partition number and a type code.

List Partition Types   Several dozen partition type codes exist, so it's easy to forget what they are. Type **l** (that's a lowercase *L*) at the main `fdisk` prompt to see a list of the most common ones. You can also get this list by typing **L** when you're prompted for the partition type when you change a partition's type code.

Mark a Partition Bootable   Some OSs, such as DOS and Windows, rely on their partitions having special bootable flags in order to boot. You can set this flag by typing **a**, whereupon `fdisk` asks for the partition number.

Get Help   Type **m** or **?** to see a summary of the main `fdisk` commands.

Exit   Linux's `fdisk` supports two exit modes. First, you can type **q** to exit the program without saving any changes; anything you do with the program is lost. This option is particularly helpful if you've made a mistake. Second, typing **w** writes your changes to the disk and exits the program.

As an example, consider deleting a primary, an extended, and a logical partition on a USB flash drive and creating a single new one in their place:

```
# fdisk /dev/sdc

Command (m for help): p

Disk /dev/sdc: 2038 MB, 2038431744 bytes
63 heads, 62 sectors/track, 1019 cylinders, total 3981312 sectors
Units = sectors of 1 * 512 = 512 bytes
Sector size (logical/physical): 512 bytes / 512 bytes
I/O size (minimum/optimal): 512 bytes / 512 bytes
Disk identifier: 0x88a46f2c

   Device Boot      Start         End      Blocks   Id  System
/dev/sdc1            2048     2099199     1048576   83  Linux
/dev/sdc2         2099200     3981311      941056    5  Extended
/dev/sdc5         2101248     3981311      940032   83  Linux

Command (m for help): d
Partition number (1-5): 5
```

```
Command (m for help): d
Partition number (1-5): 2

Command (m for help): d
Selected partition 1

Command (m for help): n
Partition type:
   p   primary (0 primary, 0 extended, 4 free)
   e   extended
Select (default p): p
Partition number (1-4, default 1): 1
First sector (2048-3981311, default 2048): 2048
Last sector, +sectors or +size{K,M,G} (2048-3981311, default 3981311):
Using default value 3981311

Command (m for help): w
The partition table has been altered!

Calling ioctl() to re-read partition table.
Syncing disks.
```

This process begins with a p command to verify that the program is operating on the correct disk. With this information in hand, the three existing partitions are deleted. Note that the first two deletions ask for a partition number, but the third doesn't, because only one partition is left. Once this is done, n is used to create a new primary partition. Once the task is complete, the w command is used to write the changes to disk and exit the program. The result of this sequence is a disk with a single primary partition (/dev/sdc1) marked as holding a Linux filesystem.

To work on a GPT disk, you can use gdisk in much the same way you use fdisk. Aside from some details, such as the lack of a prompt to create primary, extended, or logical partitions, gdisk uses the same basic commands as fdisk.

Using GNU Parted

GNU Parted (http://www.gnu.org/software/parted/) is a partitioning tool that works with MBR, GPT, APM, BSD disk labels, and other disk types. It also supports more features than fdisk and is easier to use in some ways. On the other hand, GNU Parted uses its own way of referring to partitions, which can be confusing. It's also more finicky about minor disk partitioning quirks and errors than is fdisk. Although GNU Parted isn't covered on the exam, knowing a bit about it can be handy.

You start GNU Parted much as you start fdisk, by typing its name followed by the device you want to modify, as in **parted /dev/hda** to partition /dev/hda. The result is some brief introductory text followed by a (parted) prompt at which you type commands. Type ? to see a list of commands, which are multi-character commands similar to Linux shell commands. For instance, print displays the current partition table, mkpart creates (makes) a partition, and rm removes a partition.

Some still-more-advanced partitioning capabilities appear only in flashy GUI tools, such as the GNOME Partition Editor, aka GParted (http://gparted.sourceforge.net), which is shown in Figure 3.5. Aside from its novice-friendly user interface, GParted's main claim to fame is that it enables you to easily move or resize partitions. You may need to run the program from an emergency disk to use these features, though; you can't move or resize any partition that's currently in use. Such partitions are marked with a padlock icon, as shown next to /dev/sdc1 in Figure 3.5.

FIGURE 3.5 GParted enables point-and-click partition management, including partition moving and resizing.

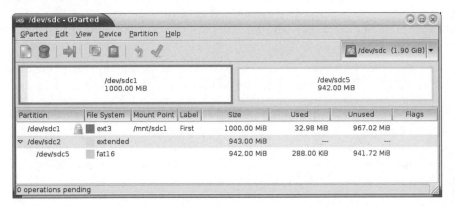

 Resizing or moving a filesystem can be dangerous. If the resizing code contains a bug or if there's a power failure during the operation, data can be lost. Thus, I strongly recommend you back up any important data before resizing or moving a partition. Also, resizing or moving your boot partition on a BIOS-based computer can render the system unbootable until you re-install your boot loader.

Preparing a Partition for Use

Once a partition is created, you must prepare it for use. This process is often called "making a filesystem" or "formatting a partition." It involves writing low-level data structures to disk. Linux can then read and modify these data structures to access and store files in the partition. You should know something about the common Linux filesystems and know how to use filesystem-creation tools to create them.

The word *formatting* is somewhat ambiguous. It can refer to either *low-level formatting,* which creates a structure of sectors and tracks on the disk media, or *high-level formatting,* which creates a filesystem. Hard disks are low-level formatted at the factory and should never need to be low-level formatted again. Floppy disks, though, can be both low- and high-level formatted. The tools described here can high-level format a floppy disk as well as a hard disk. To low-level format a floppy disk, you must use the fdformat command, as in **fdformat /dev/fd0**. This command cannot be used on a hard disk.

Common Filesystem Types

Linux supports quite a few different filesystems, both Linux-native and those intended for other OSs. Some of the latter barely work under Linux, and even when they do work reliably, they usually don't support all the features that Linux expects in its native filesystems. Thus, when preparing a Linux system, you'll use one or more of its native filesystems for most or all partitions:

Ext2fs The *Second Extended File System* (ext2fs or ext2) is the traditional Linux-native filesystem. It was created for Linux and was the dominant Linux filesystem throughout the late 1990s. Ext2fs has a reputation as a reliable filesystem. It has since been eclipsed by other filesystems, but it still has its uses. In particular, ext2fs can be a good choice for a small /boot partition, if you choose to use one, and for small (sub-gigabyte) removable disks. On such small partitions, the size of the journal used by more advanced filesystems can be a real problem, so the non-journaling ext2fs is a better choice. (Journaling is described in more detail shortly.) The ext2 filesystem type code is ext2.

On an EFI-based computer, using ext2fs, ext3fs, or ReiserFS on a separate /boot partition enables the firmware to read this partition with the help of suitable drivers. This can expand your options for boot loader configuration.

Ext3fs The *Third Extended File System* (ext3fs or ext3) is basically ext2fs with a journal added. The result is a filesystem that's as reliable as ext2fs but that recovers from power outages and system crashes much more quickly. The ext3 filesystem type code is ext3.

Ext4fs The *Fourth Extended File System* (ext4fs or ext4) is the next-generation version of this filesystem family. It adds the ability to work with very large disks (those over 16TiB, the limit for ext2fs and ext3fs) or very large files (those over 2TiB), as well as extensions intended to improve performance. Its filesystem type code is ext4.

ReiserFS This filesystem was designed from scratch as a journaling filesystem for Linux. It's particularly good at handling large numbers of small files (say, smaller than about 32KB) because ReiserFS uses various tricks to squeeze the ends of files into each other's unused spaces. This small savings can add up to a large percentage of file sizes when files are small. You can use reiserfs as the type code for this filesystem.

As of Linux kernel version 3.6.0, ReiserFS version 3.*x* is current. A from-scratch rewrite of ReiserFS, known as Reiser4, is under development, although development has slowed to the point that it's uncertain if Reiser4 will ever be included in the mainstream kernel.

JFS   IBM developed the *Journaled File System* (JFS) for its AIX OS and later re-implemented it on OS/2. The OS/2 version was subsequently donated to Linux. JFS is a technically sophisticated journaling filesystem that may be of particular interest if you're familiar with AIX or OS/2 or want an advanced filesystem to use on a dual-boot system with one of these OSs. As you might expect, this filesystem's type code is jfs.

XFS   Silicon Graphics (SGI) created its *Extents File System* (XFS) for its IRIX OS and, like IBM, later donated the code to Linux. Like JFS, XFS is a very technically sophisticated filesystem. XFS has gained a reputation for robustness, speed, and flexibility on IRIX, but some of the XFS features that make it so flexible on IRIX aren't supported well under Linux. Use xfs as the type code for this filesystem.

Btrfs   This filesystem (pronounced "butter eff ess" or "bee tree eff ess") is an advanced filesystem with features inspired by those of Sun's Zettabyte File System (ZFS). Like ext4fs, JFS, and XFS, Btrfs is a fast performer and is able to handle very large disks and files. As of the 3.6.0 kernel, Btrfs is considered experimental; however, its advanced features make it a likely successor to the current popular filesystems.

In practice, most administrators choose ext3fs, ext4fs, or ReiserFS as their primary filesystems; however, JFS and XFS also work well, and some administrators prefer them, particularly on large disks that store large files. (Ext4fs also handles large files.) Hard data on the merits and problems with each filesystem are difficult to come by, and even when they do exist, they're suspect because filesystem performance interacts with so many other factors. For instance, as just noted, ReiserFS can cram more small files into a small space than can other filesystems, but this advantage isn't very important if you'll be storing mostly larger files.

If you're using a non-*x*86 or non-*x*86-64 platform, be sure to check filesystem development on that platform. A filesystem may be speedy and reliable on one CPU but sluggish and unreliable on another.

In addition to these Linux-native filesystems, you may need to deal with some others from time to time, including the following:

FAT   The *File Allocation Table* (FAT) filesystem is old and primitive—but ubiquitous. It's the only hard disk filesystem supported by DOS and Windows 9*x*/Me. For this reason, every major OS understands FAT, making it an excellent filesystem for exchanging data on removable disks. Two major orthogonal variants of FAT exist: It varies in the size of the FAT data structure after which the filesystem is named (12-, 16-, or 32-bit pointers), and it has variants that support long filenames. Linux automatically detects the FAT size, so you shouldn't need to worry about this. To use the original FAT filenames, which are limited to eight characters with an optional three-character extension (the so-called *8.3 filenames*), use the Linux filesystem type code of msdos. To use Windows-style long filenames, use the filesystem type code of vfat. A Linux-only long filename system, known as umsdos, supports additional Linux features—enough that you can install Linux on a FAT partition, although this practice isn't recommended except for certain types of emergency disks or to try Linux on a Windows system.

NTFS   The *New Technology File System* (NTFS) is the preferred filesystem for Windows NT/200*x*/XP/Vista/7. Unfortunately, Linux's NTFS support is rather rudimentary. As of the 2.6.*x* kernel series, Linux can reliably read NTFS and can overwrite existing files, but the Linux kernel can't write new files to an NTFS partition.

 If you must have good NTFS read/write support for a dual-boot system, look into NTFS-3G (http://www.ntfs-3g.org). This is a read/write NTFS driver that resides in user space rather than in kernel space. It's used as the default NTFS driver by some Linux distributions.

HFS and HFS+   Apple has long used the *Hierarchical File System* (HFS) with its Mac OS, and Linux provides full read/write HFS support. This support isn't as reliable as Linux's read/write FAT support, though, so you may want to use FAT when exchanging files with Mac users. Apple has extended HFS to better support large hard disks and many Unix-like features with its HFS+ (aka Extended HFS). Linux 2.6.*x* and newer provide limited HFS+ support; but write support works only with the HFS+ journal disabled.

ISO-9660   The standard filesystem for CD-ROMs has long been *ISO-9660*. This filesystem comes in several levels. Level 1 is similar to the original FAT in that it supports only 8.3 filenames. Levels 2 and 3 add support for longer 32-character filenames. Linux supports ISO-9660 using its iso9660 filesystem type code. Linux's ISO-9660 support also works with the *Rock Ridge extensions*, which are a series of extensions to ISO-9660 to enable it to support Unix-style long filenames, permissions, symbolic links, and so on. Similarly, *Joliet* provides support for long filenames as implemented for Windows. If a disc includes Rock Ridge or Joliet extensions, Linux will automatically detect and use them.

UDF   The *Universal Disc Format* (UDF) is the next-generation filesystem for optical discs. It's commonly used on DVD-ROMs and recordable optical discs. Linux supports it, but read/write UDF support is still in its infancy.

As a practical matter, if you're preparing a hard disk for use with Linux, you should probably use Linux filesystems only. If you're preparing a disk that will be used for a dual-boot configuration, you may want to set aside some partitions for other filesystem types. For removable disks, you'll have to be the judge of what's most appropriate. You might use ext2fs for a Linux-only removable disk, FAT for a cross-platform disk, or ISO-9660 (perhaps with Rock Ridge and Joliet) for a CD-R or recordable DVD.

ISO-9660 and other optical disc filesystems are created with special tools intended for this purpose. Specifically, mkisofs creates an ISO-9660 filesystem (optionally with Rock Ridge, Joliet, HFS, and UDF components added), while cdrecord writes this image to a blank CD-R. The growisofs program combines both functions but works only on recordable DVD media.

Creating a Filesystem

Most filesystems, including all Linux-native filesystems, have Linux tools that can create the filesystem on a partition. Typically, these tools have filenames of the form mkfs.*fstype*, where *fstype* is the filesystem type code. These tools can also be called from a front-end tool called mkfs; you pass the filesystem type code to mkfs using its -t option:

```
# mkfs -t ext3 /dev/sda6
```

For ext2 and ext3 filesystems, the mke2fs program is often used instead of mkfs. The mke2fs program is just another name for mkfs.ext2.

This command creates an ext3 filesystem on /dev/sda6. Depending on the filesystem, the speed of the disk, and the size of the partition, this process can take anywhere from a fraction of a second to a few seconds. Most filesystem-build tools support additional options, some of which can greatly increase the time required to build a filesystem. In particular, the -c option is supported by several filesystems. This option causes the tool to perform a bad-block check—every sector in the partition is checked to be sure it can reliably hold data. If it can't, the sector is marked as bad and isn't used.

If you perform a bad-block check and find that some sectors are bad, chances are the entire hard disk doesn't have long to live. Sometimes this sort of problem can result from other issues, though, such as bad cables or SCSI termination problems.

Of the common Linux filesystems, ext2fs, ext3fs, and ext4fs provide the most options in their mkfs tools. (In fact, these tools are one and the same; the program simply creates a filesystem with the appropriate features for the name that's used to call it.) You can type **man mkfs.ext2** to learn about these options, most of which deal with obscure and unimportant features. One obscure option that does deserve mention is -m *percent*, which sets the reserved-space percentage. The idea is that you don't want the disk to completely fill up with user files; if the disk starts getting close to full, Linux should report that the disk *is* full before it really is, at least for ordinary users. This gives the root user the ability to log in and create new files, if necessary, to help recover the system.

The ext2fs/ext3fs/ext4fs reserved-space percentage defaults to 5 percent, which translates to quite a lot of space on large disks. You may want to reduce this value (say, by passing -m 2 to reduce it to 2 percent) on your root (/) filesystem and perhaps even lower (1 percent or 0 percent) on some, such as /home. Setting -m 0 also makes sense on removable disks, which aren't likely to be critical for system recovery and may be a bit cramped to begin with.

In addition to providing filesystem-creation tools for Linux-native filesystems, Linux distributions usually provide such tools for various non-Linux filesystems. The most important of these may be for FAT. The main tool for this task is called mkdosfs, but it's often linked to the mkfs.msdos and mkfs.vfat names, as well. This program can automatically adjust the size of the FAT data structure to 12, 16, or 32 bits depending on the device size. You can override this option with the -F *fat-size* option, where *fat-size* is the FAT size in bits—12, 16, or 32. No special options are required to create a FAT filesystem that can handle Windows-style (VFAT) long filenames; these are created by the OS.

In Exercise 3.1, you'll practice creating filesystems using mkfs and related utilities.

EXERCISE 3.1

Creating Filesystems

Try creating some filesystems on a spare partition or a removable disk. Even a floppy disk will do, although you won't be able to create journaling filesystems on a floppy disk. The following steps assume you're using a USB flash drive, /dev/sdc1; change the device specification as necessary. *Be sure to use an empty partition!* Accidentally entering the wrong device filename could wipe out your entire system!

This exercise uses a few commands that are described in more detail later in this chapter. To create some filesystems, follow these steps:

1. Log in as root.

2. Use **fdisk** to verify the partitions on your target disk by typing **fdisk -l /dev/sdc**. You should see a list of partitions, including the one you'll use for your tests. (If fdisk reports a single partition with ee under the Id column, the disk is a GPT disk, and you should verify the disk's partitions with gdisk rather than fdisk.)

3. Verify that your test partition is *not* currently mounted. Type **df** to see the currently mounted partitions and verify that /dev/sdc1 is not among them.

4. Type **mkfs -t ext2 /dev/sdc1**. You should see several lines of status information appear.

5. Type **mount /dev/sdc1 /mnt** to mount the new filesystem to /mnt. (You may use another mount point, if you like.)

6. Type **df /mnt** to see basic accounting information for the filesystem. On my test system with a /dev/sdc1 that's precisely 1000MiB in size, 1,007,896 blocks are present; 1,264

are used; and 955,432 blocks are available. Most of the difference between the present and available blocks is caused by the 5 percent reserved space.

7. Type **umount /mnt** to unmount the filesystem.

8. Type **mkfs -t ext2 -m 0 /dev/sdc1** to create a new ext2 filesystem on the device, but without any reserved space.

9. Repeat steps 5–7. Note that the available space has increased (to 1,006,632 blocks on my test disk). The available space plus the used space should now equal the total blocks.

10. Repeat steps 4–7, but use a filesystem type code of ext3 to create a journaling filesystem. (This won't be possible if you use a floppy disk.) Note how much space is consumed by the journal.

11. Repeat steps 4–7, but use another filesystem, such as JFS or ReiserFS. Note how the filesystem-creation tools differ in the information they present and in their stated amounts of available space.

Be aware that, because of differences in how filesystems store files and allocate space, a greater amount of available space when a filesystem is created may not translate into a greater capacity to store files.

Creating Swap Space

Some partitions don't hold files. Most notably, Linux can use a *swap partition*, which is a partition that Linux treats as an extension of memory. (Linux can also use a *swap file*, which is a file that works in the same way. Both are examples of *swap space*.) Linux uses the MBR partition type code of 0x82 to identify swap space, but as with other partitions, this code is mostly a convenience to keep other OSs from trying to access Linux swap partitions; Linux uses /etc/fstab to define which partitions to use as swap space, as described in Chapter 4, "Managing Files."

 WARNING
Solaris for *x*86 also uses an MBR partition type code of 0x82, but in Solaris, this code refers to a Solaris partition. If you dual-boot between Solaris and Linux, this double meaning of the 0x82 partition type code can cause confusion. This is particularly true when installing the OSs. You may need to use Linux's fdisk to temporarily change the partition type codes to keep Linux from trying to use a Solaris partition as swap space or to keep Solaris from trying to interpret Linux swap space as a data partition.

Although swap space doesn't hold a filesystem *per se* and isn't mounted in the way that filesystem partitions are mounted, swap space does require preparation similar to that for creation of a filesystem. This task is accomplished with the mkswap command, which you can generally use by passing it nothing but the device identifier:

```
# mkswap /dev/sda7
```

This example turns /dev/sda7 into swap space. To use the swap space, you must activate it with the swapon command:

```
# swapon /dev/sda7
```

To permanently activate swap space, you must create an entry for it in /etc/fstab, as described in Chapter 4.

Maintaining Filesystem Health

Filesystems can become "sick" in a variety of ways. They can become overloaded with too much data, they can be tuned inappropriately for your system, or they can become corrupted because of buggy drivers, buggy utilities, or hardware errors. Fortunately, Linux provides a variety of utilities that can help you keep an eye on the status of your filesystems, tune their performance, and fix them.

> **WARNING**   Many of Linux's filesystem maintenance tools should be run when the filesystem is not mounted. Changes made by maintenance utilities while the filesystem is mounted can confuse the kernel's filesystem drivers, resulting in data corruption. In the following pages, I mention when utilities can and can't be used with mounted filesystems.

Tuning Filesystems

Filesystems are basically just big data structures—they're a means of storing data on disk in an indexed method that makes it easy to locate the data at a later time. Like all data structures, filesystems include design compromises. For instance, a design feature may enable you to store more small files on disk but might chew up disk space, thus reducing the total capacity available for storage of larger files. In many cases, you have no choice concerning these compromises, but some filesystems include tools that enable you to set filesystem options that affect performance. This is particularly true of ext2fs and the related ext3fs and ext4fs. Three tools are particularly important for tuning these filesystems: dumpe2fs, tune2fs, and debugfs. The first of these tools provides information about the filesystem, and the other two enable you to change tuning options.

Obtaining Filesystem Information

You can learn a lot about your ext2 or ext3 filesystem with the dumpe2fs command. This command's syntax is fairly straightforward:

```
dumpe2fs [options] device
```

The *device* is the filesystem device file, such as /dev/sdb7. This command accepts several *options*, most of which are rather obscure. The most important option is probably -h, which causes the utility to omit information about group descriptors. (This information is helpful in very advanced filesystem debugging but not for basic filesystem tuning.) For information about additional options, consult the man page for dumpe2fs.

Unless you're a filesystem expert and need to debug a corrupted filesystem, you're most likely to want to use dumpe2fs with the -h option. The result is about three dozen lines of output, each specifying a particular filesystem option, like these:

```
Last mounted on:          <not available>
Filesystem features:      has_journal filetype sparse_super
Filesystem state:         clean
Inode count:              657312
Block count:              1313305
Last checked:             Sun Feb 26 14:23:23 2012
Check interval:           15552000 (6 months)
```

Some of these options' meanings are fairly self-explanatory; for instance, the filesystem was last checked (with fsck, described in "Checking Filesystems") on February 26, 2012. Other options aren't so obvious; for instance, the Inode count line may be puzzling. (It's a count of the number of *inodes* supported by the filesystem. Each inode contains information for one file, so the number of inodes effectively limits the number of files you can store.)

The next two sections describe some of the options you may want to change. For now, you should know that you can retrieve information about how your filesystems are currently configured using dumpe2fs. You can then use this information when modifying the configuration; if your current settings seem reasonable, you can leave them alone, but if they seem ill-adapted to your configuration, you can change them.

Unlike many low-level disk utilities, you can safely run dumpe2fs on a filesystem that's currently mounted. This can be handy when you're studying your configuration to decide what to modify.

Most other filesystems lack an equivalent to dumpe2fs, but XFS provides something with at least some surface similarities: xfs_info. To invoke it, pass the command the name of the partition that holds the filesystem you want to check:

```
# xfs_info /dev/sda7
meta-data=/dev/sda7    isize=256     agcount=88, agsize=1032192 blks
         =             sectsz=512    attr=0
data     =             bsize=4096    blocks=89915392, imaxpct=25
         =             sunit=0       swidth=0 blks, unwritten=1
naming   =version 2    bsize=4096
log      =internal     bsize=4096    blocks=8064, version=1
         =             sectsz=512    sunit=0 blks
realtime =none         extsz=65536   blocks=0, rtextents=0
```

Instead of the partition name, you can pass the mount point, such as /home or /usr/local. Unlike most filesystem tools, xfs_info requires that the filesystem be mounted. The information returned by xfs_info is fairly technical, mostly related to block sizes, sector sizes, and so on.

Another XFS tool is xfs_metadump. This program copies the filesystem's metadata (filenames, file sizes, and so on) to a file. For instance, **xfs_metadump /dev/sda7 ~/dump-file** copies the metadata to ~/dump-file. This command doesn't copy actual file contents and so isn't useful as a backup tool. Instead, it's intended as a debugging tool; if the filesystem is behaving strangely, you can use this command and send the resulting file to XFS developers for study.

Adjusting Tunable Filesystem Parameters

The tune2fs program enables you to change many of the filesystem parameters that are reported by dumpe2fs. This program's syntax is fairly simple, but it hides a great deal of complexity:

```
tune2fs [options] device
```

The complexity arises because of the large number of *options* that the program accepts. Each feature that tune2fs enables you to adjust requires its own option:

Adjust the Maximum Mount Count   Ext2fs, ext3fs, and ext4fs require a periodic disk check with fsck. This check is designed to prevent errors from creeping onto the disk undetected. You can adjust the maximum number of times the disk may be mounted without a check with the -c *mounts* option, where *mounts* is the number of mounts. You can trick the system into thinking the filesystem has been mounted a certain number of times with the -C *mounts* option; this sets the mount counter to *mounts*.

Adjust the Time Between Checks   Periodic disk checks are required based on time as well as the number of mounts. You can set the time between checks with the -i *interval* option, where *interval* is the maximum time between checks. Normally, *interval* is a number with the character d, w, or m appended, to specify days, weeks, or months, respectively.

Add a Journal   The -j option adds a journal to the filesystem, effectively converting an ext2 filesystem into an ext3 filesystem. Journal management is described in more detail in "Maintaining a Journal."

Set the Reserved Blocks   The -m *percent* option sets the percentage of disk space that's reserved for use by root. The default value is 5, but this is excessive on multi-gigabyte hard disks, so you may want to reduce it. You may want to set it to 0 on removable disks intended to store user files. You can also set the reserved space in blocks, rather than as a percentage of disk space, with the -r *blocks* option.

The options described here are the ones that are most likely to be useful. Several other options are available; consult tune2fs's man page for details.

As with most low-level disk utilities, you shouldn't use tune2fs to adjust a mounted filesystem. If you want to adjust a key mounted filesystem, such as your root (/)

filesystem, you may need to boot up an emergency disk system, such as the CD-ROM-based Parted Magic (http://partedmagic.com). Many distributions' install discs can be used in this capacity, as well.

In XFS, the xfs_admin command is the rough equivalent of tune2fs. Some options you may want to adjust include the following:

Use Version 2 Journal Format   The -j option enables version 2 log (journal) format, which can improve performance in some situations.

Obtain the Filesystem Label and UUID   You can use the -l and -u options to obtain the filesystem's label (name) and *universally unique identifier* (UUID), respectively. The name is seldom used in Linux but can be used in some cases. The UUID is a long code that is increasingly used by distributions to specify a filesystem to be mounted, as described in "Permanently Mounting Filesystems."

The blkid command can display the label and UUID of any partition's filesystem, not just an XFS partition.

Set the Filesystem Label and UUID   You can change the filesystem's label or UUID by using the -L *label* or -U *uuid* option, respectively. The label is at most 12 characters in length. You'll normally use the -U option to set the UUID to a known value (such as the UUID the partition used prior to it being reformatted); or you can use generate as the *uuid* value to have xfs_admin create a new UUID. You should *not* set the UUID to a value that's in use on another partition!

In use, xfs_admin might look something like this:

```
# xfs_admin -L av_data /dev/sda7
writing all SBs
new label = "av_data"
```

This example sets the name of the filesystem on /dev/sda7 to av_data. As with tune2fs, xfs_admin should be used only on unmounted filesystems.

Interactively Debugging a Filesystem

In addition to reviewing and changing filesystem flags with dumpe2fs and tune2fs, you can interactively modify a filesystem's features using debugfs. This program provides the abilities of dumpe2fs, tune2fs, and many of Linux's normal file-manipulation tools all rolled into one. To use the program, type its name followed by the device filename corresponding to the filesystem you want to manipulate. You'll then see the debugfs prompt:

```
# debugfs /dev/sda11
debugfs:
```

You can type commands at this prompt to achieve specific goals:

Display Filesystem Superblock Information   The show_super_stats or stats command produces superblock information, similar to what dumpe2fs displays.

Display Inode Information   You can display the inode data on a file or directory by typing **stat filename**, where *filename* is the name of the file.

Undelete a File   You can use debugfs to undelete a file by typing **undelete inode name**, where *inode* is the inode number of the deleted file and *name* is the filename you want to give to it. (You can use undel in place of undelete if you like.) This facility is of limited utility because you must know the inode number associated with the deleted file. You can obtain a list of deleted inodes by typing **lsdel** or **list_deleted_inodes**, but the list may not provide enough clues to let you zero in on the file you want to recover.

Extract a File   You can extract a file from the filesystem by typing **write internal-file external-file**, where *internal-file* is the name of a file in the filesystem you're manipulating and *external-file* is a filename on your main Linux system. This facility can be handy if a filesystem is badly damaged and you want to extract a critical file without mounting the filesystem.

Manipulate Files   Most of the commands described in Chapter 4 work within debugfs. You can change your directory with cd, create links with ln, remove a file with rm, and so on.

Obtain Help   Typing **list_requests**, **lr**, **help**, or **?** produces a summary of available commands.

Exit   Typing **quit** exits from the program.

   This summary just scratches the surface of debugfs's capabilities. In the hands of an expert, this program can help rescue a badly damaged filesystem or at least extract critical data from it. To learn more, consult the program's man page.

> Although debugfs is a useful tool, it's potentially dangerous. Don't use it on a mounted filesystem, don't use it unless you have to, and be very careful when using it. If in doubt, leave the adjustments to the experts. Be aware that the exam does cover debugfs, though.

The closest XFS equivalent to debugfs is called xfs_db. Like debugfs, xfs_db provides an interactive tool to access and manipulate a filesystem, but xfs_db provides fewer tools that are amenable to novice or intermediate use. Instead, xfs_db is a tool for XFS experts.

Maintaining a Journal

Ext2fs is a traditional filesystem. Although it's a good performer, it suffers from a major limitation: After a power failure, a system crash, or another uncontrolled shutdown, the filesystem could be in an inconsistent state. The only way to safely mount the filesystem so that you're sure its data structures are valid is to perform a full disk check on it, as described in "Checking Filesystems." This task is usually handled automatically when the system boots, but it takes time—probably several minutes, or perhaps more than an hour on a large filesystem or if the computer has many smaller filesystems.

The solution to this problem is to change to a *journaling filesystem*. Such a filesystem maintains a *journal*, which is a data structure that describes pending operations. Prior to writing data to the disk's main data structures, Linux describes what it's about to do in the journal. When the operations are complete, their entries are removed from the journal. Thus, at any given moment the journal should contain a list of disk structures that *might* be undergoing modification. The result is that, in the event of a crash or power failure, the system can examine the journal and check only those data structures described in it. If inconsistencies are found, the system can roll back or complete the changes, returning the disk to a consistent state without checking every data structure in the filesystem. This greatly speeds the disk-check process after power failures and system crashes. Today, journaling filesystems are the standard for most Linux disk partitions. Very small partitions (such as a separate /boot partition, if you use one) and small removable disks (such as Zip disks) often lack journals, though.

Five journaling filesystems are common on Linux: ext3fs, ext4fs, ReiserFS, XFS, and JFS. Of these, the last three require little in the way of journal configuration. Ext3fs is a bit different; it's basically just ext2fs with a journal added. This fact means you can add a journal to an ext2 filesystem, converting it into an ext3 filesystem. This is what the -j option to tune2fs does, as described earlier in "Adjusting Tunable Filesystem Parameters." Ext4fs is a further enhancement of this filesystem family.

> Although using tune2fs on a mounted filesystem is generally inadvisable, it's safe to use its -j option on a mounted filesystem. The result is a file called .journal that holds the journal. If you add a journal to an unmounted filesystem, the journal file will be invisible.

Adding a journal alone won't do much good, though. To use a journal, you must mount the filesystem with the correct filesystem type code—ext3 rather than ext2 for ext3fs, or ext4 for ext4fs. (The upcoming section "Mounting and Unmounting Filesystems" describes how to do this.)

The journal, like other filesystem features, has its own set of parameters. You can set these with the -J option to tune2fs. In particular, the size=*journal-size* and device=*external-journal* suboptions enable you to set the journal's size and the device on which it's stored. By default, the system creates a journal that's the right size for the filesystem and stores it on the filesystem itself.

Checking Filesystems

Tuning a filesystem is a task you're likely to perform every once in a while—say, when making major changes to an installation. Another task is much more common: checking a filesystem for errors. Bugs, power failures, and mechanical problems can all cause the data structures on a filesystem to become corrupted. The results are sometimes subtle, but if they're left unchecked, they can cause severe data loss. For this reason, Linux includes tools for verifying a filesystem's integrity and for correcting any problems that may exist. The main tool you'll use for this purpose is called fsck. This program is actually a front end to other tools, such as e2fsck (aka fsck.ext2, fsck.ext3, and fsck.ext4) or XFS's xfs_check and xfs_repair. The syntax for fsck is as follows:

```
fsck   [-sACVRTNP] [-t fstype] [--] [fsck-options]  filesystems
```

The exam objectives include both e2fsck and fsck, but because fsck is the more general tool that's useful on more filesystems, it's the form described in more detail in this book.

The more common parameters to fsck enable you to perform useful actions:

Check All Files   The -A option causes fsck to check all the filesystems marked to be checked in /etc/fstab. This option is normally used in system startup scripts.

Indicate Progress   The -C option displays a text-mode progress indicator of the check process. Most filesystem check programs don't support this feature, but e2fsck does.

Show Verbose Output   The -V option produces verbose output of the check process.

No Action   The -N option tells fsck to display what it would normally do without actually doing it.

Set the Filesystem Type   Normally, fsck determines the filesystem type automatically. You can force the type with the -t fstype flag, though. Used in conjunction with -A, this causes the program to check only the specified filesystem types, even if others are marked to be checked. If fstype is prefixed with no, then all filesystems *except* the specified type are checked.

Filesystem-Specific Options   Filesystem check programs for specific filesystems often have their own options. The fsck command passes options it doesn't understand, or those that follow a double dash (--), to the underlying check program. Common options include -a or -p (perform an automatic check), -r (perform an interactive check), and -f (force a full filesystem check even if the filesystem initially appears to be clean).

Filesystem List   The final parameter is usually the name of the filesystem or filesystems being checked, such as /dev/sda6.

Normally, you run fsck with only the filesystem device name, as in **fsck /dev/sda6**. You can add options as needed, however. Check fsck's man page for less common options.

Run fsck *only* on filesystems that are not currently mounted or that are mounted in read-only mode. Changes written to disk during normal read/write operations can confuse fsck and result in filesystem corruption.

Linux runs `fsck` automatically at startup on partitions that are marked for this in `/etc/fstab`, as described later in "Permanently Mounting Filesystems." The normal behavior of `e2fsck` causes it to perform just a quick cursory examination of a partition if it's been unmounted cleanly. The result is that the Linux boot process isn't delayed because of a filesystem check unless the system wasn't shut down properly. This rule has a couple of exceptions, though: `e2fsck` forces a check if the disk has gone longer than a certain amount of time without checks (normally six months) or if the filesystem has been mounted more than a certain number of times since the last check (normally 20). You can change these options using `tune2fs`, as described earlier in "Adjusting Tunable Filesystem Parameters." Therefore, you'll occasionally see automatic filesystem checks of ext2, ext3, and ext4 filesystems even if the system was shut down correctly.

Journaling filesystems do away with full filesystem checks at system startup even if the system wasn't shut down correctly. Nonetheless, these filesystems still require check programs to correct problems introduced by undetected write failures, bugs, hardware problems, and the like. If you encounter odd behavior with a journaling filesystem, you might consider unmounting it and performing a filesystem check—but be sure to read the documentation first. Some Linux distributions do odd things with some journaling filesystem check programs. For instance, Mandriva uses a symbolic link from `/sbin/fsck.reiserfs` to `/bin/true`. This configuration speeds system boot times should ReiserFS partitions be marked for automatic checks, but it can be confusing if you need to manually check the filesystem. If this is the case, run `/sbin/reiserfsck` to do the job. Similarly, `/sbin/fsck.xfs` is usually nothing but a script that advises the user to run `xfs_check` or `xfs_repair`.

Monitoring Disk Use

One common problem with disks is that they can fill up. To avoid this problem, you need tools to tell you how much space your files are consuming. This is the task of the `df` and `du` programs, which summarize disk use on a partition-by-partition and directory-by-directory basis, respectively.

Monitoring Disk Use by Partition

The `df` command's syntax is as follows:

`df [options] [files]`

In the simplest case, you can type the command name to see a summary of disk space used on all of a system's partitions:

```
$ df
Filesystem    1K-blocks       Used Available Use% Mounted on
/dev/sdb10      5859784    4449900   1409884  76% /
/dev/sdb12      2086264     991468   1094796  48% /opt
/dev/hda13      2541468     320928   2220540  13% /usr/local
```

```
/dev/hda9      15361340   10174596   5186744   67%  /home
/dev/hda10     22699288   13663408   7882820   64%  /other/emu
/dev/hda6        101089      22613     74301   24%  /boot
/dev/sdb5       1953216    1018752    934464   53%  /other/shared
none             256528          0    256528    0%  /dev/shm
speaker:/home   6297248    3845900   2451348   62%  /speaker/home
//win/music    17156608    8100864   9055744   48%  /win/mp3s
```

This output shows the device file associated with the filesystem, the total amount of space on the filesystem, the used space on the filesystem, the free space on the filesystem, the percentage of space that's used, and the mount point. Typically, when used space climbs above about 80 percent, you should consider cleaning up the partition. The appropriate ceiling varies from one computer and partition to another, though. The risk is greatest on partitions that hold files that change frequently—particularly if large files are likely to be created on a partition, even if only temporarily.

You can fine-tune the effects of df by passing it several options. Each option modifies the df output in a specific way:

Include All Filesystems   The -a or --all option includes pseudo-filesystems with a size of 0 in the output. These filesystems may include /proc, /sys, /proc/bus/usb, and others.

Use Scaled Units   The -h or --human-readable option causes df to scale and label its units; for instance, instead of reporting a partition as having 5859784 blocks, it reports the size as 5.6G (for 5.6GiB). The -H and --si options have a similar effect, but they use power-of-10 (1,000; 1,000,000; and so on) units rather than power-of-2 (1,024; 1,048,576; and so on) units. The -k (--kilobytes) and -m (--megabytes) options force output in their respective units.

Summarize Inodes   By default, df summarizes available and used disk space. You can instead receive a report on available and used inodes by passing the -i or --inodes option. This information can be helpful if a partition has very many small files, which can deplete available inodes sooner than they deplete available disk space.

The -i option works well for ext2, ext3, ext4, XFS, and some other filesystems that create a fixed number of inodes when the filesystem is created. Other filesystems, such as ReiserFS and Btrfs, create inodes dynamically, rendering the -i option meaningless.

Local Filesystems Only   The -l or --local option causes df to omit network filesystems. This can speed up operation.

Display Filesystem Type   The -T or --print-type option adds the filesystem type to the information df displays.

Limit by Filesystem Type   The -t *fstype* or --type=*fstype* option displays only information about filesystems of the specified type. The -x *fstype* or --exclude-type=*fstype* option has the opposite effect; it excludes filesystems of the specified type from the report.

This list is incomplete; consult df's man page for details about more options. In addition to these options, you can specify one or more *files* to df. When you do this, the program restricts its report to the filesystem on which the specified file or directory exists. For instance, to learn about the disk space used on the /home partition, you could type **df /home**. Alternatively, you can give a device filename, as in **df /dev/hda9**.

Monitoring Disk Use by Directory

The df command is helpful for finding out which partitions are in danger of becoming overloaded, but once you've obtained this information, you may need to fine-tune the diagnosis and track down the directories and files that are chewing up disk space. The tool for this task is du, which has a syntax similar to that of df:

du [*options*] [*directories*]

This command searches directories you specify and reports how much disk space each is consuming. This search is recursive, so you can learn how much space the directory and all its subdirectories consume. The result can be a very long listing if you specify directories with many files, but several options can reduce the size of this output. Others can perform helpful tasks as well:

Summarize Files As Well As Directories   Ordinarily, du reports on the space used by the files in directories but not the space used by individual files. Passing the -a or --all option causes du to report on individual files as well.

Compute a Grand Total   Adding the -c or --total option causes du to add a grand total to the end of its output.

Use Scaled Units   The -h or --human-readable option causes du to scale and label its units; for instance, instead of reporting the total disk space used as 5859784 blocks, it reports the size as 5.6G (for 5.6GiB). The -H and --si options have a similar effect, but they use power-of-10 (1,000; 1,000,000; and so on) units rather than power-of-2 (1,024; 1,048,576; and so on) units. The -k (--kilobytes) and -m (--megabytes) options force output in their respective units.

Count Hard Links   Ordinarily, du counts files that appear multiple times as hard links only once. This reflects true disk space used, but sometimes you may want to count each link independently—for instance, if you're creating a CD-R and the file will be stored once for each link. To do so, include the -l (that's a lowercase *L*) or --count-links option. (Links are described in more detail in Chapter 4.)

Limit Depth   The --max-depth=*n* option limits the report to *n* levels. (The subdirectories' contents are counted even if they aren't reported.)

Summarize   If you don't want a line of output for each subdirectory in the tree, pass the -s or --summarize option, which limits the report to those files and directories you specify on the command line. This option is equivalent to --max=depth=0.

Limit to One Filesystem   The -x or --one-file-system option limits the report to the current filesystem. If another filesystem is mounted within the tree you want summarized, its contents aren't included in the report.

This list is incomplete; you should consult du's man page for information about additional options.

As an example of du in action, consider using it to discover which of your users is consuming the most disk space in /home. Chances are you're not concerned with the details of which subdirectories within each home directory are using the space, so you'll pass the -s option to the program:

```
# du -s /home/*
12          /home/ellen
35304       /home/freddie
1760        /home/jennie
12078       /home/jjones
0           /home/lost+found
10110324    /home/mspiggy
```

In this example, the wildcard character (*) stands for all the files and directories in /home, thus producing summaries for all these subdirectories. (For more on this topic, consult Chapter 4.) Clearly, mspiggy (or whoever owns the /home/mspiggy directory) is the biggest disk space user—or at least, that directory's contents are consuming the most space. You could investigate further, say by typing **du -s /home/mspiggy/*** to learn where the disk space is being used within the /home/mspiggy directory. In the case of user files, if this space consumption is a problem, you may want to contact this user instead of trying to clean it up yourself.

WARNING   Many types of files shouldn't simply be deleted. For instance, most program files should be removed via the system's package management system, if you decide to remove them. (This topic is covered in Chapter 2, "Managing Software.") If you're not sure what a file is or how it should be removed, don't delete it—try a Web search, type *man filename*, or otherwise research it to figure out what it is.

Mounting and Unmounting Filesystems

Maintaining filesystems is necessary, but the whole reason filesystems exist is to store files—in other words, to be useful. Under Linux, filesystems are most often used by being *mounted*—that is, associated with a directory. This task can be accomplished on a one-time basis by using tools such as mount (and then unmounted with umount) or persistently across reboots by editing the /etc/fstab file.

Temporarily Mounting or Unmounting Filesystems

Linux provides the mount command to mount a filesystem to a mount point. The umount command reverses this process. (Yes, umount is spelled correctly; it's missing the first n.) In practice, using these commands isn't usually too difficult, but they support a large number of options.

Syntax and Parameters for *mount*

The syntax for mount is as follows:

```
mount [-alrsvw] [-t fstype] [-o options] [device]  [mountpoint]
```

Common parameters for mount support a number of features:

Mount All Filesystems   The -a parameter causes mount to mount all the filesystems listed in the /etc/fstab file, which specifies the most-used partitions and devices. The upcoming section "Permanently Mounting Filesystems" describes this file's format.

Mount Read-Only   The -r parameter causes Linux to mount the filesystem read-only, even if it's normally a read/write filesystem.

Show Verbose Output   As with many commands, -v produces verbose output—the program provides comments on operations as they occur.

Mount Read/Write   The -w parameter causes Linux to attempt to mount the filesystem for both read and write operations. This is the default for most filesystems, but some experimental drivers default to read-only operation. The -o rw option has the same effect.

Specify the Filesystem Type   Use the -t *fstype* parameter to specify the filesystem type. Common filesystem types are ext2 (for ext2fs), ext3 (for ext3fs), ext4 (for ext4fs), reiserfs (for ReiserFS), jfs (for JFS), xfs (for XFS), vfat (for FAT with VFAT long filenames), msdos (for FAT using only short DOS filenames), iso9660 (for CD-ROM filesystems), udf (for DVD and some CD-ROM filesystems), nfs (for NFS network mounts), and cifs (for SMB/CIFS network shares). Linux supports many others. If this parameter is omitted, Linux will attempt to auto-detect the filesystem type.

Linux requires support in the kernel or as a kernel module to mount a filesystem of a given type. If this support is missing, Linux will refuse to mount the filesystem in question.

Mount by Label or UUID   The -L *label* and -U *uuid* options tell mount to mount the filesystem with the specified label or UUID, respectively.

Additional Options   You can add many options using the -o parameter. Many of these are filesystem-specific.

Device   The *device* is the device filename associated with the partition or disk device, such as /dev/hda4, /dev/fd0, or /dev/cdrom. This parameter is usually required, but it may be omitted under some circumstances, as described shortly.

Mount Point   The *mountpoint* is the directory to which the device's contents should be attached. As with *device*, it's usually required, but it may be omitted under some circumstances.

The preceding list of mount parameters isn't comprehensive; consult the mount man page for some of the more obscure options. The most common applications of mount use few parameters because Linux generally does a good job of detecting the filesystem type and the default parameters work reasonably well. For instance, consider this example:

```
# mount /dev/sdb7 /mnt/shared
```

This command mounts the contents of /dev/sdb7 on /mnt/shared, auto-detecting the filesystem type and using the default options. Ordinarily, only root may issue a mount command; however, if /etc/fstab specifies the user, users, or owner option, an ordinary user may mount a filesystem using a simplified syntax in which only the device *or* mount point is specified, but not both. For instance, a user may type **mount /mnt/cdrom** to mount a CD-ROM if /etc/fstab specifies /mnt/cdrom as its mount point and uses the user, users, or owner option.

Most Linux distributions ship with auto-mounter support, which causes the OS to automatically mount removable media when they're inserted. In GUI environments, a file browser may also open on the inserted disk. To eject the disk, the user will need to unmount the filesystem by using umount, as described shortly, or by selecting an option in the desktop environment.

When Linux mounts a filesystem, it ordinarily records this fact in /etc/mtab. This file has a format similar to that of /etc/fstab and is stored in /etc, but it's not a configuration file you should edit. You might examine this file to determine what filesystems are mounted, though. (The df command, described in more detail in "Monitoring Disk Use by Partition," is another way to learn what filesystems are mounted.)

Options for *mount*

When you do need to use special parameters (via -o or in /etc/fstab), it's usually to add filesystem-specific options. Table 3.5 summarizes the most important filesystem options. Some of these are meaningful only in the /etc/fstab file.

TABLE 3.5 Important filesystem options for the mount command

Option	Supported filesystems	Description
defaults	All	Causes the default options for this filesystem to be used. It's used primarily in the /etc/fstab file to ensure that the file includes an options column.
loop	All	Causes the loopback device for this mount to be used. Allows you to mount a file as if it were a disk partition. For instance, **mount -t vfat -o loop image.img /mnt/image** mounts the file image.img as if it were a disk.
auto or noauto	All	Mounts or doesn't mount the filesystem at boot time or when root issues the **mount -a** command. The default is auto, but noauto is appropriate for removable media. Used in /etc/fstab.
user or nouser	All	Allows or disallows ordinary users to mount the filesystem. The default is nouser, but user is often appropriate for removable media. Used in /etc/fstab. When included in this file, user allows users to type **mount /*mountpoint*** (where /*mountpoint* is the assigned mount point) to mount a disk. Only the user who mounted the filesystem may unmount it.
users	All	Similar to user, except that any user may unmount a filesystem once it's been mounted.
owner	All	Similar to user, except that the user must own the device file. Some distributions, such as Red Hat, assign ownership of some device files (such as /dev/fd0 for the floppy disk) to the console user, so this can be a helpful option.
remount	All	Changes one or more mount options without explicitly unmounting a partition. To use this option, you issue a mount command on an already-mounted filesystem but with remount along with any options you want to change. This feature can be used to enable or disable write access to a partition, for example.
ro	All	Specifies a read-only mount of the filesystem. This is the default for filesystems that include no write access and for some with particularly unreliable write support.
rw	All read/write file systems	Specifies a read/write mount of the filesystem. This is the default for most read/write filesystems.

TABLE 3.5   Important filesystem options for the mount command *(continued)*

Option	Supported filesystems	Description
uid=*value*	Most filesystems that don't support Unix-style permissions, such as vfat, hpfs, ntfs, and hfs	Sets the owner of all files. For instance, uid=1000 sets the owner to whoever has Linux user ID 1000. (Check Linux user IDs in the /etc/passwd file.)
gid=*value*	Most filesystems that don't support Unix-style permissions, such as vfat, hpfs, ntfs, and hfs	Works like uid=*value*, but sets the group of all files on the filesystem. You can find group IDs in the /etc/group file.
umask=*value*	Most filesystems that don't support Unix-style permissions, such as vfat, hpfs, ntfs, and hfs	Sets the umask for the permissions on files. *value* is interpreted in binary as bits to be removed from permissions on files. For instance, umask=027 yields permissions of 750, or -rwxr-x---. Used in conjunction with uid=*value* and gid=*value*, this option lets you control who can access files on FAT, HPFS, and many other foreign filesystems.
dmask=*value*	Most filesystems that don't support Unix-style permissions, such as vfat, hpfs, ntfs, and hfs	Similar to umask, but sets the umask for directories only, not for files.
fmask=*value*	Most filesystems that don't support Unix-style permissions, such as vfat, hpfs, ntfs, and hfs	Similar to umask, but sets the umask for files only, not for directories.
conv=*code*	Most filesystems used on Microsoft and Apple OSs: msdos, umsdos, vfat, hpfs, and hfs	If *code* is b or binary, Linux doesn't modify the files' contents. If *code* is t or text, Linux auto-converts files between Linux-style and DOS- or Macintosh-style end-of-line characters. If *code* is a or auto, Linux applies the conversion unless the file is a known binary file format. It's usually best to leave this at its default value of binary because file conversions can cause serious problems for some applications and file types.
norock	iso9660	Disables Rock Ridge extensions for ISO-9660 CD-ROMs.
nojoliet	iso9660	Disables Joliet extensions for ISO-9660 CD-ROMs.

Some filesystems support additional options that aren't described here. The man page for mount covers some of these, but you may need to look at the filesystem's documentation for some options. This documentation may appear in /usr/src/linux/Documentation/filesystems or /usr/src/linux/fs/*fsname*, where *fsname* is the name of the filesystem.

Using *umount*

The umount command is simpler than mount. The basic umount syntax is as follows:

```
umount [-afnrv] [-t fstype] [device | mountpoint]
```

Most of these parameters have meanings similar to their meanings in mount, but some differences deserve mention:

Unmount All   Rather than unmount partitions listed in /etc/fstab, the -a option causes the system to attempt to unmount all the partitions listed in /etc/mtab, the file that holds information about mounted filesystems. On a normally running system, this operation is likely to succeed only partly because it won't be able to unmount some key filesystems, such as the root partition.

Force Unmount   You can use the -f option to tell Linux to force an unmount operation that might otherwise fail. This feature is sometimes helpful when unmounting NFS mounts shared by servers that have become unreachable.

Fall Back to Read-Only   The -r option tells umount that if it can't unmount a filesystem, it should attempt to remount it in read-only mode.

Unmount Partitions of a Specific Filesystem Type   The -t *fstype* option tells the system to unmount only partitions of the specified type. You can list multiple filesystem types by separating them with commas.

The Device and Mount Point   You need to specify only the *device* or only the *mountpoint*, not both.

As with mount, normal users can't ordinarily use umount. The exception is if the partition or device is listed in /etc/fstab and specifies the user, users, or owner option, in which case normal users can unmount the device. (In the case of user, only the user who mounted the partition may unmount it; in the case of owner, the user issuing the command must also own the device file, as with mount.) These options are most useful for removable-media devices.

WARNING   Be cautious when removing floppy disks or unplugging USB disk-like devices (USB flash drives or external hard disks). Linux caches accesses to most filesystems, which means that data may not be written to the disk until some time after a write command. Because of this, it's possible to corrupt a disk by ejecting or unplugging it, even when the drive isn't active. You must *always* issue a umount command before ejecting a mounted disk. (GUI unmount tools do this behind the scenes, so using a desktop's unmount or eject option is equivalent to using umount.) After issuing the umount command, wait for the command to return, and if the disk has activity indicators, wait for them to stop blinking to be sure Linux has finished using the device. Another way to write the cache to disk is to use the sync command; but because this command does *not* fully unmount a filesystem, it's not a substitute for umount.

Permanently Mounting Filesystems

The /etc/fstab file controls how Linux provides access to disk partitions and removable media devices. Linux supports a unified directory structure in which every disk device (partition or removable disk) is mounted at a particular point in the directory tree. For instance, you might access a USB flash drive at /media/usb. The root of this tree is accessed from /. Directories off this root may be other partitions or disks, or they may be ordinary directories. For instance, /etc should be on the same partition as /, but many other directories, such as /home, may correspond to separate partitions. The /etc/fstab file describes how these filesystems are laid out. (The filename fstab is an abbreviation for *filesystem table*.)

The /etc/fstab file consists of a series of lines that contain six fields each; the fields are separated by one or more spaces or tabs. A line that begins with a hash mark (#) is a comment and is ignored. Listing 3.1 shows a sample /etc/fstab file.

Listing 3.1:   Sample /etc/fstab file

```
#device         mount point    filesystem options        dump fsck
/dev/hda1       /              ext4       defaults          1 1
UUID=3631a288-673e-40f5-9e96-6539fec468e9 \
                /usr           reiserfs   defaults          0 0
LABEL=/home     /home          reiserfs   defaults          0 0
/dev/hdb5       /windows       vfat       uid=500,umask=0 0 0
/dev/hdc        /media/cdrom   iso9660    users,noauto      0 0
/dev/sda1       /media/usb     auto       users,noauto      0 0
server:/home    /other/home    nfs        users,exec        0 0
//winsrv/shr    /other/win     cifs       users,credentials=/etc/creds 0 0
/dev/hda4       swap           swap       defaults          0 0
```

The meaning of each field in this file is as follows:

Device   The first column specifies the mount device. These are usually device filenames that reference hard disks, floppy drives, and so on. Most distributions now specify partitions by their labels or UUIDs, as in the LABEL=/home and UUID=3631a288-673e-40f5-9e96-6539fec468e9 entries in Listing 3.1. When Linux encounters such an entry, it tries to find the partition whose filesystem has the specified name or UUID and mount it. This practice can help reduce problems if partition numbers change, but some filesystems lack these labels. It's also possible to list a network drive, as in server:/home, which is the /home export on the computer called server; or //winsrv/shr, which is the shr share on the Windows or Samba server called winsrv.

Mount Point   The second column specifies the mount point; in the unified Linux filesystem, this is where the partition or disk will be mounted. This should usually be an empty directory in another filesystem. The root (/) filesystem is an exception. So is swap space, which is indicated by an entry of swap.

Filesystem Type   The filesystem type code is the same as the type code used to mount a filesystem with the mount command. You can use any filesystem type code you can use directly with the mount command. A filesystem type code of auto lets the kernel auto-detect the filesystem type, which can be a convenient option for removable media devices. Auto-detection doesn't work with all filesystems, though.

Mount Options   Most filesystems support several mount options, which modify how the kernel treats the filesystem. You may specify multiple mount options, separated by commas. For instance, uid=500,umask=0 for /windows in Listing 3.1 sets the user ID (owner) of all files to 500 and sets the umask to 0. (User IDs and umasks are covered in more detail in Chapter 4.) Table 3.3 summarizes the most common mount options.

Backup Operation   The next-to-last field contains a 1 if the dump utility should back up a partition or a 0 if it shouldn't. If you never use the dump backup program, this option is essentially meaningless. (The dump program was once a common backup tool, but it is much less popular today.)

Filesystem Check Order   At boot time, Linux uses the fsck program to check filesystem integrity. The final column specifies the order in which this check occurs. A 0 means that fsck should *not* check a filesystem. Higher numbers represent the check order. The root partition should have a value of 1, and all others that should be checked should have a value of 2. Some filesystems, such as ReiserFS, shouldn't be automatically checked and so should have values of 0.

If you add a new hard disk or have to repartition the one you have, you'll probably need to modify /etc/fstab. You may also need to edit it to alter some of its options. For instance, setting the user ID or umask on Windows partitions mounted in Linux may be necessary to let ordinary users write to the partition.

 Real World Scenario

Managing User-Mountable Media

You may want to give ordinary users the ability to mount certain partitions or removable media, such as floppies, CD-ROMs, and USB flash drives. To do so, create an ordinary /etc/fstab entry for the filesystem, but be sure to add the user, users, or owner option to the options column. Table 3.5 describes the differences between these three options. Listing 3.1 shows some examples of user-mountable media: /media/cdrom, /media/usb, /other/home, and /other/win. The first two of these are designed for removable media and include the noauto option, which prevents Linux from wasting time trying to mount them when the OS first boots. The second pair of mount points are network file shares that are mounted automatically at boot time; the users option on these lines enables ordinary users to unmount and then remount the filesystem, which might be handy if, say, ordinary users have the ability to shut down the server.

As with any filesystems you want to mount, you must provide mount points—that is, create empty directories—for user-mountable media. Removable media are usually mounted in subdirectories of /mnt or /media.

Many modern distributions include auto-mount facilities that automatically mount removable media when they're inserted. These tools typically create mount points in /media and create icons on users' desktops to enable easy access to the media. This configuration produces effects that are familiar to users of Windows and Mac OS.

The credentials option for the /other/win mount point in Listing 3.1 deserves greater elaboration. Ordinarily, most SMB/CIFS shares require a username and password as a means of access control. Although you can use the username=*name* and password=*pass* options to smbfs or cifs, these options are undesirable, particularly in /etc/fstab, because they leave the password vulnerable to discovery—anybody who can read /etc/fstab can read the password. The credentials=*file* option provides an alternative—you can use it to point Linux at a file that holds the username and password. This file has labeled lines:

```
username=hschmidt
password=yiW7t9Td
```

Of course, the file you specify (/etc/creds in Listing 3.1) must be well protected—it must be readable only to root and perhaps to the user whose share it describes.

Summary

Most Linux tools and procedures provide a layer around the hardware, insulating you from a need to know too many details. Nonetheless, sometimes you have to dig in and configure hardware directly. Firmware settings can control onboard devices such as hard disk controllers and USB ports. USB and SCSI devices have their own quirks, and USB in particular is quickly evolving.

Hard disks are one class of hardware that's likely to require more attention than most. Specifically, you must know how to create partitions and prepare filesystems on those partitions. These tasks are necessary when you install Linux (although most distributions provide GUI tools to help guide you through this task during installation), when you add a hard disk, or when you reconfigure an existing system. You should also know something about boot managers. These programs help get Linux up and running when you turn on a computer's power, so they're unusually critical to Linux operation.

Filesystem management is basic to being able to administer or use a Linux system. The most basic of these basic tasks are filesystem tasks—the ability to mount filesystems, check their health, and repair ailing filesystems. Once a filesystem is mounted, you may want to periodically check to see how full it is, lest you run out of disk space.

Exam Essentials

Summarize BIOS essentials.   The BIOS provides two important functions: First, it configures hardware—both hardware that's built into the motherboard and hardware on many types of plug-in cards. Second, the BIOS begins the computer's boot process, passing control on to the boot loader in the MBR. The BIOS is currently being retired in favor of a new type of firmware, EFI, which performs these tasks on modern computers.

Describe what files contain important hardware information.   There are many files under the /proc filesystem. Many of these files have been mentioned throughout this chapter. Familiarize yourself with these files, such as /proc/ioports, /proc/interrupts, /proc/dma, /proc/bus/usb, and others.

Explain Linux's model for managing USB hardware.   Linux uses drivers for USB controllers. These drivers in turn are used by some device-specific drivers (for USB disk devices, for instance) and by programs that access USB hardware via entries in the /proc/bus/usb directory tree.

Summarize how to obtain information about PCI and USB devices.   The lspci and lsusb programs return information about PCI and USB devices, respectively. You can learn manufacturers' names and various configuration options by using these commands.

Identify common disk types and their features.   PATA disks were the most common type on PCs until about 2005. Since then, SATA disks, which are more easily configured, have gained substantially in popularity. SCSI disks have long been considered the top-tier disks, but their high price has kept them out of inexpensive commodity PCs.

Describe the purpose of disk partitions.   Disk partitions break the disk into a handful of distinct parts. Each partition can be used by a different OS, can contain a different filesystem, and is isolated from other partitions. These features improve security and safety and can greatly simplify running a multi-OS system.

Summarize important Linux disk partitions.   The most important Linux disk partition is the root (/) partition, which is at the base of the Linux directory tree. Other possible partitions include a swap partition, /home for home directories, /usr for program files, /var for transient system files, /tmp for temporary user files, /boot for the kernel and other critical boot files, and more.

Describe commands that help you monitor disk use.   The df command provides a one-line summary of each mounted filesystem's size, available space, free space, and percentage of space used. The du command adds up the disk space used by all the files in a specified directory tree and presents a summary by directory and subdirectory.

Summarize the tools that can help keep a filesystem healthy.   The fsck program is a front-end to filesystem-specific tools such as e2fsck and fsck.jfs. By whatever name, these programs examine a filesystem's major data structures for internal consistency and can correct minor errors.

Explain how filesystems are mounted in Linux.   The mount command ties a filesystem to a Linux directory; once the filesystem is mounted, its files can be accessed as part of the mount directory. The /etc/fstab file describes permanent mappings of filesystems to mount points; when the system boots, it automatically mounts the described filesystems unless they use the noauto option (which is common for removable disks).

Review Questions

1. What are common IRQs for RS-232 serial ports? (Select two.)

   A. 1

   B. 3

   C. 4

   D. 8

   E. 16

2. What tool would you use to disable a motherboard's sound hardware if you don't want to use it?

   A. The firmware

   B. The `alsactl` utility

   C. The `lsmod` command

   D. The `lspci` program

   E. None of the above; onboard sound devices can't be disabled

3. What is the purpose of `udev`?

   A. To aid in the development of software

   B. To unload Linux device drivers

   C. To load Linux device drivers

   D. To store devices' BIOS configurations in files

   E. To manage the `/dev` directory tree

4. You've just installed Linux on a new computer with a single SATA hard disk. What device identifier will refer to the disk?

   A. `/dev/sda`

   B. `/dev/mapper/disk1`

   C. `/dev/hda`

   D. `C:`

   E. `/dev/sda` or `/dev/hda`

5. Which files contain essential system information such as IRQs, direct memory access channels, and I/O addresses? (Select three.)

   A. `/proc/ioports`

   B. `/proc/ioaddresses`

   C. `/proc/dma`

   D. `/proc/interrupts`

   E. `/proc/hardware`

6. Typing **fdisk -1 /dev/sda** on a Linux computer with an MBR disk produces a listing of four partitions: /dev/sda1, /dev/sda2, /dev/sda5, and /dev/sda6. Which of the following is true?

   A. The disk contains two primary partitions and two extended partitions.

   B. Either /dev/sda1 or /dev/sda2 is an extended partition.

   C. The partition table is corrupted; there should be a /dev/sda3 and a /dev/sda4 before /dev/sda5.

   D. If you add a /dev/sda3 with fdisk, /dev/sda5 will become /dev/sda6 and /dev/sda6 will become /dev/sda7.

   E. Both /dev/sda1 and /dev/sda2 are logical partitions.

7. A new Linux administrator plans to create a system with separate /home, /usr/local, and /etc partitions, in addition to the root (/) partition. Which of the following best describes this configuration?

   A. The system won't boot because critical boot-time files reside in /home.

   B. The system will boot, but /usr/local won't be available because mounted partitions must be mounted directly off their parent partition, not in a subdirectory.

   C. The system will boot only if the /home partition is on a separate physical disk from the /usr/local partition.

   D. The system will boot and operate correctly, provided each partition is large enough for its intended use.

   E. The system won't boot because /etc contains configuration files necessary to mount non-root partitions.

8. Which of the following directories is *most* likely to be placed on its own hard disk partition?

   A. /bin

   B. /sbin

   C. /mnt

   D. /home

   E. /dev

9. You discover that an MBR hard disk has partitions with type codes of 0x0f, 0x82, and 0x83. Assuming these type codes are accurate, what can you conclude about the disk?

   A. The disk holds a partial or complete Linux system.

   B. The disk holds DOS or Windows 9*x*/Me and Windows NT/200*x*/XP installations.

   C. The disk holds a FreeBSD installation.

   D. The disk is corrupt; those partition type codes are incompatible.

   E. The disk holds a Mac OS X installation.

10. You run Linux's fdisk and modify your partition layout. Before exiting the program, you realize that you've been working on the wrong disk. What can you do to correct this problem?

    A. Nothing; the damage is done, so you'll have to recover data from a backup.

    B. Type **w** to exit fdisk without saving changes to disk.

    C. Type **q** to exit fdisk without saving changes to disk.

    D. Type **u** repeatedly to undo the operations you've made in error.

    E. Type **t** to undo all the changes and return to the original disk state.

11. What does the following command accomplish?

```
# mkfs -t ext2 /dev/sda4
```

    A. It sets the partition table type code for /dev/sda4 to ext2.

    B. It converts a FAT partition into an ext2fs partition without damaging the partition's existing files.

    C. Nothing; the -t option isn't valid, and so it causes mkfs to abort its operation.

    D. It converts an ext2 filesystem to an ext4 filesystem.

    E. It creates a new ext2 filesystem on /dev/sda4, overwriting any existing filesystem and data.

12. Which of the following best summarizes the differences between DOS's FDISK and Linux's fdisk?

    A. Linux's fdisk is a simple clone of DOS's FDISK but written to work from Linux rather than from DOS or Windows.

    B. The two are completely independent programs that accomplish similar goals, although Linux's fdisk is more flexible.

    C. DOS's FDISK uses GUI controls, whereas Linux's fdisk uses a command-line interface, but they have similar functionality.

    D. Despite their similar names, they're completely different tools—DOS's FDISK handles disk partitioning, whereas Linux's fdisk formats floppy disks.

    E. DOS's FDISK manages GPT disks whereas Linux's fdisk manages MBR disks.

13. What mount point should you associate with swap partitions?

    A. /

    B. /swap

    C. /boot

    D. /mem

    E. None of the above

14. Which of the following options is used with `fsck` to force it to use a particular filesystem type?

   A. `-A`

   B. `-N`

   C. `-t`

   D. `-C`

   E. `-f`

15. Which of the following pieces of information can `df` *not* report?

   A. How long the filesystem has been mounted

   B. The number of inodes used on an ext3fs partition

   C. The filesystem type of a partition

   D. The percentage of available disk space used on a partition

   E. The mount point associated with a filesystem

16. What is an advantage of a journaling filesystem over a conventional (non-journaling) filesystem?

   A. Journaling filesystems are older and better tested than non-journaling filesystems.

   B. Journaling filesystems never need to have their filesystems checked with `fsck`.

   C. Journaling filesystems support Linux ownership and permissions; non-journaling filesystems don't.

   D. Journaling filesystems require shorter disk checks after a power failure or system crash.

   E. Journaling filesystems record all transactions, enabling them to be undone.

17. To access files on a USB flash drive, you type **mount /dev/sdc1 /media/flash** as root. Which types of filesystems will this command mount?

   A. Ext2fs

   B. FAT

   C. HFS

   D. ReiserFS

   E. All of the above

18. Which of the following /etc/fstab entries will mount /dev/sdb2 as the /home directory at boot time?

   A. `/dev/sdb2 reiserfs /home defaults 0 0`

   B. `/dev/sdb2 /home reiserfs defaults 0 0`

   C. `/home reiserfs /dev/sdb2 noauto 0 0`

   D. `/home /dev/sdb2 reiserfs noauto 0 0`

   E. `reiserfs /dev/sdb2 /home noauto 0 0`

19. What filesystem options might you specify in /etc/fstab to make a removable disk (USB flash drive, Zip disk, floppy disk, and so on) mountable by an ordinary user with a UID of 1000? (Select three.)

    A. user

    B. users

    C. owner

    D. owners

    E. uid=1000

20. What is the minimum safe procedure for removing a USB flash drive, mounted from /dev/sdb1 at /media/usb, from a Linux computer?

    A. Type **umount /media/usb**, wait for the command to return and disk-activity lights to stop, and then unplug the drive.

    B. Unplug the drive, and then type **umount /media/usb** to ensure that Linux registers the drive's removal from the system.

    C. Unplug the drive, and then type **sync /dev/sdb1** to flush the caches to ensure problems don't develop.

    D. Type **usbdrive-remove**, and then quickly remove the disk before its activity light stops blinking.

    E. Type **fsck /dev/sdb1**, wait for the command to return and disk-activity lights to stop, and then unplug the drive.

Chapter

4

Managing Files

THE FOLLOWING EXAM OBJECTIVES ARE COVERED IN THIS CHAPTER:

- ✓ 1.103.3 Perform basic file management
- ✓ 1.104.4 Manage disk quotas
- ✓ 1.104.5 Manage file permissions and ownership
- ✓ 1.104.6 Create and change hard and symbolic links
- ✓ 1.104.7 Find system files and place files in the correct location

Ultimately, Linux is a collection of files stored on your hard disk. Other disk files contain all your user data. For these reasons, being able to manage the files contained on your filesystems is an important skill for any Linux system administrator. Chapter 3, "Configuring Hardware," described creating disk partitions, preparing filesystems on them, maintaining those filesystems, and mounting them. This chapter continues this topic by looking more closely at file management.

This chapter begins with an examination of the basic commands used to access and manipulate files. As a multi-user OS, Linux provides tools that enable you to restrict *who* may access your files, so I describe the Linux ownership model and the commands that are built on this model to control file access. Furthermore, Linux provides a system that enables you to restrict how much disk space individual users may consume, so I describe this feature. Finally, this chapter looks at locating files—both the formal description of where certain types of files should reside and the commands you can use to locate specific files.

Using File Management Commands

Basic file management is critical to the use of any computer. This is particularly true on Unix-like systems, including Linux, because these systems treat almost everything as a file, including most hardware devices and various specialized interfaces. Thus, being able to create, delete, move, rename, archive, and otherwise manipulate files is a basic skill of any Linux user or system administrator.

To begin, you should understand something of the rules that govern filenames and the shortcuts you can use to refer to files. With this information in hand, you can move on to learn how to manipulate files, how to manipulate directories, how to archive files, and how to manage links.

File Naming and Wildcard Expansion Rules

Linux filenames are much like the filenames on any other OS. Every OS has its filename quirks, though, and these differences can be stumbling blocks to those who move between systems—or to those who want to move files between systems.

Linux filenames can contain uppercase or lowercase letters, numbers, and even most punctuation and control characters. To simplify your life and avoid confusion, though,

I recommend restricting non-alphanumeric symbols to the dot (.), the dash (-), and the underscore (_). Some programs create backup files that end in the tilde (~), as well. Although Linux filenames can contain spaces, and although such filenames are common in some OSs, they must be escaped on the Linux command line by preceding the space with a backslash (\) or by enclosing the entire filename in quotes ("). This requirement makes spaces a bit awkward in Linux, so most Linux users substitute dashes or underscores.

A few characters have special meaning and should never be used in filenames. These include the asterisk (*), the question mark (?), the forward slash (/), the backslash (\), and the quotation mark ("). Although you *can* create files that contain all of these characters except for the forward slash (which serves to separate directory elements) by escaping them, they're likely to cause greater confusion than other symbols.

Linux filename length depends on the filesystem in use. On ext2fs, ext3fs, ext4fs, ReiserFS, XFS, and many others, the limit is 255 characters. If you've ever used DOS, you're probably familiar with the *8.3 filename* limit: DOS filenames are restricted to eight characters followed by an optional three-character extension. These two components are separated by a dot. Although one- to four-character extensions are common in Linux, Linux filenames can contain an arbitrary number of dots. In fact, filenames can *begin* with a dot. These so-called *dot files* are hidden from view by most utilities that display files, so they're popular for storing configuration files in your home directory.

If you access a File Allocation Table (FAT) filesystem on a removable disk or partition used by DOS, you can do so using either of two filesystem type codes: msdos, which limits you to 8.3 filenames; or vfat, which supports Windows-style long filenames. In addition, the umsdos filesystem type code was a Linux-only extension that supported Linux-style long filenames. UMSDOS support was discontinued after the 2.6.11 kernel.

Two filenames are particularly special. A filename that consists of a single dot (.) refers to the current directory, whereas a filename that consists of a double dot (..) refers to the parent directory. For instance, if your current directory is /home/jerry, then . refers to that directory and .. refers to /home.

One critical difference between Linux filenames and those of many other OSs is that Linux treats its filenames in a case-sensitive way; in other words, Filename.txt is different from filename.txt or FILENAME.TXT. All three files can exist in a single directory. Under Windows, all three filenames refer to the same file. Although Windows 95 and later all retain the case of the filename, they ignore it when you refer to an existing file, and they don't permit files whose names differ only in case to co-exist in a single directory. This difference isn't a major problem for most people who migrate from Windows to Linux, but you should be aware of it. It can also cause problems when you try to read a FAT disk using the Linux vfat driver because Linux has to follow the Windows rules when managing files on that disk.

You can use *wildcards* with many commands. A wildcard is a symbol or set of symbols that stands in for other characters. Three classes of wildcards are common in Linux:

?   A question mark (?) stands in for a single character. For instance, b??k matches book, balk, buck, or any other four-character filename that begins with b and ends with k.

*   An asterisk (*) matches any character or set of characters, including no character. For instance, b*k matches book, balk, and buck just as does b??k. b*k also matches bk, bbk, and backtrack.

Bracketed Values   Characters enclosed in square brackets ([]) normally match any character in the set. For instance, b[ao][lo]k matches balk and book but not back or back. It's also possible to specify a range of values; for instance, b[a-z]ck matches back, buck, and other four-letter filenames of this form whose second character is a lowercase letter. This differs from b?ck—because Linux treats filenames in a case-sensitive way and because ? matches any character (not just any lowercase letter), b[a-z]ck doesn't match bAck or b3ck, although b?ck matches both of these filenames.

Wildcards are implemented in the shell and passed to the command you call. For instance, if you type **ls b??k**, and that wildcard matches the three files balk, book, and buck, the result is precisely as if you'd typed **ls balk book buck**. The process of wildcard expansion is known as *file globbing* or simply *globbing*.

 The way wildcards are expanded can lead to undesirable consequences. For instance, suppose you want to copy two files, specified via a wildcard, to another directory, but you forget to give the destination directory. The cp command (described shortly) will interpret the command as a request to copy the first of the files over the second.

File Commands

A few file-manipulation commands are extremely important to everyday file operations. These commands enable you to list, copy, move, rename, and delete files.

The *ls* Command

To manipulate files, it's helpful to know what they are. This is the job of the ls command, whose name is short for *list*. The ls command displays the names of files in a directory. Its syntax is simple:

```
ls [options] [files]
```

The command supports a huge number of options; consult ls's man page for details. The most useful options include the following:

Display All Files   Normally, ls omits files whose names begin with a dot (.). These dot files are often configuration files that aren't usually of interest. Adding the -a or --all parameter displays dot files.

Color Listing   The --color option produces a color-coded listing that differentiates directories, symbolic links, and so on by displaying them in different colors. This works at the Linux console, in xterm windows in X, and from some types of remote logins, but some remote-login programs don't support color displays. Some Linux distributions configure their shells to use this option by default.

Display Directory Names   Normally, if you type a directory name as one of the *files*, ls displays the contents of that directory. The same thing happens if a directory name matches a wildcard. Adding the -d or --directory parameter changes this behavior to list only the directory name, which is sometimes preferable.

Long Listing   The ls command normally displays filenames only. The -l parameter (a lowercase L) produces a long listing that includes information such as the file's permission string (described in "Understanding Permissions"), owner, group, size, and creation date.

Display File Type   The -F or --file-type option appends an indicator code to the end of each name so you know what type of file it is. The meanings are as follows:

/	Directory
@	Symbolic link
=	Socket
|	Pipe

Recursive Listing   The -R or --recursive option causes ls to display directory contents recursively. That is, if the target directory contains a subdirectory, ls displays both the files in the target directory *and* the files in its subdirectory. The result can be a huge listing if a directory has many subdirectories.

Both the *options* list and the *files* list are optional. If you omit the *files* list, ls displays the contents of the current directory. You may instead give one or more file or directory names, in which case ls displays information about those files or directories, as in this example:

```
$ ls -F /usr /bin/ls
/bin/ls*

/usr:
bin/    include/  lib32/  local/  share/  X11R6/games/  lib/    lib64@
sbin/   src/
```

This output shows both the /bin/ls program file and the contents of the /usr directory. The latter consists mainly of subdirectories, but it includes one symbolic link as well. By default, ls creates a listing that's sorted by filename, as shown in this example. In the past, uppercase letters (as in X11R6) appeared before lowercase letters (as in bin); however, recent versions of ls sort in a case-insensitive manner.

One of the most common ls options is -l, which creates a long listing like this:

```
$ ls -l t*
-rwxr-xr-x  1 rodsmith users      111 Apr 13 13:48  test
-rw-r--r--  1 rodsmith users   176322 Dec 16 09:34  thttpd-2.20b-1.i686.rpm
-rw-r--r--  1 rodsmith users  1838045 Apr 24 18:52  tomsrtbt-1.7.269.tar.gz
-rw-r--r--  1 rodsmith users  3265021 Apr 22 23:46  tripwire.rpm
```

This output includes the permission strings, ownership, file sizes, and file creation dates in addition to the filenames. This example also illustrates the use of the * wildcard, which matches any string—thus, t* matches any filename that begins with t.

You can combine multiple options by merging them with a single preceding dash, as in ls -lF to get a long listing that also includes file type codes. This can save a bit of typing compared to the alternative of ls -l -F.

The *cp* Command

The cp command copies a file. Its basic syntax is as follows:

```
cp [options] source destination
```

The *source* is normally one or more files, and the *destination* may be a file (when the source is a single file) or a directory (when the source is one or more files). When copying to a directory, cp preserves the original filename; otherwise, it gives the new file the filename indicated by *destination*. The command supports a large number of options; consult its man page for more information. Some of the useful options enable you to modify the command's operation in helpful ways:

Force Overwrite   The -f or --force option forces the system to overwrite any existing files without prompting.

Use Interactive Mode   The -i or --interactive option causes cp to ask you before overwriting any existing files.

Preserve Ownership and Permissions   Normally, a copied file is owned by the user who issues the cp command and uses that account's default permissions. The -p or --preserve option preserves ownership and permissions, if possible.

Perform a Recursive Copy   If you use the -R or --recursive option and specify a directory as the *source*, the entire directory, including its subdirectories, is copied. Although -r also performs a recursive copy, its behavior with files other than ordinary files and directories is unspecified. Most cp implementations use -r as a synonym for -R, but this behavior isn't guaranteed.

Perform an Archive Copy   The -a or --archive option is similar to -R, but it also preserves ownership and copies links as is. The -R option copies the files to which symbolic links point rather than the symbolic links themselves. (Links are described in more detail later in this chapter in "Managing Links.")

Perform an Update Copy   The -u or --update option tells cp to copy the file only if the original is newer than the target or if the target doesn't exist.

This list of cp options is incomplete but covers the most useful options. Consult cp's man page for information about additional cp options.

As an example, the following command copies the /etc/fstab configuration file to a backup location in /root, but only if the original /etc/fstab is newer than the existing backup:

```
# cp -u /etc/fstab /root/fstab-backup
```

The *mv* Command

The mv command (short for *move*) is commonly used both to move files and directories from one location to another and to rename them. Linux doesn't distinguish between these two types of operations, although many users do. The syntax of mv is similar to that of cp:

```
mv [options] source destination
```

The command takes many of the same *options* as cp does. From the earlier list, --preserve, --recursive, and --archive don't apply to mv, but the others do.

To move one or more files or directories, specify the files as the *source* and specify a directory or (optionally, for a single-file move) a filename for the *destination*:

```
$ mv document.odt important/purchases/
```

This example uses a trailing slash (/) on the destination directory. This practice can help avoid problems caused by typos. For instance, if the destination directory were mistyped as important/purchase (missing the final s), mv would move document.odt into the important directory under the filename purchase. Adding the trailing slash makes it explicit that you intend to move the file into a subdirectory. If it doesn't exist, mv complains, so you're not left with mysterious misnamed files. You can also use the Tab key to avoid problems. When you press Tab in many Linux shells, such as bash, the shell tries to complete the filename automatically, reducing the risk of a typo.

The preceding command copies the document.odt file into the important/purchases subdirectory. If the move occurs on one low-level filesystem, Linux does the job by rewriting directory entries; the file's data need not be read and rewritten. This makes mv fast. When the target directory is on another partition or disk, though, Linux must read the original file, rewrite it to the new location, and delete the original. This slows down mv.

Renaming a file with mv works much like moving a file, except that the source and destination filenames are in the same directory, as shown here:

```
$ mv document.odt washer-order.odt
```

This renames document.odt to washer-order.odt in the same directory. You can combine these two forms as well:

```
$ mv document.odt important/purchases/washer-order.odt
```

This command simultaneously moves and renames the file.

You can move or rename entire directories using mv, too; just specify one or more directories as the *source* in the command. For instance, consider the following commands:

```
$ mv important critical
$ mv critical /tmp/
```

The first of these commands renames the important subdirectory as critical in the current directory. The second command moves the renamed subdirectory to the /tmp directory. (You could combine these two commands to **mv important /tmp/critical**.) The form of these commands is identical to the form of mv when used with files, although you may optionally add a trailing slash (/) to directory names.

The *rm* Command

To delete a file, use the rm command, whose name is short for *remove*. Its syntax is simple:

```
rm [options] files
```

The rm command accepts many of the same *options* as cp or mv. Of those described with cp, --preserve, --archive, and --update don't apply to rm, but all the others do. With rm, -r is synonymous with -R.

By default, Linux doesn't provide any sort of "trash-can" functionality for its rm command; once you've deleted a file with rm, it's gone and cannot be recovered without retrieving it from a backup or performing low-level disk maintenance (such as with debugfs). Therefore, you should be cautious when using rm, particularly when you're logged on as root. This is especially true when you're using the -R option, which can destroy a large part of your Linux installation! Many Linux GUI file managers do implement trash-can functionality so that you can easily recover files moved to the trash (assuming you haven't emptied the trash), so you may want to use a file manager for removing files.

The *touch* Command

Linux-native filesystems maintain three time stamps for every file:

- Last file-modification time

- Last inode change time

- Last access time

Various programs rely on these time stamps; for instance, the make utility (which helps compile a program from source code) uses the time stamps to determine which source-code files must be recompiled if an object file already exists for a particular file. Thus, sometimes you may need to modify the time stamps. This is the job of the touch command, which has the following syntax:

```
touch [options] files
```

By default, touch sets the modification and access times to the current time. You might use this if, for instance, you wanted make to recompile a particular source code file even though a newer object file existed. If the specified *files* don't already exist, touch creates them as empty files. This can be handy if you want to create dummy files—say, to experiment with other file-manipulation commands.

You can pass various *options* to touch to have it change its behavior:

Change Only the Access Time   The -a or --time=*atime* option causes touch to change the access time alone, not the modification time.

Change Only the Modification Time   The -m or --time=*mtime* option causes touch to change the modification time alone, not the access time.

Do Not Create File   If you don't want touch to create any files that don't already exist, pass it the -c or --no-create option.

Set the Time as Specified   The -t *timestamp* option sets the time to the specified *timestamp*. This value is given in the form *MMDDhhmm*[[*CC*]*YY*][.*ss*], where *MM* is the month, *DD* is the day, *hh* is the hour (on a 24-hour clock), *mm* is the minute, [*CC*]*YY* is the year (such as 2012 or 12, which are equivalent), and *ss* is the second. Another way to set a particular time is with the -r *reffile* or --reference=*reffile* option, where *reffile* is a file whose time stamp you want to replicate.

File Archiving Commands

A file archiving tool collects a group of files into a single "package" file that you can easily move around on a single system; back up to a recordable DVD, tape, or other removable media; or transfer across a network. Linux supports several archiving commands, the most prominent being tar and cpio. The dd command, although not technically an archiving command, is similar in some ways, because it can copy an entire partition or disk into a file, or vice versa.

The zip format, which is common on Windows, is supported by the Linux zip and unzip commands. Other archive formats, such as the Roshal Archive (RAR) and StuffIt, can also be manipulated using Linux utilities. These archive formats may be important in some environments, but they aren't covered on the exam.

The *tar* Utility

The tar program's name stands for "tape archiver." Despite this fact, you can use tar to archive data to other media. In fact, *tarballs* (archive files created by tar and typically compressed with gzip or bzip2) are often used for transferring multiple files between computers in one step, such as when distributing source code.

The tar program is a complex package with many options, but most of what you'll do with the utility can be covered with a few common commands. Table 4.1 lists the primary tar commands, and Table 4.2 lists the qualifiers that modify what the commands do. Whenever you run tar, you use exactly one command, and you usually use at least one qualifier.

TABLE 4.1   tar commands

Command	Abbreviation	Description
--create	c	Creates an archive
--concatenate	A	Appends tar files to an archive
--append	r	Appends non-tar files to an archive
--update	u	Appends files that are newer than those in an archive
--diff or --compare	d	Compares an archive to files on disk
--list	t	Lists an archive's contents
--extract or --get	x	Extracts files from an archive

TABLE 4.2   tar qualifiers

Qualifier	Abbreviation	Description
--directory *dir*	C	Changes to directory *dir* before performing operations
--file [*host*:]*file*	f	Uses the file called *file* on the computer called *host* as the archive file

`--listed -incremental` *file*	g	Performs an incremental backup or restore, using *file* as a list of previously archived files
`--one-file-system`	l (on old versions of tar)	Backs up or restores only one filesystem (partition)
`--multi-volume`	M	Creates or extracts a multi-tape archive
`--tape-length` *N*	L	Changes tapes after *N* kilobytes
`--same-permissions`	p	Preserves all protection information
`--absolute-paths`	P	Retains the leading / on filenames
`--verbose`	v	Lists all files read or extracted; when used with `--list`, displays file sizes, ownership, and time stamps
`--verify`	W	Verifies the archive after writing it
`--exclude` *file*	(none)	Excludes *file* from the archive
`--exclude-from` *file*	X	Excludes files listed in *file* from the archive
`--gzip` or `--ungzip`	z	Processes an archive through gzip
`--bzip2`	j (some older versions used I or y)	Processes an archive through bzip2
`--xz`	J	Processes an archive through xz

Of the commands listed in Table 4.1, the most commonly used are `--create`, `--extract`, and `--list`. The most useful qualifiers from Table 4.2 are `--file`, `--listed-incremental`, `--one-file-system`, `--same-permissions`, `--gzip`, `--bzip2`, `--xz`, and `--verbose`. If you fail to specify a filename with the `--file` qualifier, `tar` will attempt to use a default device, which is often (but not always) a tape device file.

Three compression tools—`gzip`, `bzip2`, and `xz`—are often used with `tar`, which applies compression to the tarball as a whole rather than to the individual files. This method of compressing reduces the tarball's size compared to compressing constituent files and then adding them to the archive, but it makes the archive more susceptible to damage; a single-byte error early in the archive can make it impossible to recover any subsequent data.

Of the three compression tools, gzip is the oldest and provides the least compression, bzip2 provides improved compression, and xz is the newest and provides the best compression. Typically, files compressed with these utilities have .gz, .bz2, or .xz extensions, respectively. Compressed tarballs sometimes use their own special extensions, such as .tgz for a gzip-compressed tarball or .tbz for one compressed with bzip2.

As an example of tar in use, consider archiving and compressing the my-work subdirectory of your home directory to a USB flash drive mounted at /media/pen. The following command will do the trick:

```
$ tar cvfz /media/pen/my-work.tgz ~/my-work
```

If you then transfer this flash drive to another system, mount it at /media/usb, and want to extract the archive, you can do so with another command:

```
$ tar xvfz /media/usb/my-work.tgz
```

Instead of using the compression options, you can use a pipe to connect a compression tool to tar when extracting data. For instance, **gunzip -c tarball.tgz | tar xvf -** uncompresses tarball.tgz.

The preceding command creates a subdirectory called my-work in the current working directory and populates it with the files from the archive. If you don't know what's in an archive, it's a good practice to examine it with the --list command before extracting its contents. Although tarballs usually contain a single subdirectory, sometimes tarballs contain many files without a "carrier" subdirectory. Extracting such tarballs drops these files in your current directory, which can make it difficult to determine which files come from the tarball and which were already present.

The *cpio* Utility

The cpio program is similar in principle to tar, but the details of its operation differ. As with tar, you can direct its output straight to a tape device or to a regular file. Backing up to a tape device can be a convenient way to back up the computer because it requires no intermediate storage. To restore data, you use cpio to read directly from the tape device file or from a regular file.

The cpio utility has three operating modes:

Copy-Out Mode   This mode, activated by use of the -o or --create option, creates an archive and copies files into it.

Copy-In Mode   You activate copy-in mode by using the -i or --extract option. This mode extracts data from an existing archive. If you provide a filename or a pattern to match, cpio extracts only the files whose names match the pattern you provide.

Copy-Pass Mode   This mode is activated by the -p or --pass-through option. It combines the copy-out and copy-in modes, enabling you to copy a directory tree from one location to another.

The copy-out and copy-in modes are named confusingly. Think of them as referring to copying out of or in to the computer's main directory tree, rather than the archive file.

In addition to the options used to select the mode, cpio accepts many other options, the most important of which are summarized in Table 4.3. To create an archive, you combine the --create (or -o) option with one or more of the options in Table 4.3; to restore data, you do the same, but you use --extract (or -i). In either case, cpio acts on filenames that you type at the console. In practice, you'll probably use the redirection operator (<) to pass a filename list to the program.

TABLE 4.3: Options for use with cpio

Option	Abbreviation	Description
--reset-access-time	-a	Resets the access time after reading a file so that it doesn't appear to have been read.
--append	-A	Appends data to an existing archive.
--pattern-file=*filename*	-E *filename*	Uses the contents of *filename* as a list of files to be extracted in copy-in mode.
--file=*filename*	-F *filename*	Uses *filename* as the cpio archive file; if this parameter is omitted, cpio uses standard input or output.
--format=*format*	-H *format*	Uses a specified format for the archive file. Common values for *format* include bin (the default, an old binary format), crc (a newer binary format with a checksum), and tar (the format used by tar).
N/A	-I *filename*	Uses the specified *filename* instead of standard input. (Unlike -F, this option does not redirect output data.)
--no-absolute-filenames	N/A	In copy-in mode, extracts files relative to the current directory, even if filenames in the archive contain full directory paths.
N/A	-O *filename*	Uses the specified *filename* instead of standard output. (Unlike -F, this option does not redirect input data.)
--list	-t	Displays a table of contents for the input.
--unconditional	-u	Replaces all files without first asking for verification.
--verbose	-v	Displays filenames as they're added to or extracted from the archive. When used with -t, displays additional listing information (similar to ls -l).

To use cpio to archive a directory, you must pass a list of files to the utility using standard input. You can do this with the find utility (described in more detail later in "The find Command"):

```
$ find ./my-work | cpio -o > /media/usb/my-work.cpio
```

The resulting archive file is uncompressed, though. To compress the data, you must include a compression utility, such as gzip, in the pipe:

```
$ find ./my-work | cpio -o | gzip > /media/usb/my-work.cpio.gz
```

Extracting data from an uncompressed cpio archive (say, on another computer with the media mounted at /media/usb) entails using the -i option, but no pipe is required:

```
$ cpio -i < /media/usb/my-work.cpio
```

If your cpio archive is compressed, you must first uncompress it with gunzip. By using the -c option to this command, you can pass its output to cpio in a pipe:

```
$ gunzip -c /media/usb/my-work.cpio.gz | cpio -i
```

To uncompress an archive compressed with bzip2, you would use bunzip2 -c in the pipe rather than gunzip -c. If the archive is compressed with xz, you would use unxz -b in the pipe.

The *dd* Utility

Sometimes you want to archive a filesystem at a very low level. For instance, you may want to create a representation of a CD-ROM that you can store on your hard disk or back up a filesystem that Linux can't understand. To do so, you can use the dd program. This utility is a low-level copying program, and when you give it the device file for a partition as input, it copies that partition's contents to the output file you specify. This output file can be another partition identifier, a tape device, or a regular file, to name three possibilities. The input and output files are passed with the if=*file* and of=*file* options:

```
# dd if=/dev/sda3 of=/dev/st0
```

This command backs up the /dev/sda3 disk partition to /dev/st0 (a SCSI tape drive). The result is a very low-level backup of the partition that can be restored by swapping the if= and of= options:

```
# dd if=/dev/st0 of=/dev/sda3
```

The dd utility can be a good way to create exact backups of entire partitions, but as a general backup tool, it has serious problems. It backs up the *entire* partition, including any empty space. For instance, a 2GiB partition that holds just 5MiB of files will require 2GiB of storage space. Restoring individual files is also impossible unless the backup device is a random access device that can be mounted; if you back up to tape, you must restore everything (at least to a temporary file or partition) to recover a single file. Finally, you can't easily restore data to a partition that's smaller than the original partition; and when restoring to a larger partition, you'll end up wasting some of the space available on that partition.

Despite these problems, dd can be handy in some situations. It can be a good way to make an exact copy of a removable disk (including an optical disc), for instance. You can use dd to copy a disk for which Linux lacks filesystem drivers. If you need to create multiple identical Linux installations, you can do so by using dd to copy a working installation to multiple computers, as long as they have hard disks the same size.

You can also use dd in some other capacities. For instance, if you need an empty file of a particular size, you can copy from the /dev/zero device (a Linux device that returns nothing but zeroes) to a target file. You'll need to use the bs=*size* and count=*length* options to set the block size and length of the file, though:

```
$ dd if=/dev/zero of=empty-file.img bs=1024 count=720
```

This example creates a 720KiB (1024 × 720 bytes) empty file. You might then manipulate this file by, for example, creating a filesystem on it with mkfs.

Real World Scenario

Backing Up Using Optical Media

Optical media require special backup procedures. Normally, cdrecord accepts input from a program like mkisofs, which creates an ISO-9660 or UDF filesystem—the type of filesystem that's most often found on CD-ROMs and DVDs.

One option for backing up to optical discs is to use mkisofs and then cdrecord to copy files to the disc. If you copy files "raw" this way, though, you'll lose some information, such as write permission bits. You'll have better luck if you create a tar or cpio archive on disk. You can then use mkisofs to place that archive in an ISO-9660 or UDF filesystem and then burn the image file to the optical disc. The result will be a disc that you can mount and that will contain an archive you can read with tar or cpio.

A somewhat more direct option is to create an archive file and burn it directly to the optical disc using cdrecord, bypassing mkisofs. Such a disc won't be mountable in the usual way, but you can access the archive directly by using the CD-ROM device file. On restoration, this works much like a tape restore except that you specify the optical device filename (such as /dev/cdrom) instead of the tape device filename (such as /dev/st0).

Managing Links

In Linux, a *link* is a way to give a file multiple identities, similar to shortcuts in Windows and aliases in Mac OS. Linux employs links to help make files more accessible, to give commands multiple names, to enable programs that look for the same files in different locations to access the same files, and so on. Two types of links exist: *hard links* and *symbolic links* (aka *soft links*). (Their differences are described in more detail shortly.) The ln command creates links. Its syntax is similar to that of cp:

```
ln [options] source link
```

The *source* is the original file, and the *link* is the name of the link you want to create. This command supports options that have several effects:

Remove Target Files   The -f or --force option causes ln to remove any existing links or files that have the target *link* name. The -i or --interactive option has a similar effect, but it queries you before replacing existing files and links.

Create Directory Hard Links   Ordinarily, you can't create hard links to directories. The root user can *attempt* to do so, though, by passing the -d, -F, or --directory option to ln. (Symbolic links to directories aren't a problem.) In practice, this feature is unlikely to work because most filesystems don't support it.

Create a Symbolic Link   The ln command creates hard links by default. To create a symbolic link, pass the -s or --symbolic option to the command.

A few other options exist to perform more obscure tasks; consult ln's man page for details.

By default, ln creates hard links, which are produced by creating two directory entries that point to the same file (more precisely, the same inode). Both filenames are equally valid and prominent; neither is a "truer" filename than the other, except that one was created first (when creating the file) and the other was created second. To delete the file, you must delete both hard links to the file. Because of the way hard links are created, they must exist on a single low-level filesystem; you can't create a hard link from, say, your root (/) filesystem to a separate filesystem you've mounted on it, such as /home (if it's a separate filesystem). The underlying filesystem must support hard links. All Linux-native filesystems support this feature, but some non-Linux filesystems don't.

Symbolic links, by contrast, are special file types. The symbolic link is a separate file whose contents point to the linked-to file. Linux knows to access the linked-to file whenever you try to access the symbolic link, so in most respects accessing a symbolic link works just like accessing the original file. Because symbolic links are basically files that contain filenames, they can point across low-level filesystems—you can point from the root (/) filesystem to a file on a separate /home filesystem, for instance. The lookup process for accessing the original file from the link consumes a tiny bit of time, so symbolic link access is slower than hard link access—but not by enough that you'd notice in any but very bizarre conditions or artificial tests. Long directory listings show the linked-to file:

```
$ ls -l alink.odt
lrwxrwxrwx  1 rodsmith users 8 Dec  2 15:31 alink.odt -> test.odt
```

In practice, symbolic links are more common than hard links; their disadvantages are minor, and the ability to link across filesystems and to directories can be important. Linux employs links in certain critical system administration tasks. For instance, System V (SysV) startup scripts use symbolic links in runlevel directories, as described in Chapter 5, "Booting Linux and Editing Files." Certain commands that have historically been known by multiple names are also often accessible via links. For example, the /sbin/fsck.ext2, /sbin/fsck.ext3, /sbin/fsck.ext4, and /sbin/e2fsck programs are usually links (hard links on some systems, symbolic links on others). You can often leave these links alone, but sometimes you must adjust them. Chapter 5 describes changing the SysV startup script links to affect what programs run when the system boots, for instance.

Directory Commands

Most of the commands that apply to files also apply to directories. In particular, ls, mv, touch, and ln all work with directories, with the caveats mentioned earlier. The cp command also works with directories, but only when you use a recursion option, such as -r. A couple of additional commands, mkdir and rmdir, enable you to create and delete directories, respectively.

The *mkdir* Command

The mkdir command creates a directory. This command's official syntax is as follows:

mkdir [*options*] *directory-name(s)*

In most cases, mkdir is used without *options*, but a few are supported:

Set Mode   The -m *mode* or --mode=*mode* option causes the new directory to have the specified permission mode, expressed as an octal number. (The upcoming section "Understanding Permissions" describes permission modes.)

Create Parent Directories   Normally, if you specify the creation of a directory within a directory that doesn't exist, mkdir responds with a No such file or directory error and doesn't create the directory. If you include the -p or --parents option, though, mkdir creates the necessary parent directory.

The *rmdir* Command

The rmdir command is the opposite of mkdir; it destroys a directory. Its syntax is similar:

rmdir [*options*] *directory-name(s)*

Like mkdir, rmdir supports few options, the most important of which handle these tasks:

Ignore Failures on Non-empty Directories   Normally, if a directory contains files or other directories, rmdir doesn't delete it and returns an error message. With the --ignore-fail-on-non-empty option, rmdir still doesn't delete the directory, but it doesn't return an error message.

Delete Tree   The -p or --parents option causes rmdir to delete an entire directory tree. For instance, typing **rmdir -p one/two/three** causes rmdir to delete one/two/three, then one/two, and finally one, provided no other files or directories are present.

> When you're deleting an entire directory tree filled with files, you should use rm -R rather than rmdir. This is because rm -R deletes files within the specified directory but rmdir doesn't, so rmdir can't do the job.

Managing File Ownership

Security is an important topic that cuts across many types of commands and Linux subsystems. In the case of files, security is built on file ownership and file permissions. These two topics are closely intertwined; ownership is meaningless without permissions that use it, and permissions rely on the existence of ownership.

Ownership is two-tiered: Each file has an individual owner and a group with which it's associated (sometimes called the group owner, or simply the file's group). Each group can contain an arbitrary number of users, as described in Chapter 7, "Administering the System." The two types of ownership enable you to provide three tiers of permissions to control access to files: by the file's owner, by the file's group, and to all other users. The commands to manage these two types of ownership are similar, but they aren't identical.

Assessing File Ownership

You can learn who owns a file with the ls command, which was described earlier. In particular, that command's -l option produces a long listing, which includes both ownership and permission information:

```
$ ls -l
total 1141
-rw-r--r--  1 rodsmith users 219648 Mar  8 13:06 4425ch02.doc
-rw-r--r--  1 rodsmith users 942590 Mar  6 23:31 f0201.tif
```

This long listing includes the username of the owner (rodsmith for both files in this example) and the group name of the files' groups (users for both files in this example). The permission string (-rw-r--r-- for both files in this example) is also important for file security, as described later in "Controlling Access to Files."

In most cases, the usernames associated with files are the same as login usernames. Files can, however, be owned by accounts that aren't ordinary login accounts. For instance, some servers have accounts of their own, and server-specific files may be owned by these accounts.

If you delete an account, as described in Chapter 7, the account's files don't vanish, but the account name does. Internally, Linux uses numbers rather than names, so you'll see numbers in place of the username and group name in the ls output. Depending on the file, you may want to archive it, reassign ownership to an existing user, or delete it.

Changing a File's Owner

Whenever a file is created, it's assigned an owner. The superuser can change a file's owner using the chown command, which has the following syntax:

```
chown [options] [newowner][:newgroup] filenames
```

As you might expect, the *newowner* and *newgroup* variables are the new owner and group for the file; you can provide both or omit either, but you can't omit both. For instance, suppose you want to give ownership of a file to sally and the skyhook group:

```
# chown sally:skyhook forward.odt
```

Linux's chown command accepts a dot (.) in place of a colon (:) to delimit the owner and group, at least as of the core file utilities version 8.14. The use of a dot has been deprecated, though, meaning that the developers favor the alternative and may eventually eliminate the use of a dot as a feature.

You can use several options with chown, most of which are fairly obscure. One that's most likely to be useful is -R or --recursive, which implements the ownership change on an entire directory tree. Consult the man page for chown for information about additional options.

Only root may use the chown command to change the ownership of files. If an ordinary user tries to use it, the result is an Operation not permitted error message. Ordinary users *may*, however, use chown to change the group of files that they own, provided that the users belong to the target group.

Changing a File's Group

Both root and ordinary users may run the chgrp command, which changes a file's group. (Ordinary users may only change a file's group to a group to which the user belongs.) This command's syntax is similar to, but simpler than, that of chown:

chgrp [*options*] *newgroup filenames*

The chgrp command accepts many of the same options as chown, including -R or --recursive. In practice, chgrp provides a subset of the chown functionality.

Controlling Access to Files

The bulk of the complexity in file ownership and permissions is on the permissions end of things. Linux's system of permissions is moderately complex, so understanding how it works is critical to any manipulation of permissions. With the basic information in hand, you can tackle the commands used to change file permissions.

Understanding Permissions

Linux permissions are fairly complex. In addition to providing access control for files, a few special permission bits exist, which provide some unusual features.

The Meanings of Permission Bits

Consider the following file access control string that's displayed with the -l option to ls:

```
$ ls -l test
-rwxr-xr-x  1 rodsmith users       111 Apr 13 13:48  test
```

This string (-rwxr-xr-x in this example) is 10 characters long. The first character has special meaning—it's the *file type code*. The type code determines how Linux will interpret the file—as ordinary data, a directory, or a special file type. Table 4.4 summarizes Linux type codes.

TABLE 4.4   Linux file type codes

Code	Meaning
-	Normal data file; may be text, an executable program, graphics, compressed data, or just about any other type of data.
d	Directory; disk directories are files just like any others, but they contain filenames and pointers to disk inodes.

l	Symbolic link; the file contains the name of another file or directory. When Linux accesses the symbolic link, it tries to read the linked-to file.
p	Named pipe; a pipe enables two running Linux programs to communicate with each other. One opens the pipe for reading, and the other opens it for writing, enabling data to be transferred between the programs.
s	Socket; a socket is similar to a named pipe, but it permits network and bidirectional links.
b	Block device; a file that corresponds to a hardware device to and from which data is transferred in blocks of more than one byte. Disk devices (hard disks, floppies, CD-ROMs, and so on) are common block devices.
c	Character device; a file that corresponds to a hardware device to and from which data is transferred in units of one byte. Examples include parallel port, RS-232 serial port, and audio devices.

The remaining nine characters of the permission string (rwxr-xr-x in the example) are broken up into three groups of three characters, as illustrated in Figure 4.1. The first group controls the file owner's access to the file, the second controls the group's access to the file, and the third controls all other users' access to the file (often referred to as *world permissions*).

FIGURE 4.1   The main Linux permission options are encoded in 10 bits, the last 9 of which are grouped into three groups of 3 bits each.

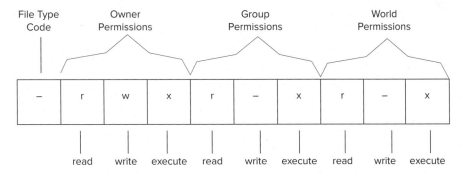

In each of these three cases, the permission string determines the presence or absence of each of three types of access: read, write, and execute. Read and write permissions are fairly self-explanatory, at least for ordinary files. If the execute permission is present, it means that the file may be run as a program. (Of course, this doesn't turn a non-program file into a program; it only means that a user may run a file if it's a program. Setting the execute bit on a non-program file will probably cause no real harm, but it could be confusing.) The absence of the permission is denoted by a dash (-) in the permission string. The presence of the permission is indicated by a letter—r for read, w for write, or x for execute.

Thus, the example permission string rwxr-xr-x means that the file's owner, members of the file's group, and all other users can read and execute the file. Only the file's owner has write permission to the file. You can easily exclude those who don't belong to the file's group, or even all but the file's owner, by changing the permission string, as described in "Changing a File's Mode" later in this chapter.

Individual permissions, such as execute access for the file's owner, are often referred to as *permission bits*. This is because Linux encodes this information in binary form. Because it's binary, the permission information can be expressed as a single 9-bit number. This number is usually expressed in octal (base 8) form because a base-8 number is 3 bits in length, which means that the base-8 representation of a permission string is three characters long, one character for each of the owner, group, and world permissions. The read, write, and execute permissions each correspond to one of these bits. The result is that you can determine owner, group, or world permissions by adding base-8 numbers: 1 for execute permission, 2 for write permission, and 4 for read permission.

Table 4.5 shows some examples of common permissions and their meanings. This table is necessarily incomplete; with 9 permission bits, the total number of possible permissions is 2^9, or 512. Most of those possibilities are peculiar, and you're not likely to encounter or create them except by accident.

TABLE 4.5   Example permissions and their likely uses

Permission string	Octal code	Meaning
rwxrwxrwx	777	Read, write, and execute permissions for all users.
rwxr-xr-x	755	Read and execute permission for all users. The file's owner also has write permission.
rwxr-x---	750	Read and execute permission for the owner and group. The file's owner also has write permission. Users who aren't the file's owner or members of the group have no access to the file.
rwx------	700	Read, write, and execute permissions for the file's owner only; all others have no access.
rw-rw-rw-	666	Read and write permissions for all users. No execute permissions for anybody.
rw-rw-r--	664	Read and write permissions for the owner and group. Read-only permission for all others.
rw-rw----	660	Read and write permissions for the owner and group. No world permissions.

rw-r--r--	644	Read and write permissions for the owner. Read-only permission for all others.
rw-r-----	640	Read and write permissions for the owner, and read-only permission for the group. No permission for others.
rw-------	600	Read and write permissions for the owner. No permission for anybody else.
r--------	400	Read permission for the owner. No permission for anybody else.

Execute permission makes sense for ordinary files, but it's meaningless for most other file types, such as device files. Directories, though, use the execute bit another way. When a directory's execute bit is set, that means that the directory's contents may be searched. This is a highly desirable characteristic for directories, so you'll almost never find a directory on which the execute bit is *not* set in conjunction with the read bit.

Directories can be confusing with respect to write permission. Recall that directories are files that are interpreted in a special way. As such, if a user can write to a directory, that user can create, delete, or rename files in the directory, even if the user isn't the owner of those files and does not have permission to write to those files. You can use the *sticky bit* (described shortly, in "Special Permission Bits") to alter this behavior.

Symbolic links are unusual with respect to permissions. This file type always has 777 (rwxrwxrwx) permissions, thus granting all users full access to the file. This access applies only to the link file itself, however, not to the linked-to file. In other words, all users can read the contents of the link to discover the name of the file to which it points, but the permissions on the linked-to file determine its file access. Changing the permissions on a symbolic link affects the linked-to file.

Many of the permission rules don't apply to root. The superuser can read or write any file on the computer—even files that grant access to nobody (that is, those that have 000 permissions). The superuser still needs an execute bit to be set to run a program file, but the superuser has the power to change the permissions on any file, so this limitation isn't very substantial. Some files may be inaccessible to root, but only because of an underlying restriction—for instance, even root can't access a hard disk that's not installed in the computer.

Special Permission Bits

A few special permission options are also supported, and they may be indicated by changes to the permission string:

Set User ID (SUID)   The *set user ID* (SUID) option is used in conjunction with executable files, and it tells Linux to run the program with the permissions of whoever owns the file rather than with the permissions of the user who runs the program. For instance, if a file is owned by root and has its SUID bit set, the program runs with root privileges and can therefore read any file on the computer. Some servers and other system programs run this way, which is often called SUID root. SUID programs are indicated by an s in the owner's execute bit position in the permission string, as in rwsr-xr-x.

Set Group ID (SGID)   The *set group ID* (SGID) option is similar to the SUID option, but it sets the group of the running program to the group of the file. It's indicated by an s in the group execute bit position in the permission string, as in rwxr-sr-x. When the SGID bit is set on a directory, new files or subdirectories created in the original directory will inherit the group ownership of the directory, rather than be based on the user's current default group.

Sticky Bit   The sticky bit has changed meaning during the course of Unix history. In modern Linux implementations (and most modern versions of Unix), it's used to protect files from being deleted by those who don't own the files. When this bit is present on a directory, the directory's files can be deleted only by their owners, the directory's owner, or root. The sticky bit is indicated by a t in the world execute bit position, as in rwxr-xr-t.

WARNING   These special permission bits all have security implications. SUID and SGID programs (and particularly SUID root programs) are potential security risks. Although some programs must have their SUID bits set to function properly, most don't, and you shouldn't set these bits unless you're certain that doing so is necessary. The sticky bit isn't dangerous this way, but because it affects who may delete files in a directory, you should consider its effect—or the effect of not having it—on directories to which many users should have write access, such as /tmp. Typically, such directories have their sticky bits set.

 Real World Scenario

Using ACLs

Unix-style permissions have served Linux well since its creation and are emphasized on the exam, but a new and improved permission system is now available. An *access control list* (ACL) is a list of users or groups and the permissions they're given. Linux ACLs, like Linux owner, group, and world permissions, consist of three permission bits, one each for read, write, and execute permissions. The file's owner can assign ACLs to an arbitrary number of users and groups, making ACLs more flexible than Linux permissions, which are limited to groups defined by the system administrator.

ACLs require support in the underlying filesystem. All the major Linux filesystems now support ACLs, but you may need to recompile your kernel (or at least the relevant kernel module) to activate this support.

ACLs require their own commands to set and view. The setfacl command sets an ACL, and the getfacl command displays the ACLs for a file. Consult these commands' man pages for more information.

Changing a File's Mode

You can modify a file's permissions using the chmod command. This command may be issued in many different ways to achieve the same effect. Its basic syntax is as follows:

chmod [*options*] [*mode*[,*mode*...]] *filename*...

The chmod options are similar to those of chown and chgrp. In particular, --recursive (or -R) changes all the files in a directory tree.

Most of the complexity of chmod comes in the specification of the file's mode. You can specify the mode in two basic forms: as an octal number or as a symbolic mode, which is a set of codes related to the string representation of the permissions.

The octal representation of the mode is the same as that described earlier and summarized in Table 4.5. For instance, to change permissions on report.tex to rw-r--r--, you can issue the following command:

$ chmod 644 report.tex

In addition, you can precede the three digits for the owner, group, and world permissions with another digit that sets special permissions. Three bits are supported (and hence they have values between 0 and 7): adding 4 sets the set user ID (SUID) bit, adding 2 sets the set group ID (SGID) bit, and adding 1 sets the sticky bit. If you omit the first digit (as in the preceding example), Linux clears all three bits. Using four digits causes the first to be interpreted as the special permissions code.

For instance, suppose you've acquired a script called bigprogram. You want to set both SUID and SGID bits (6); to make the program readable, writeable, and executable by the owner (7); to make it readable and executable by the group (5); and to make it completely inaccessible to all others (0). The following commands illustrate how to do this; note the difference in the mode string before and after executing the chmod command:

```
$ ls -l bigprogram
-rw-r--r--    1 rodsmith users    10323 Oct 31 18:58 bigprogram
$ chmod 6750 bigprogram
$ ls -l bigprogram
-rwsr-s---    1 rodsmith users    10323 Oct 31 18:58 bigprogram
```

A symbolic mode, by contrast, consists of three components: a code indicating the permission set you want to modify (the owner, the group, and so on); a symbol indicating whether you want to add, delete, or set the mode equal to the stated value; and a code specifying what the permission should be. Table 4.6 summarizes all these codes. Note that these codes are all case-sensitive.

TABLE 4.6 Codes used in symbolic modes

Permission set code	Meaning	Change type code	Meaning	Permission to modify code	Meaning
u	Owner	+	Add	r	Read
g	Group	–	Remove	w	Write
o	World	=	Set equal to	x	Execute
a	All			X	Execute only if the file is a directory or already has execute permission
				s	SUID or SGID
				t	Sticky bit
				u	Existing owner's permissions
				g	Existing group permissions
				o	Existing world permissions

To use symbolic permission settings, you combine one or more of the codes from the first column of Table 4.6 with one symbol from the third column and one or more codes from the fifth column. You can combine multiple settings by separating them with commas. Table 4.7 provides some examples of chmod using symbolic permission settings.

TABLE 4.7 Examples of symbolic permissions with chmod

Command	Initial permissions	End permissions
chmod a+x bigprogram	rw-r--r--	rwxr-xr-x
chmod ug=rw report.tex	r--------	rw-rw----
chmod o-rwx bigprogram	rwxrwxr-x	rwxrwx---
chmod g=u report.tex	rw-r--r--	rw-rw-r--
chmod g-w,o-rw report.tex	rw-rw-rw-	rw-r-----

As a general rule, symbolic permissions are most useful when you want to make a simple change (such as adding execute or write permissions to one or more classes of users) or when you want to make similar changes to many files without affecting their other permissions (for instance, adding write permissions without affecting execute permissions). Octal permissions are most useful when you want to set a specific absolute permission, such as rw-r--r-- (644). In any event, a system administrator should be familiar with both methods of setting permissions.

A file's owner and root are the only users who may adjust a file's permissions. Even if other users have write access to a directory in which a file resides and write access to the file itself, they may not change the file's permissions (but they may modify or even delete the file). To understand why this is so, you need to know that the file permissions are stored as part of the file's inode, which isn't part of the directory entry. Read/write access to the directory entry, or even the file itself, doesn't give a user the right to change the inode structures (except indirectly—for instance, if a write changes the file's size or a file deletion eliminates the need for the inode).

In Exercise 4.1, you'll experiment with the effect of Linux ownership and permissions on file accessibility.

EXERCISE 4.1

Modifying Ownership and Permissions

During this exercise, you'll need to use three accounts: root and two user accounts, each in a different group. To study these effects, follow these steps:

1. Log in three times using three virtual terminals: once as root, once as user1, and once as user2. (Use usernames appropriate for your system, though. Be sure that user1 and user2 are in different groups.) If you prefer, instead of using virtual terminals, you can open three xterm windows in an X session and use su to acquire each user's privileges.

2. As root, create a scratch directory—say, /tmp/scratch. Type **mkdir /tmp/scratch**.

3. As root, give all users read and write access to the scratch directory by typing **chmod 0777 /tmp/scratch**.

4. In the user1 and user2 login sessions, change to the scratch directory by typing **cd /tmp/scratch**.

5. As user1, copy a short text file to the scratch directory using cp, as in **cp /etc/ fstab ./testfile**.

6. As user1, set 0644 (-rw-r--r--) permissions on the file by typing **chmod 0644 testfile**. Type **ls -l**, and verify that the permission string in the first column matches this value (-rw-r--r--).

EXERCISE 4.1 (Continued)

7. As user2, try to access the file by typing **cat testfile**. The file should appear on the screen.

8. As user2, try to change the name of the file by typing **mv testfile changedfile**. The system won't produce any feedback, but if you type **ls**, you'll see that the file's name has changed. Note that user2 doesn't own the file but can rename it because user2 can write to the directory in which the file resides.

9. As user2, try to change the mode of the file by typing **chmod 0600 changedfile**. The system should respond with an Operation not permitted error because only the file's owner may change its permissions.

10. As user2, try to delete the file by typing **rm changedfile**. Depending on your configuration, the system may or may not ask for verification, but it should permit the deletion. This is true despite the fact that user2 doesn't own the file because user2 can write to the directory in which the file resides.

11. As user1, repeat step 5 to re-create the test file.

12. As user1, give the file more restrictive permissions by typing **chmod 0640**. Typing **ls -l** should reveal permissions of -rw-r-----, meaning that the file's owner can read and write the file, members of the file's group can read it, and other users are given no access.

13. As user2, repeat steps 7–10. The cat operation should fail with a Permission denied error, but steps 8–10 should produce the same results as they did the first time around. (If the cat operation succeeded, then either user2 belongs to the file's group or the file's mode is set incorrectly.)

14. Log out of the user1 and user2 accounts.

15. As root, type **rm -r /tmp/scratch** to delete the scratch directory and its contents.

If you like, you can perform tests with more file permission modes and other file-manipulation commands before step 14.

Setting the Default Mode and Group

When a user creates a file, that file has default ownership and permissions. The default owner is, understandably, the user who created the file. The default group is the user's primary group. The default permissions are configurable. These are defined by the *user mask* (umask), which is set by the umask command. This command takes as input an octal value that represents the bits to be removed from 777 permissions for directories, or from 666 permissions for files, when a new file or directory is created. Table 4.8 summarizes the effect of several possible umask values.

TABLE 4.8 Sample umask values and their effects

Umask	Created files	Created directories
000	666 (rw-rw-rw-)	777 (rwxrwxrwx)
002	664 (rw-rw-r--)	775 (rwxrwxr-x)
022	644 (rw-r--r--)	755 (rwxr-xr-x)
027	640 (rw-r-----)	750 (rwxr-x---)
077	600 (rw-------)	700 (rwx------)
277	400 (r--------)	500 (r-x------)

Note that the umask isn't a simple subtraction from the values of 777 or 666; it's a bit-wise removal. Any bit that's set in the umask is removed from the final permission for new files, but if a bit isn't set (as in the execute bit in ordinary files), its specification in the umask doesn't do any harm. For instance, consider the 7 values in several entries of Table 4.8's Umask column. This corresponds to a binary value of 111. An ordinary file might have rw- (110) permissions, but applying the umask's 7 (111) eliminates 1 values but doesn't touch 0 values, thus producing a (binary) 000 value—that is, --- permissions, expressed symbolically.

Ordinary users can enter the umask command to change the permissions on new files they create. The superuser can also modify the default setting for all users by modifying a system configuration file. Typically, /etc/profile contains one or more umask commands. Setting the umask in /etc/profile may or may not have an effect because it can be overridden at other points, such as a user's own configuration files. Nonetheless, setting the umask in /etc/profile or other system files can be a useful procedure if you want to change the default system policy. Most Linux distributions use a default umask of 002 or 022.

To find what the current umask is, type **umask** alone, without any parameters. Typing **umask -S** produces the umask expressed symbolically rather than in octal form. You may also specify a umask in this way when you want to change it, but in this case, you specify the bits that you *do* want set. For instance, **umask u=rwx,g=rx,o=rx** is equivalent to **umask 022**.

In addition to setting the default mask with umask, users can change their default group with newgrp, as in **newgrp skyhook** to create new files with the group set to the skyhook group. To use this command, the user must be a member of the specified group. The newgrp command also accepts the -l parameter, as in **newgrp -l skyhook**, which reinitializes the environment as if the user had just logged in.

Changing File Attributes

Some filesystems support attributes in addition to those described in the preceding sections. In particular, some Linux-native filesystems support several attributes that you can adjust with the chattr command:

Append Only   The a attribute sets append mode, which disables write access to the file except for appending data. This can be a security feature to prevent accidental or malicious changes to files that record data, such as log files.

Compressed   The c attribute causes the kernel to automatically compress data written to the file and uncompress it when it's read back.

Immutable   The i flag makes a file immutable, which goes a step beyond simply disabling write access to the file. The file can't be deleted, links to it can't be created, and the file can't be renamed.

Data Journaling   The j flag tells the kernel to journal all data written to the file. This improves recoverability of data written to the file after a system crash but can slow performance. This flag has no effect on ext2 filesystems.

Secure Deletion   Ordinarily, when you delete a file its directory entry is removed and its inode is marked as being available for recycling. The data blocks that make up the bulk of the file aren't erased. Setting the s flag changes this behavior; when the file is deleted, the kernel zeros its data blocks, which may be desirable for files that contain sensitive data.

No Tail-Merging   *Tail-merging* is a process in which small pieces of data at the ends of files that don't fill a complete block are merged with similar pieces of data from other files. The result is reduced disk space consumption, particularly when you store many small files rather than a few big ones. Setting the t flag disables this behavior, which is desirable if the filesystem will be read by certain non-kernel drivers, such as those that are part of the Grand Unified Boot Loader (GRUB).

No Access Time Updates   If you set the A attribute, Linux won't update the access time stamp when you access a file. This can reduce disk input/output, which is particularly helpful for saving battery life on laptops.

   This list of attributes is incomplete but includes the most useful options; consult the man page for chattr for more flags. You set the options you want using the minus (-), plus (+), or equal (=) symbol to remove an option from an existing set, add an option to an existing set, or set a precise set of options (overwriting any that already exist), respectively. For instance, to add the immutable flag to the important.txt file, you enter the following command:

```
# chattr +i important.txt
```

The result is that you'll be unable to delete the file, even as root. To delete the file, you must first remove the immutable flag:

```
# chattr -i important.txt
```

Managing Disk Quotas

Just one user of a multi-user system can cause serious problems for others by consuming too much disk space. If a single user creates huge files (say, multimedia recordings), those files can use enough disk space to prevent other users from creating their own files. To help manage this situation, Linux supports *disk quotas*—limits, enforced by the OS, on how many files or how much disk space a single user may consume. The Linux quota system supports quotas both for individual users and for Linux groups.

Enabling Quota Support

Quotas require support in both the kernel for the filesystem being used and various user-space utilities. The ext2fs, ext3fs, ReiserFS, JFS, and XFS filesystems support quotas, but this support is missing for some filesystems in early 2.6.x kernels. Try using the latest kernel if you have problems with your preferred filesystem. You must explicitly enable support via the Quota Support kernel option in the filesystem area when recompiling your kernel. Most distributions ship with this support enabled, so recompiling your kernel may not be necessary, but you should be aware of this option if you recompile your kernel.

Two general quota support systems are available for Linux. The first was used through the 2.4.x kernels and is referred to as the *quota v1 support*. The second was added with the 2.6.x kernel series and is referred to as the *quota v2 system*. This description applies to the latter system, but the former works in a similar way.

Outside of the kernel, you need support tools to use quotas. For the quota v2 system, this package is usually called quota, and it installs a number of utilities, configuration files, system startup scripts, and so on.

> You can install the support software from source code, if you like; however, this job is handled most easily using a package for your distribution. This description assumes that you install the software in this way. If you don't, you may need to create startup scripts to initialize the quota support when you boot your computer. The Quota Mini-HOWTO, at http://en.tldp.org/HOWTO/Quota.html, provides details of how to do this.

You must modify your /etc/fstab entries for any partitions on which you want to use quota support. In particular, you must add the usrquota filesystem mount option to employ user quotas and the grpquota option to use group quotas. Entries that are so configured resemble the following:

```
/dev/sdc5  /home ext3  usrquota,grpquota  1  1
```

This line activates both user and group quota support for the /dev/sdc5 partition, which is mounted at /home. Of course, you can add other options if you like.

Depending on your distribution, you may need to configure the quota package's system startup scripts to run when the system boots. Chapter 5 describes startup script management in detail. Typically, you'll type a command such as **chkconfig quota on**, but you should check on the SysV scripts installed by your distribution's quota package. Some distributions require the use of commands other than chkconfig to do this task, as described in Chapter 5. Whatever its details, this startup script runs the quotaon command, which activates quota support.

After installing software and making configuration file changes, you must activate the systems. The simplest way to do this is to reboot the computer, and this step is necessary if you had to recompile your kernel to add quota support directly into the kernel. If you didn't do this, you should be able to get by with less disruptive measures: using modprobe to install the kernel module, if necessary; running the startup script for the quota tools; and remounting the filesystems on which you intend to use quotas by typing **mount -o remount /mount-point**, where */mount-point* is the mount point in question.

Setting Quotas for Users

At this point, quota support should be fully active on your computer, but the quotas themselves aren't set. You can set the quotas by using edquota, which starts the Vi editor (described in Chapter 1, "Exploring Linux Command-Line Tools") on a temporary configuration file (/etc/quotatab) that controls quotas for the user you specify. When you exit the utility, edquota uses the temporary configuration file to write the quota information to low-level disk data structures that control the kernel's quota mechanisms. For instance, you might type **edquota sally** to edit sally's quotas. The contents of the editor show the current quota information:

```
Disk quotas for user sally (uid 21810):
Filesystem      blocks        soft        hard    inodes    soft    hard
/dev/sdc4        97104     1048576     1048576      1242       0       0
```

The temporary configuration file provides information about both the number of disk blocks in use and the number of inodes in use. (Each file or symbolic link consumes a single inode, so the inode limits are effectively limits on the number of files a user may own. Disk blocks vary in size depending on the filesystem and filesystem creation options, but they typically range from 512 bytes to 8KiB.) Changing the use information (under the blocks and inodes columns) has no effect; these columns report how many blocks or inodes the user is actually consuming. You can alter the soft and hard limits for both blocks and inodes. The hard limit is the maximum number of blocks or inodes that the user may consume; the kernel won't permit a user to surpass these limits. Soft limits are somewhat less stringent; users may temporarily exceed soft limit values, but when they do so, the system issues warnings. Soft limits also interact with a grace period; if the soft quota limit is exceeded for longer than the grace period, the kernel begins treating it like a hard limit and refuses to allow the user to create more files. You can set the grace period by using edquota with its -t option, as in **edquota -t**. Grace periods are set on a per-filesystem basis rather than a per-user basis. Setting a limit to 0 (as in the inode limits in the preceding example) eliminates the use of quotas for that value; users may consume as much disk space or create as many files as they like, up to the available space on the filesystem.

When using edquota, you can adjust quotas independently for every filesystem for which quotas are enabled and separately for every user or group. (To edit quotas for a group, use the -g option, as in **edquota -g users** to adjust quotas for the users group.)

A few more quota-related commands are useful. The first is quotacheck, which verifies and updates quota information on quota-enabled disks. This command is normally run as part of the quota package's startup script, but you may want to run it periodically (say, once a week) as a cron job. (Chapter 7 describes cron jobs.) Although theoretically not necessary if everything works correctly, quotacheck ensures that quota accounting doesn't become inaccurate. The second useful auxiliary quota command is repquota, which summarizes the quota information about the filesystem you specify or on all filesystems if you pass it the -a option. This tool can be very helpful in keeping track of disk usage. The quota command has a similar effect. The quota tool takes a number of options to have them modify their outputs. For instance, -g displays group quotas, -l omits NFS mounts, and -q limits output to filesystems on which usage is over the limit. Consult quota's man page for still more obscure options.

Locating Files

Maintaining your filesystems in perfect health, setting permissions, and so on is pointless if you can't find your files. For this reason, Linux provides several tools to help you locate the files you need to use. The first of these tools is actually a standard for where files are located; with the right knowledge, you may be able to find files without the use of any specialized programs. The second class of tools includes just such specialized programs, which search a directory tree or a database for files that meet whatever criteria you specify.

The FHS

Linux's placement of files is derived from more than 40 years of Unix history. Given that fact, the structure is remarkably simple and coherent, but it's easy for a new administrator to become confused. Some directories seem, on the surface, to fulfill similar or even identical roles, but in fact there are subtle but important differences. This section describes the Linux directory layout standards and presents an overview of what goes where.

The FSSTND and FHS

Although Linux draws heavily on Unix, Unix's long history has led to numerous splits and variants, starting with the Berkeley Standard Distribution (BSD), which was originally a set of patches and extensions to AT&T's original Unix code. As a result of these schisms within the Unix community, early Linux distributions didn't always follow identical patterns. The result was a great deal of confusion. This problem was quite severe early in Linux's history, and it threatened to split the Linux community into factions. Various measures were taken to combat this problem, one of which was the development of the *Filesystem Standard* (FSSTND), which was first released in early 1994. The FSSTND standardized several specific features, such as the following:

- Standardized the programs that reside in /bin and /usr/bin. Differences on this score caused problems when scripts referred to files in one location or the other.

- Specified that executable files shouldn't reside in /etc, as had previously been common.

- Removed changeable files from the /usr directory tree, enabling it to be mounted read-only (a useful security measure).

There have been three major versions of FSSTND: 1.0, 1.1, and 1.2. FSSTND began to rein in some of the chaos in the Linux world in 1994. By 1995, however, FSSTND's limitations were becoming apparent. Thus, a new standard was developed: the *Filesystem Hierarchy Standard* (FHS). This new standard is based on FSSTND but extends it substantially. The FHS is more than a Linux standard; it may be used to define the layout of files on other Unix-like OSs.

One important distinction made by the FHS is that between *shareable files* and *unshareable files*. Shareable files may be reasonably shared between computers, such as user data files and program binary files. (Of course, you don't *need* to share such files, but you *may* do so.) If files are shared, they're normally shared through an NFS server. Unshareable files contain system-specific information, such as configuration files. For instance, you're not likely to want to share a server's configuration file between computers.

A second important distinction used in the FHS is that between *static files* and *variable files*. The former don't normally change except through direct intervention by the system administrator. Most program executables are examples of static files. Variable files may be changed by users, automated scripts, servers, or the like. For instance, users' home directories and mail queues are composed of variable files. The FHS tries to isolate each directory into one cell of this 2×2 (shareable/unshareable $\times$ static/variable) matrix. Figure 4.2 illustrates these relationships. Some directories are mixed, but in these cases, the FHS tries to specify the status of particular subdirectories. For instance, /var is variable, and it contains some shareable and some unshareable subdirectories, as shown in Figure 4.2.

FIGURE 4.2 The FHS attempts to fit each important directory in one cell of a 2×2 matrix.

	Shareable	Unshareable
Static	/usr /opt	/etc /boot
Variable	/home /var/mail	/var/run /var/lock

Like the FSSTND, the FHS comes in numbered versions. Version 2.3, the latest version as I write, was released in January 2004. The URL for FHS's official Web page is `http://www.pathname.com/fhs/`.

 Some Linux vendors—most notably Fedora—are beginning to make changes that deviate from the FHS. For instance, Fedora 17 and later now place all binaries in /usr/bin and /usr/sbin. The /bin directory is now a symbolic link to /usr/bin, and /sbin is a symbolic link to /usr/sbin. This layout complicates some types of configurations, such as those that require a separate /usr partition.

Important Directories and Their Contents

The FHS defines some directories very precisely, but details for others are left unresolved. For instance, users' files normally go in the /home directory, but you may have reason to call this something else or to use two or more separate directories for users' files. Overall, the most common directories defined by the FHS or used by convention are the following:

/ Every Linux filesystem traces its roots to a single directory, known as / (pronounced, and often referred to, as the *root filesystem* or *root directory*). All other directories branch off this one. Linux doesn't use drive letters; instead, every filesystem is mounted at a mount point within another partition (/ or something else). Certain critical subdirectories, such as /etc and /sbin, must reside on the root partition, but others can optionally be on separate partitions. Don't confuse the root directory with the /root directory, described shortly.

/boot The /boot directory contains static and unshareable files related to the initial booting of the computer. Higher-level startup and configuration files reside in another directory, /etc. Some systems impose particular limits on /boot. For instance, older *x*86 BIOSs and older versions of the Linux Loader (LILO) may require that /boot reside below the 1,024th cylinder of the hard disk. Similarly, some EFI boot methods work best with a separate /boot partition that uses ext2fs or ReiserFS. These requirements sometimes, but not always, necessitate that the /boot directory be a separate partition.

/bin This directory contains certain critical executable files, such as ls, cp, and mount. These commands are accessible to all users and constitute the most important commands that ordinary users might issue. You won't normally find commands for big application programs in /bin (although the Vi editor is located here). The /bin directory contains static files. Although in some sense the /bin files are shareable, because they're so important to the basic operation of a computer, the directory is almost never shared—any potential clients must have their own local /bin directories.

/sbin This directory is similar to /bin, but it contains programs that are normally run only by the system administrator—tools like fdisk and e2fsck. It's static and theoretically shareable, but in practice, it makes no sense to share it.

/lib   This directory is similar to /bin and /sbin, but it contains program libraries, which are made up of code that's shared across many programs and stored in separate files to save disk space and RAM. The /lib/modules subdirectory contains kernel modules—drivers that can be loaded and unloaded as required. Like /bin and /sbin, /lib is static and theoretically shareable, although it's not shared in practice.

/usr   This directory hosts the bulk of a Linux computer's programs. Its contents are shareable and static, so it can be mounted read-only and may be shared with other Linux systems. For these reasons, many administrators split /usr off into a separate partition, although doing so isn't required. (Fedora's recent changes make this difficult with this distribution, though.) Some subdirectories of /usr are similar to their namesakes in the root directory (such as /usr/bin and /usr/lib), but they contain programs and libraries that aren't absolutely critical to the basic functioning of the computer.

/usr/local   This directory contains subdirectories that mirror the organization of /usr, such as /usr/local/bin and /usr/local/lib. The /usr/local directory hosts files that a system administrator installs locally—for instance, packages that are compiled on the target computer. The idea is to have an area that's safe from automatic software upgrades when the OS as a whole is upgraded. Immediately after Linux is installed, /usr/local should be empty except for some stub subdirectories. Some system administrators split this off into its own partition to protect it from OS reinstallation procedures that might erase the parent partition.

/usr/X11R6   This directory houses files related to the X Window System (X for short), Linux's GUI environment. Like /usr/local, this directory contains subdirectories similar to those in /usr, such as /usr/X11R6/bin and /usr/X11R6/lib. Although commonly used several years ago, most modern distributions have moved the contents of this directory to others, such as /usr/bin.

/opt   This directory is similar to /usr/local in many ways, but it's intended for ready-made packages that don't ship with the OS, such as commercial word processors or games. Typically, these programs reside in subdirectories in /opt named after themselves, such as /opt/applix. The /opt directory is static and shareable. Some system administrators break it into a separate partition or make it a symbolic link to a subdirectory of /usr/local and make that a separate partition.

/home   This directory contains users' data, and it's shareable and variable. Although the /home directory is considered optional in FHS, in practice it's a matter of the *name* being optional. For instance, if you add a new disk to support additional users, you might leave the existing /home directory intact and create a new /home2 directory to house the new users. The /home directory often resides on its own partition.

/root   This is the home directory for the root user. Because the root account is so critical and system-specific, this variable directory isn't really shareable.

/var   This directory contains transient files of various types—system log files, print spool files, mail and news files, and so on. Therefore, the directory's contents are variable. Some subdirectories are shareable, but others are not. Many system administrators put /var in its own partition, particularly on systems that see a lot of activity in /var, like major Usenet news or mail servers.

/tmp   Many programs need to create temporary (hence variable) files, and the usual place to do so is in /tmp. Most distributions include routines that clean out this directory periodically and sometimes wipe the directory clean at bootup. The /tmp directory is seldom shared. Some administrators create a separate /tmp partition to prevent runaway processes from causing problems on the root filesystem when processes create too-large temporary files. A similar directory exists as part of the /var directory tree (/var/tmp).

/mnt   Linux mounts removable-media devices within its normal directory structure, and /mnt is provided for this purpose. Some (mostly older) distributions create subdirectories within /mnt, such as /mnt/floppy and /mnt/cdrom, to function as mount points. Others use /mnt directly or even use separate mount points off /, such as /floppy and /cdrom. The FHS mentions only /mnt; it doesn't specify how it's to be used. Specific media mounted in /mnt may be either static or variable. As a general rule, these directories are shareable.

/media   This directory is an optional part of the FHS. It's like /mnt, but it should contain subdirectories for specific media types, such as /media/floppy and /media/cdrom. Many modern distributions use /media subdirectories as the default mount points for common removable disk types, often creating subdirectories on the fly.

/dev   Because Linux treats most hardware devices as if they were files, the OS must have a location in its filesystem where these device files reside. The /dev directory is that place. It contains a large number of files that function as hardware interfaces. If a user has sufficient privileges, that user may access the device hardware by reading from and writing to the associated device file. The Linux kernel supports a device filesystem that enables /dev to be an automatically created *virtual filesystem*—the kernel and support tools create /dev entries on the fly to accommodate the needs of specific drivers. Most distributions now use this facility.

/proc   This is an unusual directory because it doesn't correspond to a regular directory or partition. Instead, it's a virtual filesystem that's created dynamically by Linux to provide access to certain types of hardware information that aren't accessible via /dev. For instance, if you type **cat /proc/cpuinfo**, the system responds by displaying information about your CPU—its model name, speed, and so on.

Knowledge of these directories and their purposes is invaluable in properly administering a Linux system. For instance, understanding the purpose of directories like /bin, /sbin, /usr/bin, /usr/local/bin, and others will help you when it comes time to install a new program. Placing a program in the wrong location can cause problems at a later date. For example, if you put a binary file in /bin when it should go in /usr/local/bin, that program may later be overwritten or deleted during a system upgrade when leaving it intact would have been more appropriate.

Tools for Locating Files

You use file-location commands to locate a file on your computer. Most frequently, these commands help you locate a file by name, but sometimes you can use other criteria, such as modification date. These commands can search a directory tree (including root, which scans the entire system) for a file matching the specified criteria in any subdirectory.

The *find* Command

The find utility implements a brute-force approach to finding files. This program finds files by searching through the specified directory tree, checking filenames, file creation dates, and so on to locate the files that match the specified criteria. Because of this method of operation, find tends to be slow; but it's very flexible and is very likely to succeed, assuming the file for which you're searching exists. The find syntax is as follows:

```
find [path...] [expression...]
```

You can specify one or more paths in which find should operate; the program will restrict its operations to these paths. The *expression* is a way of specifying what you want to find. The man page for find includes information about these expressions, but some of the common enable you to search by various common criteria:

Search by Filename   You can search for a filename using the -name *pattern* expression. Doing so finds files that match the specified *pattern*. If *pattern* is an ordinary filename, find matches that name exactly. You can use wildcards if you enclose *pattern* in quotes, and find will locate files that match the wildcard filename.

Search by Permission Mode   If you need to find files that have certain permissions, you can do so by using the -perm *mode* expression. The *mode* may be expressed either symbolically or in octal form. If you precede *mode* with a +, find locates files in which *any* of the specified permission bits are set. If you precede *mode* with a -, find locates files in which all the specified permission bits are set.

Search by File Size   You can search for a file of a given size with the -size *n* expression. Normally, *n* is specified in 512-byte blocks, but you can modify this by trailing the value with a letter code, such as c for bytes or k for kilobytes.

Search by Group   The -gid *GID* expression searches for files whose group ID (GID) is set to *GID*. The -group *name* option locates files whose group name is *name*. The former can be handy if the GID has been orphaned and has no name, but the latter is generally easier to use.

Search by User ID   The -uid *UID* expression searches for files owned by the user whose user ID (UID) is *UID*. The -user *name* option searches for files owned by *name*. The former can be handy if the UID has been orphaned and has no name, but the latter is generally easier to use.

Restrict Search Depth   If you want to search a directory and, perhaps, some limited number of subdirectories, you can use the -maxdepth *levels* expression to limit the search.

There are many variant and additional options; find is a very powerful command. As an example of its use, consider the task of finding all C source code files, which normally have names that end in .c, in all users' home directories. If these home directories reside in /home, you might issue the following command:

```
# find /home -name "*.c"
```

The result will be a listing of all the files that match the search criteria.

Ordinary users may use find, but it doesn't overcome Linux's file permission features. If you lack permission to list a directory's contents, find will return that directory name and the error message Permission denied.

The *locate* Command

The locate utility works much like find if you want to find a file by name, but it differs in two important ways:

- The locate tool is far less sophisticated in its search options. You normally use it to search only on filenames, and the program returns all files that contain the specified string. For instance, when searching for rpm, locate will return other programs, like gnorpm and rpm2cpio.

- The locate program works from a database that it maintains. Most distributions include a cron job that calls utilities that update the locate database, periodically, such as once a night or once a week. (You can also use the updatedb command, which is configured via the /etc/updatedb.conf file, to do this task at any time.) For this reason, locate may not find recent files, or it may return the names of files that no longer exist. If the database-update utilities omit certain directories, files in them won't be returned by a locate query.

Because locate works from a database, it's typically much faster than find, particularly on system-wide searches. It's likely to return many false alarms, though, especially if you want to find a file with a short name. To use it, type **locate** *search-string*, where *search-string* is the string that appears in the filename.

Some Linux distributions use slocate rather than locate. The slocate program includes security features to prevent users from seeing the names of files in directories they shouldn't be able to access. On most systems that use slocate, the locate command is a link to slocate, so locate implements slocate's security features. A few distributions don't install either locate or slocate by default.

The *whereis* Command

The whereis program searches for files in a restricted set of locations, such as standard binary file directories, library directories, and man page directories. This tool does *not* search user directories or many other locations that are easily searched by find or locate. The whereis utility is a quick way to find program executables and related files like documentation or configuration files.

The whereis program returns filenames that begin with whatever you type as a search criterion, even if those files contain extensions. This feature often turns up configuration files in /etc, man pages, and similar files. To use the program, type the name of the program you want to locate. For instance, the following command locates ls:

```
$ whereis ls
ls: /bin/ls /usr/share/man/man1/ls.1.bz2
```

The result shows both the ls executable (/bin/ls) and ls's man page. The whereis program accepts several parameters that modify its behavior in various ways. These are detailed in the program's man page.

The *which* Command

Considered as a search command, which is very weak; it merely searches your path for the command that you type and lists the complete path to the first match it finds. (You can search for all matches by adding the -a option.) For instance, you might want to know where the xterm program is located:

```
$ which xterm
/usr/bin/xterm
```

Because the files that which finds are on your path, it won't help you to run these programs. Instead, it's likely to be useful if you need to know the complete path for some reason—say, because you want to call the program from a script and don't want to make assumptions about the path available to the script and so want to include the complete path in the script.

The *type* Command

This command isn't really a search command; instead, it tells you how a command you type will be interpreted—as a built-in command, an external command, an alias, and so on. For instance, you can use it to identify several common commands:

```
$ type type
type is a shell builtin
$ type cat
cat is /bin/cat
$ type ls
ls is aliased to 'ls --color'
```

This example identifies type itself as a built-in shell command, cat as a separate program stored in /bin, and ls as an alias for ls --color. You can add several options to modify the command's behavior. For instance, -t shortens the output to builtin, file, alias, or other short identifiers; and -a provides a complete list, for instance providing both the alias expansion and the location of the ultimate executable when provided with an alias name.

In Exercise 4.2, you'll use several methods of locating files.

EXERCISE 4.2

Locating Files

This exercise demonstrates several methods of locating files. You'll locate the startx program. (If your system doesn't have X installed, you can try searching for another program or file, such as pwd or fstab. You may need to change the path passed to find in step 5.) To find a file, follow these steps:

1. Log into the Linux system as a normal user.

2. Launch an xterm from the desktop environment's menu system if you used a GUI login method.

3. Type **locate startx**. The system should display several filenames that include the string startx. This search should take very little time. (A few distributions lack the locate command, so this step won't work on some systems.)

4. Type **whereis startx**. The system responds with the names of a few files that contain the string startx. Note that this list may be slightly different from the list returned by step 3 but that the search proceeds quickly.

5. Type **find /usr -name startx**. This search takes longer and, when run as an ordinary user, most likely returns several Permission denied error messages. It should also return a single line listing the /usr/bin/startx or /usr/X11R6/bin/startx program file. Note that this command searches only /usr. If you searched /usr/X11R6, the command would take less time; if you searched /, the command would take more time.

6. Type **which startx**. This search completes almost instantaneously, returning the complete filename of the first instance of startx the system finds on its path.

7. Type **type startx**. Again, the search completes very quickly. It should identify startx as an external command stored at /usr/bin/startx, /usr/X11R6/bin/startx, or possibly some other location.

Summary

File management is basic to being able to administer or use a Linux system. Various commands are useful to both users and administrators for copying, moving, renaming, and otherwise manipulating files and directories. You may also want to set up access controls, both to limit the amount of disk space users may consume and to limit who may access specific files and directories. Finally, Linux provides tools to help you locate files using various criteria.

Exam Essentials

Describe commands used to copy, move, and rename files in Linux.   The cp command copies files, as in **cp first second** to create a copy of first called second. The mv command does double duty as a file-moving and a file-renaming command. It works much like cp, but mv moves or renames the file rather than copying it.

Summarize Linux's directory-manipulation commands.   The mkdir command creates a new directory, and rmdir deletes a directory. You can also use many file-manipulation commands, such as mv and rm (with its -r option), on directories.

Explain the difference between hard and symbolic links.   Hard links are duplicate directory entries that both point to the same inode and hence to the same file. Symbolic links are special files that point to another file or directory by name. Hard links must reside on a single filesystem, but symbolic links may point across filesystems.

Summarize the common Linux archiving programs.   The tar and cpio programs are both file-based archiving tools that create archives of files using ordinary file access commands. The dd program is a file-copy program; but when it's fed a partition device file, it copies the entire partition on a very low-level basis, which is useful for creating low-level image backups of Linux or non-Linux filesystems.

Describe Linux's file ownership system.   Every file has an owner and a group, identified by number. File permissions can be assigned independently to the file's owner, the file's group, and all other users.

Explain Linux's file permissions system.   Linux provides independent read, write, and execute permissions for the file's owner, the file's group, and all other users, resulting in nine main permission bits. Special permission bits are also available, enabling you to launch program files with modified account features or alter the rules Linux uses to control who may delete files.

Summarize the commands Linux uses to modify permissions.   The chmod command is Linux's main tool for setting permissions. You can specify permissions using either an octal (base 8) mode or a symbolic notation. The chown and chgrp commands enable you to change the file's owner and group, respectively. (The chown command can do both but can be run only by root.)

Describe the prerequisites of using Linux's disk quota system.   Linux's disk quota system requires support in the Linux kernel for the filesystem on which quotas are to be used. You must also run the quotaon command, typically from a SysV startup script, to enable this feature.

Explain how quotas are set.   You can edit quotas for an individual user via the edquota command, as in **edquota larry** to edit larry's quotas. This command opens an editor on a text file that describes the user's quotas. You can change this description, save the file, and exit from the editor to change the user's quotas.

Summarize how Linux's standard directories are structured.   Linux's directory tree begins with the root (/) directory, which holds mostly other directories. Specific directories may hold specific types of information, such as user files in /home and configuration files in /etc. Some of these directories and their subdirectories may be separate partitions, which helps isolate data in the event of filesystem corruption.

Describe the major file-location commands in Linux.   The find command locates files by brute force, searching through the directory tree for files that match the criteria you specify. The locate (or slocate) command searches a database of files in publicly accessible directories. The whereis command searches a handful of important directories, and which searches the path. The type command identifies another command as a built-in shell command, a shell alias, or an external command (including the path to that command).

Review Questions

1. Why might you type **touch** *filename*?

   A. To move *filename* to the current directory

   B. To ensure that *filename*'s timestamp holds the current time

   C. To convert *filename* from DOS-style to Unix-style end-of-line characters

   D. To test the validity of *filename*'s disk structures

   E. To write cached data relating to *filename* to the disk

2. What parameter can you pass to ln to create a soft link? (Select two.)

   A. -s

   B. --soft

   C. --slink

   D. --symbolic

   E. --sl

3. You want to discover the sizes of several dot files in a directory. Which of the following commands might you use to do this?

   A. ls -la

   B. ls -p

   C. ls -R

   D. ls -d

   E. ls -F

4. You want to move a file from your hard disk to a USB flash drive. Which of the following is true?

   A. You'll have to use the --preserve option to mv to keep ownership and permissions set correctly.

   B. The mv command will adjust filesystem pointers without physically rewriting data if the flash drive uses the same filesystem type as the hard disk partition.

   C. You must use the same filesystem type on both media to preserve ownership and permissions.

   D. The mv command will delete the file on the hard disk after copying it to the flash drive.

   E. You must use the FAT filesystem on the USB flash drive; Linux-native filesystems won't work on removable disks.

5. You type **mkdir one/two/three** and receive an error message that reads, in part, No such file or directory. What can you do to overcome this problem? (Select two.)

   A. Add the --parents parameter to the mkdir command.

   B. Issue three separate mkdir commands: **mkdir one**, then **mkdir one/two**, and then **mkdir one/two/three**.

   C. Type **touch /bin/mkdir** to be sure the mkdir program file exists.

   D. Type **rmdir one** to clear away the interfering base of the desired new directory tree.

   E. Type **mktree one/two/three** instead of **mkdir one/two/three**.

6. Which of the following commands are commonly used to create archive files? (Select two.)

   A. restore

   B. vi

   C. tape

   D. cpio

   E. tar

7. You've received a tarball called data79.tar from a colleague, but you want to check the names of the files it contains before extracting them. Which of the following commands would you use to do this?

   A. tar uvf data79.tar

   B. tar cvf data79.tar

   C. tar xvf data79.tar

   D. tar rvf data79.tar

   E. tar tvf data79.tar

8. You want to create a link from your home directory on your hard disk to a directory on a CD-ROM drive. Which of the following types of links might you use?

   A. Only a symbolic link

   B. Only a hard link

   C. Either a symbolic or a hard link

   D. Only a hard link, and then only if both directories use the same low-level filesystem

   E. None of the above; such links aren't possible under Linux

9. What command would you type (as root) to change the ownership of somefile.txt from ralph to tony?

   A. chown ralph:tony somefile.txt

   B. chmod somefile.txt tony

   C. chown somefile.txt tony

   D. chmod tony:ralph somefile.txt

   E. chown tony somefile.txt

10. Typing **ls -ld wonderjaye** reveals a symbolic file mode of drwxr-xr-x. Which of the following are true? (Select two.)

    A. wonderjaye is a symbolic link.

    B. wonderjaye is an executable program.

    C. wonderjaye is a directory.

    D. wonderjaye has its SUID bit set.

    E. wonderjaye may be read by all users of the system.

11. When should programs be configured SUID root?

    A. At all times; this permission is required for executable programs

    B. Whenever a program should be able to access a device file

    C. Only when they require root privileges to do their job

    D. Never; this permission is a severe security risk

    E. Whenever the program file is owned by the root user

12. Which of the following commands would you type to enable world read access to the file myfile.txt? (Assume that you're the owner of myfile.txt.)

    A. chmod 741 myfile.txt

    B. chmod 0640 myfile.txt

    C. chmod u+r myfile.txt

    D. chmod a-r myfile.txt

    E. chmod o+r myfile.txt

13. Which of the following umask values will result in files with rw-r----- permissions?

    A. 640

    B. 210

    C. 022

    D. 027

    E. 138

14. You see the usrquota and grpquota options in the /etc/fstab entry for a filesystem. What is the consequence of these entries?

    A. Quota support will be available if it's compiled into the kernel; it will be automatically activated when you mount the filesystem.

    B. User quotas will be available, but the grpquota option is invalid and will be ignored.

    C. Quota support will be disabled on the filesystem in question.

    D. Nothing; these options are malformed and so will have no effect.

    E. Quota support will be available if it's compiled into your kernel, but you must activate it with the quotaon command.

15. Which of the following commands can be used to summarize the quota information about all filesystems?

   A. `repquota`

   B. `repquota -a`

   C. `quotacheck`

   D. `quotacheck -a`

   E. `edquota -a`

16. You've installed a commercial spreadsheet program called WonderCalc on a workstation. In which of the following directories are you *most* likely to find the program executable file?

   A. `/usr/sbin`

   B. `/etc/X11`

   C. `/boot`

   D. `/opt/wcalc/bin`

   E. `/sbin/wcalc`

17. Which of the following file-location commands is likely to take the *most* time to find a file that may be located anywhere on the computer (assuming the operation succeeds)?

   A. The `find` command.

   B. The `locate` command.

   C. The `whereis` command.

   D. The `type` command.

   E. They're all equal in speed.

18. What can the `type` command do that `whereis` can't do?

   A. Identify the command as being for *x*86 or *x*86-64 CPUs

   B. Locate commands based on their intended purpose, not just by name

   C. Identify a command as an alias, internal command, or external command

   D. Assist in typing a command by finishing typing it for you

   E. Identify a command as being a binary or a script

19. You want to track down all the files in /home that are owned by karen. Which of the following commands will do the job?

   A. `find /home -uid karen`

   B. `find /home -user karen`

   C. `locate /home -username karen`

   D. `locate /home Karen`

   E. `find /home -name karen`

20. What can you conclude from the following interaction?

```
$ which man
/usr/bin/man
```

   A. The only file called man on the computer is in /usr/bin.

   B. The /usr/bin/man program was installed by system package tools.

   C. The /usr/bin/man program will be run by any user who types **man**.

   D. The first instance of the man program, in path search order, is in /usr/bin.

   E. The user man owns the /usr/bin/man program file.

Chapter

5

Booting Linux and Editing Files

THE FOLLOWING EXAM OBJECTIVES ARE COVERED IN THIS CHAPTER:

✓ 1.101.2: Boot the system

✓ 1.101.3: Change runlevels and shutdown or reboot system

✓ 1.102.2: Install a boot manager

✓ 1.103.8: Perform basic file editing operations using vi

So far, this book has dealt largely with a running Linux system, but from time to time you'll need to boot Linux. Ordinarily this process is a painless one: You press the power button, wait a couple of minutes, and see a Linux login prompt. Sometimes, though, you'll have to intervene in this process in one way or another.

The Linux boot process can be configured to boot Linux with particular options and even to boot other operating systems, so knowing how to configure the boot process can help you accomplish your boot-related goals. Once the system is booted, you should know how to study log files related to the boot process. This can help you diagnose problems or verify that the system is operating the way it should be.

Finally, this chapter looks at editing files with Vi. Vi isn't particularly boot-related, but knowing how to edit files is vital to many administrative tasks, including editing the boot loader configuration files.

Installing Boot Loaders

The computer's boot process begins with a program called a *boot loader*. This program runs before any OS has loaded, although you normally install and configure it from within Linux (or some other OS). Boot loaders work in particular ways that depend on both the firmware you use and the OS you're booting. Understanding your boot loader's principles is necessary to properly configure them, so before delving into the details of specific boot loaders, I describe these boot loader principles.

In Linux, the most-used boot loader is the *Grand Unified Boot Loader (GRUB)*, which is available in two versions: GRUB Legacy (with version numbers up to 0.97) and GRUB 2 (with version numbers from 1.9x to 2.x, with 2.00 being the latest as I write). An assortment of alternative boot loaders is available, though, and in some cases you may need to use one of them, so I provide a brief rundown of these less common boot loaders.

This chapter describes boot loaders for *x*86 and *x*86-64 computers. Other platforms have their own boot loaders. Some of these are similar to certain *x*86/*x*86-64 boot loaders, but they aren't quite identical. You should consult platform-specific documentation if you need to reconfigure a non-*x*86 boot loader.

Boot Loader Principles

In one way or another, your computer's firmware reads the boot loader into memory from the hard disk and executes it. The boot loader, in turn, is responsible for loading the Linux kernel into memory and starting it running. Thus, configuring a hard disk (or at least your boot hard disk) isn't complete until the boot loader is configured. Although Linux distributions provide semi-automated methods of configuring a boot loader during system installation, you may need to know more, particularly if you recompile your kernel or need to set up an advanced configuration—say, one to select between several OSs.

Although the exam objectives mention only the Basic Input/Output System (BIOS) firmware, beginning in 2011 the Extensible Firmware Interface (EFI) and its Unified EFI (UEFI) variant have become increasingly important. Thus, I describe the principles upon which both BIOS and EFI computers' boot loaders are based.

BIOS Boot Loader Principles

The BIOS boot process can be a bit convoluted, in part because so many options are available. Figure 5.1 depicts a typical configuration, showing a couple of possible boot paths. In both cases, the boot process begins with the BIOS. As described in Chapter 3, "Configuring Hardware," you tell the BIOS which boot device to use—a hard disk, a floppy disk, a CD-ROM drive, or something else. Assuming you pick a hard disk as the primary boot device (or if higher-priority devices aren't bootable), the BIOS loads code from the Master Boot Record (MBR), which is the first sector on the hard disk. This code is the primary boot loader code. In theory, it could be just about anything, even a complete (if tiny) OS.

FIGURE 5.1   The *x86* boot system provides several options for redirecting the process, but ultimately an OS kernel is loaded.

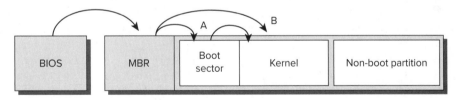

In practice, the primary boot loader does one of two things:

- It examines the partition table and locates the partition that's marked as bootable. The primary boot loader then loads the boot sector from that partition and executes it. This boot sector contains a secondary boot loader, which continues the process by locating an OS kernel, loading it, and executing it. This option is depicted by the A arrows in Figure 5.1.

- It locates an OS kernel, loads it, and executes it directly. This approach bypasses the secondary boot loader entirely, as depicted by the B arrow in Figure 5.1.

Traditionally, *x86* systems running DOS or Windows follow path A. DOS and Windows *9x*/Me ship with very simple boot loaders that provide little in the way of options. Later versions of Windows ship with a boot loader that can provide limited redirection in the second stage of the A path.

Linux's most popular BIOS boot loaders, LILO and GRUB, are both much more flexible. They support installation in either the MBR or the boot sector of a boot partition. Thus, you can either keep a DOS/Windows-style primary boot loader and direct the system to boot a kernel from a boot sector installation (path A) or bypass this step and load the kernel straight from the MBR (path B). The first option has the advantage that another OS is unlikely to wipe out LILO or GRUB, because it's stored safely in a Linux partition. Windows has a tendency to write its standard MBR boot loader when it's installed, so if you need to re-install Windows on a dual-boot system, this action will wipe out an MBR-based boot loader. If the boot loader is stored in a Linux partition's boot sector, it will remain intact, although Windows might configure the system to bypass it. To reactivate the Linux boot loader, you must use a tool such as the DOS/Windows FDISK to mark the Linux partition as the boot partition.

A drawback of placing LILO or GRUB in a partition's boot sector is that this partition must normally be a primary partition, at least with disks that use the MBR partitioning system. (An exception is if you're using some other boot loader in the MBR or in another partition. If this third-party boot loader can redirect the boot process to a logical partition, this restriction goes away.) For this reason, many people prefer to put LILO or GRUB in the hard disk's MBR.

In the end, both approaches work, and for a Linux-only installation, the advantages and disadvantages of both approaches are very minor. Some distributions don't give you an option at install time. For them, you should review your boot loader configuration and, when you must add a kernel or otherwise change the boot loader, modify the existing configuration rather than try to create a new one.

On disks that use the GUID Partition Table (GPT) partitioning system, GRUB stores part of itself in a special partition, known as the *BIOS Boot Partition*. On MBR disks, the equivalent code resides in the sectors immediately following the MBR, which are officially unallocated in the MBR scheme.

A Linux boot loader can be installed to a floppy disk or USB flash drive as well as to a hard disk. Even if you don't want to use such a disk as part of your regular boot process, you may want to create an emergency disk with your regular boot loader. You can then use it to boot Linux if something goes wrong with your regular boot loader installation.

This description provides a somewhat simplified view of boot loaders. Most Linux boot loaders are much more complex than this. They can redirect the boot process to non-Linux boot sectors and present menus that enable you to boot multiple OSs or multiple Linux kernels. You can chain several boot loaders, including third-party boot loaders such as System Commander or BootMagic. Chaining boot loaders in this way enables you to take advantage of unique features of multiple boot loaders, such as the ability of System Commander to boot several versions of DOS or Windows on a single partition.

The exam's objective 102.2 mentions the superblock. Despite its placement in an objective about boot loaders, the superblock isn't really a boot loader concept; rather, it's part of the filesystem. The superblock describes basic filesystem features, such as the filesystem's size and status. The debugfs and dumpe2fs commands, described in Chapter 3, provide some basic superblock information. On BIOS-based computers, the superblock can hold a portion of the boot loader, so damage to it can cause boot problems.

EFI Boot Loader Principles

The BIOS boot process, as just described, was designed in the 1980s, when the space available for a BIOS in the computer's firmware was tiny by today's standards. Thus, the boot process had to be very simple, and a great deal of the complexity had to be pushed into software stored on the hard disk.

The newer EFI firmware is much more complex than the older BIOS, and so its boot process can be more sophisticated. Instead of relying on code stored in boot sectors on the hard disk, EFI relies on boot loaders stored as files in a disk partition, known as the *EFI System Partition (ESP)*, which uses the File Allocation Table (FAT) filesystem. Under Linux, the ESP is typically mounted at /boot/efi. Boot loaders reside in files with .efi filename extensions stored in subdirectories named after the OS or boot loader name under the EFI subdirectory of the ESP. Thus, you might have a boot loader called /boot/efi/EFI/ ubuntu/grub.efi or /boot/efi/EFI/suse/elilo.efi.

This configuration enables you to store a separate boot loader for each OS you install on the computer. The EFI firmware includes its own program, a *boot manager*, to help you select which boot loader to launch. The resulting boot path resembles Figure 5.2. In this figure, two boot loaders (loader1.efi and loader2.efi) are available, each of which launches its own OS kernel, located on its own partition.

FIGURE 5.2   The EFI boot process begins the boot redirection from the firmware level and employs files in filesystems rather than boot code hidden in boot sectors.

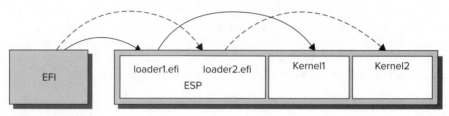

 The exam objectives use the terms *boot loader* and *boot manager* interchangeably, but this book doesn't. A boot loader loads a kernel into memory and transfers control to it, whereas a boot manager presents a menu of boot options. Many programs, including the popular GRUB, combine both functions in one program, which is the reason for the lack of clarity in many sources.

In order to work, the EFI must know about the boot loaders installed on the hard disk's ESP. This is normally done by registering the boot loaders with the firmware, either using a utility built into the firmware's own user interface or using a tool such as Linux's efibootmgr program. Alternatively, most *x86-64* EFI implementations will use a boot loader called EFI/boot/bootx64.efi on the ESP as a default if no others are registered. This is the way you boot most removable disks; you store your boot loader using this name on the removable disk's ESP.

The most popular EFI boot loaders for Linux are based on BIOS boot loaders, so they provide functionality not required by EFI boot loaders generally, such as their own boot manager features that provide the ability to chainload to another EFI boot loader. Thus, the boot process on a multi-OS computer might run a single EFI boot loader, which then chainloads other EFI boot loaders. In fact, this is sometimes a practical necessity, since many EFI implementations provide such primitive boot managers that selecting an OS must be done by a separate boot program.

Using GRUB Legacy as the Boot Loader

The Grand Unified Bootloader (GRUB) is the default boot loader for most Linux distributions; however, GRUB is really two boot loaders: GRUB Legacy and GRUB 2. Although these two boot loaders are similar in many ways, they differ in many important details. GRUB Legacy is, as you might expect, the older of the two boot loaders. It used to be the dominant boot loader for Linux, but it's been eclipsed by GRUB 2. Nonetheless, because the two boot loaders are so similar, I describe GRUB Legacy first and in more detail; the upcoming section, "Using GRUB 2 as the Boot Loader," focuses on its differences from GRUB Legacy. In the following pages, I describe how to configure, install, and interact with GRUB Legacy.

Configuring GRUB Legacy

The usual location for GRUB Legacy's configuration file on a BIOS-based computer is /boot/grub/menu.1st. Some distributions (such as Fedora, Red Hat, and Gentoo) use the filename grub.conf rather than menu.1st. The GRUB configuration file is broken into global and per-image sections, each of which has its own options. Before getting into section details, though, you should understand a few GRUB quirks.

 GRUB Legacy officially supports BIOS but not EFI. A heavily patched version, maintained by Fedora, provides support for EFI. If you're using this version of GRUB, its configuration file goes in the same directory on the ESP that houses the GRUB Legacy binary, such as /boot/efi/EFI/ redhat for a standard Fedora or Red Hat installation.

GRUB Nomenclature and Quirks

Listing 5.1 shows a sample GRUB configuration file. This file provides definitions to boot several OSs—Fedora on /dev/sda5, Debian on /dev/sda6, and Windows on /dev/sda2. Fedora and Debian share a /boot partition (/dev/sda1), on which the GRUB configuration resides.

Listing 5.1: A sample GRUB configuration file

```
# grub.conf/menu.1st
#
# Global Options:
#
default=0
timeout=15
splashimage=/grub/bootimage.xpm.gz
#
# Kernel Image Options:
#
title Fedora (3.4.1)
    root (hd0,0)
    kernel /vmlinuz-3.4.1 ro root=/dev/sda5 mem=4096M
    initrd /initrd-3.4.1
```

```
title Debian (3.4.2-experimental)
    root (hd0,0)
    kernel (hd0,0)/bzImage-3.4.2-experimental ro root=/dev/sda6
#
# Other operating systems
#
title Windows
    rootnoverify (hd0,1)
    chainloader +1
```

GRUB doesn't refer to disk drives by device filename the way Linux does. GRUB numbers drives so that instead of /dev/hda or /dev/sda, GRUB uses (hd0). Similarly, /dev/hdb or /dev/sdb is likely to be (hd1). GRUB doesn't distinguish between PATA, SATA, SCSI, and USB drives, so on a SCSI-only system, the first SCSI drive is (hd0). On a mixed system, ATA drives normally receive the lower numbers, although this isn't always the case. GRUB Legacy's drive mappings can be found in the /boot/grub/device.map file.

Additionally, GRUB Legacy numbers partitions on a drive starting at 0 instead of the 1 that is used by Linux. GRUB Legacy separates partition numbers from drive numbers with a comma, as in (hd0,0) for the first partition on the first disk (normally Linux's /dev/hda1 or /dev/sda1) or (hd0,4) for the first logical partition on the first disk (normally Linux's /dev/hda5 or /dev/sda5). Floppy devices are referred to as (fd0), or conceivably (fd1) or higher if you have more than one floppy drive. Floppy disks aren't partitioned, so they don't receive partition numbers. GRUB Legacy treats USB flash drives just like hard disks, although it relies on the firmware to access these drives, so GRUB Legacy won't boot from a USB flash drive if you're using an older computer that doesn't support this option.

GRUB Legacy defines its own root partition, which can be different from the Linux root partition. GRUB's root partition is the partition in which GRUB's configuration file (menu .lst or grub.conf) resides. Because this file is normally in Linux's /boot/grub/ directory, the GRUB root partition will be the same as Linux's root partition if you do *not* use a separate /boot or /boot/grub partition. If you split off /boot into its own partition, as is fairly common, GRUB's root partition will be the same as Linux's /boot partition. You must keep this difference in mind when referring to files in the GRUB configuration directory.

Essential Global GRUB Legacy Options

GRUB's global section precedes its per-image configurations. Typically, you'll find just a few options in this global section:

Default OS   The default= option tells GRUB which OS to boot. Listing 5.1's default=0 causes the first listed OS to be booted (remember, GRUB indexes from 0). If you want to boot the second listed operating system, use default=1, and so on, through all your OSs.

Timeout   The `timeout=` option defines how long, in seconds, to wait for user input before booting the default operating system.

Background Graphic   The `splashimage=` line points to a graphics file that's displayed as the background for the boot process. This line is optional, but most Linux distributions point to an image to spruce up the boot menu. The filename reference is relative to the GRUB root partition, so if /boot is on a separate partition, that portion of the path is omitted. Alternatively, the path may begin with a GRUB device specification, such as (hd0,5) to refer to a file on that partition.

Essential GRUB Legacy Per-Image Options

GRUB Legacy's per-image options are often indented after the first line, but this is a convention, not a requirement of the file format. The options begin with an identification and continue with options that tell GRUB how to handle the image:

Title   The `title` line begins a per-image stanza and specifies the label to display when the boot loader runs. The GRUB Legacy `title` can accept spaces and is conventionally moderately descriptive, as shown in Listing 5.1.

GRUB Root   The `root` option specifies the location of GRUB Legacy's root partition. This is the /boot partition if a separate one exists; otherwise, it's usually the Linux root (/) partition. GRUB *can* reside on a FAT partition, on a floppy disk, or on certain other OSs' partitions, though, so GRUB's root could conceivably be somewhere more exotic.

Kernel Specification   The `kernel` setting describes the location of the Linux kernel as well as any kernel options that are to be passed to it. Paths are relative to GRUB Legacy's root partition. As an alternative, you can specify devices using GRUB's syntax, such as `kernel (hd0,5)/vmlinuz ro root=/dev/sda5`. Note that you pass most kernel options on this line. Some other boot loaders split off kernel options on separate lines; but in GRUB, you incorporate these options onto the `kernel` line. The `ro` option tells the kernel to mount its root filesystem read-only (it's later remounted read/write), and the `root=` option specifies the *Linux* root filesystem. Because these options are being passed to the kernel, they use Linux-style device identifiers, when necessary, unlike other options in the GRUB configuration file.

Initial RAM Disk   Use the `initrd` option to specify an initial RAM disk, which holds a minimal set of drivers, utilities, and configuration files that the kernel uses to mount its root filesystem before the kernel can fully access the hard disk. Most Linux distributions rely heavily on the initial RAM disk as a way to keep the main kernel file small and to provide tools to the kernel at a point in the boot process before they could be loaded from the hard disk.

Non-Linux Root   The `rootnoverify` option is similar to the `root` option except that GRUB Legacy won't try to access files on this partition. It's used to specify a boot partition for OSs for which GRUB Legacy can't directly load a kernel, such as DOS and Windows.

Chainloading   The `chainloader` option tells GRUB Legacy to pass control to another boot loader. Typically, it's passed a +1 option to load the first sector of the target OS's root partition (usually specified with `rootnoverify`) and to hand over execution to this secondary boot loader.

Chainloading as just described works on BIOS computers. If you're using an EFI-enabled version of GRUB Legacy, you can chainload, but you must tell GRUB Legacy to use the ESP (typically by specifying root (hd0,0), although the device identification may differ) and then pass the name of an EFI boot loader file via the chainloader option, as in chainloader /EFI/Microsoft/boot/bootmgfw.efi.

To add a kernel to GRUB, follow these steps:

1. As root, load the menu.lst or grub.conf file into a text editor.

2. Copy a working configuration for a Linux kernel.

3. Modify the title line to give your new configuration a unique name.

4. Modify the kernel line to point to the new kernel. If you need to change any kernel options, do so.

5. If you're adding, deleting, or changing a RAM disk, make appropriate changes to the initrd line.

6. If desired, change the global default line to point to the new kernel.

7. Save your changes, and exit the text editor.

At this point, GRUB is configured to boot your new kernel. When you reboot, you should see it appear in your menu, and you should be able to boot it. If you have problems, boot a working configuration to debug the issue.

Don't eliminate a working configuration for an old kernel until you've determined that your new kernel works correctly.

Installing GRUB Legacy

The command for installing GRUB Legacy on a BIOS-based computer is grub-install. You must specify the boot sector by device name when you install the boot loader. The basic command looks like

```
# grub-install /dev/sda
```

or

```
# grub-install '(hd0)'
```

Either command will install GRUB Legacy into the first sector (that is, the MBR) of your first hard drive. In the second example, you need single quotes around the device name. If you want to install GRUB Legacy in the boot sector of a partition rather than in the MBR, you include a partition identifier, as in /dev/sda1 or (hd0,0).

If you're installing Fedora's EFI-enabled version of GRUB Legacy, you should *not* use the grub-install command; instead, copy the grub.efi file to a suitable subdirectory on your ESP, such as /boot/efi/EFI/redhat, and copy grub.conf to the same location. If you install using Fedora's grub-efi RPM file, the grub.efi file should be placed in this location by default. After copying these files, you may need to use efibootmgr to add the boot loader to the EFI's list:

```
# efibootmgr -c -l \\EFI\\redhat\\grub.efi -L GRUB
```

This command adds GRUB Legacy, stored in the ESP's /EFI/redhat directory, to the EFI's boot loader list. You must use doubled-up backslashes (\\) rather than the Linux-style forward slashes (/) as directory separators. Consult the efibootmgr utility's man page for more information.

You do *not* need to reinstall GRUB after making changes to its configuration file. (Such a reinstallation is required for some older boot loaders, though.) You need to install GRUB this way only if you make certain changes to your disk configuration, such as resizing or moving the GRUB root partition, moving your entire installation to a new hard disk, or possibly reinstalling Windows (which tends to wipe out MBR-based boot loaders). In some of these cases, you may need to boot Linux via a backup boot loader, such as GRUB installed to a floppy or USB disk.

Interacting with GRUB Legacy

The first screen the GRUB Legacy boot loader shows you is a list of all the operating systems you specified with the title option in your GRUB configuration file. You can wait for the timeout to expire for the default operating system to boot. To select an alternative, use your arrow keys to highlight the operating system that you want to boot. Once your choice is highlighted, press the Enter key to start booting.

Follow these steps when you want to change or pass additional options to your operating system:

1. Use your arrow keys to highlight the operating system that most closely matches what you want to boot.

2. Press the E key to edit this entry. You'll see a new screen listing all the options for this entry.

3. Use your arrow keys to highlight the kernel option line.

4. Press the E key to edit the kernel options.

5. Edit the kernel line to add any options, such as 1 to boot to single-user mode. GRUB Legacy passes the extra option to the kernel.

6. Press the Enter key to complete the edits.

7. Press the B key to start booting.

You can make whatever changes you like in step 5, such as using a different init program. You do this by appending init=/bin/bash (or whatever program you want to use) to the end of the kernel line.

Using GRUB 2 as the Boot Loader

In principle, configuring GRUB 2 is much like configuring GRUB Legacy; however, some important details differ. First, the GRUB 2 configuration file is /boot/grub/grub.cfg. (Some distributions place this file in /boot/grub2, enabling simultaneous installations of GRUB Legacy and GRUB 2.) GRUB 2 adds a number of features, such as support for loadable modules for specific filesystems and modes of operation, that aren't present in GRUB Legacy. (The insmod command in the GRUB 2 configuration file loads modules.) GRUB 2 also supports conditional logic statements, enabling loading modules or displaying menu entries only if particular conditions are met.

If you merely want to add or change a single OS entry, you'll find the most important changes are to the per-image options. Listing 5.2 shows GRUB 2 equivalents to the image options shown in Listing 5.1.

Listing 5.2: GRUB 2 image configuration examples

```
#
# Kernel Image Options:
#
menuentry "Fedora (3.4.1)" {
    set root=(hd0,1)
    linux /vmlinuz-3.4.1 ro root=/dev/sda5 mem=4096M
    initrd /initrd-3.4.1
}
menuentry "Debian (3.4.2-experimental)" {
    set root=(hd0,1)
    linux (hd0,1)/bzImage-3.4.2-experimental ro root=/dev/sda6
}
#
# Other operating systems
#
menuentry "Windows" {
    set root=(hd0,2)
    chainloader +1
}
```

Important changes compared to GRUB Legacy include the following:

- The title keyword is replaced by menuentry.
- The menu title is enclosed in quotation marks.
- An opening curly brace ({) follows the menu title, and each entry ends with a closing curly brace (}).

- The set keyword precedes the root keyword, and an equal sign (=) separates root from the partition specification.

- The rootnoverify keyword has been eliminated; you use root instead.

- Partitions are numbered starting from 1 rather than from 0. A similar change in disk numbering is *not* implemented. This change can be very confusing if you're used to GRUB Legacy, but it makes partition numbering mix-ups when "translating" from Linux-style partition numbering less likely. The most recent versions of GRUB 2 also support a more complex partition identification scheme to specify the partition table type, as in (hd0,gpt2) to specify that the second GPT partition should be used, or (hd1,mbr3) to specify that the third MBR partition should be used.

GRUB 2 makes further changes, in that it employs a set of scripts and other tools that help automatically maintain the /boot/grub/grub.cfg file. The intent is that system administrators need never explicitly edit this file. Instead, you would edit files in /etc/grub.d, and the /etc/default/grub file, to change your GRUB 2 configuration. After making such changes, you must explicitly rebuild the grub.cfg file, as described shortly.

Files in /etc/grub.d control particular GRUB OS probers. These scripts scan the system for particular OSs and kernels and add GRUB entries to /boot/grub/grub.cfg to support those OSs. You can add custom kernel entries, such as those shown in Listing 5.2, to the 40_custom file to support your own locally compiled kernels or unusual OSs that GRUB doesn't automatically detect.

The /etc/default/grub file controls the defaults created by the GRUB 2 configuration scripts. For instance, if you want to adjust the timeout, you might change the following line:

```
GRUB_TIMEOUT=10
```

A distribution that's designed to use GRUB 2, such as Ubuntu, will automatically run the configuration scripts after certain actions, such as installing a new kernel with the distribution's package manager. If you need to make changes yourself, you can type **update-grub** or **grub-mkconfig > /boot/grub/grub.cfg** after you've edited /etc/default/grub or files in /etc/grub.d. This command re-reads these configuration files and writes a fresh /boot/grub/grub.cfg file. (Some installations use 2 after grub in command names, as in grub2-mkconfig rather than grub-mkconfig.)

Unlike GRUB Legacy, GRUB 2 is designed to work with both BIOS and EFI-based computers, as well as with a few more-exotic firmware types. When you first install Linux, the installer should set up GRUB correctly, using grub-install in much the way described for GRUB Legacy. On EFI-based computers, GRUB 2's version of grub-install should install the GRUB 2 EFI binary file where it belongs; but if you have problems, you may need to use efibootmgr, as described earlier with reference to GRUB Legacy.

Using Alternative Boot Loaders

Although GRUB Legacy and GRUB 2 dominate the Linux boot loader arena today and are the only boot loaders covered on the exam, there are several others that you may encounter and that deserve mention:

Syslinux   The Syslinux Project (http://www.syslinux.org) is actually a family of BIOS-based boot loaders, each of which is much smaller and more specialized than GRUB Legacy or GRUB 2. The most notable member of this family is ISOLINUX, which is a boot loader for use on optical discs, which have unique boot requirements. The EXTLINUX boot loader is another member of this family; it can boot Linux from an ext2, ext3, or ext4 filesystem.

LILO   The Linux Loader (LILO) was the most common Linux boot loader in the 1990s. It's primitive and limited by today's standards, and it works only on BIOS-based computers. For more information on LILO, go to http://freshmeat.net/projects/lilo/.

ELILO   The EFI Linux Loader (ELILO; http://elilo.sourceforge.net) is the oldest Linux boot loader for EFI-based computers. It's similar to LILO in its features and functionality and is used by some distributions (most notably, OpenSUSE) as the default boot loader on EFI-based computers.

The Linux Kernel   Since version 3.3.0, the Linux kernel has incorporated an EFI boot loader for x86 and x86-64 systems. On an EFI-based computer, this feature enables the kernel to serve as its own boot loader, eliminating the need for a separate tool such as GRUB 2 or ELILO.

rEFIt   This program, hosted at http://refit.sourceforge.net, is technically a boot manager, not a boot loader. It's popular on Intel-based Macs, but some builds of the program can be used on UEFI-based PCs, too. It presents a pretty graphical interface, enabling users to select their boot OS using icons rather than a text-based interface. rEFIt appears to have been abandoned; as I write, the last update was in 2010.

rEFInd   This program is derived from rEFIt so as to make it more useful on UEFI-based PCs and to extend its feature set. Like rEFIt, rEFInd is a boot manager, not a boot loader; it's intended to present a list of boot options to users. It's most useful on computers with EFI implementations that provide poor boot managers. It also provides features that are designed to work with the Linux kernel's built-in EFI boot loader, to simplify the passing of options required to get the kernel to boot. You can learn more at http://www.rodsbooks.com/refind/.

gummiboot   This is an open source EFI boot manager that's conceptually similar to rEFIt or rEFInd, but it uses a text-mode interface and fewer options. You can learn more at http://freedesktop.org/wiki/Software/gummiboot.

Although development of Linux boot loaders for BIOS-based computers has largely stabilized, with GRUB 2 now dominating this field, EFI boot loader development is quite dynamic, at least as of late 2012. This is likely to continue to be the case in the near future, since EFI-based computers are only now becoming common.

The fact that Microsoft is requiring use of a firmware feature known as *Secure Boot* is likely to have an impact on Linux boot loaders in late 2012 and 2013, too. With Secure Boot enabled, an EFI-based computer will launch a boot loader only if it's been cryptographically signed with a key whose counterpart is stored in the computer's firmware. The goal is to make it harder for malware authors to take over a computer by inserting their programs early in the boot process. The problem from a Linux perspective is that use of Secure Boot requires the signing of a Linux boot loader with Microsoft's key (since it's the only one that's guaranteed to be on most computers), the addition of a distribution-specific or locally generated key to the computer's firmware, or disabling Secure Boot. To date, Fedora has announced that it will use its own new boot loader, in conjunction with a signed version of GRUB, to launch Fedora 18 on EFI-based computers; and Ubuntu has announced that it will work with computer manufacturers to add its own key to computers and use its own signed boot loader. In practice, though, you may need to disable Secure Boot or generate your own key to boot an arbitrary Linux distribution or a custom-built kernel.

 Real World Scenario

Fixing a Damaged Boot Loader Installation

Linux systems sometimes become unbootable because the boot loader has been damaged. You can reinstall GRUB if you can manage to boot your system, but of course this is a catch-22. Most Linux distributions provide a way to resolve this problem by enabling you to boot the computer even if the on-disk boot loader isn't working. Try booting the installation disc you used to install the OS and look for an option to boot a kernel from the hard disk. Once the system is booted, you can use grub-install to reinstall GRUB. Alternatively, the installation disc may provide a recovery option that will help to automatically or semi-automatically restore a broken system.

If your distribution's install disc isn't helpful, you can try Super GRUB Disk (http://www .supergrubdisk.org), which is a bootable disc image with a variety of options to locate and use the GRUB configuration file on your hard disk. If Super GRUB Disk can find your GRUB configuration file, you can boot using it and then re-install GRUB to your hard disk.

If all else fails, you may be able to use GRUB's interactive features to locate and boot a kernel. Doing so, however, can be frustrating; a single typo can produce a failure to boot.

Understanding the Boot Process

Any time you modify the way your computer boots, the possibility exists that you won't get the results you expect. In these cases, it's useful to know where you can turn for more information about what is happening during startup. The reports you receive on a particular boot can better guide you once you understand something about what's *supposed* to happen when a Linux system boots.

Extracting Information about the Boot Process

Certain Linux kernel and module log information is stored in what is called the *kernel ring buffer*. By default, Linux displays messages destined for the kernel ring buffer during the boot process—they're those messages that scroll past too quickly to read. (Some distributions hide most or all of these messages unless you select a special option during the boot process.) You can inspect this information with this command:

dmesg

This command generates a lot of output, so you may want to pipe it through the `less` pager or redirect it to a file. Here are some examples of these commands:

dmesg | less
dmesg > boot.messages

Many Linux distributions store the kernel ring buffer to /var/log/dmesg soon after the system boots. Because new information is logged to the kernel ring buffer as the system operates and because the kernel ring buffer's size is finite, you may need to consult this log file to learn about the boot process once the system has been operating for a while. Also, because the kernel ring buffer is held in memory, its contents are cleared and generated anew with every boot of the computer.

Another source of logging information is the system logger (`syslogd`). The most useful `syslogd` file to look at is usually /var/log/messages, but /var/log/syslog and other log files in /var/log can also hold helpful information.

Some Linux distributions also log boot-time information to other files. Debian uses a daemon called `bootlogd` that, by default, logs any messages that go to /dev/console to the /var/log/boot file. Fedora and Red Hat use `syslogd` services to log information to /var/log/boot.log.

Locating and Interpreting Boot Messages

Boot messages in the kernel ring buffer or /var/log files can be cryptic to the uninitiated. Some tips can help you locate and interpret the information you find in these sources:

Use `less` and Its Search Functions   The `less` pager is a great tool for examining both the kernel ring buffer and log files. The search function (accessed by pressing the slash key, /) can help you look for particular strings.

Look for Hardware Type Names   Many boot messages, particularly in the kernel ring buffer, relate to hardware. Try searching for the name of the hardware type, such as SCSI or USB, if you're having problems with these subsystems. Remember that Linux treats many disk devices as SCSI disks, too!

Look for Hardware Chipset Names   Linux drivers sometimes log messages along with their driver names, which are usually based on the chipset in question. If you know your hardware well enough to know the chipset name, search for it or for a subset of it. For instance, searching for 8169 may turn up messages related to a RealTek 8169 Ethernet interface. Similarly, you can search for higher-level kernel module names, such as reiserfs for messages from the ReiserFS filesystem driver.

Study the Output from a Working System   Familiarize yourself with the contents of the kernel ring buffer and log files on a working system. If you know what to expect when a system is functioning correctly, you'll find it easier to identify problems when they occur.

Sometimes, a system won't boot at all. In this case, kernel boot messages (which ordinarily go into the kernel ring buffer) are displayed on the screen, which can help you identify the cause of a failure. Many modern Linux distributions hide these messages by default, but you can sometimes reveal them by pressing the Esc key during the boot process. Once the kernel boot process has completed, other systems take over, and the last few messages displayed on the screen can also provide clues—for instance, if the last message displayed mentions starting a particular server, it's possible that the server is hanging and interrupting the boot process. You may be able to disable the server by using a single-user boot mode and therefore bypass the problem.

The Boot Process

The process of taking an *x*86 computer from its initial state when the power is turned on to having a working operating system running is complex because of the way modern personal computers have evolved. The steps a computer goes through in order to boot an operating system are as follows:

1. The system is given power, and a special hardware circuit causes the CPU to look at a predetermined address and execute the code stored in that location. The firmware (BIOS or EFI) resides at this location, so the CPU runs the firmware.

2. The firmware performs some tasks. These include checking for hardware, configuring hardware, and looking for a boot loader.

3. When the boot loader takes over from the firmware, it loads a kernel or chainloads to another boot loader, as described earlier in this chapter.

4. Once the Linux kernel takes over, it performs tasks such as initializing devices, mounting the root partition, and finally loading and executing the initial program for your system. By default, this is the program /sbin/init.

5. The initial program gets the process ID (PID) of 1 because it's the first program to run on the system. In a traditional Linux boot system, /sbin/init reads the /etc/inittab

file to determine what other programs to run. On systems that use the newer Upstart or systemd startup systems, /sbin/init reads other configuration files.

How the init program and the initialization scripts work is covered next, in "Dealing with Runlevels and the Initialization Process."

If you would like more details about this boot process, read http:// www.linuxdevcenter.com/pub/a/linux/excerpts/linux_kernel/how_ computer_boots.html. This page describes the process from the computer being powered up to the kernel being loaded and launching /sbin/init.

Dealing with Runlevels and the Initialization Process

Linux relies on *runlevels* to determine what features are available. Runlevels are numbered from 0 to 6, and each one is assigned a set of services that should be active. Upon booting, Linux enters a predetermined runlevel, which you can set. Knowing what these functions are, and how to manage runlevels, is important if you're to control the Linux boot process and ongoing operations. To this end, you must understand the purpose of runlevels, be able to identify the services that are active in a runlevel, be able to adjust those services, be able to check your default and current runlevels, and be able to change the default and current runlevels.

The next few pages describe the traditional *System V (SysV)* initialization system. Upstart and systemd differ from this system, although they provide enough compatibility features that many of the tools and concepts described with respect to SysV also apply to these newer systems. Upstart and systemd provide their own additional tools, though.

Runlevel Functions

Earlier in this chapter, I described single-user mode. To get to this mode when booting Linux, you use the number 1, the letter S or s, or the word single as an option passed to the kernel by the boot loader. Single-user mode is simply an available runlevel for your system. The available runlevels on most systems are the numbers 0 through 6. The letters S and s are synonymous with runlevel 1 as far as many utilities are concerned.

Runlevels 0, 1, and 6 are reserved for special purposes; the remaining runlevels are available for whatever purpose you or your Linux distribution provider decide. Table 5.1 summarizes the conventional uses of the runlevels. Other assignments—and even runlevels outside the range of 0 to 6—are possible with some systems, but such configurations are rare. If you run into peculiar runlevel numbers, consult /etc/inittab—it defines them and often contains comments explaining the various runlevels.

TABLE 5.1   Runlevels and their purposes

Runlevel	Purpose
0	A transitional runlevel, meaning that it's used to shift the computer from one state to another. Specifically, it shuts down the system. On modern hardware, the computer should completely power down. If not, you're expected to either reboot the computer manually or power it off.
1, s, or S	Single-user mode. What services, if any, are started at this runlevel varies by distribution. It's typically used for low-level system maintenance that may be impaired by normal system operation, such as resizing partitions.
2	On Debian and its derivatives, a full multi-user mode with X running and a graphical login. Most other distributions leave this runlevel undefined.
3	On Fedora, Mandriva, Red Hat, and most other distributions, a full multi-user mode with a console (non-graphical) login screen.
4	Usually undefined by default and therefore available for customization.
5	On Fedora, Mandriva, Red Hat, and most other distributions, the same behavior as runlevel 3 with the addition of having X run with an XDM (graphical) login.
6	Used to reboot the system. This runlevel is also a transitional runlevel. Your system is completely shut down, and then the computer reboots automatically.

WARNING   Don't configure your default runlevel to 0 or 6. If you do, your system will immediately shut down or reboot once it finishes powering up. Runlevel 1 could conceivably be used as a default, but chances are you'll want to use 2, 3, or 5 as your default runlevel, depending on your distribution and use for the system.

As a general rule, distributions have been drifting toward Red Hat's runlevel set; however, there are some exceptions and holdouts, such as Debian. Distributions that use newer startup systems generally don't use runlevels natively, but they provide compatibility tools that make the computer appear to use runlevels for the benefit of scripts and programs that assume the use of runlevels.

Identifying the Services in a Runlevel

There are two main ways to affect what programs run when you enter a new SysV runlevel. The first is to add or delete entries in your /etc/inittab file. A typical /etc/inittab file contains many entries, and except for a couple of special cases, inspecting or changing the contents of this file is best left to experts. Once all the entries in /etc/inittab for your runlevel are executed, your boot process is complete, and you can log in.

The /etc/inittab file is one SysV feature that may not be used by newer startup systems, such as Upstart and systemd. Ubuntu 12.04, which uses Upstart, provides no /etc/inittab file at all. Fedora 17, which uses systemd, provides an /etc/inittab file that contains nothing but comments noting its obsolescence. OpenSUSE 12.1 is also based on systemd, and it provides an /etc/inittab file, but it's no longer used in any meaningful way. Some other distributions, such as Debian, continue to use SysV, and the exam continues to emphasize SysV (including /etc/inittab).

Basics of the */etc/inittab* File

Entries in /etc/inittab follow a simple format. Each line consists of four colon-delimited fields:

```
id:runlevels:action:process
```

Each of these fields has a specific meaning:

Identification Code   The *id* field consists of a sequence of one to four characters that identifies its function.

Applicable Runlevels   The *runlevels* field consists of a list of runlevels for which this entry applies. For instance, 345 means the entry is applicable to runlevels 3, 4, and 5.

Action to Be Taken   Specific codes in the *action* field tell init how to treat the process. For instance, wait tells init to start the process once when entering a runlevel and to wait for the process's termination, and respawn tells init to restart the process whenever it terminates (which is great for login processes). Several other actions are available; consult the man page for inittab for details.

Process to Run   The *process* field is the process to run for this entry, including any options and arguments that are required.

The part of /etc/inittab that tells init how to handle each runlevel looks like this:

```
l0:0:wait:/etc/init.d/rc 0
l1:1:wait:/etc/init.d/rc 1
l2:2:wait:/etc/init.d/rc 2
l3:3:wait:/etc/init.d/rc 3
l4:4:wait:/etc/init.d/rc 4
l5:5:wait:/etc/init.d/rc 5
l6:6:wait:/etc/init.d/rc 6
```

These lines start with codes that begin with an l (a lowercase letter *L*, not a number 1) followed by the runlevel number—for instance, l0 for runlevel 0, l1 for runlevel 1, and so on. These lines specify scripts or programs that are to be run when the specified runlevel is entered. In the case of this example, all the scripts are the same (/etc/init.d/rc), but the script is passed the runlevel number as an argument. Some distributions call specific programs for certain runlevels, such as shutdown for runlevel 0.

The upcoming section "Checking and Changing Your Default Runlevel" describes how to tell `init` what runlevel to enter when the system boots.

The SysV Startup Scripts

The `/etc/init.d/rc` or `/etc/rc.d/rc` script performs the crucial task of running all the scripts associated with the runlevel. The runlevel-specific scripts are stored in `/etc/rc.d/rc?.d`, `/etc/init.d/rc?.d`, `/etc/rc?.d`, or a similar location. (The precise location varies between distributions.) In all these cases, *?* is the runlevel number. When entering a runlevel, `rc` passes the `start` parameter to all the scripts with names that begin with a capital S and passes the `stop` parameter to all the scripts with names that begin with a capital K. These *SysV startup scripts* start or stop services depending on the parameter they're passed, so the naming of the scripts controls whether they're started or stopped when a runlevel is entered. These scripts are also numbered, as in `S10network` and `K35smb`.

The `rc` program runs the scripts in numeric order. This feature enables distribution designers to control the order in which scripts run by giving them appropriate numbers. This control is important because some services depend on others. For instance, network servers must normally be started after the network is brought up.

In reality, the files in the SysV runlevel directories are symbolic links to the main scripts, which are typically stored in `/etc/rc.d`, `/etc/init.d`, or `/etc/rc.d/init.d` (again, the exact location depends on the distribution). These original SysV startup scripts have names that lack the leading S or K and number, as in `smb` instead of `K35smb`.

You can also start services by hand. Run them with the `start` option, as in **/etc/init.d/smb start** to start the smb (Samba) server. Other useful options are `stop`, `restart`, and `status`. Most scripts support all these options.

To determine which services are active in a runlevel, search the appropriate SysV startup script directory for scripts with filenames that begin with an S. Alternatively, you can use a runlevel management tool, as described next.

Distributions based on Upstart and systemd often provide startup scripts that are named and work much like on SysV-based computers; however, when the computer boots, it may use other startup methods, as described later, in "Using Alternative Boot Systems." The SysV scripts are provided mainly for backward compatibility to help system administrators who are familiar with the SysV startup method and for the benefit of administrative scripts that might rely on SysV scripts. Fedora is notable in that it provides very few such compatibility scripts (at least as of Fedora 17); you may need to use native systemd methods rather than SysV if you use Fedora.

Managing Runlevel Services

The SysV startup scripts in the runlevel directories are symbolic links back to the original script. This is done so you don't need to copy the same script into each runlevel directory.

Instead, you can modify the original script without having to track down its copies in all the SysV runlevel directories. You can also modify which programs are active in a runlevel by editing the link filenames. Numerous utility programs are available to help you manage these links, such as chkconfig, update-rc.d, and rc-update. I describe the first of these tools because it's supported on many distributions. If your distribution doesn't support these tools, you should check distribution-centric documentation. These tools may provide impaired functionality on systems that don't use SysV natively; you may need to locate Upstart- or systemd-specific tools instead.

To list the services and their applicable runlevels with chkconfig, use the --list option. The output looks something like this but is likely to be much longer:

```
# chkconfig --list
pcmcia       0:off   1:off   2:on    3:on    4:on    5:on    6:off
nfs-common   0:off   1:off   2:off   3:on    4:on    5:on    6:off
xprint       0:off   1:off   2:off   3:on    4:on    5:on    6:off
setserial    0:off   1:off   2:off   3:off   4:off   5:off   6:off
```

This output shows the status of the services in all seven runlevels. For instance, you can see that nfs-common is inactive in runlevels 0–2, active in runlevels 3–5, and inactive in runlevel 6.

If you're interested in a specific service, you can specify its name:

```
# chkconfig --list nfs-common
nfs-common   0:off   1:off   2:off   3:on    4:on    5:on    6:off
```

To modify the runlevels in which a service runs, use a command like this:

```
# chkconfig --level 23 nfs-common on
```

The previous example is for Debian-based systems. On Red Hat and similar systems, you would probably want to target runlevels 3, 4, and 5 with something like --level 345 rather than --level 23.

You can set the script to be on (to activate it), off (to deactivate it), or reset (to set it to its default value).

If you've added a startup script to the main SysV startup script directory, you can have chkconfig register it and add appropriate start and stop links in the runlevel directories. When you do this, chkconfig inspects the script for special comments to indicate default runlevels. If these comments are in the file and you're happy with the suggested levels, you can add it to these runlevels with a command like this:

```
# chkconfig --add nfs-common
```

This command adds the nfs-common script to those managed by chkconfig. You would, of course, change nfs-common to your script's name. This approach may not work if the script lacks the necessary comment lines with runlevel sequence numbers for chkconfig's benefit.

Checking Your Runlevel

Sometimes it's necessary to check your current runlevel. Typically, you'll do this prior to changing the runlevel or to check the status if something isn't working correctly. Two different runlevel checks are possible: checking your default runlevel and checking your current runlevel.

Checking and Changing Your Default Runlevel

On a SysV-based system, you can determine your default runlevel by inspecting the /etc/inittab file with the less command or opening it in an editor. Alternatively, you may use the grep command to look for the line specifying the initdefault action. On a Debian system, you'll see something like this:

```
# grep :initdefault: /etc/inittab
id:2:initdefault:
```

If grep returns nothing, chances are you've either mistyped the command or your computer is using Upstart, systemd, or some other initialization tool. On some systems, the second colon-delimited field will contain a 3, 5, or some value other than the 2 shown here.

You may notice that the id line doesn't define a process to run. In the case of the initdefault action, the process field is ignored.

If you want to change the default runlevel for the next time you boot your system, edit the initdefault line in /etc/inittab and change the runlevel field to the value you want. If your system lacks an /etc/inittab file, create one that contains *only* an initdefault line that specifies the runlevel you want to enter by default.

If your system doesn't use SysV, you'll need to adjust the default runlevel in some other way, as described later in "Using Alternative Boot Systems."

Determining Your Current Runlevel

If your system is up and running, you can determine your runlevel information with the runlevel command:

```
# runlevel
N 2
```

The first character is the previous runlevel. When the character is N, this means the system hasn't switched runlevels since booting. It's possible to switch to different runlevels on a running system with the init and telinit programs, as described next. The second character in the runlevel output is your current runlevel.

Both Upstart and systemd provide `runlevel` commands for compatibility with SysV. These alternatives don't technically use runlevels, though, so the information is a sort of "translation" of what the startup system is using to SysV terms.

Changing Runlevels on a Running System

Sometimes you may want to change runlevels on a running system. You might do this to get more services, such as going from a console to a graphical login runlevel, or to shut down or reboot your computer. This can be accomplished with the `init` (or `telinit`), `shutdown`, `halt`, `reboot`, and `poweroff` commands.

Changing Runlevels with *init or telinit*

The `init` process is the first process run by the Linux kernel, but you can also use it to have the system reread the `/etc/inittab` file and implement changes it finds there or to change to a new runlevel. The simplest case is to have it change to the runlevel you specify. For instance, to change to runlevel 1 (the runlevel reserved for single-user or maintenance mode), you would type this command:

```
# init 1
```

To reboot the system, you can use `init` to change to runlevel 6 (the runlevel reserved for reboots):

```
# init 6
```

A variant of `init` is `telinit`. This program can take a runlevel number just like `init` to change to that runlevel, but it can also take the Q or q option to have the tool reread `/etc/inittab` and implement any changes it finds there. Thus, if you've made a change to the runlevel in `/etc/inittab`, you can immediately implement that change by typing **telinit q**.

The man pages for these commands indicate slightly different syntaxes; but `telinit` is sometimes a symbolic link to `init`, and in practice `init` responds just like `telinit` to the Q and q options.

The Upstart and systemd tools provide `init` and `telinit` commands that work much as they do on SysV-based computers.

Changing Runlevels with *shutdown*

Although you can shut down or reboot the computer with `init`, doing so has some problems. One issue is that it's simply an unintuitive command for this action. Another is that changing runlevels with `init` causes an immediate change to the new runlevel. This may cause other users on your system some aggravation because they'll be given no warning about the shutdown. Thus, it's better to use the shutdown command in a multi-user environment when you want to reboot, shut down, or switch to single-user mode. This command supports extra options that make it friendlier in such environments.

The shutdown program sends a message to all users who are logged into your system and prevents other users from logging in during the process of changing runlevels. The shutdown command also lets you specify when to effect the runlevel change so that users have time to exit editors and safely stop other processes they may have running.

When the time to change runlevels is reached, shutdown signals the init process for you. In the simplest form, shutdown is invoked with a time argument like this:

```
# shutdown now
```

This changes the system to runlevel 1, the single-user or maintenance mode. The now parameter causes the change to occur immediately. Other possible time formats include *hh:mm*, for a time in 24-hour clock format (such as 6:00 for 6:00 a.m. or 13:30 for 1:30 p.m.), and *+m* for a time *m* minutes in the future.

You can add extra parameters to specify that you want to reboot or halt (that is, power off) the computer. Specifically, -r reboots the system, -H halts it (terminates operation but doesn't power it off), and -P powers it off. The -h option may halt or power off the computer, but usually it powers it off. For instance, you can type **shutdown -r +10** to reboot the system in 10 minutes.

To give people some warning about the impending shutdown, you can add a message to the end of the command:

```
# shutdown -h +15 "system going down for maintenance"
```

If you schedule a shutdown but then change your mind, you can use the -c option to cancel it:

```
# shutdown -c "never mind"
```

Upstart and systemd provide shutdown commands of their own that function like the shutdown command of SysV. You may want to check your computer's man page for shutdown to verify that it works in the way described here; with development active in the realm of startup systems, you may find some surprises!

Changing Runlevels with the *halt, reboot,* and *poweroff* Commands

Three additional shortcut commands are halt, reboot, and poweroff. (In reality, reboot and poweroff are usually symbolic links to halt. This command behaves differently depending on the name with which it's called.) As you might expect, these commands halt the system (shut it down without powering it off), reboot it, or shut it down and (on hardware that supports this feature) turn off the power, respectively. As with `telinit` and `shutdown`, these commands are available in SysV, Upstart, and systemd.

In Exercise 5.1, you'll experiment with some of the methods of changing runlevels just described.

EXERCISE 5.1

Changing Runlevels

This exercise will demonstrate the effects of changing the runlevel in various ways on a working system. Be aware that some of the effects will be different from one system to another, depending on both the distribution and the system-specific configuration of the computer. Also, in the course of running this exercise, you'll reboot the computer, so you shouldn't do it on a system that anybody else is using. To manage your runlevels, follow these steps:

1. Log in as root, or acquire root privileges by using su or by using sudo with each of the following commands. Use a text-mode or remote login; some of the exercise activities will shut down X.

2. Type **runlevel** to learn your current runlevel. Recall that the first character returned refers to the previous runlevel (N denotes no previous runlevel; it hasn't been changed since the system booted). The second output character is the current runlevel. This is likely to be 2 on Debian or Debian-derived systems and 3 or 5 on Red Hat or Red Hat–derived systems.

3. If your system reports it's in runlevel 5, type **telinit 3** to switch to runlevel 3. Chances are your X server will stop working. (Pressing Alt+F7 from a text-mode console will show a blank text-mode screen rather than the X display this keystroke would normally reveal.)

4. If your system initially reported a runlevel of 3, type **telinit 5** to switch to runlevel 5. This will probably start X; however, if X is misconfigured, the screen is likely to blink two or three times and possibly display an error message. If X isn't installed, nothing much will happen, aside from a display about a few services being stopped and started. If X starts, you can get back to your text-mode console by pressing Ctrl+Alt+F1.

5. If your system reported that it was in runlevel 2, you can try other runlevels, such as 3, 4, or 5; however, this isn't likely to have much effect. You can temporarily start or stop X by typing **/etc/init.d/gdm start** or **/etc/init.d/gdm stop**. (You may need to change gdm to xdm, mdm, or kdm.)

6. Return to your original runlevel using `telinit`, as in **telinit 5**.

7. If your distribution uses /etc/inittab and sets the default runlevel to 5, edit that file and change the default runlevel by changing the number in the line that reads id:*n*:initdefault:. The number, *n*, is likely to be either 3 or 5; change it to the other

value. (It's wise to make a backup of /etc/inittab before editing it!) If your distribution doesn't use /etc/inittab or sets a default runlevel of 2, don't make any changes to this file, and skip ahead to step 11.

8. Reboot the computer by typing **reboot now** or **shutdown -r now**.

9. Log in as root again, and type **runlevel** to verify that you're running in the runlevel you specified in step 7.

10. Edit /etc/inittab to restore it to its original state, or restore it from its backup.

11. Type **telinit 6**. This enters runlevel 6, which reboots the system. The computer should now be running as it was before you began this exercise.

Using Alternative Boot Systems

The preceding sections have described the traditional Linux boot and runlevel system, based on SysV scripts. In recent years, however, Linux developers have begun experimenting with several alternatives to SysV, and some of these have become popular. Two in particular, Upstart and systemd, are worth describing. Both include compatibility features to ease the transition from SysV, but they provide unique features of their own.

Configuring Upstart

Several modern Linux distributions, including recent versions of Ubuntu, now use an init process called Upstart (http://upstart.ubuntu.com) rather than the venerable SysV startup system. Broadly speaking, Upstart does the same job as the SysV scripts, but Upstart is designed to better handle today's dynamically changing *hotplug* hardware, which can be connected to and disconnected from a computer while it's still running. Upstart provides SysV compatibility features, so you should be familiar with the SysV methods described earlier; however, it also has its own unique scripts and differs in some important ways. In particular, Upstart does away with /etc/inittab, instead providing an integrated set of startup scripts that can, in principle, completely replace the SysV-style /etc/inittab and runlevel-specific startup scripts. Upstart scripts also support starting or stopping services based on a wider variety of actions than do SysV startup scripts; for instance, Upstart can launch a service whenever a particular hardware device is attached.

Using Upstart-Native Methods

A system that uses nothing but Upstart and its native scripts replaces both /etc/inittab and the runlevel-specific SysV startup script directories with scripts in the /etc/init directory. (This directory was called /etc/event.d on earlier versions of Upstart.) You may want to check the contents of this directory on your own Upstart-based system.

As I write, Upstart is under heavy development, and its configuration file format is subject to change. Thus, you may find differences from what is described in these pages.

To change the runlevels in which a particular service runs, you'll have to edit its configuration file in a text editor. Locate the script (typically /etc/init/*name*.conf, where *name* is the name of the service), and load it into a text editor. Look for lines that include the text start on and stop on, as in the following example:

```
start on (filesystem
          and started hal
          and tty-device-added KERNEL=tty7
          and (graphics-device-added or stopped udevtrigger))
stop on runlevel [016]
```

Locate any runlevel specification and adjust it for your needs. For instance, you might change the preceding example's stop on runlevel specification to read stop on runlevel [0126] to include runlevel 2 in the list of runlevels on which the service is to be stopped.

After you make such a change, you can use the start or stop command to immediately start or stop the service, as in **stop gdm** to shut down the gdm server. Before changing your runlevel (as described earlier, in "Changing Runlevels on a Running System"), you should type **initctl reload** to have Upstart reread its configuration files.

If you upgrade the package that provides the Upstart configuration script, you may need to reconfigure it.

Using SysV Compatibility Methods

Because the SysV startup script system has been so common for so long, a large number of software packages include SysV startup scripts. To accommodate such packages, Upstart provides a compatibility mode: It runs SysV startup scripts in the usual locations (/etc/rc.d/rc?.d, /etc/init.d/rc?.d, /etc/rc?.d, or a similar location). Thus, if you install a package that doesn't yet include an Upstart configuration script, it should still launch in the usual way. Furthermore, if you've installed utilities such as chkconfig, you should be able to use them to manage your SysV-based services just as you would on a SysV-based system.

You may find, however, that chkconfig and other SysV-based tools no longer work for some services. As time goes on, this is likely to be true for more and more services, because the developers of distributions that favor Upstart may convert their packages' startup scripts to use Upstart-native methods.

Using systemd

The systemd startup package (http://www.freedesktop.org/wiki/Software/systemd/) is a second major contender to replace SysV scripts. It's intended to provide faster and more flexible startup compared to SysV scripts. This is accomplished by enabling parallel startup of services and startup of services based on external activation (as opposed to starting items linearly according to fixed runlevels).

Fedora 15 and newer, Mandriva 2011 and newer, and OpenSUSE 12.1 and newer all use systemd by default. Some other distributions, such as Debian and Gentoo, provide systemd as an option but don't use it by default.

Most systemd configuration files reside in /etc/systemd and its subdirectories. The /etc/rc.conf file is also sometimes used, although it's absent by default on Fedora 17 and OpenSUSE 12.1 installations. These configuration files consist of sections identified by names in brackets, followed by assignments of values to variables, as in the following:

```
[Manager]
LogLevel=info
#LogTarget=syslog-or-kmsg
LogColor=yes
```

A hash mark (#) identifies a comment; lines beginning with this symbol are ignored. Chances are you'll find most lines in a default configuration are commented out in this way.

To control services on a systemd-based computer, either you can use SysV compatibility startup scripts (if provided) or you can use the systemctl utility. This tool takes a large number of options and commands, and you must also typically pass it a *unit* name, which is the name of a service upon which it acts. Table 5.2 summarizes the most important systemctl commands.

TABLE 5.2 systemctl commands

systemctl command name	Explanation
list-units	Displays the current status of all configured units.
start *name*	Starts the named unit.
stop *name*	Stops the named unit.
reload *name*	Causes the named unit to reload its configuration file.
restart *name*	Causes the named unit to shut down and restart.
status *name*	Displays the status of the named unit. (You can pass a PID value rather than a name, if you like.)
enable *name*	Configures the unit to start when the computer next boots.
disable *name*	Configures the unit to not start when the computer next boots.

Table 5.2 is incomplete; `systemctl` is a very complex tool with numerous commands and options. You should consult its man page to learn more about it. The commands presented in Table 5.2 will help you get started, though; they will help you to perform some of the most common tasks you'll want to do with it. As you can see, these commands provide the same basic features that SysV provides in its startup scripts and tools to manage them, such as `chkconfig`.

The `systemctl` unit names aren't quite identical to the SysV startup script names. Typically, services have the string `.service` appended. For instance, if you wanted to halt the `sendmail` service, you would type

```
# systemctl stop sendmail.service
```

Editing Files with Vi

Vi was the first full-screen text editor written for Unix. It's designed to be small and simple. Vi is small enough to fit on tiny, floppy-based emergency boot systems. For this reason alone, Vi is worth learning; you may need to use it in an emergency recovery situation. Vi is, however, a bit strange, particularly if you're used to GUI text editors. To use Vi, you should first understand the three modes in which it operates. Once you understand those modes, you can begin learning about the text-editing procedures Vi implements. You'll also examine how to save files and exit Vi.

 Most Linux distributions ship with a variant of Vi known as Vim, or "Vi Improved." As the name implies, Vim supports more features than the original Vi does. The information presented here applies to both Vi and Vim. Most distributions that ship with Vim support launching it by typing **vi**, as if it were the original Vi.

Understanding Vi Modes

At any given moment, Vi is running in one of three modes:

Command Mode   This mode accepts commands, which are usually entered as single letters. For instance, i and a both enter insert mode, although in somewhat different ways, as described shortly, and o opens a line below the current one.

Ex Mode   To manipulate files (including saving your current file and running outside programs), you use ex mode. You enter ex mode from command mode by typing a colon (:), typically directly followed by the name of the ex-mode command you want to use. After you run the ex-mode command, Vi returns automatically to command mode.

Insert Mode   You enter text in insert mode. Most keystrokes result in text appearing on the screen. One important exception is the Esc key, which exits insert mode and returns to command mode.

> If you're not sure what mode Vi is in, press the Esc key. Doing so returns you to command mode, from which you can reenter insert mode, if necessary.

Unfortunately, terminology surrounding Vi modes is inconsistent at best. For instance, command mode is sometimes referred to as normal mode, and insert mode is sometimes called edit mode or entry mode. Ex mode often isn't described as a mode at all but is referred to as *colon commands*.

Exploring Basic Text-Editing Procedures

As a method of learning Vi, consider the task of editing /etc/fstab to add a new disk to the computer. Listing 5.3 shows the original fstab file used in this example. If you want to follow along, enter it using a text editor with which you're already familiar, and save it to a file on your disk. Alternatively, copy your own computer's /etc/fstab file to a temporary location and make analogous changes to it.

Listing 5.3 Sample /etc/fstab file

```
/dev/sda2   /          ext4     defaults        1 1
/dev/sda1   /boot      ext4     defaults        1 2
/dev/sda4   /home      ext4     defaults        1 2
/dev/sda3   swap       swap     defaults        0 0
tmpfs       /dev/shm   tmpfs    defaults        0 0
devpts      /dev/pts   devpts   gid=5,mode=620  0 0
sysfs       /sys       sysfs    defaults        0 0
proc        /proc      proc     defaults        0 0
```

> Don't try editing your *real* /etc/fstab file as a learning exercise; a mistake could render your system unbootable! You might put your test fstab file in your home directory for this exercise.

The first step to using Vi is to launch it and have it load the file. In this example, type **vi fstab** while in the directory holding the file. The result should resemble Figure 5.3, which shows Vi running in an Xfce Terminal window. The tildes (~) down the left side of the display indicate the end of the file. (This feature is absent on some systems, though.) The bottom line shows the status of the last command—an implicit file-load command because you specified a filename when launching the program.

FIGURE 5.3   The last line of a Vi display is a status line that shows messages from the program.

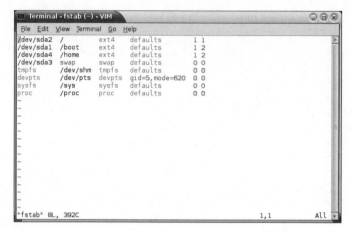

You can add a new entry to `fstab` using Vi either by typing it in its entirety or by duplicating an existing line and then modifying one copy. To do it the first way, follow these steps:

1. Move the cursor to the beginning of the /dev/sda3 line by using the arrow keys.

2. Press the O (letter O, not number 0) key. This opens a new line immediately below the current line, moves the cursor to that line, and enters insert mode.

> Although Vi's commands may seem arcane, many of them are mnemonic in their own way—that is, they're designed to be easily remembered, as in the letter *O* standing for *open line.*

3. Type a new entry, such as the following:

```
/dev/sdb1   /home2     ext4      defaults          0 0
```

4. Press the Esc key to return to command mode.

To practice making changes by modifying an existing entry, follow these steps:

1. Move the cursor to the beginning of the /dev/sdb1 line you just created by using the arrow keys, if necessary; you should see the cursor resting on the first / of /dev/sdb1.

> You can use the h, j, k, and 1 keys to move left, down, up, and right, respectively, if you prefer not to use the arrow keys.

2. You must now *yank* one line of text. This term is used much as *copy* is used in most text editors—you copy the text to a buffer from which you can later paste it back into the file. To yank text, you use the yy command, preceded by the number of lines you want to yank. Thus, type **1yy** (*do not* press the Enter key, though). The dd command

works much like yy, but it deletes the lines as well as copying them to a buffer. Both yy and dd are special cases of the y and d commands, respectively, which yank or delete text in amounts specified by the next character, as in dw to delete the next word.

3. Move the cursor to the line *before* the one where you want the new line to appear.

4. Type **p** (again, without pressing the Enter key). Vi pastes the contents of the buffer starting on the line after the cursor. The file should now have two identical /dev/sdb1 lines. The cursor should be resting at the start of the second one. If you want to paste the text into the document starting on the line *before* the cursor, use an uppercase P command.

5. Move the cursor to the 1 in /dev/sdb1 on the line you've just pasted. You're about to begin customizing this line.

6. Until now, you've operated Vi in command mode. You can use any of several commands to enter insert mode. At this point, the most appropriate is R, which enters insert mode so that it's configured for text replacement rather than insertion. If you prefer to insert text rather than overwrite it, you can use i or a (the latter advances the cursor one space, which is sometimes useful at the end of a line). For the purposes of these instructions, type **R** to enter insert mode. You should see -- REPLACE -- appear in the status line.

7. Type **2** to change /dev/sdb1 to /dev/sdb2.

8. Use the arrow keys to move the cursor to the 2 in /home2. You must modify this mount point name.

9. Type **3** to change /home2 to /home3.

 You can make more extensive changes to the fstab file, if you like, but be
WARNING sure to work from a *copy* of the file!

10. Exit insert mode by pressing the Esc key.

11. Save the file and quit by typing **:wq**. This is an ex mode command, as described shortly. (The ZZ command is equivalent to :wq.)

Many additional commands are available that you may want to use in some situations. Here are some of the highlights:

Change Case   Suppose you need to change the case of a word in a file. Instead of entering insert mode and retyping the word, you can use the tilde (~) key in command mode to change the case. Position the cursor on the first character you want to change, and press ~ repeatedly until the task is done.

Undo   To undo any change, type **u** in command mode.

Open Text   In command mode, typing **o** (a lowercase letter O) opens text—that is, it inserts a new line immediately below the current one and enters insert mode on that line.

Search To search forward for text in a file, type **/** in command mode, followed immediately by the text you want to locate. Typing **?** searches backward rather than forward.

Change Text The c command changes text from within command mode. You invoke it much like the d or y command, as in cw to change the next word or cc to change an entire line.

Go to a Line The G key brings you to a line that you specify. The H key "homes" the cursor—that is, it moves the cursor to the top line of the screen. The L key brings the key to the bottom line of the screen.

Replace Globally To replace all occurrences of one string with another, type **:%s/*original*/*replacement*/g**, where *original* is the original string and *replacement* is its replacement. Change % to a starting line number, comma, and ending line number to perform this change on a small range of lines.

   Vi offers a great deal more depth than is presented here; the editor is quite capable, and some Linux users are very attached to it. Entire books have been written about Vi. Consult one of these, or a Vi Web page like http://www.vim.org, for more information.

Saving Changes

To save changes to a file, type **:w** from command mode. This enters ex mode and runs the w ex-mode command, which writes the file using whatever filename you specified when you launched Vi. Related commands enable other functions:

Edit a New File The :e command edits a new file. For instance, **:e /etc/inittab** loads /etc/inittab for editing. Vi won't load a new file unless the existing one has been saved since its last change or unless you follow :e with an exclamation mark (!).

Include an Existing File The :r command includes the contents of an old file in an existing one.

Execute an External Command The ex-mode command :! executes the external command that you specify. For instance, typing **:!ls** runs ls, enabling you to see what files are present in the current directory.

Quit Use the :q command to quit the program. As with :e, this command won't work unless changes have been saved or you append an exclamation mark to the command (as in :q!).

You can combine ex commands such as these to perform multiple actions in sequence. For instance, typing **:wq** writes changes and then quits from Vi. (ZZ is the equivalent of :wq.)

Summary

Although Linux distributions are designed to boot painlessly and reliably once installed, understanding the boot process will help you overcome problems and maintain your system. Most Linux systems employ a boot loader known as GRUB (either GRUB Legacy or GRUB 2). These programs both fit themselves into the standard BIOS boot system, enabling the computer to load the Linux kernel. GRUB 2, and some patched versions of GRUB Legacy, also work on EFI-based computers. The kernel then runs the `init` program, which in turn reads various configuration files to boot all the services that make a running Linux system.

Modifying your GRUB configuration enables you to boot different Linux kernels or non-Linux OSs. You can also pass new boot options to Linux. Once the system is booted, you can use the `dmesg` command or log files to study the boot process in order to verify that it went correctly or to find clues as to why it didn't.

You can use the Vi editor to edit your GRUB configuration file, your system initialization scripts and configuration files, or any other plain-text file on your computer. Although Vi is old-fashioned in many ways, it's small and fits on emergency disk systems. Every administrator should be familiar with Vi, even if it's not your editor of choice for day-to-day operations.

Exam Essentials

Describe how GRUB Legacy is configured and used.   GRUB Legacy uses the `menu.lst` or `grub.conf` configuration file in `/boot/grub`. This file contains global and per-image options. Use the `grub-install` program to install the boot loader. When GRUB boots, it presents a menu of OS options that you select using the keyboard arrow keys.

Describe how GRUB 2 is configured and used.   GRUB 2 uses the `/boot/grub/grub.cfg` configuration file; however, system administrators are discouraged from editing it directly. Instead, they should rely on automatic configuration scripts and set system-specific defaults in `/etc/defaults/grub` and the files in `/etc/grub.d`. As with GRUB Legacy, you can install GRUB 2 using the `grub-install` program.

Describe the boot process.   The CPU runs the firmware, the firmware loads and runs a boot loader, the boot loader loads and runs secondary boot loaders (if needed) and the Linux kernel, the Linux kernel loads and runs the initial system program (`init`), and `init` starts the rest of the system services via startup scripts that are specific to the startup system (SysV, Upstart, systemd, or something more exotic). BIOS-based computers look for boot loaders in various boot sectors, including the MBR of a hard drive or the boot sector of a disk partition or floppy disk. EFI-based computers look for boot loaders in files on the ESP.

Summarize where to look for boot-time log information.   The `dmesg` command prints out logs from the kernel ring buffer, which holds boot-time and other kernel messages. Other useful log information can be found in `/var/log/messages` and other files in `/var/log`.

Summarize the role of /sbin/init.   The `init` program is responsible for starting many programs and services on your Linux operating system. This is done by running processes that are listed in `/etc/inittab`, including an `rc` script that runs the SysV initialization scripts.

Explain how runlevels are configured.   The default runlevel is specified with a line like id:2:initdefault: in the /etc/inittab file. Use commands such as chkconfig, update-rc.d, ntsysv, and systemctl to change which services are started when switching to specific runlevels. Runlevels 0, 1, and 6 are reserved for shutdown, single-user mode, and rebooting, respectively. Runlevels 3, 4, and 5 are the common user runlevels on Red Hat and most other distributions, and runlevel 2 is the usual user runlevel on Debian systems.

Describe how to change runlevels.   The programs init and telinit can be used to change to other runlevels. shutdown, halt, poweroff, and reboot are also useful when shutting down, rebooting, or switching to single-user mode.

Describe Vi's three editing modes.   You enter text using insert mode, which supports text entry and deletion. The command and ex modes are used to perform more complex commands or to run outside programs to operate on the text entered or changed in insert mode.

Review Questions

1. Where might the BIOS find a boot loader?

   A. RAM

   B. /dev/boot

   C. MBR

   D. /dev/kmem

   E. The swap partition

2. You want to boot a Linux system into single-user mode. What option might you add to a Linux kernel's options list at a boot loader to accomplish this task?

   A. `one`

   B. `single-user`

   C. `1`

   D. `telinit 6`

   E. `telinit 1`

3. After booting, one of your hard disks doesn't respond. What might you do to find out what's gone wrong?

   A. Check the `/var/log/diskerror` log file to see what's wrong.

   B. Verify that the disk is listed in `/mnt/disks`.

   C. Check the contents of `/etc/inittab` to be sure it's mounting the disk.

   D. Type **dmesg | less**, and peruse the output for disk-related messages.

   E. Check the `menu.1st`, `grub.conf`, or `grub.cfg` configuration file.

4. What is the first program that the Linux kernel runs once it's booted in a normal boot process?

   A. `dmesg`

   B. `init`

   C. `startup`

   D. `rc`

   E. `lilo`

5. Which of the following is the GRUB 2 boot loader configuration file?

   A. `/dev/grub`

   B. The MBR

   C. `/boot/grub/grub.conf`

   D. `/boot/grub/grub.cfg`

   E. `/boot/grub/menu.1st`

6. How might you identify an initial RAM disk file in GRUB 2?

    A. `initrd /boot/initrd-3.4.2`

    B. `initrd=/boot/initrd-3.4.2`

    C. `initramfs /boot/initrd-3.4.2`

    D. `initramfs=/boot/initrd-3.4.2`

    E. `ramdisk=/boot/initrd-3.4.2`

7. Which command is used to install GRUB Legacy into the MBR of your first SATA hard drive?

    A. `grub (hd0,1)`

    B. `grub-install /dev/sda1`

    C. `lilo /dev/sda`

    D. `grub-install /dev/sda`

    E. `grub-legacy /dev/sda1`

8. The string `root (hd1,5)` appears in your `/boot/grub/menu.1st` file. What does this mean?

    A. GRUB Legacy tells the kernel that the kernel's root partition is the fifth partition of the first disk.

    B. GRUB Legacy looks for files on the sixth partition of the second disk.

    C. GRUB Legacy looks for files on the fifth partition of the first disk.

    D. GRUB Legacy installs itself in `/dev/hd1,5`.

    E. GRUB Legacy installs itself in `/dev/sdb5`.

9. What line in `/etc/inittab` would indicate that your default runlevel is 5?

    A. `ca:12345:ctrlaltdel:/sbin/shutdown -t1 -a -r now`

    B. `id:5:initdefault:`

    C. `si:5:sysinit:/etc/init.d/rcS`

    D. `15:5:wait:/etc/init.d/rc 5`

    E. `1:2345:respawn:/sbin/getty 38400 tty1`

10. Which runlevels are reserved by `init` for reboot, shutdown, and single-user mode purposes? (Select three.)

    A. 0

    B. 1

    C. 2

    D. 5

    E. 6

11. You type the following command:

    `$ runlevel`

    5 3

    What can you tell about your runlevel status? (Select two.)

    A. The current runlevel is 5.

    B. The current runlevel is 3.

    C. The previous runlevel is 5.

    D. The previous runlevel is 3.

    E. The runlevel is in the process of changing.

12. A system administrator types the following command:

    `# shutdown -c`

    What is the effect of this command?

    A. A previously scheduled shutdown is cancelled.

    B. The system shuts down and reboots immediately.

    C. The system shuts down and halts immediately.

    D. The system asks for confirmation and then shuts down.

    E. The system closes all open windows in X without shutting down.

13. Which of the following commands may *not* be used instead of `shutdown` in certain circumstances (with appropriate options added to one or the other command)?

    A. `reboot`

    B. `halt`

    C. `poweroff`

    D. `telinit`

    E. `takedown`

14. You want to change to single-user mode on a running system. What command might you use to do this?

    A. `runlevel 1`

    B. `telinit 1`

    C. `shutdown -1`

    D. `single-user`

    E. `halt to 1`

15. What does runlevel 4 do?

    A. It reboots the computer.

    B. It starts a multi-user system without X running.

    C. It starts a multi-user system with X and an X-based login running.

    D. It starts the computer into single-user mode.

    E. Its purpose isn't standardized, so it can be used for anything you like.

16. How would you remove two lines of text from a file using Vi?

    A. In command mode, position the cursor on the first line, and type **2dd**.

    B. In command mode, position the cursor on the last line, and type **2yy**.

    C. In insert mode, position the cursor at the start of the first line, hold down the Shift key while pressing the Down arrow key twice, and press the Delete key on the keyboard.

    D. In insert mode, position the cursor at the start of the first line, and press Ctrl+K twice.

    E. Using your mouse, select both lines, and then press the Delete or Backspace key.

17. In Vi's command mode, you type **:q!**. What is the effect?

    A. Nothing; this isn't a valid Vi command.

    B. The text :q! is inserted into the file you're editing.

    C. The program terminates and saves any existing files that are in memory.

    D. The program terminates without saving your work.

    E. An exclamation point (!) overwrites the character under the cursor in the text.

18. What is an advantage of Vi over Emacs?

    A. Vi is X-based and so is easier to use than Emacs.

    B. Vi encodes text in EBCDIC, which is more flexible than Emacs' ASCII.

    C. Vi's mode-based operations permit it to handle non-English languages.

    D. Vi includes a built-in Web browser and email client; Emacs doesn't.

    E. Vi is smaller and so can fit on compact emergency systems and embedded devices.

19. From Vi's command mode, you want to enter insert mode. How might you do this? (Select three.)

    A. Type **R**.

    B. Type **i**.

    C. Type **a**.

    D. Type **:**.

    E. Press Esc.

20. How do you exit Vi's insert mode in order to type command-mode commands?

A. Press the ~ key.

B. Press the Esc key.

C. Type Ctrl+X followed by Ctrl+C.

D. Press the F10 key.

E. Press the Shift+Insert key combination.

Exam 2

PART

II

Chapter
6

Configuring the X Window System, Localization, and Printing

THE FOLLOWING EXAM OBJECTIVES ARE COVERED IN THIS CHAPTER:

✓ 1.106.1 Install and configure X11

✓ 1.106.2 Set up a display manager

✓ 1.106.3 Accessibility

✓ 1.107.3 Localization and internationalization

✓ 1.108.4 Manage printers and printing

Major modern desktop OSs all provide some form of *graphical user interface* (GUI), which provides the windows, menus, dialog boxes, flexible fonts, and so on, with which you're probably familiar. In Linux, the main GUI is known as the X *Window System* (or X for short). X configuration is either very easy or moderately hard; most distributions today provide auto-detection and easy configuration options during installation, and these usually work correctly. When they don't or when you want to tweak the configuration, you must delve into the X configuration file or use a GUI X configuration tool. Doing either requires that you know how X treats the video hardware, among other things.

Beyond basic X configuration are a few extra topics. These include fonts, GUI login tools, user desktop environments, using X for remote access, and localization. Each of these topics is closely associated with basic X configuration, but they all go beyond it in one way or another, extending X's capabilities or providing more features for users, as described in this chapter.

The X display can be considered one form of output. Another is printing, and this chapter covers that topic, as well. With a properly configured printer, you can obtain hard copies of the documents you create and edit using both X and text-based applications.

Configuring Basic X Features

Basic X configuration specifies features such as the mouse used, the keyboard layout, the screen resolution, the video refresh rate, the display color depth, and the video card you're using. Some of these options require telling X about what hardware you have installed, whereas others enable you to adjust settings on your hardware. In any event, before you proceed with actual configuration you should know something about the X servers that are available for Linux, because your selection will determine what additional tools are available and what files you may need to adjust manually. GUI and text-mode configuration utilities can help you configure X; but sometimes you must delve into the configuration files, so knowing their format is important. This requires that you know what the major option groups do so you can adjust them.

X Server Options for Linux

Although X is by far the dominant GUI for Linux, several implementations of X are available:

XFree86   The dominant X server in Linux until 2004 was XFree86 (http://www.xfree86.org). This open source server supports a wide array of video cards and input devices, and most Linux software was originally designed with XFree86 in mind. As I write, the most recent version is 4.8.0. Significant changes occurred between 3.3.6 and the 4.*x* series, and some older utilities work only with the 3.3.6 and earlier versions of XFree86. Although a tiny number of elderly systems must run XFree86 3.3.6 or earlier for driver support reasons, most systems today run XFree86 4.*x* or X.org-X11; the latter is more common on distributions released since 2004.

X.org-X11   In 2004, most Linux distributions shifted from XFree86 to X.org-X11 because of licensing changes to XFree86. X.org-X11 6.7.0 was based on XFree86 4.3.99, but it's developed independently up to the current version, 7.7. Because X.org-X11 is based on XFree86, the two are virtually identical in most important respects. One significant difference is the name of the configuration file; another is the default location for fonts. Subsequent sections of this chapter point out these differences. You can learn more at http://www.x.org/wiki/.

Accelerated-X   The commercial Accelerated-X server from Xi Graphics (http://www.xig.com) is an alternative to the open source XFree86 and X.org-X11. In practice, running Accelerated-X is seldom necessary, but if you have problems getting your video card working, you may want to look into Accelerated-X; its driver base is independent of the more popular open source choices, so it's possible you'll have better luck with it. The Accelerated-X configuration tools and files are completely different from those described in "Methods of Configuring X" and "X Configuration Options," so you'll need to consult its documentation for help. The rest of this chapter's topics still apply to Accelerated-X.

In practice, it's usually easiest to stick with whatever X server your distribution provides. For modern distributions, this is most often X.org-X11. For a handful of elderly video cards, you may need to run the equally elderly XFree86 3.3.6 rather than a more recent version.

 Real World Scenario

Using Manufacturer-Provided Video Drivers

One of X's functions is to provide drivers that control the video card. XFree86, X.org-X11, and Accelerated-X all ship with a wide variety of drivers that support most video cards. Some cards, though, have weak support in the stock packages. Other cards are supported by the standard drivers, but those drivers don't support all of the video device's features. XFree86 4.*x* and X.org-X11 both support a modular driver architecture, which means you can drop in a driver module for your card and use it with minimal changes to your X configuration. Both AMD (formerly ATI) and nVidia provide Linux video card drivers designed to work with XFree86 and X.org-X11. (Both X servers can use the same drivers.) Thus, if you have problems with the standard X video drivers, you may want to check with your video card manufacturer and the video card chipset manufacturers for Linux drivers.

Installing and using the manufacturer-provided video drivers is usually a matter of extracting files from a tarball and running an installation script. Consult the documentation that comes with the driver for details. Many of these drivers are particularly helpful for enabling 3D acceleration features of modern cards. These features were first used by games but are increasingly being used by desktop environments and other non-game software.

One problem with manufacturer-supplied drivers is that they're often proprietary. You might not have source code, which means the drivers might not work on more exotic CPUs, and the drivers could cease working with a future upgrade to your X server. The AMD and nVidia drivers also both include Linux kernel drivers as a necessary component, so you'll need to reinstall the drivers if you upgrade your kernel.

Methods of Configuring X

Configuring X has traditionally been a difficult process because the X configuration file includes many arcane options. The task is made simpler if you can use a configuration utility, and most Linux distributions now run such a utility as part of the installation process. If the configuration utility doesn't do everything you want it to do, though, you may need to delve into the X configuration file to set options manually, so knowing something about its format will help a lot. You must also know how to go about restarting X in order to test your changes.

 The upcoming section "X Configuration Options" describes in more detail the major X features and how to control them.

X Configuration Utilities

Several configuration tools for XFree86 4.*x* and X.org-X11 are available:

The X Server Itself   The X server itself includes the capacity to query the hardware and produce a configuration file. To do this, type **XFree86 -configure** (for XFree86) or **Xorg -configure** (for X.org-X11) as root when no X server is running. The result should be a file called /root/XF86Config.new (for XFree86) or /root/xorg.conf.new (for X.org-X11). This file may not produce optimal results, but it's at least a starting point for manual modifications.

Distribution-Specific Tools   Many modern distributions ship with their own custom X configuration tools. These include Red Hat's (and Fedora's) Display Settings tool (accessible from the default desktop menu or by typing **system-config-display** in an xterm) and SUSE's YaST and YaST2. These tools frequently resemble the distribution's install-time X configuration tools, which can vary substantially.

xf86cfg or xorgcfg   This utility is named differently for XFree86 vs. X.org-X11. It's deprecated, meaning it's no longer supported; but if it's present on your system, it can help you tweak settings once X is at least partially running.

All of these utilities gather the same type of information needed to manually configure X. Your best bet for understanding these tools and what they want is to understand the underlying X configuration file's format and contents.

If you're using the old XFree86 3.3.6, the tools just described don't work. Instead, you'll need to use a tool such as xf86config, Xconfigurator, or XF86Setup; or you can configure X manually. Because so few systems today use anything as old as XFree86 3.3.6, I don't describe these tools in this book.

The X Configuration File Format

The X configuration file's name and location vary with the version of X being run:

X.org-X11   This server's configuration file is called xorg.conf, and it's usually stored in /etc/X11, although /etc and several other locations are also acceptable to the server.

Many modern X.org-X11 configurations omit the X configuration file entirely, instead relying on run-time auto-detection of hardware. This often works fine, but if X doesn't work or if some of its features are set incorrectly, you may need to generate an xorg.conf file by typing **Xorg -configure** when X is *not* running and edit the file manually, as described in subsequent sections.

XFree86 4.*x*   The XFree86 4.*x* configuration file is called XF86Config-4 or XF86Config, which is found in /etc/X11 or sometimes in /etc. This file's format is the same as for the X.org-X11 configuration file.

XFree86 3.3.6 and earlier   The X configuration file's name is XF86Config, and the file is most commonly located in /etc/X11 or /etc. Although the filename can be the same as for XFree86 4.*x*, the file format is slightly different. This book, like the exam, covers the newer format used by X.org-X11 and XFree86 4.*x*.

All three of these classes of X server use configuration files that are broken down into multi-line sections, one section for each major feature. These sections begin with a line consisting of the keyword `Section` and the section name in quotes and end with the keyword `EndSection`:

```
Section "InputDevice"
    Identifier    "Keyboard0"
    Driver        "kbd"
    Option        "XkbModel" "pc105"
    Option        "XkbLayout" "us"
    Option        "AutoRepeat" "500 200"
EndSection
```

This section tells X about the keyboard—its model, layout, and so on. Details for the sections you're most likely to need to adjust are described shortly, in "X Configuration Options."

For the most part, the different X servers support the same sections and most of the same option names. A few exceptions to this rule do exist, though:

- The `Option` keyword isn't used in XFree86 3.3.6 and earlier. Instead, the option name (such as `XkbLayout` or `AutoRepeat` in the preceding example) appears without quotes as the first word on the line.

- XFree86 3.3.6 and earlier don't use the `ServerLayout` section, described later in "Putting It All Together."

- XFree86 3.3.6 and earlier lack the `Identifier` and `Driver` lines, which are common in the XFree86 4.x and X.org-X11 configuration files.

- Some section-specific features vary between versions. I describe the most important of these in the coming pages.

The X Configure-and-Test Cycle

If your X configuration isn't working correctly, you need to be able to modify that configuration and then test it. Many Linux distributions configure the system to start X automatically; but starting X automatically can make it difficult to test the X configuration. To a new Linux administrator, the only obvious way to test a new configuration is to reboot the computer.

A better solution is to kick the system into a mode in which X is *not* started automatically. On Red Hat, Fedora, and similar distributions, this goal can be achieved by typing **telinit 3**. This action sets the computer to use runlevel 3, in which X normally doesn't run. Chapter 5, "Booting Linux and Editing Files," covers runlevels in more detail.

Some distributions, such as Debian, Ubuntu, and Gentoo, don't use runlevels as a signal for whether to start X. With such distributions, you must shut down the GUI login server by typing **/etc/init.d/xdm stop**. (You may need to change xdm to gdm, kdm, mdm, or lightdm, depending on your configuration.)

Once the X session is shut down, you can log in using a text-mode login prompt and tweak your X settings manually, or you can use text-based X configuration programs. You can then type **startx** to start the X server again. If you get the desired results, quit from X (typically by selecting a "log out" option in your desktop environment) and type **telinit 5** (**/etc/init.d/xdm start** in Debian and other distributions that don't use runlevels to start the GUI login prompt) to restore the system to its normal X login screen. If after typing **startx** you don't get the results you want, you can end your X session and try modifying the system some more.

If X is working minimally but you want to modify it using X-based configuration tools, you can do so after typing **startx** to get a normal X session running. Alternatively, you can reconfigure the system before taking it out of the X-enabled runlevel.

Another approach to restarting X is to leave the system in its X-enabled runlevel and then kill the X server. The Ctrl+Alt+Backspace keystroke does this on many systems, or you can do it manually with the `kill` command after finding the appropriate process ID with the ps command, as shown here:

```
# ps ax | grep X
1375 ?    S  6:32 /usr/bin/X -auth /var/gdm/:0.Xauth
# kill 1375
```

This approach works better on systems that don't map the running of X to specific runlevels, such as Debian and its derivatives.

X Configuration Options

When editing the X configuration file, the best approach is usually to identify the feature that's not working and zero in on the section that controls this feature. You can then edit that section, save your changes, and test the new configuration. In XFree86 4.*x* and X.org-X11, the major sections described here are called `Module`, `InputDevice`, `Monitor`, `Device`, `Screen`, and `ServerLayout`. You're likely to have two `InputDevice` sections, one for the keyboard and one for the mouse. (In XFree86 3.3.6 and earlier, the mouse is handled by a separate `Pointer` section.) The section order doesn't matter.

Fonts are a complex enough topic that they're described in more detail later, in "Configuring X Fonts." Part of this configuration is handled in the `Files` section.

Loading Modules

The `Module` section controls the loading of X server modules—drivers for specific features or hardware. A typical example looks like this:

```
Section "Module"
    Load  "dbe"
    Load  "extmod"
    Load  "fbdevhw"
    Load  "glx"
```

```
    Load   "record"
    Load   "freetype"
    Load   "type1"
    Load   "dri"
EndSection
```

Each module is named (dbe, extmod, and so on) and is loaded by name using the Load option. Most of these module names can be deciphered with a bit of knowledge about the features they control. For instance, freetype and type1 handle TrueType and Adobe Type 1 font rendering, respectively. If you're perusing your Module section and see modules you don't understand, you shouldn't worry about it; generally speaking, modules that are configured automatically are necessary for normal operation, or at least they do no harm.

For the most part, if an X configuration works, you shouldn't try to adjust the Module section, even if you want to tweak the X configuration. Sometimes, though, you'll need to add lines to or remove lines from this section. This is particularly likely to be necessary if you're activating 3D acceleration support or some sort of exotic feature. In such cases, you should consult the documentation for the feature you want to activate.

Setting the Keyboard

The keyboard is one of two common input devices configured via an InputDevice section:

```
Section "InputDevice"
    Identifier   "Keyboard0"
    Driver       "kbd"
    Option       "XkbModel" "pc105"
    Option       "XkbLayout" "us"
    Option       "AutoRepeat" "500 200"
EndSection
```

The Identifier line provides a label that's used by another section (ServerLayout, described in "Putting It All Together"). The string given on this line is arbitrary, but for a keyboard, a descriptive name such as this example's Keyboard0 will help you understand the file.

The Driver line tells X what driver to use to access the keyboard. This should be kbd, Keyboard, or evdev, depending on your X server. The kbd and Keyboard drivers are, as you might expect, keyboard-specific drivers. The evdev driver, by contrast, is a generic input device driver that works with many types of input devices. Unless your keyboard isn't working at all, you shouldn't adjust this line.

The Option lines set various options that adjust keyboard features, such as the model, the layout, and the repeat rate. For the most part, the defaults work well; however, you may want to change the AutoRepeat option or add it if it's not present. This option tells X when to begin repeating characters when you hold down a key and how often to repeat them. It takes two numbers as values, enclosed in quotes: the time until the first repeat and the time between subsequent repeats, both expressed in milliseconds (ms). In the preceding example, the system waits 500ms (half a second) for the first repeat and then 200ms for each subsequent repeat (that is, five repeats per second).

 Many desktop environments and other user-level utilities provide tools to set the keyboard repeat rate. Thus, the options you set in the X configuration file are used as defaults only and may be overridden by users' settings.

Setting the Mouse

A second `InputDevice` section controls how X treats the mouse:

```
Section "InputDevice"
    Identifier  "Mouse0"
    Driver      "mouse"
    Option      "Protocol" "IMPS/2"
    Option      "Device" "/dev/input/mice"
    Option      "Emulate3Buttons" "no"
    Option      "ZAxisMapping" "4 5"
EndSection
```

As with the keyboard, the `Identifier` line is used in the `ServerLayout` section to tell X which input device to use. The `Driver` line identifies the driver to use: `mouse`. (Many modern systems use `evdev` for the mouse.) The `Option` lines set mouse control options. The most important of these are `Device` and `Protocol`.

The `Device` line tells X what Linux device file to read to access the mouse. In this example, it's `/dev/input/mice`, but other possibilities include `/dev/mouse` (a pointer to the real mouse device, whatever its name), `/dev/psaux` (for the PS/2 mouse port), `/dev/usb/usbmouse` (an old identifier for USB mice), `/dev/ttyS0` (the first RS-232 serial port mouse), and `/dev/ttyS1` (the second RS-232 serial port mouse). If your mouse is working at all (even if its motions are erratic), don't change this line. If your mouse isn't working, you may need to experiment.

The `Protocol` option tells X what signals to expect from the mouse for various movements and button presses. The `Auto` protocol causes X to try to guess the mouse's protocol, which usually works correctly. If it doesn't work, you can try more specific protocols, such as `IMPS/2` and `ExplorerPS/2`, which are very similar in practice. (Note that "PS/2" is both a hardware interface and a software protocol; many USB mice use the PS/2 mouse protocol even though they don't use the PS/2 mouse port.) If your mouse has a scroll wheel, chances are you should use one of these protocols. If your mouse is older, you may need to try an older protocol, such as `PS/2`, `Microsoft`, or `Logitech`.

Additional options are usually less critical than the `Device` and `Protocol` options. The `Emulate3Buttons` option tells X whether to treat a *chord* (that is, a simultaneous press) of both buttons on a two-button mouse as if it were a middle-button press. This option is usually disabled on three-button mice and scroll mice (the scroll wheel does double duty as a middle mouse button). The ZAxisMapping option in the preceding example maps the scroll wheel actions to the fourth and fifth buttons, because X must treat scroll wheels as if they were buttons. When you scroll up or down, these "button" presses are generated. Software can detect this and take appropriate actions.

Setting the Monitor

Some of the trickiest aspects of X configuration relate to the monitor options. You set these in the Monitor section, which can sometimes be quite large. A modest Monitor section looks like this:

```
Section "Monitor"
    Identifier   "Monitor0"
    ModelName    "AOC e2343Fk"
    HorizSync    30.0 - 83.0
    VertRefresh  55.0 - 75.0
    # My custom 1920x1080 mode
    Modeline "1920x1080"   138.50   1920 1968 2000 2080   1080 1083 1088 1111
EndSection
```

As in the keyboard and mouse configurations, the Identifier option is a free-form string that contains information that's used to identify a monitor. The Identifier can be just about anything you like. Likewise, the ModelName option can be anything you like; it's used mainly for your own edification when reviewing the configuration file.

As you continue down the section, you'll see the HorizSync and VertRefresh lines, which are extremely critical; they define the range of horizontal and vertical refresh rates that the monitor can accept, in kilohertz (kHz) and hertz (Hz), respectively. Together, these values determine the monitor's maximum resolution and refresh rate. Despite the name, the HorizSync item alone doesn't determine the maximum horizontal refresh rate. Rather, this value, the VertRefresh value, and the resolution determine the monitor's maximum refresh rate. X selects the maximum refresh rate that the monitor will support given the resolution you specify in other sections. Some X configuration utilities show a list of monitor models or resolution and refresh rate combinations (such as "1024 × 768 at 72Hz"). You select an option, and the utility then computes the correct values based on that selection. This approach is often simpler to handle, but it's less precise than entering the exact horizontal and vertical sync values. You should enter these values from your monitor's manual.

WARNING   Don't set random horizontal and vertical refresh rates; on older hardware, setting these values too high can damage a monitor. (Modern monitors ignore signals presented at too high a refresh rate.)

To settle on a resolution, X looks through a series of *mode lines*, which are specified via the Modeline option. Computing mode lines is tricky, so I don't recommend you try it unless you're skilled in such matters. The mode lines define combinations of horizontal and vertical timing that can produce a given resolution and refresh rate. For instance, a particular mode line might define a 1024 × 768 display at a 90Hz refresh rate, and another might represent 1024 × 768 at 72Hz.

Some mode lines represent video modes that are outside the horizontal or vertical sync ranges of a monitor. X can compute these cases and discard the video modes that a monitor can't support. If asked to produce a given resolution, X searches all the mode lines that accomplish the job, discards those that the monitor can't handle, and uses the remaining mode line that creates the highest refresh rate at that resolution. (If no mode line supports the requested resolution, X drops down to another specified resolution, as described shortly, and tries again.)

Although you can include an arbitrary number of `Modeline` entries in your `Monitor` section, most such files lack these entries. The reason is that XFree86 4.x and X.org-X11 support a feature known as *Data Display Channel (DDC)*. This is a protocol that enables monitors to communicate their maximum horizontal and vertical refresh rates and appropriate mode lines to the computer. You may need to create a `Modeline` if this feature fails, though. Try performing a Web search on the keywords *modeline* (or *mode line*) and your desired video resolution; or try the XFree86 Modeline Generator Web site (`http://xtiming.sourceforge.net/cgi-bin/xtiming.pl`), which can generate a `Modeline` for any resolution and refresh rate you specify.

Setting the Video Card

Your monitor is usually the most important factor in determining your maximum refresh rate at any given resolution, but X sends data to the monitor only indirectly, through the video card. Because of this, it's important that you be able to configure this component correctly. An incorrect configuration of the video card is likely to result in an inability to start X.

In the past, video hardware was almost always implemented as a plug-in card. Most modern computers include video hardware on the motherboard, though. Despite this fact, it's common to refer to a *video card*, even if the computer lacks a separate plug-in card.

Choosing the Driver

Sometimes X, and particularly modern versions of X.org-X11, can pick the optimum video driver automatically. Other times, though, you must provide that information in the `XF86Config` or `xorg.conf` file. In particular, the driver module is set by a line in the `Device` section, which resembles the following:

```
Driver "nv"
```

This line sets the name of the driver. The drivers reside in the `/usr/X11R6/lib/modules/drivers/` or `/usr/lib/xorg/modules/drivers/` directory. (On some systems, `lib` becomes `lib64`.) Most of the drivers' filenames end in `_drv.o`, and if you remove this portion, you're left with the driver name. For instance, `nv_drv.o` corresponds to the nv driver.

Some X configuration utilities provide a large list of chipsets and specific video card models, so you can select the chipset or board from this list to have the utility configure this detail.

If you type **Xorg -configure** to create an initial configuration, the resulting file is likely to include multiple Device sections, each for a different driver. Some of these, such as fbdev and vesa, are generic drivers that work—but not optimally—on a wide variety of video cards. Today, you're most likely to use the nv or nouveau drivers (both of which work on nVidia cards), the radeon driver (which works on ATI/AMD cards), or the intel driver (which works on Intel cards). You'll need to know something about your video hardware to pick the best one. If you're in doubt, you can try using each one in turn, by specifying each Device section in turn in the Screen section, as described later, in "Setting the Resolution and Color Depth."

Setting Card-Specific Options

The Device section of the xorg.conf file sets various options related to specific X servers. A typical Device section resembles the following:

```
Section "Device"
    Identifier   "Videocard0"
    Driver       "nv"
    VendorName   "nVidia"
    BoardName    "GeForce 6100"
    VideoRam     131072
EndSection
```

The Identifier line provides a name that's used in the subsequent Screen section to identify this particular Device section. The VendorName and BoardName lines provide information that's useful mainly to people reading the file.

The VideoRam line is unnecessary with most boards because the driver can detect the amount of RAM installed in the card. With some devices, however, you may need to specify the amount of RAM installed in the card, in kilobytes. For instance, the preceding example indicates a card with 128MB of RAM installed.

Many drivers support additional driver-specific options. They may enable support for features such as hardware cursors (special hardware that enables the card to handle mouse pointers more easily) or caches (using spare memory to speed up various operations). Consult the XF86Config or xorg.conf man page or other driver-specific documentation for details.

Setting the Resolution and Color Depth

The Screen section tells X about the combination of monitors and video cards you're using. XFree86 4.*x* and X.org-X11 support multiple video cards and monitors on one system. This can be handy if you're testing a new monitor or video card driver. In any event, the Screen section looks something like this:

```
Section "Screen"
    Identifier "Screen0"
    Device      "Videocard0"
    Monitor     "Monitor0"
    DefaultDepth  24
    SubSection "Display"
        Depth     24
        Modes     "1920x1080" "1280x1024" "1024x768"
    EndSubSection
    SubSection "Display"
        Depth     8
        Modes     "1024x768" "800x600" "640x480"
    EndSubSection
EndSection
```

The `Device` and `Monitor` lines refer to the `Identifier` lines in your `Device` and `Monitor` sections, respectively. The `Screen` section includes one or more `Display` subsections, which define the video modes that X may use. This example creates two such displays. The first uses a color depth of 24 bits (`Depth 24`) and possible video mode settings of 1920x1080, 1280x1024, and 1024x768. (These video modes are actually names that refer to the mode lines defined in the `Monitor` section or to standard mode lines.) The second possible display uses an 8-bit color depth (`Depth 8`) and supports 1024x768, 800x600, and 640x480 video modes.

To choose between the `Display` subsections, you include a `DefaultDepth` line. In this example, X uses the 24-bit display if possible, unless it's overridden by other options when starting X.

Graphical video modes require a certain amount of RAM on the video card. (On some laptop computers and computers with video hardware integrated into the motherboard, a portion of system RAM is reserved for this use by the BIOS.) The total amount of RAM required is determined by an equation:

$$R = xres \times yres \times bpp \div 8{,}388{,}608$$

In this equation, R is the RAM in megabytes, $xres$ is the x resolution in pixels, $yres$ is the y resolution in pixels, and bpp is the bit depth. For instance, consider a 1280×1024 display at 24-bit color depth:

$$R = 1280 \times 1024 \times 24 \div 8{,}388{,}608 = 3.75\text{MB}$$

All modern video cards have at least 32MB of RAM—usually much more. This is more than enough to handle even very high resolutions at 32-bit color depth (the greatest depth possible). Thus, video RAM shouldn't be a limiting factor in terms of video mode selection, at least not with modern video hardware. Very old video cards can impose limits, so you should be aware of them.

Modern video cards ship with large amounts of RAM to support 3D acceleration features. X supports such features indirectly through special 3D acceleration packages, but 3D acceleration support is limited compared to basic video card support. If 3D acceleration is important to you, you should research the availability of this support.

Putting It All Together

XFree86 4.*x* and X.org-X11 require a section that's not present in the XFree86 3.3.6 configuration file: ServerLayout. This section links together all the other components of the X configuration:

```
Section "ServerLayout"
    Identifier      "single head configuration"
    Screen          "Screen0" 0 0
    InputDevice     "Mouse0" "CorePointer"
    InputDevice     "Keyboard0" "CoreKeyboard"
EndSection
```

Typically, this section identifies one Screen section and two InputDevice sections (for the keyboard and the mouse). Other configurations are possible, though. For instance, XFree86 4.*x* and X.org-X11 support *multi-head displays*, in which multiple monitors are combined to form a larger desktop than either one alone would support. In these configurations, the ServerLayout section includes multiple Screen sections.

 Real World Scenario

If All Goes Well....

In practice, you may not need to edit the X configuration file. As already noted, most Linux distributions configure X automatically at installation. Indeed, most distributions now rely on launch-time auto-configuration of X along with user settings for features such as resolution, keyboard repeat rate, and so on.

Desktop environments typically provide a dialog box, such as the one shown in Figure 6.1, that enable you to set the resolution, refresh rate, and sometimes other display options. Look for such options in the desktop environment's main settings tool, typically under a title such as *Display* or *Monitor*.

FIGURE 6.1   Modern desktop environments provide easy-to-use but limited X configuration options.

Obtaining X Display Information

Sometimes it's helpful to know about the capabilities of your display, as it's managed by X. The tool for this job is xdpyinfo. When you type **xdpyinfo**, the result is copious information about the current display, such as the X version number, the resolution and color depth of all the current displays, and so on. Much of this information is highly technical in nature, so you may not understand it all. That's OK. I recommend you run this program and peruse the output to see what you can learn from it. If you should later want to obtain similar information on another computer's display, you'll know how to obtain it.

For still more technical information, you can use the -ext *extension* option to xpdyinfo. The *extension* is the name of an X extension, which is a software module that provides extended capabilities to X. (The basic xpdyinfo command, without any options, lists all the available extensions.)

You can obtain detailed technical information about a specific window with the xwininfo command. In basic use, you type **xwininfo**, move the mouse cursor over a window, and click. The result is a list of assorted data about the window you clicked, such as the following:

```
Absolute upper-left X:   1171
Absolute upper-left Y:   611
Relative upper-left X:   6
Relative upper-left Y:   25
Width: 657
Height: 414
Depth: 32
```

```
Visual Class: TrueColor
Border width: 0
Class: InputOutput
Colormap: 0x2800003 (not installed)
Bit Gravity State: NorthWestGravity
Window Gravity State: NorthWestGravity
Backing Store State: NotUseful
Save Under State: no
Map State: IsViewable
Override Redirect State: no
Corners:  +1171+611  -92+611  -92-55  +1171-55
-geometry 80x24-86-49
```

Some of this information, such as the window's position and size, is easy to interpret. Other information, such as the color map and gravity state, is highly technical, and I don't describe it further here. You can pass various options to xwininfo to modify the information it displays or how you select a window, including the following:

Alternate Window Selection Methods   The -id *id* and -name *name* options enable you to identify a window by an ID number or by its name (normally displayed in the window's border), respectively. The -root option selects the root window—that is, the entire display.

Window Relationships   Like processes, windows can have parents and children. You can identify these relationships with the -children option. The -tree option works in a similar way, but it works recursively—that is, it displays information on the children of a window's children, and so on.

Basic Information   The -stats option is used by default. You can restrict the output by using the -bits option, which limits output to information on the window's bit states.

Additional Information   The -events option produces information on the events that the window processes; -size displays information on sizing hints; -wm displays window manager data; -shape is much like -stats but adds information on the window and border shapes; -frame modifies the display to include information on the window manager's frame; -metric adds measures in millimeters (mm) to the regular pixel-based measures; -english adds measures in feet and inches; and -all displays all available information.

Windows in X are created and managed by several programs. One of these, the *window manager*, handles the window's borders and enables you to drag the window around the screen and resize it. Some xwininfo statistics relate to the window *excluding* the window manager's elements, but others *include* these elements. Options such as -frame and -wm can modify this output or display information on the window manager's features specifically.

Real World Scenario

Wayland: The Future?

An entirely new method of managing displays, known as Wayland (http://wayland .freedesktop.org), is nearing readiness as I write. Wayland is intended to address many of the problems with X, which suffers from a design dating back to the 1980s, before many modern video features became available. Thus, X is hobbled by legacy features such as a font model that's been largely replaced by add-on font libraries.

Wayland-native applications won't use X at all, which will theoretically result in simpler application design, better speed, and fewer video problems, particularly for certain graphics-intensive applications. Existing X applications will continue to work via an X server to be included with Wayland. Essentially, X will run as a process within Wayland, although ideally this will be a stopgap measure.

The developers of several major Linux distributions, including Fedora and Ubuntu, have expressed an intention to support Wayland, either as an option or as the default graphics system. The timetable for such a change is uncertain, though. Furthermore, Wayland has yet to be accepted by users; if Wayland presents unexpected problems, it may flounder. You should watch for future developments concerning this software.

Configuring X Fonts

Fonts have long been a trouble spot for Linux (or more precisely, for X). X was created at a time when available font technologies were primitive by today's standards, and although X has been updated in various ways to take advantage of newer technologies, these updates have been lacking compared to the font subsystems in most competing OSs. X's core font system can be set up from the X configuration file. Alternatively, you can configure a *font server*—a program that delivers fonts to one or many computers using network protocols—to handle the fonts. The latest Linux font technology sets up fonts in a way that's more independent of X and that produces more pleasing results, at least to most people's eyes.

Some applications don't rely on either X or any other standard library to handle fonts; they manage their own fonts themselves. This practice is particularly common in word processors. If you configure your fonts as described here but find that an important program doesn't see the changes you've made, consult its documentation; you may need to tell the program where to look to use the fonts you've added.

Font Technologies and Formats

Font technologies can be classified as falling into one of two broad categories:

Bitmap Fonts   The simplest type of font format is the *bitmap font*, which represents fonts much like bitmap graphics, in which individual pixels in an array are either active or inactive. Bitmap fonts are fairly easy to manipulate and display, from a programming perspective, which makes them good for low-powered computers. The problem is that each font must be optimized for display at a particular resolution. For instance, a font that's 20 pixels high will appear one size on the screen (typically 72 to 100 dots per inch, or dpi) but will be much smaller when printed (typically at 300 to 1200 dpi). Similarly, you need multiple files to display a single font at multiple sizes (such as 9 point versus 12 point). This means a single font, such as Times, requires potentially dozens of individual files for display at different sizes and on different display devices. If you lack the correct font file, the result will be an ugly scaled display.

Outline Fonts   Most modern fonts are distributed as *outline fonts* (aka *scalable fonts*). This type of format represents each character as a series of lines and curves in a high-resolution matrix. The computer can scale this representation to any font size or for any display resolution, enabling a single font file to handle every possible use of the font. The main problem with outline fonts is that this scaling operation is imperfect; scalable fonts often look slightly worse than bitmap fonts, particularly at small sizes. Scaling and displaying the fonts also takes more CPU time than displaying a bitmap font. This factor used to be important, but on modern CPUs it's not much of an issue.

Both bitmap and outline fonts come in several different formats. X ships with a number of basic bitmap and outline fonts, and you're unlikely to need to deal explicitly with bitmap fonts or their formats, so I don't describe them in any detail. Outline fonts are another matter, though. The two main formats are Adobe's *PostScript Type 1* (Type 1 for short) and Apple's *TrueType*. Fonts available on the Internet and on commercial font CDs come in one or both of these formats.

XFree86 3.3.6 and earlier supported Type 1 fonts but not TrueType fonts. XFree86 4.*x* and X.org-X11 support both Type 1 and TrueType fonts.

Configuring X Core Fonts

X core fonts are those that are handled directly by X. To configure these fonts, you must do two things: prepare a font directory that holds the fonts, and add the font directory to X's font path.

Preparing a Font Directory

The first step to installing fonts is to prepare a directory in which to store them. XFree86 has traditionally stored its fonts in subdirectories of /usr/X11R6/lib/X11/fonts/, but X.org-X11 changes this to /usr/share/fonts or /usr/share/X11/fonts. In either case, if you're adding fonts you've downloaded from the Internet or obtained from a commercial font CD-ROM, you may want to store these additional fonts elsewhere, such as /opt/fonts or /usr/local/fonts. (Chapter 4, "Managing Files," includes information about the logic behind Linux's directory system.) You may want to create separate subdirectories for fonts in different formats or from different sources.

When you're installing Type 1 fonts, Linux needs the font files with names that end in .pfa or .pfb; these files contain the actual font data. (The .pfa and .pfb files store the data in slightly different formats, but the two file types are equivalent.) Additional files distributed with Type 1 fonts aren't necessary for Linux. TrueType fonts come as .ttf files, and that's all you need for Linux.

Linux uses fonts in the same format that Mac OS X, Windows, OS/2, and most other OSs use. Earlier versions of Mac OS used font files in special Macintosh-only "suitcases," which Linux can't use directly. If you want to use such fonts in Linux, you must convert them. The FontForge program (http://fontforge.sourceforge.net) can do this conversion, among other things.

Once you've copied fonts to a directory, you must prepare a summary file that describes the fonts. This file is called fonts.dir, and it begins with a line that specifies the number of fonts that are described. Subsequent lines provide a font filename and an *X logical font description (XLFD)*, which is a tedious-looking description of the font. A complete fonts.dir line can be rather intimidating:

```
courb.pfa -ibm-Courier-bold-r-normal--0-0-0-0-m-0-iso8859-1
```

Fortunately, you needn't create this file manually; programs exist to do so automatically. In XFree86 4.3 and later and in X.org-X11, the simplest way to do the job is to use mkfontscale and mkfontdir:

```
# mkfontscale
# mkfontdir
```

The mkfontscale program reads all the fonts in the current directory and creates a fonts.scale file, which is just like a fonts.dir file but describes only outline fonts. The mkfontdir program combines the fonts.scale file with the fonts.dir file, creating it if it doesn't already exist.

Other programs to perform this task also exist. Most notably, ttmkfdir creates a fonts.dir file that describes TrueType fonts, and type1inst does the job for Type 1 fonts. The mkfontscale program is preferable because it handles both font types, but if you're using an older distribution that lacks this program or if it's not doing a satisfactory job, you can try one of these alternative programs.

Adding Fonts to X's Font Path

Once you've set up fonts in a directory and created a fonts.dir file describing them, you must add the fonts to the X font path. You do this by editing the Files section of the XF86Config or xorg.conf file:

```
Section "Files"
    FontPath  "/usr/share/fonts/100dpi:unscaled"
    FontPath  "/usr/share/fonts/Type1"
    FontPath  "/usr/share/fonts/truetype"
    FontPath  "/usr/share/fonts/URW"
    FontPath  "/usr/share/fonts/Speedo"
    FontPath  "/usr/share/fonts/100dpi"
EndSection
```

If your Files section contains FontPath lines that refer to unix:/7100 or unix:/-1 but that don't list conventional directories, read the section "Configuring a Font Server"; your system is configured to rely on an X font server for its core fonts. In this case, you may want to modify your font server configuration rather than change the X core fonts directly, although you can add font directories to have X both use the font server and directly handle your new fonts. If your X server configuration lacks a Files section, it uses a hard-coded default font path. You can add your own complete Files section to add new font paths.

To add your new font directory to the font path, duplicate one of the existing FontPath lines, and change the directory specification to point to your new directory. The order of these directories is significant; when matching font names, X tries each directory in turn, so if two directories hold fonts of the same name, the first one takes precedence. Thus, if you want your new fonts to override any existing fonts, place the new directory at the top of the list; if you want existing fonts to take precedence, add your directory to the end of the list.

The :unscaled string in the first entry in the preceding example tells X to use bitmap fonts from this directory only if they exactly match the requested font size. Without this string, X will attempt to scale bitmap fonts from a font directory (with poor results). Typically, bitmap directories are listed twice: once near the top of the font path with the :unscaled specification and again near the bottom of the list without it. This produces quick display of matching bitmapped fonts, followed by any matching scalable fonts, followed by scaled bitmap fonts.

Once you've added your font directory to X's font path, you should test the configuration. The most reliable way to do this is to shut down X and restart it. (If your system boots directly into X, consult "Running an XDMCP Server" for information on doing this.) A quicker approach, but one that presents some opportunity for error, is to add the font path to a running system by using the xset program:

```
$ xset fp+ /your/font/directory
$ xset fp rehash
```

The first of these commands adds */your/font/directory* to the end of the font path. (Substitute +fp for fp+ to add the directory to the start of the existing font path.) The second command tells X to re-examine all the font directories to rebuild the list of available fonts. The result is that you should now be able to access the new fonts. (You'll need to restart any programs that should use the new fonts.) One program to quickly test the matter is xfontsel. This program enables you to select an X core font for display so you can check to be sure the fonts you've added are available and display as you expect.

Configuring a Font Server

Prior to the release of XFree86 4.0, several Linux distributions began using TrueType-enabled font servers to provide TrueType font support. Most distributions have now abandoned this practice, but some haven't, and font servers can be useful in some environments.

A font server is a handy way to deliver fonts to many computers from a central location. This can be a great time-saver if you want to add fonts to many computers—set them up to use a font server and then tweak that server's font configuration. To use a font server, X must list that server in its font path:

```
Section "Files"
    FontPath   "unix:/7100"
    FontPath   "tcp/fount.pangaea.edu:7100"
EndSection
```

The first line in this example specifies a local font server. (Using unix:/-1 rather than unix:/7100 also works in some cases.) The second line specifies that the font server on the remote system fount.pangaea.edu is to be used. If your computer is already configured to use a font server, you needn't change the X configuration to add or delete fonts; instead, you can modify the font server's configuration. (You *can* still modify the X font configuration directly, but it may be cleaner to manage all the local fonts from one configuration file.)

To add fonts to a font server, you should first install the fonts on the system, as described earlier in "Preparing a Font Directory." You should then modify the font server's configuration file, /etc/X11/fs/config. Rather than a series of FontPath lines, as in the main X configuration file, the font server's configuration lists the font path using the catalogue keyword as a comma-delimited list:

```
catalogue = /usr/share/fonts/100dpi:unscaled,
            /usr/share/fonts/Type1,
            /usr/share/fonts/truetype,
```

```
/usr/share/fonts/URW,
/usr/share/fonts/Speedo,
/usr/share/fonts/100dpi
```

The `catalogue` list may span several lines or just one. In either event, all of the entries are separated by commas, but the final entry ends without a comma. You can add your new font directory anywhere in this list.

Once you've saved your changes, you must restart the font server. Typically, this is done via SysV startup scripts (described in more detail in Chapter 5):

 # /etc/init.d/xfs restart

At this point, you should restart X or type **xset fp rehash** to have X re-examine its font path, including the fonts delivered via the font server.

Although X core fonts and font servers were once very important, most modern X applications now emphasize an entirely different font system: Xft. You can add the same fonts as both X core fonts and Xft fonts, but the Xft configuration requires doing things in a new way.

Configuring Xft Fonts

X core fonts (including fonts delivered via a font server) have several important drawbacks:

- They aren't easy to integrate between the screen display and printed output. This makes them awkward from the point of view of word processing or other applications that produce printed output.

- They're server-based. This means applications may not be able to directly access the font files because the fonts may be stored on a different computer than the application. This can exacerbate the printing integration problem.

- They provide limited or no support for kerning and other advanced typographic features. Again, this is a problem for word processing programs and other programs that must generate printed output.

- They don't support *font smoothing* (aka *anti-aliasing*). This technology employs gray pixels (rather than black or white pixels) along curves to create an illusion of greater resolution than the display can produce.

These problems are deeply embedded in the X core font system, so developers have decided to bypass that system. The result is the Xft font system, which is based in part on the FreeType library (`http://www.freetype.org`), an open source library for rendering TrueType and Type 1 fonts. Xft is a client-based system, meaning that applications access font files on the computer on which they're running. Xft also supports font smoothing and other advanced font features. Overall, the result is greatly improved font support. The cost, though, is that Linux now has *two* font systems: X core fonts and Xft fonts.

Fortunately, you can share the same font directories through both systems. If you've prepared a font directory as described earlier, in "Preparing a Font Directory," you can add it to Xft. Load the `/etc/fonts/local.conf` file into a text editor. Look for any lines in this file that take the following form:

`<dir>/font/directory</dir>`

If such lines are present, duplicate one of them and change the duplicate to point to your new font directory. If such lines don't exist, create one just before the </fontconfig> line. Be sure not to embed your new font directory specification within a comment block, though. Comments begin with a line that reads <!-- and end with a line that reads -->.

> If you create a font directory that holds several subdirectories, you can add just the main directory to local.conf. For instance, if you created /opt/fonts/tt and /opt/fonts/type1, adding /opt/fonts to local.conf will be sufficient to access all the fonts you installed on the system.

Once you've made these changes, type **fc-cache** as root. This command causes Xft to run through its font directories and create index files. These files are similar to the fonts.dir file in principle, but the details differ. If you fail to take this step, you'll still be able to access these fonts, but each user's private Xft cache file will contain the lists of fonts. Generating these files can take some time, thus degrading performance.

To test your Xft fonts, use any Xft-enabled program. Most modern X-based Linux programs are so enabled, so loading a GUI text editor, word processor, Web browser, or other tool that enables you to adjust fonts should do the trick.

Managing GUI Logins

Linux can boot into a purely text-based mode in which the console supports text-based logins and text-mode commands. This configuration is suitable for a system that runs as a server computer or for a desktop system for a user who dislikes GUIs. Most desktop users, though, expect their computers to boot into a friendly GUI. For such users, Linux supports a login system that starts X automatically and provides a GUI login screen. Configuring and managing this system requires you to understand a bit of how the system works, how to run it, and how to change the configuration.

The X GUI Login System

As described later in this chapter, in "Using X for Remote Access," X is a network-enabled GUI. This fact has many important consequences, and one of these relates to Linux's GUI login system. This system employs a network login protocol, the *X Display Manager Control Protocol (XDMCP)*. To handle remote logins, an XDMCP server runs on a computer and listens for connections from remote computers' X servers. To handle local logins, an XDMCP server runs on a computer and starts the local computer's X server. The XDMCP server then manages the local X server's display—that is, it puts up a login prompt like that shown in Figure 6.2.

FIGURE 6.2   An XDMCP server manages local GUI logins to a Linux system.

Five XDMCP servers are common on Linux: the X Display Manager (XDM), the KDE Display Manager (KDM), the GNOME Display Manager (GDM), the MDM Display Manager (MDM; a recursive acronym), and the Light Display Manager (LightDM). A few more exotic XDMCP servers are also available, but these five are the most important. Of these, the exam objectives explicitly cover the first three, so they're the ones described here. As you may guess by their names, KDM and GDM are associated with the KDE and GNOME projects, respectively. MDM is a derivative of GDM. XDM is the oldest and least feature-heavy of these display managers. LightDM aims to be compact and compatible with multiple desktop environments. You can change which desktop manager your system uses if you don't like the default.

Although KDM and GDM are associated with KDE and GNOME, respectively, neither limits your choice of desktop environment. In fact, it's possible, and often necessary, to run programs associated with one desktop environment inside another one. This works fine, although it increases the memory load.

Running an XDMCP Server

Several methods exist to start an XDMCP server. The two most common are to launch it more or less directly from `init`, via an entry in `/etc/inittab` or its ancillary configuration files; or to launch it as part of a runlevel's startup script set, via a system startup script.

Chapter 5 describes both init and system startup scripts in general, so consult it for information about these processes.

Whichever method is used, many distributions configure themselves to run their chosen XDMCP server when they start in runlevel 5 but not when they start in runlevel 3. This is the only difference between these two runlevels in most cases. Thus, changing from runlevel 3 to runlevel 5 starts X and the XDMCP server on many distributions, and switching back to runlevel 3 stops X and the XDMCP server. As described in more detail in Chapter 5, you can change runlevels as root with the telinit command:

```
# telinit 5
```

Permanently changing the runlevel on a SysV-based system requires editing the /etc/ inittab file and, in particular, its id line:

```
id:5:initdefault:
```

Change the number (5 in this case) to the runlevel you want to use as the default. Most distributions that use Upstart or systemd start the XDMCP server via methods more akin to the methods traditionally used by Debian, as described next.

A few distributions—most notably Gentoo, Debian, and Debian's derivatives (including the popular Ubuntu)—attempt to start an XDMCP server in all runlevels (or don't do so at all). This is done through the use of a SysV startup script called xdm, kdm, or gdm. Thus, you can temporarily start or stop the XDMCP server by running this script and passing it the start or stop option. To permanently enable or disable the XDMCP server, you should adjust your SysV startup scripts, as described in Chapter 5.

In addition to the question of whether to run an XDMCP server is the question of *which* XDMCP server to run. Most distributions set a default XDMCP server in one way or another. Two common methods exist:

Selection via Configuration File   Some distributions hide the XDMCP server choice in a configuration file, often in the /etc/sysconfig directory. In Fedora, the /etc/ sysconfig/desktop file sets the DISPLAYMANAGER variable to the path to the executable, as in DISPLAYMANAGER=/bin/xdm. In openSUSE, /etc/sysconfig/displaymanager sets the DISPLAYMANAGER variable to the display manager's name in lowercase letters, as in DISPLAYMANAGER="xdm".

Selection via Startup Script   In Debian and derivative distributions, such as Ubuntu, the display manager is set via a SysV, Upstart, or systemd startup script—use the gdm script to use GDM, kdm to use KDM, and so on. By default, only one XDMCP server (and associated startup script) is installed, so if you want to change your XDMCP server, you may need to install your desired server. Chapter 5 describes how to configure specific startup scripts to run automatically.

Unfortunately, distribution maintainers have had a habit of changing the details of how XDMCP servers are launched from time to time, and the settings are often buried in poorly documented configuration files. Thus, you may need to go digging through the files in your /etc directory to find the correct setting. If you can't find the setting, try using grep to search for strings such as DISPLAYMANAGER or the name of the XDMCP server that's currently running.

Configuring an XDMCP Server

XDMCP servers, like most programs, can be configured. Unfortunately, this configuration varies from one server to another, although there are some commonalities. In the following pages, I provide some details for configuring XDM, KDM, and GDM.

Configuring XDM

XDM is the simplest of the major XDMCP servers. It accepts usernames and passwords but doesn't enable users to perform other actions, such as choose which desktop environment to run. (This must be configured through user login files.)

XDM's main configuration file is /etc/X11/xdm/xdm-config. Most distributions ship with a basic xdm-config file that should work fine for a local workstation. If you want to enable the computer to respond to remote login requests from other X servers on the network or if you want to verify that the system is *not* so configured, you should pay attention to this line:

```
DisplayManager.requestPort: 0
```

This line tells XDM to not access a conventional server port. To activate XDM as a remote login server, you should change 0 to 177, the traditional XDMCP port. You must then restart XDM. When so configured, users on other computers can initiate remote X-based logins to your computer via XDMCP. This can be handy on local networks, but it's also a security risk, which is why the default is to not enable such access.

The /etc/X11/xdm/Xaccess file is another important XDM configuration file. If XDM is configured to permit remote access, this file controls who may access the XDM server and in what ways. A wide-open system contains lines that use an asterisk (*) to denote that anybody may access the system:

```
*
* CHOOSER BROADCAST
```

The first line tells XDM that anybody may connect, and the second line tells XDM that anybody may request a *chooser*—a display of local systems that accept XDMCP connections. To limit the choices, you should list individual computers or groups of computers instead of using the asterisk wildcard:

```
*.pangaea.edu
tux.example.com
*.pangaea.edu CHOOSER BROADCAST
```

This example lets any computer in the pangaea.edu domain connect or receive a chooser, and it also lets tux.example.com connect but not receive a chooser.

Many additional options are set in the /etc/X11/xdm/Xresources file; it hosts X *resources*, which are similar to environment variables but apply only to X-based programs. For instance, you can change the text displayed by XDM by altering the xlogin*greeting resource in this file.

Configuring KDM

KDM is based partly on XDM and so shares many of its configuration options. Unfortunately, the location of the KDM configuration files is unpredictable; sometimes KDM uses the XDM configuration files, other times they're stored in /etc/X11/kdm or /etc/kde/kdm, and sometimes they're stored in a truly strange location such as /usr/lib/kde4/libexec/.

If you can't find the KDM configuration files, try using your package management tools, described in Chapter 2, "Managing Software." Try obtaining lists of files in the kdm or kdebase package or some other likely candidate, and look for the KDM configuration files.

KDM expands on XDM by enabling users to select a session type when they log in, to shut down the computer from the main KDM prompt, and so on. Most of these extra options are set in the kdmrc file, which appears in the same directory as the other KDM configuration files. Some of these options override the more common XDM configuration options for the same features. In particular, the [Xdmcp] section provides options relating to network operation. The Enable option in that section should be set to true if you want to support network logins.

Configuring GDM

GDM is more of a break from XDM than is KDM. GDM doesn't use the conventional XDM configuration files or similar files. Instead, it uses configuration files that are usually stored in /etc/X11/gdm or /etc/gdm. In the past, the most important of these files was gdm.conf, and it had a format similar to the kdmrc file. More recent versions of GDM, however, place this file elsewhere and give it a new format. With these versions, you can set local options in the custom.conf file in the GDM configuration directory. This file typically starts with no options, but the ones you set override the defaults. As with KDM, you should set the enable option to yes in the [xdmcp] section if you want to enable remote logins.

A GUI control tool for GDM exists on some systems but is missing from others. Type **gdmconfig** or **gdmsetup** as root to launch this program, which enables you to set GDM options using a point-and-click interface.

Like KDM, GDM provides extra options over those of XDM. These options include the ability to choose your login environment and shut down the computer. GDM is a bit unusual in that it prompts for the username and only then presents a prompt for the password. XDM and KDM both present fields for the username and password simultaneously.

Using X for Remote Access

As noted earlier, in "The X GUI Login System," X is a network-enabled GUI. This fact enables you to run Linux programs remotely—you can set up a Linux system with X programs and run them from other Linux (or even non-Linux) computers. Similarly, you can use a Linux computer as an access terminal for X programs that run on a non-Linux Unix computer, such as one running Solaris. To do this, you should first understand something of X's network model, including where the client and server systems are located, how X controls access to itself, and so on. You can then proceed to perform the remote accesses.

X Client-Server Principles

Most people think of servers as powerful computers hidden away in machine rooms, and of clients as the desktop systems that ordinary people use. Although this characterization is often correct, it's very wrong when it comes to X. X is a server, meaning that the X server runs on the computer at which the user sits. X clients are the programs that users run—xterm, xfontsel, KMail, LibreOffice, and so on. In most cases, the X server and its clients reside on the same computer, so this peculiar terminology doesn't matter; but when you use X for remote access, you must remember that the X server runs on the user's computer, while the X clients run on the remote system.

To make sense of this peculiarity, think of it from the program's point of view. For instance, consider a Web browser such as Firefox. This program accesses Web pages stored on a Web server computer. The Web server responds to requests from Firefox to load files. Just as Firefox loads files, it displays files on the screen and accepts input from its user. From the program's point of view, this activity is much like retrieving Web pages, but it's handled by an X server rather than a Web server. This relationship is illustrated in Figure 6.3.

FIGURE 6.3   From a program's point of view, the X server works much like a conventional network server such as a Web server.

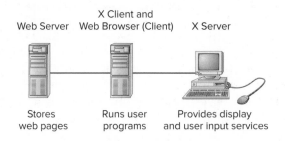

Ordinarily, Linux is configured in such a way that its X server responds only to local access requests as a security measure. Thus, if you want to run programs remotely, you must make some changes to have Linux lower its defenses—but not too far, lest you let anybody access the X server, which could result in security breaches.

Using Remote X Clients

Suppose your local network contains two machines. The computer called zeus is a powerful machine that hosts important programs, like a word processor and data analysis utilities. The computer called apollo is a much less powerful system, but it has an adequate monitor and keyboard. Therefore, you want to sit at apollo and run programs that are located on zeus. Both systems run Linux. To accomplish this task, follow these steps:

1. Log into apollo and, if it's not already running X, start it.

2. Open a terminal (such as an xterm) on apollo.

3. Type **xhost +zeus** in apollo's terminal. This command tells apollo to accept for display in its X server data that originates on zeus.

4. Log into zeus from apollo. You might use Telnet or Secure Shell (SSH), for instance. The result should be the ability to type commands in a shell on zeus.

5. On zeus, type **export DISPLAY=apollo:0.0**. (This assumes you're using bash; if you're using tcsh, the command is **setenv DISPLAY apollo:0.0**.) This command tells zeus to use apollo for the display of X programs. (Chapter 9, "Writing Scripts, Configuring Email, and Using Databases," describes environment variables, such as DISPLAY, in greater detail.)

6. Type whatever you need to type to run programs at the zeus command prompt. For instance, you could type **loffice** to launch LibreOffice. You should see the programs open on apollo's display, but they're running on zeus—their computations use zeus's CPU, they can read files accessible on zeus, and so on.

7. After you're done, close the programs you've launched, log off zeus, and type **xhost -zeus** on apollo. This tightens security so that a miscreant on zeus won't be able to modify your display on apollo.

Sometimes, you can skip some of these steps. For instance, depending on how it's configured, SSH can forward X connections, meaning that SSH intercepts attempts to display X information and passes those requests on to the system that initiated the connection. When this happens, you can skip steps 3 and 5, as well as the xhost command in step 7. (See the Real World Scenario sidebar "Encrypting X Connections with SSH.")

Real World Scenario

Encrypting X Connections with SSH

The SSH protocol is a useful remote-access tool. Although it's often considered a text-mode protocol, SSH also has the ability to *tunnel* network connections—that is, to carry another protocol through its own encrypted connection. This feature is most useful for handling remote X access. You can perform the steps described in "Using Remote X Clients" but omit steps 3 and 5 and the xhost command in step 7. This greatly simplifies the login process and adds the benefits of SSH's encryption, which X doesn't provide. On the other hand, SSH's encryption is likely to slow down X access, although if you enable SSH's compression features, this problem may be reduced in severity. Overall, tunneling X through SSH is the preferred method of remote X access, particularly when any network in the process isn't totally secure.

SSH tunneling does require that certain options be set. In particular, you must either use the -X or -Y option to the ssh client program or set the ForwardX11 or ForwardX11Trusted option to yes in /etc/ssh_config on the client system. You must also set the X11Forwarding option to yes in the /etc/sshd_config file on the SSH server system. These options enable SSH's X forwarding feature; without these options, SSH's X forwarding won't work.

As an added security measure, many Linux distributions today configure X to ignore true network connections. If your distribution is so configured, the preceding steps won't work; when you try to launch an X program from the remote system, you'll get an error message. To work around this problem, you must make an additional change, depending on how X is launched:

GDM   On older versions of GDM, check the GDM configuration file (typically /etc/X11/gdm/gdm.conf): look for the line DisallowTCP=true, and change it to read DisallowTCP=false. On newer versions of GDM, edit /etc/gdm/custom.conf, and add a line that reads DisallowTCP=false to the [security] section (adding it if required).

KDM or XDM   These two XDMCP servers both rely on settings in the Xservers file (in /etc/X11/xdm for XDM, and in this location or some other highly variable location for KDM). Look for the line that begins with :0. This line contains the command that KDM or XDM uses to launch the X server. If this line contains the string -nolisten tcp, remove that string from the line. Doing so eliminates the option that causes X to ignore conventional network connections.

Special openSUSE Configuration   In openSUSE, you must edit /etc/sysconfig/displaymanager and set the DISPLAYMANAGER_XSERVER_TCP_PORT_6000_OPEN option to yes.

X Launched from a Text-Mode Login   If you log in using text mode and type **startx** to launch X, you may need to modify the **startx** script itself, which is usually stored in

/usr/bin. Search this script for the string -nolisten tcp. Chances are this string will appear in a variable assignment (such as to defaultserverargs) or possibly in a direct call to the X server program. Remove the -nolisten tcp option from this variable assignment or program call.

Once you've made these changes, you'll need to restart X as described earlier in "Running an XDMCP Server." Thereafter, X should respond to remote access requests.

WARNING   If X responds to remote network requests, the risk of an intruder using a bug or misconfiguration to trick users by displaying bogus messages on the screen is greatly increased. Thus, you should disable this protection only if you're sure that doing so is necessary. You may be able to use an SSH link without disabling this protection.

Another option for running X programs remotely is to use the Virtual Network Computing (VNC) system (http://www.realvnc.com). VNC runs a special X server on the computer that's to be used from a distance, and a special VNC client runs on the computer at which you sit. You use the client to directly contact the server. This reversal of client and server roles over the normal state of affairs with conventional X remote access is beneficial in some situations, such as when you're trying to access a distant system from behind certain types of firewall. VNC is also a cross-platform protocol; it's possible to control a Windows or Mac OS system from Linux using VNC, but this isn't possible with X. (X servers for Windows and Mac OS are available, enabling you to control a Linux system from these non-Linux OSs.)

X Accessibility

Historically, most computers have been designed for individuals with normal physical capabilities. As computers have become everyday tools, though, the need for people with various disabilities to use computers has risen. Linux provides tools to help with this task. Some basic X settings (controlled in xorg.conf or XF86Config) can help in this respect—for instance, you can adjust the keyboard repeat rate to prevent spurious key repeats for individuals who may keep keys pressed longer than average. Other settings are unusual and may require the use of unique accessibility tools to set. Some options must be set in specific desktop environments (KDE or GNOME, for example).

Keyboard and Mouse Accessibility Issues

You can set many keyboard and mouse options using ordinary desktop environment tools for personalizing keyboard and mouse responses. Other options are more exotic, such as onscreen keyboards.

Standard Keyboard and Mouse Options

Most Linux desktop environments include keyboard and mouse control panel options. For instance, in a standard Fedora 17 GNOME installation, you can find the keyboard options in the Keyboard item of the System Settings control panel, and you can find the mouse options in the Mouse and Touchpad item. The AccessX utility is an older program that works in any desktop environment to provide similar features. Figure 6.4 shows AccessX in operation. Because the locations of such options can be customized from one distribution to another and can change from one release to another, you may need to hunt for the options in your menus.

FIGURE 6.4   AccessX and desktop environment control panels provide accessibility options.

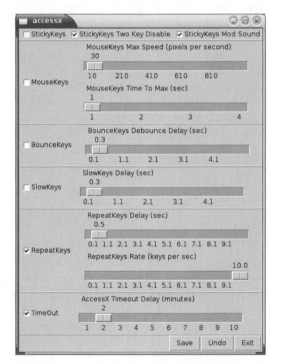

   The exam objectives mention AccessX; however, this package is not available in most distributions and appears to be abandoned. Its functionality has been folded into desktop environment control panels. Thus, although I describe AccessX's features, chances are you'll need to look for equivalents in your desktop environment's control panel.

Keyboard and mouse accessibility features that you can set with AccessX or similar tools in desktop environments include the following (sometimes under slightly different names):

Sticky Keys   When enabled, this option causes keyboard modifier keys (Ctrl, Alt, and Shift) to "stick" when pressed, affecting the next regular key to be pressed even after release of the sticky key. This can be useful for users who have difficulty pressing multiple keys simultaneously. Some tools, including AccessX, provide additional options that affect the details of how sticky keys work.

Mouse Keys   This option enables you to use the cursor keypad on your keyboard to emulate a mouse.

Bounce (or Debounce) Keys   If a user tends to accidentally press a single key multiple times, the bounce keys option may be able to compensate for this tendency. (Aging keyboards also sometimes produce keybounce.)

Slow Keys   When activated, this option requires a key to be pressed for longer than a specified period of time before it registers as a keypress. This feature is useful for individuals who tend to accidentally press keys.

Keyboard Repeat Rate   The repeat delay and rate can be set using sliders. These settings override those set in the X configuration file; but if you use a bare window manager, you may need to set these options in the X configuration file. Disabling keyboard repeat or setting a very long delay may be necessary for some users.

Time Out   In AccessX, the TimeOut option sets a time after which its accessibility options will be disabled.

Mouse Tracking and Click Options   The ordinary mouse tracking and click options can be adjusted to unusual values for those who have special needs. (This and the next two options are not provided by AccessX but are provided by many desktop environments.)

Simulated Mouse Clicks   Some environments let you configure the mouse to simulate a click whenever the mouse pointer stops moving or to simulate a double click whenever the mouse button is pressed for an extended period.

Mouse Gestures   Gestures are similar to keyboard shortcuts but are for mice; they permit you to activate program options by moving your mouse in particular ways.

Using Onscreen Keyboards

If a user has difficulty using a regular keyboard but can use a mouse, that user can employ an onscreen keyboard. This is an application that displays an image of a keyboard. Using the mouse to press the keys on the keyboard image works much like using a real keyboard. Some other keyboards require the user to enter text into their own buffers and then cut and paste the text from the keyboard application into the target program.

Browse the menus for your desktop environment to locate the onscreen keyboards available on your system. If you can't find one, or if you don't like it, use your package manager to search for such programs—searching on *keyboard* should turn up some options.

The GNOME On-Screen Keyboard (GOK) deserves special mention as a particularly powerful tool in this category. This program provides not only an onscreen keyboard but also tools that provide shortcuts for various mouse, menu, and toolbar features of other programs, as well as tools to help users navigate the GNOME desktop. You can launch

GOK by typing **gok** at a command prompt. You can learn more at the main GOK Web page, `http://library.gnome.org/users/gnome-access-guide/stable/gok.html`.

Screen Display Settings

Users with poor eyesight can benefit from adjustments to screen settings and applications. These include font options, contrast settings, and screen magnification tools.

Adjusting Default Fonts

Most desktop environments provide options to set the default fonts used on the screen. Figure 6.5 shows the System Settings dialog box provided with KDE. You can access this by typing **systemsettings** in a terminal window or by selecting Configure Desktop from the main menu and then selecting Application Appearance from the options in the window that appears. A similar tool is available in Xfce, accessible from the Appearance item in its System Settings panel.

FIGURE 6.5   Linux desktop environments usually provide control panels with font options.

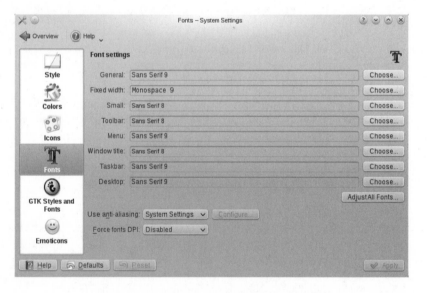

To adjust the fonts, click the Choose button to the right of the font for each of the main categories, such as General and Menu in Figure 6.5. The result is a font selection dialog box, in which you can select the font family (Sans, Times, and so on), the font style (normal, bold, and so on), and the font size in points. Adjust these options until you find a setting that works well. You'll have to adjust the font for each of the categories, or at least for those that are most important.

Dyslexic users often benefit from a special font that weights the bottoms of the characters more heavily than the tops. One such font is available from http://dyslexicfonts.com.

Unfortunately, although many applications take their cues on fonts from the desktop environment's settings, others don't. Thus, you may need to adjust options in at least some individual applications, as well as in the desktop environment as a whole.

Adjusting Contrast

Desktop environments provide various themes—settings for colors, window manager decorations, and so on. Some themes are better than others in terms of legibility. For instance, some themes are very low in contrast, and others are high in contrast.

Monitors have their own contrast controls. You can adjust these for best legibility, of course, but the contrast adjustments afforded by desktop environment settings are independent of a monitor's contrast settings.

In KDE, you can set themes in the same System Settings preferences dialog box in which you set the fonts (Figure 6.5); you click the Colors icon in the left pane and select the theme you want to use. The Workspace Appearance item (accessible by clicking Overview from the screen shown in Figure 6.5) provides additional options. Xfce provides similar options in its Appearance control panel.

Using Magnifier Tools

A screen magnifier application enlarges part of the screen—typically the area immediately surrounding the mouse. One common screen magnifier is KMag, which is part of the KDE suite. (You can use KMag even in GNOME, Xfce, or other desktop environments, though.) To use it, type **kmag** or select it from your desktop menus. The result is the KMag window on the screen, which enlarges the area around the cursor by default.

Using Additional Assistive Technologies

In addition to keyboard, mouse, and conventional display tools, some programs can help those with special needs. Most notably, screen readers and Braille displays can help those who can't read conventional displays.

Configuring Linux to Speak

Computer speech synthesis has existed for decades. Today, several speech synthesis products are available for Linux, including these:

Orca This program, which is based at http://live.gnome.org/Orca, is a screen reader that's been integrated into GNOME 2.16 and later.

Emacspeak   Similar to Orca in many respects, this program aims to enable those with visual impairments to use a Linux computer. You can learn more at `http://emacspeak .sourceforge.net`.

Using Braille Displays

A Braille display is a special type of computer monitor. Rather than display data visually, it creates a tactile display of textual information in Braille. As such, a Braille display is an efficient way for those with visual impairments to access text-mode information, such as that displayed at a Linux text-mode console. Many Linux text-mode programs can manage a Braille display with no changes.

To use a Braille display, special Linux software is required. The BRLTTY (`http://www .mielke.cc/brltty/`) project provides a Linux daemon that redirects text-mode console output to a Braille display. It includes features that support scrollback, multiple virtual terminals, and even speech synthesis.

Linux kernels since 2.6.26 include direct support for Braille displays. If you're familiar with Linux kernel compilation, you should check the Accessibility Support options in the Device Drivers area of the kernel configuration.

Configuring Localization and Internationalization

Linux is an international OS. Its developers and users reside in many countries around the world. Therefore, Linux supports a wide variety of character sets, keyboards, date/time display formats, and other features that can vary from one region to another. Many of these features are set up when you answer questions during installation, but knowing about them—and how to change them—can help you manage your system, particularly if you need to change these options for any reason.

Setting Your Time Zone

When you communicate with other computers (by sending email, transferring files, and so on), those other computers may reside in the same city or around the world. For this reason, it's helpful for your computer to know something about its time zone. This can help keep files' time stamps set sensibly and avoid weird temporal problems when exchanging data. For the most part, you need to be concerned with just one time zone setting for a Linux computer; but sometimes you may want to set the time zone one way for one account or login and another way for another account or login. Thus, I describe both methods of setting a time zone.

Setting a Linux Computer's Time Zone

Linux uses *Coordinated Universal Time* (UTC) internally. This is the time in Greenwich, England, uncorrected for daylight saving time. When you write a file to disk on a Linux-native filesystem, the time stamp is stored in UTC. When you use tools such as cron (described in Chapter 7, "Administering the System"), they "think" in UTC. Chances are, though, that you use local time. Thus, a Linux computer must be able to translate between local time and UTC.

To perform this translation, Linux needs to know your time zone. Linux looks to the /etc/localtime file for information about its local time zone. This file is one of the rare configuration files that's *not* a plain-text file, so you shouldn't try editing it with a text editor. This file could be a file of its own, or it could be a symbolic or hard link to another file. If it's a symbolic link, you should be able to determine your time zone by performing a long file listing to see the name of the file to which localtime links:

```
$ ls -l /etc/localtime
lrwxrwxrwx  1 root root 36 May 14  2008 /etc/localtime -> ↵
/usr/share/zoneinfo/America/New_York
```

If /etc/localtime is a regular file and not a symbolic link or if you want further confirmation of your time zone, try using the date command by itself:

```
$ date
Mon Sep  3 12:50:58 EDT 2012
```

The result includes a standard three-letter time zone code (EDT in this example). Of course, you'll need to know these codes, or at least the code for your area. For a list of time zone abbreviations, consult http://www.timeanddate.com/library/abbreviations/timezones/. Note that the time zone codes vary depending on whether daylight saving time is active, but the Linux time zone files don't change with this detail. Part of what these files do is describe when to change the clock for daylight saving time. If you need to change your time zone, you should copy or link a sample file from a standard directory location to the /etc/localtime file:

1. Log in as root or acquire root privileges.

2. Change to the /etc directory.

3. View the contents of the /usr/share/zoneinfo directory. This directory contains files for certain time zones named after the zones or the regions to which they apply, such as GMT, Poland, and Japan. Most users will need to look in subdirectories, such as /usr/share/zoneinfo/US for the United States or /usr/share/zoneinfo/America for North and South America. These subdirectories contain zone files named after the regions or cities to which they apply, such as Eastern or Los_Angeles. (The US subdirectory contains files named after time zones or states, whereas the America subdirectory holds files named after cities.) Identify the file for your time zone. Note that you might use a zone file named after a city other than the one in which you reside but that's in the

same time zone as you. For instance, the New_York file works fine if you're in Boston, Philadelphia, Cincinnati, or any other city in the same (Eastern) time zone as New York.

4. If a localtime file exists in /etc, delete it or rename it. (For instance, type **rm localtime**.)

5. Create a symbolic link from your chosen time zone file to the /etc/localtime file. For instance, you can type **ln -s /usr/share/zoneinfo/US/Eastern localtime** to set up a computer in the U.S. Eastern time zone. Alternatively, you can copy a file (cp) rather than create a symbolic link (ln -s). If /etc and your target file are on the same filesystem, you can create a hard link rather than a symbolic link if you like.

At this point, your system should be configured to use the time zone you've selected. If you changed time zones, you should be able to see the difference by typing **date**, as described earlier. The time zone code on your system should change compared to issuing this command before you changed the /etc/localtime file or link. The time should also change by the number of hours between the time zones you've selected (give or take a bit for the time it took you to change the time zone files).

In addition to /etc/localtime, some distributions use a secondary file with text-mode time zone data. This file is called /etc/timezone on Debian and its derivatives. On Fedora and related distributions, it's /etc/sysconfig/clock. This file contains a line or two with the name of the time zone, sometimes in the form of a variable assignment. For instance, the /etc/timezone file on my Ubuntu system looks like this:

```
America/New_York
```

This file provides a quick way to check your time zone. It should also be updated when you change your time zone, lest higher-level configuration tools become confused.

Some distributions provide text-mode or GUI tools to help make time zone changes. Look for a program called tzsetup, tzselect, tzconfig, or something similar. Typically, these programs ask you for your location in several steps (starting with your continent, then your nation, and perhaps then your state or city) and create an appropriate symbolic link.

Setting an Individual Login's Time Zone

One final wrinkle on time zone issues is the TZ environment variable. (Chapter 9 covers environment variables in more detail.) This environment variable holds time zone information in any of three formats:

- The most common format on Linux is :*filename*, as in :/usr/share/zoneinfo/Europe/London. This tells the system that the time zone is the one described in the specified file.

- A second format, common on non-Linux systems, is *std offset*, where *std* is a three-character or longer time zone name (such as EST) and *offset* is a time relative to UTC, with positive values representing offsets west of the Prime Meridian and negative values being east of it. For instance, EST+5 specifies U.S. Eastern Time. This format is used when daylight saving time is not in effect.

- If daylight saving time *is* in effect, a variant on the preceding method is possible: *std offset dst[offset]*,*start[/time]*,*end[time]*. This specification adds the daylight saving time code as well as encoded start and end dates (and optionally times). For instance, EST+5EDT,M3.10.0/2,M11.3.0/2 specifies US Eastern Time with daylight saving time encoded with dates for 2013.

In the vast majority of cases, you won't need to use the TZ environment variable. It can be useful, though, in the event that you're using a computer remotely—say, if you're logging into a work computer that's physically located in San Francisco while you're traveling to London. Using TZ will enable programs that use this variable to display the correct local date and time in London, despite the fact that the computer's global time zone is (presumably) set for San Francisco.

In practice, the easiest way to use TZ for a single login is to issue a command like the following:

```
$ export TZ=:/usr/share/zoneinfo/Europe/London
```

This example sets the time zone to London for a single session but only from the shell at which you type this command. You can add this command to a user startup script if you want to use it regularly. You should *not* use this method if all a computer's programs should use the target time zone; instead, set it by adjusting the /etc/localtime file, as described earlier in "Setting a Linux Computer's Time Zone."

Querying and Setting Your Locale

To localize your computer, you must first understand what a locale is in Linux parlance. Once you understand the basics, you can identify your current locale and other locales available to you. If necessary, you may need to install another locale's data. You can then set your computer to use that locale.

What Is a Locale?

In Linux, a *locale* is a way of specifying the computer's (or user's) language, country, and related information for purposes of customizing displays. A single locale takes the following form:

[language[_territory][.codeset][@modifier]]

Each part of this string has a set of specific acceptable forms. For instance, *language* can be en (English), fr (French), ja (Japanese), and so on. These are two- or three-letter codes for languages.

The *territory* can be US (United States), FR (France), JP (Japan), and so on. These are codes for specific regions—generally nations.

The *codeset* can be ASCII, UTF-8, or other encoding names. The *American Standard Code for Information Interchange* (ASCII) is the oldest and most primitive encoding method; it supports 7-bit encodings (generally stored in 8-bit bytes) that can handle English, including common punctuation and symbols. ASCII can't handle characters used in many non-English languages, though, so it's awkward at best for international use. *ISO-8859* was an early attempt to extend ASCII; it employs an eighth bit to extend ASCII by 128 characters, giving room for the characters needed by a small number of non-Roman alphabets. ISO-8859 is broken down into many substandards, each of which handles one language or small group of languages. ISO-8859-1 covers Western European languages and ISO-8859-5 provides Cyrillic support, for instance.

The latest language codeset is the *8-bit Unicode Transformation Format* (UTF-8). Like ISO-8859, UTF-8 starts with ASCII, but it extends it by supporting variable-byte extensions so that a single character can take anywhere from one to four bytes to be encoded. This provides the ability to encode text in any language supported by *Unicode*, which is a character set designed to support as many languages as possible. The big advantage of UTF-8 over ISO-8859 is that there's no need to specify a substandard, such as ISO-8859-1 or ISO-8859-5; UTF-8 handles all of its writing systems automatically.

The *modifier* is a locale-specific code that modifies how it works. For instance, it may affect the sort order in a language-specific manner.

What Is Your Locale?

A locale code can be assigned to one or more of several environment variables. To learn how these are set on your system, issue the `locale` command without any arguments:

```
$ /usr/bin/local
LANG=en_US.UTF-8
LC_CTYPE="en_US.UTF-8"
LC_NUMERIC="en_US.UTF-8"
LC_TIME="en_US.UTF-8"
LC_COLLATE="en_US.UTF-8"
LC_MONETARY="en_US.UTF-8"
LC_MESSAGES="en_US.UTF-8"
LC_PAPER="en_US.UTF-8"
LC_NAME="en_US.UTF-8"
LC_ADDRESS="en_US.UTF-8"
LC_TELEPHONE="en_US.UTF-8"
LC_MEASUREMENT="en_US.UTF-8"
LC_IDENTIFICATION="en_US.UTF-8"
LC_ALL=
```

As you can see, quite a few locale variables exist. When programs pay attention to these variables, they adjust themselves appropriately for your locale. For instance, a word processor may default to using common U.S. paper sizes (such as 8.5×11 inches) when the *territory* code in LC_PAPER is set to US, but European paper sizes (such as A4, 210×297 mm) when *territory* is set to a code for a country where these paper sizes are more common.

Most of the locale variables set specific and obvious features, such as LC_PAPER (paper size), LC_MEASUREMENT (measurement units), and so on. The LC_ALL variable is a sort of master override—if it's set, it overrides all the other LC_* variables.

A related environment variable is LANG. It takes the same type of locale specification as the LC_* variables. It sets the locale in case the LC_* variables aren't set.

While you're using the `locale` command, you should try it with the -a option, which identifies all the locales that are available to you:

```
$ locale -a
C
en_US.utf8
POSIX
```

In this example (from an Ubuntu system), very few locales are installed. Some systems may have many more; one of my computers has hundreds of locales available.

Changing Your Locale

If you want to change your locale, you should first verify that an appropriate one is available to you by using `locale -a`, as just described. If you don't see appropriate codes, you may need to install additional packages. Unfortunately, names for these packages aren't standardized. Your best bet is to use a GUI package manager such as yumex or Synaptic (described in Chapter 2) to search on package names and descriptions that include `locale` or `language`. In the case of an Ubuntu system that provided just a few locales, many more could be installed from packages called `language-support-??`, where *??* is a two-character language code.

To temporarily change your locale, the simplest method is to set the LC_ALL environment variable. For safety, you should also set LANG. For instance, to use the locale for Great Britain rather than the United States, you can type

```
$ export LANG=en_GB.UTF-8
$ export LC_ALL=en_GB.UTF-8
```

The result should be that all the locale variables change for that session. There will also be changes in the output of programs that honor locales. Note that this change affects only the current shell and the programs launched from it; you won't see changes in programs that are already running or that you launch from another shell.

To permanently change your locale, you can adjust your bash startup script files, such as ~/.bashrc or /etc/profile, as described in Chapter 1, "Exploring Linux Command-Line Tools." (Shell scripting is described in more detail in Chapter 9, but setting or adjusting the LANG and LC_ALL environment variables is fairly straightforward.)

X's configuration file (xorg.conf or XF86Config) includes an option called XkbLayout in the keyboard's InputDevice section. This option takes a partial or complete locale specification but converted to lowercase—for instance, us or en_us.utf-8. Adjusting this option can provide you with access to language- or country-specific keys. After changing this option, you'll have to restart X for the changes to take effect.

Some programs and sets of programs may require you to set the language independent of the overall system locale. Thus, you may need to adjust the language for certain specific programs. If a program doesn't seem to respond to the overall locale setting, check its documentation or browse through its menus to find a way to adjust its defaults.

One setting requires special mention: LANG=C. When you set LANG to C, programs that see this environment variable display output without passing it through locale translations. This can be helpful in some cases if a program's output is being corrupted by the locale—say by having conversions to UTF-8 change characters that need to be preserved as 8-bit entities. Thus, setting LANG=C can help to avoid some types of problems, particularly in pipelines and scripts that pass one program's data to another program in binary form.

 Localization support is, to some extent or another, the responsibility of each program's author. It's entirely possible to write a program that supports just one language or a small subset of languages. Thus, you won't be able to get every program to support your desired language, particularly if it's an unusual one.

Modifying Text-File Locales

Sometimes it's necessary to access textual data that originated on a system that used one encoding but process the data with a program that doesn't support that encoding. For instance, your preferred text editor might support UTF-8 but not ISO-8859. If you deal exclusively with English text files in ASCII, this isn't a problem; but if you receive an ISO-8859-1 text file with a few non-Roman characters, such as characters with umlauts, your editor might display those characters strangely.

To overcome this problem, the iconv utility converts between character sets. Its syntax is as follows:

```
iconv -f encoding [-t encoding] [inputfile]...
```

The -f and -t options specify the source and destination encodings. (You can obtain a list of encodings by typing **iconv --list**.) If you omit the target encoding, iconv uses your current locale for guidance. The program sends output to standard output, so if you want to store the data in a file, you must redirect it:

```
$ iconv -f iso-8859-1 -t UTF-8 umlautfile.txt > umlautfile-utf8.txt
```

Configuring Printing

Most Linux desktop users work with X, but many also work with another output medium: printed pages. Printing in Linux is a cooperative effort involving several tools. Applications submit print jobs as PostScript documents. Because most Linux systems aren't connected directly to true PostScript printers, a program called Ghostscript converts the print job into a form that the system's printer can actually handle. The print queue, which is managed by software known as the Common Unix Printing System (CUPS), then sends the job to the printer. At various stages, administrators and users can examine the contents of a print queue and modify the queue. Understanding the tools used to create and manage print queues will help you to manage Linux printing.

Conceptualizing the Linux Printing Architecture

Linux printing is built around the concept of a *print queue*. This is a sort of holding area where files wait to be printed. A single computer can support many distinct print queues. These frequently correspond to different physical printers, but it's also possible to configure several queues to print in different ways to the same printer. For instance, you might use one queue to print single-sided and another queue for double-sided printing on a printer that supports duplexing.

Users submit print jobs by using a program called 1pr. Users can call this program directly, or they may let another program call it. In either case, 1pr sends the print job into a specified queue. This queue corresponds to a directory on the hard disk, typically in a subdirectory of the /var/spool/cups directory. The CUPS daemon runs in the background, watching for print jobs to be submitted. The printing system accepts print jobs from 1pr or from remote computers, monitors print queues, and serves as a sort of "traffic cop," directing print jobs in an orderly fashion from print queues to printers.

The exam emphasizes the CUPS printing system, which is the most common printing system on modern Linux systems. Older systems used the BSD Line Printer Daemon (LPD) or the similar LPRng printing system. Many of the CUPS tools are workalikes of the LPD tools. If you ever use a system that runs LPD or LPRng, you'll find that user commands such as 1pr work in the way you expect, but configuring the printer must be done in a very different way.

One important and unusual characteristic of Linux printing is that it's highly network-oriented. As just noted, Linux printing tools can accept print jobs that originate from remote systems as well as from local ones. Even local print jobs are submitted via network protocols, although they don't normally use network hardware, so even a computer with no network connections can print. In addition to being a server for print jobs, CUPS can function as a client, passing print jobs to other computers that run the same protocols.

Applications can query CUPS about a printer's capabilities—its paper sizes, whether it supports color, and so on. The older LPD and LPRng printing systems didn't support such bidirectional communication. Thus, support for these features still isn't universal; some programs make assumptions about a printer's capabilities or must be told things that other programs can figure out by themselves.

Understanding PostScript and Ghostscript

If you've configured printers under Windows, Mac OS, OS/2, or certain other OSs, you're probably familiar with the concept of a *printer driver*. In these OSs, the printer driver stands between the application and the printer queue. In Linux, the printer driver is part of Ghostscript (http://www.cs.wisc.edu/~ghost/), which exists as part of the printer queue, albeit a late part. This relationship can be confusing at times, particularly because not all applications or printers need Ghostscript. Ghostscript serves as a way to translate PostScript, a common printer language, into forms that can be understood by many different printers. Understanding Ghostscript's capabilities, and how it fits into a printer queue, can be important for configuring printers.

PostScript: The De Facto Linux Printer Language

PostScript printers became popular as accessories for Unix systems in the 1980s. Unix print queues weren't designed with Windows-style printer drivers in mind, so Unix programs that took advantage of laser printer features were typically written to produce PostScript output directly. As a result, PostScript developed into the de facto printing standard for Unix and, by inheritance, Linux. Where programs on Windows systems were built to interface with the Windows printer driver, similar programs on Linux generate PostScript and send the result to the Linux printer queue.

Some programs violate this standard. Most commonly, many programs can produce raw text output. Such output seldom poses a major problem for modern printers, although some PostScript-only models choke on raw text. Some other programs can produce either PostScript or *Printer Control Language (PCL)* output for Hewlett-Packard laser printers or their many imitators. A very few programs can generate output that's directly accepted by other types of printers.

The problem with PostScript as a standard is that it's uncommon on the low- and mid-priced printers with which Linux is often paired. Therefore, to print to such printers using traditional Unix programs that generate PostScript output, you need a translator and a way to fit that translator into the print queue. This is where Ghostscript fits into the picture.

Ghostscript: A PostScript Translator

When it uses a traditional PostScript printer, a computer sends a PostScript file directly to the printer. PostScript is a programming language, albeit one that's oriented toward the goal of producing a printed page as output. Ghostscript is a PostScript interpreter that runs on a computer. It takes PostScript input, parses it, and produces output in any of dozens of different bitmap formats, including formats that can be accepted by many non-PostScript printers. This makes Ghostscript a way to turn many inexpensive printers into Linux-compatible PostScript printers at very low cost.

One of Ghostscript's drawbacks is that it produces large output files. A PostScript file that produces a page filled with text may be just a few kilobytes in size. If this page is to be printed on a 600 dots per inch (dpi) printer using Ghostscript, the resulting output file could be as large as 4MB—assuming it's black and white. If the page includes color, the size could be much larger. In some sense, this is unimportant because these big files will be stored on your hard disk only briefly. They do still have to get from the computer to the printer, though, and this process can be slow. Also, some printers (particularly older laser printers) may require memory expansion to operate reliably under Linux.

For information about what printers are supported by Ghostscript, check the Ghostscript Web page or the OpenPrinting database Web page (http://www.openprinting.org/printers).

Squeezing Ghostscript into the Queue

Printing to a non-PostScript printer in Linux requires fitting Ghostscript into the print queue. This is generally done through the use of a *smart filter*. This is a program that's called as part of the printing process. The smart filter examines the file that's being printed, determines its type, and passes the file through one or more additional programs before the printing software sends it on to the printer. The smart filter can be configured to call Ghostscript with whatever parameters are appropriate to produce output for the queue's printer.

CUPS ships with its own set of smart filters, which it calls automatically when you tell the system what model printer you're using. CUPS provides a Web-based configuration tool, as described in the upcoming section "Using the Web-Based CUPS Utilities." This system, or distribution-specific GUI printer configuration tools, can make setting up a printer for CUPS fairly straightforward.

The end result of a typical Linux printer queue configuration is the ability to treat any supported printer as if it were a PostScript printer. Applications that produce PostScript output can print directly to the queue. The smart filter detects that the output is PostScript and runs it through Ghostscript. The smart filter can also detect other file types, such as plain-text and various graphics files, and it can send them through appropriate programs instead of or in addition to Ghostscript in order to create a reasonable printout.

If you have a printer that can process PostScript, the smart filter is usually still involved, but it doesn't pass PostScript through Ghostscript. In this case, the smart filter passes PostScript directly to the printer, but it still sends other file types through whatever processing is necessary to turn them into PostScript.

Running a Printing System

Because Linux printing systems run as daemons, they must be started before they're useful. This task is normally handled automatically via startup scripts in /etc/rc.d, /etc/init.d, or /etc/rc?.d (where ? is a runlevel number). Look for startup scripts that contain the string cups (or lpd or lprng for older systems) in their names to learn what your system is running. If you're unsure if a printing system is currently active, use the ps utility to search for running processes by these names, as in

```
$ ps ax | grep cups
 1896 ?        Ss     0:01 cupsd
```

This example shows that cupsd, the CUPS daemon, is running, so the system is using CUPS for printing. If you can't find any running printing system, consult your distribution's documentation to learn what is available and check that the appropriate package is installed. All major distributions include startup scripts that should start the appropriate printing daemon when the computer boots.

Configuring CUPS

CUPS uses various configuration files in the /etc/cups directory and its subdirectories to manage its operation. You can edit these files directly, and you may need to do so if you want to share printers or use printers shared by other CUPS systems. The simplest way to add printers to CUPS, though, is to use the tool's Web-based configuration utility.

Editing the CUPS Configuration Files

You can add or delete printers by editing the /etc/cups/printers.conf file, which consists of printer definitions. Each definition begins with the name of a printer, identified by the string DefaultPrinter (for the default printer) or Printer (for a nondefault printer) in angle brackets (<>), as in the following:

```
<DefaultPrinter okidata>
```

This line marks the beginning of a definition for a printer queue called okidata. The end of this definition is a line that reads </Printer>. Intervening lines set assorted printer options, such as identifying strings, the printer's location (its local hardware port or network location), its current status, and so on. Additional options are stored in a *PostScript Printer Definition (PPD)* file that's named after the queue and stored in the /etc/cups/ppd subdirectory. PPD files follow an industry-standard format. For PostScript printers, you can obtain a PPD file from the printer manufacturer, typically from a driver CD-ROM or from the manufacturer's Web site. CUPS and its add-on driver packs also ship with a large number of PPD files that are installed automatically when you use the Web-based configuration utilities.

As a general rule, you're better off using the CUPS Web-based configuration tools to add printers rather than adding printers by directly editing the configuration files. If you like, though, you can study the underlying files and tweak the configurations using a text editor to avoid having to go through the full Web-based tool to make a minor change.

One exception to this rule relates to configuring the CUPS Web-based interface tool itself and CUPS' ability to interface with other CUPS systems. One of the great advantages of CUPS is that it uses a new network printing protocol, known as the *Internet Printing Protocol (IPP)*, in addition to the older LPD protocol used by BSD LPD and LPRng. IPP supports a feature it calls *browsing*, which enables computers on a network to automatically exchange printer lists. This feature can greatly simplify configuring network printing. You may need to change some settings in the main CUPS configuration file, /etc/cups/cupsd .conf, to enable this support.

The /etc/cups/cupsd.conf file, which is structurally similar to the Apache Web server configuration file, contains a number of configuration blocks that specify which other systems should be able to access it. Each block controls access to a particular location on the server. These blocks look like this:

```
<Location /printers>
Order Deny,Allow
Deny from All
BrowseAllow from 127.0.0.1
BrowseAllow from 192.168.1.0/24
BrowseAllow from @LOCAL
Allow from 127.0.0.1
Allow from 192.168.1.0/24
Allow from @LOCAL
</Location>
```

 If you're configuring a workstation with a local printer that you don't want to share or if you want to configure a workstation to use printers shared via LPD or some other non-IPP printing protocol, you shouldn't need to adjust /etc/cups/cupsd.conf. If you want to access remote IPP printers, however, you should at least activate browsing by setting the directive Browsing On, as described shortly. You shouldn't have to modify your location definitions unless you want to share your local printers.

The /printers location, shown here, controls access to the printers themselves. The following list includes features of this example:

Directive Order The Order Deny,Allow line tells CUPS in which order it should apply allow and deny directives—in this case, allow directives modify deny directives.

Default Policy The Deny from All line tells the system to refuse all connections except those that are explicitly permitted.

Browsing Control Lines The BrowseAllow lines tell CUPS from which other systems it should accept browsing requests. In this case, it accepts connections from itself (127.0.0.1), from systems on the 192.168.1.0/24 network, and from systems connected to local subnets (@LOCAL).

Access Control Lines The Allow lines give the specified systems non-browse access to printers—that is, those systems can print to local printers. In most cases, the Allow lines are the same as the BrowseAllow lines.

You can also create a definition that uses Allow from All and then creates BrowseDeny and Deny lines to limit access. As a general rule, though, the approach shown in this example is safer. Locations other than the /printers location can also be important. For instance, there's a root (/) location that specifies default access permissions to all other locations and an /admin location that controls access to CUPS administrative functions.

Before the location definitions in `cupsd.conf` are a few parameters that enable or disable browsing and other network operations. You should look for the following options specifically:

Enabling Browsing   The `Browsing` directive accepts `On` and `Off` values. The CUPS default is to enable browsing (`Browsing On`), but some Linux distributions disable it by default.

Browsing Access Control   The `BrowseAddress` directive specifies the broadcast address to which browsing information should be sent. For instance, to broadcast data on your printers to the 192.168.1.0/24 subnet, you'd specify `BrowseAddress 192.168.1.255`.

Once you've configured a CUPS server to give other systems access to its printers via appropriate location directions and once you've configured the client systems to use browsing via `Browsing On`, all the systems on the network should auto-detect all the printers on the network. You don't need to configure the printer on any computer except the one to which it's directly connected. All printer characteristics, including their network locations and PPD files, are propagated automatically by CUPS. This feature is most important in configuring large networks with many printers or networks on which printers are frequently added and deleted.

Obtaining CUPS Printer Definitions

Most Linux distributions ship with CUPS smart filter support for a variety of printers. If you can't find support for your printer, you can look for additional printer definitions. These definitions may consist of PPD files, appropriate behind-the-scenes "glue" to tell CUPS how to use them, and possibly Ghostscript driver files. You can obtain these printer definitions from several sources:

Your Linux Distribution   Many distributions ship extra printer definitions under various names, so check your distribution for such a package. Many distributions include some of the driver packages described next.

Foomatic   The Linux Printing Web site hosts a set of utilities and printer definitions known collectively as Foomatic (`http://www.linuxfoundation.org/en/OpenPrinting/Database/Foomatic`). These provide many additional printer definitions for CUPS (as well as for other printing systems).

Gutenprint   The Gutenprint drivers, originally known as GIMP Print, after the GNU Image Manipulation Program (GIMP), support a wide variety of printers. Check `http://gimp-print.sourceforge.net` for more information.

CUPS DDK   The CUPS Driver Development Kit (DDK) is a set of tools designed to simplify CUPS driver development. It ships with a handful of drivers for Hewlett-Packard and Epson printers and is included with the CUPS source code.

Printer Manufacturers   Some printer manufacturers offer CUPS drivers for their printers. These may be nothing more than Foomatic, Gutenprint, or other open source drivers; but a few provide proprietary drivers, some of which support advanced printer features that the open source drivers don't support.

Chances are good that you'll find support for your printer in your standard installation, particularly if your distribution has installed the Foomatic or Gutenprint package. If you start configuring printers and can't find your model, though, you should look for an additional printer definition set from one of the preceding sources.

Using the Web-Based CUPS Utilities

The CUPS IPP printing system is closely related to the Hypertext Transfer Protocol (HTTP) used on the Web. The protocol is so similar, in fact, that you can access a CUPS daemon by using a Web browser. You need only specify that you want to access the server on port 631—the normal printer port. To do so, enter **http://localhost:631** in a Web browser on the computer running CUPS. (You may be able to substitute the hostname or access CUPS from another computer by using the server's hostname, depending on your **cupsd.conf** settings.) This action brings up a list of administrative tasks you can perform. Click Printers or Manage Printers to open the printer management page, shown in Figure 6.6.

FIGURE 6.6   CUPS provides its own Web-based configuration tool.

▼ Queue Name ▼	Description	Location	Make and Model	Status
hp4000	HP 4000 laser printer	Closet	HP LaserJet 4000 Series Postscript (recommended)	Idle - "Data file sent successfully."
Stylus_Photo_RX500	EPSON Stylus Photo RX500		Epson Stylus Photo RX500 - CUPS+Gutenprint v5.2.7	Idle

If you're configuring a stand-alone computer or the only one on a network to use CUPS, the printer list may be empty, unlike the one shown in Figure 6.6. If other computers on your network use CUPS, you may see their printers in the printer list, depending on their security settings. Many modern distributions auto-configure USB printers when you plug them in or turn them on, so they may not need to be added, either.

You can add, delete, or modify printer queues using the CUPS Web control system. To add a printer, follow these steps:

1. From the Administration tab, click Add Printer.

> CUPS is likely to ask for a username and password at this point. Type **root** as the username and your root password as the password. The need to pass your root password unencrypted is one reason you should be cautious about configuring printers from a remote computer.

2. The system displays a page that shows options for printers to add in each of three categories: *local printers*, *discovered network printers*, and *other network printers*. One or more of these categories may be empty. If you're trying to add a local printer and the *local printers* category is empty, either it was auto-detected or CUPS can't detect any likely printer interface hardware. Check your cables and drivers, and then restart CUPS and reload its Web page. If you see an option for the printer you want to add, select it and click Continue.

3. If you entered a network printer, the result is a page in which you enter the complete path to the device. Type the path, such as **lpd://printserv/brother** to print to the brother queue on the printserv computer. Click Continue when you're done.

4. CUPS displays a page in which you enter the printer's name, description, and location. You'll use the name to specify the printer in both command-line and GUI tools, so a short one-word name is best. The description and location fields are both descriptive expansions to help users positively identify the printer. You can also click the Share This Printer check box if you want to share the printer definition with other CUPS-using computers on the network.

5. You'll now see a list of manufacturers. Select one, and click Continue. Alternatively, you can point directly to a PPD file if you have one handy. If you do this, you'll skip the next step.

6. CUPS now displays a complete list of printer models in the class you selected in step 5. Select an appropriate model, and click Add Printer. Alternatively, you can provide a PPD file if you have one.

7. You should now see a page on which you can set default options, such as the paper size and print resolution. The details of what options are available depend on the printer model you selected. Change any options you like and click Set Default Options. Your printer is now defined.

If you click the Printers item at the top of the page, you should be returned to the printers list (Figure 6.6), but your new printer should be listed among the existing queues. You can print a test page by clicking the link to the printer and then selecting Print Test Page from the button selector that reads Maintenance by default. If all goes well, a test page will emerge from your printer. If it doesn't, go back and review your configuration by selecting Modify Printer from the button selector that reads Administration by default. This action takes you through the steps for adding a printer but with your previous selections already entered as the defaults. Try changing some settings until you get the printer to work.

Printing to Network Printers

If your network hosts many Windows computers, you may use the Server Message Block/ Common Internet File System (SMB/CIFS) for file and printer sharing among Windows systems. Linux's Samba server also implements this protocol and so can be used for sharing printers from Linux.

On the flip side, you can print to an SMB/CIFS printer queue from a Linux system. To do so, you select an SMB/CIFS queue in the printer configuration tool. Under CUPS, it's called Windows Printer via SAMBA in step 2 in the preceding procedure. You must then provide your username, password, server name, and share name, but the format isn't obvious from the Web-based configuration tool:

`smb://username:password@SERVER/SHARE`

This is a URI for an SMB/CIFS share. You must substitute appropriate values for *username*, *password*, *SERVER*, and *SHARE*, of course. Once this is done and you've finished the configuration, you should be able to submit print jobs to the SMB/CIFS share.

 SMB/CIFS printers hosted by Windows systems are usually non-PostScript models, so you must select a local Linux smart filter and Ghostscript driver, just as you would for a local printer. Printers hosted by Linux systems running Samba, by contrast, are frequently configured to act like PostScript printers, so you should select a PostScript driver when connecting to them.

If you want to print to a Unix or Linux server that uses the old LPD protocol, the URI format is similar but omits a username and password:

`lpd://hostname/queue`

You can use the same format, but substitute `ipp://` for `lpd://`, to print to a CUPS server if browsing is disabled on your network.

In practice, you may be faced with a decision: Should you use LPD, IPP, or SMB/CIFS for submitting print jobs? To be sure, not all print servers support all three protocols, but a Linux server might support them all. As a general rule, IPP is the simplest to configure because it supports browsing, which means that CUPS clients shouldn't need explicit configuration to handle specific printers. This makes IPP the best choice for Linux-to-Linux printing, assuming both systems run CUPS. When CUPS isn't in use, LPD is generally easier to configure than SMB/CIFS, and it has the advantage of not requiring the use of a username or password to control access. Because SMB/CIFS security is password-oriented, clients typically store passwords in an unencrypted form on the hard disk. This fact can become a security liability, particularly if you use the same account for printing as for other tasks. On the other hand, sometimes using a password on the server provides more of a security benefit than the risk of storing that password on the client. Generally speaking, if clients are few and well protected, whereas the server is exposed to the Internet at large, using passwords can be beneficial. If clients are numerous and exposed to the Internet, whereas the print server is well protected, a password-free security system that relies on IP addresses may be preferable.

Monitoring and Controlling the Print Queue

You can use several utilities to submit print jobs and to examine and manipulate a Linux print queue. These utilities are lpr, lpq, lprm, and lpc. All of these commands can take the -P parameter to specify that they operate on a specific print queue.

Printing Files with *lpr*

Once you've configured the system to print, you probably want to start printing. As mentioned earlier, Linux uses the lpr program to submit print jobs. This program accepts many options that you can use to modify the program's action:

Specify a Queue Name   The -P*queuename* option enables you to specify a print queue. This is useful if you have several printers or if you've defined several queues for one printer. If you omit this option, the default printer is used.

In the original BSD version of lpr, there should be no space between the -P and the *queuename*. LPRng and CUPS are more flexible in this respect; you can insert a space or omit it as you see fit.

Delete the Original File   Normally, lpr sends a copy of the file you print into the queue, leaving the original unharmed. Specifying the -r option causes lpr to delete the original file after printing it.

Suppress the Banner   The -h option suppresses the banner for a single print job. Early versions of CUPS didn't support this option, but recent versions do.

Specify a Job Name   Print jobs have names to help identify them, both while they're in the queue and once they're printed (if the queue is configured to print banner pages). The name is normally the name of the first file in the print job, but you can change it by including the -J *jobname* option. The -C and -T options are synonymous with -J.

Notify a User by Email   The -m *username* option causes lpd to send email to *username* when the print job is complete. This option was unavailable in early versions of CUPS but is available in recent versions.

Specify the Number of Copies   You can specify the number of copies of a print job by using the -# *number* option, as in -# 3 to print three copies of a job.

Suppose you have a file called report.txt that you want to print to the printer attached to the lexmark queue. This queue is often busy, so you want the system to send email to your account, ljones, when it's finished so you know when to pick up the printout. You can use the following command to accomplish this task:

```
$ lpr -Plexmark -m ljones report.txt
```

The lpr command is accessible to ordinary users as well as to root, so anybody may print using this command. It's also called from many programs that need to print directly, such as graphics programs and word processors. These programs typically give you some way to adjust the print command so that you can enter parameters such as the printer name. For instance, Figure 6.7 shows Firefox's Print dialog box, which features a list of available print queues, Range options to enable you to print a subset of the document's pages, and a Copies field so that you can print multiple copies. Additional tabs enable you to set more options. Some programs provide a text entry field in which you type some or all of an lpr command instead of selecting from a list of available queues and options. Consult the program's documentation if you're not sure how it works.

FIGURE 6.7   Most Linux programs that can print do so by using lpr, but many hide the details of the lpr command behind a dialog box.

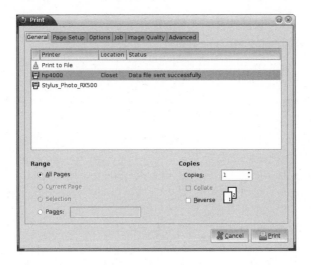

Sometimes you want to process a file in some way prior to sending it to the printer. Chapter 1 covers some commands that can do this, such as fmt and pr. Another handy program is mpage, which reads plain-text or PostScript files and reformats them so that each printed sheet contains several reduced-size pages from the original document. This can be a good way to save paper if you don't mind a reduction in the document's text or image size. In the simplest case, you can use mpage much as you'd use lpr:

```
$ mpage -Plexmark report.ps
```

This command prints the report.ps file reduced to fit four pages per sheet. You can change the number of source pages to fit on each printed page with the -1, -2, -4, and -8 options, which specify one, two, four, or eight input pages per output page, respectively. Additional mpage options exist to control features such as the paper size, the font to be used for plain-text input files, and the range of input file pages to be printed. Consult the man page for mpage for more details.

Displaying Print Queue Information with *lpq*

The lpq utility displays information about the print queue—how many files it contains, how large they are, who their owners are, and so on. By entering the user's name as an argument, you can also use this command to check on any print jobs owned by a particular user. To use lpq to examine a queue, you can issue a command like the following:

```
$ lpq -Php4000
hp4000 is ready and printing
Rank    Owner   Job     File(s)                 Total Size
active  rodsmit 1630    file:///                90112 bytes
```

Of particular interest is the job number—1630 in this example. You can use this number to delete a job from the queue or reorder it so that it prints before other jobs. Any user may use the lpq command.

Removing Print Jobs with *lprm*

The lprm command removes one or more jobs from the print queue. You can issue this command a couple of ways:

- If lprm is used with a number, that number is understood to be the job ID (as shown in lpq's output) of the job that's to be deleted.

- If a user runs the BSD or CUPS lprm and passes a dash (-) to the program, it removes all the jobs belonging to the user.

This program may be run by root or by an ordinary user; but as just noted, its capabilities vary depending on who runs it. Ordinary users may remove only their own jobs from the queue, but root may remove anybody's print jobs.

Controlling the Print Queue

In the original BSD LPD system, the lpc utility starts, stops, and reorders jobs within print queues. Although CUPS provides an lpc command, it has few features. Instead of using lpc, you should use the CUPS Web interface, which provides point-and-click print queue management:

- You can disable a queue by clicking the Stop Printer link for the printer on the CUPS Web interface. When you do so, this link changes to read Start Printer, which reverses the effect when clicked. The Jobs link also provides a way to cancel and otherwise manage specific jobs.

- You can use a series of commands, such as cupsenable, cupsdisable, and lpmove, to control the queue. These commands enable a queue, disable a queue, or move a job from one queue to another. Moving a job can be handy if you must shut down a queue for maintenance and want to redirect the queue's existing jobs to another printer.

In Exercise 6.1, you'll practice using Linux's printing capabilities.

EXERCISE 6.1

Printing with Linux

To perform this exercise, you must have a printer connected to your Linux computer—either a local printer or a network model. To perform some of the steps, you must also have root access to your computer so that you can manage the queue. To begin, follow these steps:

1. Launch a Web browser, enter http://localhost:631 as the URI, and then click the Printers tab. This should produce a list of printers, as in Figure 6.6. If the list is empty, you'll need to define at least one printer queue, as described earlier, before proceeding. If printers are defined, take note of their names. For purposes of this exercise, I'll assume a queue named hp4000 exists; change this name as necessary in the following steps.

2. Type **lpr -Php4000 /etc/fstab** to obtain a printout of this system configuration file. Verify that it printed correctly.

3. Type **lpq -Php4000** to view the contents of the hp4000 queue. If you're using a single-user computer, chances are the queue will be empty at this point.

4. Type **lpr -Php4000 /etc/fstab; lpq -Php4000**. This command prints another copy of /etc/fstab and immediately displays the contents of the print queue. It should not be empty this time, since the job will have been submitted but won't have had time to clear the queue by the time lpq executes.

5. In another shell, type **su** to obtain root access.

6. In your root shell, type **cupsdisable hp4000**. This action disables the queue; it will still accept jobs, but they won't print.

7. Type **lpr -Php4000 /etc/fstab** to obtain yet another printout of /etc/fstab. Because the queue is disabled, it won't print.

8. Type **lpq -Php4000** to view the contents of the printer queue. Note that, instead of hp4000 is ready, lpq reports hp4000 is not ready; however, the job you submitted should appear in the queue. Suppose it has a job number of 497.

9. Type **lprm -Php4000** *497* (changing the job number for your system).

10. Type **lpq -Php4000** again to verify that the job has been removed from the queue.

11. Type **cupsenable hp4000** in your root shell. This should re-enable the queue.

12. Type **lpr -Php4000 /etc/fstab** to print another copy of this file and verify that the printer is actually working again.

Using cupsdisable and cupsenable in this exercise has two purposes: to give you experience using these commands and to give you a chance to delete a job from the queue. A short file such as /etc/fstab can be printed so quickly that you might not have time to remove it from the queue before it disappears because it's sitting in the printer's out tray!

Summary

X is Linux's GUI system. In part because of Linux's modular nature, X isn't a single program; you have your choice of X servers to run on Linux. Fortunately, most Linux distributions use the same X server as all others (X.org-X11). Both X.org-X11 and its main competitor, XFree86, are configured in much the same way, using the xorg.conf (for X.org-X11) or XF86Config configuration file. Whatever its name, this file consists of several sections, each of which controls one X subsystem, such as the mouse, the keyboard, or the video card. This file also controls X's core fonts system, but you can use a font server in addition to this system; and most modern programs are now emphasizing an entirely new font system, Xft, instead of X core fonts. For this reason, Linux font configuration can be complex.

X's GUI login system uses an XDMCP server, which starts X and manages the X display. Several XDMCP servers are in common use in Linux, the most important being XDM, KDM, and GDM. They all perform the same basic tasks, but configuration details differ. (XDM is also less sophisticated than KDM and GDM.) X is a network-enabled GUI, which means you can use an X server to access programs running on another computer. Doing so requires performing a few steps for each login session. You can also tunnel X accesses through SSH, which greatly improves the security of the connection.

An assortment of tools can help make Linux more accessible to users with visual or motor impairments. You can adjust font size, screen contrast, and other display features to improve legibility; use screen magnifiers to help users read part of a larger screen; or even bypass a visual display entirely and use a screen reader for auditory output or a Braille display for tactile output. On the input side, you can adjust keyboard repeat rates, use sticky keys, or modify the mouse tracking speed and click sensitivity to improve users' ability to input data accurately. You can even have a mouse stand in for a keyboard or vice versa by using appropriate software.

The second main visual output tool on computers is a printer, and Linux provides sophisticated printer support. The CUPS package manages printers in Linux by accepting local or remote print jobs, passing them through a smart filter for processing, and queuing the jobs so that they print in a reasonable order. Most CUPS configuration is best handled via its own Web interface, but some options (particularly security features) can be set via text configuration files.

Exam Essentials

Name the major X servers for Linux.   XFree86 has been the traditional standard Linux X server, but in 2004 X.org-X11 (which was based on XFree86) rapidly gained prominence as the new standard Linux X server. Accelerated-X is a commercial X server that sometimes supports video cards that aren't supported by XFree86 or X.org-X11.

Describe the X configuration file format.   The XFree86 and X.org-X11 configuration file is broken into multiple sections, each of which begins with the keyword `Section` and ends with `EndSection`. Each section sets options related to a single X feature, such as loading modules, specifying the mouse type, or describing the screen resolution and color depth.

Summarize the differences between X core fonts, a font server, and Xft fonts.   X core fonts are managed directly by X, and they lack modern font features such as font smoothing. Font servers integrate with the X core fonts but run as separate programs and may optionally deliver fonts to multiple computers on a network. Xft fonts bypass the X core font system to provide client-side fonts in a way that supports modern features such as font smoothing.

Explain the role of an XDMCP server.   An XDMCP server, such as XDM, KDM, or GDM, launches X and controls access to X via a login prompt—that is, it serves as Linux's GUI login system. XDMCP servers are also network-enabled, providing a way to log in remotely from another X server.

Describe X's client-server model.   An X server runs on the user's computer to control the display and accept input from the keyboard and mouse. Client programs run on the same computer or on a remote computer to do the bulk of the computational work. These client programs treat the X server much as they treat other servers, requesting input from and sending output to them.

Explain the benefits of using SSH for remote X access.   SSH can simplify remote X-based network access by reducing the number of steps required to run X programs from a remote computer. More important, SSH encrypts data, which keeps information sent between the X client and X server secure from prying eyes.

Summarize X accessibility features.   You can adjust keyboard and mouse options to help those with motor impairments to use keyboards and mice or to substitute one device for the other. Font size, contrast, and magnification tools can help those with visual impairments. Finally, text readers and Braille displays can enable blind individuals to use a Linux system.

Describe how to set a time zone in Linux.   Linux uses a binary file, `/etc/localtime`, to describe the features of the time zone. This file is copied or linked from a repository of such files at system installation, but you can replace the file at any time.

Explain the role of Ghostscript in Linux printing.   PostScript is the standard Linux printing language, and Ghostscript converts PostScript into bitmap formats that are acceptable to non-PostScript printers. Thus, Ghostscript is a critical translation step in many Linux print queues, although it's not required for PostScript printers.

Summarize how print jobs are submitted and managed under Linux.   You use `lpr` to submit a print job for printing, or an application program may call `lpr` itself or implement its functionality directly. The `lpq` utility summarizes jobs in a queue, and `lprm` can remove print jobs from a queue.

Review Questions

1. When you configure an X server, you need to make changes to configuration files and then start or restart the X server. Which of the following can help streamline this process?

    A. Shut down X by switching to a runlevel in which X doesn't run automatically, and then reconfigure it and use `startx` to test X startup.

    B. Shut down X by booting into single-user mode, and then reconfigure X and use `telinit` to start X running again.

    C. Reconfigure X, and then unplug the computer to avoid the lengthy shutdown process before restarting the system and X along with it.

    D. Use the `startx` utility to check the X configuration file for errors before restarting the X server.

    E. Connect the Linux computer's network port directly to the X server, without using any intervening routers, in order to reduce network latency.

2. Which of the following summarizes the organization of the X configuration file?

    A. The file contains multiple sections, one for each screen. Each section includes subsections for individual components (keyboard, video card, and so on).

    B. Configuration options are entered in any order desired. Options relating to specific components (keyboard, video card, and so on) may be interspersed.

    C. The file begins with a summary of individual screens. Configuration options are preceded by a code word indicating the screen to which they apply.

    D. The file is broken into sections, one or more for each component (keyboard, video card, and so on). The file also has one or more sections that define how to combine the main sections.

    E. The file is a rare binary configuration file that must be accessed using SQL database tools.

3. A monitor's manual lists its range of acceptable synchronization values as 27–96kHz horizontal and 50–160Hz vertical. What implications does this have for the resolutions and refresh rates the monitor can handle?

    A. The monitor can run at up to 160Hz vertical refresh rate in all resolutions.

    B. The monitor can handle up to 160Hz vertical refresh rate depending on the color depth.

    C. The monitor can handle up to 160Hz vertical refresh rate depending on the resolution.

    D. The monitor can handle vertical resolutions of up to 600 lines (96,000 ÷ 160), but no more.

    E. The monitor can handle horizontal resolutions of up to 600 columns (96,000 ÷ 160), but no more.

4. In what section of `XF86Config` or `xorg.conf` do you specify the resolution that you want to run?

   A. In the `ServerLayout` section, using the `Screen` option

   B. In the `Monitor` section, using the `Modeline` option

   C. In the `Device` section, using the `Modeline` option

   D. In the `DefaultResolution` section, using the `Define` option

   E. In the `Screen` section, subsection `Display`, using the `Modes` option

5. What is an advantage of a font server?

   A. It provides faster font displays than are otherwise possible.

   B. It can simplify font maintenance on a network with many X servers.

   C. It's the only means of providing TrueType support for XFree86 4.*x*.

   D. It enables the computer to turn a bitmapped display into an ASCII text file.

   E. It enables X to use font smoothing, which isn't possible with core fonts.

6. What methods do Linux distributions use to start X automatically when the system boots? (Select two.)

   A. Start an XDMCP server from the `Start` folder.

   B. Start an XDMCP server from an `~/.xinitrc` script.

   C. Start an XDMCP server via a system startup script.

   D. Start an XDMCP server via a boot manager.

   E. Start an XDMCP server from `init`.

7. How would you change the text displayed by XDM as a greeting?

   A. Click Configure ➢ Greeting from the XDM main menu, and edit the text in the resulting dialog box.

   B. Pass `greeting="`*text*`"` as a kernel option in the boot loader, changing *text* to the new greeting.

   C. Edit the `/etc/X11/xorg.conf` file, and change the `Greeting` option in the xdm area.

   D. Run `xdmconfig`, and change the greeting on the Login tab.

   E. Edit the `/etc/X11/xdm/Xresources` file, and change the text in the `xlogin*greeting` line.

8. Which of the following features do KDM and GDM provide that XDM doesn't?

   A. An encrypted remote X-based access ability, improving network security

   B. The ability to accept logins from remote computers, once properly configured

   C. The ability to select the login environment from a menu on the main login screen

   D. A login screen that shows the username and password simultaneously rather than sequentially

   E. An option to log into text mode if X should fail to start

9. Which of the following commands tells the X server to accept connections from `penguin`
    `.example.com`?

    A. `xhost +penguin.example.com`

    B. `export DISPLAY=penguin.example.com:0`

    C. `telnet penguin.example.com`

    D. `xaccess penguin.example.com`

    E. `ssh penguin.example.com`

10. To assist an employee who has trouble with keyboard repeat features, you've disabled this
    function in `/etc/X11/xorg.conf`. Why might this step not be sufficient to the goal of
    disabling keyboard repeat?

    A. GNOME, KDE, or other desktop environment settings for keyboard repeat may
       override those set in `xorg.conf`.

    B. The `xorg.conf` file has been deprecated; you should instead adjust the `/etc/X11/`
       `XF86Config` file.

    C. Keyboard settings in `xorg.conf` apply only to PS/2 keyboards; you must use
       `usbkbrate` to adjust keyboard repeat for USB keyboards.

    D. You must also locate and reset the DIP switch on the keyboard to disable keyboard
       repeat.

    E. The keyboard repeat options in `xorg.conf` work only if the keyboard's nationality is
       set incorrectly, which it often is not.

11. Which of the following programs may be used to provide computer-generated speech for
    users who have trouble reading computer displays? (Select two.)

    A. SoX

    B. Braille

    C. Orca

    D. `talk`

    E. Emacspeak

12. You manage a computer that's located in Los Angeles, California, but the time zone is
    misconfigured as being in Tokyo, Japan. What procedure can you follow to fix this
    problem? (Select two.)

    A. Run `hwclock --systohc` to update the clock to the correct time zone.

    B. Delete `/etc/localtime`, and replace it with an appropriate file from `/usr/share/`
       `zoneinfo`.

    C. Edit the `/etc/tzconfig` file so that it specifies `North_America/Los_Angeles` as the
       time zone.

    D. Edit `/etc/localtime`, and change the three-letter time zone code on the TZ line.

    E. Use the `tzselect` program to select a new (Los Angeles) time zone.

13. You're configuring a Linux system that doesn't boot any other OS. What is the recommended time to which the computer's hardware clock should be set?

   A. Helsinki time

   B. Local time

   C. US Pacific time

   D. UTC

   E. Internet time

14. You've developed a script that uses several Linux commands and edits their output. You want to be sure that the script runs correctly on a computer in Great Britain, although you're located elsewhere, since the output includes features such as currency symbols and decimal numbers that are different from one nation to another. What might you do to test this?

   A. Enter the BIOS, locate and change the location code, reboot into Linux, and run the script.

   B. Edit /etc/locale.conf, change all the LC_* variables to en_GB.UTF-8, and then reboot and run the script.

   C. Type **export LC_ALL=en_GB.UTF-8**, and run the script from the same shell you used to type this command.

   D. Type **locale_set Great_Britain**, and run the script from the same shell you used to type this command.

   E. Type **export TZ=:/usr/share/zoneinfo/Europe/London**, and run the script from the same shell you used to type this command.

15. Which character set encoding is the preferred method on modern Linux systems?

   A. UTF-8

   B. ASCII

   C. ISO-8859-1

   D. ISO-8859-8

   E. ATASCII

16. Which of the following describes the function of a smart filter?

   A. It improves the legibility of a print job by adding font smoothing to the text.

   B. It detects information in print jobs that may be confidential as a measure against industrial espionage.

   C. It sends email to the person who submitted the print job, obviating the need to wait around the printer for a printout.

   D. It detects and deletes prank print jobs that are likely to have been created by miscreants trying to waste your paper and ink.

   E. It detects the type of a file and passes it through programs to make it printable on a given model of printer.

17. What information about print jobs does the lpq command display? (Select two.)

   A. The name of the application that submitted the job

   B. A numerical job ID that can be used to manipulate the job

   C. The amount of ink or toner left in the printer

   D. The username of the person who submitted the job

   E. The estimated time to finish printing the job

18. You've submitted several print jobs, but you've just realized that you mistakenly submitted a huge document that you didn't want to print. Assuming you can identify which job this was, that it's not yet printing, and that its job ID number is 749, what command would you type to delete it from the okidata print queue?

   A. The answer depends on whether you're using BSD LPD, LPRng, or CUPS.

   B. Type **lpdel -Pokidata 749**.

   C. Type **lprm -Pokidata 749**.

   D. Type **cupsdisable -Pokidata 749**.

   E. None of the above; the task is impossible.

19. Which of the following is generally true of Linux programs that print?

   A. They send data directly to the printer port.

   B. They produce PostScript output for printing.

   C. They include extensive collections of printer drivers.

   D. They can print only with the help of add-on commercial programs.

   E. They specify use of the Verdana font.

20. What tool might you use to print a four-page PostScript file on a single sheet of paper?

   A. PAM

   B. mpage

   C. 4Front

   D. route

   E. 411toppm

Chapter

7

Administering the System

THE FOLLOWING EXAM OBJECTIVES ARE COVERED IN THIS CHAPTER:

- ✓ 1.107.1 Manage user and group accounts and related system files

- ✓ 1.107.2 Automate system administration tasks by scheduling jobs

- ✓ 1.108.1 Maintain system time

- ✓ 1.108.2 System logging

Much of Linux system administration deals with handling mundane day-to-day tasks. Many of these tasks relate to users and groups: adding them, deleting them, configuring their environments, and so on. On a small system you might perform such tasks infrequently, but on a busy system you might adjust accounts frequently. In any event, you must know how to do these things. Another class of day-to-day tasks involves managing and reviewing *log files*. These are files that record details of system operations, such as remote logins. Log files can be invaluable debugging resources, but even if you aren't experiencing a problem, you should review them periodically to be sure everything is working as it should.

Many Linux tasks relate to time. Linux keeps time somewhat differently than some other OSs, and understanding how Linux treats time is important. So are the skills needed to set the time in Linux. (Some automated tools can be very helpful, but you must know how to configure them.) You can also tell Linux to run particular jobs at specific times in the future. This can be handy to help automate repetitive tasks, such as synchronizing data with other systems on a regular basis.

Managing Users and Groups

Linux is a multi-user system that relies on *accounts*—data structures and procedures used to identify individual users of a computer. Managing these accounts is a basic but important system administration skill. Before delving into the details, I describe a few basic concepts you should understand about user and group administration. With that out of the way, I describe the tools and configuration files that you employ to manage users and groups.

Understanding Users and Groups

Chances are you have a good basic understanding of accounts already. Fundamentally, Linux accounts are like accounts on Windows, Mac OS, and other OSs. Some Web sites use accounts, too. Nonetheless, a few details deserve explanation. These include Linux username conventions, the nature of Linux groups, and the way Linux maps the numbers it uses internally to the usernames and group names that people generally use.

Understanding Linux Usernames

Linux is fairly flexible about its usernames, although details vary from one utility to another. The most liberal Linux naming rules require usernames to begin with a letter and to be no more than 32 characters in length. Aside from the first character, numbers and most punctuation symbols are permitted, as are both upper- and lowercase characters. In practice, though, some important utilities, such as the useradd program described in "Adding Users," impose more restrictive rules. These rules disallow uppercase letters and most punctuation characters, although you can sometimes get away with an underscore (_) or dot (.), and a dollar sign ($) as the last character is permitted. Furthermore, some utilities truncate usernames longer than 8 characters; for this reason, many administrators try to limit username length to 8 characters.

Assuming you can create accounts with mixed-case usernames, Linux treats usernames in a case-sensitive way. Therefore, a single computer can support both ellen and Ellen as separate users. This practice can lead to a great deal of confusion, so it's best to avoid creating accounts whose usernames differ only in case. The traditional practice is to use entirely lowercase letters in Linux usernames, such as sally, sam, ellen, and george. Usernames don't need to be based on first names, of course—you could use sam_jones, s.jones, sjones, jones, jones17, or d76, to name just a few possibilities. Most sites develop a standard method of creating usernames, such as using the first initial and the last name. Creating and following such a standard practice can help you locate an account that belongs to a particular individual. If your computer has many users, though, you may find a naming convention produces duplicates, particularly if your standard is to use initials to shorten usernames. You may be forced to deviate from the standard or incorporate numbers to distinguish between all the Davids or Smiths of the world, because each account requires a unique username.

Linking Users Together for Productivity via Groups

Linux uses *groups* as a means of organizing users. In many ways, groups parallel users. In particular, they're defined in similar configuration files, have names similar to usernames, and are represented internally by numbers (as are accounts).

Groups are *not* accounts, however. Rather, groups are a means of organizing collections of accounts, largely as a security measure. Every file on a Linux system is associated with a specific user and a specific group, and various permissions can be assigned to members of that group. For instance, group members (such as faculty at a university) may be allowed to read a file, but others (such as students) may be disallowed such access. Because Linux provides access to most hardware devices (such as scanners and tape backup units) through files, you can also use this same mechanism to control access to hardware.

Every group has anywhere from no members to as many members as there are users on the computer. Group membership is controlled through the /etc/group file. This file contains a list of groups and the members belonging to each group. The details of this file's contents are described in the section "Configuring Groups."

In addition to membership defined in /etc/group, each user has a default or *primary* group. The user's primary group is set in the user's configuration in /etc/passwd (the file that defines accounts). When users log onto the computer, their group membership is set to their primary group. When users create files or launch programs, those files and running programs are associated with a single group—the current group membership. A user can access files belonging to other groups as long as the user belongs to that group and the group access permissions permit the access. To run programs or create files with a group other than the primary one, however, the user must run the newgrp command to switch current group membership. For instance, to change to the project2 group, you might type the following:

```
$ newgrp project2
```

If the user typing this command is listed as a member of the project2 group in /etc/ group, the user's current group membership changes. Thereafter, files created by that user will be associated with the project2 group. Alternatively, users can change the group associated with an existing file by using the chgrp or chown command, as described in Chapter 4, "Managing Files."

This group structure enables you to design a security system that permits different collections of users to easily work on the same files while simultaneously keeping other users of the same computer from prying into files they should not be able to access. In a simple case, you may create groups for different projects, classes, or workgroups, with each user restricted to one of these groups. A user who needs access to multiple groups can be a member of each of these groups—for instance, a student who takes two classes can belong to the groups associated with each class, or a supervisor may belong to all the supervised groups.

Mapping UIDs and GIDs to Users and Groups

As mentioned earlier, Linux defines users and groups by numbers, referred to as *user IDs (UIDs)* and *group IDs (GIDs)*, respectively. Internally, Linux tracks users and groups by these numbers, not by name. For instance, the user sam may be tied to UID 523, and ellen may be UID 609. Similarly, the group project1 may be GID 512, and project2 may be GID 523. For the most part, these details take care of themselves—you use names, and Linux uses /etc/passwd or /etc/group to locate the number associated with the name. You may occasionally need to know how Linux assigns numbers when you tell it to do something, though. This is particularly true when you're troubleshooting or if you have cause to manually edit /etc/passwd or /etc/group.

Linux distributions reserve at least the first 100 user and group IDs (0–99) for system use. The most important of these is 0, which corresponds to root (both the user and the group). Subsequent low numbers are used by accounts and groups that are associated with specific Linux utilities and functions. For instance, UID 2 and GID 2 may be the daemon account and group, respectively, which are used by various servers; and UID 8 and GID 12 might be the mail account and group, which can be used by mail-related servers and utilities. Not all account and group numbers from 0 to 99 are in use; usually, only one or two dozen accounts and a dozen or so groups are used in this way. You can check your /etc/passwd and /etc/group files to determine which user and group IDs are so used.

Aside from UID 0 and GID 0, UID and GID numbers aren't fully standardized. For instance, although UID 2 and GID 2 map to the daemon account and daemon group on Red Hat and SUSE, on Debian UID 2 and GID 2 map to the bin account and bin group; the daemon account and group correspond to UID 1 and GID 1. If you need to refer to a particular user or group, use the name rather than the number.

The first normal user account is usually assigned a UID of 500 or (more often) 1000. When you create additional accounts, the system typically locates the next-highest unused number, so the second user you create is UID 1001, the third is 1002, and so on. When you remove an account, that account's ID number may be reused, but the automatic account-creation tools typically don't do so if subsequent numbers are in use, leaving a gap in the sequence. This gap causes no harm unless you have so many users that you run out of ID numbers. (The limit is 65,536 users with the 2.2.*x* kernels and more than 4.2 billion with the 2.4.*x* and later kernels, including root and other system accounts. The limit can be set lower in configuration files or because of limits in support programs.) In fact, reusing an ID number can cause problems if you don't clear away the old user's files—the new user will become the owner of the old user's files, which can lead to confusion.

Account numbering limits are set in the /etc/login.defs file. In particular, UID_MIN and UID_MAX define the minimum and maximum UID values for ordinary user accounts. In modern distributions, these values are generally 1000 and 60000, respectively.

Typically, GID 100 is users—the default group for some distributions. On any but a very small system with few users, you'll probably want to create your own groups. Because different distributions have different default ways of assigning users to groups, it's best that you familiarize yourself with your distribution's way of doing this and plan your own group-creation policies with this in mind. For instance, you may want to create your own groups within certain ranges of IDs to avoid conflicts with the distribution's default user- and group-creation processes.

It's possible to create multiple usernames that use the same UID or multiple group names that use the same GID. In some sense, these are different accounts or groups; they have different entries in /etc/passwd or /etc/group, so they can have different home directories, different passwords, and so on. Because these users or groups share IDs with other users or groups, though, they're treated identically in terms of file permissions. Unless you have a compelling reason to do so, you should avoid creating multiple users or groups that share an ID.

Intruders sometimes create accounts with UID 0 to give themselves root privileges on the systems they invade. *Any* account with a UID of 0 is effectively the root account, with all the power of the superuser. If you spot a suspicious account in your /etc/passwd file with a UID of 0, your system has probably been compromised.

Configuring User Accounts

How frequently you'll do user maintenance depends on the nature of the system you administer. Some systems, such as small personal workstations, need changes very rarely. Others, such as multi-user servers that see heavy user turnover, may require daily maintenance. The latter situation would seem to require more knowledge of user account configuration tools, but even in a seldom-changing system, it's useful to know how to add, modify, or delete accounts so that you can do so quickly and correctly when you do need to do so.

Some security-related account issues are covered in Chapter 10, "Securing Your System."

This chapter describes the traditional text-based tools for account creation and maintenance. Most modern Linux distributions ship with GUI tools that accomplish the same goals. These tools vary from one distribution or environment to another, so they're hard to summarize for Linux as a whole. The exam also emphasizes the text-based tools. Overall, the text-based tools provide the greatest flexibility and are most broadly applicable, but you can certainly use the GUI tools if you like.

Adding Users

Adding users can be accomplished through the useradd utility. (This program is called adduser on some distributions.) Its basic syntax is as follows:

```
useradd [-c comment] [-d home-dir] [-e expire-date] [-f inactive-days]↵
 [-g default-group] [-G group[,...]]   [-m [-k skeleton-dir] | -M]↵
 [-p password] [-s shell]   [-u UID [-o]] [-r] [-n] username
```

Some of these parameters modify settings that are valid only when the system uses shadow passwords. This is the standard configuration for most distributions today.

In its simplest form, you may type just **useradd** *username*, where *username* is the username you want to create. The rest of the parameters are used to modify the default values for the system, which are stored in the file /etc/login.defs.

The parameters for the useradd command modify the program's operation in various ways:

Comment   The -c *comment* parameter passes the comment field for the user. Some administrators store public information such as a user's office or telephone number in this field. Others store just the user's real name or no information at all.

Home Directory   You specify the account's home directory with the -d *home-dir* parameter. This defaults to /home/*username* on most systems.

Account Expiration Date   Set the date on which the account will be disabled, expressed in the form *YYYY-MM-DD*, with the -e *expire-date* option. (Many systems accept alternative forms, such as *MM-DD-YYYY*, as well.) The default is for an account that doesn't expire.

Inactive Days   An account becomes completely disabled a certain number of days after a password expires. The -f *inactive-days* parameter sets the number of days. A value of -1 disables this feature and is the default.

Default Group   You set the name or GID of the user's default group with the -g *default-group* option. The default for this value varies from one distribution to another.

Additional Groups   The -G *group*[,...] parameter sets the names or GIDs of one or more groups to which the user belongs. These groups need not be the default group, and you can specify more than one by separating them with commas.

Home Directory Options   The system automatically creates the user's home directory if -m is specified. Normally, default configuration files (including subdirectories) are copied from /etc/skel, but you may specify another template directory with the -k *skeleton-dir* option. Many distributions use -m as the default when running useradd.

No Home Directory Creation   The -M option forces the system to *not* automatically create a home directory, even if /etc/login.defs specifies that this action is the default. You might use this option, often in conjunction with -u (described shortly) and -d (described earlier) if a new account is for a user who's taking over the home directory of an existing user—say, because a new employee is replacing one who is leaving.

Encrypted Password Specification   The -p *encrypted-password* parameter passes the *pre-encrypted* password for the user to the system. The *encrypted-password* value is added, *unchanged*, to the /etc/passwd or /etc/shadow file. This means that if you type an unencrypted password, it won't work as you probably expect. In practice, this parameter is most useful in scripts, which can encrypt a password (using crypt) and then send the encrypted result through useradd. The default value disables the account, so you must run passwd to change the user's password.

Default Shell   Set the name of the user's default login shell with the -s *shell* option. On most systems, this defaults to /bin/bash, but you can specify another shell or even a program that's not traditionally a shell. For instance, some systems include a shutdown account that calls /sbin/shutdown. Logging into this account immediately shuts down the computer.

UID   The -u *UID* parameter creates an account with the specified user ID value (*UID*). This value must be a positive integer, and it's normally greater than 1000 for user accounts. (Some distributions permit user account UIDs as low as 500, though.) System accounts typically have numbers less than 200, and often less than 100. The -o option allows the number to be reused so that two usernames are associated with a single UID.

System Account Creation   The -r parameter specifies the creation of a system account—an account with a value less than UID_MIN, as defined in /etc/login.defs. The useradd command doesn't create a home directory for system accounts.

No User Group   In some distributions, such as Red Hat, the system creates a group with the same name as the specified username. The -n parameter disables this behavior.

Suppose you've added a hard disk and mounted it as /home2. You want to create an account for a user named Sally in this directory and place her home directory on the new disk. You want to make the new user a member of the project1 and project4 groups, with default membership in project4. The user has also requested tcsh as her default shell. The following commands accomplish this goal:

```
# useradd -m -d /home2/sally -g project4 -G project1,project4 -s /bin/tcsh sally
# passwd sally
Changing password for user sally
New UNIX password:
Retype new UNIX password:
passwd: all authentication tokens updated successfully
```

The passwd command asks for the password twice, but it does not echo what you type. This prevents somebody who sees your screen from reading the password. passwd is described in more detail shortly, in "Setting a Password."

Modifying User Accounts

User accounts may be modified in many ways: You can directly edit critical files such as /etc/passwd, modify user-specific configuration files in the account's home directory, or use system utilities like those used to create accounts. You usually modify an existing user's account at the user's request or to implement some new policy or system change, such as moving home directories to a new hard disk. Sometimes, though, you must modify an account immediately after its creation in order to customize it in ways that aren't easily handled through the account-creation tools or because you realize you forgot a parameter to useradd.

Setting a Password

Although useradd provides the -p parameter to set a password, this tool isn't very useful when directly adding a user because it requires a pre-encrypted password. Therefore, it's usually easiest to create an account in disabled form (by not using -p with useradd) and set the password after creating the account. You can do this with the passwd command, which has the following syntax:

passwd [-k] [-l] [-u [-f]] [-d] [-S] [*username*]

Although passwd is frequently used to set or change passwords, some of its actions don't prompt you for a password. Instead, they modify the password in predictable ways, as described shortly. Other uses produce a password prompt at which you must type a new password (twice, to guard against typos).

The parameters to this command enable you to modify its behavior:

Update Expired Accounts   The -k parameter indicates that the system should update an expired account.

Lock Accounts   The -l parameter locks an account by prefixing the encrypted password with an exclamation mark (!). The result is that the user can no longer log into the account, but the files are still available, and the change can be easily undone. This parameter is particularly handy if you want to temporarily suspend user access to an account—say, because you've spotted some suspicious activity involving the account or because you know a user won't be using the account for a while and you want to minimize the chance of it being abused in the interim.

Unlock Accounts   The -u parameter unlocks an account by removing a leading exclamation mark. useradd creates accounts that are locked and have no password, so using this command on a fresh account results in an account with no password. Normally, passwd doesn't allow this—it returns an error if you attempt it. Adding -f forces passwd to turn the account into one with no password.

Remove an Account's Password   The -d parameter removes the password from an account, rendering it password-less.

Display Account Information   The -S option displays information about the password for an account—whether it's set and what type of encryption it uses.

Ordinary users may use passwd to change their passwords, but many passwd parameters may be used only by root. Specifically, -l, -u, -f, and -d are all off-limits to ordinary users. Similarly, only root may specify a username to passwd. When ordinary users run the program, they should omit their usernames; passwd will change the password for the user who ran the program. As a security measure, passwd asks for a user's old password before changing the password when an ordinary user runs the program. This precaution is *not* taken when root runs the program so that the superuser may change a user's password without knowing the original password. This is necessary because the administrator normally doesn't know the user's password. It also provides a way for the system administrator to help a user who's forgotten a password—the administrator can type **passwd** *username* and then enter a new password for the user.

Linux passwords may consist of letters, numbers, and punctuation. Linux distinguishes between upper- and lowercase letters in passwords, which means you can use mixed-case passwords, numbers, and punctuation to improve security.

Chapter 10 provides information about selecting good passwords.

Exercise 7.1 provides you with practice in creating accounts on a Linux system.

EXERCISE 7.1

Creating User Accounts

This exercise explores the process of creating user accounts. After performing this exercise, you should be familiar with the text-mode Linux account-creation tools and be able to create new accounts, including preparing new users' home directories. To add and test a new account, follow these steps:

1. Log into the Linux system as a normal user.

2. Launch an xterm from the desktop environment's menu system, if you used a GUI login method.

3. Acquire root privileges. You can do this by typing **su** in an xterm, by selecting Session ➤ New Root Console from a Konsole, or by using sudo (if it's configured) to run the commands in the following steps.

4. Type **useradd -m *username***, where *username* is the name you want to be associated with the account. This command creates an account. The -m parameter tells Linux to create a home directory for the user and fill it with default account configuration files.

5. Type **passwd *username***. You'll be asked to enter a password for the user and to type it a second time. Enter a random string or select a password as described in "Setting a Password."

6. Press Ctrl+Alt+F2 to go to a fresh text-mode login screen. (If you're already using multiple virtual terminals, you may need to use a function key number greater than F2.)

7. Try logging in as the new user to verify that the account works properly.

In practice, creating accounts on a production system may require variations on this procedure. You may need to use additional options in step 4, for instance; consult the section "Adding Users" or the useradd man page for details on these options. Furthermore, setting the password may require changes. On a small system with few users, you may be able to create accounts in the presence of their future users, in which case the user can type the password in step 5. On other systems, you may need to generate passwords yourself and then give them to users in some way.

Using *usermod*

The usermod program closely parallels useradd in its features and parameters. This utility changes an existing account instead of creating a new one, though. The major differences between useradd and usermod are as follows:

- usermod allows the addition of a -m parameter when used with -d. The -d parameter alone changes the user's home directory, but it doesn't move any files. Adding -m causes usermod to move the user's files to the new location.

- usermod supports a -l parameter, which changes the user's login name to the specified value. For instance, typing **usermod -l sjones sally** changes the username from sally to sjones.

- You may lock and unlock a user's password with the -L and -U options, respectively. These options duplicate functionality provided by passwd.

The usermod program changes the contents of /etc/passwd or /etc/shadow, depending on the option used. If -m is used, usermod also moves the user's files, as already noted.

WARNING　　Changing an account's characteristics while the owner is logged in can have undesirable consequences. This is particularly true of the -d -m combination, which can cause the files a user is working on to move. Most other changes, such as changes to the account's default shell, don't take effect until the user has logged out and back in again.

If you change the account's UID, this action does *not* change the UIDs associated with a user's existing files. Because of this, the user may lose access to these files. You can manually update the UIDs on all files by using the chown command, as described in Chapter 4. Specifically, a command like the following, issued after changing the UID on the account sally, restores proper ownership on the files in sally's home directory:

```
# chown -R sally /home/sally
```

This action does *not* change the ownership of files that aren't in sally's home directory. If you believe such files exist, you may need to track them down with the find command, as you'll see in the upcoming section "Deleting Accounts." Also, this command blindly changes ownership of *all* files in the /home/sally directory. This is probably OK, but it's conceivable that some files in that directory *should* be owned by somebody else—say, because sally and another user are collaborating on a project.

When using the -G option to add a user to new groups, be aware that any groups *not* listed will be removed. The gpasswd command, described in the upcoming section "Using gpasswd," provides a way to add a user to one or more specific groups without affecting existing group memberships, and so it's generally preferable for this purpose.

Using *chage*

The chage command enables you to modify account settings relating to account expiration. It's possible to configure Linux accounts so that they automatically expire if either of two conditions is true:

- The password hasn't been changed in a specified period of time.
- The system date is past a predetermined time.

These settings are controlled through the chage utility, which has the following syntax:

```
chage [-l] [-m mindays] [-M maxdays] [-d lastday]  [-I inactivedays]↵
 [-E expiredate] [-W warndays] username
```

The program's parameters modify the command's actions:

Display Information　　The -l option causes chage to display account expiration and password aging information for a particular user.

Set the Minimum Time Between Password Changes   The -m *mindays* parameter sets the minimum number of days between password changes. 0 indicates that a user can change a password multiple times in a day, 1 means that a user can change a password once a day, 2 means that a user may change a password once every two days, and so on.

Set the Maximum Time Between Password Changes   The -M *maxdays* parameter sets the maximum number of days that may pass between password changes. For instance, 30 requires a password change approximately once a month.

 If the user changes a password before the deadline, the counter is reset from the password-change date.

Set the Last Password Change Date   The -d *lastday* parameter sets the last day a password was changed. This value is normally maintained automatically by Linux, but you can use this parameter to artificially alter the password change count. *lastday* is expressed in the format *YYYY/MM/DD* or as the number of days since January 1, 1970.

Set the Maximum Inactive Days   The -I *inactivedays* parameter sets the number of days between password expiration and account disablement. An expired account may not be used or may force the user to change the password immediately upon logging in, depending on the distribution. A disabled account is completely disabled.

Set the Expiration Date   You can set an absolute expiration date with the -E *expiredate* option. For instance, you might use **-E 2013/05/21** to have an account expire on May 21, 2013. The date may also be expressed as the number of days since January 1, 1970. A value of –1 represents no expiration date.

Set the Number of Warning Days   The -W *warndays* option sets the number of days before account expiration that the system will warn the user of the impending expiration. It's generally a good idea to use this feature to alert users of their situation, particularly if you make heavy use of password-change expirations. Note that these warnings are usually shown only to text-mode login users; GUI login users, file-share users, and so on usually don't see these messages.

The chage command can normally be used only by root. The one exception to this rule is if the -1 option is used; this feature allows ordinary users to check their account-expiration information.

Directly Modifying Account Configuration Files

You can directly modify user configuration files. The /etc/passwd and /etc/shadow files control most aspects of an account's basic features. Both files consist of a set of lines, one line per account. Each line begins with a username and continues with a set of fields, delimited by colons (:). Many of these items may be modified with usermod or passwd. A typical /etc/passwd entry resembles the following:

```
sally:x:1029:100:Sally Jones:/home/sally:/bin/bash
```

Each field has a specific meaning, as follows:

Username   The first field in each /etc/passwd line is the username (sally in this example).

Password   The second field has traditionally been reserved for the password. Most Linux systems, however, use a shadow password system in which the password is stored in /etc/shadow. The x in the example's password field is an indication that shadow passwords are in use. In a system that doesn't use shadow passwords, an encrypted password appears here instead.

UID   Following the password is the account's user ID (1029 in this example).

Primary GID   The default login group ID is next in the /etc/passwd line for an account. The example uses a primary GID of 100.

Comment   The comment field may have different contents on different systems. In the preceding example, it's the user's full name. Some systems place additional information here, in a comma-separated list. Such information may include the user's telephone number, office number, title, and so on.

Home Directory   The user's home directory is next up in the list.

Default Shell   The default shell is the final item on each line in /etc/passwd. This is normally /bin/bash, /bin/tcsh, or some other common command shell. It's possible to use something unusual here, though. For instance, many systems include a shutdown account with /bin/shutdown as the shell. If you log into this account, the computer immediately shuts down. You can create user accounts with a shell of /bin/false, which prevents users from logging in as ordinary users but leaves other utilities intact. Users can still receive mail and retrieve it via a remote mail retrieval protocol like POP or IMAP, for instance. A variant on this scheme uses /bin/passwd so that users may change their passwords remotely but can't log in using a command shell.

You can directly modify any of these fields, although in a shadow password system, you probably do *not* want to modify the password field; you should make password-related changes via passwd so that they can be properly encrypted and stored in /etc/shadow. As with changes initiated via usermod, it's best to change /etc/passwd directly only when the user in question isn't logged in, to prevent a change from disrupting an ongoing session.

Like /etc/passwd, /etc/shadow may be edited directly. An /etc/shadow line resembles the following:

```
sally:$6$EmoFkLZPkHkpczVN2XRcMdyj8/ZeeT5UnTQ:15505:0:-1:7:-1:-1:
```

Most of these fields correspond to options set with the chage utility, although some are set with passwd, useradd, or usermod. The meaning of each colon-delimited field on this line is as follows:

Username   Each line begins with the username. Note that the UID is *not* used in /etc/shadow; the username links entries in this file to those in /etc/passwd.

Password   The password is stored in encrypted form, so it bears no obvious resemblance to the actual password. An asterisk (*) or exclamation mark (!) denotes an account with no password (that is, the account doesn't accept logins—it's locked). This is common for accounts used by the system itself. When you lock a user account via the -L option to usermod, the utility prepends an exclamation mark (!) to the password field. Removing the exclamation mark unlocks the account, restoring the original password.

If you've forgotten the root password for a computer, you can boot with an emergency recovery system and copy the contents of a password field for an account whose password you do remember. You can then boot normally, log in as root, and change the password. In a real pinch, you can delete the contents of the password field, which results in a root account with *no* password (that is, none is required to log in). If you do this, be *sure* to *immediately* change the root password after rebooting!

Last Password Change   The next field (15505 in this example) is the date of the last password change. This date is stored as the number of days since January 1, 1970.

Days Until a Change Is Allowed   The next field (0 in this example) is the number of days before a password change is allowed.

Days Before a Change Is Required   This field is the number of days after the last password change before another password change is required.

Days of Warning Before Password Expiration   If your system is configured to expire passwords, you may set it to warn the user when an expiration date is approaching. A value of 7, as in the preceding example, is typical.

Days Between Expiration and Deactivation   Linux allows for a gap between the expiration of an account and its complete deactivation. An expired account either can't be used or requires that the user change the password immediately after logging in. In either case, its password remains intact. A deactivated account's password is erased, and the account can't be used until it's reactivated by the system administrator.

Expiration Date   This field shows the date on which the account will expire. As with the last password change date, the date is expressed as the number of days since January 1, 1970. This option is helpful in the case of students, interns, auditors, contract staff, seasonal workers, and similar temporary users.

Special Flag   This field is reserved for future use and normally isn't used or contains a meaningless value. This field is empty in the preceding example.

For fields relating to day counts, a value of -1 or 99999 indicates that the relevant feature has been disabled. The /etc/shadow values are generally best left to modification through the usermod and chage commands because they can be tricky to set manually—for instance, it's easy to forget a leap year or the like when computing a date as the number of days since January 1, 1970. Similarly, because of its encrypted nature, the password field can't be edited effectively except through passwd or similar utilities. You can cut and paste a value from a compatible file or use crypt, but it's generally easier to use passwd. Copying encrypted passwords from other systems is also somewhat risky because it means that the users will have the same passwords on both systems, and this fact will be obvious to anybody who's acquired both encrypted password lists.

The /etc/shadow file is normally stored with very restrictive permissions, such as rw------- (600), with ownership by root. (Precise permissions vary from one distribution to another, though.) This fact is critical to the shadow password system's utility because it keeps non-root users from reading the file and obtaining the password list, even in an encrypted form. By contrast, /etc/passwd must be readable by ordinary users and usually has rw-r--r-- (644) permissions. If you manually modify /etc/shadow, be sure it has the correct permissions when you're done.

Network Account Databases

Many networks employ network account databases. Such systems include the Network Information System (NIS), an update to this system called NIS+, the Lightweight Directory Access Protocol (LDAP), Kerberos realms, Windows NT 4.0 domains, and Active Directory (AD) domains. All of these systems move account database management onto a single centralized computer (often with one or more backup systems). The advantage of this approach to account maintenance is that users and administrators need not deal with maintaining accounts independently on multiple computers. A single account database can handle accounts on dozens (or even hundreds or thousands) of different computers, greatly simplifying day-to-day administrative tasks and simplifying users' lives. Using such a system, though, means that most user accounts won't appear in /etc/passwd and /etc/shadow, and groups may not appear in /etc/group. (These files will still hold information on local system accounts and groups, though.)

Linux can participate in these systems. In fact, some distributions provide options to enable such support at OS installation time. Typically, you must know the name or IP address of the server that hosts the network account database, and you must know what protocol that the server uses. You may also need a password or some other protocol-specific information, and the server may need to be configured to accept accesses from the Linux system you're configuring.

Activating use of such network account databases after installing Linux is a complex topic. It involves installing appropriate software, modifying the /etc/nsswitch.conf file, and modifying the Pluggable Authentication Module (PAM) configuration files in /etc/pam.d. Such systems often alter the behavior of tools such as passwd and usermod in subtle or not-so-subtle ways. If you need to use such a system, you'll have to consult documentation specific to the service you intend to use. My book *Linux in a Windows World* (O'Reilly, 2005) covers this topic for Windows NT 4.0 domains, LDAP, and Kerberos; and Mark Minasi and Dan York's *Linux for Windows Administrators* (Sybex, 2002) covers this topic for Windows NT 4.0 domains and NIS.

Deleting Accounts

On the surface, deleting user accounts is easy. You may use the userdel command to do the job of removing a user's entries from /etc/passwd and, if the system uses shadow passwords, /etc/shadow. The userdel command takes just three parameters:

Remove User Files   The -r or --remove parameter causes the system to remove all files from the user's mail spool and home directory, as well as the home directory.

Force Deletion   You can force deletion of the account while a user is logged in by using the -f or --force option in conjunction with -r. This option also forces removal of the mail spool even if it's owned by another user and forces removal of the home directory even if another user uses the same home directory.

Get Help   The -h or --help option summarizes userdel options.

As an example, removing the sally account is easily accomplished with the following command:

```
# userdel -r sally
```

You may omit the -r parameter if you want to preserve the user's files. Be aware of one potential complication: Users may create files *outside* their home directories. For instance, many programs use the /tmp directory as "scratch space," so user files often wind up there. These files are deleted automatically after a certain period, but you may have other directories in which users may store files. To locate all such files, you can use the find command with its -uid parameter (or -user, if you use find before deleting the account). For instance, if sally was UID 1029, you can use the following command to locate all her files:

```
# find / -uid 1029
```

The result is a list of files owned by UID 529 (formerly sally). You can then go through this list and decide what to do with the files—change their ownership to somebody else, delete them, back them up to CD-R, or what have you. It's wise to do *something* with these files, or they may be assigned ownership to another user if Sally's UID is reused. This can become awkward if the files exceed the new user's disk quota or if they contain information that the new user should not have—such a person may mistakenly be accused of indiscretions or even crimes.

A few servers—most notably Samba—keep their own list of users. If you run such a server, it's best to remove the user's entry from that server's user list when you remove the user's main account. In the case of Samba, this is normally done by manually editing the smbpasswd file (usually located in /etc, /etc/samba, or /etc/samba.d) and deleting the line corresponding to the user in question or by using the smbpasswd command and its -x option, as in **smbpasswd -x sally** to delete the sally account from Samba's database.

Configuring Groups

Linux provides group configuration tools that parallel those for user accounts in many ways. Groups are not accounts, however, so many features of these tools differ. Likewise, you can create or modify groups by directly editing the configuration files in question. Their layout is similar to that for account control files, but the details differ.

Adding Groups

Linux provides the groupadd command to add a new group. This utility is similar to useradd but has fewer options. The groupadd syntax is as follows:

```
groupadd [-g GID [-o]] [-r] [-f] groupname
```

The parameters to this command enable you to adjust its operation:

Specify a GID   You can provide a specific GID with the -g *GID* parameter. If you omit this parameter, groupadd uses the next available GID. Normally, the GID you specify must be unused by other groups, but the -o parameter overrides this behavior, enabling you to create multiple groups that share one GID.

Create a System Group   The -r parameter instructs groupadd to create a group with a GID of less than SYS_GID_MIN, as defined in /etc/login.defs. Groups with GIDs in this range are considered *system groups*, which are analogous to system accounts—they're normally used by system tools or to help control access to system resources, such as hardware device files. Not all distributions support this option; it was added by Red Hat and has been used on some related distributions. Red Hat uses GIDs of 500 and greater for user private groups (that is, groups named after individual users), which is the reason for the -r parameter.

Force Creation   Normally, if you try to create a group that already exists, groupadd returns an error message. The -f parameter suppresses that error message. Not all versions of groupadd support this parameter.

In most cases, you'll create groups without specifying any parameters except for the group name itself:

```
# groupadd project3
```

This command creates the project3 group, giving it whatever GID the system finds convenient—usually the highest existing GID plus 1. Once you've done this, you can add users to the group, as described in the next section. When you add new users, you can add them directly to the new group with the -g and –G parameters to useradd, described earlier.

Modifying Group Information

Group information, like user account information, may be modified either by using utility programs or by directly editing the underlying configuration file, /etc/group. There are fewer options for modifying groups than for modifying accounts, and the utilities and configuration files are similar. In fact, usermod is one of the tools that's used to modify groups.

Using *groupmod* and *usermod*

The groupmod command modifies an existing group's settings. Its syntax is as follows:

```
groupmod [-g GID [-o]] [-n newgroupname] oldgroupname
```

The options to this command modify its operation:

Specify a GID Specify the new group ID using the -g *GID* option. groupmod returns an error if you specify a new group ID that's already in use, unless you include the -o parameter, in which case you can create two groups that share a single GID.

Specify a Group Name Specify a new group name with the -n *newgroupname* option.

One of the most common group manipulations you'll perform is not handled through groupmod; it's done with usermod. Specifically, usermod enables you to add a user to a group with its -G parameter. For instance, the following command sets sally to be a member of the users, project1, and project4 groups, and it removes her from all other groups:

```
# usermod -G users,project1,project4 sally
```

Be sure to list all the user's current groups in addition to any groups to which you want to add the user. Omitting any of the user's current groups will remove the user from those groups. You can discover the groups to which a user currently belongs with the groups command, as in **groups sally**. To avoid accidentally omitting a group, many system administrators prefer to modify the /etc/group file in a text editor or use gpasswd. Both options enable you to add users to groups without specifying a user's existing group memberships.

Using *gpasswd*

The gpasswd command is the group equivalent to passwd. The gpasswd command also enables you to modify other group features and to assign *group administrators*—users who may perform some group-related administrative functions for their groups. The basic syntax for this command is as follows:

```
gpasswd [-a user] [-d user] [-R] [-r] [-A user[,...]] [-M user[,...]] group
```

The options for this command modify its actions:

Add a User The -a *user* option adds the specified user to the specified group.

Delete a User The -d *user* option deletes the specified user from the specified group.

Disallow newgrp Additions The -R option configures the group to not allow anybody to become a member through newgrp.

Remove Password The -r option removes the password from a group.

Add Group Administrators The root user may use the -A *user[,...]* parameter to specify group administrators. Group administrators may add members to and remove members from a group and change the group password. Using this parameter completely overwrites the list of administrators, so if you want to add an administrator to an existing set of group administrators, you must specify *all* of their usernames.

Add Users The -M *user*[, . . .] option works like -A, but it also adds the specified user(s) to the list of group members.

If entered without any parameters except a group name, gpasswd changes the password for the group. Group passwords enable you to control temporary membership in a group, as granted by newgrp. Ordinarily, members of a group may use newgrp to change their current group membership (affecting the group of files they create). If a password is set, even those who aren't members of a group may become temporary group members; newgrp prompts for a password that, if entered correctly, gives the user temporary group membership.

Unfortunately, some of these features aren't implemented correctly in all distributions. In particular, password entry by non-group members sometimes does *not* give group membership—the system responds with an access denied error message. The -R option also sometimes doesn't work correctly—group members whose primary group membership is with another group may still use newgrp to set their primary group membership.

Directly Modifying Group Configuration Files

Group information is stored primarily in the /etc/group file. Like account configuration files, the /etc/group file is organized as a set of lines, one line per group. A typical line in this file resembles the following:

```
project1:x:501:sally,sam,ellen,george
```

Each field is separated from the others by a colon. The meanings of the four fields are as follows:

Group Name The first field (project1 in the preceding example) is the name of the group.

Password The second field (x in the preceding example) is the group password. Distributions that use shadow passwords typically place an x in this field; others place the encrypted password directly in this field.

GID The group ID number (in this example's case, 501) goes in this field.

User List The final field is a comma-delimited list of group members.

Users may also be members of a group based on their own /etc/passwd file primary group specification. For instance, if user george has project1 listed as his primary group, he need not be listed in the project1 line in /etc/group. If user george uses newgrp to change to another group, though, he won't be able to change back to project1 unless he's listed in the project1 line in /etc/group.

Systems with shadow passwords also use another file, /etc/gshadow, to store shadow password information about groups. This file stores the shadow password and information for group administrators, as described earlier in "Using gpasswd."

If you configure Linux to use a network account database, the /etc/group file is present and may define groups important for the system's basic operation. As with /etc/passwd and /etc/shadow, though, important user groups are likely to be defined only on the network account server, not in /etc/group.

Deleting Groups

Deleting groups is done via the groupdel command, which takes a single parameter: a group name. For instance, **groupdel project3** removes the project3 group. You can also delete a group by editing the /etc/group file (and /etc/gshadow, if present) and removing the relevant line for the group. It's generally better to use groupdel, because groupdel checks to see whether the group is any user's primary group. If it is, groupdel refuses to remove the group; you must change the user's primary group or delete the user account first.

As with deleting users, deleting groups can leave orphaned files on the computer. You can locate them with the find command, which is described in more detail in Chapter 4. For instance, if a deleted group used a GID of 1003, you can find all the files on the computer with that GID by using the following command:

```
# find / -gid 1003
```

Once you've found any files with the deleted group's ownership, you must decide what to do with them. In some cases, leaving them alone won't cause any immediate problems; but if the GID is ever reused, it can lead to confusion and even security breaches. Therefore, it's usually best to delete the files or assign them other group ownership using the chown or chgrp command.

Tuning User and System Environments

Text-mode user environments are controlled through shell configuration files. For bash, these files include /etc/profile, /etc/bash.bashrc, ~/.profile, ~/.bashrc, ~/.bash_profile, and ~/.profile. The files in /etc are global configuration files, which affect all users; those in users' home directories (which are usually copied from the skeleton directory at account creation, as described earlier) affect individual users' accounts and can be customized by individual users. These files control the various bash options, including environment variables—named variables that hold data for the benefit of many programs. For instance, you might set the $EDITOR environment variable to the name of your favorite text editor. Some (but not all) programs that launch editors pay attention to this environment variable and launch the editor you specify.

As a system administrator, you can change the system-wide bash configuration files to add, remove, or change the environment variables that all users receive. Generally speaking, you should do so because the documentation for a specific program indicates that it uses particular environment variables. You can also see all your current environment variables by typing **env**. (The list is rather long, so you may want to pipe it through less, as in **env | less**.)

In addition to setting default environment variables and otherwise modifying users' text-mode login environment by adjusting their bash configuration files, you can adjust the default set of files created by useradd. As described earlier, in "Adding Users," useradd copies files from the *skeleton directory* (/etc/skel by default) into a newly created home directory. Typically, /etc/skel contains a handful of user configuration files, such as .bashrc. You can add files (and even directories) to this directory, including user configuration files, a starting directory tree, a README file for new users, and anything else you like. Because these files are copied into users' home directories and users are given ownership of the copies, the users can read, change, and even delete their copies of these files. Thus, you shouldn't place any options in these files that are sensitive from a security point of view or that users should not be able to change. (In truth, entries you place in global bash configuration files can easily be overridden by individual users via manual bash commands or other configuration files, too.) Also, be aware that any changes you make to the global files won't automatically be moved into existing users' copies of these files; changes will affect only the files received by new users. This fact makes the global files (such as /etc/profile) preferable to /etc/skel for any changes to system defaults you want to implement system-wide, particularly if you expect you'll ever want to modify your changes.

Various programs set environment variables themselves, and some are maintained automatically by bash. For instance, bash maintains the PWD environment variable, so you shouldn't try to set it in a configuration script. Also, be aware that adjusting the bash configuration files affects only bash. If a user's default shell is something else or if a user doesn't use a text-mode shell (say, if the user logs into X and launches programs from a GUI menu), setting environment variables in the bash configuration files will do no good.

Using System Log Files

Linux maintains log files that record various key details about system operation. You may be able to begin using log files immediately, but knowing how to change the log file configuration can also be important. You do this by configuring the syslogd *daemon* (a daemon is a program that runs continuously in the background waiting for an event to trigger it to perform some action). Some servers and other programs perform their own logging and so must be configured independently of syslogd. You may even want to configure one computer to send its log files to another system as a security measure. You should also be aware of issues surrounding log file rotation; if your computer doesn't properly manage existing log files, they can grow to consume all your available disk space, at least on the partition on which they're stored. In addition to configuring logging, you must be able to use the log files that the system generates.

Understanding *syslogd*

Most Linux systems employ a special daemon to handle log maintenance in a unified way. The traditional Linux system logger is syslogd, which is often installed from a package called sysklogd. The syslogd daemon handles messages from servers and other user-mode programs. It's usually paired with a daemon called klogd, which is generally installed from the same sysklogd package as syslogd. The klogd daemon manages logging of kernel messages.

Other choices for system loggers exist. For instance, syslog-ng is a replacement that supports advanced filtering options, and metalog is another option. Recent versions of Fedora and Ubuntu use rsyslogd. This chapter describes the traditional syslogd logger. Others are similar in principle, and even in some specific features, but differ in many details.

The basic idea behind a system logger is to provide a unified means of handling log files. The daemon runs in the background and accepts data delivered from servers and other programs that are configured to use the log daemon. The daemon can then use information provided by the server to classify the message and direct it to an appropriate log file. This configuration enables you to consolidate messages from various servers in a handful of standard log files, which can be much easier to use and manage than potentially dozens of log files from the various servers running on the system.

In order to work, of course, the log daemon must be configured. In the case of syslogd, this is done through the /etc/syslog.conf file. (The rsyslogd configuration file is /etc/rsyslog.conf and is similar to syslog.conf.) The next section describes the syslog.conf file's format in more detail.

Setting Logging Options

The format of the /etc/syslog.conf file is conceptually simple but provides a great deal of power. Comment lines, as in many Linux configuration files, are denoted by a hash mark (#). Non-comment lines take the following form:

```
facility.priority    action
```

In this line, the *facility* is a code word for the type of program or tool that generated the message to be logged; the *priority* is a code word for the importance of this message; and the *action* is a file, remote computer, or other location that's to accept the message. The *facility* and *priority* are often referred to collectively as the *selector*.

Valid codes for the *facility* are auth, authpriv, cron, daemon, kern, lpr, mail, mark, news, security, syslog, user, uucp, and local0 through local7. Many of these names refer to specific servers or program classes. For instance, mail servers and other mail-processing tools typically log using the mail facility. Most servers that aren't covered by more-specific codes use the daemon facility. The security facility is identical to auth, but auth is the preferred name. The mark facility is reserved for internal use. An asterisk (*) refers to all facilities. You can specify multiple facilities in one selector by separating the facilities with commas (,).

Valid codes for the *priority* are debug, info, notice, warning, warn, error, err, crit, alert, emerg, and panic. The warning priority is identical to warn, error is identical to err, and emerg is identical to panic. The error, warn, and panic priority names are deprecated; you should use their equivalents instead. Other than these identical pairs, these priorities represent ascending levels of importance. The debug level logs the most information; it's intended, as the name implies, for debugging programs that are misbehaving. The emerg priority logs the most important messages, which indicate very serious problems. When a program sends a message to the system logger, it includes a priority code; the logger logs the message to a file if you've configured it to log messages of that level or higher. Thus, if you specify a *priority* code of alert, the system will log messages that are classified as alert or emerg but not messages of crit or below. An exception to this rule is if you precede the priority code by an equal sign (=), as in =crit, which describes what to do with messages of crit priority *only*. An exclamation mark (!) reverses the meaning of a match. For instance, !crit causes messages *below* crit priority to be logged. A *priority* of * refers to all priorities.

You can specify multiple selectors for a single action by separating the selectors with a semicolon (;). Note that commas are used to separate multiple facilities within a single selector, whereas semicolons are used to separate multiple selectors as a whole. Examples of complete selectors appear shortly.

Most commonly, the *action* is a filename, typically in the /var/log directory tree. The messages, syslog, and secure files in this directory are three common and important log files, although not all distributions use all of these files. Other possible logging locations include a device filename for a console (such as /dev/console) to display data on the screen, a remote machine name preceded by an at sign (@) to log data to the specified system, and a list of usernames of individuals who should see the message if they're logged in. For the last of these options, an asterisk (*) means all logged-in users.

Some examples should help clarify these rules. First is a fairly ordinary and simple entry:

```
mail.*          /var/log/mail
```

This line sends all log entries identified by the originating program as related to mail to the /var/log/mail file. Most of the entries in a default /etc/syslog.conf file resemble this one. Together, they typically cover all of the facilities mentioned earlier. Some messages may be handled by multiple rules. For instance, another rule might look like this one:

```
*.emerg         *
```

This line sends all emerg-level messages to the consoles of all users who are logged into the computer using text-mode tools. If this line and the earlier mail.* selector are both present, emerg-level messages related to mail will be logged to /var/log/mail *and* displayed on users' consoles.

A more complex example logs kernel messages in various ways, depending on their priorities:

```
kern.*                 /var/log/kernel
kern.crit              @logger.pangaea.edu
kern.crit              /dev/console
kern.info;kern.!err    /var/log/kernel-info
```

The first of these rules logs all kernel messages to /var/log/kernel. The second line sends critical messages to logger.pangaea.edu. (This computer must be configured to accept remote logs, which is a topic not covered in this book.) The third line sends a copy of critical messages to /dev/console, which causes them to be displayed on the computer's main text-mode console display. Finally, the last line sends messages that are between info and err in priority to /var/log/kernel-info. Because err is the priority immediately above crit and because info is the lowest priority, these four lines cause all kernel messages to be logged two or three times: once to /var/log/kernel as well as either to the remote system and the console *or* to /var/log/kernel-info.

Most distributions ship with reasonable system logger settings, but you may want to examine these settings and perhaps adjust them. If you change them, be aware that you may need to change some other tools. For instance, all major distributions ship with tools that help rotate log files. If you change the files to which syslogd logs messages, you may need to change your log file rotation scripts as well. This topic is covered in the next section.

In addition to the system logger's options, you may be able to set logging options in individual programs. For instance, you may tell programs to record more or less information or to log routine information at varying priorities. Some programs also provide the means to log via the system log daemon or via their own mechanisms. Details vary greatly from one program to another, so you should consult the program's documentation for details.

 Most programs that use the system log daemons are servers and other system tools. Programs that individuals run locally seldom log data via the system log daemon, although there are some exceptions to this rule, such as the Fetchmail program for retrieving email from remote servers.

Manually Logging Data

For the most part, the system logger accepts log entries from system tools, such as servers. Occasionally, though, you may want to manually create a log entry or have a script do so. The tool for this job is known as logger, and it has the following syntax:

```
logger [-isd] [-f file] [-p pri] [-t tag] [-u socket] [message ...]
```

Options to logger permit changing its default function:

Record `logger` **PID**   The `-i` option records the process ID (PID) of the `logger` process along with other data.

Output to Standard Error   You can echo data to standard error, as well as to the log file, by using the `-s` option. An interactive script might use this feature to alert users to problems.

Log Using Datagrams   The `-d` option causes `logger` to use datagrams rather than a stream connection to the system logger socket. This is an advanced feature that you should use only if you're instructed to do so in documentation or if you understand the networking issues involved.

Log a File   You can log the contents of a file by using the `-f` *file* option. Be cautious with this option; if *file* is big, your system log file can grow to ridiculous size!

Identify a Priority   The `-p` *pri* option specifies a priority, as described earlier.

Log Tags   By default, `logger` includes its name in the log file as a tag. You can change this tag with the `-t` *tag* option. This is useful if you want to identify a script or other program that created the log entry and don't care to record the fact that `logger` was involved in the process.

Specify a Socket   Ordinarily, `logger` calls the default system log tools to do its job. You can log directly to a network socket using the `-u` *socket* option if you prefer.

Specify a Message   If you don't specify a file using `-f` *file*, `logger` will log whatever you type after other options as the message to be logged. If you don't provide a message on the command line, `logger` accepts input you type on subsequent lines as information to be logged. You should terminate such input by pressing Ctrl+D.

As an example, suppose you want to log the message "shutting down for system mainte-nance" to the system log. You can do so by typing the following command:

```
$ logger shutting down for system maintenance
```

The result will be an entry like the following, probably in /var/log/messages:

```
Jul 29 14:09:50 nessus logger: shutting down for system maintenance
```

Adding parameters changes the details of what's logged, as just described. You can place a call to `logger` in a script as a way of documenting the script's activities. For instance, a system backup script might use `logger` to record details such as its start and stop times and the number and size of the files it has backed up.

Rotating Log Files

Log files are intended to retain information about system activities for a reasonable period of time, but system logging daemons provide no means to control the size of log files. Left unchecked, log files can therefore grow to consume all the available space on the partition on which they reside. To avoid this problem, Linux employs *log file rotation* tools. These tools rename and optionally compress the current log files, delete old log files, and force the logging system to begin using new log files.

The most common log rotation tool is a package called logrotate. This program is typically called on a regular basis via a cron job. (The upcoming section "Running Jobs in the Future" describes cron jobs in more detail.) The logrotate program consults a configuration file called /etc/logrotate.conf, which includes several default settings and typically refers to files in /etc/logrotate.d to handle specific log files. A typical /etc/logrotate.conf file includes several comment lines, denoted by hash marks (#), as well as lines to set various options, as illustrated by Listing 7.1.

Listing 7.1: Sample /etc/logrotate.conf File

```
# Rotate logs weekly
weekly
# Keep 4 weeks of old logs
rotate 4
# Create new log files after rotation
create
# Compress old log files
compress
# Refer to files for individual packages
include /etc/logrotate.d
# Set miscellaneous options
notifempty
nomail
noolddir
# Rotate wtmp, which isn't handled by a specific program
/var/log/wtmp {
    monthly
    create 0664 root utmp
    rotate 1
}
```

Most of the lines in Listing 7.1 set options that are fairly self-explanatory or that are well explained by the comments that immediately precede them—for instance, the weekly line sets the default log rotation interval to once a week. If you see an option in your file that you don't understand, consult the man page for logrotate.

Because log file rotation is handled by cron jobs that typically run late at night, it won't happen if a computer is routinely turned off at the end of the day. This practice is common with Windows workstations but is uncommon with servers. Linux workstations should either be left running overnight as a general practice or be given special tools to enable log rotation despite routine shutdowns. The anacron utility, described in the upcoming section "Using anacron," is particularly well suited to the latter task.

The last few lines of Listing 7.1 demonstrate the format for the definition of a specific log file. These definitions begin with the filename for the file (multiple filenames may be listed, separated by spaces), followed by an open curly brace ({). They end in a close curly brace (}). Intervening lines set options that may override the defaults. For instance, the /var/log/wtmp definition in Listing 7.1 sets the monthly option, which tells logrotate to rotate this log file once a month, overriding the default weekly option. Such definitions are common in the individual files in /etc/logrotate.d, which are typically owned by the packages whose log files they rotate. The following are examples of features that are often set in these definitions:

Rotated Filenaming   Ordinarily, rotated log files acquire numbers, such as messages.1 for the first rotation of the messages log file. Using the dateext option causes the rotated log file to obtain a date code instead, as in messages-20130210 for the rotation performed on February 10, 2013.

Compression Options   As already noted, compress causes logrotate to compress log files to save space. This is done using gzip by default, but you can specify another program with the compresscmd keyword, as in compresscmd bzip2 to use bzip2. The compressoptions keyword enables you to pass options to the compression command (say, to improve the compression ratio).

Creation of New Log Files   The create option causes logrotate to create a new log file for use by the system logger or program. This option takes a file mode, an owner, and a group as additional options. Some programs don't work well with this option, though. Most of them use the copytruncate option instead, which tells logrotate to copy the old log file to a new name and then clear all the data out of the original file.

Time Options   The daily, weekly, and monthly options tell the system to rotate the log files at the specified intervals. These options aren't always used; some configurations use a size threshold rather than a time threshold for when to rotate log files.

Size Options   The size keyword sets a maximum size for a log file. It takes a size in bytes as an argument (adding k, M, or G to the size changes it to kilobytes, megabytes, or gigabytes, respectively). For instance, size 100k causes logrotate to rotate the file when it reaches 100kB in size.

Rotation Options   The rotate x option causes x copies of old log files to be maintained. For instance, if you set rotate 2 for the /var/log/messages file, logrotate will maintain /var/log/messages.1 and /var/log/messages.2 in addition to the active /var/log/messages file. When that file is rotated, /var/log/messages.2 is deleted, /var/log/messages.1 is renamed to /var/log/messages.2, /var/log/messages becomes /var/log/messages.1, and a new /var/log/messages is created.

Mail Options   If you use mail *address*, logrotate will email a log file to the specified address when it's rotated out of existence. Using nomail causes the system to not send any email; the log is quietly deleted.

Scripts   The prerotate and postrotate keywords both begin a series of lines that are treated as scripts to be run immediately before or after log file rotation, respectively. In both cases, these scripts end with the endscript keyword. These commands are frequently used to force syslogd or a server to begin using a new log file.

In most cases, servers and other programs that log data either do so via the system logging daemon or ship with a configuration file that goes in /etc/logrotate.d to handle the server's log files. These files usually do a reasonable job, but you may want to double-check them. For instance, you might discover that your system is configured to keep too many or too few old log files for your taste, in which case adjusting the rotate option is in order. You should also check the /var/log directory and its subdirectories every now and then. If you see huge numbers of files accumulating or if files are growing to unacceptable size, you may want to check the corresponding logrotate configuration files. If an appropriate file doesn't exist, create one. Use a working file as a template, modifying it for the new file. Pay particular attention to the prerotate and postrotate scripts; you may need to consult the documentation for the program that's creating the log file to learn how to force that program to begin using a new log file.

In most cases, log files remain on the computer that recorded them. Sometimes, though, you may want to copy such files off-site. The easiest way to do this may be to reconfigure the log daemon to send the messages you want to archive to another system, as described in "Setting Logging Options." Another possibility is to create a cron job (as described later, in "Running Jobs in the Future") to copy files to another system using a network share, ssh, or some other network tool. You can also manually copy log files onto removable disks, if you like. There are few technical reasons to archive log files for more than a few weeks—only if a problem escapes your notice for a long time will they be useful. Managers or lawyers may want to keep them around for the long term for business or legal reasons, though.

Reviewing Log File Contents

Log files do no good if they simply accumulate on the system. Their purpose is to be used as a means of identifying problems or documenting normal activity. When a server isn't responding as you expect, when a computer refuses logins it should be accepting (or accepting logins it should be refusing), or when a system's network interface isn't coming up (to name just three types of problems), you should check your log files as part of your troubleshooting procedures. Log files can also be useful in less troublesome situations, such as helping you to identify the load on a server so as to plan upgrades. Several procedures, many of which involve tools described elsewhere in this book, can help you access your log files:

Paging Through Whole Log Files   You can use a pager program, such as less (described in Chapter 1, "Exploring Linux Command-Line Tools"), to view the entire contents of a log file. A text editor can fill the same role.

Searching for Keywords   You can use grep (described in Chapter 1) to pull lines that contain keywords out of log files. This can be particularly handy when you don't know which log file is likely to hold an entry. For instance, typing **grep eth0 /var/log/*** locates all lines in all files in the /var/log directory that contain the string eth0.

Examining the Start or End of a File   You can use the head or tail command (described in Chapter 1) to examine the first or last several lines of a log file. The tail command is particularly handy; you can use it to look at the last few entries just after you take some action that you expect to produce some diagnostic log file entries.

Monitoring Log Files   In addition to checking the last few lines of a log file, `tail` can monitor a file on an ongoing basis, echoing lines to the screen as they're added to the file. You do this with the `-f` option to `tail`, as in **`tail -f /var/log/messages`**.

Using Advanced Log Analysis Tools   Various packages exist expressly for the purpose of analyzing log files. For instance, there's Logcheck, which is part of the Sentry Tools package (`http://sourceforge.net/projects/sentrytools/`). This package comes with some distributions, such as Mandriva and Debian. Unfortunately, it requires a fair amount of customization for your own system, so it's most easily implemented if it comes with your distribution, preconfigured for its log file format.

Log file analysis is a skill that's best learned through experience. Many log file messages are cryptic, and they can be cryptic in different ways for different programs. For instance, consider these entries:

```
Apr 14 23:17:00 speaker /USR/SBIN/CRON[6026]: (george) CMD
 (/usr/bin/fetchmail -f /home/george/.fetchmailrc > /dev/null)
Apr 14 23:17:52 speaker sshd[6031]: Accepted publickey for george from
 ::ffff:192.168.1.3 port 48139 ssh2
```

These two lines relate to two entirely different events, but they have a similar format. Both entries begin with a time stamp and the name of the computer on which the activity occurred (`speaker` in this example). Next on each line is an identifier for the program that logged the activity, including its PID number: `/USR/SBIN/CRON[6026]` and `sshd[6031]` in this example. Note that these names are generated by the programs that create the activity, so they aren't necessarily consistent or even fully accurate. For instance, there is no /USR/SBIN/CRON program, although there *is* a /usr/sbin/cron program. (Recall that Linux has a case-sensitive filesystem.)

All of this information helps you identify what program logged the entry and when it did so. The rest of the log entry contains the actual logged data. The first entry in this example is from the `cron` utility, and it identifies a program run on behalf of `george`—specifically, `cron` ran the `fetchmail` program, passed it the name of a configuration file via the `-f` option, and redirected the output to /dev/null. The second entry (for `sshd`) identifies a login from 192.168.1.3 on port 48139, again involving the user `george`.

You can use entries like these to help identify malfunctioning servers, spot security breaches, and otherwise debug your system. Doing so, though, requires at least some familiarity with the normal log file contents as well as other system details. For instance, in the preceding example, if your system has no `george` account, these entries should both be suspicious but you must be familiar enough with the format of the entries to spot that `george` is a username (or be able to work it out). You must also know that your system should have no `george` account.

Overall, you should probably examine your log files from time to time to become familiar with their contents. This will help you spot abnormalities when the system begins misbehaving or when you want to use log files to help track down an unwelcome visitor.

Log file entries can be conspicuous by their absence as well as by suspicious content within them. Intruders often try to cover their tracks by editing log files to remove the entries that betray their unauthorized accesses. Sometimes, though, they're sloppy about this and just delete all the log entries from the time in question. If you notice unusual gaps in your log files, such as a space of an hour with no entries on a system that normally logs a couple dozen entries in that period, you may want to investigate further.

Maintaining the System Time

Linux depends on its system clock more than many OSs. Tools such as cron and at (described later, in "Running Jobs in the Future") run programs at specified times, the make development tool uses files' time stamps to determine which ones need attention, and so on. Thus, you should be familiar with how Linux deals with time, how to set the time zone, how to set the time, and how to keep the clock accurate.

Linux Time Concepts

The *x*86 and *x*86-64 computers that most often run Linux, as well as most other comput-ers of this general class, have two built-in clocks. The first of these clocks, sometimes called the *hardware clock*, maintains the time while the computer is turned off. When you boot Linux, it reads the hardware clock and sets the *software clock* to the value it retrieves. The software clock is what Linux uses for most purposes while it's running.

Most desktop OSs, such as Windows and pre-X versions of Mac OS, set their clocks to the local time. This approach is simple and convenient for people who are used to dealing mainly with local time, but for purposes of networking, it's inadequate. When it's 4:00 a.m. in New York, it's 1:00 a.m. in Los Angeles, so network protocols that rely even partly on time can become confused (or at the very least, create confusing log entries) when they operate across time zones. Linux, like other Unix-like OSs, sets its clock to *Coordinated Universal Time (UTC)*, which for most purposes is identical to *Greenwich Mean Time (GMT)*—the time in Greenwich, England, unadjusted for daylight saving time. This approach means that Linux systems in New York and Los Angeles (and London and Moscow and Tokyo) should have identical times, assuming all are set correctly. For communicating with users, though, these systems need to know their time zones. For instance, when you type ls -l to see a file listing complete with time stamps, Linux reads the time stamp in UTC and then adds or subtracts the appropriate amount of time so that the time stamp appears in your local time. Of course, all of this means that you must be able to set the computer's time zone. On most systems, this is done at system installation; the distribution's installer asks you for your time zone and sets things up correctly. If you erred during installation or if you need to change the time zone for any reason, refer to Chapter 6, "Configuring the X Window System, Localization, and Printing," which describes how to set your time zone.

> The exam's objective 108.1 includes the files /usr/share/zoneinfo, /etc/timezone, and /etc/localtime. These files are also included under objective 107.3 and are described in Chapter 6, which covers that objective.

Linux's internal use of UTC can complicate setting the hardware clock. Ideally, the hardware clock should be set to UTC; but if your system multi-boots between Linux and an OS that expects the hardware clock to be in local time, you'll have to set the hardware clock to local time and configure Linux to deal with this fact. For the most part, this configuration works well, but you may have to watch the clock the first time you reboot in the spring or fall after changing your clocks because of a daylight saving time. Depending on your Linux and other OS's settings, your hardware clock may be reset in a way one OS or the other doesn't expect.

Both the hardware clock and the software clock are notoriously unreliable on standard *x*86 and *x*86-64 hardware; both clocks tend to drift, so your clock can easily end up being several minutes off the correct time within a month or two of being set. To deal with this problem, Linux supports various network protocols for setting the time. The most popular of these is the *Network Time Protocol (NTP)*, which is described in the upcoming section "Using NTP."

Manually Setting the Time

You can manually set your system's clock—or more precisely, its *clocks*, because as noted earlier, Linux maintains two clocks: the hardware clock and the software clock. The main tool to set the software clock is date, which has the following syntax when setting the clock:

```
date [-u|--utc|--universal] [MMDDhhmm[[CC]YY][.ss]]
```

Used without any options, this command displays the current date and time. If you pass a time to the program, it sets the software clock to that time. This format contains a month, a day, an hour, and a minute at a minimum, all in two-digit codes (*MMDDhhmm*). You can optionally add a 2- or 4-digit year and the seconds within a minute if you like. You should specify the time in a 24-hour format. For instance, to set the time to 3:02 p.m. on October 27, 2013, you'd type the following command:

```
# date 102715022013
```

By default, date assumes you're specifying the time in local time. If you want to set the clock in UTC, include the -u, --utc, or --universal option.

Because *x*86 and *x*86-64 hardware maintains both software and hardware clocks, Linux provides tools to synchronize the two. Specifically, the hwclock utility enables you to set the hardware clock from the software clock, or vice versa, as well as do a few other things. Its syntax is fairly straightforward:

```
hwclock [options]
```

You can specify options to accomplish several goals:

Show the Hardware Clock   To view the hardware clock, pass the -r or --show option. The time is displayed in local time, even if the hardware clock is set to UTC.

Set the Hardware Clock Manually   To set the hardware clock to a date you specify, you need two options: --set and --date=*newdate*. The *newdate* is in the date format that the date program accepts.

Set the Hardware Clock Based on the Software Clock   If you've set the software clock, you can synchronize the hardware clock to the same value with the --systohc option.

Set the Hardware Clock Based on the Hardware Clock   If your hardware clock is accurate but your software clock isn't, you can use the --hctosys option to set the software clock to the hardware clock's value. This option is often used in a SysV startup script to set the system clock when the computer first boots.

Specify UTC or Local Time   You can tell Linux to treat the hardware clock as storing UTC by using the --utc option or to treat it as holding local time by using the --localtime option. The default is whichever was last used when the hardware clock was set.

Ordinarily, you won't use hwclock directly very often. You may need to use it after a daylight saving time shift if you maintain your hardware clock in local time, but most distributions include scripts that manage this task automatically. You may also want to use it once in a while to keep the hardware clock from drifting too far from an accurate time; but again, many distributions do this automatically as part of the system shutdown procedure.

You can also set the hardware clock via your computer's firmware setup utility. Consult your motherboard or computer hardware manual for details. You must reboot the system to do this, typically pressing the Delete or some other key at a critical time early in the boot process (before your boot loader takes over). You must then find the time option and set it appropriately. If Linux is using UTC, remember to set the clock to UTC rather than local time.

Using NTP

Typically, a clock on an isolated computer needn't be set with any great precision. It doesn't really matter if the time is off by a few seconds, or even a few minutes, so long as the time is reasonably consistent on that one computer for the purpose of cron, other scheduling tools, and time stamps. Sometimes, though, maintaining a truly accurate system time is important. This is true for a few scientific, business, and industrial applications (such as astronomical measurements or determining the start and stop times for television broadcasts). In a networked environment, maintaining the correct time can be more important. Time stamps on files may become confused if a file server and its clients have different times, for instance. Worse, a few protocols, such as the Kerberos security suite, embed time stamps in their packets and rely on those time stamps for normal system functioning. If two computers using Kerberos have wildly different times, they may not be able to communicate. For these reasons, several protocols exist to synchronize the clocks of multiple systems. Of these, NTP is the most popular and flexible, so I describe it. You should first understand the basic principles of NTP operation. You can then go on to configuring an NTP server for your network and setting up other systems as NTP clients.

Understanding NTP Basics

One of the most popular, flexible, and accurate network time tools is NTP. This protocol creates a tiered hierarchy of time sources, as illustrated in Figure 7.1. At the top of the structure are one or more highly accurate time sources—typically atomic clocks or radio receivers that pull their times from broadcast time signals based on atomic clocks. These are referred to as *stratum 0* time servers, but they aren't directly accessible to any but the *stratum 1* time servers to which they're connected. These stratum 1 computers run NTP servers that deliver the time to *stratum 2* servers, which deliver the time to *stratum 3* servers, and so on, for an arbitrary number of strata.

FIGURE 7.1   NTP enables an expanding pyramid of computers to set their clocks to a highly accurate source signal.

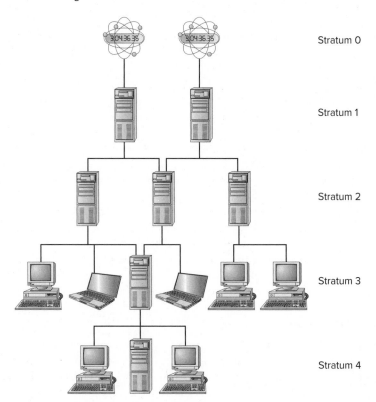

Other time-setting protocols include one built into the Server Message Block/Common Internet File System (SMB/CIFS) used for Windows file sharing and implemented in Linux by Samba and a protocol used by the rdate utility in Linux.

The key to NTP is the fact that each server can deliver time to an expanding number of clients. For instance, if a stratum 1 server has 1,000 clients, each of which has 1,000 clients, and so on, stratum 3 will consist of 1,000,000 systems, and stratum 4 will contain 1,000,000,000 systems. Each increase in the stratum number slightly decreases the accuracy of the time signal, but not by much; even a stratum 4 system's clock should be accurate to well under a second, which is accurate enough for almost all purposes. More important, if you run a network, you can set aside one computer as an NTP server and set all your other computers' clocks from that one server. Even if your primary NTP server's clock is off by a second, all the clocks on your network should be set to within a tiny fraction of each other, which is the most important consideration for time-dependent network protocols such as Kerberos.

NTP works by measuring the round-trip time for packets between the server and the client. The two systems exchange packets with embedded time stamps; the client then adjusts its time so that it is synchronized with the source's time stamp but adds a bit to the time reported by the source to account for the packet's estimated travel time. For this reason, when you select an NTP source (as described next, in "Locating a Time Source"), you should pick one with the shortest possible network time delay, all other things being equal. (In truth, several measures of reliability exist, and the NTP programs try to take them all into account.)

The main Linux NTP server program functions as both a server and a client; it sets its clock based on the time of the server to which it's pointed, and it enables other systems to set their clocks based on its own. Even the end points in the NTP hierarchy (the stratum 4 and some stratum 3 servers in Figure 7.1) often run the full NTP server package. The reason is that this software runs constantly and can monitor for and adjust the clock drift that's common in *x*86 and other computers' clocks, resulting in much more consistent timekeeping than is possible with a program that simply sets the clock and then ignores it until the next time the program is run. In other words, NTP doesn't just reset the system clock periodically; the server improves the accuracy of the system clock. In part, this is done through the ntp.drift file, which is usually buried in /var/lib/ntp but is sometimes stored in /etc. This file holds information about the software clock's inaccuracies and so can be used to correct for them. A full NTP server, even when it's functioning only as an NTP client, periodically checks with its source systems to keep the system time set correctly and to update the ntp.drift file.

Locating a Time Source

You may think that locating an NTP server with a low stratum number (such as stratum 1) is ideal. Although it's true that your own system will have a minutely more accurate clock when using such a source, the best approach in most cases is to synchronize with a stratum

2 or lower system. The reason is that this practice will help keep the load on the stratum 1 servers low, thus improving the overall performance of the NTP network as a whole. An exception might be if you're configuring an NTP server that will itself deliver the time to hundreds or more computers.

To locate an NTP server, you should consult one or more of several sources:

Your ISP   Many Internet service providers (ISPs), including business networks and universities, operate NTP servers for the benefit of their users. These servers are usually very close to your own in a network sense, making them good choices for NTP. You should consult your ISP or the networking department at your organization to learn if such a system is available.

Your Distribution's NTP Server   Some Linux distributions operate NTP servers for their users. If you happen to be close to these servers in a network sense, they can be good choices; however, chances are this isn't the case, so you may want to look elsewhere.

Public NTP Server Lists   Lists of public NTP servers are maintained at `http://support .ntp.org/bin/view/Servers/WebHome`. These servers can be good choices, but you'll need to locate the one closest to you in a network sense and perhaps contact the site you choose to obtain permission to use it.

Public NTP Server Pool   The `pool.ntp.org` subdomain is dedicated to servers that have volunteered to function as public NTP servers. These servers are accessed in a round-robin fashion by hostname, so you can end up using different servers each time you launch NTP. Thus, using the public NTP server pool can be a bit of a gamble, but the results are usually good enough for casual users or if you don't want to spend time checking and maintaining your NTP configuration. To use the pool, you can configure your NTP server to use either the `pool.ntp.org` subdomain name or a numbered host within that domain, such as `0.pool.ntp.org`. You can narrow the list geographically by adding a geographic name to the domain name, as in `north-america.pool.ntp.org` for servers located in North America. Consult `http://support.ntp.org/bin/view/Servers/NTPPoolServers` for details.

The closest server in a network sense may not be the closest computer in a geographic sense. For instance, a national ISP may route all traffic through just one or two hub sites. The result can be that traffic from, say, Atlanta, Georgia, to Tampa, Florida, may go through Chicago, Illinois. Such a detour is likely to increase round-trip time and decrease the accuracy of NTP. In such a situation, a user in Atlanta may be better off using a Chicago NTP server than one in Tampa, even though Tampa is much closer geographically.

Once you've located a few possible time servers, try using `ping` to determine the round-trip time for packets to this system. If any systems have very high `ping` times, you may want to remove them from consideration.

Configuring NTP Servers

When you're setting up a network to use NTP, select one system (or perhaps two for a network with several dozen or more computers) to function as the primary NTP server. This computer needn't be very powerful, but it must have always-up access to the Internet. You can then install the NTP server and configure it.

Most Linux distributions ship the NTP software in a package called ntp or ntpd. Look for this package and, if it's not already installed, install it. If you can't find this package, check http://www.ntp.org/downloads.html. This site hosts NTP source code, which you can compile and install. If you don't install your distribution's own NTP package, you'll need to create your own SysV startup script or start the NTP daemon in some other way.

Once NTP is installed, look for its configuration file, /etc/ntp.conf. This file contains various NTP options, but the most important are the server lines:

```
server clock.example.com
server ntp.pangaea.edu
server time.luna.edu
```

Each of these lines points to a single NTP server. When your local NTP daemon starts up, it contacts all the servers specified in /etc/ntp.conf, measures their accuracy against each other, and settles on one as its primary time source. Typically, you list about three upstream time servers for a system that's to serve many other computers. This practice enables your server to weed out any servers that deliver a bad time signal, and it also gives automatic fallback in case an upstream server becomes temporarily or permanently unavailable. If your NTP server won't be serving many computers itself, you may want to configure it for three servers initially and then drop the ones your system isn't using as its primary time source after a day or two. This will reduce the load on these servers.

You may want to peruse your configuration file for entries to remove. For instance, the configuration file may contain references to servers you'd rather not use or other odd options with associated comments that make you think they're inappropriate. Generally speaking, you shouldn't adjust entries in the ntp.conf file other than the reference server lines, but special circumstances or odd default files may require you to make changes.

Once you've made your changes, start or restart your NTP daemon. Typically, this is done via a SysV startup script:

```
# /etc/init.d/ntpd restart
```

You may need to change the path to the file, the SysV script filename, or the option (change restart to start if you're starting NTP for the first time). Most distributions configure NTP to start whenever the system boots once you install the server. Consult Chapter 5, "Booting Linux and Editing Files," for details of changing this configuration.

To verify that NTP is working, you can use ntpq, which is an interactive program that accepts various commands. Figure 7.2 shows it in operation, displaying the output of the peers command, which displays the servers to which your NTP server is connected. In Figure 7.2, three external servers are listed, plus LOCAL(0), which is the last-resort reference source of the computer's own clock. The refid column shows the server to which each system is synchronized, the st column shows the stratum of the server, and additional columns show more technical information. The server to which yours is synchronized is denoted by an asterisk (*), other servers with good times are indicated by plus signs (+), and most other symbols (such as x and -) denote servers that have been discarded from consideration for various reasons. You can obtain a server list by passing -p or --peers to ntpq, as in **ntpq -p**, without entering interactive mode. Consult ntpq's man page for more information about its operation.

FIGURE 7.2   The ntpq program enables you to verify that an NTP server is functioning correctly.

```
 - ○ ⌥                     rodsmith@speaker:~ - Shell - Konsole               ᵖ □ ✕

  Session  Edit  View  Bookmarks  Settings  Help

$ ntpq
ntpq> peers
     remote           refid      st t when poll reach   delay   offset  jitter
==============================================================================
+clock.example.c 128.227.205.3    2 u  186 1024  377   23.016   -0.624  10.787
*ntp.pangaea.edu 172.17.1.243     2 u  269 1024  377   41.464    4.139   2.553
+time.luna.edu   18.145.0.30      2 u  186 1024  377   20.183   -0.293   0.366
 LOCAL(0)        LOCAL(0)        10 l   23   64  377    0.000    0.000   0.001
ntpq>

  🖼 ■ Shell                                                                   💻
```

 You won't see a server selected as the source until a few minutes after you restart the NTP daemon. The reason is that your local NTP process takes a while to determine which of the sources is providing the best signal.

Configuring NTP Clients

Once you've configured one or more NTP servers, you can configure the rest of your computers to point to them. Their configuration is done just like the NTP server configuration, with a couple of exceptions:

- You set your NTP clients to refer to the NTP server (or servers) you've just config-ured rather than to an outside NTP source. This way, your local systems won't put an unnecessary burden on the outside NTP server you've selected.

- You may want to ensure that your NTP clients can't be accessed as servers. This is a security measure. You can do this with an iptables firewall rule or by using the restrict default ignore line in ntp.conf. This line tells the server to ignore all incoming NTP requests. Ideally, you should use both methods.

Once you've configured a client, restart its NTP daemon. You can then use ntpq to check its status. You should see that it refers only to your network's own NTP server or servers. These systems should be listed as belonging to a stratum with a number one higher than the servers to which they refer.

In some cases, a simpler way to set the time on a client is to use ntpdate. This program is part of the NTP suite, and it performs a one-time clock setting. To use it, type the command name followed by the hostname or IP address of an NTP server:

```
# ntpdate clock.example.com
```

Some NTP packages include a call to ntpdate in their NTP daemon startup scripts in order to ensure that the system is set to the correct time when it starts. The ntpdate command, however, has been deprecated and could disappear from the NTP package at any time. Instead, you can start ntpd with its -g option, which enables it to perform a one-time clock setting to a value that's wildly divergent from the current time. (Ordinarily, ntpd exits if the time server's time differs from the local time by more than a few minutes.)

 Real World Scenario

Serving Time to Windows Systems

If your network hosts both Linux and Windows computers, you may want to use a Linux system as a time source for Windows clients or conceivably even use a Windows server as a time source for Linux clients. One way to do this is to run NTP on Windows. Consult http://www.meinberg.de/english/sw/ntp.htm or perform a Web search to locate NTP software for Windows systems. For Windows NT/200x/XP/Vista, you can type **NET TIME /SETSNTP:time.server**, where *time.server* is the name of your local NTP time server. This command performs a one-time setting of the clock but doesn't run in the background like the full NTP package does on Linux. Running this command in a Windows login script may be adequate for your purposes. Windows 7 users can type **W32TM /CONFIG /MANUALPEERLIST:time.server** instead of the NET TIME command.

For older Windows 9x/Me systems, you can type **NET TIME \\SERVER /SET /YES** to have the system set the time to the time maintained by *SERVER*, which must be a Windows or Samba file or print server. This command doesn't use NTP, but if you have a Linux system that runs both NTP and Samba, it can be a good way to get the job done.

Running Jobs in the Future

Some system maintenance tasks should be performed at regular intervals and are highly automated. For instance, the /tmp directory (which holds temporary files created by many users) tends to collect useless data files, which you might want to delete. Linux provides a means of scheduling tasks to run at specified times to handle such issues. This tool is the cron program, which runs what are known as *cron jobs*. A related tool is at, which enables you to run a command on a one-time basis at a specified point in the future as opposed to doing so on a regular basis, as cron does.

Understanding the Role of *cron*

The cron program is a daemon, so it runs continuously, looking for events that cause it to spring into action. Unlike most daemons, which are network servers, cron responds to temporal events. Specifically, it "wakes up" once a minute, examines configuration files in the /var/spool/cron and /etc/cron.d directories and the /etc/crontab file, and executes commands specified by these configuration files if the time matches the time listed in the files.

There are two types of cron jobs: *system cron jobs* and *user cron jobs*. System cron jobs are run as root and perform system-wide maintenance tasks. By default, most Linux distributions include system cron jobs that clean out old files from /tmp, perform log rotation (as described earlier, in "Rotating Log Files"), and so on. You can add to this repertoire, as described shortly. Ordinary users can create user cron jobs, which might run some user program on a regular basis. You can also create a user cron job as root, which might be handy if you need to perform some task at a time not supported by the system cron jobs, which are scheduled rather rigidly.

One of the critical points to remember about cron jobs is that they run unsupervised. Therefore, you shouldn't call any program in a cron job if that program requires user input. For instance, you wouldn't run a text editor in a cron job, but you might run a script that automatically manipulates text files, such as log files.

Creating System *cron* Jobs

The /etc/crontab file controls system cron jobs. This file normally begins with several lines that set environment variables, such as $PATH and $MAILTO (the former sets the path, and the latter is the address to which programs' output is mailed). The file then contains several lines that resemble the following:

```
02 4 * * * root run-parts /etc/cron.daily
```

This line begins with five fields that specify the time. The fields are, in order, the minute (0–59), the hour (0–23), the day of the month (1–31), the month (1–12), and the day of the week (0–7; both 0 and 7 correspond to Sunday). For the month and day-of-the-week values, you can use the first three letters of the name rather than a number, if you like.

A useful mnemonic for the order of the time fields is that the first four fields are ordered in increasing unit size. The day of the week doesn't fit neatly within this pattern and so is placed outside of it—that is, in the fifth field.

In all cases, you can specify multiple values in several ways:

- An asterisk (*) matches all possible values.
- A list separated by commas (such as 0,6,12,18) matches any of the specified values.
- Two values separated by a dash (-) indicate a range, inclusive of the end points. For instance, 9-17 in the hour field specifies a time of from 9:00 a.m. to 5:00 p.m.

- A slash, when used in conjunction with some other multi-value option, specifies stepped values—a range in which some members are skipped. For instance, */10 in the minute field indicates a job that's run every 10 minutes.

After the first five fields, /etc/crontab entries continue with the account name to be used when executing the program (root in the preceding example) and the command to be run (run-parts /etc/cron.daily in this example). The default /etc/crontab entries generally use run-parts, cronloop, or a similar utility that runs any executable scripts within a directory. Thus, the preceding example runs all the scripts in /etc/cron.daily at 4:02 a.m. every day. Most distributions include monthly, daily, weekly, and hourly system cron jobs, each corresponding to scripts in a directory called /etc/cron.*interval*, where *interval* is a word associated with the run frequency. Others place these scripts in /etc/cron.d/*interval* directories.

The exact times chosen for system cron jobs to execute vary from one distribution to another. Normally, though, daily and longer-interval cron jobs run early in the morning—between midnight and 6:00 a.m. Check your /etc/crontab file to determine when your system cron jobs run.

To create a new system cron job, you may create a script to perform the task you want performed (as described in Chapter 9, "Writing Scripts, Configuring Email, and Using Databases") and copy that script to the appropriate /etc/cron.*interval* directory. When the runtime next rolls around, cron will run the script.

Before submitting a script as a cron job, test it thoroughly. This is particularly important if the cron job will run when you're not around. You don't want a bug in your cron job script to cause problems by filling the hard disk with useless files or producing thousands of email messages when you're not present to quickly correct the problem.

If you need to run a cron job at a time or interval that's not supported by the standard /etc/crontab, you can either modify that file to change or add the cron job runtime or create a user cron job, as described shortly. If you choose to modify the system cron job facility, model your changes after an existing entry, changing the times and script storage directory as required.

System cron job storage directories should be owned by root, and only root should be able to write to them. If ordinary users can write to a system cron directory, unscrupulous users can write scripts to give themselves superuser privileges and place them in the system cron directory. The next time cron runs those scripts, the users will gain full administrative access to the system.

Creating User *cron* Jobs

To create a user cron job, you use the crontab utility, not to be confused with the /etc/crontab configuration file. The syntax for crontab is as follows:

crontab [-u *user*] [-l | -e | -r] [*file*]

If given without the -u *user* parameter, crontab modifies the cron job file (or *user crontab*) associated with the current user.

 The word *crontab* has three related but distinct meanings: It can refer to the crontab program, to the /etc/crontab file, or to the file that holds user cron jobs. This multiplicity of meanings can obviously be confusing. In this book, I refer to the program by using a monospaced code font, I always include the complete path to /etc/crontab, and I do *not* use a monospaced font when referring to user crontabs. A user's crontab file can define multiple cron jobs.

The crontab utility can become confused by the use of su to change the current user identity, so if you use this command, it's safest to also use -u *user*, even when you're modifying your own crontab.

If you want to work directly on a crontab, use the -l, -r, or -e option. The -l option causes crontab to display the current crontab; -r removes the current crontab; and -e opens an editor so that you can edit the current crontab. (Vi is the default editor, but you can change this by setting the VISUAL or EDITOR environment variable.)

Alternatively, you can create a cron job configuration file and pass the filename to crontab using the *file* parameter. For instance, **crontab -u tbaker my-cron** causes the crontab program to use my-cron for tbaker's cron jobs—that is, it copies tbaker's my-cron file into the directory in which it stores user crontabs, making a few minor changes along the way.

Whether you create a crontab file and submit it via the *file* parameter or edit it via -e, the format of the user crontab file is similar to that described earlier. You can set environment variables by using the form *VARIABLE=value*, or you can specify a command preceded by five numbers or wildcards to indicate when the job is to run. In a user crontab, you do *not* specify the username used to execute the job, as you do with system cron jobs. That information is derived from the owner of the crontab. Listing 7.2 shows a sample user crontab file. This file runs two programs at different intervals: The fetchmail program runs every 30 minutes (on the hour and half hour), and clean-adouble runs on Mondays at 2:00 a.m. Both programs are specified via complete paths, but you can include a PATH environment variable and omit the complete path specifications.

Listing 7.2: A Sample User crontab File

```
SHELL=/bin/bash
MAILTO=tbaker
HOME=/home/tbaker
0,30 * * * * /usr/bin/fetchmail -s
0 2 * * mon /usr/local/bin/clean-adouble $HOME
```

Ultimately, user crontab files are stored in the /var/spool/cron, /var/spool/cron/tabs, or /var/spool/cron/crontabs directory. Each file in this directory is named after the user under whose name it runs; for example, tbaker's file might be called /var/spool/cron/tabs/tbaker. You shouldn't directly edit the files in this directory; instead, use crontab to make changes.

Access to the cron facility may be restricted in several ways:

Executable Permissions The permissions on the cron and crontab programs may be restricted using standard Linux permissions mechanisms, as described in Chapter 4. Not all distributions configure themselves in this way, but for those that do, users who should be able to schedule jobs using cron should be added to the appropriate group. This group is often called cron, but you should check the group owner and permissions on the /usr/sbin/cron and /usr/bin/crontab program files to be sure.

Allowed Users List The /etc/cron.allow file contains a list of users who should be permitted access to cron. If this file is present, only users whose names appear in the file may use cron; all others are denied access. If this file isn't present, anybody may use cron, assuming access isn't restricted by executable permissions or a disallowed-users list.

Disallowed-Users List The /etc/cron.deny file contains a list of users who should be denied access to cron. If this file is present, any user whose name appears in the file is denied access to cron, but all others may use it, assuming executable permissions and the allowed-users list don't restrict access.

Exercise 7.2 guides you through the process of creating user cron jobs.

EXERCISE 7.2

Creating User cron Jobs

cron jobs can be a useful way to run programs at regular times. In this exercise, you'll create a simple user cron job that will mail you the output of an ifconfig command on a daily basis. This exercise assumes that you're authorized to use cron as an ordinary user. To configure your cron job, follow these steps:

1. Log into the Linux system as a normal user.

2. Launch an xterm from the desktop environment's menu system, if you used a GUI login method.

3. Create and edit a file called cronjob in your home directory. Use your favorite text editor for this purpose. The file should contain the following lines:

```
SHELL=/bin/bash
MAILTO=yourusername
00 12 * * * /sbin/ifconfig
```

> Be sure to type these lines exactly; a typo will cause problems. One exception: Substitute your email address on the Linux system or elsewhere for *yourusername*; cron uses the MAILTO environment variable to determine to whom to email the output of cron jobs.

4. Type **crontab cronjob** to install the cronjob file as a cron job. Note that this command replaces any existing user crontabs that may exist. If you've already defined user crontabs for your account, you should edit your existing cronjob file to add the line calling ifconfig rather than create a new file, or type **crontab -e** to edit its copy from the crontab storage directory.

5. Wait for noon (00 12 in the cron time format). When this time rolls around, you should have a new email waiting for you with the contents of the ifconfig output.

Instead of waiting for noon, you can substitute a time that's a couple of minutes in the future. Remember that cron specifies minutes first, followed by the hour in a 24-hour format. For instance, if you create the file at 3:52 p.m., you might enter 54 15 as the first two numbers on the final line of the file; this will cause the cron job to execute at 15:54 on a 24-hour clock, or 3:54 p.m.

Using *anacron*

Although cron is a great tool for performing certain tasks, such as rotating log files, on systems that are up most or all of the time, it's a much less useful tool on systems that are frequently shut down, such as notebook computers or even many desktop systems. Frequently, late-night cron jobs are never executed on such systems, which can lead to bloated log files, cluttered /tmp directories, and other problems.

One solution to such problems is anacron (http://anacron.sourceforge.net). This program is designed as a supplement to cron to ensure that regular maintenance jobs are executed at reasonable intervals. It works by keeping a record of programs it should execute and how frequently it should do so, in days. Whenever anacron is run, it checks to see when it last executed each of the programs it's configured to manage. If a period greater than the program's execution interval has passed, anacron runs the program. Typically, anacron itself is run from a system startup script, and perhaps from a cron job. You can then reconfigure your regular system cron jobs as anacron jobs and be sure they'll execute even on systems that are regularly shut down for long stretches of time.

Like cron, anacron is controlled through a configuration file named after itself: /etc/anacrontab. This file consists of three main types of lines: comment lines (denoted by a leading hash mark, #), environment variable assignments (as in SHELL=/bin/bash), and job definition lines. This last type of line contains four fields:

period delay identifier command

The *period* is how frequently, in days, the command should be run. The *delay* is a delay period, in minutes, between the time anacron starts and the time the command is run, if it should be run. This feature is intended to help keep the system from being overloaded if anacron determines it needs to run many commands when it starts up; you can specify different *delay* times to stagger the running of the jobs. The *identifier* is a string that identifies the command. You can pass it to anacron on the command line to have anacron check and, if necessary, run only that one command. Finally, *command* is the command to be run. This is a single command or script name, optionally followed by any parameters it may take.

Listing 7.3 shows a sample /etc/anacrontab file. This file sets a couple of environment variables; PATH is particularly important if any scripts call programs without specifying their complete paths. The three job definition lines tell anacron to run the run-parts command, passing it the name of a different directory for each line. This command is used on some distributions to run cron jobs, so the effect of calling it from anacron is to take over cron's duties. The first line, run once a day, causes anacron to run (via run-parts) the scripts in /etc/cron.daily; the second line causes the scripts in /etc/cron.weekly to be run once a week; and the third, run once every 30 days, runs the scripts in /etc/cron .monthly.

Listing 7.3: Sample /etc/anacrontab File

```
SHELL=/bin/bash
PATH=/usr/local/sbin:/usr/local/bin:/sbin:/bin:/usr/sbin:/usr/bin
# format: period delay job-identifier command
1       5       cron.daily      run-parts /etc/cron.daily
7       10      cron.weekly     run-parts /etc/cron.weekly
30      15      cron.monthly    run-parts /etc/cron.monthly
```

Of course, to do any good, anacron must be called itself. This is typically done in one of two ways:

Via a Startup Script   You can create a startup script to run anacron. A simple SysV startup script that takes no options but that runs anacron should do the job if configured to run from your regular runlevel. Alternatively, you can place a call to anacron in a local startup script, such as Fedora and Red Hat's /etc/rc.d/rc.local or SUSE's /etc/boot.d/boot .local.

Via a cron Job   You can create a cron job to run anacron. Typically, this call will replace your regular system cron job entries (in /etc/crontab), and you'll probably want to call anacron on a daily basis or more frequently.

The startup script approach is best employed on systems that are shut down and started up frequently, such as laptops or desktop systems that are regularly shut down at the end of the day. One drawback to this approach is that it can cause sluggish performance when the system is booted if anacron needs to run a time-consuming task. Calling anacron via a cron job can shift the burden to off-hours, but if cron can reliably run anacron, cron can as easily and reliably run the jobs that anacron runs. Typically, you use a cron job if the system is sometimes, but not always, left running overnight. This ensures that anacron and the jobs it handles are run fairly frequently, if not on a completely regular basis. Alternatively, you can call anacron more frequently than once a day. For instance, if it's called once every six hours, it will almost certainly be called during a typical eight-hour workday.

 For a desktop system, you might try calling anacron via a cron job at the user's typical lunch break. This will help minimize the disruption caused by any resource-intensive programs that anacron must run.

No matter how you run anacron, you should be sure to disable any cron jobs that anacron now handles. If you don't do so, those tasks will be performed twice, which may needlessly burden your system. Because anacron measures its run intervals in days, it's not a useful utility for running hourly cron jobs. Thus, you shouldn't eliminate any hourly system cron jobs when you edit your cron configuration for anacron.

Using *at*

Sometimes cron and anacron are overkill. You may simply want to run a single command at a specific point in the future on a one-time basis rather than on an ongoing basis. For this task, Linux provides another command: at. In ordinary use, this command takes a single option (although options to fine-tune its behavior are also available): a time. This time can take any of several forms:

Time of Day   You can specify the time of day as *HH:MM*, optionally followed by AM or PM if you use a 12-hour format. If the specified time has already passed, the operation is scheduled for the next occurrence of that time—that is, for the next day.

noon, midnight, or teatime   These three keywords stand for what you'd expect (teatime is 4:00 p.m.).

Day Specification   To schedule an at job more than 24 hours in advance, you must add a date specification after the time-of-day specification. This can be done in numeric form, using the format *MMDDYY, MM/DD/YY* or *DD.MM.YY*. Alternatively, you can specify the date as *month-name day* or *month-name day year*.

A Specified Period in the Future   You can specify a time using the keyword now, a plus sign (+), and a time period, as in now + 2 hours to run a job in two hours.

 The at command relies on a daemon, atd, to be running. If your system doesn't start atd automatically, you may need to configure a startup script to do so.

When you run at and give it a time specification, the program responds with its own prompt, at>, which you can treat much like your normal bash or other command shell prompt. When you're done typing commands, press Ctrl+D to terminate input. Alternatively, you can pass a file with commands by using the -f parameter to at, as in **at -f commands .sh noon** to use the contents of commands.sh as the commands you want to run at noon.

The at command has several support tools. The most important of these is atd, the at daemon. This program must be running for at to do its work. If it's not, check for its presence using ps. If it's not running, look for a startup script and ensure that it's enabled, as described in Chapter 5.

Other at support programs include atq, which lists pending at jobs; atrm, which removes an at job from the queue; and batch, which works much like at but executes jobs when the system load level drops below 0.8. These utilities are all fairly simple. To use atq, simply type its name. (The program does support a couple of options, but chances are you won't need them; consult atq's man page for details.) To use atrm, type the program name and the number of the at job, as returned by atq. For instance, you might type **atrm 12** to remove at job number 12.

The at facility supports access restrictions similar to those of cron. Specifically, the /etc/at.allow and /etc/at.deny files work analogously to the /etc/cron.allow and /etc/cron.deny files. There are a few wrinkles with at, though. Specifically, if neither at.allow nor at.deny exists, only root may use at. If at.allow exists, the users it lists are granted access to at; if at.deny exists, everybody *except* those mentioned in this file is granted access to at. This differs from cron, in which everybody is granted access if neither access-control file is present. This tighter default security on at means that the program is seldom installed with restrictive execute permissions, but of course you can use program file permissions to deny ordinary users the ability to run at if you want an extra layer of security.

Summary

Routine system administration involves a variety of tasks, many of which center around user management. Adding, deleting, and modifying user accounts and groups are critical tasks that all system administrators must master. Also related to users, you should know where to go to modify the default user environment.

System log files are critical troubleshooting tools that are maintained by the system. You should be able to configure what data is logged to what files and know how to use these log files.

Time management is important in Linux. Setting the Linux clocks (both hardware and software) and configuring NTP to keep the software clock accurate are important tasks. Tools that rely on the time include cron, anacron, and at, which enable the system to run programs in the future. These tools are used for many common system tasks, including rotating log files.

Exam Essentials

Summarize methods of creating and modifying user accounts.   Accounts can be created or modified with the help of tools designed for the purpose, such as useradd and usermod. Alternatively, you can directly edit the /etc/passwd and /etc/shadow files, which hold the account information.

Describe the function of groups in Linux.   Linux groups enable security features to be applied to arbitrary groups of users. Each group holds an arbitrary collection of users, and group permissions can be set on files, giving all group members the same access rights to the files.

Explain the purpose of the skeleton files.   Skeleton files provide a core set of configuration files that should be present in users' home directories when those directories are created. They provide a starting point for users to modify their important shell and other configuration files.

Summarize how to configure system logging.   System logging is controlled via the /etc/syslog.conf file. Lines in this file describe what types of log data, generated by programs, are sent to log files and to which log files the log messages should go.

Describe how log rotation is managed.   Log rotation is controlled via the /etc/logrotate.conf file (which typically refers to files in /etc/logrotate.d). Entries in these files tell the system whether to rotate logs at fixed intervals or when they reach particular sizes. When a log rotates, it's renamed (and possibly compressed), a new log file is created, and the oldest archived log file may be deleted.

Explain the two types of clocks in *x*86 and *x*86-64 hardware.   The hardware clock keeps time when the computer is powered down, but it isn't used by most programs while the computer is running. Such programs refer to the software clock, which is set from the hardware clock when the computer boots.

Summarize the function of NTP.   The Network Time Protocol (NTP) enables a computer to set its clock based on the time maintained by an NTP server system. NTP can function as a tiered protocol, enabling one system to function as a client to an NTP server and as a server to additional NTP clients. This structure enables a single highly accurate time source to be used by anywhere from a few to (theoretically) billions of computers via a tiered system of links.

Explain the difference between system and user cron jobs.   System cron jobs are controlled from /etc/crontab, are created by root, and may be run as any user (but most commonly as root). System cron jobs are typically run at certain fixed times on an hourly, daily, weekly, or monthly basis. User cron jobs may be created by any user (various security measures permitting), are run under the authority of the account with which they're associated, and may be run at just about any repeating interval desired.

Review Questions

1. Which of the following is a legal Linux username that will be accepted by `useradd`?

   A. `larrythemoose`

   B. `4sale`

   C. `PamJones`

   D. `Samuel_Bernard_Delaney_the_Fourth`

   E. `ted cho`

2. Why are groups important to the Linux user administration and security models?

   A. They can be used to provide a set of users with access to files without giving *all* users access to the files.

   B. They enable you to set a single login password for all users within a defined group.

   C. Users may assign file ownership to a group, thereby hiding their own creation of the file.

   D. By deleting a group, you can quickly remove the accounts for all users in the group.

   E. They enable you to link together the account databases in a group of two or more computers, simplifying administration.

3. An administrator types **chage -M 7 time**. What is the effect of this command?

   A. The `time` account's password must be changed at least once every seven days.

   B. All users must change their passwords at least once every seven days.

   C. All users are permitted to change their passwords at most seven times.

   D. The `time` account's age is set to seven months.

   E. The account database's time stamp is set to seven months ago.

4. What is wrong with the following /etc/passwd file entry? (Select two.)

   `4sally:x:1029:Sally Jones:/home/myhome:/bin/passwd`

   A. The default shell is set to `/bin/passwd`, which is an invalid shell.

   B. The username is invalid; Linux usernames can't begin with a number.

   C. The home directory doesn't match the username.

   D. Either the UID or the GID field is missing.

   E. The encrypted password is missing.

5. You want `sally`, `tom`, and `dale` to be members of the group `managers` (GID 501). How would you edit the `managers` entry in /etc/group to accomplish this goal?

   A. `managers:501:sally tom dale`

   B. `managers:501:sally:tom:dale`

   C. `managers:x:501:sally:tom:dale`

    D. `managers:x:501:dale,sally,tom`

    E. `managers:501:x:dale\sally\tom`

6. What types of files might you expect to find in `/etc/skel`? (Select three.)

    A. A copy of the `/etc/shadow` file

    B. An empty set of directories to encourage good file management practices

    C. A README or similar welcome file for new users

    D. A starting `.bashrc` file

    E. The RPM or Debian package management database

7. What would a Linux system administrator type to remove the `nemo` account and its home directory?

    A. `userdel nemo`

    B. `userdel -f nemo`

    C. `userdel -r nemo`

    D. `rm -r /home/nemo`

    E. `usermod -D nemo`

8. Which of the following system logging codes represents the *highest* priority?

    A. `info`

    B. `warning`

    C. `crit`

    D. `debug`

    E. `emerg`

9. Which of the following configuration files does the `logrotate` program consult for its settings?

    A. `/etc/logrotate.conf`

    B. `/usr/sbin/logrotate/logrotate.conf`

    C. `/usr/src/logrotate/logrotate.conf`

    D. `/etc/logrotate/.conf`

    E. `~/.logrotate`

10. You want to create a log file entry noting that you're manually shutting down the system to add a new network card. How might you create this log entry, just prior to using `shutdown`?

    A. `dmesg -l "shutting down to add network card"`

    B. `syslog shutting down to add network card`

    C. `rsyslogd "shutting down to add network card"`

    D. `logger shutting down to add network card`

    E. `wall "shutting down to add network card"`

11. Your manager has asked that you configure `logrotate` to run on a regular, unattended basis. What utility/feature should you configure to make this possible?

    A. at

    B. logrotate.d

    C. cron

    D. inittab

    E. ntpd

12. You've set your system (software) clock on a Linux-only computer to the correct time, and now you want to set the hardware clock to match. What command might you type to accomplish this goal?

    A. date --sethwclock

    B. ntpdate

    C. sysclock --tohc

    D. time --set –hw

    E. hwclock --utc --systohc

13. As root, you type **date 12110710**. What will be the effect?

    A. The software clock will be set to 7:10 a.m. on December 11 of the current year.

    B. The software clock will be set to 12:11 p.m. on October 7 of the current year.

    C. The software clock will be set to 7:10 a.m. on November 12 of the current year.

    D. The software clock will be set to 12:11 p.m. on July 10 of the current year.

    E. The software clock will be set to July 10 in the year 1211.

14. What will be the effect of a computer having the following two lines in /etc/ntp.conf?

    ```
    server pool.ntp.org
    server tardis.example.org
    ```

    A. The local computer's NTP server will poll a server in the public NTP server pool; the first `server` option overrides subsequent `server` options.

    B. The local computer's NTP server will poll the `tardis.example.org` time server; the last `server` option overrides earlier server options.

    C. The local computer's NTP server will poll both a server in the public NTP server pool and `tardis.example.org` and use whichever site provides the cleanest time data.

    D. The local computer's NTP server will refuse to run because of a malformed `server` specification in /etc/ntp.conf.

    E. The local computer's NTP server will poll a computer in the public NTP server pool but will fall back on `tardis.example.org` if and only if the public pool server is down.

15. You've configured one computer (gateway.pangaea.edu) on your five-computer network as an NTP server that obtains its time signal from ntp.example.com. What computer(s) should your network's other computers use as their time source(s)?

   A. You should consult a public NTP server list to locate the best server for you.

   B. Both gateway.pangaea.edu and ntp.example.com.

   C. Only ntp.example.com.

   D. Only gateway.pangaea.edu.

   E. None; NTP should be used on the Internet, not on small local networks.

16. Which of the following tasks are most likely to be handled by a cron job? (Select two.)

   A. Starting an important server when the computer boots

   B. Finding and deleting old temporary files

   C. Scripting supervised account creation

   D. Monitoring the status of servers and emailing a report to the superuser

   E. Sending files to a printer in an orderly manner

17. Which of the following lines, if used in a user cron job, will run /usr/local/bin/cleanup twice a day?

   A. 15 7,19 * * * tbaker /usr/local/bin/cleanup

   B. 15 7,19 * * * /usr/local/bin/cleanup

   C. 15 */2 * * * tbaker /usr/local/bin/cleanup

   D. 15 */2 * * * /usr/local/bin/cleanup

   E. 2 * * * * /usr/local/bin/cleanup

18. You're installing Linux on a laptop computer. Which of the following programs might you want to add to ensure that log rotation is handled correctly?

   A. tempus

   B. anacron

   C. crontab

   D. ntpd

   E. syslog-ng

19. What do the following commands accomplish? (The administrator presses Ctrl+D after typing the second command.)

   ```
   # at teatime
   at> /usr/local/bin/system-maintenance
   ```

   A. Nothing; these commands aren't valid.

   B. Nothing; teatime isn't a valid option to at.

   C. Nothing; you may only type valid bash built-in commands at the at> prompt.

    D. Nothing; at requires you to pass it the name of a script, which `teatime` is not.

    E. The `/usr/local/bin/system-maintenance` program or script is run at 4:00 p.m.

20. How might you schedule a script to run once a day on a Linux computer? (Select two.)

    A. Place the script, or a link to it, in `/etc/cron.daily`.

    B. Use the at command to schedule the specified script to run on a daily basis at a time of your choosing.

    C. Create a user `cron` job that calls the specified script once a day at a time of your choosing, and install that `cron` job using `crontab`.

    D. Use `run-parts` to schedule the specified script to run on a daily basis.

    E. Type **crontab -d *scriptname***, where *scriptname* is the name of your script

Chapter
8

Configuring Basic Networking

THE FOLLOWING EXAM OBJECTIVES ARE COVERED IN THIS CHAPTER:

- ✓ 1.109.1 Fundamentals of internet protocols
- ✓ 1.109.2 Basic network configuration
- ✓ 1.109.3 Basic network troubleshooting
- ✓ 1.109.4 Configure client-side DNS

Most Linux systems are connected to a network, either as clients or as servers (and often as both). Even home computers and dedicated appliances such as smart phones usually connect to the Internet. For this reason, setting up Linux's basic networking tools is necessary for fully configuring Linux. To begin this task, you must first understand the basics of modern networking, such as the nature of network addresses and the types of tools that are commonly used on networks. From there, you can move on to Linux network configuration, including tasks such as setting a computer's address, routing, and name resolution. Unfortunately, network configuration sometimes goes wrong; understanding the tools and techniques used to diagnose and fix network problems is a necessary part of network configuration, so this chapter covers the basics of network troubleshooting.

Understanding TCP/IP Networking

Networking involves quite a few components that are built atop one another. These include network hardware, data packets, and protocols for data exchange. Together, these components make up a *network stack*. The most common network stack today is the *Transmission Control Protocol/Internet Protocol* (TCP/IP) stack, but this isn't the only stack available. Nonetheless, understanding the basics of TCP/IP theory will help you to configure and manage networks.

Knowing the Basic Functions of Network Hardware

Network hardware is designed to enable two or more computers to communicate with one another. Modern computers have network interfaces built into their motherboards, but internal (PCI, PCIe, or similar) network cards and external (USB, PC Card, and similar) network interfaces are also available. Many networks rely on wires or cables to transmit data between machines as electrical impulses, but network protocols that use radio waves or even light to do the job are growing rapidly in popularity.

Sometimes the line between network hardware and peripheral interface ports can be blurry. For instance, a parallel port normally isn't considered a network port; but when it's used with the Parallel Line Interface Protocol (PLIP; http://tldp.org/HOWTO/PLIP .html), the parallel port becomes a network device. In the past, a USB or RS-232 serial port frequently became a network interface when used with the *Point-to-Point Protocol* (PPP), typically in conjunction with a telephone modem. Such connections are rare today, but they're still possible. If you need to know how to configure a PPP connection, consult your distribution's documentation or the PPP HOWTO (`http://tldp.org/HOWTO/PPP-HOWTO/`).

At its core, network hardware is hardware that facilitates the transfer of data between computers. Hardware that's most often used for networking includes features that help this transfer in various ways. For instance, such hardware may include ways to address data intended for specific remote computers, as described later in the section "Addressing Hardware." When basically non-network hardware is pressed into service as a network medium, the lack of such features may limit the utility of the hardware or require extra software to make up for the lack. If extra software is required, you're unlikely to notice the deficiencies as a user or system administrator because the protocol drivers handle the work, but this makes the hardware more difficult to configure and more prone to sluggishness or other problems than dedicated network hardware.

Investigating Types of Network Hardware

Linux supports several types of common network hardware. The most common of these is Ethernet, which comes in several varieties. Most modern Ethernet hardware uses *twisted-pair* cabling, which consists of pairs of wires twisted around each other to minimize interference. Such varieties of Ethernet are identified by a *-T* suffix to the Ethernet variety name, as in 10Base-T or 100Base-T. The numbers denote the speed of the protocol in megabits per second (Mbps). In the late 1990s, 100Base-T took over from 10Base-T as the standard in office and even home networks. More recently, 1000Base-T and Ethernet variants that use optical cabling and that are capable of 1000Mbps speeds (that is, *gigabit Ethernet*) have become the standard, with 10-gigabit Ethernet the new emerging standard.

Other types of network hardware exist, but most are less common than Ethernet. These include Token Ring, LocalTalk, Fiber Distributed Data Interface (FDDI), High-Performance Parallel Interface (HIPPI), and Fibre Channel. Token Ring was common on some IBM-dominated networks in the 1990s but has been steadily losing ground to Ethernet for years. Likewise, LocalTalk was the favored medium for early Macintoshes, but modern Macs ship with Ethernet instead of LocalTalk. FDDI, HIPPI, and Fibre Channel are all high-speed interfaces that are used in high-performance applications. Some of these protocols support significantly greater maximum cable lengths than does Ethernet, which makes them suitable for linking buildings that are many yards, or even miles, apart.

Wireless networking (aka Wi-Fi) is an exception to Ethernet's dominance. Common wireless protocols include 802.11a, 802.11b, 802.11g, and 802.11n. These protocols support maximum speeds of 11Mbps (for 802.11b), 54Mbps (for 802.11a and 802.11g), or 300 Mbps (for 802.11n). With the exception of the rarely used 802.11a, Wi-Fi protocols are compatible with one another, albeit at the speed of the slowest protocol in use. Wireless networking is particularly useful for laptop computers, but it's even handy for desktop computers in homes and small offices that don't have adequate wired network infrastructures in place.

WARNING   If you use a wireless protocol, your data are transmitted via radio waves, which are easily intercepted. Wireless protocols include optional encryption, but this feature is sometimes disabled by default, and some varieties of wireless encryption are notoriously poor. If you use wireless network products, be sure to enable Wi-Fi Protected Access (WPA) or, better, WPA2 encryption. The weaker Wired Equivalent Privacy (WEP) encryption is easily broken. For added protection, use a strong encryption protocol, such as the Secure Shell (SSH) login tool or Secure Sockets Layer (SSL) encryption, when transferring any data that's even remotely sensitive; and be extra cautious about security on networks that support wireless access. In a typical configuration, an intruder who can break into your wireless access point looks to the rest of your network like any other local user, so protecting that access point is extremely important.

In addition to the network hardware in your computers, you need network hardware outside the computers. With the exception of wireless networks, you need some form of network cabling that's unique to your hardware type. (For 100Base-T Ethernet, get cabling that meets at least Category 5, or Cat-5, specifications. Gigabit Ethernet works best with Cat-5e or optical cables.) Many network types, including twisted-pair Ethernet, require the use of a central device known as a *hub* or *switch*. You plug every computer on a local network into this central device, as shown in Figure 8.1. The hub or switch then passes data between the computers.

FIGURE 8.1   Many networks link computers together via a central device known as a hub or switch.

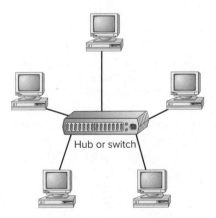

As a general rule, switches are superior to hubs. Hubs mirror all traffic to all computers, whereas switches are smart enough to send packets only to the intended destination. Switches also allow *full-duplex* transmission, in which both parties can send data at the same time (like two people talking on a telephone). Hubs permit only *half-duplex* transmission, in which the two computers must take turns (like two people using walkie-talkies). The result is that switches let two pairs of computers engage in full-speed data transfers with each other; with a hub, these two transfers would interfere with each other.

Computers with Wi-Fi adapters can be configured to communicate directly with one another, but it's more common to employ a wireless router, which links together both wireless and Ethernet devices. Such routers also provide connections to an outside network—typically the Internet, sometimes via a broadband connection.

Understanding Network Packets

Modern networks operate on discrete chunks of data known as *packets*. Suppose you want to send a 100KiB file from one computer to another. Rather than send the file in one burst of data, your computer breaks it down into smaller chunks. The system might send 100 packets of 1KiB each, for instance. This way, if there's an error sending one packet, the computer can resend just that one packet rather than the entire file. (Many network protocols include error-detection procedures.)

When the recipient system receives packets, it must hold on to them and reassemble them in the correct order to re-create the complete data stream. It's not uncommon for packets to be delayed or even lost in transmission, so error-recovery procedures are critical for protocols that handle large transfers. Some types of error recovery are handled transparently by the networking hardware.

There are several types of packets, and they can be stored within each other. For instance, Ethernet includes its own packet type (known as a *frame*), and the packets generated by networking protocols that run atop Ethernet, such as those described in the next section, are stored within Ethernet frames. All told, a data transfer can involve several layers of wrapping and unwrapping data. With each layer, packets from the adjacent layer may be merged or split up.

Understanding Network Protocol Stacks

It's possible to think of network data at various levels of abstractness. For instance, at one level, a network carries data packets for a specific network type (such as Ethernet); the data packets are addressed to specific computers on a local network. Such a description, while useful for understanding a local network, isn't very useful for understanding higher-level network protocols, such as those that handle email transfers. These high-level protocols are typically described in terms of commands sent back and forth between computers, frequently without reference to packets. The addresses used at different levels also vary, as explained in the upcoming section "Using Network Addresses."

A *protocol stack* is a set of software that converts and encapsulates data between layers of abstraction. For instance, the stack can take the commands of email transfer protocols, and the email messages that are transferred, and package them into packets. Another layer of the stack can take these packets and repackage them into Ethernet frames. There are several layers to any protocol stack, and they interact in highly specified ways. It's often possible to swap out one component for another at any given layer. For instance, at the top of each stack is a program that uses the stack, such as an email client. You can switch from one email client to another without too much difficulty; both rest atop the same stack. Likewise, if you change a network card, you have to change the driver for that card, which constitutes a layer very low in the stack. Applications above that driver can remain the same.

Each computer in a transaction requires a compatible protocol stack. When they communicate, the computers pass data down their respective stacks and then send data to the partner system, which passes the data up its stack. Each layer on the receiving system sees the data as packaged by its counterpart on the sending computer.

Protocol stacks are frequently represented graphically in diagrams like Figure 8.2, which shows the configuration of the TCP/IP protocol stack that dominates the Internet today. As shown in Figure 8.2, client programs at the application layer initiate data transfers. These requests pass through the transport, internet, and link layers on the client computer, whereupon they leave the client system and pass to the server system. (This transfer can involve a lot of complexity not depicted in Figure 8.2.) On the server, the process reverses itself, with the server program running at the application layer replying to the client program. This reply reverses the journey, traveling down the server computer's stack, across the network, and up the stack on the client. A full-fledged network connection can involve many back-and-forth data transfers.

FIGURE 8.2 Information travels "down" and "up" protocol stacks, being checked and re-packed at each step of the way.

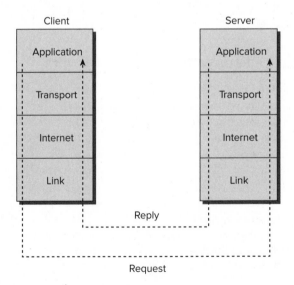

When spelled with an uppercase *I*, the word *Internet* refers to the globe-spanning network of networks with which you're no doubt familiar. When spelled with a lowercase *i*, however, the word *internet* refers to any collection of networks. An internet in this sense could be a couple of small networks in somebody's basement with no outside connections. Internet networking protocols such as TCP/IP can work on any internet, up to and including *the* Internet.

Each component layer of the sending system is equivalent to a layer on the receiving system, but these layers need not be absolutely identical. For instance, you can have different models of network card at the link layer, or you can even use entirely different network hardware types, such as Ethernet and Token Ring, if some intervening system translates between them. The computers may run different OSs and hence use different—but logically equivalent—protocol stacks. What's important is that the stacks operate in compatible ways.

Linux was designed with TCP/IP in mind, and the Internet is built atop TCP/IP. Other protocol stacks are available, though, and you may occasionally run into them. In particular, NetBEUI was the original Microsoft and IBM protocol stack for Windows, AppleTalk was Apple's initial protocol stack, and the Internet Packet Exchange/Sequenced Packet Exchange (IPX/SPX) was Novell's favored protocol stack. All three are now fading in importance, but you may still need to use them in some environments. Linux supports AppleTalk and IPX/SPX but not NetBEUI.

Knowing TCP/IP Protocol Types

Within TCP/IP, several different protocols exist. Each of these protocols can be classified as falling on one of the four layers of the TCP/IP stack, as shown in Figure 8.2. The most important of the internet- and transport-layer protocols are the building blocks for the application-layer protocols with which you interact more directly. These important internet- and transport-layer protocols include the following:

IP   The *Internet Protocol* (IP) is the core protocol in TCP/IP networking. Referring to Figure 8.2, IP is an internet-layer (aka a network-layer or layer 2) protocol. IP provides a "best effort" method for transferring packets between computers—that is, the packets aren't guaranteed to reach their destination. Packets may also arrive out of order or corrupted. Other components of the TCP/IP stack must deal with these issues and have their own ways of doing so. IP is also the portion of TCP/IP with which IP addresses are associated. (The Real World Scenario sidebar "The Coming of IPv6" describes a change in the IP portion of TCP/IP that's underway.)

ICMP   The *Internet Control Message Protocol* (ICMP) is a simple protocol for communicating data. ICMP is most often used to send error messages between computers—for instance, to signal that a requested service isn't available. This is often done by modifying an IP packet and returning it to its sender, which means that ICMP is technically an internet-layer protocol, although it relies upon IP. In most cases, you won't use programs that generate ICMP packets on demand; they're created behind the scenes as you use other protocols. One exception is the ping program, which is described in more detail in "Testing Basic Connectivity."

UDP The *User Datagram Protocol* (UDP) is the simplest of the common transport-layer (aka layer 3) TCP/IP protocols. It doesn't provide sophisticated procedures to correct for out-of-order packets, guarantee delivery, or otherwise improve the limitations of IP. This fact can be a problem, but it also means that UDP can be faster than more-sophisticated tools that provide such improvements to IP. Common application-layer protocols that are built atop UDP include the Domain Name System (DNS), the Network File System (NFS), and many streaming-media protocols.

TCP The *Transmission Control Protocol* (TCP) may be the most widely used transport-layer protocol in the TCP/IP stack. Unlike UDP, TCP creates full connections with error checking and correction as well as other features. These features simplify the creation of network protocols that must exchange large amounts of data, but the features come at a cost: TCP imposes a small performance penalty. Most of the application-layer protocols with which you may already be familiar, including the Simple Mail Transfer Protocol (SMTP), the Hypertext Transfer Protocol (HTTP), and the File Transfer Protocol (FTP), are built atop TCP.

You may notice that the name of the TCP/IP stack is built up of two of the stack's protocol names: TCP and IP. This is because these two protocols are so important for TCP/IP networking generally. TCP/IP, though, is much more than just these two protocols; it includes additional protocols, most of which (below the application layer) are rather obscure. On the other hand, a TCP/IP exchange need not use both TCP and IP—it could be a UDP or ICMP exchange, for instance.

The Coming of IPv6

The IP portion of TCP/IP has been at version 4 for many years. A major upgrade to this is underway, however, and it goes by the name *IPv6*, for IP version 6. Its most important improvements over IPv4 include the following:

- IPv4 supports a theoretical maximum of about 4 billion addresses. Although this may sound like plenty, those addresses have not been allocated as efficiently as possible. Therefore, as the Internet has expanded, the number of truly available addresses has been shrinking at a rapid rate—in fact, the global pool is already exhausted, although IPv4 addresses remain available from local registries in many parts of the world, as of late 2012. IPv6 raises the number of addresses to 2^{128}, or 3.4×10^{38}. This is enough to give every square millimeter of land surface on Earth 2.2×10^{18} addresses.

- IPv6 makes *multicasting*—the simultaneous transmission of data from one computer to multiple recipients—part of the basic IP specification, compared to an optional (albeit commonly implemented) part of IPv4.

- IPv6 includes a new feature, known as *stateless address auto-configuration (SLAAC)*, which simplifies initial network setup. This feature is similar in some ways to the Dynamic Host Configuration Protocol (DHCP) that's commonly used on IPv4. (DHCP can also be used on IPv6; which works best depends on the local network's configuration.)

- IPv6 originated the *Internet Protocol Security (IPsec)* tools, which can improve the security of Internet connections. IPsec has since been back-ported to IPv4.

- IPv6 has streamlined some data structures, enabling quicker processing by routers.

More obscure differences also exist. Check http://en.wikipedia.org/wiki/IPv6 or http://www.ipv6forum.com for detailed information about IPv6.

IPv6 is starting to emerge as a real networking force in many parts of the world. The United States, though, is lagging behind on IPv6 deployment. The Linux kernel includes IPv6 support, and most distributions now attempt to automatically configure IPv6 networking in addition to IPv4. Chances are that by the time the average office will need IPv6, it will be standard. Configuring a system for IPv6 is somewhat different from configuring it for IPv4, which is what this chapter emphasizes.

Understanding Network Addressing

In order for one computer to communicate with another over a network, the computers need to have some way to refer to each other. The basic mechanism for doing this is provided by a network address, which can take several different forms, depending on the type of network hardware, protocol stack, and so on. Large and routed networks pose additional challenges to network addressing, and TCP/IP provides answers to these challenges. Finally, to address a specific program on a remote computer, TCP/IP uses a *port number*, which identifies a specific running program, something like the way a telephone extension number identifies an individual in a large company. The following sections describe all these methods of addressing.

Using Network Addresses

Consider an Ethernet network. When an Ethernet frame leaves one computer, it's normally addressed to another Ethernet card. This addressing is done using low-level Ethernet features, independent of the protocol stack in question. Recall, however, that the Internet is composed of many different networks that use many different low-level hardware components. A user may have a dial-up telephone connection (through a serial port) but connect to one server that uses Ethernet and another that uses Token Ring. Each of these devices uses a different type of low-level network address. TCP/IP requires something more to integrate across different types of network hardware. In total, three types of addresses are important when you're trying to understand network addressing: network hardware addresses, numeric IP addresses, and text-based hostnames.

Addressing Hardware

One of the characteristics of dedicated network hardware such as Ethernet or Token Ring cards is that they have unique *hardware addresses*, also known as *Media Access Control (MAC) addresses*, programmed into them. In the case of Ethernet, these addresses are 6 bytes in length, and they're generally expressed as hexadecimal (base 16) numbers separated by colons. You can discover the hardware address for an Ethernet card by using the ifconfig command. Type **ifconfig eth*n***, where *n* is the number of the interface (0 for the first card, 1 for the second, and so on). You'll see several lines of output, including one like the following:

```
eth0      Link encap:Ethernet  HWaddr 00:A0:CC:24:BA:02
```

This line tells you that the device is an Ethernet card and that its hardware address is 00:A0:CC:24:BA:02. What use is this, though? Certain low-level network utilities and hardware use the hardware address. For instance, network switches use it to direct data packets. The switch detects that a particular address is connected to a particular wire, and so it sends data directed at that address *only* over the associated wire. The *Dynamic Host Configuration Protocol* (DHCP), which is described in the upcoming section "Configuring with DHCP," is a means of automating the configuration of specific computers. It has an option that uses the hardware address to consistently assign the same IP address to a given computer. In addition, advanced network diagnostic tools are available that let you examine packets that come from or are directed to specific hardware addresses.

For the most part, though, you don't need to be aware of a computer's hardware address. You don't enter it in most utilities or programs. It's important for what it does in general.

Linux identifies network hardware devices with type-specific codes. With most distributions, Ethernet hardware is eth*n*, where *n* is a number from 0 up. The first Ethernet device is eth0, the second is eth1, and so on. (Fedora uses a more complex Ethernet naming system, though.) Wireless devices have names of the form wlan*n*. Unlike most Linux hardware devices, network devices don't have entries in /dev; instead, low-level network utilities take the device names and work with them directly.

Managing IP Addresses

Earlier, I said that TCP/IP, at least in its IPv4 incarnation, supports about 4 billion addresses. This figure is based on the size of the *IP address* used in TCP/IP: 4 bytes (32 bits). Specifically, $2^{32} = 4,294,967,296$. For IPv6, 16-byte (128-bit) addresses are used. Not all of these addresses are usable; some are overhead associated with network definitions, and some are reserved.

The 4-byte IPv4 address and 6-byte Ethernet address are mathematically unrelated. This can be the case for IPv6, too, although the IPv6 standard allows the IPv6 address to be built, in part, from the computer's MAC address. In any event, the TCP/IP stack converts between the MAC address and the IP address using the *Address Resolution Protocol* (ARP) for IPv4 or the *Neighbor Discovery Protocol* (NDP) for IPv6. These protocols enable a computer to send a *broadcast* query—a message that goes out to all the computers on the local network. This query asks the computer with a given IP address to identify itself. When a reply comes in, it includes the hardware address, so the TCP/IP stack can direct traffic for a given IP address to the target computer's hardware address.

 The procedure for computers that aren't on the local network is more complex. For such computers, a router must be involved. Local computers send packets destined for distant addresses to routers, which send the packets on to other routers or to their destination systems.

IPv4 addresses are usually expressed as four base-10 numbers (0–255) separated by periods, as in 172.30.9.102. If your Linux system's protocol stack is already up and running, you can discover its IP address by using ifconfig, as described earlier. The output includes a line like the following, which identifies the IP address (inet addr):

```
inet addr:172.30.9.102   Bcast:172.30.255.255    Mask:255.255.0.0
```

Although it isn't obvious from the IP address alone, this address is broken into two components: a network address and a computer address. The network address identifies a block of IP addresses that are used by one physical network, and the computer address identifies one computer within that network. The reason for this breakdown is to make the job of routers easier—rather than record how to direct packets destined for each of the 4 billion IP addresses, routers can be programmed to direct traffic based on packets' network addresses, which is a much simpler job. Ordinarily, a computer can directly communicate only with computers on its local network segment; to communicate outside of this set of computers, a router must be involved.

IPv6 addresses work in a similar way, except that they're larger. Specifically, IPv6 addresses consist of eight groups of four-digit hexadecimal numbers separated by colons, as in fed1:0db8:85a3:08d3:1319:8a2e:0370:7334. If one or more groups of four digits is 0000, that group or those groups may be omitted, leaving two colons. Only one such group of zeroes can be compressed in this way, because if you removed two groups, there would be no way of telling how many sets of zeroes would have to be replaced in each group.

The *network mask* (also known as the *subnet mask* or *netmask*) is a number that identifies the portion of the IP address that's a network address and the part that's a computer address. It's helpful to think of this in binary (base 2) because the netmask uses binary 1 values to represent the network portion of an address and binary 0 values to represent the computer address. The network portion ordinarily leads the computer portion. Expressed in base 10, these addresses usually consist of 255 or 0 values, 255 being a network byte and 0 being a computer byte. If a byte is part network and part computer address, it will have some other value. Figure 8.3 illustrates this relationship, using the IP address 172.30.9.102 and the netmask 255.255.0.0.

FIGURE 8.3   TCP/IP addresses are combined with a netmask to isolate the network address.

IP Address	172.30.9.102	10101100 00011110 00001001 01100110
Netmask	255.255.0.0	11111111 11111111 00000000 00000000
Network Address	172.30.0.0	10101100 00011110 00000000 00000000

Another way of expressing a netmask is as a single number representing the number of network bits in the address. This number usually follows the IP address and a slash. For instance, 172.30.9.102/16 is equivalent to 172.30.9.102 with a netmask of 255.255.0.0—the last number shows the network portion to be two solid 8-bit bytes and hence is 16 bits. The longer notation showing all 4 bytes of the netmask is referred to as *dotted quad* notation. IPv6 netmasks work just like IPv4 netmasks, except that larger numbers are involved, and IPv6 favors hexadecimal over decimal notation.

On modern IPv4 networks, netmasks are often described in *Classless Inter-Domain Routing* (CIDR) form. Such network masks can be broken at any bit boundary for any address. For instance, 192.168.1.7 could have a netmask of 255.255.0.0, 255.255.255.0, 255.255.255.128, or various other values. (Keeping each byte at 0 or 255 reduces the odds of human error causing problems but sometimes isn't practical, depending on the required or desired sizes of subnets.) Traditionally, though, IPv4 networks have been broken into one of several classes, as summarized in Table 8.1. Classes A, B, and C are for general networking use. Class D addresses are reserved for *multicasting*—sending data to multiple computers simultaneously. Class E addresses are reserved for future use. There are a few special cases within most of these ranges. For instance, the 127.*x.y.z* addresses are reserved for use as *loopback* (aka *localhost*) devices—these addresses refer to the computer on which the address is entered. Addresses in which all the machine bits are set to 1 refer to the network block itself—they're used for broadcasts. The ultimate broadcast address is 255.255.255.255, which sends data to all computers on a network segment. (Routers normally block packets directed to this address. If they didn't, the Internet could easily be brought to its knees by a few people flooding the network with broadcast packets.)

TABLE 8.1   IPv4 network classes and private network ranges

Class	Address range	Reserved private addresses
A	1.0.0.0–127.255.255.255	10.0.0.0–10.255.255.255
B	128.0.0.0–191.255.255.255	172.16.0.0–172.31.255.255

C	192.0.0.0–223.255.255.255	192.168.0.0–192.168.255.255
D	224.0.0.0–239.255.255.255	none
E	240.0.0.0–255.255.255.255	none

Within each of the three general-use network classes is a range of addresses reserved for private use. Most IP addresses must be assigned to individual computers by a suitable authority, lest two systems on the Internet both try to use a single address. Anybody can use the reserved private address spaces, though. (These address blocks are sometimes referred to as RFC1918 addresses, after the standards document—RFC1918—in which they're defined.) The caveat is that routers normally drop packets sent to these addresses, effectively isolating them from the Internet as a whole. The idea is that these addresses may be safely used by small private networks. Today, they're often used behind Network Address Translation (NAT) routers, which enable arbitrary numbers of computers to "hide" behind a single system. The NAT router substitutes its own IP address on outgoing packets and then directs the reply to the correct system. This is very handy if you want to connect more computers to the Internet than you have IP addresses.

I generally use reserved private addresses for examples in this book. Unless otherwise specified, these examples work equally well on conventional assigned (non-private) IP addresses.

IPv6 has its equivalent to private addresses. IPv6 site-local addresses may be routed within a site but not off-site. They begin with the hexadecimal number fec, fed, fee, or fef. Link-local addresses are restricted to a single network segment; they shouldn't be routed at all. These addresses begin with the hexadecimal number fe8, fe9, fea, or feb.

IPv4 address classes were designed to simplify routing; but as the Internet evolved, they became restrictive. Thus, today they serve mainly as a way to set default netmasks, such as 255.0.0.0 for Class A addresses or 255.255.255.0 for Class C addresses. Most configuration tools set these netmasks automatically, but you can override the settings if necessary.

IP addresses and netmasks are extremely important for network configuration. If your network doesn't use DHCP or a similar protocol to assign IP addresses automatically, you must configure your system's IP address manually. A mistake in this configuration can cause a complete failure of networking or more subtle errors, such as an inability to communicate with just some computers.

Non-TCP/IP stacks have their own addressing methods. NetBEUI uses machine names; it has no separate numeric addressing method. AppleTalk uses two 16-bit numbers. These addressing schemes are independent from IP addresses.

Broadcasting Data

Earlier, I mentioned broadcasts. A broadcast is a type of network transmission that's sent to all the computers on a local network, or occasionally all of the computers on a remote network. Under TCP/IP, a broadcast is done by specifying binary 1 values in all the machine bits of the IP address. The network portion of the IP address may be set to the network's regular value, and this is required for directed broadcasts—that is, those that are sent to a remote network. (Many routers drop directed broadcasts, though.) In many cases, broadcasts are specified by the use of 255.255.255.255 as an IP address. Packets directed at this address are sent to all the machines on a local network.

Because the broadcast address for a network is determined by the IP address and netmask, you can convert between the broadcast address and netmask, given one of these and a computer's IP address. If the netmask happens to consist of whole-byte values (expressed as 0 or 255 in dotted quad notation), the conversion is easy: Replace the IP address components that have 0 values in the dotted quad netmask with 255 values to get the broadcast address. For instance, consider a computer with an IP address of 172.30.9.102 and a netmask of 255.255.0.0. The final two elements of the netmask have 0 values, so you swap in 255 values for these final two elements in the IP address to obtain a broadcast address of 172.30.255.255.

In the case of a CIDR address that has non-255 and non-0 values in the netmask, the situation is more complex because you must resort to binary (base 2) numbers. For instance, consider a computer with an IP address of 172.30.9.102 and a netmask of 255.255.128.0 (that is, 172.30.0.0/17). Expressed in binary, these numbers are

```
10101100 00011110 00001001 01100110
11111111 11111111 10000000 00000000
```

To create the broadcast address, you must set the top (network address) values to 1 when the bottom (netmask) value is 0. In this case, the result is

```
10101100 00011110 01111111 11111111
```

Converted back into base 10 notation, the resulting broadcast address is 172.30.127.255. Fortunately, you seldom need to perform such computations. When configuring a computer, you can enter the IP address and netmask and let the computer do the binary computations.

Understanding Hostnames

Computers work with numbers, so it's not surprising that TCP/IP uses numbers as computer addresses. People, though, work better with names. For this reason, TCP/IP includes a way to link names for computers (known as *hostnames*) to IP addresses. In fact, there are *several* ways to do this, some of which are described in the next section, "Resolving Hostnames."

As with IP addresses, hostnames are composed of two parts: *machine names* and *domain names*. The former refers to a specific computer and the latter to a collection of computers. Domain names are not equivalent to the network portion of an IP address, though; they're completely independent concepts. Domain names are registered for use by an individual or organization, which may assign machine names within the domain and link those machine names to any arbitrary IP address desired. Nonetheless, there is frequently some correspondence between domains and network addresses because an individual or organization that controls a domain is also likely to want a block of IP addresses for the computers in that domain.

Internet domains are structured hierarchically. At the top of the hierarchy are the top-level domains (TLDs), such as .com, .edu, and .uk. These TLD names appear at the *end* of an Internet address. Some correspond to nations (such as .uk and .us, for the United Kingdom and the United States, respectively), but others correspond to particular types of entities (such as .com and .edu, which stand for commercial and educational organizations, respectively). Within each TLD are various domains that identify specific organizations, such as sybex.com for Sybex or loc.gov for the Library of Congress. These organizations may optionally break their domains into *subdomains*, such as cis.upenn.edu for the Computer and Information Science department at the University of Pennsylvania. Even subdomains may be further subdivided into their own subdomains; this structure can continue for many levels but usually doesn't. Domains and subdomains include specific computers, such as www.sybex.com, Sybex's Web server.

When you configure your Linux computer, you may need to know its hostname. This will be assigned by your network administrator and will be a machine name within your organization's domain. If your computer isn't part of an organizational network (say, if it's a system that doesn't connect to the Internet at all or if it connects only via a dial-up account), you'll have to make up a hostname. Alternatively, you can register a domain name, even if you don't use it for running your own servers. Check http://www.icann.org/registrar-reports/accredited-list.html for pointers to accredited domain registrars. Most registrars charge between $10 and $15 per year for domain registration. If your network uses DHCP, it may or may not assign your system a hostname automatically.

If you make up a hostname, choose an invalid domain name. This will guarantee that you don't accidentally give your computer a name that legitimately belongs to somebody else. Such a name conflict might prevent you from contacting that system, and it could cause other problems as well, such as misdirected email. Four TLDs—.example, .invalid, .localhost, and .test—are reserved for such purposes. Three second-level domains—.example.com, .example.net, and .example.org— are also reserved and so may be safely used.

Resolving Hostnames

The *Domain Name System* (DNS) is a distributed database of computers that converts between IP addresses and hostnames. Every domain must maintain at least two DNS servers that can either provide the names for every computer within the domain or redirect a DNS query to another DNS server that can better handle the request. Therefore, looking up a hostname involves querying a series of DNS servers, each of which redirects the search until the server that's responsible for the hostname is found. In practice, this process is hidden from you because most organizations maintain DNS servers that do all the tedious work of chatting with other DNS servers. You need only point your computer to your organization's DNS servers. This detail may be handled through DHCP, or it may be information you need to configure manually, as described later in the section "Configuring Linux for a Local Network."

Sometimes, you need to look up DNS information manually. You might do this if you know the IP address of a server through non-DNS means and suspect your DNS configuration is delivering the wrong address or to check whether a DNS server is working. Several programs can be helpful in performing such checks:

nslookup This program performs DNS lookups (on individual computers by default) and returns the results. It also sports an interactive mode in which you can perform a series of queries. This program is officially deprecated, meaning that it's no longer being maintained and will eventually be dropped from its parent package (bind-utils or bind-tools on most distributions). Thus, you should get in the habit of using host or dig instead of nslookup.

host This program serves as a replacement for the simpler uses of nslookup, but it lacks an interactive mode, and of course many details of its operation differ. In the simplest case, you can type **host target.name**, where *target.name* is the hostname or IP address you want to look up. You can add various options that tweak the program's basic operation; consult host's man page for details.

dig This program performs more complex DNS lookups than host. Although you can use it to find the IP address for a single hostname (or a hostname for a single IP address), it's more flexible than host.

whois You can look up information on a domain as a whole with this command. For instance, typing **whois sybex.com** reveals who owns the sybex.com domain, who to contact in case of problems, and so on. You may want to use this command with -H, which omits the lengthy legal disclaimers that many domain registries insist on delivering along with whois information. Check the man page for whois for information on additional options.

Exercise 8.1 illustrates the use of the nslookup, host, and dig tools.

EXERCISE 8.1

Practice Resolving Hostnames

The differences between nslookup, host, and dig are best illustrated by example. In this exercise, you'll practice using these three tools to perform both forward and reverse DNS lookups. To do so, follow these steps:

1. Log into a Linux text-mode session or launch a terminal window in a GUI session.

2. Type **nslookup www.google.com**. You may substitute another hostname; however, one key point of this hostname is that it resolves to multiple IP addresses, which nslookup

shows on multiple Name: and Address: lines. This practice is common on extremely popular sites because the load can be balanced across multiple computers. Note also that nslookup reports the IP address of the DNS server it uses, on the Server: and Address: lines. (The latter includes the port number, as described later, in "Network Ports."

3. Type **host www.google.com**. The output of this command is likely to be somewhat briefer than that of the nslookup command, but it should report the same IP addresses for the server. Although host doesn't report the DNS server's address, it is IPv6-enabled, so it reports an IPv6 address, as well as the site's IPv4 addresses.

4. Type **dig www.google.com**. This output is significantly longer than that of either nslookup or host. In fact, it closely resembles the format of the configuration files used to define a domain in a DNS server. In the case of www.google.com, that hostname is defined as a CNAME record that points to www.1.google.com, which in turn has several A-record entries that point to specific IP addresses. (This structure could change by the time you read this, though, and of course it's likely to be different if you examine other hostnames.) You'll also see several NS records that point to the domain's name servers, and you'll see additional A records that point to the name servers' IP addresses.

5. Perform nslookup, host, and dig queries on IP addresses, such as one of those returned by your lookups on www.google.com. (This is known as a *reverse lookup*.) In each case, the tool should return a hostname. Note, however, that the hostname might not match the one you used originally. This is because multiple hostnames can point to the same IP address, and the owner of that IP address decides which hostname to link to the IP address for reverse lookup purposes. In some cases, the tool will return an NXDOMAIN error, which means that the IP address's owner hasn't configured reverse lookups.

6. Perform similar queries on other computers, such as ones associated with your school, employer, or ISP. Most hostnames have just one IP address associated with them, and you may see other differences, too.

Sometimes DNS is overkill. For instance, you might just need to resolve a handful of hostnames. This may be because you're configuring a small private network that's not connected to the Internet at large or because you want to set up a few names for local (or even remote) computers that aren't in the global DNS database. For such situations, /etc/hosts may be just what you need. This file holds mappings of IP addresses to hostnames, on a one-line-per-mapping basis. Each mapping includes at least one name, and sometimes more:

```
127.0.0.1     localhost
192.168.7.23  apollo.luna.edu   apollo
```

In this example, the name localhost is associated with the 127.0.0.1 address, and the names apollo.luna.edu and apollo are tied to 192.168.7.23. The first of these linkages is standard; it should exist in any /etc/hosts file. The second linkage is an example that you can modify as you see fit. The first name is a full hostname, including the domain portion; subsequent names on the line are aliases—typically the hostname without its full domain specification.

Once you've set up an /etc/hosts file, you can refer to computers listed in the file by name, whether or not those names are recognized by the DNS servers the computer uses. One major drawback to /etc/hosts is that it's a purely local file; setting a mapping in one computer's /etc/hosts file affects name lookups performed by that computer alone. Thus, to do good on an entire network, you must modify the /etc/hosts files on all of the computers on the network.

Linux normally performs lookups in /etc/hosts before it uses DNS. You can modify this behavior by editing the /etc/nsswitch.conf file, which configures the Name Service Switch (NSS) service. More specifically, you must adjust the hosts line. This line lists the order of the files and dns options, which stand for /etc/hosts and DNS, respectively:

```
hosts:       files dns
```

Reverse the order of the files and dns options to have the system consult DNS before it consults /etc/hosts.

The /etc/nsswitch.conf file supports many more options. For instance, you can perform name resolution using Windows NetBIOS calls or a Lightweight Directory Access Protocol (LDAP) server by adding appropriate options to the hosts line, along with the necessary support software. The passwd, shadow, and group lines control how Linux authenticates users and manages groups. You should not attempt to change these configurations unless you understand the systems involved, but you should be aware of the importance of /etc/nsswitch.conf generally.

In addition to /etc/hosts, Linux supports a file called /etc/networks. It works much like /etc/hosts, but it applies to network addresses, and it reverses the order of the names and the IP address on each line:

```
loopback 127.0.0.0
mynet 192.168.7.0
```

This example sets up two linkages: the loopback name to the 127.0.0.0/8 network and mynet for the 192.168.7.0/24 network. It's seldom necessary to edit this file.

Network Ports

Contacting a specific computer is important, but one additional type of addressing is left: The sender must have an address for a specific program on the remote system. For instance, suppose you're using a Web browser. The Web server computer may be running more servers than just a Web server—it may also be running an email server or an FTP server, to name just two of many possibilities. Another number beyond the IP address enables you to direct traffic to a specific program. This number is a network port number, and programs that access a TCP/IP network typically do so through one or more ports.

 Port numbers are features of the UDP and TCP protocols. Some protocols, such as ICMP, don't use port numbers.

When they start up, servers tie themselves to specific ports, which by convention are associated with specific server programs. For instance, port 25 is associated with email servers, and port 80 is used by Web servers. Table 8.2 summarizes the purposes of several important ports. A client can direct its request to a specific port and expect to contact an appropriate server. The client's own port number isn't fixed; it's assigned by the OS. Because the client initiates a transfer, it can include its own port number in the connection request, so clients don't need fixed port numbers. Assigning client port numbers dynamically also enables one computer to easily run several instances of a single client because they won't compete for access to a single port.

TABLE 8.2   Port numbers, their purposes, and typical Linux servers

Port number	TCP or UDP	Purpose	Example Linux servers
20	TCP	File Transfer Protocol (FTP) data	ProFTPd, vsftpd
21	TCP	FTP	ProFTPd, vsftpd
22	TCP	Secure Shell (SSH)	OpenSSH, Dropbear
23	TCP	Telnet	in.telnetd
25	TCP	Simple Mail Transfer Protocol (SMTP)	Sendmail, Postfix, Exim, qmail
53	TCP and UDP	Domain Name System (DNS)	Berkeley Internet Name Domain (BIND; aka named), dnsmasq, djbdns
67	UDP	Dynamic Host Configuration Protocol (DHCP)	Internet Software Consortium (ISC) DHCP (dhcpd), dnsmasq
80	TCP	Hypertext Transfer Protocol (HTTP)	Apache, Roxen, thttpd
110	TCP	Post Office Protocol version 3 (POP-3)	Dovecot, Qpopper, popa3d

TABLE 8.2 Port numbers, their purposes, and typical Linux servers *(continued)*

Port number	TCP or UDP	Purpose	Example Linux servers
111	TCP and UDP	Portmapper	NFS, NIS, other RPC-based services
113	TCP	auth/ident	identd
119	TCP	Network News Transfer Protocol (NNTP)	InterNetNews (INN), Diablo, Leafnode
139	TCP	NetBIOS Session (Windows file sharing)	Samba
143	TCP	Interactive Mail Access Protocol (IMAP)[1]	Dovecot, Cyrus IMAP, UW-IMAP
161	UDP	Simple Network Management Protocol (SNMP)	Net-SNMP
177	UDP	XDMCP	XDM, KDM, GDM
389	TCP	LDAP	OpenLDAP
443	TCP	HTTP over SSL (HTTPS)	Apache, Roxen
445	TCP	Microsoft Directory Services (DS)	Samba
465	TCP	SMTP over SSL; or URL Rendezvous Directory (URD)[2]	Sendmail, Postfix, Exim, qmail; or network routers
631	TCP	Internet Printing Protocol (IPP)	Common Unix Printing System (CUPS)
993	TCP	IMAP over SSL	Dovecot, Cyrus IMAP, UW-IMAP
995	TCP	POP-3 over SSL	Dovecot, Qpopper, popa3d
5900+	TCP	Remote Framebuffer (RFB)	Virtual Network Computing (VNC): OpenVNC, TightVNC, TigerVNC
6000–6007	TCP	The X Window System (X)	X.org-X11, XFree86

[1]Some sources expand *IMAP* as *Internet Message Access Protocol* or *Internet Mail Access Protocol*.

[2]Port 465 is officially registered for URD; however, it's also commonly used as a secure email delivery port, although this isn't the officially designated purpose of this port.

One key distinction in TCP/IP ports is that between *privileged ports* and *unprivileged ports*. The former have numbers less than 1024. Unix and Linux systems restrict access to privileged ports to `root`. The idea is that a client can connect to a privileged port and be confident that the server running on that port was configured by the system administrator and can therefore be trusted. Unfortunately, on today's Internet, this trust would be unjustified based solely on the port number, so this distinction isn't very useful. Port numbers greater than 1024 may be accessed by ordinary users.

Clients and Servers

An important distinction is the one between clients and servers. A *client* is a program that initiates a network connection to exchange data. *A server* listens for such connections and responds to them. For instance, a Web browser, such as Firefox or Opera, is a client program. You launch the program and direct it to a Web page, which means that the Web browser sends a request to the Web (HTTP) server at the specified address. The Web server sends back data in reply to the request. Clients can also send data, like when you enter information in a Web form and click a Submit or Send button.

The terms *client* and server can also be applied to entire computers that operate mostly in one or the other role. Thus, a phrase such as *Web server* is somewhat ambiguous—it can refer either to the Web server program or to the computer that runs that program. When this distinction is important and unclear from context, I clarify it (for instance, by referring to "the Web server program").

Fortunately, for basic functioning, you need to do nothing to configure ports on a Linux system. You may have to deal with this issue if you run unusual servers, though, because you may need to configure the system to link the servers to the correct ports. This can sometimes involve editing the /etc/services file, which maps port numbers to names, enabling you to use names in server configurations and elsewhere. This file consists of lines that begin with a name and end with a port number, including the type of protocol it uses (TCP or UDP):

```
ssh      22/tcp      # SSH Remote Login Protocol
ssh      22/udp      # SSH Remote Login Protocol
telnet   23/tcp
smtp     25/tcp
```

Configuring Linux for a Local Network

Now that you know something about how networking functions, the question arises: How do you implement networking in Linux? Most Linux distributions provide you with the means to configure a network connection during system installation. Therefore, chances are good that networking already functions on your system. In case it doesn't, though, the following sections summarize what you must do to get the job done. Actual configuration can be done using either the automatic DHCP tool or static IP addresses. Linux's underlying network configuration mechanisms rely on startup scripts and their configuration files, but you may be able to use GUI tools to do the job instead.

Network Hardware Configuration

The most fundamental part of network configuration is getting the network hardware up and running. In most cases, this task is fairly automatic—most distributions ship with system startup scripts that auto-detect the network card and load the correct driver module. If you recompile your kernel, building the correct driver into the main kernel file will also ensure that it's loaded at system startup.

If your network hardware isn't correctly detected, though, subsequent configuration (as described in the upcoming sections "Configuring with DHCP" and "Configuring with a Static IP Address") won't work. To correct this problem, you must load your network hardware driver. You can do this with the modprobe command:

```
# modprobe tulip
```

You must know the name of your network hardware's kernel module (tulip in this example). Chapter 3, "Configuring Hardware," describes the task of hardware configuration and activation in more detail.

Configuring with DHCP

One of the easiest ways to configure a computer to use a TCP/IP network is to use DHCP, which enables one computer on a network to manage the settings for many other computers. It works like this: When a computer running a DHCP client boots up, it sends a broadcast in search of a DHCP server. The server replies (using nothing but the client's hardware address) with the configuration information the client needs to enable it to communicate with other computers on the network—most important, the client's IP address and netmask and the network's gateway and DNS server addresses. The DHCP server may also give the client a hostname and provide various other details about the network. The client then configures itself with these parameters. The IP address isn't assigned permanently; it's referred to as a *DHCP lease*, and if it's not renewed, the DHCP server may give the lease to another computer. Therefore, from time to time the client checks back with the DHCP server to renew its lease.

Three DHCP clients are in common use on Linux: pump, dhclient, and dhcpcd (not to be confused with the DHCP server, dhcpd). Some Linux distributions ship with just one of these, but others ship with two or even all three. All distributions have a default DHCP client—the one that's installed when you tell the system you want to use DHCP at system installation time. Those that ship with multiple DHCP clients typically enable you to swap out one for another simply by removing the old package and installing the new one.

Ideally, the DHCP client runs at system bootup. This is usually handled either by its own startup script, as described in Chapter 5, "Booting Linux and Editing Files," or as part of the main network configuration startup file (typically a startup script called `network` or `networking`). The system often uses a line in a configuration file to determine whether to run a DHCP client. For instance, Red Hat and Fedora set this option in a file called `/etc/sysconfig/network-scripts/ifcfg-`*name*, where *name* is the name of the network interface, such as p2p1. The line in question looks like this:

```
BOOTPROTO="dhcp"
```

Recall that most distributions use eth0 to refer to the computer's first Ethernet port, eth1 for the second (if present), and so on. Fedora names its interfaces differently, though, and in a way that's inconsistent from one computer to another.

If the `BOOTPROTO` variable is set to something else, changing it as shown here will configure the system to use DHCP. It's usually easier to use a GUI configuration tool to set this option, though.

Ubuntu uses the `/etc/network/interfaces` file for a similar purpose, but the details differ. On a system that uses DHCP, a line like the following appears:

```
iface eth0 inet dhcp
```

Details may vary, of course; for instance, the interface name (eth0) may be something else. You may prefer to use the GUI system configuration tools to adjust these options.

Once a DHCP client is configured to run when the computer boots, the configuration task is done—at least, if everything works as it should. On very rare occasions, you may need to tweak DHCP settings to work around client-server incompatibilities or to have the DHCP client do something unusual. Consult the `man` page for your DHCP client if you need to make changes. You'll then have to modify its startup script or a file to which it refers in order to change its operation.

If you need to manually run a DHCP client, you can usually do so by typing its name (as root), optionally followed by a network identifier, as in **dhclient eth0** to have the DHCP client attempt to configure eth0 with the help of any DHCP server it finds on that network.

Configuring with a Static IP Address

If a network lacks a DHCP server, you must provide basic network configuration options manually. You can set these options using interactive commands, as described shortly; but to set them in the long term, you adjust a configuration file such as `/etc/sysconfig/network-scripts/ifcfg-`*name* or `/etc/network/interfaces`. Listing 8.1 shows a typical ifcfg-*name* file, configured to use a static IP address. (Note that this file's exact location and name may vary from one distribution to another.)

Listing 8.1: A sample network configuration file

```
DEVICE="p2p1"
BOOTPROTO="static"
IPADDR="192.168.29.39"
NETMASK="255.255.255.0"
NETWORK="192.168.29.0"
BROADCAST="192.168.29.255"
GATEWAY="192.168.29.1"
ONBOOT="yes"
```

Several specific items are required, or at least helpful, for static IP address configuration:

IP Address   You can set the IP address manually via the ifconfig command (described in more detail shortly) or via the IPADDR item in the configuration file.

Network Mask   The netmask can be set manually via the ifconfig command or via the NETMASK item in a configuration file.

Gateway Address   You can manually set the gateway via the route command. To set it permanently, you need to adjust a configuration file, which may be the same configuration file that holds other options or another file, such as /etc/sysconfig/network/routes. In either case, the option is likely to be called GATEWAY. The gateway isn't necessary on a computer that isn't connected to a wider network—that is, if the computer works *only* on a local network that contains no routers.

DNS Settings   In order for Linux to use DNS to translate between IP addresses and hostnames, you must specify at least one DNS server in the /etc/resolv.conf file. Precede the IP address of the DNS server by the keyword nameserver, as in nameserver 192.168.29.1. You can include up to three nameserver lines in this file. Adjusting this file is all you need to do to set the name server addresses; you don't have to do anything else to make the setting permanent. You can also set your computer's local domain name in this file using the domain option, as in domain luna.edu to set the domain to luna.edu.

The network configuration script may hold additional options, but most of these are related to others. For instance, Listing 8.1 has an option specifying the interface name (DEVICE="p2p1"), another that tells the computer to assign a static IP address (BOOTPROTO="static"), and a third to bring up the interface when the computer boots (ONBOOT="yes"). The NETWORK and BROADCAST items in Listing 8.1 are derived from the IPADDR and NETMASK items, but you can change them if you understand the consequences.

Unfortunately, these configuration details vary from one distribution to another. For instance, if you use Ubuntu, you would edit /etc/network/interfaces rather than /etc/sysconfig/network-scripts/ifcfg-eth0. The precise layout and formatting of information in the two files differs, but the same basic information is present in both of them. You may need to consult distribution-specific documentation to learn about these details. Alternatively, GUI tools are usually fairly easy to figure out, so you can look for these.

If you aren't sure what to enter for the basic networking values (the IP address, network mask, gateway address, and DNS server addresses), you should consult your network administrator. *Do not* enter random values or values you make up that are similar to those used by other systems on your network. Doing so is unlikely to work at all, and it could conceivably cause a great deal of trouble—say, if you mistakenly use an IP address that's reserved for another computer.

As just mentioned, the ifconfig program is critically important for setting both the IP address and netmask. This program can also display current settings. Basic use of ifconfig to bring up a network interface resembles the following:

ifconfig *interface up addr* netmask mask

For instance, the following command brings up eth0 (the first Ethernet device on most distributions) using the address 192.168.29.39 and the netmask 255.255.255.0:

```
# ifconfig eth0 up 192.168.29.39 netmask 255.255.255.0
```

This command links the specified IP address to the device so that the computer responds to the address and claims to be that address when sending data. It doesn't, though, set up a route for traffic beyond your current network. For that, you need to use the route command:

```
# route add default gw 192.168.29.1
```

Substitute your own gateway address for 192.168.29.1. (Routing and the route command are described in more detail shortly, in "Configuring Routing.") Both ifconfig and route can display information on the current network configuration. For ifconfig, omit up and everything that follows; for route, omit add and everything that follows. For instance, to view interface configuration, you might issue the following command:

```
# ifconfig eth0
eth0  Link encap:Ethernet  HWaddr 00:A0:CC:24:BA:02
      inet addr:192.168.29.39  Bcast:192.168.29.255   Mask:255.255.255.0
      UP BROADCAST RUNNING MULTICAST  MTU:1500  Metric:1
      RX packets:10469 errors:0 dropped:0 overruns:0 frame:0
      TX packets:8557 errors:0 dropped:0 overruns:0 carrier:0
      collisions:0 txqueuelen:100
      RX bytes:1017326 (993.4 Kb)  TX bytes:1084384 (1.0 Mb)
      Interrupt:10 Base address:0xc800
```

When configured properly, ifconfig should show a hardware address (HWaddr), an IP address (inet addr), and additional statistics. There should be few or no errors, dropped packets, or overruns for both received (RX) and transmitted (TX) packets. Ideally, few (if any) collisions should occur, but some are unavoidable if your network uses a hub rather than a switch. If collisions total more than a few percent of the total transmitted and received packets, you may want to consider replacing a hub with a switch. To use route for diagnostic purposes, you might try the following:

```
# route -n
Kernel IP routing table
Destination  Gateway       Genmask       Flags Metric Ref  Use Iface
192.168.29.0 *             255.255.255.0 U     0      0      0 eth0
127.0.0.0    *             255.0.0.0     U     0      0      0 lo
0.0.0.0      192.168.29.1  0.0.0.0       UG    0      0      0 eth0
```

The -n option to route causes it to not attempt to find the hostnames associated with IP addresses. Although hostnames are often useful, this lookup can be slow or fail altogether if your DNS configuration is broken, so using -n with route is sometimes necessary.

This shows that data destined for 192.168.29.0 (that is, any computer with an IP address between 192.168.29.1 and 192.168.29.254) goes directly over eth0. The 127.0.0.0 network is a special interface that "loops back" to the originating computer. Linux uses this for some internal networking purposes. The last line shows the *default route*, which describes what to do with everything that doesn't match any other entry in the routing table. This line specifies the default route's gateway system as 192.168.29.1. If it's missing or misconfigured, some or all traffic destined for external networks, such as the Internet, won't make it beyond your local network segment.

As with DHCP configuration, it's almost always easier to use a GUI configuration tool to set up static IP addresses, at least for new administrators. The exact locations of the configuration files differ from one distribution to another, so the examples listed earlier may not apply to your system.

Configuring Routing

As explained earlier, routers pass traffic from one network to another. You configure your Linux system to directly contact systems on the local network. You also give the computer a router's address, which your system uses as a gateway to the Internet at large. Any traffic that's not destined for the local network is directed at this router, which passes it on to its destination. In practice, there are likely to be a dozen or more routers between you and most Internet sites. Each router has at least two network interfaces and keeps a table of rules concerning where to send data based on the destination IP address. Your own Linux computer has such a table, but it's probably very simple compared to those on major Internet routers.

Linux can function as a router, which means it can link two or more networks together, directing traffic between them on the basis of its routing table. This task is handled, in part, by the route command. This command can be used to do much more than specify a single gateway system, though, as described earlier. A simplified version of the route syntax is as follows:

```
route {add | del} [-net | -host] target [netmask nm] [gw gw] ↵
 [reject] [[dev] interface]
```

You specify add or del along with a *target* (a computer or network address) and optionally other parameters. The -net and -host options force route to interpret the target as a network or computer address, respectively. The netmask option lets you set a netmask as you desire, and gw lets you specify a router through which packets to the specified *target* should go. (Some versions of route use gateway rather than gw.) The reject keyword installs a blocking route, which refuses all traffic destined for the specified network. (This is *not* a firewall, though.) Finally, although route can usually figure out the interface device (for instance, eth0) on its own, you can force the issue with the dev option.

As an example, consider a network in which packets destined for the 172.20.0.0/16 subnet should be passed through the 172.21.1.1 router, which isn't the default gateway system. You can set up this route with the following command:

```
# route add -net 172.20.0.0 netmask 255.255.0.0 gw 172.21.1.1
```

Incorrect routing tables can cause serious problems because some or all computers won't respond. You can examine your routing table by typing **route** alone and compare the results to what your routing table should be. (Consult a network administrator if you're not sure what your routing table should contain.) You can then delete incorrect routes and add new ones to replace them, if necessary. Ultimately, of course, changing your configuration files is the best solution, but typing a couple of route commands will do the trick in the short term.

One more thing you may need to do if you're setting up a router is enabling routing. Ordinarily, a Linux system won't forward packets it receives from one system that are directed at another system. If Linux is to act as a router, though, it must accept these packets and send them on to the destination network (or at least to an appropriate gateway). To enable this feature, you must modify a key file in the /proc filesystem:

```
# echo "1" > /proc/sys/net/ipv4/ip_forward
```

This command enables IP forwarding. Permanently setting this option requires modifying a configuration file. Some distributions set it in /etc/sysctl.conf:

```
net.ipv4.ip_forward = 1
```

Other distributions use other configuration files and options, such as /etc/sysconfig/ sysctl and its IP_FORWARD line. If you can't find it, try using grep to search for ip_forward or IP_FORWARD, or modify a local startup script to add the command to perform the change.

Using GUI Configuration Tools

Most distributions include their own GUI configuration tools for network interfaces. For instance, Fedora and Red Hat ship with a custom GUI tool called Network Configuration (system-config-network), and SUSE has a text-mode and GUI tool called YaST. The details of operating these programs differ, but the GUI configuration tool provides a means to enter the information described earlier.

Although the exam doesn't cover GUI network configuration tools, they're generally easier to locate and use than the configuration files in which settings are stored. Thus, you may want to look for your distribution's tool and learn to use it. Once you understand the principles of network configuration (IP addresses, DHCP, and so on), you shouldn't have trouble entering the necessary information in the GUI fields.

The precise details of how to configure a Linux system using GUI tools differ from one distribution to another. For instance, SUSE's YaST doesn't lay out its options in precisely the same way as Fedora's Network Configuration tool. The basic principles are the same, though; you must choose whether to use static IP address assignment or an automatic system such as DHCP and enter a number of key options, depending on what configuration method you choose.

Using the *ifup* and *ifdown* Commands

Most Linux distributions today ship with two commands, ifup and ifdown, that combine the functions of several other network commands, most notably ifconfig and route. In their simplest forms, they bring interfaces up or shut them down based on information in whatever files your distribution uses to store network configuration data:

```
# ifup eth0
Determining IP information for eth0... done.
```

After you issue this command, eth0 will be fully configured, including all routing information, assuming you've properly configured it by using your distribution's network configuration tools or by manually editing configuration files such as /etc/network /interfaces and /etc/sysconfig/network-scripts/ifcfg-*name*. You can bring the interface down with equal ease by typing **ifdown eth0**.

The ifup and ifdown commands are useful for verifying that the network settings are configured properly for the next time the computer boots. They're also useful if you want to quickly take down the network or bring it back up again, because you can type fewer commands and you don't need to remember all the details of IP addresses, routes, and so on. If you need to experiment or debug a problem, though, using ifconfig and route individually is preferable, because they give you finer control over the process.

The ifup and ifdown commands are implemented as scripts that consult the configuration files and run the relevant low-level commands behind the scenes.

Configuring Hostnames

The hostnames described earlier (in "Resolving Hostnames") are configured in a couple of ways:

On DNS   Your network administrator should be able to add an entry for your system to your network's DNS server. This entry should make your computer addressable by name from other computers on your local network, and perhaps from the Internet at large. Alternatively, remote systems' /etc/hosts files can be modified to include your system.

On Your Local Computer   Various local programs should know your computer's name. For instance, you may want to have your hostname displayed as part of a command prompt or entered automatically in email messages. For this task, you must set your hostname locally. Note that this is entirely independent of your DNS hostname. In theory, you can set the two to very different values, but this practice is likely to lead to confusion and perhaps even failure of some programs to operate properly.

The most basic tool for setting your hostname locally is called, appropriately enough, hostname. Type the command alone to see what your hostname is, or type it with a new name to set the system's hostname to that name:

```
# hostname nessus.example.com
```

Similar commands, domainname and dnsdomainname, display or set the computer's domain name (such as example.com). The domainname command sets the domain name as used by Network Information System (NIS), whereas dnsdomainname sets the domain name as used by DNS. These commands don't affect remote servers—just the name given to programs that use calls designed for these servers.

Many Linux distributions look in the /etc/hostname or /etc/HOSTNAME file for a hostname to set at boot time. Thus, if you want to set your hostname permanently, you should look for these files, and if one is present, you should edit it. Fedora uses /etc/sysconfig/network for this purpose, among others. If you can't find one of these files, consult your distribution's documentation; it's conceivable that your distribution stores its hostname in some unusual location.

In Exercise 8.2, you'll familiarize yourself with some of the tools used to configure basic network settings. You'll use these tools both to study and to change your network configuration.

EXERCISE 8.2

Configuring a Network Connection

In this exercise, the assumption is that the computer is correctly configured to use an IPv4 Ethernet network, including both local network access and access to a larger network (probably the Internet) via a router.

Some of the procedures in this exercise can easily break your network connectivity if something goes wrong. If this happens, typing **ifdown** followed by **ifup** is one way to recover. If this fails, rebooting the computer is almost certain to work, although it's a radical solution.

EXERCISE8.2 *(continued)*

To study and modify your system's network configuration, follow these steps:

1. Log into the Linux system as a normal user.

2. Launch an xterm from the desktop environment's menu system, if you used a GUI login method.

3. Acquire root privileges. You can do this by typing **su** in an xterm or by using sudo (if it's configured) to run the commands in the following steps.

4. Type **ifconfig**. This command displays information about your local network settings for all your network interfaces. Most systems have both a loopback interface (lo) and an Ethernet interface (eth0). Look for a line in the Ethernet section that includes the string inet addr:. The following 4-byte number is your IP address. Write it down, as well as the value of your netmask (Mask:). Study the other information in this output, too, such as the number of received (RX) and transmitted (TX) packets, the number of errors, the number of collisions, and the Ethernet adapter's hardware address.

5. Type **route -n**. The output is your computer's routing table information. This normally includes information about the loopback network address (127.0.0.0/24), the local net-work address, and a default route (identified as the route for 0.0.0.0). Some systems may display fewer or additional lines, depending on local configuration. The default route includes an IP address under the Gateway column. Write down that address.

6. Use ping to test connectivity to both local and remote computers. (This command is described in more detail shortly, in "Testing Basic Connectivity.") You need the name or IP address of at least one local computer and at least one distant computer (beyond your local router). Type **ping** *address*, where *address* is the name or IP address of each test machine. Perform this test for localhost or 127.0.0.1, your own machine (use the IP address you noted in step 4), your local router (use the IP address you noted in step 5), and a distant computer (if you're connected to the Internet, you can use an Internet-accessible site, such as www.linux.org). All of these ping tests should be successful. Note, however, that some computers are configured to ignore packets sent by ping. Thus, some of these tests may fail if you run into such systems. You can learn the configuration of local computers from their administrators, but for Internet sites, you may want to simply try another site if the first one you test fails.

7. Bring down the local Ethernet connection by typing **ifconfig eth0 down**.

8. Repeat steps 4–6. Note that the eth0 interface is no longer shown when you type ifconfig, all routes associated with it have been removed from the routing table, and pinging systems accessible from the interface no longer works. (Linux retains some information about its former Ethernet link, so you may still be able to ping the computer itself via its former eth0 address.)

9. Bring the local Ethernet connection back up by typing **ifconfig eth0 up** *address* **netmask** *mask*, where *address* is the original IP address and *mask* is the original netmask, both as identified in step 4.

10. Repeat steps 4–6. Note that the ifconfig command automatically added back your local network to the routing table but that the default route is still missing. As a result,

you can't contact any systems that are located off the local network. If your DNS server is such a system, this means your ability to contact even local machines by name may be impaired as well.

11. Restore the default route by typing **route add default gw** *gateway*, where *gateway* is the router address you identified in step 5.

12. Repeat steps 4–6. If your network configuration is typical, all connectivity should be restored. (Some more exotic systems may still be lacking certain routes.)

 Real World Scenario

Using PPP with DSL

Broadband users, and particularly those with Digital Subscriber Line (DSL) connections, sometimes have to use a variant of PPP to make their connections. PPP is a login-based way to access the Internet—you use a PPP utility to initiate a connection to a remote computer, which includes an exchange of a username and a password. A decade ago, PPP was used in dial-up Internet access (and it's still used in this capacity), but some DSL providers have adapted PPP for their own purposes. In the case of DSL, this configuration method is called PPP over Ethernet (PPPoE).

In many cases, the simplest way to use a PPPoE configuration is to purchase a broadband router. This device attaches to the DSL modem and makes the PPPoE connection. The broadband router then works just like an ordinary Ethernet or Wi-Fi router, as far as your local computers are concerned, so you can configure Linux as you would on any other local network.

If you must connect a Linux system directly to a DSL network that uses PPPoE, you must use a Linux PPPoE client. Most Linux distributions ship with such clients, but configuration details vary from one distribution to another. Your best bet is to look for your distribution's GUI network configuration tool; chances are, you'll be able to find a set of options that are clearly labeled as applying to DSL or PPPoE.

Diagnosing Network Connections

Network configuration is a complex task, and unfortunately, things don't always work as planned. Fortunately, there are a few commands you can use to help diagnose a problem. Five of these are `ping`, `traceroute`, `tracepath`, `netstat`, and `tcpdump`. Each of these commands exercises the network in a particular way and provides information that can help you track down the source of a problem. You can also use some common network programs that aren't primarily debugging tools in your debugging efforts.

Testing Basic Connectivity

The most basic network test is the ping command, which sends a simple ICMP packet to the system you name (via IP address or hostname) and waits for a reply. In Linux, ping continues sending packets once every second or so until you interrupt it with a Ctrl+C keystroke. (You can instead specify a limited number of tests via the -c *num* option.) Here's an example of its output:

```
$ ping -c 4 speaker
PING speaker (192.168.1.1) 56(84) bytes of data.
64 bytes from speaker.example.com (192.168.1.1): icmp_seq=1 ttl=64 time=0.194ms
64 bytes from speaker.example.com (192.168.1.1): icmp_seq=2 ttl=64 time=0.203ms
64 bytes from speaker.example.com (192.168.1.1): icmp_seq=3 ttl=64 time=0.229ms
64 bytes from speaker.example.com (192.168.1.1): icmp_seq=4 ttl=64 time=0.217ms
--- speaker ping statistics ---
4 packets transmitted, 4 received, 0% packet loss, time 3002ms
rtt min/avg/max/mdev = 0.194/0.210/0.229/0.022 ms
```

This command sent four packets and waited for their return, which occurred quite quickly (in an average of 0.210ms) because the target system was on the local network. By pinging systems on both local and remote networks, you can isolate where a network problem occurs. For instance, if you can ping local computers but not remote systems, the problem is most probably in your router configuration. If you can ping by IP address but not by name, the problem is with your DNS configuration.

Tracing a Route

A step up from ping is the traceroute command, which sends a series of three test packets to each computer between your system and a specified target system. The result looks something like this:

```
$ traceroute -n 10.1.0.43
traceroute to 10.1.0.43 (10.1.0.43), 30 hops max, 52 byte packets
 1   192.168.1.1   1.021 ms   36.519 ms   0.971 ms
 2   10.10.88.1   17.250 ms   9.959 ms   9.637 ms
 3   10.9.8.173   8.799 ms   19.501 ms   10.884 ms
 4   10.9.8.133   21.059 ms   9.231 ms   103.068 ms
 5   10.9.14.9   8.554 ms   12.982 ms   10.029 ms
 6   10.1.0.44   10.273 ms   9.987 ms   11.215 ms
 7   10.1.0.43   16.360 ms   *   8.102 ms
```

The -n option to this command tells it to display target computers' IP addresses rather than their hostnames. This can speed up the process a bit, particularly if you're having DNS problems, and it can sometimes make the output easier to read—but you may want to know the hostnames of problem systems because that can help you pinpoint who's responsible for a problem.

This sample output shows a great deal of variability in response times. The first hop, to 192.168.1.1, is purely local; this router responded in 1.021, 36.519, and 0.971 milliseconds (ms) to its three probes. (Presumably the second probe caught the system while it was busy with something else.) Probes of most subsequent systems are in the 8–20ms range, although one is at 103.068ms. The final system has only two times; the middle probe never returned, as the asterisk (*) on this line indicates.

Using traceroute, you can localize problems in network connectivity. Highly variable times and missing times can indicate a router that's overloaded or that has an unreliable link to the previous system on the list. If you see a dramatic jump in times, it typically means that the physical distance between two routers is great. This is common in intercontinental links. Such jumps don't necessarily signify a problem unless the two systems are close enough that a huge jump isn't expected.

What can you do with the traceroute output? Most immediately, traceroute is helpful in determining whether a problem in network connectivity exists in a network for which you're responsible. For instance, the variability in the first hop of the preceding example could indicate a problem on the local network, but the lost packet associated with the final destination most likely is not a local problem. If the trouble link is within your jurisdiction, you can check the status of the problem system, nearby systems, and the network segment in general.

 Some routers are configured in such a way that traceroute isn't a useful tool; these routers block all traceroute data, either to themselves only or for all packets that pass through them. If your traceroute output contains one or two lines of all asterisks but everything else seems OK, chances are you've run into such a system. If you see nothing but asterisks after a certain router but diagnostic tools such as ping still work, a router is probably blocking all traceroute operations.

The tracepath program is an alternative to traceroute. In basic operation, it's similar, although it produces one line of output for each test packet and so yields longer outputs than traceroute. There are also fewer tracepath options than there are traceroute options.

Checking Network Status

Another useful diagnostic tool is netstat. This is something of a Swiss Army knife of network tools because it can be used in place of several others, depending on the parameters it's passed. It can also return information that's not easily obtained in other ways. Examples include the following:

Interface Information   Pass netstat the --interface or -i parameter to obtain information about your network interfaces similar to what ifconfig returns. (Some versions of netstat return information in the same format, but others display the information differently.)

Routing Information   You can use the --route or -r parameter to obtain a routing table listing similar to what the route command displays.

Masquerade Information   Pass netstat the --masquerade or -M parameter to obtain information about connections mediated by Linux's NAT features, which often go by the name *IP masquerading*. NAT enables a Linux router to "hide" a network behind a single IP address. This can be a good way to stretch limited IPv4 addresses.

Program Use   Some versions of netstat support the --program (or -p) parameter, which attempts to provide information about the programs that are using network connections. This attempt isn't always successful, but it often is, so you can see what programs are making outside connections.

Open Ports   When used with various other parameters, or without any parameters at all, netstat returns information about open ports and the systems to which they connect.

All Connections   The --all or -a option is used in conjunction with others. It causes netstat to display information about the ports that server programs open to listen for network connections, in addition to already-open connections. This use of netstat is described in more detail in Chapter 10, "Securing Your System."

Keep in mind that netstat is a very powerful tool, and its options and output aren't entirely consistent from one distribution to another. You may want to peruse its man page and experiment with it to learn what it can do.

Examining Raw Network Traffic

One advanced network troubleshooting tool is tcpdump. This utility is a *packet sniffer*, which is a program that can intercept network packets and log them or display them on the screen. Packet sniffers can be useful diagnostic tools because they enable you to verify that a computer is actually receiving data from other computers. They also enable you to examine the data in its raw form, which can be useful if you understand enough of the protocol's implementation details to spot problems.

WARNING   Although packet sniffers are useful diagnostic tools, they can also be abused. For instance, unscrupulous individuals can run packet sniffers to capture passwords that others send over the network. Depending on your network configuration, this trick can work even if the packet sniffer isn't running on either the sending or the receiving computer. For this reason, many organizations have policies forbidding the use of packet sniffers except under limited circumstances. Thus, before running a packet sniffer, you should obtain written permission to use such a program from an individual who is authorized to grant such permission. Failure to do so can lead you into serious trouble, possibly up to losing your job or even being sued.

In its most basic form, you can use tcpdump by typing its name:

```
# tcpdump
tcpdump: verbose output suppressed, use -v or -vv for full protocol decode
listening on eth0, link-type EN10MB (Ethernet), capture size 96 bytes
19:31:55.503759 IP speaker.example.com.631 > 192.168.1.255.631: UDP, ↵
 length: 139
19:31:55.505400 IP nessus.example.com.33513 > speaker.example.com.domain: ↵
 46276+ PTR? 255.1.168.192.in-addr.arpa. (44)
19:31:55.506086 IP speaker.example.com.domain > nessus.example.com.33513: ↵
 46276 NXDomain* 0/1/0 (110)
```

The first thing to note about this command is that you must run it as root; ordinary users aren't allowed to monitor network traffic in this way. Once it's run, tcpdump summarizes what it's doing and then begins printing lines, one for each packet it monitors. (Some of these lines can be quite long and so may take more than one line on your display.) These lines include a time stamp, a stack identifier (IP in all of these examples), the origin system name or IP address and port, the destination system name or IP address and port, and packet-specific information. Ordinarily, tcpdump keeps displaying packets indefinitely, so you must terminate it by pressing Ctrl+C. Alternatively, you can pass it the -c *num* option to have it display *num* packets and then quit.

Even this basic output can be very helpful. For instance, consider the preceding example of three packets, which was captured on nessus.example.com. This computer successfully received one broadcast packet (addressed to 192.168.1.255) from speaker.example.com's UDP port 631, sent a packet to speaker.example.com, and received a packet from that system directed at nessus.example.com rather than sent as a broadcast. This sequence verifies that at least minimal communication exists between these two computers. If you were having problems establishing a connection, you could rule out a whole range of possibilities based on this evidence, such as faulty cables or a firewall that was blocking traffic.

If you need more information, tcpdump provides several options that enhance or modify its output. These include -A to display packet contents in ASCII, -D to display a list of interfaces to which tcpdump can listen, -n to display all addresses numerically, -v (and additional -v options, up to -vvv) to display additional packet information, and -w *file* to write the captured packets to the specified *file*. Consult tcpdump's man page for more details on these options and for additional options.

Using Additional Tools

In addition to specialized network diagnostic programs, you can use some common user programs as debugging tools. One of the most useful of these may be Telnet. This program and protocol is mainly a remote login tool; type the program name followed by the name of a remote system to receive a login prompt on that system:

```
$ telnet speaker
Trying 192.168.1.1...
Connected to speaker.
Escape character is '^]'.
speaker login: harry
Password:
Last login: Mon Apr 25 21:48:44 from nessus.example.com
Have a lot of fun...
harry@speaker:~>
```

WARNING   Telnet is a poor choice as a remote login protocol because it's entirely unencrypted. As a general rule, you should remove the Telnet server from your system and never use the telnet client program. It can be a useful lowest-common-denominator protocol on sufficiently protected private networks, though, and the telnet client can also be a handy tool for debugging, as described next. Chapter 10 describes SSH, which is a much safer alternative to Telnet.

You can use Telnet to debug network protocols; if you give it a port number after the remote hostname, the telnet program connects to that port, enabling you to interact with the server:

```
$ telnet speaker 25
Trying 192.168.1.1...
Connected to speaker.
Escape character is '^]'.
220 speaker.example.com ESMTP Postfix
HELO nessus.example.com
250 speaker.example.com
```

This example connects to port 25, which is used by email servers. After connecting, I entered a HELO command, which is used by SMTP to identify a client; the remote system responded with a 250 code, which indicates an accepted command.

Of course, to use Telnet in this way, you must know a great deal about the protocol. Even without this knowledge, though, you can use Telnet to test whether a server is running: If you try to connect but get a Connection refused error message, you know that a remote server isn't running or is inaccessible for some reason (say, because it's being blocked by a firewall). If you get in (to the Escape character message shown in the earlier example or beyond), the server is running, although it may not be working correctly. This test works only for protocols that use TCP. Some tools use UDP instead, and Telnet won't connect with them.

Sometimes the File Transfer Protocol (FTP) can be a useful diagnostic tool, as well. This program, as its name suggests, enables you to transfer files between systems. To use it, type the program name followed by the FTP server's name. You'll then see a login prompt and be able to issue FTP commands:

```
$ ftp speaker
Connected to speaker.
220 (vsFTPd 1.2.1)
Name (speaker:harry): harry
530 Please login with USER and PASS.
SSL not available
331 Please specify the password.
Password:
230 Login successful.
Remote system type is UNIX.
Using binary mode to transfer files.
ftp> get zathras.wav
local: zathras.wav remote: zathras.wav
200 PORT command successful. Consider using PASV.
150 Opening BINARY mode data connection for zathras.wav (109986 bytes).
226 File send OK.
109986 bytes received in 0.104 secs (1e+03 Kbytes/sec)
ftp> quit
221 Goodbye.
```

This example retrieves a single file, `zathras.wav`, from the remote computer. The basic `ftp` client displays a file size, transfer time, and transfer rate (`1e+03 Kbytes/sec`—in other words, 1×103 KiB/s, or 1000 KiB/s). This can be a useful way to test your network transfer speed, although you'll get more reliable results with files that are several hundred kilobytes or larger in size. In addition to `get`, which retrieves files, you can issue commands such as `put` to upload a file; `ls` or `dir` to display the remote system's directory contents; `cd` to change directories on the remote system; `delete` to remove a file; and `quit` or `exit` to exit from the program. You can use the `help` or `?` command to see a list of available `ftp` commands.

Like Telnet, FTP is a poor choice of protocol for security reasons. The same SSH protocol that can substitute for Telnet can also handle most FTP duties. One important exception exists to the rule not to use FTP, though: Anonymous FTP sites are a common method of distributing public files on the Internet. You can download Linux itself from anonymous FTP sites. These sites typically take a username of `anonymous` and any password (your email address is the conventional reply) and give you read access to their contents. In most cases, you can't upload files to anonymous FTP sites, and you can access only a limited number of files.

You can access public FTP sites using a Web browser. Enter a URL that begins with `ftp://`, such as `ftp://downloads.example.org`, and the Web browser connects to the site using FTP rather than HTTP.

Summary

Linux is a network-enabled OS, and it relies on its networking features more than most OSs do. This networking is built around TCP/IP, so you should understand the basics of this protocol stack, including IP addresses, hostnames, and routing. Most Linux distributions provide tools to configure networking during system installation, but if you want to temporarily or permanently change your settings, you can do so. Tools such as `ifconfig` and `route` can temporarily change your network configuration, and editing critical files or running distribution-specific utilities enables you to make your changes permanent.

Exam Essentials

Describe the information needed to configure a computer on a static IP network. Four pieces of information are important: the IP address, the netmask (aka the network mask or subnet mask), the network's gateway address, and the address of at least one DNS server. The first two are required, but if you omit either or both of the latter two, basic networking will function, but you won't be able to connect to the Internet or use most DNS hostnames.

Determine when using /etc/hosts rather than DNS makes the most sense. The /etc/hosts file provides a static mapping of hostnames to IP addresses on a single computer. Therefore, maintaining this file on a handful of computers for a small local network is fairly straightforward, but when the number of computers rises beyond a few or when IP addresses change frequently, running a DNS server to handle local name resolution makes more sense.

Summarize tools you can use to translate between hostnames and IP addresses. The `nslookup` program can perform these translations in both directions using either command-line or interactive modes, but this program has been deprecated. You're better off using `host` for simple lookups or `dig` for more complex tasks.

Describe the function of network ports. Network ports enable packets to be directed to specific programs; each network-enabled program attaches itself to one or more ports, sending data from that port and receiving data directed to the port. Certain ports are assigned to be used by specific servers, enabling client programs to contact servers by directing requests at specific port numbers on the server computers.

Explain when you should use static IP addresses or DHCP. Static IP address configuration involves manually entering the IP address and other information and is used when a network lacks a Dynamic Host Configuration Protocol (DHCP) server or when a computer shouldn't be configured by that server (say, because the computer *is* the DHCP server). DHCP configuration is easier to set up on the client but works only if the network has a DHCP server system.

Explain what the route command accomplishes. The route command displays or modifies the routing table, which tells Linux how to direct packets based on their destination IP addresses.

Describe some basic network diagnostic tools. The ping program tests basic network connectivity, and traceroute and tracepath perform similar but more complex tests that can help you localize where on a route between two systems a problem exists. The netstat utility is a general-purpose network status tool that can report a wide variety of information about your network configuration. Packet sniffers such as tcpdump provide detailed information about the network packets "seen" by a computer, which can be a useful way to verify that certain packet types are actually being sent or received.

Review Questions

1. Which types of network hardware does Linux support? (Select three.)

   A. Token Ring

   B. Ethernet

   C. DHCP

   D. NetBEUI

   E. Fibre Channel

2. Which of the following is a valid IPv4 address for a single computer on a TCP/IP network?

   A. 202.9.257.33

   B. 63.63.63.63

   C. 107.29.5.3.2

   D. 98.7.104.0/24

   E. 255.255.255.255

3. You want to set up a computer on a local network via a static TCP/IP configuration, but you lack a gateway address. Which of the following is true?

   A. Because the gateway address is necessary, no TCP/IP networking functions will work.

   B. TCP/IP networking will function, but you'll be unable to convert hostnames to IP addresses or vice versa.

   C. You'll be able to communicate with machines on your local network segment but not with other systems.

   D. Since a gateway is needed only for IPv6, you'll be able to use IPv4 but not IPv6 protocols.

   E. Without a gateway address available, you'll be unable to use DHCP to simplify configuration.

4. Using a packet sniffer, you notice a lot of traffic directed at TCP port 22 on a local computer. What protocol does this traffic use, assuming it's using the standard port?

   A. HTTP

   B. SMTP

   C. Telnet

   D. SSH

   E. NNTP

5. What network port would an IMAP server normally use for IMAP exchanges?

    A. 21

    B. 25

    C. 110

    D. 143

    E. 443

6. Which of the following are *not* Linux DHCP clients? (Select two.)

    A. pump

    B. dhcpcd

    C. dhcpd

    D. dhclient

    E. ifconfig

7. Which of the following types of information are returned by typing `ifconfig eth0`? (Select two.)

    A. The names of programs that are using eth0

    B. The IP address assigned to eth0

    C. The hardware address of eth0

    D. The hostname associated with eth0

    E. The kernel driver used by eth0

8. Which of the following programs is conventionally used to perform a DNS lookup?

    A. host

    B. dnslookup

    C. pump

    D. ifconfig

    E. netstat

9. Which of the following commands should you type to add to host 192.168.0.10 a default gateway to 192.168.0.1?

    A. `route add default gw 192.168.0.10 192.168.0.1`

    B. `route add default gw 192.168.0.1`

    C. `route add 192.168.0.10 default 192.168.0.1`

    D. `route 192.168.0.10 gw 192.168.0.1`

    E. `route host gw 192.168.0.1`

10. Which of the following commands might bring up an interface on eth1? (Select two.)

    A. dhclient eth1

    B. ifup eth1

    C. ifconfig eth1

    D. network eth1

    E. netstat -up eth1

11. What is the purpose of /etc/hostname, if it's present on the system?

    A. It holds the hostname of a package repository server.

    B. It holds a list of servers that resolve hostnames.

    C. It holds a list of IP addresses and associated hostnames.

    D. It holds the hostname of the local gateway computer.

    E. It holds the computer's default hostname.

12. Network accesses to parts of the Internet work fine, but several common sites have stopped responding (even when addressed via raw IP addresses). Which of the following tools will be most helpful in diagnosing the source of this problem?

    A. netstat

    B. ping

    C. traceroute

    D. ifconfig

    E. dig

13. The ping utility responds normally when you use it with an IP address but not when you use it with a hostname that you're positive corresponds to this IP address. What might cause this problem? (Select two.)

    A. The target computer may be configured to ignore packets from ping.

    B. Your computer's DNS configuration may be broken.

    C. The DNS configuration on the target system may be broken.

    D. The route between your computer and its DNS server may be incorrect.

    E. Your computer's hostname may be set incorrectly in /etc/hostname.

14. How can you learn what programs are currently accessing the network on a Linux system?

    A. Type ifconfig -p eth0.

    B. Examine /proc/network/programs.

    C. Type netstat -p.

    D. Examine /etc/xinetd.conf.

    E. Type dmesg | less.

15. To diagnose a problem with an IMAP server (`imap.example.com`), you type **`telnet imap`** **`.example.com 143`** from a remote client. How can this procedure help you? (Select two.)

   A. You can verify basic connectivity between the client computer and the server program.

   B. By examining the output, you can locate intermediate routers that are misbehaving.

   C. By using an encrypted protocol, you ensure that problems aren't caused by a packet-sniffing intruder.

   D. Once connected, you can type IMAP commands to test the server's response to them.

   E. Once you've logged into the remote system, you can examine its IMAP log files.

16. You're configuring a new system, and your network administrator scribbles its IP address (172.25.78.89), netmask (255.255.255.0), gateway address (172.25.79.1), and DNS server address (10.24.89.201) on a piece of paper. You enter this information into your configuration files and type **`ifup eth0`**, but you find that you can't access the Internet with this computer. Which of the following is definitely true?

   A. Because the DNS server is on a completely different network, it won't function properly for your system. You should ask for the local network's DNS server's IP address.

   B. The netmask identifies the gateway as being on a different network segment than the computer you're configuring, so the two can't communicate directly. You most likely misread one address.

   C. Because the IP addresses involved are private IP addresses, there's no way for them to access the Internet. You must ask for public IP addresses for this system or use only your local private network.

   D. The computer's IP address is a Class B address, but the netmask is for a Class C address. This combination can't work together, so you must obtain a new IP address or netmask.

   E. The `ifup` utility works only for computers that use DHCP, so the use of a static IP address as specified in the question won't work correctly.

17. What is the purpose of the `-n` option to `route`?

   A. It causes no operation to be performed; `route` reports what it would do if `-n` were omitted.

   B. It precedes specification of a netmask when setting the route.

   C. It limits `route`'s output to descriptions of non-Internet routes.

   D. It forces interpretation of a provided address as a network address rather than a host address.

   E. It causes machines to be identified by IP address rather than hostname in output.

18. What is the purpose of `/etc/resolv.conf`?

   A. It holds the names of network protocols and the port numbers with which they're associated.

   B. It controls whether the computer's network options are configured statically or via a DHCP server.

   C. It specifies the IP address of a DHCP server from which the computer attempts to obtain an IP address.

   D. It holds the routing table for the computer, determining the route that network packets take to other computers.

   E. It sets the computer's default search domain and identifies (by IP address) the name servers that the computer may use.

19. Which of the following entries are found in the `/etc/hosts` file?

   A. A list of hosts allowed to remotely access this one

   B. Mappings of IP addresses to hostnames

   C. A list of users allowed to remotely access this host

   D. Passwords for remote Web administration

   E. A list of port numbers and their associated protocols

20. How can you reconfigure Linux to use DNS queries prior to consulting `/etc/hosts`?

   A. Edit the `/etc/resolv.conf` file, and be sure the `nameserver dns` line comes before the `nameserver files` line.

   B. As root, type **nslookup dns**.

   C. Edit the `/etc/named.conf` file, and change the `preferred-resolution` option from `files` to dns.

   D. Edit `/etc/nsswitch.conf`, and change the order of the `files` and `dns` options on the `hosts:` line.

   E. As root, type **dig local dns**.

Chapter

9

Writing Scripts, Configuring Email, and Using Databases

THE FOLLOWING EXAM OBJECTIVES ARE COVERED IN THIS CHAPTER:

- ✓ 1.105.1 Customize and use the shell environment
- ✓ 1.105.2 Customize or write simple scripts
- ✓ 1.105.3 SQL data management
- ✓ 1.108.3 Mail Transfer Agent (MTA) basics

This chapter covers a number of miscellaneous topics. The first of these relate to shell management and scripting. Linux shells (introduced in Chapter 1, "Exploring Linux Command-Line Tools") can be customized in various ways. Knowing how to do this will help you be productive when using Linux. You may even need to set various options to use particular programs, and you may need to make similar changes on a global level so that all your users can work effectively. Managing your shell environment is done, essentially, by modifying standard shell startup scripts, so this chapter covers scripting next. You can write scripts to help automate tedious repetitive tasks or to perform new and complex tasks. Many of Linux's startup functions (described in Chapter 5, "Booting Linux and Editing Files") are performed by scripts, so mastering scripting will help you manage the startup process.

The next major topic of this chapter is Structured Query Language (SQL) data management. Many Linux installations rely on a SQL database to store information, and so you may need at least a minimal grounding in how to interact with SQL databases.

Finally, this chapter describes the basics of email management under Linux. Several Linux email packages exist, and you're not expected to understand the details of their configuration for the exam; however, you should know how to configure mail forwarding, examine mail queues, and otherwise interact with a Linux mail server that's already basically working.

Managing the Shell Environment

Chapter 1 introduced Linux shell use, including topics such as command completion, history, redirection, and the basics of environment variables. Now it's time to go further, with more details about environment variables, aliases, and configuration files. Using this information, you'll be able to customize your shell environment to suit your personal tastes or change the default environment for all the users on your system.

Reviewing Environment Variables

As described in Chapter 1, environment variables provide the means to pass named data (variables) to programs launched from a shell. Shells themselves also rely on environment variables. For instance, $HOSTNAME conventionally holds the computer's name, such as carson.example.com. A program that needs to know the computer's name can refer to $HOSTNAME to obtain this information.

You set an environment variable manually via an equal-sign assignment operator. To make the variable available to programs you launch from your shell, you then use the export command:

```
$ HOSTNAME=carson.example.com
$ export HOSTNAME
```

You can combine these two commands into one for brevity:

```
$ export HOSTNAME=carson.example.com
```

On a bash command line, you can refer to an environment variable by using the echo command to examine a single variable (as in **echo $HOSTNAME**) or by typing **env** to display all the environment variables.

> Environment variable names are usually preceded by a dollar sign ($) in scripts and on shell command lines, except when they're assigned. Getting this detail wrong can produce results you weren't expecting; for instance, typing **echo HOSTNAME** produces the output HOSTNAME rather than the computer's hostname.

Setting an environment variable as just described sets it permanently for the shell or (when used with export) for all programs you launch from it. If you want to set an environment variable for just one program, you can do so with env:

```
$ env DISPLAY=seeker.example.com:0.0 nedit
```

This command launches the nedit program such that it attempts to use the :0.0 display on seeker.example.com rather than the default local display (or whatever the original DISPLAY environment variable specifies; for more on this variable, see the next section). This particular command is not guaranteed to work, though, since it depends on the configuration of seeker.example.com to work. It's actually possible to omit the env command in most cases; however, env can take options that require its use. Most notably, -i or --ignore-environment begins with a completely empty environment, and -u *VARNAME* or --unset=*VARNAME* unsets the specified variable, $*VARNAME*.

Although you can set environment variables manually at a bash prompt, a more common approach is to set them in a global or local bash startup script. These scripts are described in more detail shortly, in "Modifying Shell Configuration Files."

Understanding Common Environment Variables

You may encounter many common environment variables on your system. You can find out how environment variables are configured by typing **env** alone. When it's typed without options, env returns all the environment variables that are currently set, in a format similar to that of bash environment variable assignments:

```
$ env | grep HOSTNAME
```
HOSTNAME=carson.example.com

Of course, the variables you see and their values will be unique to your system and even your account—that's the whole point of environment variables. Table 9.1 summarizes common variables you may see in this output.

TABLE 9.1 Common environment variables and their meanings

Variable name	Explanation
USER or USERNAME	This is your current username. It's a variable that's maintained by the system.
SHELL	This variable holds the path to the current command shell.
PWD	This is the present working directory. This environment variable is maintained by the system. Programs may use it to search for files when you don't provide a complete pathname.
HOSTNAME	This is the current TCP/IP hostname of the computer.
PATH	This is an unusually important environment variable. It sets the *path* for a session, which is a colon-delimited list of directories in which Linux searches for executable programs when you type a program name. For instance, if PATH is /bin:/usr/bin and you type **ls**, Linux looks for an executable program called ls in /bin and then in /usr/bin. If the command you type isn't on the path, Linux responds with a command not found error. The PATH variable is typically built up in several configuration files, such as /etc/profile and the .bashrc file in the user's home directory.
HOME	This variable points to your home directory. Some programs use it to help them look for configuration files or as a default location in which to store files.
MAIL	This variable holds the location of the user's mail spool. It's usually /var/spool/mail/*username*.
LANG	The system holds your current language, specified as a locale, using this variable. Locales are described further in Chapter 6, "Configuring the X Window System, Localization, and Printing."
TZ	You can set this environment variable to your own time zone, which is most useful if that's different than the computer's time zone—for instance, if you're using a computer remotely. Chapter 6 describes the formats you can use when setting the time zone in this way.

LD_LIBRARY_PATH   A few programs use this environment variable to indicate directories in which library files may be found. It works much like PATH.

PS1   This is the default prompt in bash. It generally includes variables of its own, such as \u (for the username), \h (for the hostname), and \W (for the current working directory). This value is frequently set in /etc/profile, but it's often overridden by users.

TERM   This variable is the name of the current terminal type. To move a text-mode cursor and display text effects for programs like text-mode editors, Linux has to know what commands the terminal supports. The TERM environment variable specifies the terminal in use. This information is combined with data from additional files to provide terminal-specific code information. TERM is normally set automatically at login, but in some cases you may need to change it.

DISPLAY   This variable identifies the display used by X. It's usually :0.0, which means the first (numbered from 0) display on the current computer. When you use X in a networked environment, though, this value may be preceded by the name of the computer at which you're sitting, as in machine4.luna.edu:0.0. This value is set automatically when you log in, but you may change it if necessary. You can run multiple X sessions on one computer, in which case each one gets a different DISPLAY number—for instance, :0.0 for the first session and :1.0 for the second.

EDITOR   Some programs launch the program pointed to by this environment variable when they need to call a text editor for you to use. Thus, changing this variable to your favorite editor can help you work in Linux. It's best to set this variable to a text-mode editor, though; GUI editors may cause problems if they're called from a program that was launched from a text-mode login.

WARNING   The PATH variable sometimes includes the current directory indicator (.) so that you can easily run programs in the current directory. This practice poses a security risk, though, because a miscreant can create a program with the same name as some other program (such as ls) and trick another user into running it by simply leaving it in a directory the victim frequents. Even the root user may be victimized this way. For this reason, it's best to omit the current directory from the PATH variable, especially for the super-user. If it's really needed for ordinary users, put it at the end of the path.

Any given system is likely to have several other environment variables set, but these are fairly esoteric or relate to specific programs. If a program's documentation says that it needs certain environment variables set, you can set them system-wide in /etc/profile or some other suitable file, or you can set them in user configuration files, as you deem appropriate.

Although you can see the entire environment by typing **env**, this output can be long enough to be intimidating. If you just want to know the value of one variable, you can use the echo command, which echoes to the screen what you type. If you pass it a variable name preceded by a dollar sign ($), echo returns the value of the variable. Here's an example:

```
$ echo $PS1
[\u@\h \W]\$
```

This command reveals that the PS1 environment variable is set to [\u@\h \W]\$, which in turn produces a bash prompt like [david@penguin homes]$. Exercise 9.1 illustrates how you can change your bash prompt.

EXERCISE 9.1

Changing Your bash Prompt

This exercise describes how to change your bash prompt to show the current time and number of jobs managed by the shell. To accomplish this task, follow these steps:

1. Log into the Linux system as a normal user.

2. Launch an xterm from the desktop environment's menu system, if you used a GUI login method.

3. Type **export PS1="\T; \j jobs> "**. The backslash (\) is an escape character that denotes special data to be inserted into the prompt when used in the PS1 environment variable. \T is expanded into the current time in 12-hour format, and \j is expanded into the number of jobs the shell manages. The man page for bash has a complete list of expansions the PS1 variable accepts. The result of typing this command should be an immediate change in your prompt to resemble something like 04:42; 0 jobs>.

4. Wait for a minute, and then run a program in the background by typing its name and appending an ampersand (&). For instance, you can type **xeyes &** to run the xeyes program from an xterm. You should see the number of jobs increase, and the time should change.

5. To make this change permanent, edit the .bashrc file in your home directory. Load this file into your favorite editor, and add a line to its end that reads export PS1="\T; \j jobs> ". Save the file, and exit the editor. (Shell configuration files are described in more detail shortly, in "Modifying Shell Configuration Files.")

6. To test your change to .bashrc, log out and then log back in again. Instead of your distribution's default prompt, you should see the new one.

7. If you don't like the new prompt, edit .bashrc again and delete the line you added in step 5.

Using Aliases

Most Linux shells, including bash, support command *aliases*, which are new names you can give to regular commands. Typically, you'll use aliases to assign easier-to-remember names to obscure commands, to implement desirable command options as the default for commands, or to create a shortened version of a command to minimize the amount of typing you must do. You can define aliases in a one-off fashion at any bash prompt, but they're typically included in your bash startup scripts, as described shortly in "Modifying Shell Configuration Files."

To implement an alias, you use the following syntax:

```
alias alias_name='commands'
```

The *alias_name* is what you want to type at the command prompt, and the shell substitutes *commands* for whatever you type. As an example, consider the ls command, which lists the contents of a directory. A popular option for this command is --color, which color-codes the output, giving directories, links, and other special files particular colors to make them stand out. If you want to use this option as the default, you can use alias:

```
$ alias ls='ls --color'
```

In this example, ls becomes an alias for an extended version of itself. This doesn't result in recursion—that is, the ls to the right of the equal sign is *not* expanded. After you type this alias command, typing **ls** will work as if you'd typed **ls --color**. In fact, this particular alias is popular enough that it's included as a standard part of many distributions' bash startup scripts.

You can use an alias name that's unrelated to the original command name. For instance, suppose you want to type bye instead of logout to terminate a text-mode login session. You can do so with alias:

```
$ alias bye='logout'
```

In practice, this particular alias isn't likely to be useful if you type it manually at a command prompt, because you'll log out of a session only once. You might want to include it in a bash startup script, though. If you do that, then you won't need to type the alias manually at each session; it will be created automatically whenever you log in.

Modifying Shell Configuration Files

Configuring shells requires editing shell configuration files. These files can be classified in a couple of ways. First, files may be global files that affect all users of a shell or local files that affect just one user. Second, files may be login files that are launched only by a login process (such as a text-mode console login) or non-login files that are launched by other processes (such as when starting an xterm window). The result is a 2 × 2 matrix of configuration files, as shown in Table 9.2. (This table shows only bash configuration files; consult your shell's documentation if you're using another shell.)

TABLE 9.2   Common bash configuration files

Type of file	Login file location	Non-login file location
Global	`/etc/profile` and files in `/etc/profile.d`	`/etc/bashrc` or `/etc/bash.bashrc`
User	`~/.bash_login`, `~/.profile`, or `~/.bash_profile`	`~/.bashrc`

Precisely which of these files are used differs from one distribution to another. No matter the name, though, these files are shell scripts. Shell scripting is described in more detail later, in "Writing Scripts," but most bash startup scripts contain a series of commands. These commands may include both built-in bash commands and external commands.

Global configuration files affect all users of a system; however, their settings may be overridden by individual users, either in user configuration files or in commands the users type themselves. Thus, you shouldn't rely on global configuration files to set options that shouldn't be changed by users. For that, you should look to global security features, such as permissions on executable files.

The `/etc/skel` directory holds files that are copied to individual users' home directories when their accounts are created. These files are sometimes called *skeleton files*. Typically, this set of files includes local bash startup files. You can examine these files and, if necessary, alter them to suit your local needs. Changes to these files affect only new accounts, not existing accounts. If you want to make a change that affects both existing and new users, you should edit a global configuration file instead.

Just as shells have startup scripts, they may also have logout scripts—scripts that run when the user logs out. For bash, this script is `~/.bash_logout`. Most distributions don't create this script as part of users' default home directories, but individual users can do so. The logout script might execute programs to clean up temporary directories, remove security keys from memory, clear the screen, or perform other tasks that are appropriate when a user logs out.

WARNING   One problem with logout scripts is that they may not work well when users log in multiple times. If you regularly have multiple sessions open, such as logins in multiple Linux virtual terminals, be careful about what you do in a logout script lest you wipe out important temporary files when you log out of just one session.

Another bash configuration file is `~/.inputrc`, which helps customize your keyboard configuration. It consists of lines that look like this:

```
M-Control-u: universal-argument
```

This line maps the Meta-Ctrl+U keystroke to the `universal-argument` action. The Meta key is usually the Esc key on *x*86 or *x*86-64 systems, and the `universal-argument` action is one of many possible actions defined by the readline library, which is one of the basic text-mode input libraries used by Linux.

In most cases, there's no need to adjust the ~/.inputrc file, because the default readline mappings work well for *x*86 systems with standard keyboards. If you find that certain key-strokes don't work the way they should in text mode, though, you may want to research this configuration file further.

X uses its own keyboard input routines, so ~/.inputrc doesn't affect pro-grams run in X, even text-mode programs run inside xterm windows.

Writing Scripts

You'll do much of your work on a Linux system by typing commands at a shell prompt. As you use Linux, though, you're likely to find some of these tasks to be repetitive. If you need to add 100 new users to the system, for instance, typing **useradd** 100 times can be tedious. Fortunately, Linux includes a way to cut through the tedium: *shell scripts*. These are simple programs written in an interpreted computer language that's embedded in the Linux shell you use to type commands.

Most Linux systems use bash by default, so shell scripts are often written in the bash shell scripting language; but tcsh and other shell scripting languages are similar. In fact, it's not uncommon to see shell scripts that run in any common Linux shell. You're not restricted to running shell scripts written in your default shell, however; the first line of a shell script identifies the shell that should be used to run it.

Many Linux startup scripts, including SysV startup scripts, are in fact shell scripts. Therefore, understanding shell scripting is necessary if you want to modify a Linux startup script.

Like any programming task, shell scripting can be quite complex. Conse-quently, this chapter barely scratches the surface of what can be accom-plished through shell scripting. Consult a book on the topic, such as Cameron Newham's *Learning the Bash Shell, 3rd Edition* (O'Reilly, 2005) or Richard Blum and Christine Bresnahan's *Linux Command Line and Shell Scripting Bible, 2nd Edition* (Wiley, 2011), for more information.

To create a shell script, you must first know how to begin editing one. Once you do so, you'll find that one of the easiest tasks to do is to call external commands. More advanced tasks include using variables and using conditional expressions.

Beginning a Shell Script

Shell scripts are plain-text files, so you create them in text editors. A shell script begins with a line that identifies the shell that's used to run it, such as the following:

```
#!/bin/sh
```

The first two characters are a special code that tells the Linux kernel that this is a script and to use the rest of the line as a pathname to the program that's to interpret the script. (This line is sometimes called the *shebang, hashbang, hashpling,* or *pound bang* line.) Shell scripting languages use a hash mark (#) as a comment character, so the script utility ignores this line, although the kernel doesn't. On most systems, /bin/sh is a symbolic link that points to /bin/bash, but it can point to some other shell. Specifying the script as using /bin/sh guarantees that any Linux system will have a shell program to run the script; but if the script uses any features specific to a particular shell, you should specify that shell instead—for instance, use /bin/bash or /bin/tcsh instead of /bin/sh.

When you're done writing the shell script, you should modify it so that it's executable. You do this with the chmod command, as described in Chapter 4, "Managing Files." Specifically, you use the +x option to add execute permissions, probably in conjunction with a to add these permissions for all users. For instance, to make a file called my-script executable, you should issue the following command:

```
$ chmod a+x my-script
```

You'll then be able to execute the script by typing its name, possibly preceded by ./ to tell Linux to run the script in the current directory rather than searching the current path. If you fail to make the script executable, you can still run the script by running the shell program followed by the script name (as in **bash my-script**), but it's generally better to make the script executable. If the script is one you run regularly, you may want to move it to a location on your path, such as /usr/local/bin. When you do that, you won't have to type the complete path or move to the script's directory to execute it; you can just type **my-script**.

> **WARNING**   It's possible to set a script's SUID or SGID bits. (See Chapter 4 for information about the SUID and SGID bits.) Doing so is potentially dangerous, particularly if the script is owned by root, for reasons described in Chapter 4. You should therefore be very cautious about applying the SUID bit to scripts.

Another way to run a script requires mention: *sourcing* it. You can source a script by using the source keyword or a dot (.), as follows:

```
$ source my-script
$ . my-script
```

Sourcing a script causes it to run *in the current shell*, as opposed to launching a new instance of the shell, as occurs when you run a script by typing its name alone or using the exec command, as described in Chapter 1. This has some important implications:

- When you source a script, it will have access to environment variables set in the calling shell, even if you haven't exported them. Ordinarily, only environment variables that you explicitly export become available to scripts you run.

- If you source a script and if that script sets an environment variable, that variable will become available (or will be changed) in the calling shell. If you run the script normally, any environment variables it sets will remain local to it and to the programs that it calls, even if the script exports the variables.

- Running a script in the normal ways imposes overhead costs associated with launching the new shell. These costs are normally negligible, but if a script calls itself recursively or calls many other scripts, sourcing those scripts within the first script may improve performance.

- Sourcing a script causes it to execute in the calling shell's language, whereas running a script normally causes it to use the shell language specified on the hashbang line.

Using Commands

One of the most basic features of shell scripts is the ability to run commands. You can use both shell internal commands and external commands. Most of the commands you type in a shell prompt are external commands—they're programs located in /bin, /usr/bin, and other directories on your path. You can run such programs, as well as internal commands, by including their names in the script. You can also specify parameters to such programs in a script. For instance, suppose you want a script that launches two xterm windows and the KMail mail reader program. Listing 9.1 presents a shell script that accomplishes this goal.

Listing 9.1: A simple script that launches three programs

```
#!/bin/bash
/usr/bin/xterm &
/usr/bin/xterm &
/usr/bin/kmail &
```

Aside from the first line that identifies it as a script, the script looks just like the commands you might type to accomplish the task manually, except for one fact: The script lists the complete paths to each program. This is usually not strictly necessary, but listing the complete path ensures that the script will find the programs even if the PATH environment variable changes. On the other hand, if the program files move (say, because you upgrade the package from which they're installed and the packager decides to move them), scripts that use complete paths will break.

Each program-launch line in Listing 9.1 ends in an ampersand (&). This character tells the shell to go on to the next line without waiting for the first to finish. If you omit the ampersands in Listing 9.1, the effect will be that the first xterm will open but the second won't open until the first is closed. Likewise, KMail won't start until the second xterm terminates.

Although launching several programs from one script can save time in starting your working environment and some other situations, scripts are also frequently used to run a series of programs that manipulate data in some way. Such scripts typically do *not* include the ampersands at the ends of the commands because one command must run after another or may even rely on output from the first. A comprehensive list of such commands is impossible because you can run any program you can install in Linux as a command in a script—even another script. A few commands that are commonly used in scripts include the following:

Normal File Manipulation Commands   The file manipulation commands, such as ls, mv, cp, and rm, are often used in scripts. You can use these commands to help automate repetitive file maintenance tasks.

grep   This command is described in Chapter 1. It locates files that contain specific strings.

find   Where grep searches for patterns within the contents of files, find does so based on filenames, ownership, and similar characteristics. This command is described in Chapter 4.

cut   This command extracts text from fields in a file. It's frequently used to extract variable information from a file whose contents are highly patterned. To use it, you pass it one or more options that specify what information you want, followed by one or more filenames. For instance, users' home directories appear in the sixth colon-delimited field of the /etc/passwd file. You can therefore type **cut -f 6 -d ":" /etc/passwd** to extract this information. The same command in a script will extract this information, which you'll probably save to a variable or pass to a subsequent command via a pipe.

sed   This program is described in Chapter 1. It provides many of the capabilities of a conventional text editor but via commands that can be typed at a command prompt or entered in a script.

echo   Sometimes a script must provide a message to the user; echo is the tool to accomplish this goal. You can pass various options to echo or just a string to be shown to the user. For instance, echo "Press the Enter key" causes a script to display the specified string.

mail   The mail command can be used to send email from within a script. Pass it the -s *subject* parameter to specify a subject line, and give it an email address as the last argument. If used at the command line, you then type a message and terminate it with a Ctrl+D keystroke. If used from a script, you might omit the subject entirely, pass it an external file as the message using input redirection, or use a here document to pass text to the mail command as input. (Chapter 1 describes input redirection and here documents.) You might want to use this command to send mail to the superuser about the actions of a startup script or a script that runs on an automated basis. This command is described in more detail later in this chapter.

Many of these commands are extremely complex, and completely describing them is beyond the scope of this chapter. You can consult these commands' man pages for more information. A few of them are described elsewhere in this book.

Even if you have a full grasp of how to use some key external commands, simply executing commands you might when typing them at a command prompt is of limited utility. Many administrative tasks require you to modify what you type at a command, or even what commands you enter, depending on information from other commands. For this reason, scripting languages include additional features to help you make your scripts useful.

Using Variables

Variables can help you expand the utility of scripts. A variable is a placeholder in a script for a value that will be determined when the script runs. Variables' values can be passed as parameters to scripts, generated internally to the scripts, or extracted from the script's environment.

Variables that are passed to the script are frequently called *parameters*. They're represented by a dollar sign ($) followed by a number from 0 to 9—$0 stands for the name of the script, $1 is the first parameter to the script, $2 is the second parameter, and so on. To understand how this might be useful, consider the task of adding a user. As described in Chapter 7, "Administering the System," creating an account for a new user typically involves running at least two commands—useradd and passwd. You may also need to run additional site-specific commands, such as commands that create unusual user-owned directories aside from the user's home directory.

The shift command shifts the parameter variables so that what would ordinarily be $2 becomes $1, what would be $3 becomes $2, and so on. Adding a number, as in shift 3, shifts the assignments by that number of units. The shift command does not alter the $0 variable, though. You can use shift in conjunction with a loop (described later, in "Using Loops") to examine all of the parameters passed to a script, in case their order or number is unknown when you write the script.

As an example of how a script with a parameter variable can help in such situations, consider Listing 9.2. This script creates an account and changes the account's password (you'll be prompted to enter the password when you run the script). It creates a directory in the /shared directory tree corresponding to the account, and it sets a symbolic link to that directory from the new user's home directory. It also adjusts ownership and permissions in a way that may be useful, depending on your system's ownership and permissions policies.

Listing 9.2: A script that reduces account-creation tedium

```
#!/bin/sh
useradd -m $1
passwd $1
mkdir -p /shared/$1
chown $1.users /shared/$1
chmod 775 /shared/$1
ln -s /shared/$1 /home/$1/shared
chown $1.users /home/$1/shared
```

If you use Listing 9.2, you need type only three things: the script name with the desired username and the password (twice). For instance, if the script is called mkuser, you can use it like this:

```
# mkuser ajones
Changing password for user ajones
New password:
Retype new password:
passwd: all authentication tokens updated successfully
```

Most of the scripts' programs operate silently unless they encounter problems, so the interaction (including typing the passwords, which don't echo to the screen) is a result of just the passwd command. In effect, Listing 9.2's script replaces seven lines of commands with one. Every one of those lines uses the username, so by running this script, you also reduce the chance of a typo causing problems.

Another type of variable is assigned within scripts—for instance, such variables can be set from the output of a command. These variables are also identified by leading dollar signs, but they're typically given names that at least begin with a letter, such as $Addr or $Name. (When values are assigned to variables, the dollar sign is omitted, as illustrated shortly.) You can then use these variables in conjunction with normal commands as if they were command parameters, but the value of the variable is passed to the command.

For instance, consider Listing 9.3, which checks to see whether the computer's router is up with the help of the ping utility. This script uses two variables. The first is $ip, which is extracted from the output of route using the grep, tr, and cut commands. (These commands are described in Chapter 1.) When you're assigning a value to a variable from the output of a command, that command should be enclosed in back-tick characters (`), which appear on the same key as the tilde (~) on most keyboards. These are *not* ordinary single quotes, which appear on the same key as the regular quote character (") on most keyboards. The second variable, $ping, simply points to the ping program. It can easily be omitted, with subsequent uses of $ping replaced by the full path to the program or simply by ping (relying on the $PATH environment variable to find the program). Variables like this are sometimes used to make it easier to modify the script in the future. For instance, if you move the `ping` program, you need only modify one line of the script. Variables that point to binaries can also be used in conjunction with conditionals to ensure that the script works on more systems—for instance, if `ping` were called something else on some systems.

Listing 9.3: Script demonstrating assignment and use of variables

```
#!/bin/sh
ip=`route -n | grep UG | tr -s " " | cut -f 2 -d " "`
ping="/bin/ping"
echo "Checking to see if $ip is up..."
$ping -c 5 $ip
```

In practice, you use Listing 9.3 by typing the script's name. The result should be the message Checking to see if *192.168.1.1* is up (with *192.168.1.1* replaced by the computer's default gateway system) and the output from the `ping` command, which should attempt to send five packets to the router. If the router is up and is configured to respond to pings, you'll see five return packets and summary information. If the router is down, you'll see error messages to the effect that the host was unreachable.

Listing 9.3 is of limited practical use and contains bugs. For instance, the script identifies the computer's gateway merely by the presence of the string UG in the router's output line from route. If a computer has two routers defined, this won't work correctly, and the result is likely to be a script that misbehaves. The point of Listing 9.3 is not to be a flawless program but to demonstrate how variables can be assigned and used.

Scripts like Listing 9.3, which obtain information from running one or more commands, are useful in configuring features that rely on system-specific information or information that varies with time. You can use a similar approach to obtain the current hostname (using the `hostname` command), the current time (using `date`), the total time the computer's been running (using `uptime`), free disk space (using `df`), and so on. When combined with conditional expressions (described shortly), variables become even more powerful because then your script can perform one action when one condition is met, and another in some other case. For instance, a script that installs software can check free disk space and abort the installation if insufficient disk space is available.

In addition to assigning variables with the assignment operator (=), you can read variables from standard input using `read`, as in `read response` to read input for subsequent access as `$response`. This method of variable assignment is useful for scripts that must interact with users. For instance, instead of reading the username from the command line, Listing 9.2 may be modified to prompt the user for the username. Listing 9.4 shows the result. To use this script, you type its name *without* typing a username on the command line. The script will then prompt for a username, and after you enter one, the script will attempt to create an account with that name.

Listing 9.4: Modified version of Listing 9.2 that employs user interaction

```
#!/bin/sh
echo -n "Enter a username: "
read name
useradd -m $name
passwd $name
mkdir -p /shared/$name
chown $name.users /shared/$name
chmod 775 /shared/$name
ln -s /shared/$name /home/$name/shared
chown $name.users /home/$name/shared
```

One special type of variable was mentioned earlier in this chapter: environment variables, described in "Managing the Shell Environment." Environment variables are assigned and accessed just like shell script variables. The difference is that the script or command that sets an environment variable uses the export command (in bash) to make the value of the variable accessible to programs launched from the shell or shell script that made the assignment. In other words, you can set an environment variable in one script and use it in another script that the first script launches. Environment variables are most often set in shell startup scripts, but the scripts you use can access them. For instance, if your script calls X programs, it might check for the presence of a valid $DISPLAY environment variable and abort if it finds that this variable isn't set. By convention, environment variable names are all uppercase, whereas non-environment shell script variables are all lowercase or mixed case.

Using Conditional Expressions

Scripting languages support several types of *conditional expressions*. These expressions enable a script to perform one of several actions contingent on some condition—typically the value of a variable. One common command that uses conditional expressions is if, which allows the system to take one of two actions depending on whether some condition is true. The if keyword's conditional expression appears in brackets after the if keyword and can take many forms. For instance, -f *file* is true if *file* exists and is a regular file; -s *file* is true if *file* exists and has a size greater than 0; and *string1* == *string2* is true if the two strings have the same values. (Typically, one or both strings is a variable.) Conditionals may be combined together with the logical and (&&) or logical or (||) operators. When conditionals are combined with &&, both sides of the operator must be true for the condition as a whole to be true. When || is used, if either side of the operator is true, the condition as a whole is true.

To better understand the use of conditionals, consider the following code fragment:

```
if [ -s /tmp/tempstuff ]
   then
```

```
      echo "/tmp/tempstuff found; aborting!"
      exit
fi
```

This fragment causes the script to exit if the file /tmp/tempstuff is present and is larger than 0 bytes. The then keyword marks the beginning of a series of lines that execute only if the conditional is true, and fi (if backward) marks the end of the if block. Such code may be useful if the script creates and then later deletes this file, because its presence indicates that a previous run of the script didn't succeed or is still underway.

An alternative form for a conditional expression uses the test keyword rather than square brackets around the conditional:

```
if test -s /tmp/tempstuff
```

You can also test a command's return value by using the command as the condition:

```
if [ command ]
   then
       additional-commands
fi
```

In this example, the *additional-commands* will be run only if *command* completes successfully. If *command* returns an error code, the *additional-commands* won't be run. Conditional expressions may be expanded by use of the else clause:

```
if [ conditional-expression ]
   then
       commands
   else
       other-commands
fi
```

Code of this form causes either *commands* or *other-commands* to execute, depending on the evaluation of *conditional-expression*. This is useful if *something* should happen in a part of the program but precisely what should happen depends on some condition. For instance, you may want to launch one of two different file archiving programs depending on a user's input.

What do you do if more than two outcomes are possible—for instance, if a user may provide any one of four possible inputs? You can nest several if/then/else clauses, but this gets awkward very quickly. A cleaner approach is to use case:

```
case word in
   pattern1) command(s) ;;
   pattern2) command(s) ;;
   ...
esac
```

For a case statement, a *word* is likely to be a variable, and each *pattern* is a possible value of that variable. The patterns can be expanded much like filenames, using the same wildcards and expansion rules (* to stand for any string, for instance). You can match an arbitrary number of patterns in this way. Each set of commands must end with a double semicolon (;;), and the case statement as a whole ends in the string esac (case backward).

Upon execution, bash executes the commands associated with the first pattern to match the *word*. Execution then jumps to the line following the esac statement; any intervening commands don't execute. If no patterns match the word, no code within the case statement executes. If you want to have a default condition, use * as the final *pattern*; this pattern matches any *word*, so its commands will execute if no other *pattern* matches.

Using Loops

Conditional expressions are sometimes used in *loops*. Loops are structures that tell the script to perform the same task repeatedly until some condition is met (or until some condition is no longer met). For instance, Listing 9.5 shows a loop that plays all the .wav audio files in a directory.

Listing 9.5: A script that executes a command on every matching file in a directory

```
#!/bin/bash
for d in `ls *.wav` ; do
    aplay $d
done
```

The aplay command is a basic audio file player that works with the Advanced Linux Sound Architecture (ALSA) audio drivers. On some systems, you may need to use play or some other command instead of aplay.

The for loop as used here executes once for every item in the list generated by ls *.wav. Each of those items (filenames) is assigned in turn to the $d variable and so is passed to the aplay command.

The seq command can be useful in creating for loops (and in other ways, too): This command generates a list of numbers starting from its first argument and continuing to its last one. For instance, typing **seq 1 10** generates 10 lines, each with a number between 1 and 10. You can use a for loop beginning for x in `seq 1 10` to have the loop execute 10 times, with the value of $x incrementing with each iteration. If you pass just one parameter to seq, it interprets that number as an ending point, with the starting point being 1. If you pass three values to seq, it interprets them as a starting value, an increment amount, and an ending value.

Another type of loop is the while loop, which executes for as long as its condition is true. The basic form of this loop type is like this:

```
while [ condition ]
do
    commands
done
```

The `until` loop is similar in form, but it continues execution for as long as its condition is *false*—that is, until the condition becomes true.

Using Functions

A *function* is a part of a script that performs a specific subtask and that can be called by name from other parts of the script. Functions are defined by placing parentheses after the function name and enclosing the lines that make up the function within curly braces:

```
myfn() {
    commands
}
```

The keyword `function` may optionally precede the function name. In either event, the function is called by name as if it were an ordinary internal or external command.

Functions are very useful in helping to create modular scripts. For instance, if your script needs to perform half a dozen distinct computations, you may place each computation in a function and then call them all in sequence. Listing 9.6 demonstrates the use of functions in a simple program that copies a file but aborts with an error message if the target file already exists. This script accepts a target and a destination filename and must pass those filenames to the functions.

Listing 9.6: A script demonstrating the use of functions

```
#/bin/bash
doit() {
   cp $1 $2
}
function check() {
  if [ -s $2 ]
     then
         echo "Target file exists! Exiting!"
         exit
  fi
}
check $1 $2
doit $1 $2
```

If you enter Listing 9.6 and call it safercp, you can use it like this, assuming the file original.txt exists and dest.txt doesn't:

```
$ ./safercp original.txt dest.txt
$ ./safercp original.txt dest.txt
Target file exists! Exiting!
```

The first run of the command succeeded because dest.txt didn't exist. When the command was run a second time, though, the destination file did exist, so the program terminated with the error message.

Note that the functions aren't run directly and in the order in which they appear in the script. They're run only when called in the main body of the script (which in Listing 9.6 consists of just two lines, each corresponding to one function call).

Shell scripts are useful tools, and creating them requires practice. Exercise 9.2 begins your exploration of shell scripts, but in the long run you'll need to learn to design your own shell scripts by doing more than copying examples from a book.

EXERCISE 9.2

Creating a Simple Script

This exercise presents a shell script that gives you the option of using less to read every text file (with a name ending in .txt) in the current directory. To begin with this script, follow these steps:

1. Log into the Linux system as a normal user.

2. Launch an xterm from the desktop environment's menu system, if you used a GUI login method.

3. Start an editor, and tell it to edit a file called testscript.

4. Type the following lines into the editor:

   ```
   #!/bin/bash
   for file in `ls *.txt` ; do
     echo -n "Display $file? "
     read answer
     if [ $answer == 'y' ]
       then
           less $file
     fi
   done
   ```

   Be sure you've typed every character correctly; any mistake may cause the script to misbehave. One common error is mistyping the back-tick characters (`` ` ``) on the second line as ordinary single-quote characters (').

5. Save the file, and exit the editor.

6. Type **chmod a+x testscript** to add the executable bit to the file's permissions.

7. Type **./testscript** to run the script. If there are no text (*.txt) files in your current directory, the script displays a no such file or directory error message; but if any text files are present, the script gives you the option of viewing each one in turn via less.

This example script is extremely limited, but it illustrates several important script features, such as variable assignment and use, for loops, and if/then conditional expressions.

Managing Email

Email is one of the most important network services. What's more, Linux relies on email even in a completely non-networked environment—certain Linux subsystems, such as cron (described in Chapter 7), may use email to notify you of activities. For this reason, most Linux distributions ship with email server software installed and configured for basic activities, and you should have a basic understanding of how to use these servers to accomplish various tasks. You should understand the basics of email and be able to identify the specific email server package your system is running. You should also be able to set up email aliases (alternate names for users) and forwarding (to send mail for a user to another destination). Finally, you should understand the security implications of email so that you can prevent problems or identify them when they occur.

Understanding Email

Several protocols exist to manage email. The most common of these is the *Simple Mail Transfer Protocol* (SMTP), which is designed as a push mail protocol, meaning that the sending system initiates the transfer. This design is good for sending data, so SMTP is used through most of a mail delivery system. The final stage, though, often employs a pull mail protocol, such as the *Post Office Protocol* (POP) or the *Internet Message Access Protocol* (IMAP). With these protocols, the receiving system initiates the transfer. This is useful when the receiving system is an end user's workstation, which may not be powered on at all times or able to receive incoming connections.

SMTP was designed to enable a message to be relayed through an arbitrary number of computers. For instance, an end user may compose a message, which is sent to the local SMTP server. (SMTP servers are also known as mail transfer agents, or MTAs.) This server looks up a recipient system using the Domain Name System (DNS) and sends the message to that computer. This system may use its own internal routing table to redirect the message to another local computer, from which the message may be read, either directly or via a POP or IMAP server. This arrangement is illustrated in Figure 9.1. Bear in mind that the number of links in this chain is variable and depends on how each system is configured. In the simplest case, local email stays on just one system. In theory, an arbitrarily large number of computers can be involved in an email exchange, although in practice it's rare to see email pass through more than half a dozen systems.

At each step in a relay chain, email is altered. Most important, each server adds a *header* to the email, which is a line that provides information about the message. In particular, mail servers add Received: headers to document the path the mail has taken. In theory, this enables you to trace the email back to its source. Unfortunately, spammers and other email abusers have learned to forge email headers, which greatly complicates such analysis.

FIGURE 9.1   Email typically traverses several links between sender and recipient.

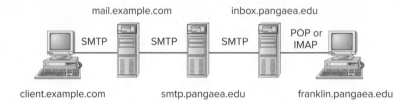

Because an SMTP server can function as both a server (receiving mail from other systems) and a client (sending mail to other systems), you must deal with both sides of the configuration equation. For the most part, this chapter and the exam don't cover all these details, though, just a few of them. Sometimes a computer never functions in one role or the other, which can simplify matters—but you must then be careful not to accidentally configure the computer incorrectly. In particular, *open relay* configurations, in which a mail server relays mail from anybody, should be avoided. This and other security implications of running an SMTP server are covered in "Securing Your Email Server."

On Linux, email is tied intricately to user accounts. The mail server holds incoming messages for each user, typically in a file in /var/spool/mail—for instance, /var/spool/mail/benf holds mail for the user benf. Some email servers store incoming mail in subdirectories of the users' home directories, though. This incoming mail file or directory is referred to as the user's mail spool.

You may recall that the userdel command, described in Chapter 7, includes options related to the handling of users' mail spools. If you delete a user account but leave the user's mail spool intact, the mail can still be accessed. If the mail server software stores mail in /var/spool/mail, leftover mail spools can cause problems if you eventually re-use an old username. Email can be sent as well as received. The traditional Linux approach to sending email is to have local programs contact the local mail server to send email. The local mail server then contacts its outgoing email server, as in Figure 9.1. Most Linux email clients (aka mail user agents, or MUAs), as well as similar programs on other platforms, provide the option to directly contact a remote SMTP server when sending email. Such a configuration slightly simplifies the email path but can make operation unreliable if the local network link goes down. If your email client talks to an SMTP server that runs locally, the email can be queued for delivery by the SMTP server even if the network is temporarily down.

Choosing Email Software

Linux supports quite a few email servers. Chances are, one of the major servers will be installed on your system by default. If not and if you want to install one, you'll have to pick one. You may also want to change your email server if you need to configure it in advanced ways; some servers are easier to configure than others or support specific options that others don't. Four email servers are most popular on Linux:

Sendmail   The sendmail program (http://www.sendmail.org) was for many years the dominant email server package on the Internet. In recent years it's lost some of its dominance to the other servers described here, as well as to Windows email servers. Nonetheless, sendmail remains a popular server. It's very powerful, but it's also difficult to configure because its configuration file formats are rather arcane.

Postfix   Postfix (http://www.postfix.org) was designed as a modular replacement for sendmail—rather than a single program that does everything (as sendmail is designed), Postfix uses multiple programs, each of which handles its own specific small task. This design improves security, at least in theory. Postfix tends to be easier to configure than sendmail, and it's become the default email server on many Linux distributions.

Exim   Although Exim (http://www.exim.org) is a monolithic server, like sendmail, it has a much simpler configuration file format and so is easier to configure. A few Linux distributions use Exim as the default email server.

qmail   The fourth major Linux email server, qmail (http://www.qmail.org), is a modular server with security as a major design goal. Like Postfix and Exim, qmail is easier to configure than sendmail. It's not the standard email server in any Linux distribution because its license is a bit strange and complicates qmail distribution with Linux; however, many system administrators like qmail enough that they replace their distributions' standard email servers with qmail.

You learn which email server your Linux distribution runs have several ways to. The two most reliable are to use ps (described in Chapter 2, "Managing Software") to look for running processes or to use your package management tools (also described in Chapter 2) to see which package is installed. In either case, you may need to check for each of the programs in turn. For instance, you might see results like these:

```
$ ps ax | grep send
31129 pts/2    R+     0:00 grep send
$ ps ax | grep post
 7778 ?        Ss     0:45 /usr/lib/postfix/master
31132 pts/2    S+     0:00 grep post
```

The search for a process containing the string *send* failed, but the search for *post* returned a process called /usr/lib/postfix/master—thus, it appears that Postfix is running on this system.

You can also look for executable filenames for each email server in /usr/bin or /usr/sbin; but be aware that most Linux email servers include a program called sendmail. This is done for compatibility reasons; because the original sendmail program was once ubiquitous, providing a compatible interface for scripts and administrators helps other SMTP servers work.

In addition to the SMTP server, a fully functional Linux email system is likely to include other software:

Pull Mail Servers Two pull mail protocols, POP and IMAP, are popular. If a Linux system should function as a mail server from which users can read their email remotely, chances are you'll install a POP or an IMAP server package, such as Cyrus IMAP (http://cyrusimap.web.cmu.edu/) or Dovecot (http://www.dovecot.org).

Fetchmail This program, based at http://fetchmail.berlios.de, fills an odd gap in the email-delivery chain. If you run a small site that relies on an external ISP for email delivery, chances are the ISP supports only POP or IMAP. If you want to use a variety of email clients, you may want to run your own SMTP server, and perhaps your own POP or IMAP server, to deliver mail locally. To do this, you need a program that pulls mail using POP or IMAP and then injects it into a local SMTP mail queue. This is the job of Fetchmail. Most sites don't need it, but for those that do, it's indispensable.

Mail readers The final link in the email chain is the mail reader. Examples in Linux include Evolution (http://projects.gnome.org/evolution/), KMail (http://userbase .kde.org/KMail), Thunderbird (http://www.mozilla.org/en-US/thunderbird/), and mutt (http://www.mutt.org). The mail utility, which is installed on most Linux systems by default, is the lowest-common-denominator email utility. It's described shortly, in "Sending and Receiving Email." Most Linux email clients enable reading either from a local mail queue or from a remote POP or IMAP mail server. A multi-user system is likely to have multiple email clients installed, enabling each user to choose which client to use.

Neither this book nor the exam covers pull mail servers, Fetchmail, or mail readers in any detail. As a practical matter, you may need to learn how to configure any or all of these packages, depending on your site's needs. Fortunately, mail reader configuration, which is the most common task, is usually fairly straightforward, as long as you have information on the hostnames of your outgoing (SMTP) and incoming (POP, IMAP, or local queue) email servers.

Working with Email

Although setting up an email server for a site is beyond the scope of this book and the exam, managing a few common email server administrative tasks is not. I therefore describe some common administrative tasks involving sending and receiving mail using the mail utility, email queue management, configuring aliases, and forwarding email.

Sending and Receiving Email

Linux supports a wide variety of email clients, some of which were mentioned earlier, in "Choosing Email Software." Chances are, you'll use a full-fledged email client for your personal email; however, you should also know how to use the mail program. This tool is a very basic command-line email utility. It has the advantage of being usable from a script, so you can write a script to automatically handle some email tasks, and perhaps even run that script automatically. For instance, you might write a script to check for user passwords that are about to expire and then email the users about this impending event so that they can change their passwords before their accounts are locked.

> Some Linux systems ship with a program called nail rather than mail. The nail program supports additional features compared to the original mail, such as the ability to add attachments, but the two programs are very similar in basic operation. Typically, a link with the name mail points to nail, so you can call nail as mail.

The mail program is intended to be used on the command line to send or receive messages. The basic syntax for mail, including its most useful options, is as follows:

```
mail [-v] [-s subject] [-c cc-addr] [-b bcc-addr] to-addr
mail [-v] [-f [name] | -u user]
```

The first of these syntax lines is used for sending email; the second is used for reading email. (Unlike most email readers, mail only supports reading the local email queue, not email stored on remote servers and read via POP or IMAP.) You can achieve various goals with the options to mail:

Use Verbose Operation As with many commands, the -v option produces more verbose output. This may be helpful if you need to debug problems.

Specify a Subject Line The -s subject option enables you to specify a subject line.

Set a Carbon Copy Address You can send a message to multiple people by sending a *carbon copy* using the -c cc-addr or -b bcc-addr options. These options vary in that the -b option produces a "blind" carbon copy, meaning that the recipient's address doesn't appear in the address list. This is useful if you want to discreetly send a copy of an email to somebody, but some spam filters may delete such emails.

Set the Recipient's Address The main recipient's email address terminates the mail command's line for an outgoing email.

Read Email To read your email, pass the -f option to the program, optionally followed by the name of the mail spool file. Alternatively, you can use the -u *user* option to read the mail of the specified user.

This list of options is incomplete, but it includes the most important features. You should consult the man page for mail to learn about more exotic options. Remember that some systems use mail whereas others use nail, and available options differ for these two programs. The preceding options have the same effect for both programs; but some options, such as -a, have different meanings for the two programs. (The -a option enables you to insert an arbitrary email header in the original mail, but in nail it's how you attach a file to an outgoing message.)

As an example of mail in action, consider the task of sending a quick email message. Suppose you want to send an email to two recipients informing them of a meeting. You can do so as follows:

```
$ mail -s "Meeting reminder" -c benf@example.com sallyg@example.com
Remember the meeting at 4:00 today!
Cc: benf@example.com
```

After you type the mail command, the program waits for input via standard input, but there's no prompt. You signal the end of the message by pressing Ctrl+D. This example shows a simple one-line message. After you press Ctrl+D, the program displays the Cc: line to verify this option. You can still change the address at this point, but if you don't want to, you can press the Enter key and the message will be on its way.

To use mail in a script, you can use input redirection to pass it the contents of a file to be mailed:

```
mail -s "Automated alert!" < /tmp/alert.txt benf@example.com
```

This line, if included in a script, sends the contents of /tmp/alert.txt to benf@example .com with the specified subject.

You can use mail to read incoming email, too, but only if it's stored on a local Linux mail spool. In this case, you'll normally use mail interactively. Type mail, and you'll see the contents of your mail spool. Each message has a summary line that lists the sender, date, and subject, among other things:

```
0046 sally@luna.edu  Sun Jan 13 18:27 116/4262  Priorities
```

This is message number 46; it's from sally@luna.edu; it arrived on January 13 at 18:27 (6:27 p.m.); it has 116 lines and 4262 bytes (including headers); and its subject is Priorities. To read a message, type its number. You can then delete the message by typing **d** or reply to it by typing **r**.

As a practical matter, most people prefer to use more-sophisticated mail readers for their day-to-day mail reading. You'll probably find mail more useful for the scripted sending of email than for reading email or sending personal email.

Checking the Email Queue

An email server manages a queue of email messages that it must deliver. This queue is similar in some respects to the queue of print jobs that the Linux printing system handles, as described in Chapter 6. Instead of sending jobs to a printer, though, the email server sends email messages to another computer or stores them in local users' mail spools. This task may sound simple, but it can be surprisingly complex. The server may be asked to deliver many messages in a very short period of time, and thus it may need to delay delivery of some messages while it works on others. Furthermore, any number of problems can lead to temporary or permanent inability to deliver messages. When a problem seems to be temporary, such as a network routing failure, the email server must store the message and try to deliver it again later. Thus, a Linux computer's email queue may contain undelivered messages. Knowing how to identify these messages and manage the queue can help you keep your Linux computer's email subsystem working smoothly.

The `mailq` program is the main tool to help in email queue management. This program was originally part of the sendmail package, but Postfix, Exim, qmail, and other Linux SMTP servers have all implemented compatible commands. Unfortunately, command options differ between implementations. The basic command, without any options, shows the contents of the email queue on all systems:

```
$ mailq
-Queue ID- --Size-- ----Arrival Time---- -Sender/Recipient-------
5B42F963F*      440 Fri Jan 18 13:58:19  sally@example.com
                                          benf@luna.edu
-- 0 Kbytes in 1 Request.
```

This example, taken from a system running Postfix, shows one message in the queue, along with relevant identifying information. The exact display format varies from one SMTP server to another. In most cases, typing **mailq** is equivalent to typing **sendmail -bp**.

If your network connection goes down temporarily or if an upstream email server goes down for a while, email messages can pile up in the queue. Your SMTP server will ordinarily attempt redelivery at a later date; but if your network connection has come up again and you want to clear the queue immediately, you can do so. Typing **sendmail -q** will do the job with most SMTP servers, and some have other equivalent commands, such as postqueue in Postfix or runq in Exim.

All email servers offer a wide variety of advanced options to prioritize email delivery, accept messages on the command line, delete specific messages from the queue, debug email connections, and so on. Unfortunately, commands and procedures to use these features vary from one email server to another. Thus, you should consult your server's documentation to learn how to use these features.

Redirecting Email

Email *aliases* enable one address to stand in for another one. For instance, all email servers are supposed to maintain an account called `postmaster`. Email to this account should be read by somebody who's responsible for maintaining the system. One way to do this is to set up an alias linking the `postmaster` name to the name of a real account. You can do this by editing the `aliases` file, which usually resides in /etc or sometimes in /etc/mail.

The `aliases` file format is fairly straightforward. Comment lines begin with hash marks (#), and other lines take the following form:

name: *addr1*[,*addr2*[,...]]

The *name* that leads the line is a local name, such as postmaster. Each address (*addr1*, *addr2*, and so on) can be the name of a local account to which the messages are forwarded, the name of a local file in which messages are stored (denoted by a leading slash), a command through which messages are piped (denoted by a leading vertical bar character), the name of a file whose contents are treated as a series of addresses (denoted by a leading :include: string), or a full email address (such as fred@example.com).

A typical default configuration includes a few useful aliases for accounts such as postmaster. Most such configurations map most of these aliases to root. Reading mail as root is inadvisable, though—doing so increases the odds of a security breach or other problem because of a typo or bug in the mail reader. Thus, you may want to set up an alias line like the following:

```
root: yourusername
```

This redirects all of root's mail, including mail directed to root via another alias, to *yourusername*, which can take any of the forms just described (it's most likely to be a local username or a valid remote email address). Some mail servers, including sendmail, Postfix, and qmail, require you to compile /etc/aliases into a binary file that can be processed more quickly. To do so, use the newaliases command:

```
# newaliases
```

 Exim has a newaliases command for compatibility with sendmail, but it doesn't do anything by default.

Another approach to redirecting mail is to do so on the user level. In particular, you can edit the ~/.forward file in a user's home directory to have mail for that user sent to another address. Specifically, the ~/.forward file should contain the new address—either a username on the current computer or an entire email address on another computer. This approach has the advantage that it can be employed by individual users—say, to consolidate email from multiple systems into one account without bothering system administrators. A drawback is that it can't be used to set up aliases for nonexistent accounts or for accounts that lack home directories. The ~/.forward file can also be changed or deleted by the account owner, which might not be desirable if you want to enforce a forwarding rule that the user shouldn't be able to override.

Securing Your Email Server

Like any server, an email server is a potential security risk. Broadly speaking, this risk takes two forms:

Bugs Bugs in the email server can expose your computer to danger. In theory, a bug might enable somebody to gain access to your system by sending an email or by connecting to the SMTP port (25) via a Telnet client and typing SMTP commands to trigger the bug. For this reason, many Linux distributions today limit access to the email server to the local computer only.

Misconfiguration   Poor configuration of an email server can cause problems. Email servers aren't designed to provide login access, so they aren't likely to be abusable to gain full login access. Instead, the big risk is a configuration that will make your system a menace to the Internet. The most common misconfiguration of this nature is an open relay, which is a computer that will relay mail from any computer to any other computer. In the past, spammers made heavy use of open relays as a way to help hide their true identities, but spammers today have largely moved on to other techniques. Nonetheless, some spammers still abuse open relays.

To guard against bugs, you should ensure that your email server is upgraded to the latest version. Chapter 2 describes software management, so you should consult it for advice on keeping your system software up to date.

Major Linux distributions configure their email servers so that they aren't open relays; however, a misconfiguration can open your email server. Various Web sites provide tests for such misconfigurations. Check `http://www.abuse.net/relay.html` or `http://www.spam help.org/shopenrelay/` to test your system to verify that it's not an open relay. These sites, and others like them, run a series of tests, attempting to relay email through your server. If your server is properly configured, the page will report that it was unable to connect or that it was unable to relay email. If the testing site was able to relay email, though, you'll need to learn more to properly configure your server. Unfortunately, the steps needed to secure an open relay vary from one email server to another, and they require relatively advanced configuration, which is beyond the scope of this book or the exam. You can learn about closing open relay configurations in your email server's documentation.

Managing Data with SQL

The Structured Query Language (SQL), as its expanded name suggests, is a language used for retrieving data from a database. In practice, SQL is implemented in several different database products. Thus, you should know a little about the SQL products that are available for Linux. With a SQL package installed, you can begin learning about the principles of SQL use and move on to actual data storage and retrieval.

Picking a SQL Package

SQL is a language for accessing data, and specific SQL packages implement that language. This distinction is similar to that between a network protocol (such as SMTP) and the servers that implement it (such as sendmail, Postfix, and Exim). In principle, you can use any SQL package to satisfy your SQL database needs. In practice, specific products that store data using SQL may work better with (or even require) particular packages. Some common choices in Linux include the following:

MySQL   Oracle owns this SQL implementation, which has been released under the GPL. Most major Linux distributions include MySQL in their package databases. For a complete installation, you'll probably need to install multiple packages, such as a client, a server, and perhaps development tools. You can learn more at http://www.mysql.com

PostgreSQL   This SQL implementation evolved from the earlier Ingres software (the name *PostgreSQL* is a compressed form of *post-Ingres SQL*). It's available under the BSD license and is available as multiple packages in most Linux distributions. As with MySQL, you'll most likely have to install a client, a server, and perhaps additional support packages. PostgreSQL is headquartered at http://www.postgresql.org.

SQLite   This package, based at http://www.sqlite.org, is a library that implements SQL. As such, it's not a stand-alone database; instead, it's intended as a way to provide programs with a way to store data using a SQL interface within the program. If you install a program that uses SQLite, your distribution's package manager should install the relevant libraries for you. If you want to write a program that requires database access and you don't want to install a complete client-server SQL package such as MySQL or PostgreSQL, SQLite may be just what you need.

There are dozens more SQL database products for Linux. For the purpose of learning SQL, MySQL or PostgreSQL should do fine, or you can use another full implementation if you prefer. If you have a specific purpose in mind for using SQL, though, you should research SQL packages in more detail. You may need a particular product for compatibility with other software, or you may need a SQL package that provides specific features.

As just noted, some SQL packages, including MySQL and PostgreSQL, operate on a client-server model: One program (the server) manages the database, while another (the client) provides users and programs with access to the database. Such implementations can work over a network, enabling users at multiple client systems to access a centralized database server.

Understanding SQL Basics

SQL is a tool for accessing databases, and more specifically, relational databases. Figure 9.2 illustrates data in a relational database. Each row (sometimes known as a tuple) represents a single object or other item, and each column (sometimes referred to as an attribute or field) represents a specific feature. The combination of rows and columns is referred to as a table. Each database may contain multiple tables, and SQL supports multiple databases. Thus, to access data, you must first select a database and a table, as described in more detail shortly.

FIGURE 9.2   A relational database stores data in a table, with each row representing one object or item and each column representing specific attributes.

attributes (columns)

lizard	green	5 inches	soft	$10
tree	green	10 feet	medium	$200
pillow	white	18 inches	soft	$5
brick	red	8 inches	hard	$1
banana	yellow	8 inches	soft	$0.10

tuples (rows)

The data in a table are unordered, at least conceptually. (In practice, of course, data will be stored in some order on disk, but this order is arbitrary.) You can impose an order on query results, as described shortly; for instance, you may retrieve data from the database represented by Figure 9.2 and order the results according to cost (the final column).

A database enables retrieval of information that matches specific criteria. You can search for all the green objects in Figure 9.2, for instance. You can also insert, delete, and update information in a table. SQL supports multiple tables, so you can have, for instance, different tables for property in your office and for employees who work in your office.

Columns (attributes) in a database hold specific types of data, and swapping them around makes little sense. For instance, it's clear that the second column in Figure 9.2 is a color, whereas the final column is a price or value, expressed in dollars. It would make little sense to enter green as a price or $1.00 as a color. The restrictions placed on what may appear in a column are known as a *domain* or a *data type*: The domain for the second column is a set of color names, whereas the domain for the final column is a numeric value expressed in dollars. Table 9.3 summarizes some common SQL data types.

TABLE 9.3   Common SQL data type

Data Type Name	Purpose
INTEGER (**aka** INT)	4-byte integer value
SMALLINT	2-byte integer value
DECIMAL	Precision storage of decimal values
NUMERIC	Precision storage of decimal values
FLOAT	Floating-point number
DOUBLE PRECISION	Floating-point number stored with twice the precision of FLOAT
DATETIME	A date and time
DATE	A date
TIME	A time, in *HH*:*MM*:*SS* format; may be a time of day or a period of time
CHAR	One or more characters
VARCHAR	A variable number of characters
ENUM	An enumerated list, such as one of small, medium, or large
SET	Data that may have zero or more values, as in any of the set of nuts, sprinkles, fudge, and cherry for ice cream toppings

Additional data types exist; Table 9.3 is intended to give you a feel for what's available and to list some of the data types you're likely to encounter. Some implementations support unique data types, too. Each of these data types has its own features. For instance, the numeric data types (INTEGER, DECIMAL, and so on) can be manipulated by mathematic operators.

Using MySQL

To learn about SQL, you should have access to a SQL database. For purposes of demonstration, I'm using MySQL as a reference. Other SQL implementations are similar to what I describe here, but some details differ. One of these details is how to start the database. In the case of MySQL, your distribution should include a SysV or other startup script for the SQL server. This server may also need to be configured with its own root password.

Debian and related distributions will prompt for this when you install the package, but you may need to set this manually with other distributions.

Starting to Use MySQL

To begin a SQL session, you should first ensure that the server is running, as just described. You can then start the SQL client. In the case of MySQL, this program is called `mysql`:

```
$ mysql
```

If you've just installed MySQL for learning purposes, it may have no databases defined. To learn what's defined, you can use the SHOW DATABASES command:

```
mysql> SHOW DATABASES;
+--------------------+
| Database           |
+--------------------+
| information_schema |
+--------------------+
1 row in set (0.00 sec)
```

> **NOTE** This example illustrates an important feature of SQL: Commands are terminated by semicolons (;). There are a few exceptions to this rule, but if you forget the semicolon, you're likely to see a new prompt that reads -> rather than mysql>, at least in MySQL. You can use this fact to split your commands across multiple lines, if you like. If you forget the semicolon that terminates a command, you can enter it by itself on the -> prompt line. SQL commands are conventionally shown in uppercase, but SQL commands are case-insensitive, so you can type your commands in uppercase, lowercase, or any mixture of case you like.

In this example, one database is already defined: `information_schema`. Some installations define a database called `test`. If you see such a database, you can probably use it for your own tests; however, other users may be able to see and modify this database, so don't store important data in it. If you're not in charge of the SQL installation, you should double-check with whoever is in charge of it to be sure you can use the `test` database—or any other database, for that matter.

Creating Databases and Tables

If no database for testing purposes exists, you can create one with the CREATE DATABASE command, which takes a database name as an option:

```
mysql> CREATE DATABASE test;
Query OK, 1 row affected (0.00 sec)
```

NOTE   Although SQL commands are case-insensitive, database names are not. Thus, be sure to create the database name using whatever case you intend to use to refer to it in the future.

If you type **SHOW DATABASES;**, you'll see the test database in addition to any that already existed. Regardless of whether test (or some other testing database) existed when you first started MySQL or had to be created, you can begin using it with the USE command:

```
mysql> USE test;
```

Within each database, tables must be created and selected for use. The commands to do so are similar to the commands used to create and select databases. In a newly created database, no tables exist:

```
mysql> SHOW TABLES;
Empty set (0.00 sec)
```

The response Empty set denotes an empty database. To fill the database with data, you must first decide on a table structure—what sort of data you want to record. For instance, Figure 9.2 shows various attributes of common objects: their names, colors, sizes, hardnesses, and values in dollars. To create a table that includes columns for these five attributes, you use a CREATE TABLE command, passing it various details:

```
mysql> CREATE TABLE objects (name VARCHAR(30), color VARCHAR(20),
    -> size FLOAT, hardness ENUM('soft','medium','hard'),
    -> value DECIMAL(10,2));
Query OK, 0 rows affected (0.01 sec)
```

This example creates a table with five columns: name, color, size, hardness, and value. Each column has an associated data type, as described in Table 9.3. A few points worth noting about this table definition are as follows:

- The name and color columns are both VARCHAR examples, but with different sizes: The name may be up to 30 characters, whereas the color may be up to 20 characters. If these were defined as CHARs, each name would have to be precisely 30 characters in size, with each color precisely 20 characters. A limited set of colors can be specified by using an ENUM rather than a VARCHAR. Presumably you wouldn't want to limit object names this way.

- The size column is a FLOAT, which is less precise than an integer data type, but a FLOAT can hold real (non-integer) numbers. Figure 9.2 includes sizes in inches and feet, but in practice you'll need to convert everything to one unit—probably inches in this case.

- Note the syntax for defining the ENUM: The list of values as a whole is enclosed in parentheses (()), and each enumerated value is enclosed in single quotes (') and separated from other values by a comma (,).

- The DECIMAL value includes a specification of the number of digits (10 in this example) and the number of digits after the decimal point (2 in this example), separated by a comma. Some implementations support a MONEY data type that can be used in this case, but MySQL lacks this data type, so DECIMAL is the best choice for the job. A DECIMAL type is better for currency than FLOAT because a FLOAT type is likely to introduce rounding errors because of the way numbers are encoded in a FLOAT value. Such errors are typically unacceptable in currency, although they may be tolerable in some applications.

If you need to create a table with other types of values, you should consult the documentation for your specific SQL implementation to see what data types it supports.

With the table created, you may want to verify that it's been created correctly. You can do so by typing **DESCRIBE objects;**. The result should be a summary of the fields you've just created for the objects table.

Storing Data

You can now begin storing data in your database. To do so, use the INSERT INTO command:

```
mysql> INSERT INTO objects
    -> VALUES('lizard','green',6,'soft',10.00);
```

This example creates an entry for the first row of Figure 9.2 (but with one error, which is deliberate). You can verify that the database now holds this information by typing **SELECT * FROM objects;**. The result is a listing of all the data in the objects table, which in this case should be just the one entry. (The next section, "Retrieving Data," covers data retrieval in more detail.)

This example entered incorrect data for one field: The lizard is entered in the table as being 6 inches in size, rather than 5. You can correct this error by using UPDATE:

```
mysql> UPDATE objects SET size=5 WHERE name='lizard';
Query OK, 1 row affected (0.00 sec)
Rows matched: 1  Changed: 1  Warnings: 0
```

This example begins with the keyword UPDATE and the table name (objects). The example then tells MySQL what to update: SET size=5—in other words, set the size field to 5. The WHERE keyword begins a specification of which rows to change. In this case, with only one row present, you can use any data or even omit WHERE and the rest of the line up to the semicolon. In most cases, though, you must provide enough criteria to uniquely identify the column you want to change. In this example, the name of the object is used—hence name='lizard', which tells MySQL to change the data for all rows for which the name field is lizard.

Before you continue with data retrieval activities, you should complete a database. Exercise 9.3 will guide you through this process.

EXERCISE 9.3

Creating a SQL Database

In this exercise, you'll continue creating a small database. This exercise assumes you've performed the steps described in "Creating Databases and Tables" and "Storing Data" and that you therefore have a SQL database called test, which contains a table called objects, which contains one entry based on the first line in the matrix in Figure 9.2. To complete this database, follow these steps:

1. If you're not currently running MySQL, do so by typing **mysql**.

2. If you're not already using the test database, type **USE test;** to begin using the test database.

3. Type **INSERT INTO objects VALUES('tree', 'green', 120, 'medium', 200);**. (You may split this command across lines, if you like.) This entry is based on the second row of Figure 9.2, but note that the size value has been expressed in inches.

4. Verify that you entered the data correctly by typing **SELECT * FROM objects;** and verifying that the new entry is present.

5. Repeat step 3 (and step 4, if you like) for the remaining rows in Figure 9.2.

If you like, you can continue and enter more data; however, if you do so, some subsequent examples may not work as described.

Retrieving Data

The whole point of having a database is to be able to retrieve data from it. The main command for doing so has already been described: SELECT. This command's power lies in its ability to accept specifications of *what* to select. You can use a variety of keywords to select data that matches various criteria, such as exact matches or matches to a range of values. The overall form of SELECT may be described in this way:

```
SELECT field(s) FROM table [ WHERE conditions ] [ORDER BY field]
```

Previous uses of SELECT have used an asterisk (*) as field(s), meaning that the command returns all the columns that match the remaining criteria. You can instead specify columns by name. For instance, suppose you're interested only in the colors and values of objects. You can view this restricted set of data using SELECT:

```
mysql> SELECT value,color FROM objects;
+--------+--------+
| value  | color  |
+--------+--------+
|  10.00 | green  |
| 200.00 | green  |
```

```
|    5.00 | white  |
|    1.00 | red    |
|    0.10 | yellow |
+--------+--------+
5 rows in set (0.00 sec)
```

The *field(s)* criteria appears as a comma-separated list of columns. In this example, the criteria were listed in the reverse order from their order in the database, and so they appear in the reverse order in the output.

A more interesting way to retrieve data is to use WHERE *conditions*. This tool has already been mentioned, in reference to updating data. You can use *conditions* to retrieve specific data in several ways:

Exact Matches   Using a column name, an equal sign, and a value to match returns only those rows that match the specified value. For instance, typing **SELECT * FROM objects WHERE color='green';** returns the two entries for green objects (lizard and tree).

Numeric Tests   You can retrieve data that match certain numeric criteria. For instance, to retrieve data on all objects that are greater than 10 inches in size, you can type **SELECT * FROM objects WHERE size>10;**.

Alphabetic Tests   The greater-than (>) and less-than (<) operators work on letters as well as numbers. This fact can be used to retrieve data based on the first letter of a string, as in **SELECT * FROM objects WHERE name>'b';** to retrieve records for which the name begins with b or later letters in the alphabet. (Although this example uses a greater-than operator, it does in fact match the letter b.)

Multiple Tests   You can combine multiple criteria using the AND and OR operators. For instance, to retrieve data on soft objects valued at more than $7.50, you can type **SELECT * FROM objects WHERE hardness='soft' AND value>7.50;**.

You can have MySQL return the data as an ordered list by specifying a field name after the ORDER BY keyword:

```
mysql> SELECT * FROM objects WHERE hardness='soft' ORDER BY value;
+--------+--------+------+----------+-------+
| name   | color  | size | hardness | value |
+--------+--------+------+----------+-------+
| banana | yellow |    8 | soft     |  0.10 |
| pillow | white  |   18 | soft     |  5.00 |
| lizard | green  |    5 | soft     | 10.00 |
+--------+--------+------+----------+-------+
3 rows in set (0.00 sec)
```

Combining Data from Multiple Tables

As noted earlier, a database may contain multiple tables. This feature of SQL enables you to create tables for different functions. For instance, Figure 9.2 might represent a database of object characteristics that are of interest for some reason. You might also have a database containing the locations and conditions (on a 10-point scale) of different objects, as shown in Table 9.4. Sometimes you might want to combine these two tables to create a master table on which you can perform queries. In order to do so, though, the two tables must have one matching field that can be used to bind the two tables together, and each table must have one field whose value uniquely identifies each row. This uniquely identifying field is known as a *primary key*. In the case of Figure 9.2, the first column (called name) can serve as a primary key. In the case of Table 9.4, the Object ID column will do the job.

TABLE 9.4   Data on object locations and conditions

Object ID	Object name	Location	Condition
1	banana	kitchen	9
2	banana	kitchen	8
3	tree	back yard	2
4	brick	garage	10
5	brick	garage	9
6	brick	back yard	9
7	lizard	living room	8

You can create this table much as you created the first one:

```
mysql> CREATE TABLE locations (id INTEGER, name VARCHAR(30),
    -> location VARCHAR(30), cond INTEGER);
mysql> INSERT INTO locations VALUES(1, 'banana', 'kitchen', 9);
```

Additional INSERT operations will fill out the table. At this point, you can use the SELECT operator to select data based on fields from both tables. For instance, suppose you want to know where all the green objects are located. The first table (objects) contains color data but not locations, whereas the second table (locations) holds locations but not color data. You can accomplish the goal by using a few tricks:

```
mysql> SELECT objects.name, objects.color, locations.location
    -> FROM objects, locations
    -> WHERE objects.name=locations.name AND objects.color='green';
+--------+-------+------------+
| name   | color | location   |
+--------+-------+------------+
| tree   | green | back yard  |
| lizard | green | living room |
+--------+-------+------------+
2 rows in set (0.00 sec)
```

MySQL automatically combines the two tables and produces output based on the criteria you specify. The final output in this example includes the name, color, and location of the objects, even though each table has just two of those three values.

A second way to combine data from multiple tables is to use JOIN. This approach is very similar to the preceding one, but you specify one table using FROM and the other using JOIN:

```
mysql> SELECT objects.name, objects.color, locations.location
    -> FROM objects
    -> JOIN locations
    -> WHERE objects.name=locations.name AND objects.color='green';
```

Combining data enables you to simplify the structure of your database in certain situations. The examples used here illustrate this fact, albeit with very small data sets. The data in the objects table describes objects generically, whereas the data in the locations table describes objects specifically. A retail business might use similar tables to describe its inventory—something analogous to the objects table can hold descriptions of products, whereas something like the locations table can specify where each box holding a particular product is shelved, perhaps even across multiple warehouses or stores. This design enables each table to be relatively small. If all the data were stored in a single table, that table would require multiple entries for each item, duplicating a lot of data. By splitting the data across tables, each table can be much smaller, thus reducing storage space.

A retrieval command that requires special mention is GROUP BY. This command is used in conjunction with mathematical operators, such as SUM(), to restrict the operation of the operator to the specified columns. For instance, suppose you want to know the total value of all the objects in the database, grouped by object type. You can do so as follows, combining data from both tables:

```
mysql> SELECT objects.name, objects.value, SUM(value)
    -> FROM objects, locations
    -> WHERE locations.name=objects.name
    -> GROUP BY value;
```

The result is a summary of the values of all the objects by type. Omitting the GROUP BY clause produces an error message in MySQL.

Deleting Data

Sometimes your data need to be deleted. Table 9.4 suggests that the tree in the back yard is ill—its condition rating is just 2 on a 10-point scale. Perhaps you'll decide to cut it down and therefore remove it from the locations database. To do so, you'll use the DELETE command, which takes the following form:

```
DELETE FROM table WHERE conditions
```

For instance, to delete that now-removed tree, you can type the following command:

```
mysql> DELETE FROM locations
    -> WHERE name='tree' AND location='back yard' ;
Query OK, 1 row affected (0.05 sec)
```

In this specific case, the WHERE condition is more detailed than it needs to be, because the back yard tree is the only one in the table. As usual when deleting any sort of data on a computer, though, it's better to be overly cautious than sloppy.

> Before deleting data, try using SELECT to see what data your WHERE conditions match. Doing this will help you prevent accidentally deleting too much data.

You can delete all the data from a table by using a variant of the DELETE command: **DELETE * from locations;**. This command deletes all the table's data without deleting the table itself. This may be useful if the table is hopelessly messed up from experimentation. An even more drastic deletion operation is DROP: **DROP TABLE locations;**. This example completely eliminates the locations table. Naturally, this is an extremely dangerous command, but you may want to use it when cleaning up your own SQL practice session.

Learning More About SQL

SQL is a very complex topic, and this chapter can only scratch the surface. For more information, you should read more from various sources. Your own SQL package's documentation can be a good starting point, particularly if you need to use features that are unique to your implementation. Books on SQL, such as Alan Beaulieu's *Learning SQL, 2nd Edition* (O'Reilly, 2009) and Alex Kriegel's *SQL Bible* (Wiley, 2008), are also worth reading if you need to do more than trivial SQL work.

Summary

Serious Linux administrators must have at least a basic understanding of shell scripts. Many configuration and startup files are in fact shell scripts, and being able to read them, and perhaps modify them, will help you administer your system. Being able to create new shell scripts is also important, because doing so will help you simplify tedious tasks and create site-specific tools by gluing together multiple programs to accomplish your goals. Email server administration is another task with which you must have at least a passing familiarity. Although most Linux systems don't operate as email servers in the sense of computers whose primary duty is to handle email, most Linux installations do include email servers for processing locally generated email and sometimes to send email to outside systems or even to receive email for local users. You can configure email forwarding and perform a few other tweaks without delving too heavily into email server configuration.

The final topic of this chapter, SQL use, will help you manage simple databases stored using the SQL language. Many programs rely on SQL for their operation, so being able to perform simple SQL queries will help you work with these programs. You may even decide to set up databases to help manage your own tasks, such as tracking where you keep things in your office or home.

Exam Essentials

Explain the function of environment variables. Environment variables are used to store information on the system for the benefit of running programs. Examples include the PATH environment variable, which holds the locations of executable programs, and HOSTNAME, which holds the system's hostname.

Describe how a shell script can be useful. A shell script combines several commands, possibly including conditional expressions, variables, and other programming features, to make the script respond dynamically to a system. Therefore, a shell script can reduce administrative effort by performing a series of repetitive tasks at one command.

Describe the purpose of shell aliases. Aliases enable you to create a command "shortcut"—a simple command that can stand in for a different or longer command. Aliases are typically defined in shell startup scripts as a way to create a shortened version of a command, to have useful options for a command be used as new defaults, or to create an easier-to-remember version of a command.

Summarize the major SMTP servers for Linux. Sendmail was the most common SMTP server a decade ago and is still very popular today. Postfix and Exim are often supplied as the default mail servers on modern distributions, whereas qmail is sometimes installed by administrators but isn't the default for any major distribution. Postfix and qmail use modular designs, whereas sendmail and Exim are monolithic.

Explain the difference between an email alias and email forwarding.   An email alias is configured systemwide, typically in /etc/aliases. It can set up forwarding for any local address, even if that address doesn't correspond to a real account; and if the system is properly configured, only root may edit /etc/aliases and therefore modify aliases. Email forwarding, on the other hand, is handled by the ~/.forward file in a user's home directory; it's intended as a means for users to control their own email forwarding without bothering the system administrator.

Summarize the structure of a SQL database.   Each SQL installation consists of a number of named databases, each of which in turn may contain multiple tables. Each table can be thought of as a two-dimensional array of data. Each row in a table describes some object or concept (inventory items, employees, movies in a personal DVD collection, and so on), and each column in a table holds data about these objects or concepts (model number, salary, or director, for example).

Describe the commands used to enter data in a SQL database.   The INSERT command inserts a single entry into a database. It requires a table name and a set of values, as in **INSERT INTO movies VALUES('Brazil', 'Terry Gilliam', 1985);**. The UPDATE command can be used in a similar way to update an existing entry, but you must use SET to specify the column to set and WHERE to identify the row or rows to be modified.

Explain the commands used to extract data from a SQL database.   The SELECT command retrieves data from a SQL database. It can be used with a variety of additional options, such as FROM, JOIN, and WHERE, to identify the table or tables from which data should be retrieved and to locate specific values of interest.

Review Questions

1. Where is the best location for the current directory indicator (.) to reside in root's PATH environment variable?

    A. Before all other directories

    B. After all other directories

    C. At any location *except* the last one

    D. Wherever is convenient

    E. Nowhere; it shouldn't be in root's path

2. You want to create a shortcut for the command cd ~/papers/trade. Which of the following lines, if entered in a bash startup script, will accomplish this goal?

    A. `alias cdpt='cd ~/papers/trade'`

    B. `export cdpt='cd ~/papers/trade'`

    C. `cd ~/papers/trade`

    D. `shortcut cdpt "cd ~/papers/trade"`

    E. `env cdpt ` ``cd ~/papers/trade`` `

3. What is the purpose of the EDITOR environment variable?

    A. Set to Y (the default), the shell environment permits editing of commands; set to N, such editing is disallowed.

    B. It specifies the filename of the text editor that bash uses by default while you're entering commands at its prompt.

    C. If you type **edit filename** at a command prompt, the program specified by EDITOR will be launched.

    D. Set to GUI, programs call a GUI editor; set to TEXT, programs call a text-based editor.

    E. Some programs refer to EDITOR to determine what external editor to launch when they need to launch one.

4. In what environment variable is the current working directory stored?

    A. PATH

    B. CWD

    C. PWD

    D. PRESENT

    E. WORKING

5. Which of the following commands, if typed in a bash shell, will create an environment variable called MYVAR with the contents mystuff that will be accessible to subsequently launched programs?

    A. `export MYVAR='mystuff'`

    B. `MYVAR='mystuff'`

    C. `$MYVAR==mystuff`

    D. `echo $MYVAR mystuff`

    E. `setenv MYVAR mystuff`

6. What file might a user modify to alter his or her own bash environment?

    A. `~/.startup`

    B. `/etc/bashrc`

    C. `/home/.bashrc`

    D. `/home/profilerc`

    E. `~/.bashrc`

7. What commands might you use (along with appropriate options) to learn the value of a specific environment variable? (Select two.)

    A. env

    B. DISPLAY

    C. export

    D. echo

    E. cat

8. After using a text editor to create a shell script, what step should you take before trying to use the script?

    A. Set the SUID bit using chmod.

    B. Copy the script to the /usr/bin/scripts directory.

    C. Compile the script by typing **bash scriptname**, where *scriptname* is the script's name.

    D. Run a virus checker on the script to be sure it contains no viruses.

    E. Set one or more executable bits using chmod.

9. Describe the effect of the following short script, cp1, if it's called as cp1 big.c big.cc:

    ```
    #!/bin/bash
    cp $2 $1
    ```

    A. It has the same effect as the cp command—copying the contents of big.c to big.cc.

    B. It compiles the C program big.c and calls the result big.cc.

    C. It copies the contents of big.cc to big.c, eliminating the old big.c.

    D. It converts the C program big.c into a C++ program called big.cc.

    E. It interprets the big.c and big.cc files as bash scripts.

10. What is the purpose of conditional expressions in shell scripts?

    A. They prevent scripts from executing if license conditions aren't met.

    B. They display information about the script's computer environment.

    C. They enable the script to take different actions in response to variable data.

    D. They enable scripts to learn in a manner reminiscent of Pavlovian conditioning.

    E. They improve code quality by improving its readability.

11. Which of the following lines identify valid shell scripts on a normally configured system? (Select two.)

    A. `#!/bin/script`

    B. `#!/bin/bash`

    C. `!#/bin/tcsh`

    D. `#!/bin/sh`

    E. `!#/bin/zsh`

12. Which of the following are valid looping statements in `bash` shell scripting? (Select three.)

    A. `for`

    B. `while`

    C. `goto`

    D. `until`

    E. `case`

13. Your SMTP email server, `mail.luna.edu`, receives a message addressed to `postmaster@mail.luna.edu`. There is no `postmaster` account on this computer. Assuming the system is properly configured, how should the email server respond?

    A. Accept the message, but do so very slowly so as to tie up the sender's resources.

    B. Bounce the message so that the sender knows the account doesn't exist.

    C. Hold the message in the local mail queue until the `postmaster` account is created.

    D. Delete the message without bouncing it so as to reduce email clutter.

    E. Deliver the email to another account, either locally or on another computer.

14. Which of the following is *not* a popular SMTP server for Linux?

    A. Postfix

    B. Sendmail

    C. Fetchmail

    D. Exim

    E. qmail

15. You see the following line in a script:

```
mail -s "Error" -c abort < /tmp/msg root
```

What is the effect of this line, if and when it executes?

A. An email is sent to the user `Error`, the script is aborted using `root` privileges, and error messages are written to `/tmp/msg`.

B. An email with the subject of `Error` and the contents from `/tmp/msg` is sent to the local users `root` and `abort`.

C. An email with the subject of `Error` and the contents of `/tmp/msg` is sent to the local user `root`, and then the script is aborted.

D. An email is sent with `Error` priority to the local user `root`, and the email system is then shut down with error messages being stored in `/tmp/msg`.

E. An email with the subject of `Error` and contents of `/tmp/msg` is sent to `root`, and information on this is logged with priority `abort`.

16. Your Internet connection has gone down for several hours. What is true of email sent by your users to off-site recipients via a properly configured local SMTP server?

A. The SMTP server will refuse to accept email from local clients during the outage.

B. Email will be neither delayed nor lost.

C. All email sent during the outage will be lost.

D. Email will be delayed by a few hours but not lost.

E. Recipients will have to retrieve the mail via POP or IMAP.

17. You examine your `/etc/aliases` file and find it contains the following line:

```
root: jody
```

What can you conclude from this?

A. Email addressed to `jody` on this system will be sent to the local user `root`.

B. Email addressed to `root` on this system will be sent to the local user `jody`.

C. The local user `jody` has broken into the system and acquired `root` privileges.

D. The local user `jody` has permission to read email directly from `root`'s mail queue.

E. The administrator may log in using either username: `root` or `jody`.

18. You've just installed MySQL and run it by typing `mysql`. How would you create a database called `fish` to store data on different varieties of fish?

A. Type **NEW DATABASE fish;** at the mysql> prompt.

B. Type **CREATE DATABASE fish;** at the mysql> prompt.

C. Type **NEW DATABASE FISH;** at the mysql> prompt.

D. Type **DATABASE CREATE fish;** at the mysql> prompt.

E. Type **DB CREATE fish;** at the mysql> prompt.

19. Which of the following are true statements about SQL tables? (Select two.)

   A. Multiple tables may exist in a single SQL database.

   B. Tables may be combined for cross-table searches using the DROP command.

   C. Tables consist of rows, each of which holds attributes, and columns, each of which defines a specific database item.

   D. Careful table design can reduce the amount of data entry and database storage size.

   E. Tables are stored on disk using a lossy compression algorithm.

20. What is the effect of the following SQL command, assuming the various names and data exist?

   ```
   mysql> UPDATE stars SET magnitude=2.25 WHERE starname='Mintaka';
   ```

   A. It returns database entries from the stars table for all stars with magnitude of 2.25 and starname of Mintaka.

   B. It sets the value of the stars field in the magnitude set to Mintaka, using a precision of 2.25.

   C. It sets the value of the magnitude field to 2.25 for any item in the stars table with the starname of Mintaka.

   D. It combines the stars and magnitude=2.25 tables, returning all items for which starname is Mintaka.

   E. It updates the stars database, creating a new entry with a starname of Mintaka and a magnitude of 2.25.

Chapter

10

Securing Your System

THE FOLLOWING EXAM OBJECTIVES ARE COVERED IN THIS CHAPTER:

- ✓ 1.110.1 Perform security administration tasks
- ✓ 1.110.2 Set up host security
- ✓ 1.110.3 Securing data with encryption

Chances are, you take basic security measures in your daily life—locking the door to your house, avoiding unsafe neighborhoods, keeping valuables out of sight in your car, and so on. Such measures can minimize the risk of a theft or even personal injury, and similar measures on a computer can help protect the computer from compromise. This chapter covers several security issues: restricting access to the computer by port number, managing the security of individual programs, managing passwords, setting miscellaneous account security options, and using encryption to secure data. Understanding these basics will help you begin to secure your computer.

There is no such thing as a 100 percent secure computer. You can take steps to improve security, but no one step or set of steps will absolutely guarantee that you'll have no problems. You must decide for yourself (or the organization for which you work must decide) just how much effort to put into securing your systems and live with the level of threat that remains. This chapter's security information can help you start securing your computer; but if you need more than very basic security, you'll have to learn and do more than I can describe here.

Administering Network Security

Linux systems are often used as server computers, or at least they're connected to the Internet more or less directly. On such systems, network security is particularly important, because incorrectly configured servers can provide miscreants with a way into your computer to do whatever damage they like. Several methods of protecting networked computers from unwanted outside access exist. Some of the simplest of these methods involve shutting down or restricting access to network servers by controlling the network ports they use. (Network ports are described in Chapter 8, "Configuring Basic Networking.") You can check for existing network connections, check for open ports (that is, ports that are in use by a server program), use super server restrictions to limit access, and disable servers you're not using.

The popular media uses the term *hacker* to refer to computer criminals. This word has an older meaning, though: It refers to individuals who are skilled with computers (and particularly with programming), who enjoy these activities, and who use their skills to productive and legal ends. Many Linux programmers consider themselves hackers in this positive sense. Therefore, I use another term, *cracker*, to refer to computer criminals.

Using Super Server Restrictions

Many network server programs open network ports and listen for connections directly. Some programs, though, work through an intermediary: a *super server*. This is a program that listens for network connections on behalf of another program and then, when a connection is initiated, hands off control of that connection to the intended server. This activity may sound like pointless complication, but it actually has several advantages over a more direct connection. For instance, using a super server can reduce memory load if the super server handles several servers that are seldom used—most of the time, only the super server and perhaps one or two of the servers it handles will be in memory. Another advantage is security: You can employ security checks in the super server to protect all the servers that the super server manages. In the following pages, I describe the basics of configuring Linux's two major super servers, inetd and xinetd, with particular emphasis on their security features. In the case of inetd, security is handled by a package called TCP Wrappers. xinetd's security features are built into xinetd itself, by contrast.

Whenever possible, apply redundant access controls. For instance, you can use both a server's own security features and TCP Wrappers or xinetd to block unwanted access. Doing this helps protect against bugs and misconfiguration—if a problem emerges in the super server configuration, for instance, the secondary block will probably halt the intruder. If you configure the system carefully, such an access will also leave a log file message that you'll see, so you'll be alerted to the fact that the super server didn't do its job.

Configuring *inetd*

The inetd package was once the standard super server in Linux, and it's still used on some systems. Over the past decade, though, xinetd has gained substantial ground, so your system may use xinetd instead. Type **ps ax | grep inetd** to see which super server is running on your system—the output should include a line with either the inetd or xinetd command. Some systems run neither super server, though. If your system has inetd installed, the next few pages cover it.

Setting Up *inetd*

You control servers that launch via inetd through the /etc/inetd.conf file or files in /etc/inetd.d. The /etc/inetd.conf file consists of a series of lines, one for each server. A typical line resembles the following:

```
ftp stream tcp nowait root /usr/sbin/tcpd /usr/sbin/in.ftpd -l
```

 This and several subsequent examples refer to in.ftpd, an FTP server that was once quite popular but that's been replaced on many systems by other FTP servers. Some of these servers cannot be run from a super server.

Instead of using a single monolithic /etc/inetd.conf file, recent versions of inetd enable you to split the configuration into several files in the /etc/inetd.d directory. Doing so enables you to easily add or delete server configurations by adding or deleting their configuration files. For brevity, the following paragraphs refer only to /etc/inetd.conf, but the description applies to files in /etc/inetd.d, as well.

Each line in /etc/inetd.conf consists of several fields separated by one or more spaces. The meanings of these fields are as follows:

Service Name   The first field (ftp in the preceding example) is the name of the service as it appears in the /etc/services file.

Socket Type   The socket type entry tells the system what type of connection to expect—a reliable two-way connection (stream), a less reliable connection with less overhead (dgram), a low-level connection to the network (raw), or various others. The differences between these types are highly technical; your main concern in editing this entry should be to correctly type the value specified by the server's documentation.

Protocol   This is the TCP/IP transport-layer protocol used, usually tcp or udp.

Wait/No Wait   For dgram socket types, this entry specifies whether the server connects to its client and frees the socket (nowait) or processes all its packets and then times out (wait). Servers that use other socket types should specify nowait in this field.

User   This is the username used to run the server. The root and nobody users are common choices, but others are possible as well. As a general rule, you should run servers with a low-privilege user whenever possible as a security precaution. Some servers require root access, though. Consult the server's documentation for details.

Server Name   This is the filename of the server. In the preceding example, the server is specified as /usr/sbin/tcpd, which is the TCP Wrappers binary. As described shortly in "Controlling Access via TCP Wrappers," this program is an important security tool and should usually be included as the means of launching programs via inetd.

Parameters   Everything after the server name consists of parameters that are passed to the server. If you use TCP Wrappers, you pass the name of the true target server (such as /usr/sbin/in.ftpd) in this field, along with its parameters.

The hash mark (#) is a comment symbol for /etc/inetd.conf. Therefore, if a server is running via inetd and you want to disable it, you can place a hash mark at the start of the line. If you want to add a server to inetd.conf, you need to create an entry for it. Most servers that can be run from inetd include sample entries in their documentation. Many distributions ship with inetd.conf files that include entries for common servers as well, although many of them are commented out; remove the hash mark at the start of the line to activate the server.

After modifying inetd.conf, you must restart the inetd super server. You can generally restart it by using your startup script system, as described in Chapter 5, "Booting Linux and Editing Files." On most computers, typing something similar to the following should work:

```
# /etc/init.d/inetd restart
```

Alternatively, you can tell inetd to reload its configuration by using a reload parameter rather than restart. The restart option shuts down the server and then starts it again. When you use reload, the server never stops running; it just rereads the configuration file and implements any changes. As a practical matter, the two are similar. Using restart is more likely to correctly implement changes, but it's also more likely to disrupt existing connections.

Instead of using the SysV startup scripts, you can use kill or killall (described in Chapter 2, "Managing Software") to pass the SIGHUP signal to inetd. This signal causes many servers, including inetd, to reload their configuration files. For instance, you can type **kill -HUP** *pid* if you know the process ID (PID) of inetd, or you can type **killall -HUP inetd** to have all instances of inetd reload their configuration files. (Ordinarily, only one instance of inetd runs on a system.) In practice, this should work very much like the reload option to the SysV startup script—in fact, such scripts often use this technique to implement this option.

It's generally wise to disable as many servers as possible in inetd.conf (or the xinetd configuration files, if you use xinetd). As a general rule, if you don't understand what a server does, disable it. This will improve the security of your system by eliminating potentially buggy or misconfigured servers from the equation.

Controlling Access via TCP Wrappers

The TCP Wrappers package provides a program known as tcpd. Instead of having inetd call a server directly, inetd calls tcpd, which does two things: It checks whether a client is authorized to access the server, and if the client has this authorization, tcpd calls the server program.

TCP Wrappers is configured through two files: /etc/hosts.allow and /etc/hosts.deny. The first of these specifies computers that are allowed access to the system in a particular way, the implication being that systems not listed are not permitted access. By contrast, hosts.deny lists computers that are not allowed access; all others are granted access to the system. If a computer is listed in both files, hosts.allow takes precedence.

Both files use the same basic format. The files consist of lines of the following form:

daemon-list : *client-list*

The *daemon-list* is a list of servers, using the names for the servers that appear in /etc/services. Wildcards are also available, such as ALL for all servers.

The *client-list* is a list of computers to be granted or denied access to the specified daemons. You can specify computers by name or by IP address, and you can specify a network by using a leading or trailing dot (.) when identifying networks by name or IP address block, respectively. For instance, .luna.edu blocks all computers in the luna.edu domain, and 192.168.7. blocks all computers in the 192.168.7.0/24 network. You can also use wildcards in the *client-list*, such as ALL (all computers). EXCEPT creates an exception. For instance, when placed in hosts.deny, 192.168.7. EXCEPT 192.168.7.105 blocks all computers in the 192.168.7.0/24 network except for 192.168.7.105.

The man pages for hosts.allow and hosts.deny (they're actually the same document) provide additional information about more advanced features. You should consult them as you build TCP Wrappers rules.

WARNING   Remember that not all servers are protected by TCP Wrappers. Normally, only those servers that inetd runs via tcpd are so protected. Such servers often include, but are not limited to, Telnet, FTP, TFTP, rlogin, finger, POP, and IMAP servers. A few servers can independently parse the TCP Wrappers configuration files, though; consult the server's documentation if in doubt.

Configuring *xinetd*

The xinetd program is an extended super server. It provides the functionality of inetd plus security options that are similar to those of TCP Wrappers. Modern versions of Fedora, Mandriva, Red Hat, SUSE, and a few other distributions use xinetd by default. Other distributions may use it in the future. If you like, you can replace inetd with xinetd on any distribution.

Setting Up *xinetd*

The /etc/xinetd.conf file controls xinetd. On distributions that use xinetd by default, this file contains only global default options and a directive to include files stored in /etc/xinetd.d. Each server that should run via xinetd then installs a file in /etc/xinetd.d with its own configuration options.

Whether the entry for a server goes in /etc/xinetd.conf or a file in /etc/xinetd.d, it contains information similar to that in the inetd.conf file. The xinetd configuration file, though, spreads the information across multiple lines and labels it more explicitly. Listing 10.1 shows an example that's equivalent to the earlier inetd.conf entry from "Setting Up inetd." This entry provides precisely the same information as the inetd.conf entry except that it doesn't include a reference to /usr/sbin/tcpd, the TCP Wrappers binary. Because xinetd includes similar functionality, it's generally not used with TCP Wrappers.

Listing 10.1: Sample `xinetd` configuration entry

```
service ftp
{
        socket_type     = stream
        protocol        = tcp
        wait            = no
        user            = root
        server          = /usr/sbin/in.ftpd
        server_args     = -l
}
```

One additional `xinetd.conf` parameter is commonly present: `disable`. If you include the line `disable = yes` in a service definition, `xinetd` ignores the entry. Some server packages install startup files in `/etc/xinetd.d` that have this option set by default; you must edit the file and change the entry to read `disable = no` to enable the server. You can also disable a set of servers by listing their names in the `defaults` section of the main `xinetd.conf` file on a line called `disabled`, as in `disabled = ftp shell`.

As with `inetd`, after you make changes to `xinetd`'s configuration, you must restart the super server. You do this by typing a command similar to the one used to restart `inetd`. As with that command, you can use either `reload` or `restart`, with similar effects:

```
# /etc/init.d/xinetd restart
```

Also as with `inetd`, you may pass the SIGHUP signal to `xinetd` via the `kill` or `killall` command to have it reload its configuration file. This approach may be preferable if you're using a distribution that doesn't use a conventional SysV startup script to launch `xinetd`.

Controlling Access via *xinetd*

Security is handled on a server-by-server basis through the use of configuration parameters in `/etc/xinetd.conf` or the server-specific configuration files. Some of these options are similar to the function of `hosts.allow` and `hosts.deny`:

Network Interface   The `bind` option tells `xinetd` to listen on only one network interface for the service. For instance, you can specify `bind = 192.168.23.7` on a router to have it listen only on the Ethernet card associated with that address. This feature is extremely useful in routers, but it isn't as useful in computers with just one network interface. You can, however, use this option to bind a server only to the loopback interface, 127.0.0.1, if a server should be available only locally. You might do this with a configuration tool like the Samba Web Administration Tool (SWAT). A synonym for this option is `interface`.

Allowed IP or Network Addresses   You can use the `only_from` option to specify IP addresses, networks (as in `192.168.78.0/24`), or computer names on this line, separated by spaces. The result is that `xinetd` will accept connections only from these addresses, similar to TCP Wrappers' `hosts.allow` entries.

Disallowed IP or Network Addresses   The `no_access` option is the opposite of `only_from`; you list computers or networks here that you want to blacklist. This is similar to the `hosts.deny` file of TCP Wrappers.

Access Times   The access_times option sets times during which users may access the server. The time range is specified in the form *hour*:*min*-*hour*:*min*, using a 24-hour clock. Note that this option affects only the times during which the server will *respond*. If the xinetd access_times option is set to 8:00-17:00 and somebody logs in at 4:59 p.m. (one minute before the end time), that user may continue using the system well beyond the 5:00 p.m. cutoff time.

You should enter these options into the files in /etc/xinetd.d that correspond to the servers you want to protect. Place the lines between the opening brace ({) and closing brace (}) for the service. If you want to restrict *all* your xinetd-controlled servers, you can place the entries in the defaults section in /etc/xinetd.conf.

Some servers provide access control mechanisms similar to those of TCP Wrappers or xinetd. For instance, Samba provides hosts allow and hosts deny options that work much like the TCP Wrappers file entries. These options are most common on servers that are awkward or impossible to run via inetd or xinetd.

 Real World Scenario

Configuring a Firewall

Although the exam objectives don't mention firewalls, you should be familiar with the concept. A *firewall* is a computer that restricts access to other computers or software that runs on a single computer to protect it alone. Broadly speaking, two types of firewalls exist: *packet-filter firewalls*, which work by blocking or permitting access based on low-level information in individual data packets (such as source and destination IP addresses and ports), and *proxy filters*, which partially process a transaction (such as a Web page retrieval) and block or deny access based on high-level features in this transaction (such as the filename of an image in the Web page).

In Linux, the kernel includes packet-filter firewall capabilities, which can be programmed via the iptables program. You can set up rules by typing **iptables** followed by various options that define specific restrictions, such as limits on the IP addresses that may access a specific network port. Creating an effective firewall requires learning iptables in detail and writing a script that calls this program repeatedly to set up specific rules.

Many distributions make things easier by providing a generic firewall script that you can configure using a GUI tool. These tools are generally designed for protecting a single computer against unwanted outside access. Check your distribution's GUI system administration options for a firewall configuration tool. You may be able to set security based on a few levels (high, medium, and low security, for instance) or in a somewhat more refined manner.

Linux can also function as a firewall computer that protects an entire network; however, such a configuration is likely to require in-depth knowledge of iptables, as well as topics such as configuring Linux as a router.

Disabling Unused Servers

Quite a few server programs ship with most Linux distributions, which can be a great advantage—you don't need to hunt for servers you want to run. On the other hand, this very advantage can be a drawback; if you're not careful, you can end up running a server and not even realize it's installed! For this reason, you should periodically search for servers and shut down any you find that aren't really necessary. You must begin this task by locating unwanted servers. Several tools to do so exist, such as netstat, lsof, and remote network scanners. You can also search your local configuration files for clues about what may be running. Disabling unused servers can be done by uninstalling the package or by reconfiguring the server.

Using *netstat*

One way to begin diagnosing network security is to look for network activity or open ports on a computer. One tool that can help in this respect is netstat. This program is the Swiss Army knife of network status tools; it provides many different options and output formats to deliver information about routing tables, interface statistics, and so on. For spotting unnecessary servers, you can use netstat with its -a and -p options, as shown here:

```
# netstat -ap
Active Internet connections (servers and established)
Proto Recv-Q Send-Q Local Address          Foreign Address          State↵
PID/Program name
tcp       0      0 *:ftp                    *:*                      LISTEN↵
690/inetd
tcp       0      0 teela.rodsbooks.com:ssh nessus.rodsbooks.:39361 ESTABLISHED↵
787/sshd
```

> **NOTE** I've trimmed most of the entries from this output to make it manageable as an example. Also, netstat can be run as an ordinary user, but it may not return as much information. Specifically, only root and a process's owner see the PID and program name of a process.

This version of the netstat command shows active network connections, which can reveal the presence of servers that are running on your computer. The Local Address and Foreign Address columns specify the local and remote addresses, including both the hostname or IP address and the port number or associated name from /etc/services. The first of the two entries shown here isn't actively connected, so the local address, the foreign address, and the port number are all listed as asterisks (*). This entry does specify the local port, though: ftp. This line indicates that a server is running on the ftp port (TCP port 21). The State column specifies that the server is listening for a connection. The final column in this output, under the PID/Program name heading, indicates that the process with a process

ID (PID) of 690 is using this port. In this case, it's inetd. In other words, this server is running and listening for connections, but nobody is currently connected to it.

The second output line indicates that a connection has been established between teela.rodsbooks.com and nessus.rodsbooks.com (the second hostname is truncated). The local system (teela) is using the ssh port (TCP port 22), and the client (nessus) is using port 39361 on the client system. The process that's handling this connection on the local system is sshd, running as PID 787.

It may take some time to peruse the output of netstat, but doing so will leave you with a much-improved understanding of your computer's network connections. If you spot servers listening for connections that you didn't realize were active, you should investigate the matter further. Some servers may be innocent or even necessary. Others may be pointless security risks.

When you use the -p option to obtain the name and PID of the process using a port, the netstat output is wider than 80 columns. You may want to open an extra-wide terminal window to handle this output or redirect it to a file that you can study in a text editor capable of displaying more than 80 columns. To quickly spot servers listening for connections, type **netstat -lp** rather than **netstat -ap**. The result will show all servers that are listening for connections, omitting client connections and specific server instances that are already connected to clients.

Exercise 10.1 demonstrates the use of netstat to monitor network port use.

EXERCISE 10.1

Monitor Network Port Use

To get started with netstat, follow these steps:

1. Log into the Linux system as a normal user. (Acquiring root privileges will produce more complete output, as described earlier, but isn't strictly necessary for this exercise.)

2. Launch a terminal from the desktop environment's menu system if you used a GUI login method.

3. Type **netstat -ap | less**, and page through the output. Chances are, you'll see quite a few entries for servers that are listening for connections and for established connections to local servers or from local clients to remote servers. Pay particular attention to servers that are listening for new connections—that is, those that list LISTEN in the State column of the output.

4. Type **netstat -ap | grep ssh** to find connections involving SSH. Depending on your configuration and the servers you have running, you may see no output or many lines of output.

5. In another login session or xterm window, initiate an SSH connection to another computer. For instance, type **ssh *remote.luna.edu*** to connect to *remote.luna.edu*.

6. Type **netstat -ap | grep ssh** in your original session (not in your SSH connection). Compare the output to that which you obtained in step 4. The output should have an additional line, reflecting the session you initiated in step 5.

7. Log out of the SSH session you initiated.

8. Type **netstat -ap | grep ssh** again. The output should be missing the line for the session you've now closed.

If you're using a multi-user system, additional SSH sessions may come and go during the course of this exercise, reflecting the activities of other users.

Using *lsof*

The lsof program nominally lists open files. It can be used to identify what files are open in a directory, find who's accessing them, and so on. The definition of *file* used by lsof is broad, though; it includes network connections. Thus, you can use lsof instead of netstat for some tasks, including locating servers that are in use. In its most basic form in this role, you should pass the -i parameter to lsof:

```
# lsof -i
COMMAND    PID         USER    FD    TYPE  DEVICE SIZE NODE NAME
ssh        2498    rodsmith    3u    IPv4 3292662       TCP↲
nessus.rodsbooks.com:53106->seeker.rodsbooks.com:ssh (ESTABLISHED)
exim4      4827 Debian-exim    5u    IPv4 3369596       TCP *:smtp (LISTEN)
sshd       4997        root    3u    IPv4   13273       TCP *:ssh (LISTEN)
```

As in the output of netstat shown earlier, this output is truncated for brevity's sake. This example shows two types of connections. The first non-header line, which begins with ssh, shows an outgoing connection from nessus.rodsbooks.com (the system on which the command was typed) to the ssh port on seeker.rodsbooks.com. Such connections are identified by the existence of two hostnames in the NAME column and by the keyword ESTABLISHED in the same column. The next two lines, which begin with exim4 and sshd, show two servers that are listening for connections on the smtp and ssh ports, respectively. These lines are identified by the fact that the NAME column takes the form *:*service* (LISTEN), where *service* is the service name or port number. Other columns in the output reveal additional information, such as the PID and username associated with the port access.

If you type **lsof -i** as an ordinary user, you'll see only your own network connections; thus, in order for this command to be a useful diagnostic for system security, you must run it as root.

You can restrict the output of lsof by including an address after the -i option. The address takes the following form:

[46][*protocol*][*@hostname|hostaddr*][*:service|port*]

The digit 4 or 6 represents an IPv4 or IPv6 connection, the protocol is the protocol type (TCP or UDP), the *hostname* or *hostaddr* is the computer hostname or IP address associated with the remote system, the *service* is a service name (from /etc/services), and the *port* is the port number. For instance, suppose you want to verify that no FTP server is running on a computer. You can search for any connections associated with the FTP port:

```
# lsof -i :ftp
```

Alternatively, you can replace ftp with 21, because 21 is the port number associated with the FTP port. (Table 8.2 in Chapter 8 summarizes the common network port numbers.) In either case, this command returns a list of all processes associated with FTP connections, both incoming and outgoing. If no such connections exist, the command returns no output; the system simply produces a new command prompt. Be sure to note which output lines are linked with server as opposed to client processes. Even if you're not running an FTP server locally, the preceding command may produce dozens of lines of output if users on the computer are making use of FTP clients.

To perform a general audit of your system's network connections, you should type **lsof -i** by itself, without restricting the output. You'll probably want to pipe the output through less or use a terminal's scroll buffer to review the output. Piping the output through grep to search for the string LISTEN can be a shortcut to find active servers:

```
# lsof -i | grep LISTEN
```

Paging through the raw output (without using grep to search for LISTEN) will provide you with a better idea of your system's overall network use. You could conceivably spot something suspicious, such as an outgoing network connection to a sensitive computer that the client shouldn't be contacting. This network activity may indicate active cracking attempts by a user of the client, intrusion by an outsider, or the work of an automated worm or Trojan horse program.

If you identify programs that shouldn't be running, such as unnecessary servers, you can use the command name, PID, and other information to help shut them down. The preceding section "Disabling Unused Servers" describes how to do this in more detail.

Another use of lsof is in identifying who's accessing files. This might be handy if you need to unmount a filesystem (including a network filesystem) but can't because of in-use files or if you suspect inappropriate activities involving file access.

Using Remote Network Scanners

Network scanners, such as Nmap (http://www.insecure.org/nmap/) or Nessus (http://www.nessus.org), can scan for open ports on the local computer or on other computers. The more sophisticated scanners, including Nessus, check for known vulnerabilities, so they can tell you whether a server may be compromised should you decide to leave it running.

Network scanners are used by crackers to locate likely target systems, as well as by network administrators for legitimate purposes. Many organizations have policies forbidding the use of network scanners except under specific conditions. Therefore, you should check these policies and obtain explicit permission, signed and in writing, to perform a network scan. Failure to do so could cost you your job or even result in criminal charges, even if your intentions are honorable.

Nmap is capable of performing a basic check for open ports. Pass the -sT parameter and the name of the target system to it, as shown here:

```
$ nmap -sT seeker.rodsbooks.com
Starting Nmap 4.53 ( http://insecure.org ) at 2008-09-04 15:38 EDT
Interesting ports on seeker.rodsbooks.com (192.168.1.6):
Not shown: 1704 closed ports
PORT      STATE SERVICE
22/tcp    open  ssh
80/tcp    open  http
2049/tcp  open  nfs
3306/tcp  open  mysql
Nmap done: 1 IP address (1 host up) scanned in 0.100 seconds
```

As with the output of netstat and lsof shown earlier, this output has been trimmed for brevity's sake.

This output shows four open ports: 22, 80, 2049, and 3306, used by ssh, http, nfs, and mysql, respectively. If you weren't aware that these ports were active, you should log into the scanned system and investigate further, using netstat, lsof, or ps to locate the programs using these ports and, if desired, shut them down. The -sT option specifies a scan of TCP ports. A few servers, though, run on UDP ports, so you need to scan them by typing **nmap -sU *hostname*.** (This usage requires root privileges, unlike scanning TCP ports.)

Nmap is capable of more-sophisticated scans, including "stealth" scans that aren't likely to be noticed by most types of firewalls, ping scans to detect which hosts are active, and more. The Nmap man page provides details. Nessus, which is built atop Nmap, provides a GUI and a means of performing automated and still-more-sophisticated tests. Nessus comes as separate client and server components; the client enables you to control the server, which does the actual work.

When you use a network scanner, you should consider the fact that the ports you see from your test system may not be the same as those that might be visible to an attacker. This issue is particularly important if you're testing a system that resides behind a firewall from another system that's behind the same firewall. Your test system is likely to reveal accessible ports that would not be accessible from the outside world. On the other hand, a cracker on your local network would most likely have access similar to your own, so you shouldn't be complacent because you use a firewall. Nonetheless, firewalls can be important tools for hiding servers without shutting them down.

You can use a stand-alone Linux boot CD-ROM to perform security checks on a network. Tools intended for this purpose, such as BackTrack (http://www.backtrack-linux.org), provide easy access to Nmap and other network security tools, enabling quick checks of network security even if no computer on that network regularly runs Linux.

Examining Configuration Files

Most Linux server packages include configuration files. Thus, you may be able to spot installed but unwanted servers by looking for their configuration files. On most systems, two classes of files are important: those controlling startup scripts and those controlling your super server.

Startup scripts are described in Chapter 5, so review that chapter for details of how they're managed. Generally speaking, you'll look in /etc/rc?.d, /etc/init.d/rc?.d, or /etc/rc.d/rc?.d, where ? is your default runlevel number, for SysV startup scripts whose names take the form S##*server*, where ## is a number and *server* is the name of the server. If you find such a script for a server you know you don't want to run, you should disable it using your SysV startup script editing tools, as described in Chapter 5. If your distribution uses Upstart or systemd, though, you'll need to look elsewhere to find the relevant startup files.

Be aware that many startup scripts start entire subsystems that aren't directly network-related. Thus, you'll probably see startup scripts that you don't recognize. You shouldn't automatically disable these scripts, because they may be necessary even if you don't recognize the name. If in doubt, leave it in place until you can research the matter further.

Try doing a Web search on the name of the startup script (minus the S and sequence number or other components unique to your startup system), possibly in conjunction with "Linux" or "startup script." Chances are, you'll find a helpful reference.

The other major configuration-file class you should examine is the super server configuration. Thus, you should check your inetd or xinetd configuration files for unwanted servers. Also, unlike system startup scripts, super servers launch network servers only, not non-network services. Therefore, you should take a more aggressive approach to disabling entries you don't recognize from your super server configuration than you do with system startup scripts.

On computers using the SysV startup system, /etc/inittab deserves examination. This file, described in Chapter 5, controls some of the earliest stages of the startup process. Of greatest interest from a security point of view is the fact that older /etc/inittab installations started the processes used to accept text-mode logins, as well as similar processes used to accept logins via dial-up modems and RS-232 serial ports. These processes are called getty or some variant of this, such as mingetty. Ordinarily, a Linux machine must have at least one such process running, and it's controlled via an /etc/inittab entry such as the following:

```
1:2345:respawn:/sbin/mingetty --noclear tty1
```

The first character of this line (1) specifies the virtual terminal (VT) it controls. Most Linux distributions include similar lines for the first six VTs, and there's usually no need to adjust these lines. Lines that begin with S#, where # is a number, control login via RS-232 serial ports and modems:

```
S0:2345:respawn:/usr/sbin/mgetty -F -s 57600 /dev/ttyS0
```

If you want to use a modem with the computer but don't want to enable remote logins via the modem, you should ensure that /etc/inittab does *not* have such lines.

Modern systems that lack /etc/inittab or have only very basic /etc/inittab files typically move these functions into other files, such as SysV startup scripts or files in /etc/init. You won't ordinarily need to modify such configurations, but you may want to check to be sure your system isn't listening for dial-up modem connections unnecessarily. Files called /etc/init/tty# (where # is a number) control local login access, whereas /etc/init/ttyS# files control RS-232 serial or modem access.

Uninstalling or Reconfiguring Servers

Once you've identified an unnecessary server, your task becomes one of shutting it down. Broadly speaking, two options exist:

- You can disable the server by changing its startup script configuration or by disabling it in your system's super server. Consult Chapter 5 and the preceding sections on inetd and xinetd for details on how to perform these tasks. Disabling the server in this way has the advantage that you can easily reactivate the server in the future if you decide to do so. It has the disadvantage that the server's files will continue to consume disk space, and the server might be *accidentally* reactivated in the future.

- You can completely uninstall the server using your distribution's package management tools or by otherwise deleting its files. Chapter 2, "Managing Software," describes this task. Completely uninstalling software has the advantage of reducing the risk of accidental reactivation, but it has the drawback that it will take more effort to reactivate the server should you decide to do so in the future.

Overall, completely removing the server is generally preferable unless you merely want to temporarily disable a server. If you decide to reactivate the server in the future, you can always re-install it.

Administering Local Security

Security isn't limited to networking—local security issues can be as much of a threat as remote intruders. Thus, you should attend to some local security matters: securing passwords, limiting root access to the computer, setting user limits, and tracking down SUID/SGID files.

Securing Passwords

A default Linux configuration relies heavily on passwords. Users' passwords are their keys into the system, and careless handling of passwords is much like careless handling of physical keys—security breaches can result. Understanding these risks is critical to maintaining system security, but this is one task for which you *must* enlist the help of your users; after all, they're the ones who are in possession of their passwords! You should also be aware of some of the tools Linux provides to help keep passwords secure. (Most of the details concerning password-related commands are described in Chapter 7, "Administering the System.")

Password Risks

Passwords can end up in crackers' hands in various ways, and you must take steps to minimize these risks. Steps you can take to improve your system's security include the following:

Use Strong Passwords   Users should employ good passwords, as described shortly in "Choosing a Good Password." This practice won't eliminate all risk, though.

Change Passwords Frequently   You can minimize the chance of damage due to a compromised password by changing passwords frequently. Some Linux tools can help to enforce such changes, as described briefly in "Tools for Managing Passwords" and in more detail in Chapter 7.

Use Shadow Passwords   If a cracker who's broken into your system through an ordinary user account can read the password file or if one of your regular users is a cracker who has access to the password file, that individual can run any of several password-cracking programs on the file. For this reason, you should use shadow passwords stored in /etc/shadow whenever possible. All major Linux distributions use shadow passwords by default. If yours doesn't, consult the upcoming section "Tools for Managing Passwords" for information about enabling this feature.

Keep Passwords Secret   You should remind your users not to reveal their passwords to others. Such trust is sometimes misplaced, and sometimes even a well-intentioned password recipient may slip up and let the password fall into the wrong hands. This can happen by writing the password down, storing it in electronic form, or sending it by email or other electronic means. Users shouldn't email their own passwords even to themselves, because email can be intercepted.

Use Secure Remote Login Protocols   Certain remote login protocols are inherently insecure; all data traverse the network in an unencrypted form. Intervening computers can be configured to snatch passwords from such sessions. Because of this, it's best to disable Telnet, FTP, and other protocols that use cleartext passwords in favor of protocols that encrypt passwords, such as SSH.

Be Alert to Shoulder Surfing   If your users log in using public terminals, as is common on college campuses, in Internet cafes, and the like, it's possible that others will be able to watch them type their passwords—a practice sometimes called *shoulder surfing*. Users should be alert to this possibility and minimize such logins if possible.

Use Each Password on Just One System   If one computer's password database is compromised and if users of that system reuse their passwords on other systems, those other systems can be compromised. For this reason, it's best to use each password just once. Unfortunately, the proliferation of Web sites that require passwords for access makes this rule almost impossible to enforce, at least without violating the rule of not writing the password down. (Modern Web browsers can remember passwords for you, but this is done by storing them in a file—essentially, writing them down.) A reasonable compromise might be to use one password for the least-sensitive Web sites (such as online newspapers) and unique passwords for sensitive Web sites (such as banking sites) and login accounts.

Be Alert to Social Engineering   Crackers often use *social engineering* to obtain passwords. This practice involves tricking individuals into giving up their passwords by pretending to be a system administrator or by otherwise misleading victims. Amazingly, a large percentage of people fall for this ploy. A related practice is *phishing*, in which an attacker puts up a fake Web site or sends an email pretending to be from somebody else. The victim is then lured into revealing sensitive data (such as credit card numbers).

Some of these steps are things you can do, such as replacing insecure remote login protocols with encrypted ones. Others are things your users must do. This illustrates the importance of user education, particularly on systems with many users.

Choosing a Good Password

As a general rule, people tend to be lazy when it comes to security. In computer terms, this means users tend to pick passwords that are easy to guess, and they change those passwords infrequently. Both these conditions make a cracker's life easier, particularly if the cracker knows the victim. Fortunately, Linux includes tools to help make your users select good passwords and change them regularly.

Poor but common passwords include those based on the following:

- The names of family members, friends, and pets
- Favorite books, movies, television shows, or the characters in any of these
- Telephone numbers, street addresses, or Social Security numbers
- Any other meaningful personal information
- Any single word that's found in a dictionary (in *any* language)
- Any simple keyboard or alphanumeric combination, such as `qwerty` or `123456`

The best possible passwords are random collections of letters, digits, and punctuation. Unfortunately, such passwords are difficult to remember. A reasonable compromise is to build a password in two steps:

1. Choose a base that's easy to remember but difficult to guess.

2. Modify that base in ways that increase the difficulty of guessing the password.

One approach to building a base is to use two *unrelated* words, such as *bun* and *pen*. You can then merge these two words (bunpen). Another approach, and one that's arguably better than the first, is to use the first letters of a phrase that's meaningful to the user. For instance, the first letters of "yesterday I went to the dentist" become yiwttd. In both cases, the base should not be a word in any language. As a general rule, the longer the password, the better. Older versions of Linux could handle passwords of no more than eight characters, but those limits have been lifted by the use of the MD5 and SHA password hashes, which are the standard on modern Linux distributions. Many Linux systems require passwords to be at least four to six characters in length; the passwd utility won't accept anything shorter than the distribution's minimum.

With the base in hand, it's time to modify it to create a password. The user should apply at least a couple of several possible modifications:

Adding Numbers or Punctuation   One important modification is to insert random numbers or punctuation in the base. This step might yield, for instance, bu3npe&n or y#i9wttd. As a general rule, add at least two symbols or numbers.

Mixing Case   Linux uses case-sensitive passwords, so jumbling the case of letters can improve security. Applying this rule might produce Bu3nPE&n and y#i9WttD, for instance.

Reversing Order   A change that's very weak by itself but that can add somewhat to security when used in conjunction with the others is to reverse the order of some or all letters. You might apply this to just one word of a two-word base. This could yield Bu3nn&EP and DttW9i#y, for instance.

Growing the Haystack   A would-be intruder's task of discovering a password has been likened to finding a needle in a haystack. One way to make this task harder is to increase the size of the haystack. In password terms, this means making a password longer. You can do this by using longer words or phrases, of course, but this can make a password harder to remember and type. Even a size increase that simply repeats a single character can be helpful. Thus, you might turn the passwords into Bu3nn&EPiiiiiiiiiii or Dtt::::::::::W9i#y.

Your best tool for getting users to pick good passwords is to educate them. Tell them that passwords can be guessed by malicious individuals who know them or even who target them and look up personal information in telephone books, on Web pages, and so on. Tell them that, although Linux encrypts its passwords internally, programs exist that feed entire dictionaries through Linux's password encryption algorithms for comparison to encrypted passwords. If a match is found, the cracker has found the password. Therefore, using a password that's not in a dictionary, and that isn't a simple variant of a dictionary word, improves security substantially. Tell your users that their accounts might be used as a first step toward compromising the entire computer or as a launching point for attacks on other computers. Explain to your users that they should *never* reveal their passwords to others, even people claiming to be system administrators—this is a common scam, but real system administrators don't need users' passwords. You should also warn them not to use the same password on multiple systems because doing so quickly turns a compromised account on one system into a compromised account on all the systems. Telling your users these things will help them understand the reasons for your concern, and it's likely to help motivate at least some of them to pick good passwords.

If your users are unconcerned after being told these things (and in any large installation, some will be), you'll have to rely on the checks possible in `passwd`. Most distributions' implementations of this utility require a minimum password length (typically four to eight characters). They also usually check the password against a dictionary, thus weeding out some of the absolute worst passwords. Some require that a password contain at least one or two digits or punctuation.

WARNING Password-cracking programs, such as John the Ripper (`http://www.open wall.com/john/`), are easy to obtain. You might consider running such programs on your own encrypted password database to spot poor passwords, and in fact, this is a good policy in many cases. It's also grounds for dismissal in many organizations and can even result in criminal charges being brought, at least if done without authorization. If you want to weed out bad passwords this way, discuss the matter with your superiors and obtain written permission from a person with the authority to grant it before proceeding. Take extreme care with the files involved, too; it's best to crack the passwords on a computer with no network connections.

Another password security issue is password changes. Frequently changing passwords minimizes the window of opportunity for crackers to do damage; if a cracker obtains a password but it changes before the cracker can use it (or before the cracker can do further damage using the compromised account), the password change has averted disaster. As described shortly, you can configure accounts to require periodic password changes. When so configured, an account will stop accepting logins after a time if the password isn't changed periodically. (You can configure the system to warn users when this time is approaching.) This is a very good option to enable on sensitive systems or those with many users. Don't set the expire time too low, though—if users have to change their passwords too frequently, they'll probably just switch between a couple of passwords or pick poor ones. Precisely what "too low" a password change time is depends on the environment. For most systems, one to six months is probably a reasonable change time, but for some it may be longer or shorter.

Tools for Managing Passwords

Most Linux distributions use shadow passwords by default, and for the most part, this chapter is written with the assumption that this feature is active. In addition to providing extra security by moving hashed passwords out of the world-readable `/etc/passwd` file and into the more secure `/etc/shadow` file, shadow passwords add extra account information.

One of the advantages of shadow passwords is that they support password aging and account expiration features. These features enable you to enforce password changes at regular intervals or to automatically disable an account after a specified period of time. You can enable these features and set the times using the chage command, which is described in more detail in Chapter 7.

The usermod utility, described in Chapter 7, can be used to adjust some shadow password features, such as account expiration dates. The chage command is more thorough with respect to account security features, but usermod can adjust more non-security account features.

Limiting *root* Access

Because root can do anything on a Linux computer, access to that account must of course be limited. On a system with a single administrator, this can be accomplished by having the administrator set a unique root password that nobody else knows. This user can then log in directly as root or use su to acquire root privileges. The su command's name stands for *switch user*, and it's used to change a user's apparent identity. Typing su alone results in a prompt for the root password. If the user types that password correctly, the session effectively becomes a root session. You can also type a username after su to acquire that user's privileges. When root does so, no password is required. (This is sometimes handy for investigating problems reported by a single user.) To run a single program with root privileges, use -c to specify the program name, as in **su -c "lsof -i"** to run lsof -i as root.

Logging in directly as root is generally discouraged for several reasons: No record of who typed the password appears in log files; the root password can be intercepted in various ways; and if the user leaves the terminal, a passerby can hijack the computer. Using su is somewhat better than a direct login from a security point of view, because use of su generally leaves a trace in system logs of who became root.

A method of acquiring root access that is somewhat more secure than either direct logins or su is sudo. This program runs a single command as root; for instance, to run lsof -i as root, you type

```
$ sudo lsof -i
[sudo] password for georgia:
```

In this example, the computer prompts for the *user's* (georgia's) password, not for the root password. The idea behind sudo is that you first configure the computer to accept certain users as sudo users. Those users may then use *their own* passwords to perform superuser tasks, even if those users don't have the root password. (Some sudo configurations require users to enter the superuser's password rather than their own password, though.) You can even fine-tune what tasks users may perform. This is done via the /etc/sudoers configuration file. You must edit this configuration file via visudo, which is a variant of Vi (described in Chapter 5) that's used only to edit /etc/sudoers.

The /etc/sudoers file consists of two types of entries: aliases and user specifications. Aliases are basically variables; you can use them to define groups of commands, groups of users, and so on. User specifications link users to machines and commands (possibly using aliases for some or all options). Thus, you can configure sudoers such that georgia can run network programs with root privileges but not account maintenance tools, whereas george can run account maintenance tools but not network programs.

Your default /etc/sudoers file probably includes several examples. Consider the following lines:

```
## Storage
Cmnd_Alias STORAGE = /sbin/fdisk, /sbin/sfdisk, /sbin/parted,↵
/sbin/partprobe, /bin/mount, /bin/umount
## Processes
Cmnd_Alias PROCESSES = /bin/nice, /bin/kill, /usr/bin/kill, /usr/bin/killall
%sys ALL = STORAGE, PROCESSES
%disk ALL = STORAGE
%wheel ALL=(ALL) ALL
```

This example defines two command aliases, STORAGE and PROCESSES, each of which stands in for a set of commands. Users who are members of the sys group may use both sets of commands; users who are members of the disk group may use the STORAGE commands but not the PROCESSES commands; and members of the wheel group may use all commands, whether or not they're explicitly mentioned in /etc/sudoers.

Some distributions, such as Ubuntu, make heavy use of sudo; these distributions are designed to be administered exclusively via sudo, and they set up an /etc/sudoers file that provides at least one user with easy access to all system utilities. Other distributions don't rely on sudo this way, although you can tweak your sudo configuration to enable administration via sudo if you like.

Setting Login, Process, and Memory Limits

Sometimes you may want to impose limits on how many times users may log in, how much CPU time they can consume, how much memory they can use, and so on. Imposing such limits is best done through a Pluggable Authentication Modules (PAM) module called pam_limits. Most major Linux distributions use this module as part of their standard PAM configuration, so chances are you won't need to add it; however, you will still need to configure pam_limits. You do so by editing its configuration file, /etc/security/limits .conf. This file contains comments (denoted by a hash mark, #) and limit lines that consist of four fields:

domain type item value

Each of these fields specifies a particular type of information:

The Domain   The *domain* describes the entity to which the limit applies. It can be a username; a group name, which takes the form *@groupname*; or an asterisk (*) wildcard, which matches everybody.

Hard or Soft Limits The *type* field specifies the limit as hard or soft. A hard limit is imposed by the system administrator and cannot be exceeded under any circumstances, whereas a soft limit may be temporarily exceeded by a user. You can also use a dash (-) to signify that a limit is both hard and soft.

The Limited Item The *item* field specifies what type of item is being limited. Examples include core (the size of core files), data (the size of a program's data area), fsize (the size of files created by the user), nofile (the number of open data files), rss (the resident set size), stack (the stack size), cpu (the CPU time of a single process in minutes), nproc (the number of concurrent processes), maxlogins (the number of simultaneous logins), and priority (the process priority). The data, rss, and stack items all relate to memory consumed by a program. These and other measures of data capacity are measured in kilobytes.

The Value The final field specifies the value that's to be applied to the limit.

As an example, consider a system on which certain users should be able to log in and perform a limited number of actions but not stay logged in indefinitely and consume vast amounts of CPU time. You can use a configuration like this one:

```
@limited  hard  cpu  2
```

This configuration applies a hard CPU limit of two minutes to the limited group. Members of this group can log in and run programs; but if one of those programs consumes more than two minutes of CPU time, it will be terminated.

NOTE CPU time and total system access time are two entirely different things. CPU time is calculated based on the amount of time the CPU is actively processing a user's data. Idle time (for instance, when a user's shell is active but no CPU-intensive tasks are running) doesn't count. Thus, a user can log in and remain logged in for hours even with a very low hard CPU time limit. This limit is intended to prevent problems caused by users who run very CPU-intensive programs on systems that shouldn't be used for such purposes.

Another way to set limits on system resource use is via the ulimit command. This command is a bash built-in command, so it affects only bash and programs launched from it. The ulimit syntax is as follows:

```
ulimit [options [limit]]
```

The *options* define what is being limited:

Core File Limits The -c option limits the size of *core dumps*, which are files created for debugging purposes in certain types of program crashes.

File Limits The -f option limits the size of files that may be created by the shell, and -n limits the number of open file descriptors. (Most systems don't honor the -n limits, though.)

Process Limits The -u option limits the number of processes a user may run, and -t limits the total CPU time in seconds.

Memory Limits   The -v option sets the total amount of virtual memory available to the shell, -s sets the maximum stack size, -m sets the maximum resident set size, -d limits programs' data set size, and -1 sets the maximum size that may be locked into memory.

Hard and Soft Limits   The -H and -S options modify other options, causing them to be set as *hard* or *soft* limits, respectively. Hard limits may not be subsequently increased, but soft limits may be. If neither option is provided, ulimit sets both the hard and soft limits for the feature specified.

Current Settings   Passing -a causes ulimit to report its current settings.

The *limit* is typically a numeric value associated with the limit. The ulimit command is often found in system or user bash startup scripts, typically as ulimit -c 0, in order to prevent creation of core files, which can sometimes clutter a filesystem. If your users perform software development, you may want to ensure that you do *not* set this limit, or at least set it as a soft limit (as in ulimit -Sc 0) so users may override it when necessary.

WARNING   Because ulimit is a bash built-in command, its utility as a system security tool is limited. If users have access to GUI login tools or can log into the system in any way that bypasses bash (such as via SSH, depending on how it's configured), restrictions imposed by ulimit become meaningless. Thus, you should treat ulimit as a way to prevent problems because of accidental, rather than intentional, abuse of the system.

One particularly radical approach to security is to use the /etc/nologin file. If this file is present, only root may log into the computer. Other users are shown the contents of this file when they attempt to log in. In many respects, this is like setting critical system limits to 0 for all other users. This file is most likely to be useful on dedicated server systems that have no regular console or remote shell users.

Locating SUID/SGID Files

Chapter 4, "Managing Files," describes the SUID and SGID bits. In brief, these are special flags that may be applied to executable program files, causing Linux to treat the program as if it were run by the program file's owner (for SUID) or by the file's group (for SGID) rather than by the individual who actually ran the program. For instance, if a program's SUID bit is set and if the program file is owned by bruce, the program, when run by anybody, will be able to access all the files owned by bruce and otherwise behave as if bruce had run it.

The SUID and SGID bits are frequently associated with the root account in order to enable them to perform tasks that require special privilege. For instance, the passwd program (described in Chapter 7) is SUID root because only root may modify the Linux password database. Thus, for an ordinary user to change a password, some mechanism must exist to run a process as root. That mechanism, in the case of passwd, is the SUID bit.

The problem with all of this is that the SUID and SGID bits can be security risks. For instance, suppose the rm program's SUID bit was set. This program is normally owned by root, so setting the SUID bit on rm would mean that any user could delete any file on the computer. Although no Linux distribution sets the SUID bit on rm by default, the SUID bit can be set inappropriately. This can happen by accident (say, a mistyped command by root), by malice (if a cracker gains access to the system), or because of a more subtle misconfiguration by the distribution maintainer (the SUID bit set unnecessarily on a program for which it's less blatantly inappropriate than rm). Even if the SUID or SGID bit is set appropriately, a bug in the program can become more serious because the bug executes as root. If the bug enables users to write files, for example, any user can exploit the bug to overwrite critical system configuration files. For these reasons, you should periodically review your system to find all the SUID programs and, if appropriate, change their configuration.

To do this, you can use the find command, which is described in detail in Chapter 4. In particular, you can use the -perm *mode* option, which searches for files with the specified permission mode. To search for SUID and SGID files, you should pass a *mode* of +6000. The symbolic representation for the SUID and SGID bits is 6000, and the plus sign (+) tells find to locate any file with any of the specified bits set. (You could search for SUID files alone by passing +4000 or SGID alone by passing +2000.) You may also want to pass -type f, which restricts the search to regular files. (Directories use the SUID and SGID bits differently, as described in Chapter 4.) Thus, to search the entire computer for SUID and SGID programs, you type this:

```
# find / -perm +6000 -type f
```

The result is a list of files, one per line, that have either the SUID or the SGID bits set. Programs that are likely to be present in this list include su, ping, mount, passwd, umount, and sudo. These programs all have a legitimate need to be so configured. Most systems have additional SUID and SGID programs, some of which may seem trivial. For instance, some games are associated with the games group and set the SGID bit. This configuration enables users to modify the games' system-wide high-score files. If you have doubts about whether the program really needs SUID or SGID status, you should investigate further. Try verifying the package integrity using your package management tools and perform a Web search on the program name and "SUID" or "SGID," as appropriate. You can also try changing the SUID status of the program using chmod, as described in Chapter 4, and see if it still works as it should when run by a normal user.

WARNING   Programs that are SUID or SGID root, but that shouldn't be, can be a sign of system compromise. Crackers might reconfigure programs this way in order to more easily do their dirty work. Thus, if you find such programs, investigate the overall integrity of the system. On the other hand, if a distribution maintainer set the SUID or SGID bit unnecessarily, this isn't cause for concern about a break-in, although you may want to fix the matter. Likewise, accidental misconfiguration by you or another administrator isn't cause for massive system upheaval—but you'll need to dig a bit deeper to ascertain whether such a change was accidental or a sign of a deeper problem.

Configuring SSH

In the past, Telnet was the remote text-mode login protocol of choice on Linux and Unix systems. Unfortunately, Telnet is severely lacking in security features. Thus, in recent years SSH has grown in popularity, and it is now the preferred remote login tool. SSH can also handle file transfer tasks similar to those of FTP. For these reasons, knowing how to configure SSH can be very helpful. This task requires knowing a bit about SSH generally and about the SSH configuration file under Linux. As is usual in this chapter, I conclude the look at SSH with information about the security implications of running the server.

SSH is complex enough that I can't cover more than its basics in this chapter. Consult OpenSSH's documentation or a book on the topic, such as *SSH, The Secure Shell: The Definitive Guide, Second Edition,* by Daniel J. Barrett, Richard Silverman, and Robert G. Byrnes (O'Reilly, 2005) or *SSH Mastery: OpenSSH, PuTTY, Tunnels and Keys* (CreateSpace, 2012) by Michael W. Lucas, for more details.

SSH Basics

Linux supports remote login access through several different servers, including Telnet, Virtual Network Computing (VNC), and even X. Unfortunately, most of these methods suffer from a major drawback: They transfer all data over the network in unencrypted form. This fact means that anybody who can monitor network traffic can easily snatch sensitive data, often including passwords. (VNC and a few other protocols encrypt passwords but not other data.) This limitation puts a serious dent in the utility of these remote login tools; after all, if using a remote access protocol means you'll be giving away sensitive data or compromising your entire computer, it's not a very useful protocol.

Non-encrypting remote access tools are particularly risky for performing work as root, either by logging in directly as root or by logging in as an ordinary user and then using su, sudo, or other tools to acquire root privileges.

   SSH was designed to close this potentially major security hole by employing strong encryption techniques for all parts of the network connection. SSH encrypts the password exchange and all subsequent data transfers, making it a much safer protocol for remote access.

   In addition to encryption, SSH provides file transfer features and the ability to *tunnel* other network protocols—that is, to enable non-encrypted protocols to piggyback their data over an SSH connection, thus delivering SSH's encryption advantages to other protocols. This feature is frequently employed in conjunction with X, enabling encrypted remote GUI access, as described in Chapter 6, "Configuring the X Window System, Localization, and Printing."

Of course, SSH's advantages don't come without a price. The main drawback of SSH is that the encryption and decryption consume CPU time. This fact slows down SSH connections compared to those of direct connections and can degrade overall system performance. This effect is modest, though, particularly for plain text-mode connections. If you tunnel a protocol that transfers much more data, such as X, you may see a greater performance drop when using SSH. Even in this case, the improved security is generally worth the slight speed cost.

Several SSH servers are available for Linux, but the most popular by far is the OpenSSH server (http://www.openssh.org). This program was one of the first open source implementations of the SSH protocol, which was developed by the commercial SSH Communications Security (http://www.ssh.com), whose server is now sold under the name SSH Tectia. OpenSSH, SSH Tectia, and other SSH products can interoperate with one another, assuming they're all configured to support at least one common level of the SSH protocol. OpenSSH 6.1, the latest version as I write, supports SSH levels 1.3, 1.5, and 2.0, with 2.0 being the preferred level because of known vulnerabilities in the earlier versions.

OpenSSH is closely associated with the OpenBSD OS, so its Web site has an OpenBSD bias. If you visit the site, you may want to click the Linux link under the For Other OS's heading. You can find Linux-compatible source code and binaries from that site, and OpenSSH now ships with most Linux distributions.

OpenSSH may be launched via either a super server (inetd or xinetd) or a SysV startup script. The latter method is preferred because the server may need to perform CPU-intensive tasks upon starting, so if it's started from a super server OpenSSH may be sluggish to respond to connection requests, particularly on systems with weaker CPUs. Most distributions deliver suitable startup scripts with their SSH packages. If you make changes to your SSH configuration, you may need to pass the reload or restart option to the startup script, as in **/etc/init.d/sshd reload**. (Chapter 5 covers startup scripts in more detail.) However it's launched, the OpenSSH server binary name is sshd—the same as the binary name for SSH Tectia.

Setting SSH Options for Your Computer

For the most part, SSH works reasonably well when it's first installed, so you may not need to make any changes to its configuration. If you do need to make changes, though, these are mostly handled through the main SSH configuration file, /etc/ssh/sshd_config. You can also edit some additional files to limit access to the SSH server or to change how SSH manages the login process.

Configuring Basic SSH Features

The /etc/ssh/sshd_config file consists mainly of option lines that take the following form:

Option value

WARNING   Don't confuse the sshd_config file with the ssh_config file. The former controls the OpenSSH server, whereas the latter controls the SSH client program, ssh.

In addition to configuration lines, the sshd_config file holds comments, which are denoted by hash marks (#). Most sample configuration files include a large number of SSH options that are commented out; these lines specify the default values, so uncommenting the lines without otherwise changing them will have no effect. If you want to change an option, uncomment the line and change it. Most options' default values are suitable for most systems. The following list includes some that you may want to check and, perhaps, change:

Protocol   This option specifies the protocol levels OpenSSH understands. Possible values are 1 and 2. You can configure OpenSSH to support both protocols by separating them by a comma, as in 1,2 or 2,1, which are equivalent. Given the fact that OpenSSH protocol level 1 has been compromised, the safest configuration is to set Protocol 2. This limits the server's ability to communicate with older clients, though.

PermitRootLogin   By default, this option is set to yes, which enables OpenSSH to accept direct logins by root. This is safer than a similar configuration under Telnet, but for a bit of added security, set this value to no. The result will be that anybody wanting to perform remote work as root will need to first log in as an ordinary user, which means that an intruder who has somehow acquired the root password will also need a regular username and its password. (If the computer is configured to allow an ordinary user to work via sudo, though, a compromise of that user's account would also effectively be a compromise of the root account.)

X11Forwarding   This option specifies whether OpenSSH's X tunneling features should be active. If you want to enable remote users to run X programs via SSH, you must set this option to yes. Doing so can slightly degrade security of the client's X display, though, depending on certain other options; hence the conservative default value of no.

For information about additional options, consult the man page for sshd_config. If you make changes to the SSH configuration, remember to restart it using the server's SysV startup script.

SSH Keys

Part of SSH's security involves *encryption keys*. Each server system and each user have a unique number, or key, for identification purposes. In fact, SSH uses a security system that involves two keys: a *public key* and a *private key*. These two keys are mathematically linked in such a way that data encrypted with a particular public key may be decrypted only with the matching private key. When establishing a connection, each side sends its public key to the other. Thereafter, each side encrypts data with the other side's public key, ensuring that the data can be decrypted only by the intended recipient. In practice, this is just the first step of the process, but it's critical. What's more, SSH clients typically retain the public keys of servers they've contacted. This enables them to spot changes to the public key. Such changes can be signs of tampering, so if a client detects such a change, it will warn its user of this fact.

Most OpenSSH server startup scripts include code that looks for stored public and private keys and, if they're not present, generates them. In total, four to six keys are needed: public and private keys for two or three encryption tools SSH supports. These keys are normally stored in /etc/ssh and are called ssh_host_rsa_key and ssh_host_dsa_key for private keys, with .pub filename extensions added for public keys. Some systems add ssh_host_rsa1_key and its associated public key. If your system doesn't have these keys and you can't get the SSH server to start up, you can try generating the keys with the ssh-keygen command:

```
# ssh-keygen -q -t rsa1 -f /etc/ssh/ssh_host_key -C '' -N ''
# ssh-keygen -q -t rsa -f /etc/ssh/ssh_host_rsa_key -C '' -N ''
# ssh-keygen -q -t dsa -f /etc/ssh/ssh_host_dsa_key -C '' -N ''
```

Each of these commands generates both a private key (named in the -f parameter) and a public key (with the same name but with .pub appended).

Don't run these ssh-keygen commands if the SSH key files already exist. Replacing the working files will cause clients who've already connected to the SSH server to complain about the changed keys and possibly refuse to establish a connection.

WARNING   Be sure the private keys are suitably protected; if an intruder obtains one of these keys, the intruder can impersonate your system. Typically, these files should have 0600 (-rw-------) permissions and be owned by root. The public key files (with .pub filename extensions) should be readable by all users, though.

When you configure a client system, you may want to consider creating a global cache of host keys. As already noted, the ssh program records host keys for each individual user. (It stores these in the ~/.ssh/known_hosts file.) When you set up the client, you can populate the global ssh_known_hosts file, which is normally stored in /etc or /etc/ssh. Doing so ensures that the public key list is as accurate as the sources you use to populate the global file. It also eliminates confirmation messages when users connect to the hosts whose keys you've selected to include in the global file.

How do you create this file? One simple way is to copy the file from a user account that's been used to connect to the servers you want to include. For instance, you can type `cp /home/ecernan/.ssh/known_hosts /etc/ssh/ssh_known_hosts` to use ecernan's file.

> In the past, you could review SSH's known hosts file in a text editor, since it's a text-mode file. Today, though, OpenSSH 4.0 and newer support hashing of the data in this file. When this feature is enabled, the information is *hashed* (that is, encrypted using a one-way encryption algorithm) and stored in hashed form. The idea is that you'll still be able to authenticate SSH servers to which you connect, because a hash of the typed hostname will match a hash of the stored hostname; but if an intruder steals your known hosts file, the intruder will be unable to determine the identities of the computers to which you've been connecting. An unfortunate side effect of this hashing is that you can't tell what servers it describes yourself.

Controlling SSH Access

You can limit who may access an SSH server in various ways. The most obvious and basic method is via password authentication. The usual SSH authentication method is to employ a username and password, much as Telnet does. (The `ssh` client program sends the username automatically or as part of the command line, so you won't see a username prompt when logging in via `ssh`.)

Beyond password authentication, SSH supports several other types of limitations:

TCP Wrappers   If you run SSH from a super server or if the server was compiled with TCP Wrappers support, you can use the `/etc/hosts.allow` and `/etc/hosts.deny` files to limit access by IP address. Note that if you launch SSH via a system startup script, this approach works only if the server was compiled to support it. This support may or may not be present in your distribution's standard SSH package.

Firewalls   As with all servers, you can restrict access by using a firewall. SSH uses TCP port 22. Technically, this isn't an SSH feature, but it's certainly useful for protecting an SSH server.

/etc/nologin   If this file is present, SSH honors it. As described earlier, this file's presence means that only `root` may log in. When a non-`root` user tries to log in locally, the file's contents are displayed as an error message; however, OpenSSH doesn't do this.

Copying Files via SSH

Most users employ the `ssh` client program, which provides remote login access—type **ssh** *othersystem* to log into *othersystem* using the same username you're using on the client system; or add a username, as in **ssh** **user@*othersystem***, to log in using another username.

SSH includes a file-copying command, too: `scp`. This command works much like the `cp` command for copying files locally; however, you must specify the target computer, and optionally the username, just before the target filename. For instance, to copy the file masterpiece.c to the lisa account on leonardo.example.com, you would type

```
$ scp masterpiece.c lisa@leonardo.example.com:
```

The colon (:) that terminates this command is extremely important; if you omit it, you'll find that scp works like cp, and you'll end up with a file called lisa@leonardo.example.com on the original system. If you want to rename the file, you can do so by including the new name following the colon. Likewise, you can place the file in a particular directory in the same way, as follows:

```
$ scp masterpiece.c lisa@leonardo.example.com:~/art/mona.c
```

This example copies masterpiece.c to the ~/art directory on the target computer and renames it mona.c. If the specified directory doesn't exist, an error results, and the file is not transferred. If you specify a directory *without* a trailing slash or filename and you mistype the directory name, scp will copy the file and rename it to your mistyped directory name. (scp works just like cp in this respect.)

Configuring Logins Without Passwords

If you use SSH a lot or if you use it in automated tools, you'll no doubt become annoyed by the need to type a password with every connection. There is a way around this requirement: You can set up the SSH client with keys and give the client's public key to the server computer. With this configuration, the SSH client computer can identify itself, possibly obviating the need for you to type a password.

Configuring SSH to operate without the use of passwords is convenient, but it does increase security risks. If somebody you don't trust ever gains access to your account on the SSH client system, that person will be able to log into the SSH server system as you without the benefit of your password. Thus, you should create a password-less login only from a client that's very well protected, if at all. Configuring access to the root account in this way is particularly risky.

To configure SSH to not require a password, follow these steps:

1. Log into the SSH client system as the user who will be performing remote access.

2. Type the following command to generate a version 2 SSH key:

   ```
   $ ssh-keygen -q -t rsa -f ~/.ssh/id_rsa -C '' -N ''
   ```

Step 2 generates a version 2 key. You can instead generate a version 1 key by typing ssh-keygen -q -t dsa -f ~/.ssh/id_dsa -C '' -N ''. This generates id_dsa and id_dsa.pub files. This procedure is not recommended because SSH version 1 is not as secure as version 1; however, you may need to use version 1 to connect to some servers.

3. Step 2 generates two files: id_rsa and id_rsa.pub. Transfer the second of these files to the SSH server computer in any way that's convenient—via a USB flash drive, by using scp, or by any other means. Copy the file under a temporary name, such as temp.rsa.

4. Log into the SSH server system. If you use SSH, you'll need to type your password.

5. Add the contents of the file you've just transferred to the end of the ~/.ssh /authorized_keys file. (This file is sometimes called ~/.ssh/authorized_keys2, so you should check to see which is present. If neither is present, you may need to experiment.) Typing **cat ~/temp.rsa >> ~/.ssh/authorized_keys** should do this job, if you stored the original file as ~/temp.rsa.

6. On some systems, you may need to modify permissions on the ~/.ssh/authorized_ keys file and on the directories leading to it. The authorized_keys file may require 0600 permissions, and you may need to remove write permissions for any but the account's owner on your home directory and on the ~/.ssh directory.

If you now log out of the SSH server system and try to log in again via SSH from the client, you shouldn't be prompted for a password; the two computers handle the authentication automatically. If this doesn't work, chances are the ~/.ssh/authorized_keys file needs another name, as described earlier. You may also want to check that the file includes a line matching the contents of the original public-key file on the client. Some older clients may require you to specify that you use version 2 of the SSH protocol by including the -2 option:

```
$ ssh -2 server
```

Using *ssh-agent*

Another SSH authentication option is to use the ssh-agent program. This program requires a password to initiate connections, so it's more secure than configuring logins without passwords; however, ssh-agent remembers your password, so you need type it only once per local session. To use ssh-agent, follow these steps:

1. Follow the procedure for enabling no-password logins described in "Configuring Logins Without Passwords," but with one change: Omit the -N '' option from the ssh-keygen command in step 2. You'll be asked for a passphrase at this step. This passphrase will be your key for all SSH logins managed via ssh-agent.

2. On the SSH client system, type **ssh-agent /bin/bash**. This launches ssh-agent, which in turn launches bash. You'll use this bash session for subsequent SSH logins.

3. In your new shell, type **ssh-add ~/.ssh/id_rsa**. This adds your RSA key to the set that's managed by ssh-agent. You'll be asked to type your SSH passphrase at this time.

From this point on, whenever you use SSH to connect to a remote system to which you've given your public key, you won't need to type a password. You *will*, however, have to repeat steps 2 and 3 whenever you log out, and the benefits will accrue only to the shell launched in step 2 or any shells you launch from that one.

If you make heavy use of this facility, you can insert ssh-agent into your normal login procedure. For instance, you can edit /etc/passwd so that ssh-agent /bin/bash is your login shell. For a GUI login, you can rename your normal GUI login script (for instance, change ~/.xsession to ~/.xsession-nossh) and create a new GUI login script that calls ssh-agent with the renamed script as its parameter. Either action inserts ssh-agent at the root of your user process tree so that any call to SSH uses ssh-agent.

Using SSH Login Scripts

Ordinarily, an SSH text-mode login session runs the user's configured shell, which runs the shell's defined login scripts. The OpenSSH server also supports its own login script, sshrc (normally stored in /etc or /etc/ssh). The OpenSSH server runs this script using /bin/sh, which is normally a symbolic link to bash, so you can treat it as an ordinary bash script.

Setting Up SSH Port Tunnels

SSH has the ability to extend its encryption capabilities to other protocols, but doing so requires extra configuration. The way this is done is known as *tunneling.* Chapter 6 described a special type of SSH tunneling involving X, but the process can work for other protocols.

Figure 10.1 illustrates the basic idea behind an SSH tunnel. The server computer runs two server programs: a server for the tunneled protocol (Figure 10.1 uses the Internet Mail Access Protocol, IMAP, as an example) and an SSH server. The client computer also runs two clients: one for the tunneled protocol and one for SSH. The SSH client also listens for connections for the tunneled protocol; it's effectively both a client and a server. When the SSH client receives a connection from the tunneled protocol's client, the result is that the tunneled protocol's connection is encrypted using SSH, tunneled to the SSH server, and then directed to the target server. Thus, data pass over the network in encrypted form, even if the target protocol doesn't support encryption.

FIGURE 10.1   An SSH tunnel extends SSH's encryption benefits to other protocols.

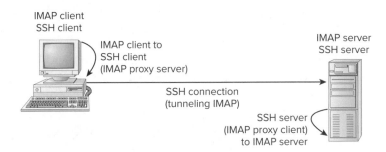

Of course, all of this requires special configuration. The default configuration on the server enables tunneling; but to be sure, check the /etc/ssh/sshd_config file on the server for the following option:

```
AllowTcpForwarding no
```

If this line is present, change no to yes. If it's not present or if it's already set to yes, you shouldn't need to change your SSH server configuration.

On the client side, you must establish a special SSH connection to the server computer. You do this with the normal `ssh` client program, but you must pass it several parameters. An example will help illustrate this use of `ssh`:

```
# ssh -N -f -L 142:mail.luna.edu:143 benf@mail.luna.edu
```

The -N and -f options tell `ssh` to not execute a remote command and to execute in the background after asking for a password, respectively. These options are necessary to create a tunnel. The -L option specifies the local port on which to listen, the remote computer to which to connect, and the port on the remote computer to which to connect. This example listens on the local port 142 and connects to port 143 on `mail.luna.edu`. (You're likely to use the same port number on both ends; I changed the local port number in this example to more clearly distinguish between the local and remote port numbers.) The final parameter (`benf@mail.luna.edu` in this example) is the remote username and computer to which the tunnel goes. Note that this computer need not be the same as the target system specified via -L.

If you want SSH on the client system to listen to a privileged port (that is, one numbered below 1024), you must execute the `ssh` program as root, as shown in the preceding example. If listening to a non-privileged port is acceptable, the `ssh` client can be run as a normal user.

With the tunnel established, you can use the client program to connect to the local port specified by the first number in the -L parameter (port 142 in the preceding example). For instance, this example is intended to forward IMAP traffic, so you'd configure a mail reader on the client to retrieve IMAP email from port 142 on `localhost`. When the email reader does this, SSH kicks in and forwards traffic to the SSH server, which then passes the data on to the SSH server computer's local port 143, which is presumably running the real IMAP server. All of this is hidden from the email reader program; as far as it's concerned, it's retrieving email from a local IMAP server.

SSH Security Considerations

SSH is intended to solve security problems rather than create them. Indeed, on the whole using SSH is superior to using Telnet for remote logins, and SSH can also take over FTP-like functions and tunnel other protocols. Thus, SSH is a big security plus compared to using less-secure tools.

Like all servers, though, SSH can be a security liability if it's run unnecessarily or inappropriately. Ideally, you should configure SSH to accept only protocol level 2 connections and to refuse direct root logins. If X forwarding is unnecessary, you should disable this feature. If possible, use TCP Wrappers or a firewall to limit the machines that can contact an SSH server. As with all servers, you should keep SSH up to date; there's always the possibility of a bug causing problems.

You should consider whether you really need a remote text-mode login server. Such a server can be a great convenience—often enough to justify the modest risk involved. For extremely high-security systems, though, using the computer exclusively from the console may be an appropriate approach to security.

One unusual security issue with SSH is its keys. As noted earlier, the private-key files are extremely sensitive and should be protected from prying eyes. Remember to protect the backups of these files, as well—don't leave a system backup tape lying around where it can be easily stolen.

Using GPG

SSH is designed to encrypt interactive login sessions and file transfers. Sometimes, though, another type of encryption is desirable: You may want to encrypt email messages or files sent to another person via some other means. Email was never designed as a secure data transfer tool, and most email messages pass through several email servers and network routers. A compromise at any one of these points enables a cracker to sniff email traffic and extract sensitive data, such as credit card or Social Security numbers. Encrypting your email keeps such details private.

The usual tool for encrypting email is the GNU Privacy Guard (GPG or GnuPG; http://www.gnupg.org) package. This package is an open source re-implementation of the proprietary Pretty Good Privacy (PGP). In addition to encrypting entire messages, GPG enables you to digitally "sign" messages. Used in this way, messages can be read by recipients who lack the GPG software or appropriate keys; but those who have these tools can verify that the contents haven't been tampered with.

Generating Keys

To begin using GPG, you should first install the software. Chances are, your distribution includes it as a standard package, so you can install it that way. Once this is done, you must generate keys. GPG keys are conceptually similar to SSH keys: You need a private key (aka a secret key) and a public key. As the names imply, the private key is kept private, but the public key is publicly available. You can sign your messages with your private key, and readers can verify it with your public key; or you can encrypt a message with another user's public key, and it can be decrypted only with that user's private key.

To generate keys, you use the gpg program with its --gen-key option:

```
$ gpg --gen-key
```

The program will ask you a series of questions. In most cases, answering with the defaults should work well, although you may have to type in your full name and email address. The keys are stored in a *keyring* (a file that holds keys) in the ~/.gnupg directory.

Once you've generated your keys, you can *export* your public key:

```
$ gpg --export name > gpg.pub
```

This command saves the public key associated with *name* in the file gpg.pub. You can use your email address as *name*. (If you create additional public keys or add others' public keys to your keyring, you can specify their names to export those keys.) You can then make your public key available to others so that they may encrypt email messages sent to you or verify your signed messages. Adding the --armor option produces ASCII output, which may be preferable if you intend to email the key. You can make the file accessible on your Web site, transfer it as an email attachment, or distribute it in various other ways.

One important method of distributing your public key is via a *keyserver*. This is a network server that functions much like a keyring. To send your public key to a keyserver, you can use the --keyserver *hostname* and --send-keys *keyname* options to gpg, as follows:

```
$ gpg --keyserver pgp.mit.edu --send-keys jennie@luna.edu
```

This example sends the public key for jennie@luna.edu from your public keyring to the server at pgp.mit.edu. Thereafter, anybody who wants to can retrieve the key from that server. (pgp.mit.edu is a popular site for hosting PGP public keys.)

Importing Keys

To encrypt email you send to others, you must obtain their public keys. Ask your correspondents how to obtain them. Once you've done so, you can add their keys to your *keyring* (that is, the set of keys GPG maintains):

```
$ gpg --import filename
```

This command adds *filename* to your set of public keys belonging to other people.

Although public keys are, by definition, public, there are security concerns relating to them. Specifically, you should be sure you use a *legitimate* public key. Hypothetically, a miscreant could publish a fake public key in order to obtain sensitive communications or fake a signed email. For instance, George might distribute a fake GPG public key that claimed to be from Harold. George could then either sign messages claiming to be from Harold or intercept email sent to Harold that was encrypted using the fake key. Thus, you should use as secure a communication method as possible to distribute your public key and to receive public keys from others.

Once you've created your own key and, perhaps, imported keys from others, you can see what keys are available by using the --list-keys option to gpg:

```
$ gpg --list-keys
/home/gjones/.gnupg/pubring.gpg
-------------------------------
pub    1024D/190EDB2E 2008-09-05
```

```
uid                     George A. Jones <gjones@example.com>
sub   2048g/0D657AC8 2008-09-05
pub   1024D/A8B2061A 2008-09-05
uid                     Jennie Martin <jennie@luna.edu>
sub   2048g/4F33EF6B 2008-09-05
```

The uid lines contain identifiers you'll use when encrypting or decrypting data, so you should pay particular attention to that information.

Revoking a Key

Sometimes, you might have cause to revoke a public key. For instance, suppose you've stored a copy of your private key on a laptop computer and that laptop is stolen, or perhaps some employees have left your organization and you no longer want those individuals to be able to use the keys associated with their employee accounts. To revoke a key, you use the --gen-revoke *keyname* option to gpg:

```
$ gpg --gen-revoke jennie@luna.edu
```

The program asks you to answer a few questions, such as the reason for revoking the key. It then generates a key block, such as the following:

```
-----BEGIN PGP PUBLIC KEY BLOCK-----Version: GnuPG v2.0.19 ↵
(GNU/Linux)Comment: A revocation certificate should follow
iEwEIBECAAwFAlBPvbkFHQBG28bACgkQbBimvBMO2y4uzwCeQiLkZx8jl2jk+↵
hnOOKUl3EznmBQAn2WvtuQW+AP6wlvOvNU/qYi8a7t8=sO/s
-----END PGP PUBLIC KEY BLOCK-----
```

You should copy this text into a file (say, revocation.gpg) and import the file to your keyring:

```
$ gpg --import revocation.gpg
```

If you've distributed public keys associated with the revoked key, you should distribute this revocation, too. If you've sent your public keys to a GPG keyserver, you can pass your revocation along in the same way you sent your original public key:

```
$ gpg --keyserver pgp.mit.edu --send-keys jennie@luna.edu
```

Once this is done, you can generate and distribute a new set of keys, if desired.

Encrypting and Decrypting Data

To encrypt data, you use gpg with its --out and --encrypt options and, optionally, --recipient and --armor:

```
$ gpg --out encrypted-file --recipient uid --armor --encrypt original-file
```

You can use the UID from a gpg --list-keys output, or just the email address portion, as the *uid* in this command. If you haven't signed the recipient's key, you'll have to verify that you want to use that key. The result is a new file, *encrypted-file*, which holds an encrypted version of *original-file*. If you omit the --armor option, the resulting file is a binary file; if you send it as email, you'll need to send it as an attachment or otherwise encode it for transmission over the text-based email system. If you include the --armor option, the output is ASCII, so you can cut and paste the encrypted message into an email or send it as an attachment.

If you receive a message or file that was encrypted with your public key, you can reverse the encryption by using the --decrypt option:

```
$ gpg --out decrypted-file --decrypt encrypted-file
```

You'll be asked to enter your passphrase. The result should be a decrypted version of the original file.

In practice, GPG can be even easier to use than this description may make you think. GPG is primarily used to secure and verify email, so most Linux email clients provide GPG interfaces. These options call gpg with appropriate options to encrypt, sign, or decrypt messages. Details vary from one email client to another, so you should consult your email client's documentation for details.

Signing Messages and Verifying Signatures

As noted earlier, GPG can be used to sign messages so that recipients know they come from you. To do so, use the --sign or --clearsign option to gpg:

```
$ gpg --clearsign original-file
```

The --sign option creates a new file with the same name as the original, but with .gpg appended to the filename. This file is encrypted using your private key so that it may be decrypted only with your public key. This means that anybody with your public key may read the message, but anybody who can read it knows it's from you. The --clearsign option works similarly, but it leaves the message text unencrypted and only adds an encrypted signature that can be verified using your public key. The --clearsign option creates a file with a name that ends in .asc.

If you receive a signed message, you can verify the signature using the --verify option to gpg:

```
$ gpg --verify received-file
```

If any of the keys in your keyring can decode the message or verify the signature, gpg displays a Good signature message. To read a message that was encrypted via the --sign option, you must decrypt the message via the --decrypt option, as described earlier.

Summary

Maintaining system security is both important and time-consuming. A great deal of security emphasis is on network security, and for this, configuring your super server and disabling unused servers will go a long way. Attending to passwords and performing miscellaneous tasks to keep your local accounts from becoming security risks are also important security tasks.

Encryption is a hot topic in security. SSH is a protocol and tool that can handle many network encryption tasks by encrypting two-way connections between computers. Typically used as a remote login protocol, SSH can also be used to transfer files or encrypt other protocols. When you want to encrypt data sent to another individual via a tool such as email, you can do so with the help of GPG. This package enables you to encrypt individual files, which can then be attached to or embedded in email messages and decrypted by the recipient.

Exam Essentials

Identify the purpose of a super server.   Super servers, such as `inetd` and `xinetd`, manage incoming network connections for multiple servers. They can add security and convenience features, and they can help minimize the memory load imposed by seldom-accessed servers.

Explain the function of super server port access controls.   Super servers or programs called by them (such as TCP Wrappers) can restrict access to ports for the servers they manage. These restrictions occur at a higher level than a firewall's restrictions, and they apply only to the servers managed by the super server.

Summarize the tools you can use to identify the servers running on a computer.   The `netstat` and `lsof` programs both provide options to list all (or a subset of) the open network connections, as well as programs that are listening for connections. Remote network scanners, such as Nmap, can probe another computer for open network ports. Perusal of local configuration files can also provide clues to what's running on a computer.

Describe why SUID and SGID programs are potentially risky.   The set user ID (SUID) and set group ID (SGID) bits tell Linux to run the program as the user or group that owns the file. This is particularly risky when `root` owns the program file because it essentially elevates all users to `root` for the purposes of running the file, making bugs in the program more dangerous and raising the possibility of a clever user abusing the program to acquire full `root` privileges or otherwise wreaking havoc.

Explain why shadow passwords are important.   Shadow passwords store password hashes in a file that can't be read by ordinary users, thus making it harder for miscreants on the local system to read the hashed passwords and use brute-force attacks to discover other users' passwords. Modern Linux distributions use shadow passwords by default.

Explain how to generate a good password. Ideally, passwords should be random. Failing that, one good approach is to generate a base that's hard to guess and then modify it by adding digits and punctuation, changing the case of some characters, changing letter order, and significantly increasing the length of the password (even with repeated characters).

Explain why SSH is the preferred remote text-mode login tool. The Secure Shell (SSH) protocol provides encryption for all traffic, including both the password exchange and all subsequent data exchanges, whereas older tools, such as Telnet, do not. This makes SSH much safer (if not 100 percent safe) for the exchange of sensitive data, particularly over untrusted networks such as the Internet.

Identify the most important SSH configuration file. The SSH server is controlled through the /etc/ssh/sshd_config file. The SSH client configuration file is /etc/ssh/ssh_config; don't confuse the two.

Describe the function of GPG. GPG enables public-key encryption of individual files or email messages. You can use GPG to encrypt sensitive data for transmission over email or other insecure means.

Review Questions

1. Typing **lsof -i | grep LISTEN** as root produces three lines of output, corresponding to the sendmail, sshd, and proftpd servers. What can you conclude about the security of this system?

    A.   Everything's OK; the presence of sshd ensures that data are being encrypted via SSH.

    B.   The sendmail and sshd servers are OK, but the FTP protocol used by proftpd is insecure and should never be used.

    C.   The sendmail server should be replaced by Postfix or qmail for improved security, but sshd and proftpd are fine.

    D.   Because sendmail and proftpd both use unencrypted text-mode data transfers, neither is appropriate on a network-connected computer.

    E.   No conclusion can be drawn without further information; the listed servers may or may not be appropriate or authentic.

2. As part of a security audit, you plan to use Nmap to check all the computers on your network for unnecessary servers. Which of the following tasks should you do prior to running your Nmap check?

    A.   Back up /etc/passwd on the target systems to eliminate the possibility of its being damaged.

    B.   Obtain the root passwords to the target systems so that you can properly configure them to accept the Nmap probes.

    C.   Obtain written permission from your boss to perform the Nmap sweep.

    D.   Configure /etc/sudoers on the computer you intend to use for the sweep, to give yourself the ability to run Nmap.

    E.   Disable any firewall between the computer that's running Nmap and the servers you intend to scan.

3. Your login server is using PAM, and you want to limit users' access to system resources. Which configuration file will you need to edit?

    A.   /etc/limits.conf

    B.   /etc/pam/limits.conf

    C.   /etc/security/limits.conf

    D.   /etc/security/pam/limits.conf

    E.   /usr/local/limits.conf

4. Which of the following tools might you use to check for open ports on a local computer? (Select three.)

    A.   Nmap

    B.   netstat

    C.   lsof

    D.   portmap

    E.   services

5. Which of the following commands will locate all program files on a computer on which the SUID bit is set?

   A. `find / -type SUID`

   B. `find / -perm +4000 -type f`

   C. `find / -perm +SUID -type f`

   D. `find / -type +4000`

   E. `find / -suid`

6. The `/etc/sudoers` file on a computer includes the following line. What is its effect?

   `%admin ALL=(ALL) ALL`

   A. Members of the `admin` group may run all programs with `root` privileges by using `sudo`.

   B. Users in the `admin` user alias, defined earlier in the file, may run all programs with `root` privileges by using `sudo`.

   C. The `admin` user alias is defined to include all users on the system.

   D. The `admin` command alias is defined to include all commands.

   E. The user `admin` may run all programs on the computer as `root` by using `sudo`.

7. Which command would you type, as `root`, to discover all the open network connections on a Linux computer?

   A. `lsof -c a`

   B. `netstat -ap`

   C. `ifconfig eth0`

   D. `nmap -sT localhost`

   E. `top -net`

8. A server/computer combination appears in both `hosts.allow` and `hosts.deny`. What's the result of this configuration when TCP Wrappers runs?

   A. TCP Wrappers refuses to run and logs an error in `/var/log/messages`.

   B. The system's administrator is paged to decide whether to allow access.

   C. `hosts.deny` takes precedence; the client is denied access to the server.

   D. `hosts.allow` takes precedence; the client is granted access to the server.

   E. The client is granted access to the server *if* no other client is currently accessing it.

9. When is the `bind` option of `xinetd` most useful?

   A. When you want to run two servers on one port

   B. When you want to specify computers by name rather than IP address

   C. When `xinetd` is running on a system with two network interfaces

   D. When resolving conflicts between different servers

   E. When `xinetd` manages a DNS server program

10. You've discovered that the Waiter program (a network server) is running inappropriately on your computer. You therefore locate its SysV startup script and shut it down by removing that script from your default runlevel. How can you further reduce the risk that the Waiter program will be abused by outsiders? (Select two.)

    A. By blocking the Waiter program's port using a firewall rule

    B. By reading the Waiter program's documentation to learn how to run it in stealth mode

    C. By tunneling the Waiter program's port through SSH

    D. By uninstalling the Waiter package

    E. By uninstalling any clients associated with Waiter from the server computer

11. You want to use `xinetd` access controls to limit who may access a server that's launched via `xinetd`. Specifically, only users on the 192.168.7.0/24 network block should be able to use that server. How may you do this?

    A. Enter `hosts_allow = 192.168.7.0/24` in the `/etc/xinetd.d` configuration file for the server in question.

    B. Enter `only_from = 192.168.7.0/24` in the `/etc/xinetd.d` configuration file for the server in question.

    C. Enter `server : 192.168.7.`, where *server* is the server's name, in the `/etc/hosts.allow` file.

    D. Enter `server : 192.168.7.`, where *server* is the server's name, in the `/etc/hosts.deny` file.

    E. Type **iptables -L 192.168.7.0** to enable only users of 192.168.7.0/24 to access the server.

12. Of the following, which is the best password?

    A. `Odysseus`

    B. `iA710ci^My~~~~~`

    C. `pickettomato`

    D. `Denver2Colorado`

    E. `123456`

13. Which of the following types of attacks involves sending bogus email to lure unsuspecting individuals into divulging sensitive financial or other information?

    A. Phishing

    B. Script kiddies

    C. Spoofing

    D. Ensnaring

    E. Hacking

14. Ordinary users report being unable to log onto a computer, but `root` has no problems doing so. What might you check for to explain this situation?

    A. A misbehaving `syslogd` daemon

    B. A `login` process that's running as `root`

    C. The presence of an `/etc/nologin` file

    D. The presence of an SUID bit on `/bin/login`

    E. Inappropriate use of shadow passwords

15. Which servers might you consider retiring after activating an SSH server? (Select two.)

    A. SMTP

    B. Telnet

    C. FTP

    D. NTP

    E. Samba

16. You find that the `ssh_host_dsa_key` file in `/etc/ssh` has 0666 (`-rw-rw-rw-`) permissions. Your SSH server has been in operation for several months. Should you be concerned?

    A. Yes

    B. No

    C. Only if the `ssh_host_dsa_key.pub` file is also world-readable

    D. Only if you're launching SSH from a super server

    E. Only if you're using a laptop computer

17. For best SSH server security, how should you set the `Protocol` option in `/etc/ssh/sshd_config`?

    A. `Protocol 1`

    B. `Protocol 2`

    C. `Protocol 1,2`

    D. `Protocol 2,1`

    E. `Protocol *`

18. Why is it unwise to allow `root` to log on directly using SSH?

    A. Disallowing direct `root` access means that the SSH server may be run by a non-`root` user, improving security.

    B. The `root` password should never be sent over a network connection; allowing `root` logins in this way is inviting disaster.

    C. SSH stores all login information, including passwords, in a publicly readable file.

    D. When logged on using SSH, `root`'s commands can be easily intercepted and duplicated by undesirable elements.

    E. Somebody with the `root` password but no other password can then break into the computer.

19. You've downloaded a GPG public key from a Web site, into the file `fredkey.pub`. What must you do with this key to use it?

    A. Type `inspect-gpg fredkey.pub`.

    B. Type `gpg --readkey fredkey.pub`.

    C. Type `import-gpg fredkey.pub`.

    D. Type `gpg --import fredkey.pub`.

    E. Type `gpg-import fredkey.pub`.

20. You want to send an encrypted message to an email correspondent. You both have GPG. What do you need to exchange before you can send your encrypted message?

    A. Your correspondent must obtain your GPG public key.

    B. Your correspondent must obtain your GPG private key.

    C. You must exchange private keys with your correspondent.

    D. You must obtain your correspondent's GPG private key.

    E. You must obtain your correspondent's GPG public key.

Appendix A

Answers to Review Questions

Chapter 1: Exploring Linux Command-Line Tools

1. D. Any of these approaches will work, or at least *might* work. (You might err when performing any of them.) Option B or C is likely to be the most efficient approach; with a long filename to type, option A is likely to be tedious.

2. E. The echo command is implemented internally to bash, although an external version is also available on most systems. The cat, less, tee, and sed commands are not implemented internally to bash, although they can be called from bash as external commands.

3. E. The echo command echoes what follows to standard output, and $PROC is an environment variable. Thus, **echo $PROC** displays the value of the $PROC environment variable, meaning that it must have been set to the specified value by you, one of your configuration files, or a program you've run. Although many environment variables are set to particular values to convey information, $PROC isn't a standard environment variable that might be associated with information described in options A, B, C, or D.

4. A. The pwd command prints (to standard output) the name of the current working directory. The remaining options are simply incorrect, although option B describes the cd command, and various tools can be used to reformat wide text for display or printing in fewer columns, as in option C.

5. D. The exec command causes the rest of the command to replace the current shell. Thus, when you exit from gedit in this scenario, the result will be the same as if you'd terminated the shell; namely, the xterm window will close. The exec command doesn't raise the execution privilege, so option A is incorrect. (The su and sudo commands can raise execution privilege, though.) Because the xterm window closes, option B is incorrect. X won't ordinarily terminate when a single xterm does, and definitely not if that xterm was launched from a window manager, so option C is incorrect. The exec command does not cause re-execution of the command after the first instance terminates, so option E is incorrect.

6. A. The dot (.) character refers to the current working directory, and the slash (/) is a directory separator. Thus, preceding a program name by ./ unambiguously identifies the intention to run the program that's stored in the current directory. Option B will run the first instance of the program that's found on the current path. Because paths often omit the current directory for security reasons, this option is likely to fail. The run command isn't a standard Linux command, so option C is unlikely to do anything, much less what the question specifies. Option D would be correct except that it reverses the order of the two characters. The effect is to attempt to run the .myprog file in the root (/) directory. This file probably doesn't exist, and even if it did, it's not the file the question specifies should be run. Option E runs the first instance of myprog found on the path, and additionally it runs the program in the background. (Chapter 2 covers background execution in more detail.)

7. E. By default, man uses the `less` pager to display information on most Linux systems, so option E is correct. Although an X-based version of man does exist (xman), the basic man doesn't use a custom X-based application (option A), nor does it use Firefox (option B) or the Vi editor (option D). The `info` command is a competing documentation system to man, so option C is incorrect.

8. C. The > redirection operator stores a command's standard output in a file, overwriting the contents of any existing file by the specified name, so option C is correct. Option A specifies the standard input redirection so that `ifconfig` will take the contents of `file .txt` as input. Option B is almost correct; the >> redirection operator redirects standard output, as requested, but it appends data to the specified file rather than overwriting it. Option D specifies a pipe; the output of `ifconfig` is sent through the `file.txt` program, if it exists. (Chances are it doesn't, so you'd get a `command not found` error message.) Option E redirects standard error, rather than standard output, to `file.txt`, and so is incorrect.

9. C. The &> redirection operator sends both standard output and standard error to the specified file, as option C states. (The name of the file, `input.txt`, is intentionally deceptive, but the usage is still valid.) Option A mentions standard error but describes it as if it were an input stream, which it's not; it's an output stream. Option B mentions standard input, but the &> operator doesn't affect standard input. Because only option C is correct, neither option D nor E can be correct.

10. E. In principle, you can pipe together as many commands as you like. (In practice, of course, there will be limits based on input buffer size, memory, and so on, but these limits are far higher than the 2, 3, 4, or 16 commands specified in options A, B, C, and D.)

11. B. The tee command sends its output both to standard output and to a named file. Thus, placing the tee command (with an output filename) after another command and a pipe will achieve the desired effect. Options A and D redirect gabby's output to a file, which means you won't be able to see the output and interact with it. Option C sends the contents of `gabby-out.txt` to gabby as input, which isn't what's desired, either. Option E attempts to run `gabby-out.txt` as a program and use its output as command-line arguments to gabby, which is not what's desired.

12. C. The 2> redirection operator redirects standard error only, leaving standard output unaffected. Sending standard error to `/dev/null` gets rid of it. Thus, option C is correct. Option A pipes the standard output of verbose through the quiet program, which isn't a standard Linux program. Option B sends both standard output and standard error to `/dev/null`, so you won't be able to interact with the program, as the question specifies you must be able to do. Option D redirects standard output only to the `junk.txt` file, so once again, interaction will be impossible—and you'll see the unwanted error messages on the screen. Option E's quiet-mode program is fictitious (or at least non-standard), so this option is incorrect.

13. A. Option A correctly describes the difference between these two redirection operators. Option B is almost correct, but the >> operator will create a new file if one doesn't already exist. The >> operator does not redirect standard error (as stated in option C) or standard input (as stated in option D). Both operators will create a new file if one doesn't already exist, contrary to what option E states.

14. C. The `tail` command displays the final 10 lines of a file, so option C is correct. (You can change the number of lines displayed with the -n option.) The `uniq` command (option A) removes duplicate lines from a list. The `cut` command (option B) echoes the specified characters or fields from an input text file. The `wc` command (option D) displays counts of the number of characters, words, and lines in a file. The `fmt` command (option E) is a plain-text formatter.

15. A. The `pr` program takes a text file as input and adds formatting features intended for printing, such as a header and blank lines to separate pages. The command also pipes the output through `lpr` (which is a Linux printing command). Option A describes these effects and so is correct. Option B describes the effect of the `cat` program, and so is incorrect. The conversion of tabs to spaces can be done by the `expand` program, so option C is incorrect. Although the specified command does print `report.txt`, error messages are not stored in the `lpr` file, so option D is incorrect. Because option A is correct, option E is incorrect.

16. B, C, D. The `nl` command numbers lines, so it does this task without any special options, and option B is correct. (Its options can fine-tune the way it numbers lines, though.) The `cat` command can also number lines via its -b and -n options; -b numbers non-blank lines, whereas -n numbers all lines (including blank lines). Thus, options C and D are both correct. Neither the `fmt` command nor the `od` command will number the lines of the input file, so options A and E are both incorrect.

17. C. The `sed` utility can be used to "stream" text and change one value to another. In this case, the `s` option is used to replace `dog` with `mutt`, making option C correct. The syntax in option A is incorrect, and choices B and D are incorrect because `grep` doesn't include the functionality needed to make the changes. Option E combines `fmt`, `cut`, and redirection in a way that simply won't work to achieve the desired goal.

18. B. The `fmt` command performs the desired task of shortening long lines by inserting carriage returns. It sends its results to standard output, so option B uses output redirection to save the results in a new file. The `sed` command of option A won't accomplish anything useful; it only replaces the string `Ctrl-M` with the string `NL`. Although these strings are both sometimes used as abbreviations for carriage returns or new lines, the replacement of these literal strings isn't what's required. Option C creates an exact copy of the original file, with the long single-line paragraphs intact. Although option D's `pr` command is a formatting tool, it won't reformat individual paragraphs. It will also add headers that you probably don't want. Option E's `grep` command searches for text within files; it won't reformat text files.

19. A. The `grep` utility is used to find matching text within a file and print those lines. It accepts regular expressions, which means you can place in brackets the two characters that differ in the words for which you're looking. Thus, option A is correct. The syntax for `sed`, `od`, `cat`, and `find` wouldn't perform the specified task, so options B through E are all incorrect.

20. C. The bracket expression within the `d[o-u]g` regular expression in option C means that any three-character string beginning in d, ending in g, and with the middle character being between o and u will match. These results meet the question's criteria. Option A's dot matches any single character, so d.g matches all three words. The bracket expression [ou] in option B matches the characters o and u, but no other values. Since the question specifies that some other matches will be made, this option is incorrect. Option D's di*g matches dig; diig; diiig; or any other word that begins with d, ends with g, and contains any number of i letters in between. Thus, option D matches dig but not dog or dug as required. Option E, like Option A, uses a dot to match any character, so it will actually match certain four-letter words, but not dog or dug.

Chapter 2: Managing Software

1. D. Because they must be compiled prior to installation, source packages require *more* time to install than binary packages do, contrary to option D's assertion, thus making this option correct. The other options all describe advantages of source packages over binary packages.

2. A. The two systems use different databases, which makes coordinating between them difficult. Thus, using them both simultaneously is inadvisable, making option A correct. Package management systems don't share information, but neither do their databases actively conflict, so option B is incorrect. Installing the same libraries using both systems would almost guarantee that the files served by both systems would conflict with one another, making option C incorrect. Actively using both RPM and Debian packages isn't common on any distribution, although it's possible with all of them, so option D is incorrect. The alien program converts between package formats. Although it requires that both systems be installed to convert between them, alien is not required to install both these systems. Thus, option E is incorrect.

3. E. RPMs are usually portable across distributions, but occasionally they contain incompatibilities, so option E is correct. The package format and software licensing have nothing to do with one another, so option A is incorrect. There is no --convert-distrib parameter to rpm, so option B is incorrect. Although recompiling a source package can help work around incompatibilities, this step is not always required, so option C is incorrect. Binary packages can't be rebuilt for another CPU architecture, so option D is incorrect, although source packages may be rebuilt for any supported architecture provided the source code doesn't rely on any CPU-specific features.

4. B. The -i operation installs software, so option B is correct. (The -v and -h options cause a status display of the progress of the operation, which wasn't mentioned in the option.) Uninstallation is performed by the -e operation, and rebuilding source RPMs is done by the --rebuild operation (to either rpm or rpmbuild, depending on the RPM version), so options A and C are incorrect. Although the filename megaprog.rpm is missing several conventional RPM filename components, the rpm utility doesn't use the filename as a package validity check, so option D is incorrect. Option E describes a package upgrade, which is handled by the -U operation, not -i as in the question, so option E is incorrect.

5. A. The `rpm2cpio` program extracts data from an RPM file and converts it into a `cpio` archive that's sent to standard output. Piping the results through `cpio` and using the `-i` and `--make-directories` options, as in option A, will extract those files to the current directory. Option B creates a `cpio` file called `make-directories` that contains the files from the RPM package. Option C will uninstall the package called `myfonts.rpm` (but not the `myfonts` package). The `alien` utility has no `--to-extract` target, so option D is invalid. The `rpmbuild` utility builds a source RPM into a binary RPM, making option E incorrect.

6. E. An uppercase `-P` invokes the purge operation, which completely removes a package and its configuration files, so option E is correct. The `-e` parameter uninstalls a package for `rpm`, but not for `dpkg`, so option A is incorrect. The lowercase `-p` causes `dpkg` to print information about the package's contents, so option B is incorrect. The `-r` parameter removes a package but leaves configuration files behind, so options C and D are both incorrect. (Option D also specifies a complete filename, which isn't used for removing a package—you should specify only the shorter package name.)

7. C. You can specify Debian package archive sites in `/etc/apt/sources.list`, and then you can type **apt-get update** and **apt-get upgrade** to quickly update a Debian system to the latest packages, so option C is correct. GUI package management tools for Debian and related distributions exist, but they aren't `apt-get`, so option A is incorrect. The `alien` program can convert a tarball and install the converted package on a Debian system, but `apt-get` can't do this, so option B is incorrect. `dpkg` and `apt-get` both come with all Debian-based distributions, so option D is incorrect. The `dpkg` program can install only Debian packages on Debian-based systems, but `apt-get` can work with both package systems, so option E is backward.

8. E. The `--get-selections` action to `dpkg` displays the names of all installed packages, making option E correct. There is no `showall` option to `apt-get`, so option A is incorrect. The `showpkg` subcommand to `apt-cache` displays information about a named package; when used without a package name, as in option B, it displays no data. The `dpkg -r` action removes a package, so option C would remove the package called `allpkgs` if it were installed. The `dpkg -i` action installs a package, so option D is incorrect—and that option doesn't list a package name, which the `-i` action requires.

9. D. The `update` option to `apt-get` causes retrieval of new information, as described in option D. This option is perfectly valid, contrary to option A's assertion. The `apt-get` program doesn't permit you to upload information to the Internet repositories, so option B is incorrect. Option C describes the effect of the `upgrade` or `dist-upgrade` options, not the `update` option. The `upgrade` or `dist-upgrade` options can upgrade APT itself, but `update` alone won't do the job, so option E is incorrect.

10. A, B. The `yum` utility's `update` and `upgrade` options are nearly identical in effect, and either can be used to upgrade an individual package, such as `unzip`, so options A and B are both correct. The primary command options to `yum` don't use dashes, so options C and D are both incorrect. The `check-update` option to `yum` checks for the availability of updates but does *not* install them, so option E is incorrect.

11. B. Yum uses files in the /etc/yum.repos.d directory to locate its repositories, so you can add to the repository list by adding files to this subdirectory, as option B specifies, typically either by installing an RPM or by adding a file manually. Option A describes a method of adding a repository to a computer that uses APT, not Yum. Option C's add-repository subcommand is fictitious. Although the /etc/yum.conf file described in options D and E is real, it doesn't store repository data.

12. B. The /etc/ld.so.conf file holds the global library path, so editing it is the preferred approach. You must then type **ldconfig** to have the system update its library path cache. Thus, option B is correct. Although you can add a directory to the library path by altering the LD_LIBRARY_PATH environment variable globally, as in option A, this approach isn't the preferred one, so this option is incorrect. Option C simply won't work. Option D also won't work, although linking individual library files would work. This method isn't the preferred one for adding a whole directory, though. The ldd utility displays information on libraries used by executable files, so option E won't have the desired effect.

13. D. Libraries are selected by programmers, not by users or system administrators. If you don't like the widgets provided by one library, you have few options, and option D is correct. (Many widget sets do provide a great deal of configurability, though, so you may be able to work around the problem in other ways.) Options A, B, and E describe fictitious options to ldconfig, rpm, dpkg, and the kernel. Option C wouldn't work; Qt-using programs would crash when they found GTK+ libraries in place of the Qt libraries they were expecting.

14. D. The kill program accepts various signals in numeric or named form (9 in this example) along with a process ID number (11287 in this example). Signal 9 corresponds to SIGKILL, which is an extreme way to kill processes that have run out of control. Thus, option D describes the effect of this command. Although you might use kill to kill network processes, you can't pass kill a TCP port number and expect it to work, so option A is incorrect. The program also won't display information about the number of processes that have been killed, making option B incorrect. To do as option C suggests, you'd need to tell kill to pass SIGHUP (signal 1), so the command would be **kill -1 11287**, and option C is incorrect. The kill program can't change the priority of a process, so option E is incorrect.

15. C, D. The top utility displays a dynamic list of processes ordered according to their CPU use along with additional system information, including load averages, so option C is correct. If you want only the load average at a specific moment, uptime (option D) may be better because it presents less extraneous information—it shows the current time, the time since the system was booted, the number of active users, and the load averages. Option A's ld command has nothing to do with displaying load averages (it's a programming tool that links together program modules into an executable program). There are no standard Linux programs called load (option B) or la (option E).

16. A. The --forest option to ps shows parent-child relationships by creating visual links between process names in the ps output, making option A correct. (Listing 2.4 shows this effect.) Options B and C are both valid ps commands, but neither creates the specified effect. Option D describes a fictitious ps option. Since options B, C, and D are incorrect, option E is also necessarily incorrect.

17. A. CPU-intensive programs routinely consume 90 percent or more of available CPU time, but not all systems run such programs. Furthermore, some types of program bugs can create such CPU loads. Thus, option A is correct, and you must investigate the matter more. What is `dfcomp`? Is it designed as a CPU-intensive program? Is it consuming this much CPU time consistently, or was this a brief burst of activity? Options B, C, D, and E all jump to conclusions or present fictitious reasons for the behavior being normal or abnormal.

18. E. The `jobs` command summarizes processes that were launched from your current shell. When no such processes are running, `jobs` returns nothing, so option E is correct. The `jobs` command doesn't check or summarize CPU load, so option A is incorrect. The `jobs` command also doesn't check for processes run from shells other than the current one, so option B is incorrect (processes running under your username could have been launched from another shell or from a GUI environment). There is no standard `jobs` shell in Linux, so option C is incorrect. Because the `jobs` output is limited to your own processes in the shell you're running, a blank output does *not* indicate a crashed system, making option D incorrect.

19. C, E. The `nice` command launches a program (`crunch` in this example) with increased or decreased priority. The default priority when none is specified is 10, and the `nice -10 crunch` command also sets the priority to 10, so options C and E are equivalent. Option A isn't a valid `nice` command because `nice` has no `--value` option. Option B is a valid `nice` command, but it sets the priority to –10 rather than 10. Despite the similarity in form of options C and D, option D is not a valid `nice` command, and so is incorrect. (When passing a numeric value to `nice`, you *must* use a preceding dash, -, or -n.)

20. D, E. Linux insulates users' actions from one another, and this rule applies to `renice`; only `root` may modify the priority of other users' processes, so option D is correct. Similarly, only `root` may increase the priority of a process, in order to prevent users from setting their processes to maximum priority, thus stealing CPU time from others, so option E is correct. Option A correctly describes `nice`, but not `renice`; the whole point of `renice` is to be able to change the priorities of existing processes. Contrary to option B, `renice` doesn't care about the shell from which `renice` or the target program was launched. Users may use `renice` to decrease their own processes' priorities, contrary to option C.

Chapter 3: Configuring Hardware

1. B, C. IRQs 3 and 4 are common defaults for RS-232 serial ports, so options B and C are both correct. IRQ 1 is reserved for the keyboard, so option A is incorrect. IRQ 8 is reserved for use by the real-time clock, so option D is incorrect. Although IRQ 16 exists on modern systems, it didn't exist on early $x86$ systems, and its purpose isn't standardized.

2. A. Modern firmware (BIOSs and EFIs) provide the means to disable many onboard devices, including sound hardware, in case you don't want to use them, so option A is correct. Although the `alsactl` utility mentioned in option B is real, it's used to load or store sound card mixer settings, not to disable the sound hardware. The `lsmod` command mentioned in option C displays information about loaded kernel modules, but it doesn't remove them or disable the hardware they use. Similarly, option D's `lspci` displays information on PCI devices but can't disable them. Contrary to option D, on-board sound hardware can usually be disabled.

3. E. The `udev` software creates and manages a dynamic `/dev` directory tree, adding entries to that directory for devices that exist on the target system, so option E is correct. The `udev` software has nothing to do with software development (option A). It doesn't unload drivers (option B) or load drivers (option C), although it does respond to the loading of drivers by creating appropriate entries in `/dev`. It also doesn't store BIOS configuration options in a file (option D).

4. E. SATA disks are *usually* handled by Linux's SCSI subsystem and so are referred to as `/dev/sdx`; however, some drivers handle these disks as if they were PATA disks and so refer to them as `/dev/hdx`. Thus, option E is correct, and both options A and C are incorrect. The `/dev/mapper` directory holds device files related to LVM and RAID configurations, not disk partition identifiers, so option B is incorrect. Option D (`C:`) is how Windows would likely refer to the first partition on the disk, but Linux doesn't use this style of disk identifier.

5. A, C, D. There are no files called `/proc/ioaddresses` or `/proc/hardware`, so options B and E are both incorrect. All the other files listed contain useful information; `/proc/ioports` holds information about I/O ports, `/proc/dma` holds information about DMA port usage, and `/proc/interrupts` holds information about IRQs.

6. B. Logical partitions are numbered 5 and up, and they reside in an extended partition with a number between 1 and 4. Therefore, one of the first two partitions must be an extended partition that houses partitions 5 and 6, making option B correct. Because one of the first two partitions is an extended partition, the other must be a primary partition, and there can be no more of either type of partition. This makes option A incorrect. Gaps in the range of partitions 1–4 are normal in MBR disks, contrary to option C. Because logical partitions are numbered starting at 5, their numbers won't change if `/dev/sda3` is subsequently added, so option D is incorrect. On MBR disks, partitions 1–4 must be primary or extended partitions; logical partitions are numbered 5 and up. Thus, option E is incorrect.

7. E. The `/etc/fstab` file contains the mapping of partitions to mount points, so `/etc` must be an ordinary directory on the root partition, not on a separate partition, making option E correct. Although option A's statement that the system won't boot is correct, the reason is not; `/home` holds user files, not critical system files. Options B and C describe restrictions that don't exist. Option D would be correct if `/etc` were not a separate partition.

8. D. The `/home` directory (option D) is frequently placed on its own partition in order to isolate it from the rest of the system and sometimes to enable use of a particular filesystem or filesystem mount options. The `/bin` and `/sbin` directories (options A and B) should *never* be split off from the root (`/`) filesystem because they contain critical executable files

that must be accessible in order to do the most basic work, including mounting filesystems. The /mnt directory (option C) often contains subdirectories used for mounting floppy disks, CD-ROMs, and other removable media or may be used for this purpose itself. It's seldom used to directly access hard disk partitions, although it can be used for this purpose. The /dev directory (option E) usually corresponds to a virtual filesystem, which holds pseudo-files but is not stored on a disk partition.

9. A. The 0x0f partition type code is one of two common partition type codes for an extended partition. (The other is 0x05.) The 0x82 code refers to a Linux swap partition, and 0x83 denotes a Linux filesystem partition. Thus, it appears that this disk holds Linux partitions, making option A correct. DOS, Windows 9x/Me, Windows NT/200x/XP, FreeBSD, and Mac OS X all use other partition type codes for their partitions, so options B, C, and E are all incorrect. (Mac OS X is also rarely installed to MBR disks.) Partitions exist, in part, to enable different OSs to store their data side-by-side on the same disk, so mixing several partition types (even for different OSs) on one disk does not indicate disk corruption, making option D incorrect.

10. C. Linux's fdisk doesn't write changes to disk until you exit the program by typing **w**. Typing **q** exits without writing those changes, so typing **q** in this situation will avert disaster, making option C correct. Typing **w** (option B) would be precisely the wrong thing to do. Because fdisk doesn't write changes until you type **w**, the damage is not yet done, contrary to option A. Typing **u** (option D) or **t** (option E) would do nothing useful because those aren't undo commands.

11. E. The mkfs command creates a new filesystem, overwriting any existing data and therefore making existing files inaccessible, as stated in option E. This command doesn't set the partition type code in the partition table, so option A is incorrect. The mkfs command is destructive, contrary to option B. The -t ext2 option tells mkfs to create an ext2 filesystem; it's a perfectly valid option, so option C is incorrect. Although mkfs could (destructively) convert ext2fs to ext4fs, the -t ext2 option clearly indicates that an ext2 filesystem is being created, so option D is incorrect.

12. B. Although they have similar names and purposes, Linux's fdisk isn't modeled after DOS's FDISK, so option B is correct and option A is not. DOS's FDISK does *not* have GUI controls, contrary to option C. Linux's fdisk does *not* format floppy disks, contrary to option D. Both programs manage MBR disks, contrary to option E.

13. E. Swap partitions aren't mounted in the way filesystems are, so they have no associated mount points, making option E correct.

14. C. The −t option is used to tell fsck what filesystem to use, so option C is correct. (If this option isn't used, fsck determines the filesystem type automatically.) The −A option (option A) causes fsck to check all the filesystems marked to be checked in /etc/fstab. The −N option (option B) tells fsck to take no action and to display what it would normally do without doing it. The −C option (option D) displays a text-mode progress indicator of the check process. The -f option (option E) is fictitious.

15. A. A default use of `df` reports the percentage of disk space used (option D) and the mount point for each filesystem (option E). The number of inodes (option B) and filesystem types (option C) can both be obtained by passing parameters to `df`. This utility does *not* report how long a filesystem has been mounted (option A), so that option is correct.

16. D. The journal of a journaling filesystem records pending operations, resulting in quicker disk checks after an uncontrolled shutdown, so option D is correct. Contrary to option A, journaling filesystems are, as a class, newer than non-journaling filesystems; in fact, the journaling ext3fs is built upon the non-journaling ext2fs. Although disk checks are quicker with journaling filesystems than with non-journaling filesystems, journaling filesystems do have `fsck` utilities, and these may still need to be run from time to time, so option B is incorrect. All Linux-native filesystems support Linux ownership and permissions; this isn't an advantage of journaling filesystems, contrary to option C. The journal of a journaling filesystem doesn't provide an unlimited "undo" feature, so option E is incorrect.

17. E. When typed without a filesystem type specification, `mount` attempts to auto-detect the filesystem type. If the media contains any of the specified filesystems, it should be detected and the disk mounted, so option E is correct.

18. B. The `/etc/fstab` file consists of lines that contain the device identifier, the mount point, the filesystem type code, filesystem mount options, the `dump` flag, and the filesystem check frequency, in that order. Option B provides this information in the correct order and so will work. Option A reverses the second and third fields but is otherwise correct. Options C, D, and E all scramble the order of the first three fields and also specify the `noauto` mount option, which causes the filesystem to not mount automatically at boot time.

19. A, B, C. The `user`, `users`, and `owner` options in `/etc/fstab` all enable ordinary users to mount a filesystem, but with slightly different implications: `user` enables anybody to mount a filesystem, and only that user may unmount it; `users` enables anybody to mount a filesystem, and anybody may unmount it; and `owner` enables only the owner of the mount point to mount or unmount a filesystem. Thus, options A, B, and C are all correct. The `owners` parameter of option D doesn't exist. The `uid=1000` parameter of option E tells Linux to set the ownership of files to UID 1000 on filesystems that lack Linux permissions features. Although this might be desirable for some disks, it doesn't enable the user with UID 1000 to mount the disk, so option E is incorrect.

20. A. Option A correctly describes the safe procedure for removing a removable medium that lacks a locking mechanism from a Linux computer. (Instead of typing **umount /media/ usb**, you could type **umount /dev/sdb1**; in this context, the two commands are equivalent.) Option B reverses the order of operations; the `umount` command *must* be typed *before* you physically remove the flash drive. Option C also has it backward; the `sync` command would need to be issued *before* removing the drive. (The `sync` command can prevent damage when removing disks, but it isn't a complete substitute for `umount`.) There is no standard `usbdrive-remove` command in Linux, and if you were to write a script that calls `umount` and call it `usbdrive-remove`, pulling the flash drive quickly, as option D describes, would be exactly the wrong thing to do. The `fsck` command of option E checks a filesystem for errors. It's not necessary to do this before removing a disk, and it won't unmount the disk, so option E is incorrect.

Chapter 4: Managing Files

1. B. The touch utility updates a file's time stamps, as option B specifies. (If the specified file doesn't exist, touch creates an empty file.) You can't move files with touch; that's the job of the mv command, so option A is incorrect. Various tools can convert end-of-line formats, but touch is not one of them, so option C is incorrect. Testing the validity of disk structures, as in option D, is normally done on a whole-filesystem basis with fsck and related tools; touch can't do this job. You can write cached data to disk for a whole filesystem by unmounting it or by using sync, but touch can't do this, so option E is incorrect.

2. A, D. The -s and --symbolic options to ln are equivalent, and both create a symbolic (aka soft) link. Thus, options A and D are both correct. Options B, C, and E are all fictitious.

3. A. The -l parameter produces a long listing, including file sizes. The -a parameter produces a listing of all files in a directory, including the dot files. Combining the two produces the desired information (along with information about other files), so option A is correct. The -p, -R, -d, and -F options don't have the specified effects, so the remaining options are all incorrect.

4. D. When moving from one partition or disk to another, mv must necessarily read and copy the file and then delete the original if that copy was successful, as stated in option D. If both filesystems support ownership and permissions, they'll be preserved; mv doesn't need an explicit --preserve option to do this, and this preservation does not rely on having exactly the same filesystem types. Thus, option A is incorrect. Although mv doesn't physically rewrite data when moving within a single low-level filesystem, this approach can't work when you're copying to a separate low-level filesystem (such as from a hard disk to a pen drive); if the data isn't written to the new location, it won't be accessible should the disk be inserted in another computer. Thus, option B is incorrect. Although not all filesystems support ownership and permissions, many do, and these attributes are preserved when moving files between them, so option C is incorrect. Although FAT is a common choice on removable media because of its excellent cross-platform support, other filesystems will work on such disks, so option E is incorrect.

5. A, B. If you try to create a directory inside a directory that doesn't exist, mkdir responds with a No such file or directory error. The --parents parameter tells mkdir to automatically create all necessary parent directories in such situations, so option A is correct. You can also manually do this by creating each necessary directory separately, so option B is also correct. (It's possible that mkdir one wouldn't be necessary in this example if the directory one already existed. No harm will come from trying to create a directory that already exists, although mkdir will return a File exists error.) Typing touch /bin/mkdir, as option C suggests, will likely result in an error message if typed as a normal user and won't help if typed as root, so this option is incorrect. Clearing away existing directories in the one/two/three tree won't help, so option D is incorrect. Option E's mktree command is fictitious.

6. D, E. The cpio and tar programs are common Linux archive-creation utilities, so options D and E are both correct. The restore command restores (but does not back up) data; its backup counterpart command is dump. Thus, option A is incorrect. The vi command launches a text editor; it's not used to create archives, so option B is incorrect. There is no standard tape command in Linux, so option C is incorrect.

7. E. With the tar utility, the --list (t) command is used to read the archive and display its contents. The --verbose (v) option creates a verbose file listing, and --file (f) specifies the filename—data79.tar in this case. Option E uses all of these features. Options A, B, C, and D all substitute other commands for --list, which is required by the question.

8. A. Symbolic links can point across filesystems, so creating a symbolic link from one filesystem (in which your home directory resides) to another (on the CD-ROM) isn't a problem, making option A correct. Hard links, as in options B, C, and D, are restricted to a single filesystem and so won't work for the described purpose. Because symbolic links will work as described, option E is incorrect.

9. E. Option E is the correct command. Typing chown ralph:tony somefile.txt, as in option A, sets the owner of the file to ralph and the group to tony. The chmod command used in options B and D is used to change file permissions, not ownership. Option C reverses the order of the filename and the owner.

10. C, E. The d character that leads the mode indicates that the file is actually a directory (option C), and the r symbol in the r-x triplet at the end of the symbolic mode indicates that all users of the system have read access to the directory (option E). Symbolic links are denoted by leading l characters, which this mode lacks, so option A is incorrect. Although the x symbols usually denote executable program files, as specified in option B, in the case of directories this permission bit indicates that the directory's contents may be searched; executing a directory is meaningless. SUID bits are indicated by an s character in place of the owner's execute bit position in the symbolic mode. Since this position holds an x in this example, option D is incorrect.

11. C. The set user ID (SUID) bit enables programs to run as the program's owner rather than as the user who ran them. This makes SUID root programs risky, so setting the SUID bit on root-owned programs should be done only when it's required for the program's normal functioning, as stated in option C. This should certainly *not* be done for all programs because the SUID bit is *not* required of all executable programs as option A asserts. Although the SUID root configuration does enable programs to access device files, the device files' permissions can be modified to give programs access to those files, if this is required, so option B is incorrect. Although SUID root programs are a security risk, as stated in option D, they're a necessary risk for a few programs, so option D goes too far. Many program files that should *not* be SUID root are owned by root, so option E is incorrect.

12. E. Using symbolic modes, the o+r option adds read (r) permissions to the world (o). Thus, option E is correct. Option A sets the mode to rwxr----x, which is a bit odd and doesn't provide world read access to the file, although it does provide world execute access. Option

B sets the mode to rw-r-----, which gives the world no access whatsoever to the file. Option C adds read access to the file for the owner (u) if the owner doesn't already have this access; it doesn't affect the world permissions. Option D *removes* read access for *all* users, so it's incorrect.

13. D. Option D, 027, removes write permissions for the group and all world permissions. (Files normally don't have execute permissions set, but explicitly removing write permissions when removing read permissions ensures reasonable behavior for directories.) Option A, 640, is the octal equivalent of the desired rw-r----- permissions; but the umask sets the bits that are to be *removed* from permissions, not those that are to be set. Option B, 210, would remove write permission for the owner, but it wouldn't remove write permission for the group, which is incorrect. This would also leave all world permissions open. Option C, 022, wouldn't remove world read permission. Option E, 138, is an invalid umask, since all the digits in the umask must be between 0 and 7.

14. E. Using quotas requires kernel support, the usrquota or grpquota (for user or group quotas) filesystem mount option, and activation via the quotaon command (which often appears in system startup scripts). Thus, option E is correct. Option A suggests that quotaon is not necessary, which is incorrect. Option B's statement that grpquota is invalid is incorrect. Option C's statement that these options *disable* quota support is backward. The usrquota and grpquota options are both valid, so option D is incorrect.

15. B. The repquota utility is used to summarize the quota information about the filesystem. When used with the -a option, it shows this information for all filesystems, so option B is correct. This command won't return useful information when typed alone, though, so option A is incorrect. The quotacheck utility checks quota information about a disk and writes corrections, so options C and D are both incorrect. The edquota utility enables you to edit quota information. It doesn't summarize quota information, and -a isn't a valid option to edquota. Thus, option E is incorrect.

16. D. The /opt directory tree exists to hold programs that aren't a standard part of a Linux distribution, such as commercial programs. These programs should install in their own directories under /opt; these directories usually have bin subdirectories of their own, although this isn't required. Thus, option D is correct (that is, it's a plausible possibility). The /usr/sbin directory holds programs that are normally run only by the system administrator, so it's not a likely location, making option A incorrect. The /etc/X11 directory holds X-related configuration files, so it's very unlikely that WonderCalc will be housed there, making option B incorrect. The /boot directory holds critical system boot files, so option C is incorrect. The /sbin directory, like /usr/sbin, is an unlikely location for user files, so option E is incorrect. (Furthermore, /sbin seldom contains subdirectories.)

17. A. The find utility (option A) operates by searching all files in a directory tree, and so it's likely to take a long time to search all of a computer's directories. The locate program uses a precompiled database, whereis searches a limited set of directories, and type searches the shell's path and built-in commands, so these commands will take less time. Thus, options B, C, D, and E are all incorrect.

18. C. The `type` command identifies a command, as executed by the shell, as being a built-in shell command, a shell alias, or an external command, whereas the `whereis` command helps find the location of external command files. Thus, option C is correct. Neither `type` nor `whereis` identifies the CPU architecture of a program file, can locate commands based on intended purpose, complete an incompletely typed command, or identify a command as a binary or a script; thus, the remaining options are all incorrect.

19. B. The `find` command includes the ability to search by username using the `-user name` option, where *name* is the username; thus, option B is correct. The `-uid` option to `find` can also locate files owned by a user, but it takes a numeric user ID (UID) number as an argument, so option A isn't quite correct. The `locate` command provides no ability to search by user, so options C and D are incorrect. Although option E is a valid `find` command, it finds all the files under /home with a *filename* of `karen`, not all files owned by the user `karen`, so this option is incorrect.

20. D. The `which` program searches the path just as `bash` does, but it prints the path to the first executable program it finds on the path. Thus, option D is correct. The `which` program doesn't conduct an exhaustive search of the system, so there could be many more files called `man` on the system, contrary to option A. System package tools and `which` aren't closely related; option B is incorrect. Although /usr/bin/man would be run when the user whose `which` output matches that in the question types **man**, this may not be true of others because the path can vary from one user to another. Thus, option C is incorrect. The `which` program doesn't reveal file ownership information, so option E is incorrect.

Chapter 5: Booting Linux and Editing Files

1. C. The Master Boot Record (MBR) can contain a boot loader that is up to 446 bytes in size, so option C is correct. If more space is required, the boot loader must load a secondary boot loader. Although the boot loader is loaded into RAM (option A), it's not stored there permanently because RAM is volatile storage. Both /dev/boot and /dev/kmem (options B and D) are references to files on Linux filesystems; they're meaningful only after the BIOS has found a boot loader and run it and lots of other boot processes have occurred. The swap partition (option E) is used as an adjunct to RAM; the BIOS won't look there for a boot loader.

2. C. Runlevel 1 is single-user mode, and adding the digit 1 to the kernel's options line in a boot loader will launch the system in this runlevel, so option C is correct. Options A and B both present invalid kernel options and so are incorrect. Although the `telinit` command specified in options D and E will change the runlevel once the computer is running and runlevel 1 is a single-user mode, these commands are *not* passed to the kernel via a boot loader, so these options are both incorrect.

3. D. The kernel ring buffer, which can be viewed by typing **dmesg** (piping this through less is a good supplement), contains messages from the kernel, including those from hardware drivers. These messages may provide a clue about why the disk didn't appear; thus, option D is correct. The /var/log/diskerror file (option A) is fictitious, as is /mnt/disks (option B). The /etc/inittab file (option C) doesn't directly control disk access and so is unlikely to provide useful information. The files specified in option C are GRUB Legacy and GRUB 2 configuration files, which don't contain information that could explain why a disk isn't responding.

4. B. Ordinarily, Linux runs init (option B) as the first program; init then runs, via various scripts, other programs. The dmesg program (option A) is a user diagnostic and information tool used to access the kernel ring buffer; it's not part of the startup process. The startup program (option C) is fictitious. The rc program (option D) is a script that some versions of init call, typically indirectly, during the startup sequence, but it's not the first program the kernel runs. LILO is an older boot loader for Linux on BIOS systems, and lilo (option E) is the command that installs this boot loader to the MBR. Since boot loaders run before the kernel loads, this option is incorrect.

5. D. Option D is the correct GRUB 2 configuration file. Option A is a fictitious file; it doesn't exist. Although some of GRUB 2's boot loader code may be written to the MBR, as implied by option B, this isn't the location of the program's configuration file. Options C and D are both possible names for the GRUB Legacy configuration file, but that name is not shared by GRUB 2.

6. A. The initrd keyword identifies an initial RAM disk file in the GRUB 2 configuration file, and a space separates this keyword from the filename. (Several variants on this syntax are possible.) Option B adds an equal sign (=), which renders the syntax incorrect. Options C, D, and E use the incorrect initramfs and ramdisk keywords instead of initrd.

7. D. You use grub-install to install the GRUB Legacy boot loader code into an MBR or boot sector. When using grub-install, you specify the boot sector on the command line. The MBR is the first sector on a hard drive, so you give it the Linux device identifier for the entire hard disk, /dev/sda. Hence, option D is correct. Option A specifies using the grub utility, which is an interactive tool, and the device identifier shown in option A is a GRUB-style identifier for what would probably be the /dev/sda3 partition in Linux. Option B is almost correct but installs GRUB to the /dev/sda1 partition's boot sector rather than the hard disk's MBR. Option C is the command to install LILO to the MBR rather than to install GRUB. Option E contains the same error as option B, and it also uses the fictitious grub-legacy command.

8. B. The root keyword in a GRUB Legacy configuration file tells the boot loader where to look for files, including its own configuration files, kernel files, and so on. Because GRUB Legacy numbers both disks and partitions starting from 0, (hd1,5) refers to the sixth partition on the second disk, as option B specifies. Option A is incorrect because you pass the Linux root partition to the kernel on the kernel line, not via the GRUB root keyword. Options A, C, and E all misinterpret the GRUB numbering scheme. The GRUB installation location is specified on the grub-install command line, so options D and E are incorrect; and /dev/hd1,5 isn't a standard Linux device file, so option D is incorrect.

9. B. The `initdefault` action specifies the default runlevel, so option B is correct. The remaining options are all taken from actual /etc/inittab files but don't have the specified meaning.

10. A, B, E. Runlevel 0 (option A) is the reserved runlevel for halting the system. Runlevel 1 (option B) is reserved for single-user mode. Runlevel 6 (option E) is reserved for rebooting. Runlevel 2 (option C) is the default runlevel on Debian and most distributions derived from it, but it does none of the things described in the question. Runlevel 5 (option D) is a regular, user-configurable runlevel, which isn't normally used for the things described in the question. (Many systems use it for a regular boot with a GUI login prompt.)

11. B, C. The first number in the `runlevel` output is the previous runlevel (the letter N is used to indicate that the system hasn't changed runlevels since booting). The second number is the current runlevel. Hence, options B and C are both correct, while options A and D are both incorrect. The runlevel changes very quickly, and the `runlevel` utility doesn't provide a code to indicate that the runlevel is in the process of being changed, so option E is incorrect.

12. A. The -c option to `shutdown` cancels a previously scheduled shutdown, as stated in option A. Options B and C describe the effects of the -r and -h options to `shutdown`, respectively. No `shutdown` option asks for confirmation before taking action, although you can delay a shutdown by specifying a shutdown time in the future, so option D is incorrect. No `shutdown` option closes open windows in X, except as a consequence of shutting down, so option E is incorrect.

13. E. There is no standard `takedown` command in Linux, so option E is correct. The `reboot` command (option A) is equivalent to `shutdown -r`, `halt` (option B) is equivalent to `shutdown -H`, `poweroff` (option C) is equivalent to `shutdown -P`, and `telinit 0` (option D) is equivalent to `shutdown -H`.

14. B. The `telinit` command is used to change runlevels; when it's passed the 1 parameter, as in option B, `telinit` changes to runlevel 1, which is single-user mode. The `runlevel` command (option A) displays the current runlevel but doesn't change runlevels. Although `telinit` can be used to shut down or reboot the computer, the `shutdown` command (option C) can't be used to change runlevels except to runlevel 0 or 6. There is no standard `single-user` command (option D). The `halt` command (option E), like `shutdown`, can't be used to change to single-user mode.

15. E. Runlevel 4 isn't standardized, and most distributions don't use it for anything specific (although in practice it will do *something* if you enter it). Thus, you can safely redefine runlevel 4 to achieve specific goals, and option E is correct. Option A describes runlevel 6. Option B describes runlevel 3 on Red Hat and related distributions. Option C describes runlevel 5 on Red Hat and related distributions. Option D describes runlevel 1.

16. A. In Vi, dd is the command-mode command that deletes lines. Preceding this command by a number deletes that number of lines. Thus, option A is correct. Although yy works similarly, it copies (yanks) text rather than deleting it, so option B is incorrect. Option C works in many more modern text editors, but not in Vi. Option D works in Emacs and similar text editors, but not in Vi. Option E works in many GUI text editors, but not in Vi.

17. D. The :q! Vi command does as option D states. Options A and E are both simply incorrect. Option B would be correct if this command were typed while in Vi's insert mode, but the question specifies that command mode is in use. To achieve option C, the command would be :wq, not :q!.

18. E. Vi is included on Linux emergency disks, embedded systems, and other systems where space is at a premium because its executable is tiny. Emacs is, in contrast, a behemoth. Thus, option E is correct. Contrary to option A, Vi isn't an X-based program (although X-based Vi variants are available); Emacs can be used in text mode or with X. Extended Binary Coded Decimal Interchange Code (EBCDIC) is an obscure 8-bit character encoding system used on some very old mainframe OSs. When run on Linux, Vi doesn't use EBCDIC; furthermore, EBCDIC offers few or no advantages over the American Standard Code for Information Interchange (ASCII). Thus, option B is incorrect. Vi's modes, referred to in option C, have nothing to do with non-English language support. Option D is backward; it's Emacs that includes a Web browser, email client, and other add-ons.

19. A, B, C. Typing R (option A) in command mode enters insert mode with the system configured to overwrite existing text. Typing i or a (options B and C, respectively) enters insert mode with the system configured to insert text. (The i and a commands differ in how they place the cursor; a advances one space.) Typing : (option D) in command mode enters ex mode (you typically type the ex-mode command on the same command line immediately after the colon). Pressing the Esc key (option E) returns Vi to command mode from insert mode.

20. B. The Esc key exits Vi's insert mode, as option B specifies. Typing a tilde (~) inserts that character into the file, so option A is incorrect. The Ctrl+X, Ctrl+C key combination exits from Emacs, but it's not a defined Vi key sequence, so option C is incorrect. The F10 key and the Shift+Insert key combination also aren't defined in Vi, so options D and E are both incorrect.

Chapter 6: Configuring the X Window System, Localization, and Printing

1. A. On most Linux systems, some runlevels don't run X by default, so using one of them along with the startx program (which starts X running) can be an effective way to quickly test changes to an X configuration, making option A correct. The telinit program changes runlevels, which is a lengthy process compared to using startx, so option B is incorrect. Unplugging the computer to avoid the shutdown process is self-defeating because you'll have to suffer through a long startup (if you use a non-journaling filesystem), and it can also result in data loss. Thus, option C is incorrect. The startx utility doesn't check the veracity of an X configuration file; it starts X running from a text-mode login, making option D incorrect. Reconfiguring an X server does not normally require network access; the X server runs on the computer at which you sit. Thus, option E is incorrect.

2. D. The XF86Config and `xorg.conf` file design enables you to define variants or multiple components and easily combine or recombine them as necessary, using the structure specified in option D. Options A, B, and C all describe fictitious structures. Option E is incorrect because the X.org-X11 and XFree86 configuration files use a text-mode structure, not a binary structure.

3. C. The vertical refresh rate range includes a maximum value, but that value may be reduced when the resolution and vertical refresh rate would demand a higher horizontal refresh rate than the monitor can handle. Thus, option C is correct. Since the resolution affects the maximum refresh rate, option A is incorrect. The color depth is irrelevant to resolution and refresh rate calculations, so option B is incorrect. The computations shown in options D and E are bogus, making these options incorrect.

4. E. Option E describes the correct location for this option. The ServerLayout section (referenced in option A) combines all the other options together but doesn't set the resolution. The Modeline option in the Monitor section (as described in option B) defines *one* possible resolution, but there may be several Modeline entries defining many resolutions, and there's no guarantee that any of them will be used. The Modeline option doesn't exist in the Device section (as suggested by option C), nor is that section where the resolution is set. There is no DefaultResolution section (as referenced in option D).

5. B. By maintaining fonts on one font server and pointing other X servers to that font server, you can reduce the administrative cost of maintaining the fonts on all the systems, so option B is correct. Font servers don't produce faster font displays than X's local font handling; if anything, the opposite is true. Thus, option A is incorrect. XFree86 4.*x* supports TrueType fonts directly, so option C is incorrect. Converting a bitmapped display into ASCII text is a function of optical character recognition (OCR) software, not a font server, so option D is incorrect. Neither X core fonts nor a font server handles font smoothing; for that, you need Xft. Thus, option E is incorrect.

6. C, E. XDMCP servers are typically launched either from a system startup script or by init (as specified in /etc/inittab), as described in options C and E. The XDMCP server then starts X. The Start folder mentioned in option A is a Windows construct, not a Linux construct. The ~/.xinitrc script mentioned in option B is an X login script used when starting X from the command line via startx; it's not used to automatically start X when the system boots. A boot manager, as described in option D, launches the kernel; it doesn't directly start X, so option D is incorrect.

7. E. The XDM greeting is a resource set in the /etc/X11/xdm/Xresources file, so option E is correct. XDM doesn't offer many options on its main screen and certainly not one to change its greeting, as described in option A. The kernel doesn't directly handle the login process, nor does it pass options directly to XDM, so option B is incorrect. Although the xorg.conf file mentioned in option C is real, this file provides no XDM configuration options because XDM is a separate program from the X server. There is no standard xdmconfig program, as mentioned in option D.

8. C. KDM and GDM add many features, one of which is a menu that enables users to select their desktop environment or window manager when they log in rather than specifying it in a configuration file, as option C states. Option A describes one of the advantages of the Secure Shell (SSH) as a remote-access protocol. Option B describes a feature common to all three XDMCP servers. Option D describes the way both KDM and XDM function; GDM is the one that presents username and password fields in series rather than simultaneously. Although a failure of X to start usually results in a fallback to a text-mode login, this feature is not provided by the XDMCP server, so option E is incorrect.

9. A. The xhost command controls various aspects of the local X server, including the remote computers from which it will accept connections, making option A correct. Option B sets the DISPLAY environment variable, which doesn't directly affect the X server (it does tell X clients which X server to use). Option C initiates a text-mode remote login session with penguin.example.com. Option D's xaccess is a fictitious program. Although logging into penguin.example.com via ssh may also initiate an X tunnel, this isn't guaranteed, and such a tunnel doesn't cause the local X server to accept *direct* connections from the remote computer, so option E is incorrect.

10. A. As stated in option A, GNOME, KDE, and other user programs often override the keyboard repeat settings in the X configuration file. Option B has it almost backward; most Linux distributions have abandoned XFree86, and therefore its XF86Config file, in favor of X.org-X11 and its xorg.conf file. Option C is pure fiction; xorg.conf settings apply to all varieties of keyboards, and there is no standard usbkbrate program. Although some keyboards do have hardware switches, they don't affect X's ability to control the keyboard repeat rate, contrary to option D. Although you can set a keyboard's nationality in xorg.conf, this option is independent of the keyboard repeat rate settings, so option E is incorrect.

11. C, E. The Orca and Emacspeak programs both provide text-to-speech conversion facilities, so options C and E are both correct. Braille is a form of writing that uses bumps or holes in a surface that can be felt by the reader. Although Linux supports Braille output devices, the question specifies computer-generated speech, which Braille is not, so option B is incorrect. SoX (option A) is an audio format converter, but it won't convert from text to speech. The talk program (option D) is an early Unix online text-mode "chat" program, but it has no built-in speech synthesis capabilities.

12. B, E. Time zones are determined by the /etc/localtime file, so replacing that one with the correct file (a selection is stored in /usr/share/zoneinfo) will fix the problem, making option B correct. (You may also need to edit /etc/timezone or some other file to keep automatic utilities from becoming confused.) Utilities such as tzselect will make these changes for you after prompting you for your location, so option E is also correct. The hwclock program mentioned in option A reads and writes data from the system's hardware clock. Although it relies on time zone data, it can't adjust your system's time zone itself. There is no standard /etc/tzconfig file, although the tzconfig program, like tzselect, can help you set the time zone. Thus, option C is incorrect. The /etc/localtime file is a binary format; you shouldn't attempt to edit it in a text editor, making option D incorrect.

13. D. Linux, like Unix, maintains its time internally in Coordinated Universal Time (UTC), so setting the computer's hardware clock to UTC (option D) is the recommended procedure for computers that run only Linux. Although Linus Torvalds spent time at the University of Helsinki, Helsinki time (as in option A) has no special place in Linux. Local time (as in option B) is appropriate if the computer dual-boots to an OS, such as Windows, that requires the hardware clock to be set to local time, but this is the second-best option for a Linux-only system. Option C's US Pacific time, like Helsinki time, has no special significance in Linux. Internet time (option E) is an obscure way to measure time that divides each day into 1,000 "beats." It's not a time zone and is not an appropriate way to set your hardware clock.

14. C. The LC_ALL environment variable (option C), when set, adjusts all the locale (LC_*) variables, so setting this and then running the script will make the programs that your script uses work as if on a British computer. The BIOS has no location code data, so option A is incorrect. There is no standard /etc/locale.conf file, so option B is incorrect. There is no standard locale_set utility, so option D is incorrect. Although setting the TZ environment variable, as in option E, will set the time zone for your local shell to that for Great Britain, this won't affect the sort of text formatting options noted in the question.

15. A. The Unicode Transformation Format 8 (UTF-8) standard can encode characters for just about any language on Earth, while looking just like ordinary ASCII to programs that only understand ASCII. Thus, UTF-8 (option A) is the preferred method for character encoding when a choice is possible. ASCII (option B) is an old standard that's adequate for English and a few other languages, but it lacks some or all characters needed by most languages. ISO-8859 (options C and D) is a standard that extends ASCII, but it requires separate encodings for different languages and so is awkward when a computer must process data from multiple languages. ATASCII (option E) is a variant of ASCII used in the 1980s by Atari for its home computers; it's obsolete and inadequate today.

16. E. The smart filter makes a print queue "smart" in that it can accept different file types (plain text, PostScript, graphics, and so on) and print them all correctly, as in option E. Font smoothing is useful on low-resolution computer monitors, but not on most printers, and adding font smoothing is not a function of a smart filter, so option A is incorrect. A smart filter doesn't detect confidential information (option B) or prank print jobs (option D). The lpr program can be given a parameter to email a user when the job finishes (option C), but the smart filter doesn't do this.

17. B, D. The job ID (option B) and job owner (option D) are both displayed by lpq. Unless the application embeds its own name (option A) in the filename, that information won't be present. Most printers lack Linux utilities to query ink or toner status (option C); certainly lpq can't do this. Although knowing when your job will finish printing (option E) would be handy, this information is well beyond lpq's capabilities to provide.

18. C. The lprm command (option C) deletes a job from the print queue. It can take the -Pqueue option to specify the queue and a print job number or various other parameters to specify which jobs to delete. BSD LPD, LPRng, and CUPS all implement the lprm command, so you can use it with any of these systems, making option A incorrect. Option

B presents the correct syntax but the wrong command name; there is no standard `lpdel` command. The `cupsdisable` command can be used to disable the whole queue, but not to delete a single print job, so option D is incorrect. Because option C is correct, option E obviously is not.

19. B. PostScript is the de facto printing standard for Unix and Linux programs, as specified in option B. Linux programs generally *do not* send data directly to the printer port (option A); on a multi-tasking, multi-user system, this would produce chaos because of competing print jobs. Although a few programs include printer driver collections, most forgo this in favor of generating PostScript, making option C incorrect. Printing utilities come standard with Linux; add-on commercial utilities aren't required, so option D is incorrect. Verdana is one of several "Web fonts" released by Microsoft. Although many Linux programs *can* use Verdana for printing if the font is installed, most Linux distributions don't install Verdana by default, and few Linux programs use it for printing by default even if it's installed, so option E is correct.

20. B. The `mpage` utility (option B) prints multiple input pages on a single output page, so it's ideally suited to the specified task. PAM (option A) is the Pluggable Authentication Modules, a tool for helping to authenticate users. 4Front (option C) is the name of a company that produces commercial sound drivers for Linux. The `route` command (option D) is used to display or configure a Linux routing table. The `411toppm` program (option E) converts files from Sony's `.411` image file format to the `.ppm` image file format; it doesn't do the specified task.

Chapter 7: Administering the System

1. A. A Linux username must contain fewer than 32 characters and start with a letter, and it may consist of letters, numbers, and certain symbols. The `useradd` utility imposes additional restrictions: Uppercase letters and most symbols are not permitted. Of these options, only option A meets all of these criteria. Option B begins with a number and so is invalid. Option C is a legal Linux username but won't be accepted by `useradd` because of its uppercase letters. Option D is too long to be legal at 33 characters, and it contains uppercase letters and underscore symbols. Option E is a legal Linux username but won't be accepted by `useradd` because of the space in the name.

2. A. Groups provide a good method of file-access control, as described in option A. Although they may have passwords, these are *not* account login passwords, as option B suggests; those passwords are set on a per-account basis. Files do have associated groups, but these are *in addition* to individual file ownership and so they can't be used to mask the file's owner, making option C incorrect. Deleting a group *does not* delete all the accounts associated with the group, so option D is incorrect. Groups are not fundamentally a cross-computer construct, contrary to option E. (This option describes the function of network account databases such as LDAP accounts or Active Directory.)

3.   A. The chage command changes various account expiration options. The -M parameter sets the maximum number of days for which a password is valid, and in the context of the given command, time is a username. Thus, option A is correct. Options B, C, D, and E are all made up.

4.   B, D. As stated in option B, Linux usernames may not begin with numbers, so the username (4sally) is invalid. The /etc/passwd entries have third and fourth fields of the UID and the GID, but this line has only one of those fields (which one is intended is impossible to determine); this example line's fourth field is clearly the fifth field of a valid entry. Thus, option D is correct. Option A is incorrect because, although /bin/passwd is an unorthodox login shell, it's perfectly valid. This configuration might be used on, say, a Samba file server or a POP mail server to enable users to change their passwords via SSH without granting login shell access. Option C is a correct observation but an incorrect answer; the username and the user's home directory name need not match. The encrypted password is officially stored in the second field (x in this example), but in practice, most Linux computers use shadow passwords, and an x value for the password is consistent with this use, so option E is incorrect.

5.   D. Option D shows a valid /etc/group entry that has the desired effect. (Note that the order of users in the comma-separated user list is unimportant.) Option A has two problems: It's missing a password field (x in the correct entry), and the usernames are separated by spaces rather than commas. Option B also has two problems: It's missing a password field, and its usernames are separated by colons rather than commas. Option C has just one problem: Its usernames are separated by colons rather than commas. Option E has two problems: Its password and GID fields are reversed, and its usernames are separated by backslashes rather than commas.

6.   B, C, D. Files in /etc/skel are copied from this directory to new users' home directories by certain account-creation tools. Thus, files you want in all new users' home directories should reside in /etc/skel. Options B, C, and D all describe reasonable possibilities, although none is absolutely required. Including a copy of /etc/shadow in /etc/skel (option A) would be a very bad idea, because this would give all users access to all other users' encrypted passwords, at least as of the moment of account creation. You wouldn't likely find package management databases (option E) in /etc/skel, since users don't need privileged access to this data, nor do they need individualized copies of it.

7.   C. The userdel command deletes an account, and the -r option to userdel (option C) causes it to delete the user's home directory and mail spool, thus satisfying the terms of the question. Option A deletes the account but leaves the user's home directory intact. Option B does the same; the -f option forces account deletion and file removal under some circumstances, but it's meaningful only when -r is also used. Option D's rm command deletes the user's home directory (assuming it's located in the conventional place, given the username) but doesn't delete the user's account. Option E's usermod command can modify accounts, including locking them, but it can't delete accounts. Furthermore, the -D option to usermod is fictitious.

8.   E. The emerg priority code (option E) is the highest code available and so is higher than all the other options. (The panic code is equivalent to emerg but isn't one of the options.) From highest to lowest priorities, the codes given as options are emerg, crit, warning, info, and debug.

9. A. The `logrotate` program consults a configuration file called `/etc/logrotate.conf` (option A), which includes several default settings and typically refers to files in `/etc/logrotate.d` to handle specific log files. The remaining options are all fictitious, at least as working log files for `logrotate`.

10. D. The `logger` utility can be used to create a one-time log file entry that you specify. In its simplest form, it takes no special arguments, just a message to be inserted in the log file, as in option D. The `dmesg` utility in option A is used to review the kernel ring buffer; it doesn't create log file entries. Option B's `syslog` command isn't a Linux user-mode command, although it is the name of the logging system generically, as well as a programming language command name. Option C's `rsyslogd` is the name of one of several system logging daemons; it maintains the system log but isn't used to manually insert log entries. Option E's `wall` command writes a message to all users' terminals. Although you might want to use wall prior to shutting down so as to alert users of this fact, it won't create a log file entry as the question requires.

11. C. The `logrotate` program can be started automatically—and unattended—on a regular basis by adding an entry for it in `cron`, so option C is correct. The `at` utility (option A) would be used if you wanted the program to run only once. `logrotate.d` (option B) defines how the program is to handle specific log files. The `inittab` file (option D) is used for services and startup and not for individual programs. The `ntpd` program (option E) is the Network Time Protocol daemon, which synchronizes the system's clock with outside time sources.

12. E. The `hwclock` utility is used to view or set the hardware clock. The `--utc` option tells it to use UTC, which is appropriate for a Linux-only system, and `--systohc` sets the hardware clock based on the current value of the software clock. Thus, option E is correct. Option A's `date` utility can be used to set the software clock but not the hardware clock; it has no `--sethwclock` option. Option B's `ntpdate` is used to set the software clock to the time maintained by an NTP server; it doesn't directly set the hardware clock. Option C's `sysclock` utility is fictitious. Option D's `time` command is used to time how long a command takes to complete; it has no `--set` or `--hw` option and does not set the hardware clock.

13. A. The format of the `date` command's date code is *[MMDDhhmm[[CC]YY][.ss]]*. Given that the question specified an eight-digit code, this means that the ordering of the items, in two-digit blocks, is month-day-hour-minute. Option A correctly parses this order, whereas options B, C, D, and E do not.

14. C. Multiple `server` entries in `/etc/ntp.conf` tell the system to poll all the named servers and to use whichever one provides the best time data. Thus, option C is correct. (The `pool.ntp.org` subdomain and numbered computers within that subdomain give round-robin access to a variety of public time servers.) Options A and B both incorrectly state that one `server` statement overrides another, when in fact this isn't the case. The `server` statements shown in the question are properly formed. These `server` entries are properly formed, so option D is incorrect. Although it is true that this configuration will result in use of `tardis.example.com` should the public-pool server be unavailable, as option E states, this is not the *only* reason the NTP server will use `tardis.example.com`; this could happen if the public-pool server provides an inferior time signal, for instance. Thus, option E is incorrect.

15. D. Once you've configured one computer on your network to use an outside time source and run NTP, the rest of your computers should use the first computer as their time reference. This practice reduces the load on the external time servers, as well as your own external network traffic. Thus, option D is correct. (Very large networks might configure two or three internal time servers that refer to outside servers for redundancy, but this isn't necessary for the small network described in the question.) Option A describes the procedure to locate a time server for the first computer configured (`gateway.pangaea.edu`) but not for subsequent computers. Although configuring other computers to use `ntp.example.com` instead of or in addition to `gateway.pangaea.edu` is possible, doing so will needlessly increase your network traffic and the load on the `ntp.example.com` server. Thus, options B and C are both incorrect. Contrary to option E, NTP is suitable for use on small local networks, and in fact it's very helpful if you use certain protocols, such as Kerberos.

16. B, D. The `cron` utility is a good tool for performing tasks that can be done in an unsupervised manner, such as deleting old temporary files (option B) or checking to see that servers are running correctly (option D). Tasks that require interaction, such as creating accounts (option C), aren't good candidates for `cron` jobs, which must execute unsupervised. Although a `cron` job could restart a crashed server, it's not normally used to start a server when the system boots (option A); that's done through system startup scripts or a super server. Sending files to a printer (option E) is generally handled by a print server such as CUPS.

17. B. User `cron` jobs don't include a username specification (`tbaker` in options A and C). The `*/2` specification for the hour in options C and D causes the job to execute every other hour; the `7,19` specification in options A and B causes it to execute twice a day, on the 7th and 19th hours (in conjunction with the 15 minute specification, that means at 7:15 a.m. and 7:15 p.m.). Thus, option B provides the correct syntax and runs the job twice a day, as the question specifies, whereas options A, C, and D all get something wrong. Option E causes the job to run once an hour, not twice a day.

18. B. The `anacron` program is a supplement to `cron` that helps ensure that log rotation, `/tmp` directory cleanup, and other traditional `cron` tasks are handled even when the computer is shut down (and, hence, when `cron` isn't running) for extended periods of time. Thus, this is the program to add to the system to achieve the stated goal, and option B is correct. There is no common Linux utility called `tempus`, so option A is incorrect. Option C's `crontab` is the name of a file or program for controlling `cron`, which is likely to be an unreliable means of log rotation on a laptop computer. The `ntpd` program (option E) is the NTP daemon, which helps keep the system clock in sync with an external source. Although running `ntpd` on a laptop computer is possible, it won't directly help with the task of scheduling log rotation. The `syslog-ng` package is an alternative system log daemon, but this program doesn't help solve the problem of potentially unreliable log rotation on laptops when using standard `cron` utilities.

19. E. The at command runs a specified program at the stated time in the future. This time may be specified in several ways, one of which is teatime, which stands for 4:00 p.m. Thus, option D is correct. The objections stated in options A, B, C, and D are all invalid. (You *may* pass a script to at with the -f parameter, but this isn't required, contrary to option D.)

20. A, C. The contents of /etc/cron.daily are automatically run on a daily basis in most Linux distributions, and the crontab utility can create user cron jobs that run programs at arbitrary time intervals, so both A and C are correct. The at command noted in option B can be used to run a program a single time, but not on a regular basis (such as daily). Option D's run-parts utility is used by some distributions as a tool to help run programs in the /etc/cron.* subdirectories, but it's not used to schedule jobs. Although the crontab program can maintain user crontabs, it's not used as shown in option E, and it has no -d parameter at all.

Chapter 8: Configuring Basic Networking

1. A, B, E. Ethernet (option B) is currently the most common type of wired network hardware for local networks. Linux supports it very well, and Linux also includes support for Token Ring (option A) and Fibre Channel (option E) network hardware. DHCP (option C) is a protocol used to obtain a TCP/IP configuration over a TCP/IP network. It's not a type of network hardware, but it can be used over hardware that supports TCP/IP. NetBEUI (option D) is a network stack that can be used instead of or in addition to TCP/IP over various types of network hardware. Linux doesn't support NetBEUI directly.

2. B. IP addresses consist of four 1-byte numbers (0–255). They're normally expressed in base 10 and separated by periods. 63.63.63.63 meets these criteria, so option B is correct. 202.9.257.33 includes one value (257) that's not a 1-byte number, so option A is incorrect. 107.29.5.3.2 includes five 1-byte numbers, so option C is incorrect. 98.7.104.0/24 (option D) is a network address—the trailing /24 indicates that the final byte is a machine identifier, and the first 3 bytes specify the network. Option E, 255.255.255.255, meets the basic form of an IP address, but it's a special case—this is a broadcast address that refers to *all* computers, rather than the *single* computer specified by the question.

3. C. The gateway computer is a router that transfers data between two or more network segments. As such, if a computer isn't configured to use a gateway, it won't be able to communicate beyond its local network segment, making option C correct. A gateway is not necessary for communicating with other systems on the local network segment, so option A is incorrect. If your DNS server is on a different network segment, name resolution via DNS won't work, as stated in option B; however, other types of name resolution, such as /etc/hosts file entries, will still work, and the DNS server might be on the local network segment, so option B is incorrect. Gateways play the same function in both IPv4 and IPv6

networking, so option D is incorrect. DHCP functions fine without a gateway, provided a DHCP server is on the same local network segment as its clients (as is normally the case), so option E is incorrect.

4. D. The Secure Shell (SSH) protocol uses port 22, so if the traffic to port 22 is using the correct protocol, it's SSH traffic, and option D is correct. The Hypertext Transfer Protocol (HTTP; option A) is conventionally bound to port 80; the Simple Mail Transfer Protocol (SMTP; option B) uses port 25; Telnet (option C) uses port 22; and the Network News Transfer Protocol (NNTP; option E) uses port 119. None of these would normally be directed to port 22.

5. D. The Interactive Mail Access Protocol (IMAP) is assigned to TCP port 143. Ports 21, 25, 110, and 443 are assigned to the File Transfer Protocol (FTP), the Simple Mail Transfer Protocol (SMTP), the Post Office Protocol version 3 (POP-3), and the Hypertext Transfer Protocol over SSL (HTTPS), respectively. Although some IMAP server programs also support POP-3 and might therefore listen to both ports 110 and 143, the question specifies IMAP exchanges, so option D is the only correct answer.

6. C, E. Option C, dhcpd, is the Linux DHCP *server*. Option E, ifconfig, can be used for network configuration but is not itself a DHCP client. The others are all DHCP clients. Any given computer will use just one DHCP client (or none at all), but from one to three of A, B, and D will be available choices.

7. B, C. When used to display information on an interface, ifconfig shows the hardware and IP addresses (options B and C) of the interface, the protocols (such as TCP/IP) bound to the interface, and statistics on transmitted and received packets. This command does *not* return information about programs using the interface (option A), the hostname associated with the interface (option D), or the kernel driver used by the interface (option E).

8. A. The host program (option A) is a commonly used program to perform a DNS lookup. There is no standard dnslookup program (option B), although the nslookup program is a deprecated program for performing DNS lookups. pump (option C) is a DHCP client. ifconfig (option D) is used for configuration of networking parameters and cards. netstat (option E) is a general-purpose network diagnostic tool.

9. B. To add a default gateway of 192.168.0.1, the command would be **route add default gw 192.168.0.1**, as in option B. Specifying the IP address of the host system (as in options A, C, and D) is not necessary and in fact will confuse the route command. Although route provides a –host option, using host (without a dash), as in option E, is incorrect. Furthermore, option E omits the critical add parameter.

10. A, B. The dhclient utility, if installed, attempts to configure and bring up the network(s) passed to it as options (or all networks if it's given no options) using a DHCP server for guidance. Thus, option A may work, although it won't work if no DHCP server is available. Option B applies whatever network options are configured using distribution-specific tools and brings up the network. Thus, options A and B both may work, although neither is guaranteed to work. Option C displays the network status of eth1, but it won't activate

eth1 if it's not already active. There is no standard `network` utility in Linux, so option D won't work. The `netstat` utility is a network diagnostic tool; it won't bring up a network interface, so option E is incorrect.

11. E. Although not all systems use /etc/hostname, option E correctly describes it for those systems that use it. The file or files that hold information on package repository servers vary from one package system to another, so option A is incorrect. Option B describes the purpose of /etc/resolv.conf. Option C describes the purpose of /etc/hosts. Option D doesn't describe any standard Linux configuration file, although the gateway computer's IP address is likely to appear in a distribution-specific configuration file.

12. C. The `traceroute` command (option C) identifies the computers that lie between your own computer and a destination computer, along with some very basic information about network packet travel time and reliability. Thus, `traceroute` can help you track down the source of the described problem—perhaps a router that's critical to reaching all of the non-responsive systems has failed. The `netstat` and `ifconfig` utilities of options A and D both provide information about local network configuration options, but they most likely won't be of much help in diagnosing a problem that affects only some sites. The `ping` utility (option B) may help you quickly identify sites that have failed but won't be of much use beyond that. You can use `dig` (option E) to obtain information on the mapping of hostnames to IP addresses, but it won't help in resolving basic connectivity problems.

13. B, D. DNS problems can manifest as an ability to connect to computers using IP addresses but not using hostnames. Thus, options B and D (and various other DNS-related problems) could create the symptoms described. If the target system were configured to ignore `ping` packets, as described in option A, then it wouldn't respond when you identified it by IP address. The target system's DNS configuration (option C) doesn't enter into the equation, because it responds to the `ping` request via IP address alone. Your own computer's locally set hostname (in /etc/hostname) isn't used by the remote system to reply, so option E is incorrect.

14. C. The `netstat` program produces various network statistics, including the process IDs (PIDs) and names of programs currently accessing the network when passed the -p parameter. Thus, option C is correct. The `ifconfig` program can't produce this information, and the -p option to this program is fictitious, so option A is incorrect. Option B's /proc/network/programs file is also fictitious. Option C's /etc/xinetd.conf file is real and may provide some information about some servers that are using the network (as described in Chapter 10); but this file won't provide information about all servers, much less about clients that are accessing the network. The `dmesg` command displays the kernel ring buffer, which doesn't contain information on programs that are currently accessing the network, so option E is incorrect.

15. A, D. If you get any response at all, you know that the basic network connection is working, including that the server is responding to the client. With basic knowledge of IMAP commands, `telnet` enables you to test the server's responses in more detail than most IMAP clients (mail readers) permit. Thus, options A and D are both correct. Option C describes the functionality of `traceroute` or `tracepath`; `telnet` provides no information about intermediate routers' functionality, so option B is incorrect. Because neither `telnet` nor IMAP on port 143 uses encryption, option C is incorrect. Furthermore, a packet sniffer

is likely to have no effect on the transfer of data; it just copies the data so that the packet sniffer's user can see it. Although `telnet` can be used for remote access in a way that could make option E correct, the question specifies using `telnet` to connect to port 143, which is the IMAP port, not the Telnet port. Thus, option E is incorrect. (Furthermore, using `telnet` for remote administration is very risky, since `telnet` is an unencrypted protocol.)

16. B. The computer's IP address (172.25.78.89) and netmask (255.255.255.0) mean that the computer can directly address computers with IP addresses in the range of 172.25.78.1 to 172.25.78.254, but the gateway address (172.25.79.1) is outside of this range. Thus, either the IP address or the gateway address is wrong, and option B is correct. Nothing about the way DNS operates necessitates that the DNS server be on the same network segment as the DNS client, so option A is incorrect. Although private IP addresses are often isolated from the Internet, as option C specifies, Network Address Translation (NAT) can get around this limitation. Thus, although there could be some truth to option C, it's not certain to be true. The class A/B/C distinctions are just guidelines that can be overridden by specific configurations. Thus, option D is incorrect. Option E's assertion that `ifup` is used only on computers that use DHCP is incorrect; `ifup` can work on computers that use static IP addresses, provided that the relevant information is entered correctly.

17. E. The `-n` option is used when you want to use `route` to display the current routing table, and it does as option E specifies. There is no `route` parameter that behaves as options A or C specify. Option B describes the purpose of the `netmask` parameter to `route`. Option D describes the purpose of the `-net` parameter to `route`.

18. E. Option E correctly identifies the function of `/etc/resolv.conf`. Option A describes the purpose of `/etc/services`. Various distribution-specific configuration files perform the function described in option B, but `/etc/resolv.conf` is not one of these files. A DHCP client sends a broadcast to locate a DHCP server; there is no client configuration file that holds the DHCP server's address, as option C describes. The routing table is maintained internally, although basic routing information may be stored in distribution-specific configuration files, so option D is also incorrect.

19. B. The `/etc/hosts` file holds mappings of IP addresses to hostnames, on a one-line-per-mapping basis. Thus, option B is correct. The file does not list the users (option C) or other hosts (option A) allowed to remotely access this one, affect remote administration through a Web browser (option D), or map port numbers to protocols (option E).

20. D. The `/etc/nsswitch.conf` file controls the order of name resolution, among other things. Option D correctly describes the procedure for changing the order in which Linux performs name resolution. The `/etc/resolv.conf` file mentioned in option A controls the DNS servers that Linux consults, but it doesn't control access to `/etc/hosts`. Option B's `nslookup` command resolves a hostname, so option B will return the IP address of the computer called `dns`, if Linux can find such a system. The `/etc/named.conf` file of option C is the configuration file for the standard name server. This server isn't likely to be installed on most Linux systems, and even if it is, the procedure described in option C is invalid. Like option B's `nslookup`, option E's `dig` looks up hostname-to-IP-address mappings, so option E will display such mappings for the computers called `local` and `dns`, if they exist.

Chapter 9: Writing Scripts, Configuring Email, and Using Databases

1. E. The current directory indicator is particularly dangerous in root's PATH environment variable because it can be used by unscrupulous local users to trick root into running programs of the unscrupulous user's design. Thus, option E is correct and all the other options are incorrect.

2. A. The alias built-in command creates a duplicate name for a (potentially much longer) command. Option A shows the correct syntax for using this built-in command; it causes the new alias cdpt to work like the much longer cd ~/papers/trade. The export command in option B creates an environment variable called cdpt that holds the value cd ~/papers/trade. This will have no useful effect. Option C, if placed in a bash startup script, will cause the user's current directory to shift to ~/papers/trade immediately after the user logs in. There is no standard shortcut command, so option D is meaningless. Although env is a valid command, it's used incorrectly in option E, and so this option is incorrect.

3. E. Some programs use the EDITOR environment variable as described in option E. Contrary to option A, the EDITOR environment variable has nothing to do with command-line editing. When you're typing at a bash command prompt, bash itself provides simple editing features, so option B is incorrect. (You can launch the editor specified by $EDITOR by typing Ctrl+X followed by Ctrl+E, though.) The edit command doesn't behave as option C suggests. (This command may be configured differently on different systems.) You can create links called GUI and TEXT to have the EDITOR environment variable behave as option D suggests, but this isn't a normal configuration.

4. C. The PWD environment variable holds the present working directory, so option C is correct. The PATH environment variable (option A) holds a colon-delimited list of directories in which executable programs are stored so that they may be run without specifying their complete pathnames. There are no standard CWD, PRESENT, or WORKING environment variables, so options B, D, and E are all incorrect.

5. A. Option A creates the desired environment variable. Option B creates a local variable—but not an environment variable—called MYVAR, holding the value mystuff. After typing option B, you can also type **export MYVAR** to achieve the desired goal, but option B by itself is insufficient. Option C isn't a valid bash shell command. Option D displays the contents of the MYVAR variable and also echoes mystuff to the screen, but it doesn't change the contents of any environment variable. Option E's setenv isn't a valid bash command, but it will set an environment variable in tcsh.

6. E. The ~/.bashrc file is a non-login bash startup script file. As such, it can be used to alter a user's bash environment, and option E is correct. There is no standard ~/.startup file for bash, so option A is incorrect. The /etc/bashrc file is a global bash startup script. Editing it will modify users' bash environments, but an individual user should not be able

to modify it, so option B is incorrect. There is no standard /home/.bashrc file; this option would be correct only if the user's home directory were set to /home, which would almost certainly be an error. Thus, option C is incorrect. Likewise, option D's /home/profilerc doesn't refer to a user's configuration file; and even if it did, profilerc isn't a valid bash configuration filename (although ~/.profile is a valid user configuration file and /etc/profile is a valid global configuration file).

7.   A, D. The env command displays all defined environment variables, so option A satisfies the question. (In practice, you might pipe the results through grep to find the value of a specific environment variable.) The echo command, when passed the name of a specific environment variable, displays its current value, so option D is also correct. DISPLAY is an environment variable, but it's not a command for displaying environment variables, so option B is incorrect. You can use the export command to create an environment variable but not to display the current settings for one, so option C is incorrect. Option E's cat command concatenates files or displays the contents of a file to the screen, but it doesn't display environment variables.

8.   E. Scripts, like binary programs, normally have at least one executable bit set, although they can be run in certain ways without this feature. Thus, you should use chmod, as in option E. You should *not*, however, use chmod to set the set-user-ID (SUID) bit, as in option A, since this would be a security risk for most scripts. There is no standard /usr/bin/ scripts directory, and scripts can reside in any directory, so option B is incorrect. Scripts are interpreted programs, which means they don't need to be compiled, making option C incorrect. (Typing **bash *scriptname*** will run the script, though.) Viruses are extremely rare in Linux, and because you just created the script, the only ways it could possibly contain a virus would be if your system was already infected or if you wrote it as a virus. Thus, option D is incorrect.

9.   C. The cp command is the only one called in the script, and that command copies files. Because the script passes the arguments ($1 and $2) to cp in reverse order, their effect is reversed—where cp copies its first argument to the second name, the cp1 script copies the second argument to the first name. Thus, option C is correct. Because the order of arguments to cp is reversed, option A is incorrect. The cp command has nothing to do with compiling (option B) or converting (option D) C or C++ programs, so neither does the script. The reference to /bin/bash in the first line of the script identifies the script itself as being a bash script; it does not cause the arguments to the script to be run as bash scripts, so option E is incorrect.

10.   C. Conditional expressions enable the script to execute different sets of instructions depending on some condition, as described in option C. They have nothing to do with license conditions (option A), the computer's environment (option B), or Pavlovian conditioning (option D). Although code readability can be influenced by proper or improper use of many programming features, including conditional expressions, this isn't the primary purpose of conditional expressions, so option E is incorrect.

11.   B, D. Valid shell scripts begin with the characters #! and the complete path to a program that can run the script. Options B and D both meet this description, because /bin/bash is a shell program that's installed on virtually all Linux systems and /bin/sh is usually a link

to /bin/bash or to some other valid shell. There is no standard /bin/script program, so option A is incorrect. Options C and E are both almost correct; /bin/tcsh and /bin/zsh are valid shells on many systems, but the order of the first two characters is reversed, so this option is incorrect.

12. A, B, D. The for, while, and until statements are all valid looping statements in bash, so options A, B, and D are all correct. There is no goto statement in bash's scripting language, so option C is incorrect. The case statement is a conditional, not a looping, statement in bash, so option E is incorrect.

13. E. All SMTP email servers are supposed to accept email to postmaster. Linux systems typically do so by using an alias to forward the email to another local user, or occasionally to a user on another computer. Thus, option E is correct. Option A would be rude and pointless in this case, although this type of response is used by some administrators when receiving mail from known spam sites, so as to degrade spammers' operations. Options B and D both describe non-delivery of the message, in violation of proper email server configuration. Option C is effectively the same as option D unless creation of the postmaster account is imminent, and an email server would have no way of knowing this.

14. C. The Fetchmail program is a tool for retrieving email from remote POP or IMAP servers and injecting it into a local (or remote) SMTP email queue. As such, it's not an SMTP server, so option C is correct. Postfix (option A), sendmail (option B), Exim (option D), and qmail (option E) are all popular SMTP email servers for Linux.

15. B. The -s option to mail sets the message subject line, and -c sets carbon copy (cc:) recipients. Input redirection (via <) reads the contents of a line into mail as a message. A mail command line normally terminates with the primary recipient. Thus, option B correctly describes the effect of the specified line. Options A, C, D, and E are all confused in their interpretation of the effects of mail parameters. Options B and D also confuse input and output redirection, and option A incorrectly suggests that a script (or the mail program) can elevate its run status to root privileges.

16. D. SMTP servers accept local email for delivery even if their Internet connections are down. If the SMTP server can't contact recipient servers, the SMTP server holds the email and attempts delivery later, so option D is correct. Because SMTP servers don't check on the availability of remote servers until after email is accepted for delivery, option A is incorrect. Option B can't possibly be correct unless the server has a backup Internet connection, which wasn't specified in the question. Option C isn't correct because the SMTP server will hold the mail and attempt delivery later. How recipients retrieve their mail is not under your control, so option E is incorrect.

17. B. The /etc/aliases file configures system-wide email forwarding. The specified line does as option B describes. A configuration like this one is common. Option A has things reversed. Option C is not a valid conclusion from this evidence alone, although an intruder may conceivably be interested in redirecting root's email; so if jody shouldn't be receiving root's email, this should be investigated further. Although the effect of option D (jody reading root's email) is nearly identical to the correct answer's effect, they are different; jody cannot directly access the file or directory that is root's email queue. Instead, the

described configuration redirects `root`'s email into `jody`'s email queue. Thus, option D is incorrect. Because `/etc/aliases` is an email configuration file, not an account configuration file, it can't have the effect described in option E.

18. B. The `CREATE DATABASE` command creates a new database with the specified name. Because SQL commands are case-insensitive, this command may be typed in uppercase or lowercase, and option B is correct. Options A and C both use the incorrect command `NEW` rather than `CREATE`, and option C specifies the database name as `FISH` rather than `fish`. (Database names *are* case-sensitive.) Option D reverses the order of the `CREATE` and `DATABASE` keywords. Option E uses the fictitious command `DB`.

19. A, D. A single database may hold multiple tables, as option A suggests. Option D is also correct; by splitting data across tables (such as into tables describing objects generically and specifically), databases can be more space-efficient. Option B is incorrect because the `DROP` command doesn't combine tables; it *deletes* a table! Option C is incorrect because it reverses the meaning of rows and columns in a SQL table. A lossy compression algorithm, as the name suggests, deliberately corrupts or loses some data—an unacceptable option for a text database, making option E incorrect. (Lossy compression is used for some audio and video file formats, though.)

20. C. The `UPDATE` command modifies existing database table entries, and in this case it does so as option C describes. Option B also describes an update operation, but in a confused and incorrect way. Options A and D both describe database retrieval operations, but `UPDATE` doesn't retrieve data. Option E mistakenly identifies `stars` as a database name, but it's a table name; and it mistakenly identifies the operation as adding a new entry (`INSERT` in SQL) rather than as modifying an existing entry (`UPDATE` in SQL).

Chapter 10: Securing Your System

1. E. The server names alone are insufficient to determine whether they're legitimate. The computer in question may or may not need to run any of these servers, and their presence may or may not be intentional, accidental, or the sign of an intrusion. Thus, option E is correct. Contrary to option A, the mere presence of an SSH server does not ensure security. Although, as option B asserts, FTP is not a secure protocol, it's still useful in some situations, so the mere presence of an FTP server is not, by itself, grounds for suspicion. Similarly, in option C, although some administrators prefer Postfix or qmail to `sendmail` for security reasons, `sendmail` isn't necessarily bad, and the names alone don't guarantee that the `sshd` and `proftpd` servers are legitimate. As option D states, `sendmail` and `proftpd` both use unencrypted text-mode transfers; but this is appropriate in some situations, so option D is incorrect.

2. C. Although Nmap and other port scanners are useful security tools, they're also used by crackers, and many organizations have policies restricting their use. Thus, you should always obtain permission to use such tools prior to using them, as option C specifies. A

port scanner can't cause damage to `/etc/passwd`, so there's no need to back it up, contrary to option A. A port scanner also doesn't need the `root` password on a target system to operate, so you don't need this information, making option B incorrect. (In fact, asking for the `root` password could be seen as extremely suspicious!) Although you could use `sudo` to run Nmap, there's no need to do so to perform a TCP scan, and you can perform a UDP scan by running Nmap as `root` in other ways (such as via a direct login or by using `su`). Thus, option D isn't strictly necessary, although you might want to tweak `/etc/sudoers` as a matter of system policy. As a firewall is part of your network's security, you probably want it running when you perform a network scan, contrary to option E. Furthermore, it would be safer to leave the firewall running and scan from behind it, if you want to test the security of the network in case of a firewall breach.

3. C. The `/etc/security/limits.conf` (option C) file holds the configuration settings that allow you to limit users' access. The other options listed don't give the correct path to this file.

4. A, B, C. Nmap (option A) is usually used to perform scans of remote computers, but it can scan the computer on which it's run, as well. The `netstat` (option B) and `lsof` (option C) utilities can both identify programs that are listening for connections (that is, open ports) on the local computer. The `portmap` program (option D) is used by the Network File System (NFS) and some other servers, but it's not used to identify open ports. There is no standard Linux services program (option E), although the `/etc/services` file holds a mapping of port numbers to common service names.

5. B. The `-perm` option to `find` locates files with the specified permissions, and +4000 is a permission code that matches SUID files. The `-type f` option restricts matches to files in order to avoid false alarms on directories. Option B uses these features correctly. Options A, C, and D use these features incorrectly. Option E specifies a fictitious `-suid` parameter to `find`.

6. A. Option A correctly describes the meaning of the specified line. A percent sign (%) identifies a Linux group name, and the remainder of the line tells `sudoers` to enable users of that group to run all programs as `root` by using `sudo`. The remaining options all misinterpret one or more elements of this configuration file entry.

7. B. The `netstat` command can do what is described in the question. To do so, the `-ap` options to the command are good choices, so option B is correct. Although `lsof` can also accomplish the job, the `-c a` option is incorrect; this option restricts output to processes whose names begin with a. Thus, option A is incorrect. Option C's `ifconfig` command doesn't display open network connections, so it's incorrect. Although option D's `nmap` command will locate ports that are open on the `localhost` interface, it doesn't locate all open *connections*, nor does it locate connections on anything but the `localhost` interface. Option D's `top` command displays a list of processes sorted by CPU use, not open network connections (and `-net` is an invalid option to `top`, as well).

8. D. Option D is correct. TCP Wrappers uses this feature to allow you to override broad denials by adding more specific explicit access permissions to `hosts.allow`, as when setting a default deny policy (`ALL : ALL`) in `hosts.deny`.

9. C. The `bind` option of `xinetd` lets you tie a server to just one network interface rather than link to them all, so option C is correct. It has nothing to do with running multiple servers on one port (option A), specifying computers by hostname (option B), resolving conflicts between servers (option D), or the Berkeley Internet Name Domain (BIND) or any other DNS server (option E).

10. A, D. Using a firewall rule to block Waiter's port, as in option A, can increase security by providing redundancy; if Waiter is accidentally run in the future, the firewall rule will block access to its port. Uninstalling the program, as in option D, improves security by reducing the risk that the program will be accidentally run in the future. Most programs don't have a "stealth" mode, so option B is incorrect. (Furthermore, *reading* the documentation isn't enough; to improve security, you must change some configuration.) Tunneling Waiter's connections might have some benefit in some situations, but this configuration requires setup on both client and server computers and by itself leaves the server's port open, so option C is incorrect. Clients associated with the server program, installed on the server computer, pose little or no risk of abuse of the associated server; it's clients on *other* computers that are most likely to be used to abuse a server program, and you can't control that. Thus, option E is incorrect.

11. B. Option B correctly describes how to accomplish this goal. Option A is incorrect because the `hosts_allow` option isn't a legal `xinetd` configuration file option. Option C correctly describes how to configure the described restriction using TCP Wrappers, which is generally used with `inetd`, but it's not the way this is done using `xinetd`. Option D also describes a TCP Wrappers description, but it reverses the meaning. Option E's `iptables` utility configures a firewall. Although a firewall rule could be a useful redundant measure, the question specifies a `xinetd` configuration; and option E's use of `iptables` is incorrect.

12. B. Ideally, passwords should be completely random but still memorable. Option B's password was generated from a personally meaningful acronym and then modified to change the case of some letters, add random numbers and symbols, and extend its length using a repeated character. This creates a password that's close to random but still memorable. Option A uses a well-known mythological figure, who is likely to be in a dictionary. Option C uses two common words, which is arguably better than option A, but not by much. Option D uses two closely related words separated by a single number, which is also a poor choice for a password. Option E uses a sequential series of numbers, which is a poor (but sadly common) password choice.

13. A. Phishing (option A) involves sending bogus email or setting up fake Web sites that lure unsuspecting individuals into divulging sensitive financial or other information. Script kiddies (option B) are intruders who use root kits. Spoofing (option C) involves pretending data is coming from one computer when it's coming from another. Ensnaring (option D) isn't a type of attack. Hacking (option E) refers to either lawful use of a computer for programming or other advanced tasks or breaking into computers.

14. C. The `/etc/nologin` file, if present, prevents logins from ordinary users; only `root` may log in. You might set this file when performing maintenance and then forget to remove it, thus explaining the symptoms in the question. Thus, option C is correct. The `syslogd` daemon mentioned in option A records system messages and is unlikely to produce the specified symptoms. The login process ordinarily runs as root and is normally SUID root, so options B and D are also incorrect. Shadow passwords, as in option E, are used on almost all modern Linux systems, and are not likely to cause these symptoms.

15. B, C. SSH is most directly a replacement for Telnet (option B), but SSH also includes file-transfer features that enable it to replace FTP (option C) in many situations. SSH is not a direct replacement for the Simple Mail Transfer Protocol (SMTP; option A), the Network Time Protocol (NTP; option D), or Samba (option E).

16. A. The ssh_host_dsa_key file holds one of three critical private keys for SSH. The fact that this key is readable (and writeable!) to the entire world is disturbing, so option A is correct. In principle, a miscreant who has acquired this file might be able to redirect traffic and masquerade as your system, duping users into delivering passwords and other sensitive data. Because of this, option B (No) is an incorrect response, and the conditions imposed by options C, D, and E are all irrelevant, making all of these options incorrect.

17. B. SSH protocol level 2 is more secure than protocol level 1; thus, option B (specifying acceptance of level 2 only) is the safest approach. Option A is the *least* safe approach because it precludes the use of the safer level 2. Options C and D are exactly equivalent in practice; both support both protocol levels. Option E is invalid.

18. E. Allowing only normal users to log in via SSH effectively requires two passwords for any remote root maintenance, improving security, so option E is correct. Whether or not you permit root logins, the SSH server must normally run as root, since SSH uses port 22, a privileged port. Thus, option A is incorrect. SSH encrypts all connections, so it's unlikely that the password, or commands issued during an SSH session, will be intercepted, so option B isn't a major concern. (Nonetheless, some administrators prefer not to take even this small risk.) SSH doesn't store passwords in a file, so option C is incorrect. Because SSH employs encryption, option D is incorrect (this option better describes Telnet than SSH).

19. D. Option D provides the correct command to import fredkey.pub prior to use. The inspect-gpg, import-gpg, and gpg-import commands of options A, C, and E are fictitious; and there is no --readkey option to gpg, as option B suggests.

20. E. The usual method of sending encrypted messages with GPG entails the sender using the recipient's public key to encrypt the message. Thus, option E is correct. Option A would be correct if your correspondent needed to send you an encrypted message, but the question only specifies your sending the encrypted message. Options B, C, and D all entail delivery of private keys, which is inadvisable at best, because private keys in the wrong hands permit the holder to impersonate the person who owns the keys.

Appendix B

About the Additional Study Tools

In this appendix:

- Additional Study Tools
- System Requirements
- Using the Study Tools
- Troubleshooting

Additional Study Tools

The following sections are arranged by category and summarize the software and other goodies you'll find from the companion Web site. If you need help with installing the items, refer to the installation instructions in the "Using the Study Tools" section of this appendix.

The additional study tools can be found at http://www.sybex.com/go/linux plus2e. Here, you will get instructions on how to download the files to your hard drive.

Sybex Test Engine

The files contain the Sybex test engine, which includes two bonus practice exams, as well as the assessment test and the chapter review questions, which are also included in the book itself.

Electronic Flashcards

These handy electronic flashcards are just what they sound like. One side contains a question, and the other side shows the answer.

PDF of Glossary of Terms

We have included an electronic version of the glossary in .pdf format. You can view the electronic version of the glossary with Adobe Reader.

Adobe Reader

We've also included a copy of Adobe Reader so you can view PDF files that accompany the book's content. For more information on Adobe Reader or to check for a newer version, visit Adobe's Web site at http://www.adobe.com/products/reader/.

System Requirements

Make sure your computer meets the minimum system requirements shown in the following list. If your computer doesn't match up to most of these requirements, you may have problems using the software and files. For the latest and greatest information, please refer to the ReadMe file located in the downloads.

Windows Users

- A PC running Microsoft Windows 98, Windows 2000, Windows NT4 (with SP4 or later), Windows Me, Windows XP, Windows Vista, or Windows 7
- An Internet connection

Linux Users

- A computer with Flash Player 9
- An Internet connection

Mac Users

- A computer with OS X or later
- An Internet connection

Using the Study Tools

To install the items on a Windows OS, follow these steps:

1. Download the .ZIP file to your hard drive, and unzip to an appropriate location. Instructions on where to download this file can be found here: http://www.sybex .com/go/linuxplus2e.

2. Click the Start.EXE file to open the study tools file.

3. Read the license agreement, and then click the Accept button if you want to use the study tools.

   The main interface appears. The interface allows you to access the content with just one or two clicks.

   To install the items on a computer running Linux, follow these steps:

1. Download the .ZIP file to your hard drive, and unzip to an appropriate location. Instructions on where to download this file can be found here: http://www.sybex .com/go/linuxplus2e.

2. Open the Start.html file in an internet browser to open the study tools file.

3. Read the license agreement, and then click the Accept button if you want to use the study tools.

To install the items on a Mac, follow these steps:

1. Download the .ZIP file to your hard drive, and unzip to an appropriate location. Instructions on where to download this file can be found here: http://www.sybex .com/go/linuxplus2e.

2. Click the image file to mount the volume to your desktop

3. Open the JWS volume on your desktop and click Start.

4. Read the license agreement, and then click the Accept button if you want to use the study tools.

Troubleshooting

Wiley has attempted to provide programs that work on most computers with the minimum system requirements. Alas, your computer may differ, and some programs may not work properly for some reason.

The two likeliest problems are that you don't have enough memory (RAM) for the programs you want to use or you have other programs running that are affecting installation or running of a program. If you get an error message such as "Not enough memory" or "Setup cannot continue," try one or more of the following suggestions and then try using the software again:

Turn off any antivirus software running on your computer.   Installation programs sometimes mimic virus activity and may make your computer incorrectly believe that it's being infected by a virus.

Close all running programs.   The more programs you have running, the less memory is available to other programs. Installation programs typically update files and programs; so if you keep other programs running, installation may not work properly.

Have your local computer store add more RAM to your computer.   This is, admittedly, a drastic and somewhat expensive step. However, adding more memory can really help the speed of your computer and allow more programs to run at the same time.

Customer Care

If you have trouble with the book's companion study tools, please call the Wiley Product Technical Support phone number at (800) 762-2974 or email them at http://sybex .custhelp.com/.

Index

Note to the Reader: Throughout this index **boldfaced** page numbers indicate primary discussions of a topic. *Italicized* page numbers indicate illustrations.

C

M

Free Online Study Tools

Register on Sybex.com to gain access to a complete set of study tools to help you prepare for your exam

Comprehensive Study Tool Package includes:

- **Assessment Test** to help you focus your study to specific objectives

- **Chapter Review Questions** for each chapter of the book

- **Two Full-Length Practice Exams** to test your knowledge of the material

- **Electronic Flashcards** to reinforce your learning and give you that last-minute test prep before the exam

- **Searchable Glossary** gives you instant access to the key terms you'll need to know for the exam

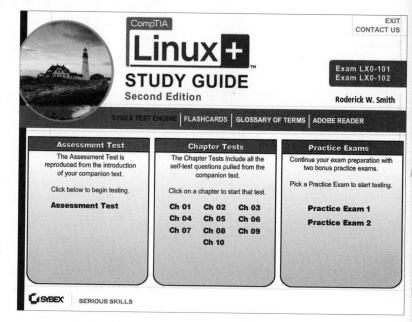

Go to **www.sybex.com/go/linuxplus2e** to register and gain access to this comprehensive study tool package.